CRITICAL TERMS FOR THE STUDY OF GENDER

CRITICAL TERMS FOR THE STUDY OF GENDER

Edited by CATHARINE R. STIMPSON
and GILBERT HERDT

THE UNIVERSITY OF CHICAGO PRESS   Chicago and London

The University of Chicago Press, Chicago 60637
The University of Chicago Press, Ltd., London
© 2014 by The University of Chicago
All rights reserved. Published 2014.
Printed in the United States of America

23 22 21 20 19 18 17 16 15 14   1 2 3 4 5

ISBN-13: 978-0-226-77480-0 (cloth)
ISBN-13: 978-0-226-77481-7 (paper)
ISBN-13: 978-0-226-01021-2 (e-book)
DOI: 10.7208/chicago/9780226010212.001.0001

Lauren Berlant's "Desire" and "Love" were first published in *Desire/
Love* (Brooklyn: Punctum Books, 2012); portions of Wendy Brown and
Joan W. Scott's "Power" appeared in "Power after Foucault" by Wendy
Brown, in *The Oxford Handbook of Political Theory*, ed. John S. Dryzek,
Bonnie Honig, and Anne Phillips (Oxford: Oxford University Press, 2006);
Judith Butler's "Regulation" was first published as "Gender Regulations"
in *Undoing Gender* (New York: Routledge, 2004); and Michael Warner's
"Public/Private" was first published as "Public and Private" in *Publics and
Counterpublics* (New York: Zone Books, 2002).

Library of Congress Cataloging-in-Publication Data

Critical terms for the study of gender / edited by Catharine R. Stimpson
and Gilbert Herdt.
   pages cm
Includes index.
ISBN 978-0-226-77480-0 (cloth : alk. paper)
ISBN 978-0-226-77481-7 (pbk. : alk. paper)
ISBN 978-0-226-01021-2 (e-book)
1. Sex (Psychology)—Teminology. 2. Gender identity—Terminology.
I. Stimpson, Catharine R., 1936– II. Herdt, Gilbert H., 1949–
HQ23.C68 2014
305.3—dc23

2013043366

♾ This paper meets the requirements of ANSI/NISO Z39.48-1992
(Permanence of Paper).

Contents

Introduction

CATHARINE R. STIMPSON AND GILBERT HERDT

In the late sixteenth century, a young Basque woman, Catalina, was about to take her final vows in a convent in her hometown of San Sebastian when she quarreled with one of the sisters. Feisty, independent, she walked out of the convent and took refuge in a chestnut grove. There she hid until she could restitch her bodice and petticoat into a suit of men's clothes. She also cut her hair, and then left town, initiating a life of adventures and scrapes as a man. In 1603 she reached Peru, one of the Spanish colonies in the Americas. At one point, she was buying wheat, grinding it, and selling it profitably as flour. One Sunday during this period, as she writes in her memoir, having "nothing better to do," she played cards with a merchant. After the game, on the way home, the merchant drew his sword, but Catalina "pulled out my own blade and we fell to fighting—we parried, but before long I ran him through and down he went" (de Erauso 1996, 40). Eventually, our tough, successful fighter reveals the secret of her sex and gender to a young bishop, then reemerges in Peru and Europe—as an intact virgin.

The story of Catalina—La Monja Alférez, the Lieutenant Nun—is rollicking and fascinating in itself. It is also a story about the fluidities of gender, about a young woman who willingly becomes a transvestite and dresses and lives as a man. This volume, *Critical Terms for the Study of Gender*, is a rich tapestry of ideas that enables us to think about both a historic Catalina and the significance of gender in our contemporary lives.

This introduction has three related purposes. The first is to outline the malleable, changing meanings of the word *gender*. The second is, briefly, to describe the evolving contemporary study of gender as the organization of sexual difference. Feminism has influenced these explorations, helping to shape perspectives that have been critical, in the senses of the word this volume uses: important, serious, questioning, challenging. The work on gender is growing rapidly. Do a database search on the topic of gender in the *Social Sciences Citation Index*. Between 1900 and 2002, you will find 47,392 results; between 2002 and November 2012, 91,054—nearly twice the previous century's output in a decade.

The third purpose of the introduction is to point to salient features of this volume. It is a collection of original essays, each of which scrutinizes a key word, a crucial term, in the study of gender. The essays have been written during a time when gender practices—in the United States and elsewhere—are as disputatious as the study of gender itself. Some of our contributors have been pioneers in the study of women and gender; all are innovative figures. We are proud that they agreed to write for this volume and grateful to them for their work and independence. They offer a range of ideas and methods, but together their essays demonstrate the centrality of the critical study of gender to our understanding of culture and society. As Gayatri Chakravorty Spivak, a founder of feminist and postcolonial criticism, wrote about her own work, "[My] method: gender as a general critical instrument rather than something to be factored into special cases" (Spivak 2003, 74). Our focus is on the United States, and inquiry there is our primary platform, but the essays range widely. We hope this book will have cross-cultural resonance and theoretical value.

Changing Meanings of the Word "Gender"

Until quite recently, many of the people who were interested in gender were students of language who related gender to grammar. Since the 1960s, however, gender has far more commonly referred to the complex ways in which societies and cultures organize and define sexual difference. In this sense, gender systems pervade and regulate human lives—in law courts and operating rooms, ballparks and poker clubs, hairdressing salons and kitchens, classrooms and playgroups, and, for a Catalina, in convents and colonized lands. Because so many different human societies have built their own gender systems, we must speak of diverse "genders" rather than a monolithic "gender." Exactly how gender works varies from culture to culture, and from historical period to historical period, but gender is very rarely *not* at work. Nor does gender operate in isolation. It is linked to other social structures and sources of identity.

Not surprisingly, the English word *gender* has a history. It comes from an older French word, *gendre*, which, in turn, derives from the Latin word *genus*. The Latin *genus* has a Greek cognate, *genos*. Both *genus* and *genos* can indicate a race, a breed, or a branch of a family, and each has an accompanying verb—in Latin *gigno*, in Greek *gignomai*—referring to birth. A second Latin verb, *generare*, means to beget, to father.

Together, the Greek and Latin sources of *gender* connote three big, complicated human activities: first, the general trait of classifying people into discrete classes, into one group or another, and then marking each group and assigning it characteristics; second, using language, a primary tool of this trait, to create and maintain sexual classifications, a specific way of marking and characterizing groups; and third, practicing a sexuality that aims to reproduce a family or group, to bring the next generation into being. Each activity reveals an interaction between nature and culture so intricate that rigidly quantifying what is nature and what is culture is a fool's task.

The evolution of *gender* in English extends these connotations. In 1971 the *Oxford English Dictionary* summarized gender's etymology to that date—as the contemporary study of gender was gaining strength. Of the various meanings in the 1971 *OED*, one, little used today, is taxonomic, that is, it signifies a kind, a category, a class. In Shakespeare's *Hamlet*, King Claudius is plotting what do about Hamlet, his stepson and nephew. He feels inhibited because of Hamlet's popularity with the mass of the people, "the great love the general gender bear him" (IV.vii.18).

Other meanings, if traditional, are still with us. One simply treats sex and gender as synonyms, a conflation and confusion to which we will return. Another signifies bringing something new into the world, either begetting offspring or "engendering" a tool or an odor or a feeling or an idea or a condition. Still another is one way of organizing grammar. Some languages—such as Bengali—dispense with gender altogether. Others, like English, use it sparingly, although English has gender-marked pronouns: *he* for a man, *she* for a woman, *it* for sexless objects. (In reaction, some feminists and transgendered persons have experimented with gender-neutral pronouns—for example, substituting *ze* for *he* and *she*, *hir* for *him* and *her*.) Still other languages, including classical Greek and Latin, strongly connect gender to grammar, labeling words as masculine, feminine, or neuter. The correlations between the laws of a language and a social world are often nonexistent. It is reasonable that in French *oncle* (uncle) should be masculine and *tante* (aunt) feminine, but why should *filament* (thread) be masculine and *auguille* (needle) feminine? Nor are gender assignments consistent across languages. A word may be masculine in one tongue, feminine in another, neuter in a third. Law, for example, is feminine in French and Spanish but neuter in German.

In the 1950s and 1960s, the US researcher John Money, in a series of observations of human infants with "a discrepancy between the gonads ... and the morphology of the external genitalia," took the term *gender* from linguistics and adapted it to the medical and psychological literature (Money 1968, 210; Person 1999, 2). Gender roles were assigned to, or "imprinted" on, these infants on the basis of an interpretation of the genitalia. This gender assignment, which shaped the rearing of the child, was firmly established about the time "he" or "she" was learning a native language.

Money's work has been controversial, but he was influential in establishing as a meaning of gender the complex organization and definition of sexual difference. The historian Joan W. Scott has argued brilliantly and most influentially that this organization consists of several elements. One is the set of culturally available symbols of femininity and masculinity. Framing these symbols are normative concepts that set and guide our interpretations of them. Inseparable, these symbols and concepts—what anthropologists would call "cultural ideologies"—are allied to kinship arrangements (families and households), the labor market, and the range of social institutions that help to embody and perpetuate gender as an organization. The dynamic interactions among all of these shape our subjective gender identities, our gendered sense of ourselves, which in turn shape our responses to the worlds in which we dwell.

One example: the Roman Catholic church permits men to become priests and prohibits women from doing so. Interwoven in this rule are tradition; church governance, theology, and canon law; and an understanding of the priestly calling as one sign of a uniquely elevated masculinity. A woman born into a faith that declares it impossible for her to become a priest—because she is a woman—will experience herself as someone with limits on her possibilities for the religious life. She may celebrate these limits, accept them without question, rebel against them openly, subvert them covertly, put on a priest's garb and masquerade, or find an alternative religious role—for example, as a mystic or a nun. But no matter what she does, she cannot experience herself as a "real" ordained priest who lawfully conducts a mass.

Socially and psychologically, an individual's "gender identification" is one crucible of a comprehensive identity (Lopata and Thorne 1978). So are other structures, processes, and forces. As a result, identities are multiple, fluid, and in flux. The African American writer and performance artist Anna Deavere Smith, in her essay about Lyle Ashton Harris, an African American photographer and performance artist, asks, "Is it possible that, now, we can look at identity as a constellation: / that each of us has inside of ourselves many fragments? / And the fragments are not / neurosis"? (Smith 2002, pt. 1). Although Meena Alexander, the postcolonial and feminist writer, uses a different metaphor, she has a similar perception of identity. In *Fault Lines*, her memoir about migrating among India, her birthplace, Sudan, Great Britain, and the United States, she writes:

> There are so many strands all running together in a bright snarl of life. I cannot unpick it, take it apart, strand by strand. That would lose the quick of things. My job is to evoke it all, altogether. For that is what my ethnicity requires, that is what America with its hotshot present tense compels me to.... What parts of my past can I hold onto when I enter this life? (Alexander 2003, 198)

To represent identity as a "constellation" or "strands ... in a bright snarl of life" is to use metaphor. Adding to the complexity of gender practices is the cultural tradition of using masculinity and femininity themselves as metaphors, which the self can then internalize. Men represent and are associated with this, women represent and are associated with that. One reason the study of gender is often hard to do incisively is gender's function as a term and category, as a historically variable social organization based on sexual differences, and as a metaphor. Linking polarized and metaphorical thinking, binary oppositions have been set up between culture, which men are said to represent, and nature, which women are said to represent; lightness, which men are said to represent, and darkness, which women are said to represent; mind, which men are said to represent, and body, which women are said to represent. Culture, lightness, and mind are clustered together around one pole, which is masculinized; nature, darkness, and body are clustered together around another, which is feminized. All this is then held to be true, factual, natural.

As Scott and others point out, gender is also a metaphor for power and politics. A wife rebelling against her husband is, in and of herself, a threat to a familial and social order, but this disobedient and upstart spouse also represents a dangerously disobedient and upstart class. Our political rhetoric also metaphorically genderizes groups and nations and then assumes that these metaphors mirror reality. For example, the United States often valorizes itself as strongly and appropriately virile, while condemning its political enemies as either weakly feminine or as repellently virile and uncivilized barbarians. Yet, demonstrating some metaphorical flexibility, the country happily imagines itself as both Uncle Sam and the sturdily feminine Statue of Liberty.

The critical study of gender has resulted in other key insights that this volume will explore. Among the most significant is the need to distinguish between sex, a biological category, and gender, a social category and construction, which in turn shapes our beliefs about biological categories. As the French writer Simone de Beauvoir put it in *The Second Sex*, a founding text of women's studies (published in French in 1949 and English in 1953), "One is not born, but rather becomes, a woman" (Beauvoir 1953, 301). English speakers often use the words *female* and *male* to refer to biological classifications, *feminine* and *masculine* for gender classifications. Over these words float *men* and *women*, sometimes signifying sex, sometimes gender, sometimes both. In the 1960s, the psychiatrist Robert Stoller, author of *Sex and Gender*, proposed that we distinguish between "core gender identity," a sense of self as female or male, and "gender identity," a sense of self as feminine or masculine.

In brief, *gender* does not mean sex but the social and sexual relationships between the sexes and the place assigned to members of each sex within these relationships. Not sex but gender has ordained that men should have control over "their" women. Not sex but gender decrees that rape might be permissible. Often, people broadly attribute the differences between men and women to "biology" or, more specifically, to differences in genetic and anatomical formations. Unfortunately, "studies" of biological femaleness and maleness have historically been riddled with error, and often risible, but despite these flaws, biology has been used to reproduce and justify normative gender arrangements by rooting them in nature.

To be sure, most females do carry the XX pair of sex chromosomes, most males the XY. The genetics of sex, however, cannot be reduced to a rigid binary. Not all humans are XX or XY; for example, a third chromosomal pattern, XO, exists in people who lack one sex chromosome. Significantly, a great number of cultures have created figures or mythological types that are neither female nor male and that have meanings specific to the cultures that recognized or invented them. Among them are the Transgendered, the Gender Queer, the Two Spirit, and the Androgyne, a word that literally unites the Greek for male and female. A contemporary idiomatic term is "gender-bending." In 1993 a political movement, the Intersex Society of North America, began in order to change the treatment of still another group, intersexed people, *intersex* defined as "the umbrella medical term to describe the presence of ambiguous or unusual genitalia at birth (conditions also classified as hermaphroditism and pseudohermaphroditism)" (Rosario 2004, 282).

To be sure, too, females share a biological reproductive capacity. So do males. However, as the anthropologist Carole Vance once cautioned, we should be wary of regarding "reproduction" as the "core" of gender and sexuality. We are more than our reproductive capacities, joy though they can bring. Reproduction is also a social construct, and its meanings go far beyond those of procreation. They include such vastly different human experiences as the ritual insemination of boys by adolescent males among the Sambia of New Guinea (to "grow" and "give birth" to masculinity in them, according to the local sexual culture); the sequence of "trial marriages" to older men that lead to adulthood among !Kung women of the Kalahari region of southern Africa; and, in the contemporary and affluent West, the employment of high-tech medical procedures to enhance fertility and childbirth.

As our examples suggest, the organization of sexual difference across cultures has varied greatly. As the story of Catalina shows, the borders within systems can be fragile or fluid. Marjorie Garber has written vividly about Catalina and category crises in culture. A category crisis is "a failure of definitional distinction, a borderline that becomes permeable, permitting border crossings from one apparent distinct category to another" (foreword to de Erauso 1996, xiv). Gender systems also change, not only from within but over time. Life—in all its messiness and contingency—and people—with all their desires, hopes, needs, and decisions—interrupt, break into, break them up. There is no universal reason why a gender system changes, partly or completely, but rather multiple reasons, multiple historical circumstances and contexts. Individuals have felt that their prescribed gender roles did not fit. The writer Jan Morris, born a male child named James Humphry Morris, tells of a moment of utmost significance in her life. "I was three or perhaps four years old when I realized that I had been born into the wrong body, and should really be a girl. I remember the moment well, and it is the earliest memory of my life" (Morris 2002, 3). Instead of such experiences of "gender dysphoria" leading only to self-hatred, they have led to questions about and changes in people's lives. Historical developments and events strain gender systems and put them under enormous pressures. In the United States, for example, because of slavery, racism, and class structures, the categories of the prevailing gender system established supposedly irrevocable differences between black men and white men, black women and white women. These demeaned and dehumanized blackness while elevating whiteness. Some white women, but no blacks, could be "proper women" and "ladies," a vicious ascription that blacks resisted. The cataclysm of World War II helped to disrupt concepts of gender and race and the connections between them. Political and social movements arose that documented the damage these systems did and that continue to work to transform them.

The striking diversity and mutability of gender systems are evident in the myths of origin that cultures offer to explain them. To contrast but three: the first, from myth, is a passage from one of Plato's most famous dialogues. *The Symposium* (ca. 384 BCE) features the Greek playwright Aristophanes telling a charming parable about the variety show of sexuality. Originally, he claims, three sexes dwelt happily on earth: one male, one female, one a union of the two. Unfortunately, they attacked the gods. Their punishment was to be cut in two. After the god Apollo healed their wounds, each half began to seek its other half, male seeking male, female seeking female, male and female seeking each other.

A second, far more powerful origin story is from the Judeo-Christian tradition. Genesis, the first book of the Old Testament, offers two narratives about the creation of the sexes. In the first, God creates male and female in his image; in the second, God forms Adam from dust, and then, so that he will not be alone, brings into being animals, birds, language, and, out of Adam's rib, a woman, Eve. After Eve disobeys God and tempts Adam to do the same, God punishes them both by expelling them from Eden and assigning them gender roles: Adam is to labor in the fields, Eve to labor in childbirth and to obey Adam.

In contrast, a third account comes from neither myth nor religion but from the modern evolutionary social sciences. In *The First Sex*, the anthropologist Helen Fisher recognizes the power of social forces but also argues that sexual and gender differences, established in prehistory, are hardwired into our brains, hormones, and genes: "Men and women emerged from the womb with some innate tendencies and proclivities bred on the grasslands of Africa millennia ago. The sexes are not the same. Each has some natural talents. Each is a living archive of its distinctive past" (Fisher 1999, xvi). To this, Fisher adds a four-stage theory of history that echoes some thinking from both nineteenth- and twentieth-century feminist and Marxist speculations. In prehistory, she surmises, women and men were "roughly equal." Then, during the Agricultural Revolution, men took on primary economic roles and assumed power over the state and their families. Women became the second sex. Next, during the Industrial Revolution, women, joining the paid labor force, became economically powerful again. Now, as we enter the twenty-first century, the "female mind" and "uniquely feminine attributes"—a talent with words, a "gift for networking and negotiating"—will dramatically influence "business, sex, and family life" (Fisher 1999, xvi–ii). As we move from prehistory to prophecy, Eve is no longer a sinner to be subdued, but a savior to be celebrated.

Despite this diversity and mutability of gender systems, and origin myths, a group that we call gender traditionalists hopes to find essential differences among the sexes that can be justified in a myth of origins, be its source legend, religion, or academic speculation. In the United States today, gender traditionalists are perhaps most vocal in their opposition to same-sex marriage, flatly declaring that marriage is between "one man and one woman," that we know what a man is and what a woman is, and that civilization itself depends on such sacrosanct unions. Gender traditionalists perform three, linked operations that add up to a suspect cultural logic of gender. The first is to maximize contrasts. For traditionalists, gender depends on fixing and sustaining sexual differences. If gender structures were to minimize differences, the structures would contract and shrivel. The second is to organize these differences into patterns of relations. If men are like this, then women must complement them by being like that. A gender system then consists of complex codependencies. One such common pattern, which we noted before, is that of polarity or binary oppositions. If men are rational, women are irrational. Deploying metaphor, if men are from Mars, then women are from Venus. These polarities are then linked to other polarities to form a worldview. The third operation of gender traditionalists is to generalize these patterns of differences so that a gender structure seems universal. Descriptions and/or studies of men and women then become both archetypal and stereotypical. An entry in the 1968 *International Encyclopedia of the Social Sciences* illustrates such thinking:

> Males as a group excel in speed and co-ordination of gross bodily movements, spatial orientation, mechanical comprehension, and arithmetic reasoning. Females excel in manual dexterity, perceptual speed and accuracy, memory, numerical computation, verbal fluency, and other tasks involving the mechanics of language. Among the principle personality differences found between the sexes are the greater aggressiveness, achievement drive, and emotional stability of the male and the stronger social orientation of the female. (Quoted in Anastasi 1968, 205)

At the turn of the millennium, gender systems in the United States were changing, unevenly perhaps, but rapidly. In 1999 the film *Boys Don't Cry* (directed by Kimberly Peirce; cowritten by Peirce and Andy Bienen) was a significant narrative about gender at that historical moment, combining diversity and mutability and resistance to both. Based on a true story (which also inspired the 1998 documentary film *The Brandon Teena Story*), *Boys Don't Cry* tells of a young woman who yearns to be a young man. Born female, given the girl's name Teena, raised as a girl, she cannot wholly escape her femaleness. She menstruates. She has breasts that she must bind and hide. Although she is stranded in the heartland of America, without money or education or status, she acts on her dream of personal transformation and performs as if she were a male, whom she calls Brandon Teena. She thus reverses both gender identity and birth name. The boy is also stranded in the heartland. He, too, lacks money or education or status. However, Brandon is a comely, romantic—if prevaricating—young man, who offers dreams to the girlfriend he finds as well as an uncanny tenderness no other "man" provides.

Sadly, claiming an identity is not the same thing as constructing a workable life. If Brandon cannot wholly escape Teena's femaleness, neither can he wholly escape from her history, which has had unsavory as well as unhappy elements. Within weeks, his dream dies hard. Unmasked as a woman, he is raped and eventually murdered by two local thugs. Boys may not cry, but his girlfriend can, and so can the audience. *Boys Don't Cry* is about love, violence, and wasted American lives. It is also a harrowing tale about gender and the fate of people who will not conform to its local rules. Except for his girlfriend, others find Brandon's gender choice at best puzzling, at worst intolerable. The two people who find it most intolerable, who rape and murder him, are themselves young men, his contemporaries, with whom he has enacted a gawky version of male bonding. They are punishing both "Teena," who has become Brandon and betrayed the norms of femininity, and "Brandon," who was once Teena and thus betrayed the norms of masculinity. For them, people who resist the local heterosexual culture in which such taxonomies of gender thrive are monsters to be destroyed.

The overarching moral narrative of the film, however, portrays these two destructive, angry gender conformists as losers, drunken louts, petty criminals before they were murderers. Though pessimistic, *Boys Don't Cry* also offers a vision of a different world in which gender nonconformity might live unthreatened, and even flourish. As such, the film's dramatization of human resilience and courage in the face of oppression shares an element with a grand project of many who study gender: to illuminate the experiences and insights of being different, to track those differences across space and time, and to identify the hesitations that appear before "different" desires become integrated into "normal" language.

Evolving Contemporary Studies of Gender

Three linked developments occurred in the West in the mid- nineteenth to the early twentieth century. First, modern ideas about subjectivity and identity, about what it means to be a person, emerged. These incorporated ideas about gender and sexuality. Second, people were categorized as "heterosexuals" or "homosexuals." Indeed, these terms first appear in the nineteenth century. Moreover, same-sex or homosexual practices began to be regarded less as a series of specific actions, a way of doing sex, than as signs of identity, a way of being. Third, great changes occurred in the roles and status of women, most forcefully expressed and supported by women's movements and their searing analyses of gender relations. Women's suffrage, the right to vote, a twentieth-century achievement in most countries (badly marred in the United States by discrimination against women of color), is but one of them.

The historian Paul Robinson calls these changes "the modernization of sex." Modernization both led to and was stimulated by the professionalization of the study of sex, often pioneered by "sexual enthusiasts" who wanted to create progress through sexual reform in the service of modernity. Among them were Richard von Krafft-Ebing, Sigmund Freud, Havelock Ellis, and Magnus Hirschfeld. During the twentieth century in the United States, this study took several, often overlapping paths. Probably the dominant early force was psychoanalysis, imported from Europe, which explored psychosexual development and provided a new vocabulary to describe sexuality and the genesis of gender differentiation.

An affirmative legacy that emerged from sexology and reacted to psychoanalysis was more empirical: the focused study of sexual behavior in human and animals, "all responses directly associated with genital stimulation and copulation, whether homosexual or heterosexual" (Phoenix 1968, 194). Counting sex acts was the high art of this approach, best known from the more than nine thousand interviews conducted by the zoologist Alfred C. Kinsey (1894–1956) and his colleagues, who published their results in *Sexual Behavior in the Human Male* (1948) and *Sexual Behavior in the Human Female* (1953). Patriarch and quantifier though Kinsey was, he had great compassion for the sexual marginals and underdogs of American society. He describes the state of the laws governing sexuality and the chronic effects of guilt for engaging in illegal activities, activities that Kinsey, in general terms, believed to be part of the "normal and natural" range of human experiences, accepted in some societies but treated as "deviations" from the norm and punished in others. Finding class differences in sexual attitudes, Kinsey suggests that the American upper and middle classes tended to organize sexual activities by moral categories while the lower classes tended to label them "natural" or "unnatural." Kinsey might be seen as both scientist and social scientist. To a degree, sex and gender were of interest to the social sciences, perhaps most famously in the work of the anthropologist Margaret Mead (1901–1978), roughly Kinsey's contemporary. In her widely read books on cultural beliefs and norms, she argues for the malleability and plasticity of gender roles. Others in the social sciences studied sex differences in intelligence and behavior; the sociologist Mirra Komarovsky, for example, explored the concept of "sex roles" and the development of "preferences and patterns of behavior" to enact them (Tyler 1968, 208).

The contemporary study of gender as the organization of sexual difference grew rapidly after the 1960s. The purposes of this activity are to use gender as a category of analysis; to render the organization of sexual differences visible and explore its complexities; and, for many, to think about change or even transformation in our gender systems. Such work has gone on within existing disciplines and in new interdisciplinary fields organized around the experiences of groups that first felt themselves to be marginal to, if not despised by, the governing structures and norms of society and the academy. Black studies was a pioneer, then women's studies, often called feminist studies, to be followed by Asian American studies, Chicano studies, Latino/Latina studies, Native American studies, the more global postcolonial studies, global studies itself, and, most recently, disability studies and animal studies. Both taking from and giving to the established academic disciplines, each has influenced the study of gender, women's studies perhaps most pervasively. Although its practitioners vary by generation, field, methodology, institution, and resources, they have reached some consensus on the validity of several theoretical frameworks. To oversimplify, one passionately argued debate was between "essentialists," who argued that women shared some universal characteristics, and "constructivists," who argued that various societies constructed and determined women's characteristics. The winners were the constructivists, although the debate lingers on. For example, Vernon A. Rosario writes that the "essentialism-versus-constructionism wars that riled us all in gay and lesbian studies in the 1980s . . . had grown tiresome" by the early 1990s. Yet, he admits, "biology soon came back to haunt us" (Rosario 2004, 280–81).

In the 1960s and 1970s, women's studies explored the question of difference between women and men in three ways, to all of which feminism provided intellectual energy and insights and a moral and political framework. The first was to expose and to transform the harmful differences between men and women that are the consequence of men's dominance over women, of hierarchical patriarchal structures, and of phallocentrism. Some societies may exist where the domain of men and the domain of women have a rough parity. Far more likely are societies in which men exert power over women, especially those in their own class and family, and often brutally so. One ironic characteristic of some societies in which women lack economic or social power is an emphasis on their sexual power and, as a consequence, their tempting and dangerous natures. In addition to a deficit in formal power, women may lack access to the tools of self-empowerment. Gender gaps exist in income, access to literacy and education, holding of public and private office, and cultural authority. Mary Hawkesworth, in "Feminist Conceptions of Power," a magisterial review, writes, "Feminist theorists of power suggest that persistent gender and racial asymmetry should be understood as a system of oppression. Imbalances of power in families, schools, workplaces, churches, temples, mosques, synagogues, and official institutions of governance are interrelated" (Hawkesworth 2011, 3).

Because of such deficits, studies of women and gender are often marred by false universalisms, ethnocentric bias, and gender blinders. Leila Ahmed, a founder of the study of women and gender in Islam, writes sardonically of professors "who have no sympathy whatever for feminism (but who) are now jumping on the bandwagon of gender studies and directing a plethora of dissertations on this or that medieval text with titles like 'Islam and Menstruation.'" But, she continues, "such dissertations should more aptly have titles along the lines of 'A Study of Medieval Male Beliefs about Menstruation'" (Ahmed 2000, 129).

The second approach to differences between men and women was to reveal what women have done and continue to do despite male dominance, to which the publication of Carol Gilligan's work on moral reasoning, *In a Different Voice* (1981), gave impetus. For women have created culture, built institutions, raised families in harsh situations, and devised mechanisms of survival. Understanding these achievements, the third approach, which women of color pioneered and which many in women's studies were late in discerning, asked about diversity, the differences *among* women—those of race, class, age, religion, sexuality, nationality, and status as citizens. This approach connects studies of race and ethnicity with those of gender. Clearly seeing the differences among women also complicates questions of gender structures and hierarchy. For a woman might be under the rule of the men in her family or class or race, but also have men and women of another class or race under hers.

Though the focus of women's studies is on women, increasingly seen in all their differences, it was hard to study women without studying men. In the late 1970s, women's studies stimulated the development of men's studies, which examined men's lives and the construction of masculinity and masculinities. An obvious step was to show the conceptual, legal, sociopolitical, and cultural relations among men and women in a gender system. In 1975 Gayle S. Rubin had written of the "sex/gender system." In 1981 Myra Jehlen called on feminist critics to be "radical comparativists," comparing male and female traditions, male and female innovations. Bringing together gender theory and Afro-American criticism, Valerie Smith showed how to read slave narratives by black men and black women in this way. Together, such individual voices and women's studies and men's studies were building blocks of gender studies as an academic field. Influencing them after 1978 was the historical exploration of sexual norms and practices closely associated with the work of the French scholar Michel Foucault and his analyses of discourses of power. However, many in women's studies feared that the rise of gender studies would eliminate women as a central focus of study and women's lives as a subject of deep, lasting social change. The summer 1987 issue of *Signs: Journal of Women in Culture and Society* focused on the theme "Within and Without: Women, Gender, and Theory." The opening sentences of its editorial reflects the tension between the fields:

> With this issue we confront the implicit question: should women's stud-ies yield to gender studies? Is women's studies, in its focus on women, on Woman, "gender-bound" and hence, ultimately, still partial in choosing its subject and in generating concepts and theory from and for that sub-ject? Or, is the study of women the best, or even the only, way to tran-scend gender because such study allows the possibility of critique from within particular women's lives and from without, as the Woman chal-lenges phallocentric reality? Support for both positions can be found in this issue, and that is appropriate since these questions are by no means settled—nor even sharply defined—yet. (*Signs* 1987, 619)

Simultaneously, as women's studies took differences more and more se-riously, the lesbian difference became more prominent, sufficiently so that lesbians began to want an institutional base of their own. Taking with them the feminist analysis of gender and gender hierarchies, they either formed lesbian studies, or joined with gay men, with whom they shared the burdens of a stigmatized sexuality, to create lesbian and gay studies. This, too, evolved and mutated. In 1984 Gayle S. Rubin published a second landmark essay, "Thinking Sex: Notes for a Radical Theory of the Politics of Sexuality," in which she suggested that the term "gender" could not adequately cover "sexuality." She also urged lesbians to real-ize that they were also "oppressed as queers and perverts" and that they shared "many of the sociological features and suffered from many of the same social penalties as have gay men, sadomasochists, transvestites, and prostitutes" (Rubin 1993, 33). Such thinking helped to shape new ac-ademic programs in sexuality studies or gender and sexuality.

By the mid-1990s, in part because of the focus on sexuality, the ear-lier rubric of lesbian and gay studies had expanded to become lesbian gay bisexual transgender (LGBT) studies (now commonly LGBTQ). LGBT studies both reflected and inquired into three human possibilities that became more socially and culturally accessible in the late twentieth cen-tury: first, that of the transsexual, who transforms her or his body into that of the opposite sex, through medical means that began to evolve in the 1950s; second, that of the bisexual, who actively desires both men and women; and third, that of the transgender person, who feels and takes on the identity of the opposite gender or floats among gender identities. In the mid-1990s, the word "transgender" became an umbrella term for transsexuals, drag queens or drag kings, transgendered people, and others who blur and cross gender boundaries, living in a psychological state now often called "gender queer."

Displaying the porous boundaries between social change and some academic work, "queer" became part of vernacular speech, the name of an active subculture and an academic field, queer studies. If feminist theory and women's studies had historically distrusted Freud and psychoanalysis, queer studies and overlapping elements of gender studies turned to the Freud who interpreted sexuality as a fluid field, the libido as polyvalenced and a site of multiple energies. Eve Kosofsky Sedgwick, a founder of queer studies and gender studies, writes, albeit with subtle skepticism, "Freud gave psychological texture and credibility to a ... universalizing mapping of ... the supposed protean mobility of sexual desire and ... the potential bisexuality of every human creature" (Sedgwick 1990, 56). Queer studies also helped confront the need to understand the terrible impact of the AIDS pandemic, now a global tragedy. In the United States, it sought to mobilize the government to change its policies regarding HIV/AIDS. Among the new social complexities it explored were those of lesbians drawn into caretaking arrangements for their gay male friends. The new AIDS activism was eventually to feed still another kind of diffuse intellectual and social activism, a feature of the post–Cold War landscape that would seek to redefine relations between public and private spheres, to expand definitions of sexual citizenship, and to claim human rights for all genders and sexual minorities.

As a result of these creations, crossings, and mutations, the academic study of gender takes place within individual academic disciplines and within interdisciplinary clusterings. We want to stress that the contributors to this volume, which seeks to be intellectually spacious, are students of gender who belong to a number of disciplines, programs, and schools of thought. The diversity of the origins and sites for the study of gender and other related subjects has helped to generate two of its primary features: first, it has a mixed intellectual and academic lineage, full of arguments and quarrels; second, kept lively by these disagreements, it is continually developing. We are keenly and happily aware that the critical terms in the study of gender will change over time. For example, the importance of terms with which to analyze the connections between gender and globalization will only increase.

Yet, some widespread agreements do exist. One is methodological. Because of the historical and cross-cultural variations in gender as word, social organization, and metaphor, the study of gender fails when it indulges in vain universalisms, overgeneralizations, biases of various sorts, and the assumption that the local gender structures that we now know are all that there was or is to know. Another, compatible consensus is that gender is not an ahistorical, primordial, stable, given structure that controls men and women cross-culturally. To be sure, the neurosciences and genetics are producing a number of studies about sex differences, but gender is not the consequence of some omnicompetent, omnipotent, intelligently designed machine-tool that uniformly manufactures men and women, though some gender traditionalists justify a particular gender structure by claiming that it is. On the contrary, gender in its several senses is largely to be constructed, negotiated, or, in the famous term of Judith Butler, "performed" again and again until it seems ahistorical, primordial, stable, and given. In brief, to turn to another but compatible theory, we "do" gender (West and Zimmerman 1987).

Salient Features of This Volume

The essays in this volume are not literature reviews but presentations of, interpretations of, and informed arguments about crucial elements of a working vocabulary for the study of gender. Each is deeply grounded in the analytic work of the field. Together, they present a series of intellectually suggestive and clarifying moments rather than a set of permanent definitions. The language of any field as hybrid, fluid, and contentious as the study of gender will itself be subject to criticism and will inevitably change over time. These critical terms—important, serious, questioning, challenging—both mark the field's development and aim to inspire further inquiry and exploration of meanings. They are capable of opening up under the pressure of inquiry.

The critical terms appear here in alphabetical order, from "bodies" to "utopia," but readers should instead think of the entries as representing expanding, interlocking, and overlapping circles of inquiry. "Body" cannot, for example, be isolated from "sex/sexuality/sexual classification," nor can "desire" from "identity." Some names will recur (among them, Sigmund Freud, Michel Foucault, Jacques Derrida, and Judith Butler), as will certain themes (for example, differences, including racial differences; relations between gender and power; and the use and influence of new reproductive technologies). Such repetitions reflect the ongoing influence of these thinkers and the consequence of these themes to the study of gender.

The first of our interlocking circles of inquiry concerns the body, for some the site of initial experiences of gender. The next circles deal with psychology and subjectivity, asking questions about identity, desire, fantasy, and love. The next circles are about culture and language, culturally enacted and regulated gender roles, culturally inscribed sexual and gender classifications, concepts of difference, myth, religion, and utopian dreams (so often flawed) about gender. The next circle concerns socially and politically governed gender arrangements, focusing on kinship and the family, ethnicity, relations of race and gender, the pervasive dichotomy between public and private spheres, justice, and power itself. These inquiries also take up questions of globalization and of human rights, since World War II a global ideal. Still another circle focuses on nature, and the interrelation of nature and culture.

Finally, one essay is about the "posthuman." The term *posthumanism* emerged from a series of conferences held by the Josiah Macy Foundation after World War II. Their purpose was to "search for a new theoretical model for biological, mechanical, and communicational processes that removed the human and *Homo sapiens* from any particularly privileged position in relation to matters, meaning, information, and cognition" (Tirosh-Samuelson 2012, 2). Like postmodernism, with which it overlaps, posthumanism asks us to be radical skeptics about a centuries-old legacy of thinking about the meaning of being human. Like some science fiction, posthumanism describes "a new form of human existence in which the boundaries between humans and nature and humans and machines are blurred, as well as a prescription for an ideal situation in which the limitations of human biology are transcended, replaced by machines" (Tirosh-Samuelson 2012, 1).

This introduction began with a narrative about a young Basque woman who crossed gender boundaries. We now end by asking if the crossing and dissolution of gender boundaries has become inseparable from the crossing and dissolution of other boundaries once thought to be fixed. We are moved by inquiry. And we are certain that the study of gender seeks to picture the full experiences of women and men as they generate, inhabit, support, regenerate, resist, and change the systems that define the meanings of being a woman, being a man, or being a bit of both. Some predict that the current century will be the arena of a gender revolution. Gender—as term, system, metaphor—is too entrenched and varied to engage in the leaps and bounds of revolutionary change, but over time, women and men may negotiate greater equality, happiness, and justice. Slowly, but without hampering our capacities for love and dreams and interpretation, gender, as a system in need of change, may cease to be such a problem for history. We hope that *Critical Terms for the Study of Gender* will provide its twenty-first-century readers with a useful tool with which to further the study of gender, to ameliorate its historic harms, and to engender creative human energies.

References

Abelove, Henry, Michèle Aina Barale, and David M. Halperin, eds. 1993. *The Lesbian and Gay Studies Reader.* New York: Routledge.

Ahmed, Leila. 2000. *A Border Passage: From Cairo to America—A Woman's Journey.* New York: Penguin.

Alexander, Meena. 2003. *Fault Lines: A Memoir.* Rev. and expanded ed. New York: Feminist Press at the City University of New York.

Anastasi, Anne. 1968. "Sex Differences." In Sills 1968, 7:200–207.

Butler, Judith. 1990. *Gender Trouble: Feminism and the Subversion of Identity.* New York: Routledge.

de Beauvoir, Simone. 1953. *The Second Sex.* Trans. H. M. Parshley. New York: Knopf.

de Erauso, Catalina.1996. *Lieutenant Nun: Memoir of a Basque Transvestite in the New World.* Trans. Michelle Stepto and Gabriel Stepto. Boston: Beacon.

Fisher, Helen. 1999. *The First Sex: The Natural Talents of Women and How They Are Changing the World.* New York: Random House.

Hawkesworth, Mary. 2011. "Feminist Conceptions of Power."In *Encyclopedia of Power*, ed. Keith M. Dowding, 1–13. Sage Publications.

Lopata, Helene Z., and Barrie Thorne. 1978. "On the Term 'Sex Roles.'" *Signs* 3 (3) (Spring): 718–21.

Money, John. 1968 "Sexual Deviation: Psychological Aspects." In Sills 1968, 14:209–15.

Morris, Jan. 2002. *Conundrum.* New York: New York Review Books.

Person, Ethel Spector. 1999. *The Sexual Century.* New Haven, CT: Yale University Press.

Phoenix, Charles H. 1968. "Animal Sexual Behavior." In Sills 1968, 14:194–201.

Rosario, Vernon A. 2004. "The Biology of Gender and the Construction of Sex?" *GLQ: A Journal of Lesbian and Gay Studies* 10 (2): 280–87.

Rubin, Gayle S. 1975. "The Traffic in Women: On the 'Political Economy' of Sex." In *Toward an Anthropology of Women*, ed. Rayna R. Reiter. New York: Monthly Review Press.

———. 1993. "Thinking Sex: Notes for a Radical Theory of the Politics of Sexuality" (1984). In Abelove, Barale, and Halperin 1993.

Scott, Joan W. 1988."Gender: A Useful Category of Historical Analysis." In *Gender and the Politics of History.* New York: Columbia University Press.

Sedgwick, Eve Kosofsky. 1990. "Epistemology of the Closet." In Abelove, Barale, and Halperin 1993.

Signs. 1987. Editorial. *Signs* 12 (4) (Summer): 619–20.

Sills, David A. ed. 1968. *International Encyclopedia of the Social Sciences.* New York: Macmillan Company/Free Press.

Smith, Anna Deavere. 2002. "Essay." *Lyle Ashton Harris.* New York: Gregory R. Miller Company/CRG Gallery.

Spivak, Gayatri Chakravorty. 1999. "History." In *A Critique of Postcolonial Reason: Toward a History of the Vanishing Present.* Cambridge, MA: Harvard University Press.

——. 2003. *Death of a Discipline*. New York: Columbia University Press.

Stanton, Domna. 1992. "Introduction: The Subject of Sexuality." In *Discourses of Sexuality*, ed. Domna C. Stanton. Ann Arbor: University of Michigan Press. (pp. 1–46.)

Tirosh-Samuelson, Hava. 2012. "Transhumanism as a Secularist Faith." *Zygon* 47 (4): 1–25.

Tyler, Leona E. 1968. "Sex Differences" In Sills 1968, 7:207–13.

West, Candace and Don H. Zimmerman. 1987. "Doing Gender." *Gender and Society* 1 (2): 125–51.

1 :: BODIES CARROLL SMITH-ROSENBERG

Bodies take form, move, are experienced, assume meanings at specific points in time, within particular material, economic, and demographic settings, in interaction with the cultural forces of their time and place in relation to other temporally located physical bodies, bodies of knowledge, fields of power—in short, in history.

Bodies fill history, marking its transformative crises and quotidian rhythms. The millions of bodies raped and killed during the Spanish "Conquest of the Indies," the millions more transported from Africa to take their places on the sugar, coffee, and tobacco plantations of North and South America. Bodies stacked like cords of wood in Nazi death camps signaled world-changing moments in the construction of knowledge and the deployment of power. More recently, the bodies of raped and murdered women figured the partition of India, the dismemberment of Yugoslavia, the ethnic conflicts in Rwanda and Darfur. On a more mundane level, images of bodies make the Industrial Revolution real to us: the bodies of half-naked women dragging carts in British mines; the stooped, pallid bodies of child laborers; the begrimed bodies of the British working-class women, photographed by Arthur Munby scrubbing the marble stoops of the bourgeoisie (Munby 2000). Today the bodies of malnourished children proffered to us in solicitations from UNICEF and Doctors without Borders embody current disparities between the global North and South. Of course, these swollen and deformed bodies constitute but one part of complex and multilayered class and regional portraits. Behind the lenses that make them real to us are the well-scrubbed bodies of bourgeois reformers intent on observing and "knowing," their bodies at home with the comforts and luxuries industrialization and imperialism make possible.

But still more bodies crowd the pages of history—resisting and protesting bodies, the bodies of maroon warriors in Saint-Domingue and

Jamaica, of Native Americans at Wounded Knee, suffragists' bodies refusing forced feeding, black and white bodies marching to Selma or "occupying" Wall Street, gay bodies at Act Up rallies, defying violent reprisals. And history incorporates still other bodies, metaphoric and discursive—social bodies and bodies politic, bodies of knowledge, of law, of ideology.

Intimate connections bind these bodies to one another. Individuals' bodily experiences depend on the bodies of language that inform those experiences, just as languages and discourses acquire their meanings through exchanges among embodied speakers at specific times and places. Ideological fictions, metaphoric abstractions, bodies politic, especially national bodies politic, are particularly dependent on actual biological bodies, for they come alive only when literal bodies, embedded in particular times and spaces, embrace them as their own true selves. But for this to happen, for the body politic to assume an integrity it has not, it must cloak itself in the rhetoric, the languages, of corporeality, must assume the characteristics of the biological body, its internal cohesion, its "naturalness." In all these varied ways, corporeal and political bodies, the bodies of the empowered and the disempowered, of women and men, of blacks and whites, browns and reds, are locked in a decentering, protean dance of constitutive interdependencies and interactions.

Feminist scholars have long explored these complex patterns of interaction and interdependency. Scholars as disparate as Mary Douglas and Joan Scott insist that there is no "natural" or timeless way to experience our selves, our identities, our bodies. They see both identities and the body as socially and discursively informed. "The social body constrains the way the physical body is perceived," Douglas argues:

> The forms it [the biological body] adopts in movement and repose express social pressures in manifold ways. The care that is given to it, in grooming, feeding and therapy, the theories about what it needs in the way of sleep and exercise, about the stages it should go through, the pains it can stand ... all the cultural categories in which it is perceived ... correlate closely with the categories in which society is seen.... Every kind of action carries the imprint of learning. (Douglas 1970, 93)

But the complex interaction of social and biological bodies is not that easily captured. Transformed by the human mind into a cultural construct, the biological body metamorphoses, becoming a reservoir of affective rhetoric that members of the social body can draw upon to express conflicted and cathected social tensions. Theories of sexuality, purification rituals, pollution fears, the valorization and degradation of body parts—all can be read as symbolic languages in which the physical body is used to speak of social anxieties and conflicts. S[...] and biological bodies fuse, refusing separation.

A cacophony of social dialects spoken by different classes, eth[...] ties, generations, professions, and genders characterizes every heteroge- neous society, a cacophony reproduced differently within the conscious- ness of different social speakers (Bakhtin 1981, 259–422). Power colors these discourses. The languages of the economically and politically domi- nant struggle to deny the legitimacy of more marginal social discourses. During periods of social transformation, when social forms crack open, social dialects proliferate among both the powerful and the powerless at the heart of the metropole and along its colonized margins. Blending and conflicting with one another, these varied discourses challenge the domi- nant discourses. At such times, ideological conflict fractures discourse. At such times, as well, sexuality and the physical body emerge as particu- larly evocative political symbols. Those aspects of human sexuality con- sidered most disorderly are evoked to represent social atomization, the overthrow of hierarchies, the uncontrollability of change. Within this discursive field, those fearful of change define the socially disorderly as sexually deviant, dangerous infections within the body politic. In this way, the fearful project onto the bodies of those they have named social misfits their own desires for social control.

A few examples may be in order. In the turbulent years following the US Civil War, with northern radicals seeking to impose a new ra- cial and political order and thousands, black and white, homeless and on the road, southern whites, fearful of these changes, constituted a met- onymic figure to stand for all the social disruptions they could not con- trol. That figure was the savage black male rapist. Disgust and desire, projection and displacement, radiated through his imagined construc- tion, a process graphically depicted in James Baldwin's "Going to Meet the Man" (Baldwin 1995, 227–49). Raging against that figure (and the lit- eral bodies "he" represented), the fearful protested against a world out of their control. Today members of America's white middle class who again feel the world beyond their understanding deploy other bodies to figure current fears—black inner-city adolescents, lesbians and gays, abort- ing women, Muslim terrorists. Effigies of fear, these bodies are anything but simple metaphors. Fetishes, they are simultaneously sentient bod- ies, whose flesh is literally scarred, whose genitals are literally mutilated, whose lives are literally destroyed by the metaphor-makers.

Conversations, by their nature, are dialogic. Defiantly displaying their own sexuality as symbols of social resistance, the marginal and the scarred also fuse sexual and social disorder, defiantly displaying their

ols of social resistance. Social disarray, discursive
bodies merge, reinforce one another; the dismem-
bolic body speaks of the dismemberment of the body
nventional meaning.

sitioned the physical body within a field of discourses,
eful not to bury it under the avalanche of words, ideolo-
phors that bombard it. The physical body possesses its own
grity. Bodily experiences can at times transcend discourse,
ry argues, pointing to the ways pain explodes beyond the ex-
ability of words to represent it (Scarry 1985). While symbolic
anthropologists and poststructural theorists argue that language constitutes desire, many feminists still insist that desire can also appear within
discourses that have not named it. Despite all our focus on the ideological
and discursive nature of our bodies and desires, the physical body refuses
to disappear from feminist discourse. Feminist philosopher Rosi Braidotti, for example, while marking the ways feminism interrogates the corporeal, insists on women's need to reconnect with their physical bodies,
to entertain a "transmobile, materialist theory of feminist subjectivity."
Insisting on "rethinking the bodily roots of subjectivity," she continues:

> The starting point for most feminist redefinitions of subjectivity is a new
> form of materialism, one that develops the notion of corporeal materi-
> ality by emphasizing the embodied and therefore sexually differentiated
> structure of the speaking subject. (Braidotti 1994, 2–4)

How, embodied in time, are we to map the interplay of these swirling
bodies when we ourselves are caught in the vortex, see and feel only as
parts of those social bodies, speak only in already existing discourses?
How can we position ourselves so that we gain the perspective from
which to chart the dynamic processes that give us form and meaning—
in time?

Bodies and Power

Michel Foucault is the preeminent cartologist of the interplay of bodies,
painstakingly tracing the ways the political and the social construct the
biological and the sexual. While Foucault's work is the subject of serious feminist criticism, he has made significant contributions to feminist
thought, mapping the ways biological bodies and sexual subjects are political constructions, centrally implicated in the rise of the modern state,
modern science, modern systems of power, and the arts of governance.
In the process, he disclosed us all as physical subjects of and to those
knowledge/power systems.

The physical body, its health, sexuality, and desires, are no more natural for Foucault than they are for Mary Douglas. Like Douglas, Foucault focuses on the discursive construction of the body. Like Douglas, he is concerned with the ways constituting the body (discursive representations, definitions and treatments of diseases, who should and who should not reproduce) forms a key component of ongoing social structures. Sexualized bodies, criminal bodies, and diseased bodies, Foucault insists, can only be understood as products of specific temporal and material settings. Universal patterns of causation tell us little about the political construction of bodies or the deployment of power, he argues. Rather, we must focus on the processes by which power, knowledge, and discourses develop and plot the historically specific conditions, the material bases of their production, the ways they then produce biological and sexual bodies, identities, and subjects. We must ask why particular bodies of knowledge, texts, institutions, and practices appear at particular moments in time, trace the ways they coincide with one another, how they overlap, interact, and multiply to produce the physical bodies and psychopolitical subjects of modernity.

But differences as well as parallels exist between Foucault's and Douglas's analyses. Douglas, working within the structuralist paradigm of the 1960s, focused on the harmonious interplay of social and symbolic systems. Foucault, writing during the intellectual, sexual, and political furor of the 1970s and 1980s, focuses on issues of social conflict and control, on the unstable aspects of the body politic, and on the proliferating, protean nature of power itself.

The relation of power to bodies, Foucault argues, began to change in fundamental ways in the eighteenth century when the focus of government shifted from securing a sovereign's power over territory to the arts of policing populations. Surveillance and control of men in all "their relations, their links, their imbrications" became the object of governance that quickly assumed the form of power over life (Foucault 1991, 92). "Power gave itself the function of administering life," Foucault argues, and "it is over life that power establishes its domination." Power, in this new sense, took two interactive forms. One revolved around economic and disciplinary discourses and practices, producing an "anatomo-politics of the human body"; the other revolved around political and medical discourses and practices that produced a "bio-politics of the population." The first "centered on the body as a machine: its disciplining, the optimization of its capabilities . . . its integration into systems of efficient and economic controls" (Foucault 1978, 138–39). The biopolitics of population, on the other hand, focused on the organization of the body in relation to reproduction. It required the state and a host of public and private institutions and groups to study and concern themselves about its health, marriage, and fertility patterns and mortality rates. Together they made biological bodies social problems and the control of those problems the source of proliferating knowledge and power. Health, fertility, and mortality became not natural processes but occasions for "infinitesimal surveillance, permanent controls, extremely meticulous orderings of space, indeterminate medical and psychological examinations,... statistical assessments"—in short, "an entire micro-power concerned with the body" (Foucault 1978, 145–46). It is interesting to think of Foucault's mapping of the operation of power over and through French bodies in relation to slave owners' comparable power over the bodies of their slaves. Foucault does not note this parallel but it was certainly very present in the eighteenth-century Atlantic world, a world in which France played a critical role.

Without doubt a host of French institutions arose to study and manage different aspects of this body—hospitals, specialized medical and scientific associations and journals, police departments and prisons, philanthropic and state welfare agencies, census bureaus, sociology and anthropology departments. Statistics were compiled and disseminated. Case studies accumulated, were analyzed, and transformed into policies that proliferated more studies, more institutions accumulating more knowledge. Classes of experts developed: professional criminologists, medical specialists, sexologists, eugenicists. All became producers of knowledge— and wielders of power. Power both generated these bodies of knowledge and flowed through them as along a giant capillary system penetrating every point in the social body, the body politic. For bodies of knowledge produce power over the bodies *they* "know"—and equally over the bodies *that* "know." For Foucault, bodies of knowledge are multidirectional, ensnaring the knowing body along with the body known. Ultimately, all became enmeshed in ever finer and more extensive systems of knowing until their self-knowledge, their bodies, their desires became parts of the body politic's ever proliferating, ever more protean "will to know." Power in its multiple forms became interconnected, inseparable, continuous (Foucault 1991, 91).

These new knowledges and mechanisms of management sexually saturated entire populations. Women's bodies—their health, their minds, their reproductive systems—became sites of disease and perversion. Childhood was similarly sexualized. From being a time of sexual innocence, childhood became a site of proliferating and perverse sexual instincts, requiring active surveillance by parents, physicians, and teachers. Parents were, themselves, sexually suspect figures. Required by the biopolitics of population to reproduce successive generations of healthy and productive worker-citizens, parents repeatedly threatened to betray their social responsibilities, engage in perverse, nonproductive sexual acts, restrict their birthrate, abort. By the mid-nineteenth century, the family had emerged as a veritable factory of perverse sexualities, "the crystal in the deployment of sexualities," a font of hysterias, venereal diseases, neuroses, sterility, frigidity, incest, and adultery (Foucault 1978, 111). Avoidance of marriage offered no escape. Proliferating sexual discourses snared the single body as well, making the refusal of heterosexuality a physiological and psychological pathology. In these ways, the "institutionalized" modern subject became his or her sexuality. Sexualities became personified as subjects—and all were embedded in specific times and places. For Foucault, the timeless, the universal, did not exist.

Bodies Diverse and Expressive

But for all Foucault's emphasis on the protean and decentered nature of sexualized discourses and bodies of knowledge, in the end he presents us with only one overarching discourse, a single "uniform truth of sex"— that initiated by the brokers of power. The multiple physical and sexual bodies he discusses are fragmented parts of one body of knowledge, one system of power. Foucault neither explored the role the marginal and the disempowered played in the multiplication of sexual discourses— nor did he read their discourses as examples of diversity or as sites of agency and resistance. Feminist, race, and postcolonial scholars have done both, seeking in proliferating sexual discourses evidence of social diversity, listening for the voices of the marginal and the disempowered, reading back from the actions of the oppressed to their theories of power (Dubois 2006).

Theories advanced by British and American symbolic anthropologists who, during the 1960s and 1970s, explored the ways divergent groups within the same society used the biological and sexual body as a reservoir of symbols and metaphors expressive of social tensions and conflicts, prove helpful in these endeavors. We have already considered Mary Douglas's trope of two bodies, her proposal that the physical body can be transformed into a symbolic representation of the social forces that created it. Symbolic anthropologist Victor Turner was equally fascinated with the ways in which the imagination, through metaphor and myth, links physical and social bodies. All symbols are bipolar, Turner argues. At one pole, we find the physical body, sensuous, gross, and timeless; at the other, we find time-specific social structures and relationships, conflicts and anxieties. Individuals and social groups, located at different points in the social body, draw upon the carnality of the physical body to form affective vocabularies expressive of their social experiences and concerns. The physical body assumes its full meaning, Turner insists, only when seen as a culturally specific construct used by specific speakers at specific times to express, reinforce, or protest their social experiences (Turner 1974, 1967).

Heterogeneous societies, especially societies in the process of rapid social transformation, Turner continues, produce a host of divergent symbolic systems in which the physical body and sexuality mark points of social contestation or dis-ease. Different social and economic groups, experiencing economic and demographic change differently, having different degrees of power with which to respond to the changes that transform their world, create differing sexual discourses, images, and fantasies, debate with and condemn one another, and depict a future of perfection or of degradation—all in graphic physical and sexual imagery. At least some of those caught in the vortex of massive and unremitting social transformations respond by attempting to capture and encapsulate such change within a new and ordered symbolic universe. When the social fabric is rent in fundamental ways, bodily and familial imagery assume ascendancy, for when the world spins out of control, the last intuitive resource of any individual is her or his own body and especially its sexual impulses. That, at least, many feel they can and must control. Others in the same society embrace change and glory in disorder, making the explosive force of the male orgasm a symbol of social disorder that they experience as liberating and empowering. Still others, battling for social power or self-expression, represent their social and political rivals as sexually violent and dangerous, sexual subjects who must be controlled. These discourses interact with one another and refuse the discourses of the socially dominant, those empowered by Foucault's proliferating bodies of sexual knowledge.

America in the first half of the nineteenth century was a world in flux. Political, social, and economic revolutions transformed modes of production, institutional arrangements, and demographic patterns. Expectations of time and space altered, as did the functions, structures, and internal dynamics of the family, gender, and generational relations. Some Americans' obsession with categorizing the physical—especially the sexual—with describing the abnormal, and with defining the legitimate, can be read as an effort to impose order upon the chaos of the nonsexual world. Other Americans developed radically different sexual discourses, especially those conventionally silenced by the formal institutions and traditional discourses of Victorian America. Women, the formerly enslaved, and young men marginal to the new industrial economy, as well as older men in marginal professions and religious radicals, used sexual imagery to express their experiences of social change and conflict (Smith-Rosenberg 1985, 79–89).

Choosing four from the vast array of nineteenth-century sexual discourses, let us explore the ways symbolic analyses can expand upon Foucault's sexualized system of power, deepen our understanding of the social body's complex structures, highlight diversity, and map the gender and generational conflicts that characterized Jacksonian America. Three of these four discourses took the form of sexual melodramas; the fourth, of comic inversion and satire. All focused on adolescence, its sexual desires and dangers. The melodramas presented the adolescent as a frail and vulnerable figure, beset by sexual enemies and dangers. Only in the satiric sexual comedy did adolescents emerge as sexually empowered, socially autonomous—and joyous. At the same time, we must remember that these speakers, these discourses, existed within a world framed by the bodies and discourses of the excluded: Native Americans, relentlessly driven to the margins of the continent; the enslaved, denied all political, social, and economic rights; defeated Mexicans, whose lands were fodder for the expansion of slavery.

Early in the 1830s fears of youthful male masturbation began to obsess bourgeois male reformers (Smith-Rosenberg 1980, 51–70). In medical and educational tracts, they constituted a sexual melodrama in which a vulnerable male adolescent emerged as the problematic figure. With puberty, powerful sexual urges tempted him to masturbate, visit prostitutes, marry early, and revolt against father and family. Sexual danger, physiological and social transgressions fused. If the young man lived outside the family, violated an elaborate system of dietary laws, adopted habits associated with the new commercial centers—his lower organs and instincts would become uncontrollable, destroy his body's hierarchical order, and lead to a progression of diseases, insanity, and death. If, on the other hand, the young man remained an obedient son within the rural, patriarchal family, or a faithful apprentice within his master's household, if he married late and limited his sexual activity within marriage to an infrequent procreative act, he would be rewarded by becoming one healthy link in an endless chain of fathers and sons, stretching unbroken into a physiological and social millennium in which health and order would reign.

A second, strikingly different—if equally fabricated—young man danced charismatically across the male Jacksonian imagination. Joyfully embracing change and christening it "progress," the autonomous young man of the frontier was the satiric image of the fragile and dependent son of the eastern reformers. Wild and rough-featured, dressed in animal skins, and pitted daily against a wild and relentless nature, Davy Crockett and his cohort of riverboat men, trappers, and backwoods squatters fought with their fathers, broke out of apprenticeships, rebelled against education, and escaped into a mythical and phallic world of rivers and rifles (Smith-Rosenberg 1982, 325–50). There they drank heavily, masturbated, whored, and experimented with homosexuality. Women, as presented in the *Crockett Almanacs,* differed little from the rowdy men. Interestingly, the almanacs neither respected nor reinscribed normative gender polarities.

Jacksonian men did not hold the stage of sexual discourse alone. Jacksonian women, neither wild frontier women nor bold Bowery girls, but pious, bourgeois women, month after month inscribed graphic and lurid stories of sexual seduction in *The Advocate of Moral Reform and Family Guardian,* their female-edited and widely read magazine (Smith-Rosenberg 1971, 562–84). (At times the US Postal Service refused to accept issues of the *Advocate,* condemning them as pornographic.)

The women's melodrama differed as radically from the men's stories as the men's differed from one another. Neither wild nor fragile male adolescents crossed their pages. Masturbation did not concern them. Rather, they obsessed over the seduction and exploitation of young girls. For twenty years, the *Advocate* told two stories about poor young women in the city. The first was an economic narrative of women forced to labor in the sweated needle trades, as washerwomen or domestics, driven by low wages into prostitution and beggary. The second told a melodramatic story of innocent and vulnerable farming daughters, seduced by wily urban men and carried off to the city, to prostitution, insanity, and death. The country, in this story, was a precommercial Eden of loving mothers and daughters. The city, in contrast, was a male preserve. Stock exchanges and men's clubs, hotels and theaters, gambling houses and brothels lined its streets. Tabooed to respectable matrons, it was a place of danger, excess, and dissipation.

The *Advocate*'s pious readers, however, did not hesitate to enter it. Representing themselves as the spiritual mothers of lost daughters, they marched into the bastions of male privilege and power—brothels and theaters, the public prints and reform podiums. At a time when bourgeois women were to remain silent and at home, these women asserted their right to public and political roles, lobbying state legislatures to reform prisons and raise the age of sexual consent. In these many ways they fought openly with bourgeois men for sexual control of their homes and social control of their cities.

But theirs was not the only story of seduction and exploitation. African American women appropriated the *Advocate*'s format to tell of their own experiences. Slavery, they argued, sexually exploited young women far more viciously than industrialization did. In *Incidents in the Life of a Slave Girl,* Harriet Jacobs painfully detailed what she claimed had been the most terrifying aspect of her slave experience. "The slave girl is reared in an atmosphere of licentiousness and fear," Jacobs wrote. "The lash and the foul talk of her master and his sons are her teachers. Resistance is hopeless." Nor was the slave girl the only victim. "The slaveholder's sons," Jacobs continued, "are ... vitiated, even white boys ... by the unclean influence everywhere around them," adding ominously, "Nor do the master's daughters ... escape" (Jacobs 2000, 51). On Jacobs's pages, the South had become a bordello, a sore on the body politic, a place of danger for women, black and white alike.

With the exception of Jacobs's narrative, these sexual scenarios were fantastical confabulations.[1] Power did not flow through their pages. They did not exert control over the sexuality of others. Yet all permitted men and women, buffeted by relentless change, to express social fears and resentments, to dream of possessing the power to alter or escape their worlds. On their pages, sex—especially sex outside of marriage and heterosexuality—symbolized the disruption of traditional social order, the thrust of change itself. Some Jacksonians embraced that change, gloried in defying tradition. The lawlessness and violence of the Crockett frontier proved especially attractive to the rootless young men of the new cities. Its unmapped wilds reflected their experiences in the new industrial cities and economies, where they too wandered mapless and outside traditional structures. The bravado, the fantasies of freedom and sexual power, offered men, at sea in a world they could neither understand nor control, a vicarious sense of power—and, yes, sovereignty. They felt momentarily that they could rule their world.

This same sexual bravado and violence alarmed male sexual and medical reformers, who sought through sexual fantasies to reconstitute an orderly and patriarchal world. Physical disarray—when the "lower organs," stimulated by pleasures associated with commerce and the new cities, gained ascendancy over the higher organs, the brain, the head, and the heart—symbolized the fragmentation of an earlier hierarchical order of deferential politics, patriarchal authority, and an urban working class under bourgeois control. Powerless either to prevent relentless economic and social change or to control young men's social and sexual behavior, the authors of the masturbation tracts sought through their sexual alarms and admonitions to give themselves a sense of controlling what was uncontrollable—young men loose from social ties, tossed about by the process of change itself.

Women's sexual melodramas differed radically from men's symbolic systems, providing us with an opportunity to study women's appropriation and transformation of already existing discourses to express their social experiences. In the process, we can also examine the costs discursive and ideological appropriations entail.

The myth of the True Woman lay at the heart of the *Advocate*'s melodrama. Originally designed by men to make women docile wives and pious rearers of children, it appeared on the pages of the *Advocate* so reworked that its affirmation of women's innate purity and piety affirmed men's innate sexual degeneracy. No longer constraining bourgeois women, it now empowered them to battle bourgeois men for domestic dominance and a public presence. But only at the personal cost of espousing a repressive, asexual subjectivity. The women traded an active sexuality for social authority and political agency.[2]

Within their complex symbolic system, prostitution (i.e., commercial sex) symbolized the dangers of the commercial economy itself. Men's unquenchable sexuality figured male power within the new economy. The powerless prostitute stood for working-class women exploited by the new wage-labor system. But more, the prostitute represented all women's powerlessness within the new capitalist economy. Middle-class women knew that a father's or husband's death or bankruptcy would expose them to the harsh realities of the working-class woman's life. The mother/daughter metaphor underscored their sense that America's emerging economic and social arrangements disempowered and oppressed all women, middle and working class—that gender united, more than class divided, women. However, mothers and daughters are not sisters, not equals. The metaphor thus suggests a unique female vision of emerging class relations, an intimate relation between working- and middle-class women, one in which bourgeois women exercised power, not over men or the male-constituted economy, but over working-class women—their domestics, mantua makers, washerwomen, the objects of their reforming philanthropy. Pious mothers, they knew what was best for working-class women and worked to constitute them in their own image.

Harriet Jacobs's appropriation of the *Advocate*'s social purity scenario adds a further layer of complexity to our picture of discursive appropriation and translation. Charges of slaveholders' sexual degeneracy and exploitation were Jacobs's most powerful critique of slavery. They helped her gain the attention and sympathy of middle-class white women. Indeed, white women's social-purity rhetoric authorized Jacobs as a political writer, as a spokeswoman for her people, and as a leading abolitionist. But social purity was a two-edged sword. Empowering Jacobs, it also branded her as a fallen daughter and denied her claims to domestic propriety. Further, it bound her, as it bound white middle-class women to an asexual sexual persona (Hartman 1997, 102–12).

Which brings us back to Foucault's linking of sex and power, his representations of sexuality as "a great surface network in which ... the incitement to discourse, the formation of special knowledges, the strengthening of controls and resistances, are linked to one another" (Foucault 1978, 105–6). But as feminist scholars, we return to Foucault only after having first explored the ways sexual discourses provide diverse groups—women as well as men, slaves as well as masters, the youthful and marginal as well as the wielders of authority—with ways to both protest and order their worlds. Sexual discourses tell us a great deal about the production and proliferation of power. They tell us even more about social diversity, conflict, and the human *imaginaire*.

Bodies Politic

Feminist scholars are critical of Foucault for failing to read the sexual discourses of the nineteenth century as maps of social complexity and conflict, and especially of the emotional life of women and other marginal groups. But they have registered a second, in some ways far more telling, criticism of Foucault's treatment of bodies in time. For all his insistence on grounding bodies in time and space, Foucault's bodies exist outside the racial and colonial categories that shape the world of modernity from the Renaissance to the present. Feminist scholars, students of race, and postcolonial theorists insist that any analysis of social bodies and bodies of knowledge must focus on the multiplicity and diversity of sexualized bodies that characterize modern heterogeneous societies. If knowledge and power, interwoven, flow through physical and sexual bodies, proliferating and penetrating the body politic, then they do so through specific constructions of gender and race, mediated always by class and colonial status. One cannot talk of modern systems of power or bodies of knowledge without simultaneously talking of race, gender, and class. Cultural historian Evelyn Brooks Higginbotham forcefully argues this point in her pathbreaking essay "African-American Women's History and the Metalanguage of Race" (Higginbotham 1992). As does legal historian Mary Frances Berry. Exploring thousands of United States appellate court decisions from Reconstruction to the present, Berry presents gender, race, and class as protean and interactive categories that assume meaning only in relation to one another as they work in tandem to inform and reform the knowledge/power grids of modernity—and our understanding and deployment of "justice" (Berry 1999).

Feminist scholars of the Renaissance and the early modern period were among the first to stress the centrality of race, gender, and colonial status to the production of modernity and especially to the sexualities and subjectivities of modernity. Early modern mappings of the imperial world, literary critic Valerie Traub insists, simultaneously inscribed routes of trade and conquest, represented Europe as the home of white patriarchal heterosexuality, and presented Africa as a site of transgressive sexual practices (Traub 2000). Literary critic Kim Hall and early modern historian Jennifer Morgan have traced the way Europe constituted itself by coloring and engendering its others, representing Africans and Americans as sexualized naked women, who both welcomed European male penetration and, through their corporal differences, reaffirmed the physical and cultural superiority of the European (Hall 1995; Morgan 1997). For four hundred years, these bodily differences were used to confirm the legitimacy of conquest, colonization, and enslavement.

Bodies in time were not only central to the emergence and justification of European colonial domination or the creation of bourgeois class structures. They also lay at the heart of what feminist political theorist Carol Pateman calls the greatest political fiction of modern times—the social contract (Pateman 1988). As European explorers and cartologists were mapping states of nature in Africa and America—and legitimating slavery in those states—European political theorists were rooting theories of popular sovereignty and republican political forms in the European man's emergence out of a state of nature. European men, renouncing the barbarism, violence, and anarchy of the state of nature, theorists like Hobbes, Pufendorf, and Locke all argued, contracted to establish republics dedicated to the protection of men's lives, liberties, and property. But only the life, liberty, and property of those men who had maintained their freedom while in the state of nature. Only they could participate in the social contract. Only they were endowed with liberty and sovereignty. While still in the state of nature, women, their bodies weaker than men's, handicapped by the care of their children, lost their freedom to dominant men. But women were not alone. Men facing death—at least those charged with capital crimes or those defeated in a just war—also resigned their natural rights, accepting a life of slavery. Significantly, within classic contractarian thought, these events did not occur in Europe, where slavery had long disappeared, but in Africa, which was seen as remaining in a state of nature, outside the promise of freedom as a natural right (Bernasconi and Mann 2005). In all these ways, gender and racial distinctions modified the more radical implications of Enlightenment liberalism—most especially its celebration of the universality of unalienable rights, its vision, in feminist scholar Nancy Stepan's words, of a liberal political body, "disembodied,"unmarked" by class, race, or gender (Stepan 1998). As a result, the new republics born of the Age of Revolution, with little or no debate, excluded women and persons of color from their revolutionary body politics. Haiti is, of course, the great exception. As Robin Blackburn argues, Haiti, the first nation in history to constitutionally outlaw slavery, redeemed the radical promise of the Age of Revolution and isolated itself from the rest of the Atlantic world (Blackburn 2010).

Central to Enlightenment thought, bodies remain critical to feminist liberal philosophers and critical legal theorists. Take Drucilla Cornell's reconstruction of liberal legal theory to confirm women as full and equal members of the republican political body. Equal inclusion and protection of rights as women cannot be achieved, Cornell insists, by focusing on gender. Within liberal discourses, gender embodies difference. Liberalism and legal systems based on liberal premises, such as the one in the United States, cannot incorporate bodily and social differences under its promise of equality, since equality presumes sameness. Full recognition of the rights of women and of persons of color can only be achieved by shifting the feminist focus from one of seeking legal and constitutional recognition of women's gendered differences and needs to one of representing women's needs in gender-neutral, universalist terms. Only by representing women's gender-specific demands as a demand for the protection of the bodily integrity and the sexual imaginary of all citizens, female and male, black and white, homosexual and heterosexual,can feminist goals be achieved (Cornell 1995, 3–27). In the process, Cornell expands her concept of bodily integrity to include not only the person's biological body and sexuality, but her/his imaginative body, indeed the entire realm of the imagination and of the language upon which imagination depends. Cornell insists that bodily integrity demands "space for the renewal of the imagination and the concomitant re-imagining of who one is and who one seeks to become" (Cornell 1995, 5). This reimagining requires equitable access to language and symbolic forms upon which the imaginary domain and one's sense of self-value depends.

But in many ways Cornell's concept of equivalent rights and gender-neutral demands pragmatically sidesteps the fundamental tension within liberalism—that between its celebration of the sameness of all persons and the universality of unalienable rights and its simultaneous acceptance of a world structured around hierarchical systems of difference. This tension, this contradiction, may have been more obvious at the birth of liberal republics during the Age of Revolution (when Thomas Jefferson could simultaneously celebrate universal rights and slavery), but, as Cornell's work demonstrates, it continues to this day. As recent Supreme Court decisions concerning affirmative action demonstrate, liberalism continues to view difference, and most especially different bodies with different needs, with alarm.

Embodying the Nation, Excluding the Other

A last, critically important body remains to be examined: the national body politic. Closely related to but distinct from the engendered and racialized political bodies we have just considered, the national body politic constitutes the foundational core of a people's identity, its members' sense of belonging to a coherent political and cultural community. Foundational, it is also fabricated. As Benedict Anderson argues, nations are imagined communities, promising a sense of connectedness and cohesion that diversity in modern heterogeneous societies renders simultaneously artificial and necessary (Anderson 2005). To create an imagined community out of the multiple diverse and heteroglossic bodies that inhabit modern nations requires the construction of a series of imagined others, whose differences from the idealized national subject overshadow the differences that divide actual citizens. National identities contrast idealized national bodies to the bodies of these others, which are excluded from the body politic as different, inferior, and dangerous. Exclusion is the key word. National bodies politic, Stuart Hall reminds us, "function as points of identification and attachment only because of their capacity to exclude, to leave out, to render 'outside,' 'abjected'" (Hall 1996). So positioned, those others become, to quote Judith Butler, "site[s] of dreaded identification," against which those of us who claim inclusion repeatedly identify ourselves (Butler 1993, 3). Depicting our national others as deformed or dangerous, we reaffirm their corporality along with the need to exclude, to expel their bodies from the national body politic. To keep these others at bay (many internal to the nation-state, but many foreign as well), we formally and informally create inadequate educational systems, do little to eliminate poverty, pass restrictive naturalization laws, build towering walls, and post border guards and guard dogs. Racist stereotyping at home, coupled with extremist anti-immigration rhetoric, give voice to these mechanisms of exclusion—which the black youths who crowd our prisons and the forty-two million stateless persons who wander the globe—or, in our imagination, clamor at our borders—literally embody.[3]

But a nation's literal and imagined others cannot be so easily expelled. The projected embodiments of our own most feared and hated qualities, they are our fanaticized discursive and psychological doubles, our own dark (self)reflections. To paraphrase Pogo, we have met the Other and he is us. Further complicating our Tar Baby relation with our national others as figures of the transgressive, they point to forbidden possibilities, tempt us down proscribed paths. Consciously and unconsciously, we seek to incorporate them into our sense of self—at times in response to deep-rooted fears of isolation and loss, at other times for qualities we imagine they have and we long to make our own. As long as we fear difference, as long as we disdain our complex patterns of gender, racial, and ethnic diversity, they will remain essential components of our national bodies politic. We need their confabulated otherness to imagine ourselves as a coherent whole. But the more we struggle to keep them at bay, the more they incite our enraged enactments of their exclusion, enactments that have found expression throughout the global North's long history of racism, xenophobia, and sexism. Caught in an intimate—sometimes deadly—embrace, we cannot separate from our others, whom we need, dread, and desire (Smith-Rosenberg 2010a).

To more fully explore this pattern of rage and desire, exclusion and introjection, let us look at the complex hate/love relation that has bound European and Native Americans together over the five hundred years we have shared a continent. One of the basic dilemmas facing European Americans is how to render coherent a fundamentally incoherent identity. On the one hand, we see ourselves as heirs of a rich European culture stretching back through Shakespeare, Chaucer, and Beowulf to classical antiquity. On the other, we see our idealized national characteristics of independence, love of liberty, and self-reliance as rooted in the American continent, its riches, and its challenges. But how do we legitimate our presence on this continent, justify our claims to the name "American"? Our anxious need to establish our Americanness (and at the same time retain our European connections) may go far to explain our relentless desire for American land. We feel the need to take the vastness, the riches, the very superabundance of America into ourselves. And not just Native American lands, but the strength and power we believe Native Americans gained from their deep connections to the land: the love of freedom that only the land's vast expanses could give; a sense of honor, uncorrupted by the niceties of refined culture; and above all, a fierce, wild courage in defense of liberty. In short, to assert our Americanness we have greedily introjected both the land and its peoples, seeking to make it/them a central component of our unstable, contradictory sense of self. Yet at the same time, we have long condemned the "red man" as savage, lazy, unproductive, drunken, and unworthy of the continent he inhabited. How else could we, as Europeans, justify our possession of his lands, claim to have replaced him as the true Americans? The desire to possess and the desire to destroy entwine within our most intense sense of being Americans. Our European American children, in their innocence, repeatedly perform our national ambivalence—dressing as Indian chiefs and princesses on Halloween, playing cowboys and Indians the rest of the year (Smith-Rosenberg 2010b).

Now, in what might well be called the Age of the Stateless Refugee, or of the Illegal Alien, a new set of other bodies alarms us, dark and threatening bodies we imagine prowling around our borders, encircling our nation. And as earlier with Native Americans, we savagely engage with those bodies, this time, however, in virtual—not literal—combat. In endless video game after endless video game, or mesmerized before the big screen in 3-D, we savagely strike back against invading aliens. Yet the end of one game marks another's beginning. Final victory forever eludes us. We never free ourselves from the bodies of our alien others. Riveted by dread and desire, we have incorporated them into our very being.

Conclusion

The modern body politic, from Locke through Foucault to Cornell, is structured around bodies—biological and discursive, imaginary and political. Inclusion and exclusion, sameness and difference, equality and freedom, political subjectivity and political oppression—all are always embodied and sexualized. To study bodies in time is to study their protean and productive interaction. Perhaps the most innovative theorist of the body in time and in motion is dance theorist Susan Foster, who, in her "Choreographies of Gender," calls on feminist theorists to take the literal body seriously, to refuse "the dichotomization of verbal and non-verbal cultural practices," to recognize "the thought-filledness of movement and the theoretical potential of bodily action." Only then will feminists disrupt "the traditional divisions of labor between verbal and nonverbal acts by fusing the experiential and 'feminine' cultivation of bodily presence to the intellectual and 'masculine' analysis of representation." Only then will feminists "impart to any body a specificity that must be acknowledged; yet ... also connect that body to other cultural orchestrations of identity." Only then will feminists truly begin to theorize gender "as an unstable, non-originary, historically specific orchestration ... of performed sociality" (Foster 1998, 28–29).

Notes

1. Scholars wonder about the accuracy of some of Jacobs's statements about her youthful sexual experiences. They point to significant omissions and silences, and while they do not question the broad outline of her story, they do suspect that she may have decided not to present full details to a critical white audience.

2. Late eighteenth-century novels of seduction, in contrast to those of the mid-nineteenth-century tales, deployed illicit sexuality to suggest alternative, empowering roles for women along with young women's desire for a public voice and a right to liberty and the pursuit

of happiness. See, for example, Hannah Webster Foster's *The Coquette* (1797) and Smith-Rosenberg (1987, 9–27).

3. Miriam Ticktin (2011) presents a fascinating discussion of the role the bodies of the stateless play in France's no-immigration policies and their enforcement.

References

Anderson, Benedict. 2005. *Imagined Communities: Reflections on the Origin and Spread of Nationalism*. London: Verso.

Bakhtin, M.M. 1981. "Discourse in the Novel." In *The Dialogic Imagination*. Ed. Michael Holquist. Trans. Caryl Emerson and Michael Holquist. Austin: University of Texas Press.

Baldwin, James. 1995. "Going to Meet the Man" (1965). In *Going to Meet the Man: Stories*. New York: Vintage.

Bernasconi, Robert, and Anika Maaza Mann. 2005. "The Contradictions of Racism: Locke, Slavery, and the Two Treatises." In *Race and Racism in Modern Philosophy*, ed. Andrew Valls, 81–108. Ithaca, NY: Cornell University Press.

Berry, Mary Frances. 1999. *The Pig Farmer's Daughter and Other Tales of American Justice: Episodes of Racism and Sexism in the Courts from 1865 to the Present*. New York: Knopf.

Blackburn, Robin. 2010. "Haiti, Slavery, and the Age of Democratic Revolution." *William and Mary Quarterly* 63:643–74.

Braidotti, Rosi. 1994. *Nomadic Subjects: Embodiment and Sexual Difference in Contemporary Feminist Theory*. New York: Columbia University Press.

Butler, Judith. 1993. *Bodies That Matter: On the Discursive Limits of Sex*. New York: Routledge.

Cornell, Drucilla. 1995. *The Imaginary Domain: Abortion, Pornography, and Sexual Harassment*. New York: Routledge.

Douglas, Mary. 1970. *Natural Symbols: Explorations in Cosmology*. New York: Routledge.

Dubois, Laurent. 2006. "An Enslaved Enlightenment: Rethinking the Intellectual History of the French Atlantic." *Social History* 31.

Foster, Susan. 1998. "Choreographies of Gender." *Signs* 24.

Foucault, Michel. 1978. *A History of Sexuality*. Vol. 1, *An Introduction*. Trans. Robert Hurley. New York: Pantheon.

———. 1991. "Governmentality." In *The Foucault Effect: Studies in Governmentality*, ed. Graham Burchell, Colin Gordon, and Peter Miller. Chicago: University of Chicago Press.

Hall, Kim. 1995. *Things of Darkness: Economies of Race and Gender in Early Modern England*. Ithaca, NY: Cornell University Press.

Hall, Stuart. 1996. "Introduction: Who Needs Identity?" In *Questions of Cultural Identity*, ed. Stuart Hall and Paul Du Gay. London: Sage.

Hartman, Saidiya. 1997. *Scenes of Subjection: Terror, Slavery, and Self-Making in Nineteenth-Century America*. New York: Oxford University Press.

Higginbotham, Evelyn Brooks. 1992. "African-American Women's History and the Metalanguage of Race." *Signs* 17:251–74.

Jacobs, Harriet. 2000. *Incidents in the Life of a Slave Girl, Written by Herself*. Ed. Maria Child, with an introduction by Jean Fagan Yallen. Cambridge, MA: Harvard University Press.

Morgan, Jennifer. 1997. "'Some Could Suckle over Their Shoulder': Male Travelers, Female

Bodies, and the Gendering of Racial Ideology, 1500–1770." *William and Mary Quarterly* 54:167–92.

Munby, Arthur. 2000. "Munby Reappraised." Special issue, *Journal of Victorian Culture* 5.

Pateman, Carol. 1988. *The Sexual Contract*. Palo Alto, CA: Stanford University Press.

Scarry, Elaine. 1985. *Bodies in Pain: The Making and Unmaking of the World*. New York: Oxford University Press.

Smith-Rosenberg, Carroll. 1971. "Beauty, the Beast, and the Militant Woman: A Case Study in Sex Roles and Social Stress in Jacksonian America." *American Quarterly* 23.

——. 1980. "Sex as a Symbol in Victorian America." *Prospects* 5.

——. 1982 "Davey Crockett as Trickster: Pornography, Liminality, and Symbolic Inversion in Victorian America." *Journal of Contemporary History* 18.

——. 1985. *Disorderly Conduct: Visions of Gender in Nineteenth-Century America*. New York: Knopf.

——. 1987. "Misprisoning Pamela: Representations of Gender and Class in Nineteenth-Century America." *Michigan Quarterly Review* 26.

——. 2010a. "Preface." In *This Violent Empire: The Birth of an American National Identity*, ix–xvii. Omohundro Institute of Early American History and Culture. Chapel Hill: University of North Carolina Press.

——. 2010b. "Dangerous Doubles." In *This Violent Empire: The Birth of an American National Identity*, 191–287. Omohundro Institute of Early American History and Culture. Chapel Hill: University of North Carolina Press.

Stepan, Nancy. 1998. "Race, Gender, Science, and Citizenship." *Gender and History* 10.

Ticktin, Miriam. 2011. *Casualties of Care: Immigration and the Politics of Humanitarianism in France*. Berkeley: University of California Press.

Traub, Valerie. 2000. "Mapping the Global Body." In *Early Modern Visual Culture: Representation, Race, and Empire in Renaissance England*, ed. Peter Erickson and Clark Hulse, 44–97. Philadelphia: University of Pennsylvania Press.

Turner, Victor. 1974. *Dramas, Fields, and Metaphors: Symbolic Action in Human Society*. Ithaca, NY: Cornell University Press.

2 :: CULTURE   KATE CREHAN

Culture, according to Raymond Williams, one of the most influential literary critics of the second half of the twentieth century, is "one of the two or three most complicated words in the English language." This, Williams explains in his invaluable *Keywords*, is mainly because the term *culture*, with "its intricate historical development, in several European languages ... has now come to be used for important concepts in several distinct intellectual disciplines and in several distinct and incompatible systems of thought" (Williams 1983, 87). The two primary meanings I shall be dealing with in this essay are the anthropological understanding of culture as a way of life characteristic of a particular group of people, and culture understood as the practice and the products of artistic creation, that is, culture as music, literature, painting, sculpture, theater, film, and so on.

The history of a term can be very revealing; how particular concepts have come to mean what they do at a given moment is always related to larger historical contexts. The meanings concepts acquire are never completely fixed but evolve continually; there is a constant back-and-forth between the relatively stable meanings they acquire over time and the uses to which people put them in particular contexts. Concepts' existing meanings have considerable power simply because to an important extent human beings cannot but perceive their world in terms of the names or concepts they have inherited.[1]

A Complicated Word

The word *culture* in English, Williams tells us, began as "a noun of process: the tending *of* something, basically crops or animals" (1983, 87; Williams's emphasis), a meaning that is still present in words like agriculture or horticulture. Later culture also began to be used to refer to a process of human development, and this became its main sense until the beginning of the nineteenth century. Very gradually, however, beginning as early as the late seventeenth century, culture began to acquire some of its modern senses. *Civilization*, a term which emerged during the eighteenth century and that by the end of that century had "behind it the general spirit of the Enlightenment, with its emphasis on secular and progressive human self-development" (1983, 58), was originally closely linked to the concept of culture. Well into the nineteenth century, civilization and culture were used as synonyms. It was specifically at the end of the eighteenth century and the beginning of the nineteenth, however, that culture assumed its modern meanings in English, which were strongly influenced by what the terms *culture* and *Cultur*, later spelled *Kultur*, were coming to mean in French and in German, respectively.

The emergence of this new cluster of meanings can be linked to the seismic historical events taking place throughout Europe at this time. This is the period when Enlightenment thinking was erupting throughout Europe, the French Revolution was overturning old hierarchies, and, a little later, Napoleon at the head of the revolutionary French army was marching through Europe redrawing national borders. To understand how these ideas and events merged together for people at the time, we might think of the cluster of associations bundled up in the notion of "modernity" today. Disentangling the concept of modernity from the history of the global North[2] and the power of contemporary capitalism is so hard that most people, in the South as well as in the North, find it almost impossible to imagine a modernity that does not in some form replay Euro-American history. Similarly, for those living through the events of the late eighteenth and early nineteenth centuries, the Enlightenment seemed inextricably bound up with France and its advancing armies. Partially as a reaction against the Enlightenment and everything it stood for, a very different current of thought emerged that became associated with the Romantic movement. In place of the Enlightenment's secular rationalism, Romantic thinkers celebrated the emotions, irrationality, and authentic "tradition." In addition, and closely linked with both Romantic and Enlightenment currents of thought (although in complicated and varying ways in different countries and at different times), various forms of nationalism asserting the "rights of nations" to their "national territory" emerged. One of the new senses that culture acquired in the context of this swirling, historical maelstrom was that of a people's way of life. And it is this meaning that the much-cited anthropologist Clifford Geertz had in mind when he declared in a famous essay that culture is the concept "around which the whole discipline of anthropology arose" (Geertz 1973a). This anthropological understanding of culture has now become one of the term's dominant meanings, and it is this meaning on which I focus for the most part in this essay.

A key figure in the genealogy of this meaning of culture is the German Romantic philosopher Johann Herder (1744–1803), who attacked the Enlightenment teleology that saw "civilized" European culture as the culmination of all human history. He insisted—and this was his radical departure—that we should not speak of "culture," in the singular, but of "cultures." For Herder, different nations and different time periods had different cultures, and even within a single nation there were different cultures associated with different social and economic groups. The larger impulse from which this claim emerged is nicely caught in this passage from his unfinished *Ideas on the Philosophy of the History of Mankind* (1784–1791) which has a very modern ring to it:

> Men of all the quarters of the globe, who have perished over the ages, you have not lived solely to manure the earth with your ashes, so that at the end of time your posterity should be made happy by European culture. The very thought of a superior European culture is a blatant insult to the majesty of Nature. (quoted in Williams 1983, 89)

In this usage, culture ceases to be a synonym for civilization, becoming instead an alternative, even an antonym. Used first by the Romantics particularly in reference to "national" and "traditional" cultures (which tended to be seen as constituting organic wholes), it came later to be used to contrast older, more "authentic" cultures, centered on the needs of human beings, with the supposedly soulless, mechanical character of emerging industrial "civilization."

Herder's insistence that different peoples have different cultures, their own ways of seeing and doing things, can be seen in part as a reaction against the universalizing claims of Enlightenment thinkers. It was argued that their stress on humanity as an undifferentiated whole, with a single history moving toward a single goal guided by universal human reason, had led to the excesses of the French Revolution. As Napoleon's revolutionary army marched through Europe, remaking it in its own Enlightenment image, resistance, including that of German intellectuals, frequently took the form of nationalist claims, according to which different "peoples" have a right to autonomy. At the same time, the ideas and language of nationalism also drew on Enlightenment thinking; the discourse of universal human rights, a legacy of the Enlightenment, and the discourse of Romanticism are entangled in complicated ways. It is in this complex historical context that the anthropological understanding of culture as referring to the ways of life of particular groups of people, each with their own culture, has its roots.

Crucially, the nationalist notions sweeping Europe shaped how cultures were imagined; cultures were seen as bounded wholes of the same broad type as nationalities. A culture, like a nationality, tended, for example, to be thought of as referring to a specific people, associated often with a specific territory and characterized by a particular worldview, expressed through a common language. It was often assumed, explicitly or implicitly, that authentic cultures were rooted in the past. Cultures, like nationalities, were seen as having a *right* to exist and to defend themselves, for instance, against a modernizing state's attempts to change them. The point here is not that all cultures were necessarily assumed to share all of these features, or to have these rights, but that this cluster of associations was carried along, even if only implicitly, with the notion of culture as it developed its distinct anthropological meanings. The circumstances of its birth, then, can be seen as having given the notion of culture "around which the whole discipline of anthropology arose" a certain shape and as having left embedded in it certain persistent traces.

Culture acquired yet another meaning in the late nineteenth and early twentieth centuries: the *products* of intellectual and, especially, artistic activity. This can be seen as extending the sense of culture as "a general process of intellectual, spiritual and aesthetic development" (Williams 1983, 90) to include all that is taken as representing this development and helping to bring it about. I shall come back to this meaning of culture in the final section of this essay. For the moment, however, I want to stay with the anthropological notion of culture and its implications for those interested in mapping the gendered contours of different societies. I will then go on to look at a rather different way of thinking about culture, the approach found in the writings of the early twentieth-century Italian political theorist and activist Antonio Gramsci.

Anthropology and Culture

Probably no anthropologist would dispute that culture has been a central concept in anthropology in both the United States and Europe since its establishment as a recognized discipline in the early twentieth century. As is common with emerging disciplines, anthropology in its early days was hospitable, albeit within certain limits, to members of groups traditionally marginalized within the elite realms of academic life, such as Jews and women. The two towering figures in the establishment of anthropology as a discipline, Franz Boas in the US and Bronislaw Malinowski in Britain, both had numerous women students, many of whom—such as Margaret Mead and Ruth Benedict in the US, and

Audrey Richards and Lucy Mair in Britain—would themselves become dominant presences within anthropology.

And not only was anthropology welcoming to women practitioners; its content, too, included women. Given that the discipline's subject matter was commonly defined as the explication of different ways of life in their entireties, and that kinship and marriage were among its central concerns, it would have been difficult for anthropologists not to pay at least *some* attention to the lives of women. Nonetheless, as second-wave feminist anthropologists would point out, while women might not be absent from anthropological accounts, they were seen, for the most part, through male eyes, their activities and perspectives marginalized. Anthropologists from the countries of the North took with them to the field preconceptions as to what was worth recording that originated in their own male-dominated societies, which themselves ignored or denigrated women's experiences. In line with this, anthropologists' accounts of other cultures, even those collected by women, tended to see things from the vantage point of those cultures' dominant men. The work of feminist anthropologists would draw attention to this taken-for-granted "male bias" within anthropology and make it increasingly difficult for any anthropologist not at least to pay lip service to the importance of this critique.[3]

Almost at once, however, the anthropological feminist critique was itself subjected to critical scrutiny by other feminists. They noted, for example, that it was too often taken for granted that a woman anthropologist, simply by virtue of being a woman, could understand the women she studied, no matter how remote her experiences from theirs, in a way that a male anthropologist could not. Such a belief, it was pointed out, rests on a highly problematic assumption that "woman" is a universal category to be found in all societies. This criticism was leveled, for instance, at an article by Sherry Ortner, one of the pioneers of feminist anthropology, that had been widely read and much praised when it appeared in 1974. In this article, "Is Female to Male as Nature Is to Culture?," Ortner sought to explain what she thought to be the universal subordination of women by men in all societies. Drawing on Simone de Beauvoir's *The Second Sex*, she argued that men were associated universally with culture and women with nature, that culture was valued more highly than nature, and that women were consequently devalued.

One problem was that this supposedly universal category, "woman," tended in practice to assume the shape of what "being a woman" meant in the anthropologist's own society. Not only, it was argued—particularly by anthropologists of color—did this overlook important differences between societies; it also ignored important differences, such as those of class and ethnicity, *within* the feminist anthropologists' own societies of the North. Along with an emphasis on the importance of not treating women as an undifferentiated category, there was an increasing awareness among feminist anthropologists that if we want to understand women we also need to study men, and to analyze the often complicated ways in which men's and women's lives are entangled. In other words, there was a shift from studying women to studying gender. By the 1990s, the study of gender was established as one of the primary concerns of anthropologists. It can be said that the work of feminist anthropologists in the last forty years has in certain important respects transformed anthropology as a field. To mention just a few examples, there are Marilyn Strathern's (1972, 1988) and Annette Weiner's (1976) gendered rethinkings of power in Melanesia; the work of Rapp (Ginsburg and Rapp 1995; Rapp 1999) and Strathern (1992) on the social impact of new reproductive technologies; and Sylvia Junko Yanagisako and Jane Fishburne Collier's feminist rethinkings of kinship theory (Collier and Yanagisako 1987).

And yet the relationship between anthropology and feminism has been, as Strathern noted in 1987, an awkward one. Part of the reason for this is that the anthropological concept of culture does not always fit very well if our concern is to map the gendered landscapes women and men inhabit. Culture, as it has been theorized by mainstream anthropology, tends to have buried within it certain implicit assumptions stemming from the conditions of its birth in the historical moment of Romanticism and nationalism that hinder rather than help this mapping. And these ghosts have proven difficult to exorcise completely, simply because they are such a foundational element within the concept of culture.

One powerful assumption, for instance, which stems ultimately, I would argue, from the Romantic notion of cultures as authentic, organic wholes, is that cultures are in some sense *systems*, not necessarily homogeneous or conflict-free assemblages, but patterned wholes of some kind; and that these wholes, in some sense, constitute discrete and bounded entities. By way of example, let me quote one of Geertz's definitions of culture:

> The culture concept to which I adhere ... denotes an historically transmitted *pattern* of meanings embodied in symbols, a *system* of inherited conceptions expressed in symbolic forms by means of which men communicate, perpetuate, and develop their knowledge about and attitudes towards life. (Geertz 1973b, 89; emphasis added)

This kind of a priori assumption of an overarching system, within which gender cleavages are contained, tends to subordinate the fractures of gender—and, indeed, other fractures such as those of race and class— to some superordinate "culture."

In recent years the idea that cultures constitute bounded wholes has been much criticized. Anthropologists nowadays often spend a lot of time emphasizing the fluid, shifting nature of cultural boundaries and the overlapping and intermingling of cultures. Nonetheless, a focus on difference, on the existence of distinct cultures, which in some sense hang together, however fluid and shifting their boundaries, remains, I would argue, a basic concern for many anthropologists.

It should be remembered that anthropology is a discipline that grew up specifically focusing on the world beyond the North and on perspectives other than those of the North and of modernity. That concern may have been implicated in the whole colonial enterprise, and have been to some extent the product of an imperialist endeavor, but it was a concern that took the South seriously and tried in some measure to understand its societies on their own terms. Understandably, anthropologists have on the whole been anxious to hold onto this attention to difference, to a view of the contemporary "globalized" world that attempts to see how things look from a perspective other than that of its hegemonic centers. Ortner, in a much-cited survey of anthropological theory written in the mid-1980s, expressed a characteristic anxiety in her critique of the then very influential political-economy approach in anthropology. What worried her was what she saw as the abandonment of anthropology's traditional concern with "other worlds" beyond the North. In her view, "The attempt to view other *systems* from ground level is the basis, perhaps the only basis, of anthropology's distinctive contribution to the human sciences" (Ortner 1984, 143; emphasis added).

Even James Clifford, a theorist whom many regard as having radically challenged accepted anthropological notions of culture, seems to want to hold on to some notion of coherence. In *Routes*, for example, we find him writing:

> *Routes* continues an argument with the concept of culture. In earlier books, especially *The Predicament of Culture* (1988), I worried about the concept's propensity to assert holism and aesthetic form, its tendency to privilege value, hierarchy, and historical continuity in notions of common "life." I argued that these inclinations neglected, and at times actively repressed, many impure, unruly processes of collective invention and survival. At the same time, *concepts of culture seemed necessary if human systems of meaning and difference were to be recognised and supported.* Claims to coherent identity were, in any event, inescapable in a contemporary world riven by ethnic absolutism. (Clifford 1997, 2–3; emphasis added)

While Clifford is unhappy with the concept of culture—in part because of its "propensity to assert holism," the assumption that cultures are bounded entities—he is unwilling to abandon it. Not only does he see the existence of "cultures" in the contemporary world as an inescapable reality, the concept of culture is for him important because it names "human systems of meaning and difference."

A very different way of thinking about culture, which does not make this kind of a priori assumption of coherence and which seems to me to have much to offer those interested in the mapping of gender, is to be found in the writings of Antonio Gramsci. Gramsci, a political activist who was one of the founders of the Italian communist party, was imprisoned in 1926 after Mussolini and his fascist party took power in Italy. During his long incarceration, Gramsci wrote what have come to be known as the prison notebooks, in which he reflects on the nature of power, analyzing how and why certain regimes of power perpetuate themselves while others are overthrown. The role of culture is a major theme. And while gender and its significance was not a major topic for Gramsci, the implications of his theorization of culture can be extremely helpful for those interested in issues of gender.

The first major translation of the prison notebooks into English appeared in the 1970s (Gramsci 1971), and they were soon being read and cited by anthropologists in both Britain and the United States. Gramsci, however, has a very different approach to culture than that associated with mainstream anthropology—something that the anthropologists who cite Gramsci have not always appreciated. I develop this argument in detail in *Gramsci, Culture and Anthropology* (2002). Here I want only to look briefly at the kind of entity culture is for Gramsci and to illustrate a little of what such an approach might mean in practice, particularly for those concerned with questions of gender.

Gramsci and Culture

While Gramsci wrote extensively about culture, his primary concern was not the mapping of different cultures. For him, the analysis of society does not, as it does for Clifford, center on tracing out the relations between "human systems of meaning and difference." Neither for Gramsci are cultures primary movers in human history, as they are in the nationalist discourse within which the concept of cultures as particular ways of life emerged. When reading Gramsci, we need always to remember that he was a Marxist and an activist; his central concern was the radical transformation of capitalist society. For him, the actors in human history are not cultures but *classes*. This is not to say, of course, that Gramsci saw classes as the *only* actors in history, just that for him it is such large groupings, of people who occupy a similar economic position in a given society, that ultimately explain large and genuinely revolutionary epochal changes, such as the emergence of the bourgeois world out of feudalism or the possibility of the overthrow of capitalist society. As a political activist, it is this kind of epochal change that was his ultimate concern. At the same time, Gramsci sees issues of culture as at the heart of any revolutionary project, since culture is for him how the inequality that is class is lived, and how people inhabit and understand their world inevitably shapes their ability to imagine how it might be changed, and whether they see such changes as desirable or feasible.

It should be stressed that the concept of class in Gramsci is both nuanced and complex, far from a simple identity defined purely by economic relations. A fundamental theme running through the prison notebooks is the profound, but hard to map, relationship between culture and basic economic relations. It is certainly true that, for Gramsci, basic economic relations provide the ultimate dynamic of history—but only *ultimately;*[4] we are talking here about a highly mediated relationship. Equally importantly, "culture" is never seen by Gramsci merely as an epiphenomenon, or simple reflection of more fundamental economic relations. While he retains throughout the prison notebooks the Marxist language of base and superstructure, in practice he transcends this overly simplified metaphor of stacked layers. Crucially, "culture" in Gramsci never represents any kind of autonomous domain; it is for him both ideational and material, both the imagined world and the hard material realities that underpin this world. And just as he does not oppose culture to some more fundamental economic base, neither does he oppose it to history; culture is, rather, a precipitate that is continually generated in the course of history. In other words, the ways of being and living in the world that we think of as culture can be seen as particular forms assumed by the interaction of a multitude of historical processes at particular moments of time—forms that are inherently in flux, however fixed and unchanging they may appear. Gramsci's whole approach to culture, therefore, is far from any kind of traditional anthropological mapping out of distinct and bounded "cultures."

To illustrate some of the implications of a Gramscian approach to culture in the context of gender, I look first at *Gender, Class and Rural Transition: Agribusiness and the Food Crisis in Senegal*, a thought-provoking study of agricultural transformation in Senegal in the 1970s by the feminist economist Maureen Mackintosh, and then more briefly at *The Woman in the Surgeon's Body*, a study of North American women surgeons by Joan Cassell. Neither study draws explicitly on Gramsci, but in different ways both begin to suggest what a Gramscian understanding of culture might look like in practice.

Class, Culture, and the Analysis of Rural Transition

The setting for Mackintosh's study is the establishment by Bud Antle, a giant American agribusiness corporation, of two large estates in Senegal in the early 1970s, on which it proposed to grow fruit and vegetables for the European market. Initially, the Senegalese government was enthusiastic. Bud's management argued that employment on the estates would provide a valuable source of income for local villagers and that the estates' dry-season operations, based on irrigation, would not compete with villagers' existing wet-season farming activities. In the event, the project turned out to be a miserable failure, and by the end of the decade Bud had abandoned its estates and Senegal. Nonetheless, for a few years Bud and its employment opportunities were dominating presences in the lives of the surrounding villagers. It is the impact of this presence that *Gender, Class and Rural Transition* explores.

Mackintosh's study is very much about class. It is not that she sees the villagers as neatly divided into distinct classes; class for her, as for Gramsci, is rather a way of naming certain kinds of patterned inequality. Neither Mackintosh nor Gramsci, it should be stressed, see these contours of inequality as translating into the realities of individuals' daily lives in any simple way. A key theme of the book is the very different, and not always predictable, implications Bud could have for different villagers; women, men, the married, the unmarried, those with access to plenty of land, those with insufficient (or no) land all experienced Bud differently. What Bud did was to create, or at the very least exacerbate, certain systematic inequalities. Not that there was necessarily a process of class formation within the villages themselves; rather, we should see the establishment of the Bud farms as contributing to the larger pattern of class formation within the Senegalese economy as a whole. Central to this process of class formation was gender.

Mackintosh's study is also very much about culture. She herself does not use the term—culture is not a central theoretical concept in her discipline, economics. Her case study, however, is certainly concerned with a people's way of life—their culture—and how this was being transformed. She tells us, for instance, that her basic argument is that "long-range changes induced in the social and economic organization of rural life and work are the most important effects of such projects [i.e., the Bud project]" (Mackintosh 1989, xiii). One of my reasons for selecting this case study is precisely that Mackintosh does not frame her study in terms of "cultural" transformation; the changes she observed were for her equally about material realities, ideas, and beliefs.

I also chose Mackintosh's book because of her approach to an issue much argued over by feminists: the relation between the inequalities of class and of gender. Mackintosh refuses to separate out these inequalities; for her, they are inextricably entangled:

> One of the most general results of feminist inspired research [i.e., since the 1970s] has been the understanding that class experience—and class change—is gender specific. This book provides evidence for the view that, not only do men's and women's experience of class differ, but changes in the relations between men and women, including the sexual division of labour, is one of the ways in which new class structures become established. (Mackintosh 1989, 35)

In one of the three villages Mackintosh studied, Ponty, the villagers—many of them migrants who had moved to Ponty because of the employment opportunities offered by Bud—no longer farmed. Ponty, she writes, "remained in economic terms an obstinately homogeneous village of wage workers" (1989, 162). This homogeneity, however, did not extend to the respective working lives of women and men. In Ponty, as in the other villages studied, domestic labor—all the crucial but unpaid tasks of child care, cooking, cleaning, care of the sick and the elderly, and so on—was, as is so often the case, the sole responsibility of women. Women usually moved to their husbands' homes on marriage, and it was these in-marrying women who were expected to take on the household's domestic labor; a new wife, for example, would be expected, and would herself expect, to take over the work of her mother-in-law. Households in Ponty may have lost the access some once had to land and the labor to work it, but membership in a household still gave its head (normally male), its male members, and sometimes some female members (female relatives of the husband were considered exempt from such domestic responsibilities) "access to the products of the domestic work of other women" (1989, 162). In the context of the new employment opportunities offered by Bud, "A familiar process was occurring whereby women's work within the household constrained their participation in the Bud labour force, thus reinforcing their subordinate place within both institutions" (1989, 163). As regards class formation, Mackintosh writes:

> The establishment of these new types of hierarchy, especially new forms of gender division, is an integral part of the process of class formation. Bud, by its presence, was contributing to the formation of a working class in Senegal, and a crucial part of that process of formation was the creation of new forms of household adapted to the economic pressures of dependence on insecure wage incomes. These adaptions spelled the end, for the people involved, of older household forms adapted to the needs of

a farming society, and the gradual stabilization of a new social organization with new sets of assumptions. And, in a manner all too familiar, this
involved the creation of a new, transformed yet still subordinate position
for women within the new class structure. (1989, 163)

This "gradual stabilization of a new social organization with new sets of
assumptions" can be seen as the emergence of a new culture—as long
as, following Gramsci, we think of cultures as how certain class positions are lived. Associated with the culture Mackintosh sees as emerging are certain broad assumptions, some of which represent continuity
with the past (e.g., domestic work is the responsibility of women) and
some of which are new (e.g., there exists a "proper" gender division of labor within wage labor, which employer and employees should respect).

One of the striking findings of Mackintosh's study is the astonishing
rapidity with which a fixed gender division of labor established itself on
the Bud estates, in what she terms "an all too familiar process: within
three years, that familiar category of 'women's work' had been created
on the estate. That is, certain jobs, classified as women's jobs, had come
to have attached to them lower pay and worse conditions than the jobs
predominantly done by men" (1989, 172). At the same time, all the jobs
classified as skilled or semiskilled, including clerical work, tractor driving, and mechanics, were defined as male jobs. Among the unskilled jobs,
too, there was a clear gender division of labor:

> Of the jobs classified as unskilled, certain were done exclusively by men:
> irrigation work, hand hoeing, melon and pepper harvesting. The others,
> packing produce and bean harvesting, were done mainly, but *not* exclu-
> sively, by women. The men's teams specifically excluded women; the jobs
> "where the women are" were sometimes done reluctantly by young men
> who could find no other work. (1989, 172; Mackintosh's italics)

There was no technological imperative for this gender division of labor. It was due in part, as Mackintosh argues, to women's domestic
responsibilities—all those responsibilities that tend to make them
"less reliable" as workers outside the home. But the gender division of
labor was also underpinned by certain taken-for-granted assumptions
about the "proper" and "appropriate" division of labor between men and
women. Both the Bud estates' managers and the local villagers tended
to agree that men ought to have privileged access to the more desirable
jobs, and that the pay for the women's jobs should be lower. The women
might complain that they were paid too little, but they did not argue that
they ought to be paid the same as the men. This is an important aspect of
the "all too familiar process" identified by Mackintosh, whereby the new

demands of a capitalist labor process, which in terms of its strictly technological needs is indifferent to workers' gender, race, ethnicity, and so on, are in practice interwoven with existing cultural expectations.

Mackintosh also saw firsthand the first embryonic stirrings of what we could term a working-class culture. During her fieldwork, there were work stoppages on both of the Bud estates. Interestingly, in both cases it was the women workers who went on strike: on one estate, over local women's claims to priority in hiring over women from elsewhere; on the other, over an attempt to impose a piecework rather than an hourly rate on women packing workers, which would have decreased their wages. In each case, the workers won at least some concessions from management. It should be emphasised, as Mackintosh is careful to do, that there is no simple cause-and-effect relationship between the establishment of enterprises like the Bud farms and the emergence of a new working-class culture. We are, as Gramsci stresses, dealing with complex historical processes, and how particular individuals and groups respond can never be predicted in any straightforward way.

Capitalist enterprises, particularly those trying to establish themselves in places not already saturated with the culture of the unencumbered "free" market and "free" labor, are normally happy to adopt those aspects of local culture that do not affect their ability to turn a profit, and that may ease their integration into the local society. For their part, the villagers learning to live with Bud were engaged in a complicated dance: they knew the power of what confronted them and that it was a reality to which they could not shut their eyes. Their concern tended to be to gain what benefit they could from it, while minimizing its adverse effects on what they held dear. The problem, as Mackintosh's study reveals, is that the cumulative effects of perfectly rational strategies on the part of individuals can set in motion long-term structural changes that are difficult to reverse.

In Kirene, another of the villages in which Mackintosh carried out fieldwork, she was able to observe this kind of structural change. In the early 1970s, when Bud first arrived on the scene, Kirene still had a reasonably viable village economy based on farming. Within this economy, there was neither a land nor a labor market: land was under the control of groups of kin and was allocated by household heads (normally male) to those within their households; claims to labor also depended on relations of marriage and kinship. A significant element of the farming system was joint fields, cultivated collectively by groups of households. Crucially, this was a farming system based on nonmonetized production relations. It did not, however, represent some age-old "traditional" pattern, unchanged since time immemorial. When land had started to be in short supply, the villagers had adapted, partly by changing their mix of crops. Like African farmers elsewhere, local people, with or without extension agents, had readily adopted new crops when these were seen to offer advantages. In Kirene, both groundnuts and vegetables were grown as cash crops, but the staple food in the village, and the heart of the local farming system, was millet, which was rarely grown for sale. It was millet that was normally grown on the collective fields.

The jointly farmed millet fields were an important safeguard against hunger in a village in which many households frequently ran short of basic foodstuffs. This kind of cooperation, however, was becoming less common. And while Bud was not the sole cause, it was an important contributing factor. Already, before Bud, there was increasing pressure on the land, and it was becoming harder for the heads of the household groupings, responsible for allocating the land for collective fields, to find the necessary land. Bud (which established its farms on land appropriated from the villagers without compensation) both increased that pressure and competed for the labor needed to work the collective fields. Mackintosh describes what happened:

> Once the collective fields disintegrated, part of the rationale for the household grouping went.... When exchange labour of this sort is based on no strict accounting of obligations, then it depends on both a sense of fairness and a concept of reciprocal obligation: people contribute when they can and benefit when they must. If people began dropping out of the work of the collectivity for their own material benefit as wage workers, then strains quickly arose. A situation of systematically uneven participation by different millet farmers in a collective field because of wage labour obligations was unlikely to continue for many years without destroying the institution, and the effects were already visible in strain and mutual resentment. (1989, 83)

This system of collective cultivation depended, we could say, on the maintenance of a culture of reciprocity. And the material basis of such a culture and its sustaining set of assumptions tend to decay together. Once such a system ceases to be practiced, it is very difficult to revive. In this case, the presence of Bud, and the Kirene villagers' attempts to adapt to it, including their readiness to take up the employment opportunities it offered, had the effect of radically undermining the reciprocal culture on which their previous farming economy depended so heavily.

What was happening in Kirene can be seen as an example of a more general and gendered process common to the commoditization of societies worldwide. Commoditization occurs when a society's production is geared toward goods for sale, rather than for direct consumption, and people obtain the things they need, or want, not through their own production but by buying them. In other words, production and consumption are mediated by the market. And what happens when there is a shift away from nonmonetized production relations in a farming system is the development of an increasingly clear divide, familiar from contemporary industrial societies, between what is recognized as "real" production (the market-based production of commodities, which for the most part takes place outside the home and uses wage labor) and noncommoditized production (the domestic labor that takes place within the world of the household and the family). In the noncommoditized world of the family, cultures of reciprocity in varying forms retain their importance. It may sound odd to some to talk about "production relations" in the context of domestic labor, but this is only because, in contemporary industrialized societies, economic production has come to be identified with the production of quantifiable value in the context of market relations. One of the major contributions of feminist economists like Mackintosh is to insist that we widen the conventional view of production and productivity to include *all* those activities that provide for its members' needs and wants, and not just those produced within market relations. The rearing of children and the care of family members may be unpaid work, but it is certainly vital and it deserves to be seen as an integral part of a society's overall production. A corollary of this is that how this (frequently unpaid) labor is organized, and who is given the responsibility for performing it, is an important dimension of any society's class landscape.

In the next section, we move from rural Senegal to North America. My focus here is on culture, gender, and power. While Gramsci himself wrote little about gender, his approach to the problem of power seems to me to have much to offer those trying to understand the lived reality of gendered power relations. The example I have chosen to illustrate this comes from a world that represents modern technological skill at its most advanced: the operating room of the contemporary American hospital. "Culture" is sometimes thought of, particularly in popular understandings, as something that only others have. Multiculturalism, for example, is rarely thought of as including mainstream white American culture in its basket of "world" cultures, and yet that too represents a way (or ways) of life.

When Women Enter the Men's House

Joan Cassell is an anthropologist who began studying the elite world of American surgeons in the 1980s. In her 1998 study *The Woman in the Surgeon's Body* she focused on the small but growing number of women surgeons. Cassell, like Mackintosh, does not make use of Gramsci, but thinking through her rich material on the perhaps changing but still at that time overwhelmingly male-dominated world of the operating room in terms of Gramsci's notion of hegemony can begin to suggest some potentially productive ways of approaching issues of power and gender.

The meaning of *hegemony* in Gramsci has been much argued over.[5] Part of the problem is that nowhere does he give us a simple definition, and in different places in the prison notebooks the term is used in apparently contradictory ways. In general, Gramsci sees a continuum of power; at one pole is direct coercion through brute force, at the other, willing consent. Often Gramsci places hegemony at the latter pole, defining it as *consent* organized by civil society, as opposed to *coercion* effected through the apparatus of state power (see, for instance, Gramsci 1971, 12). Elsewhere, however, Gramsci does not oppose civil society/hegemony and the state/coercion in this way, writing, for instance, "by 'State' should be understood not only the apparatus of government, but also the 'private' apparatus of 'hegemony' or civil society" (1971, 261). Hegemony in Gramsci is thus a highly fluid and flexible term with no single definition; rather than being a precisely bounded theoretical concept, it simply names the problem with which he is concerned: how are the power relations that underpin various forms of inequality produced and reproduced? What in any given context constitutes hegemony can only be discovered through careful empirical analysis. While Gramsci himself has little to say about the nature of power in the context of gender, his approach to the problem of power can help us understand how gendered power relations are lived.

In the 1990s, Cassell writes, being a surgeon in the United States was still seen as a quintessentially male occupation. As in other male-identified occupations—soldier, test pilot, firefighter—there were "ritualised ordeals for initiates, active male bonding, and profound distrust and exclusion of women as participants" (Cassell 1998, 18). Cassell compares the entry of women into surgery (by 1993 5 percent of US surgeons were women, up from 1 percent in 1970) to women entering the sacred all-male men's houses of New Guinea. Women surgeons in the operating room often seemed, as Cassell puts it, "bizarrely out of place to [surgery's] martial masculine practitioners" (1998, 12). These female bodies, whether consciously or not, were seen as the wrong bodies in the wrong place. One female surgeon explained the double bind in which she found herself: to the male surgeons with whom she worked, a woman surgeon, if she was good at her job, was not really a woman but rather "a dog or a lesbian"; meanwhile, any properly feminine woman was assumed to be incompetent (1998, 42). To be a *good* woman surgeon, according to this logic, is a contradiction in terms. Nor can a woman insist that she is not a woman surgeon but simply a surgeon:

> Alas, a woman surgeon who thinks of herself as "one of the guys" shows a tragicomic resemblance to Winnie-the-Pooh holding onto a balloon and floating up into the sky asking hopefully if he does not resemble a black cloud. No, you look like a bear with a balloon, Pooh is told. (1998, 210)

Cassell's study, based on participant observation in operating rooms and extensive interviews with women surgeons, leaves no doubt that the culture of the operating room in the 1990s was one in which men dominated. There was what we might term an entrenched male hegemony within the world of American surgery. But how was this hegemony enforced? To survive the brutal years of surgical training anyone, man or woman, needed to be pretty tough. Those who were not were soon weeded out. How is it, then, that the highly educated women who become surgeons, who are, in general, like their male peers, "confident, commanding and competitive" (1998, 1), seemed nonetheless to be so successfully disciplined by male power? Following Gramsci, we can see this male hegemony as involving both coercion and consent; both the iron fist that compels submission; and the apparently willing acceptance by the women themselves of surgery's macho ethos and practices. I lack space here to do more than point to a couple of examples, but I hope they will suggest something of the complex ways in which coercion and consent can be entangled.

One of the women Cassell interviewed explains how she dealt with the stress of surgical training by not allowing herself to acknowledge certain realities. She had simply refused to realize, for example,

> how sick it is to be a surgical resident. It's not even so much a gender thing as just someone so thoroughly controls your life.... You work endless hours, and you just have to suck it up. You can't ever get mad or show that—not only because that wouldn't be taken well, but because *there is nothing you can change*. You just have to put up with it. (Cassell 1998, 122; my emphasis)

I stress this woman's comment that "there is nothing you can change" because the notion of consent contained within that of hegemony does not necessarily imply enthusiastic endorsement; it is enough that people feel there is no other option, that this is how the world is and you had better get used to it.

Cassell describes a number of incidents in which women training to be surgeons were subjected to various forms of intimidation. Men, too, might be intimidated, but there were particular gendered forms used against women that played on their perceived unsuitability. Stories of individual incompetent women, for instance, were used to enforce compliance in others. Cassell writes of one woman who was continually teased by being compared to another woman, Jennifer, who had preceded her and who "was hated by everybody." Jennifer's final sin had been to become pregnant, not once but twice. According to Cassell, "Many programs seem to have a Jennifer-who-did-everything-wrong whose technical, moral, and behavioral errors are used by seniors to warn junior women: *you* had better do everything right" (Cassell 1998, 109–10). A trainee surgeon who may well have been the only woman in her program was judged, and felt herself judged, not merely as an individual but as a representative of her whole gender. Moreover, it was the senior surgeons (nearly always men) holding up the specter of "Jennifer-who-did-everything-wrong" who wielded the power that determines whether a trainee surgeon, after investing many grueling years and much money in her training, would in fact qualify. And many of them did not—a further specter that disciplined their successors into compliance. Control over conditions of employment and basic resources are important components of this kind of male hegemony.

It is not surprising that women who survive the long and rigorous years of training and do qualify as surgeons have often internalized a good deal of the macho martial ethos of their profession. They have, in other words, been socialized into the male-dominated culture of the world of surgery. However, the very fact that more women are entering the field, together with other wide-ranging changes in the organization of American medicine, may be chipping away at the image of the godlike and very male surgeon on his plinth. The culture of surgery may itself be changing. A passage from the prison notebooks in which Gramsci talks about the relation between the individual and his or her culture is relevant here. Gramsci is reflecting on how a language contains its own specific conception of the world and how we are all from our first conscious moments already within culture:

> Is it better to take part in a conception of the world mechanically imposed by the external environment, i.e. by one of the many social groups in which everyone is automatically involved from the moment of his entry into the conscious world ...? Or, on the other hand, is it better to work out consciously and critically one's own conception of the world and thus, in connection with the labours of one's own brain, choose one's sphere of activity, take an active part in the creation of the history of the world, be one's own guide, refusing to accept passively and supinely from outside the moulding of one's personality? In acquiring one's conception of the world one always belongs to a particular grouping which is that of all

the social elements which share the same mode of thinking and acting.…. We are all conformists of some conformism or other, always man-in-the-mass or collective man. (Gramsci 1971, 323–24)

Cultures here are particular groupings made up of "all the social elements which share the same mode of thinking and acting," and we all belong to various forms of grouping: "We are all conformists of some conformism or other." The crucial distinction Gramsci wants to draw here is between an unthinking, "mechanical" adoption of the culture given by the social milieu into which we are born, and a critical and conscious working out of our own "conception of the world." There is no assumption here that these different conceptions of the world constitute distinct and coherent systems; they are, rather, complex and in many ways incoherent assemblages. Also, while we can in some sense choose to belong to a culture with the potential to "take an active part in the creation of the history of the world," this always involves a struggle with external forces that act to "mold" our personality. We are of necessity social beings, always already part of various social worlds, but through conscious, critical activity we have the potential to change our culture.

Gramsci's stress on culture as individuals' critical engagement with the various social worlds into which they are born, so as to go beyond them to create new cultures, is relevant to Cassell's discussion, toward the end of her book, of the Association of Women Surgeons (AWS). Throughout her book, Cassell stresses the isolation most of the women she studied faced during their training. There were few, if any, other women in their training programs. Even when there were, it seems the women did not band together to confront the male hegemony and its frequently abusive treatment of women. The AWS would seem to offer a possible site for women surgeons to come together and take an active part in the creation of a different surgical culture that would challenge the existing male hegemony, something that is almost impossible for an individual woman to do on her own. Cultures can be transformed by the actions of individuals but only when—sometimes knowingly, sometimes unknowingly—they act in concert.

"Women's Literature"

So far I have focused on culture understood as "a way of life." In this final section of this essay I want to turn to culture's other main contemporary meaning: "the independent and abstract noun which describes the works and practices of intellectual and especially artistic activity" (Williams 1983, 90). Explorations of gender and culture in this second sense have gone in three overlapping directions. Notably, all three have included "high" culture (Shakespeare, Picasso, Beethoven), "folk" culture (storytellers, quilters, blues singers), and "popular" culture (TV comedies, comic strip artists, Madonna and other performers). The first and perhaps most common direction has been the study of *representations* of gender. How have men and women been dramatized, viewed, and portrayed? Have there been particular patterns of masculinity and of femininity? Have men been strong (except for gay men) and women weak? If women have been strong, have they been valued or feared?

The second direction comprises studies of the production and reception of culture. Who has been permitted to have access to the technologies of culture? If, for example, women are barred from movie studios, it is hard for them to become movie directors. Has the creation of culture been thought more appropriate to persons of one gender? In late nineteenth-century America, women could engage in creative work, but their domain was thought to be the more genteel arts. And does one gender have more control than the other over the judgment of culture, over the assessment of which works have greater value, beauty, and meaning?

The third direction has been the study of the history of culture, cultures, and cultural works. Have our histories accurately analyzed the work of both men and women, and of all creative men and women? To illustrate these three directions, in this section I look briefly at the shifting artistic reputation of the German novelist Sophie von La Roche (1730–1807). This is a story that takes us back to the emergence of Romanticism— a historical moment crucial to the development of the anthropological concept of culture.

My account of La Roche is taken from *The Author, Art, and the Market: Rereading the History of Aesthetics*, in which Martha Woodmansee, a historian, examines the origins of the modern meaning of art. These origins are closely linked to culture's later development as meaning creative works and practices. Woodmansee includes a short chapter that looks at the place of women in this story and at the "acts of exclusion" that rendered women producers of art invisible and established the role of women in art as primarily that of audience or muse. The case of La Roche provides a concrete instance of this process.

The new interest in women artists of all kinds, fostered by feminist scholarship, has done much to restore La Roche's reputation as a pioneering and hugely influential German novelist. Previously remembered chiefly as the "muse" of one of the major male figures of German literature, Christopher Martin Wieland (1733–1813), to whom she was briefly engaged, she was in fact Germany's first acclaimed woman novelist. Her first novel, *The Story of Fräulein von Sternheim* (*Geschichte des Fräuleins von Sternheim*), was published in 1771, when she was forty years old. The book was an immediate sensation, reprinted three times within a year of publication. Although originally published anonymously under the editorship of Wieland, with whom La Roche maintained a close friendship until her death, the book's authorship was soon revealed. It was rapidly translated into Dutch, French, Russian, and English, and La Roche became famous throughout Europe, going on to publish four more novels, numerous stories and essays, and an anthology, as well as founding a journal. Among *The Story of Fräulein von Sternheim*'s many admirers was Herder, the thinker who played such an important role in transforming "culture" into "cultures." Another was Johann Goethe (1749–1832), whose characterization of the sensitive and romantic young Werther was, according to Woodmansee, strongly influenced by *Fräulein von Sternheim*.

Wieland's original introduction reveals a lot about how women writers were regarded at the time, and who were thought to be their audience. Wieland had advised and encouraged La Roche while she was writing *Fräulein von Sternheim*, and he helped her get it published. To the modern ear, however, the introduction he wrote sounds extraordinarily defensive. He apologizes profusely for making the work public; he knows that La Roche "never intended to write for the world or to create a work of art" (quoted in Woodmansee 1994, 107), but wrote it thinking that it would never be seen by anyone but Wieland and herself, except perhaps, if he approved, their respective children. It is Wieland who has taken the step of making it public, and he hopes she will forgive him. Foreseeing that the book will have its detractors, he attempts to forestall them by himself drawing attention to its faults: "Dear as she is, considered as a work of intellect, a literary composition, indeed, even as just an ordinary German composition, your Sternheim has defects which will not go unnoticed by detractors" (quoted in Woodmansee 1994, 107). Wieland's defensiveness has been read either as a way of deflecting criticism from "a reading audience already deeply prejudiced against scribbling women" or (and this is Woodmansee's preferred reading) "with an eye to extending and deepening such prejudice" (Woodmansee 1994, 106). Whatever may have been Wieland's true motives, his introduction takes it for granted—and assumes his readers will also take it for granted—that women cannot be expected to produce great literature. If a woman is to enter the hallowed halls of literature, she needs to be carefully ushered in by a male writer, and once there should modestly take her place in some dim corner; no true "womanly" woman would ever display any eagerness to enter the public world of literature. A similar logic is found by Cassell more than two hundred years later among male surgeons who cannot accept that a "real" woman could be a good surgeon.

As Woodmansee points out, Wieland, while drawing attention to *Fräulein von Sternheim*'s aesthetic failures, is far from suggesting that La Roche should revise and improve it. Rather he assumes that, as a woman author, this is not in her power. The power of the book, he argues, is the result not of art but of nature, writing, for example, that the heroine is "something that art could never have achieved as effectively as here where nature was at work" (quoted in Woodmansee 1994, 107). This identification of women with nature, and by implication men with art, again calls to mind Ortner's 1974 essay "Is Female to Male as Nature Is to Culture?" While men, it would seem, produce art as a conscious creative act, women do not, any more than a plant produces flowers consciously.

But while women may not have been thought capable of producing great art, they *were* seen as an important audience. Wieland stresses the value of *Fräulein von Sternheim* for women readers. Justifying his decision to publish the book, he says he could not "resist the urge to present to all the virtuous mothers and charming young daughters of our nation" a book that would help teach wisdom and virtue "among [their] sex, and even among [his] own" (quoted in Woodmansee 1994, 107). Throughout Europe at this time women made up a large and important part of the reading public, particularly for novels. The novel was still a relatively new genre, and one that tended to be regarded by the guardians of high culture with a suspicion similar to that with which contemporary cultural mandarins regard video games. Those who championed the novel tended to stress its potentially valuable educational effect, particularly for women, who were in general barred from any serious, intellectually demanding education. However, arguments along these lines, like those of Wieland, can be seen, Woodmansee argues, as helping to create a particular category of literature, "women's literature." These were works that in general were considered not to be in the same class as the great works of literary art but were thought appropriate for a female readership. It is this category—one that is still with us today—to which the writings of female authors were normally assigned.

In this essay I have looked at the two main contemporary meanings of culture: as a way of life and as creative practices and works. Each of these usages is equally valid; they just belong to different conversations in different academic disciplines: anthropology and the social sciences, on the one hand, and literary studies and the humanities, on the other. The two usages do, however, overlap in some interesting ways. If we think of the literary, humanities' usage as emerging out an earlier understanding of culture as the process by which an individual develops, this suggests a range of questions about the relation between how human beings come to realize their full potential and, in Williams's phrase, "the practices of art and intelligence" that help or hinder this process. And this in turn suggests yet more questions about the relation between creative practices and works and culture in the anthropological sense, since the products of art and intelligence recognized as culture are always embedded in, and to some extent the product of, particular cultural environments.

The Senegalese women struggling to adapt to the dominant presence of the Bud estates might seem to have little in common either with the women surgeons studied by Cassell or with La Roche, struggling to win a place for herself in the literary world of eighteenth-century Germany. But La Roche, the Senegalese women, and the women surgeons were all attempting to navigate existing cultural landscapes and, through that very navigation, were bringing about changes in those landscapes. Gramsci, as I have argued, can help us to map those landscapes precisely because of his understanding of culture as fluid, often incoherent, and always in motion. Culture, for Gramsci, is the precipitate of history, always in flux, always coming into being and ceasing to be. Culture is how a society's shifting contours of inequality, including those of gender, are lived day to day. The existence of gender difference may seem fixed and inescapable, but just what this difference is thought to be in any given context is never fixed. How a woman is expected to behave, and how a man, what signifies female, what male, not only varies from society to society but, even within a single society, is continually being negotiated and renegotiated, sometimes in obvious ways, as when women surgeons challenge the masculinist definitions of their profession, and sometimes in less perceptible and more ambivalent ways, as when La Roche makes her carefully staged, modest entrance into the masculine world of literature.

Cultures confront individuals at any historical moment with a set of relatively fixed meanings but are simultaneously pulled in different directions by how those individuals live their culture. Crucially, individuals always live their culture as *gendered* beings. Whatever time and place we inhabit, we come to a realization of ourselves as women or men within a preexisting gendered landscape. This landscape confronts us with paths that, depending on our gender, are more or less open or obstructed; in treading those paths we can adhere to their existing contours, so helping to ensure their continued existence, or we can begin to tread out new ones. As Gramsci reminds us, we all, in however small a way, have the potential to "take an active part in the creation of the history of the world." And this includes the reimagining and remaking of its gendered contours. Individuals are always at one and the same time confronted by the culture of their time and place as a given, and the active producers of that culture.

Notes

1. The power bound up with the naming of social reality is discussed in Crehan (1997, 30–35).

2. The North is the preferred term nowadays for what used to be called the West, or the developed world, while what was formerly referred to as the underdeveloped, developing, or third world is now termed the South.

3. An important early article identifying this kind of male bias in anthropology is Ardener 1975. Two influential early collections edited by feminist anthropologists were *Woman, Culture, and Society* (Rosaldo and Lamphere 1974) and *Toward an Anthropology of Women* (Reiter 1975).

4. See Engels's famous 1890 letter to Joseph Bloch (Marx and Engels 1975, 394).

5. See Crehan (2002, 99–105) for a fuller discussion of the concept of hegemony.

References

Ardener, Edwin. 1975. "Belief and the Problem of Women." In *Perceiving Women*, ed. Shirley Ardener. London: Dent.

Cassell, Joan.1998. *The Woman in the Surgeon's Body.* Cambridge, MA: Harvard University Press.

Clifford, James. 1997. *Routes: Travel and Translation in the Late Twentieth Century.* Cambridge, MA: Harvard University Press.

Collier, Jane Fishburne, and Sylvia Janko Yanagisako. 1987. *Gender and Kinship: Essays toward a Unified Analysis.* Palo Alto, CA: Stanford University Press.

Crehan, Kate. 1997. *The Fractured Community: Landscapes of Power and Gender in Rural Zambia.* Berkeley: University of California Press.

———. 2002. *Gramsci, Culture and Anthropology.* Berkeley: University of California Press.

de Beauvoir, Simone. 1953. *The Second Sex.* Trans. H. M. Parshley. New York: Knopf. Orig. French ed., 1949.

Geertz, Clifford. 1973a. "Thick Description: Toward an Interpretive Theory of Culture." In *The Interpretation of Cultures.* New York: Basic Books.

———. 1973b. "Religion as a Cultural System." In *The Interpretation of Cultures.* New York: Basic Books.

Ginsburg, Faye D., and Rayna Rapp, eds. 1995. *Conceiving the New World Order: The Global Politics of Reproduction.* Berkeley: University of California Press.

Gramsci, Antonio. 1971. *Selections from the Prison Notebooks.* Ed. Quintin Hoare and Geoffrey Nowell Smith. London: Lawrence and Wishart.

Mackintosh, Maureen. 1989. *Gender, Class and Rural Transition: Agribusiness and the Food Crisis in Senegal.* New York: St. Martin's.

Marx, Karl, and Frederick Engels. 1975. *Selected Correspondence.* Moscow: Progress Publishers.

Ortner, Sherry B. 1974. "Is Female to Male as Nature Is to Culture?" In *Woman, Culture, and*

Society, ed. Michelle Zimbalist Rosaldo and Louise Lamphere. Palo Alto, CA: Stanford University Press.

———. 1984. "Theory in Anthropology since the Sixties." *Comparative Studies in Society and History* 26 (1):142–66.

Rapp, Reyna. 1999. *Testing Women, Testing the Fetus: The Social Impact of Amniocentesis in America.* New York: Routledge.

Reiter, Rayna R., ed. 1975. *Toward an Anthropology of Women.* New York: Monthly Review Press.

Rosaldo, Michelle Zimbalist, and Louise Lamphere, eds. 1974. *Woman, Culture, and Society.* Palo Alto, CA: Stanford University Press.

Strathern, Marilyn. 1972. *Women in Between: Female Roles in a Male World.* London: Seminar/Academic Press.

———. 1987. "An Awkward Relationship: The Case of Feminism and Anthropology." *Signs* 12 (2): 276–92.

———. 1988. *The Gender of the Gift: Problems with Women and Problems with Society in Melanesia.* Berkeley: University of California Press.

———. 1992. *After Nature: English Kinship in the Late Twentieth Century.* Berkeley: University of California Press.

Weiner, Annette. 1976. *Women of Value, Men of Renown.* Austin: University of Texas Press.

Williams, Raymond. 1983. *Keywords: A Vocabulary of Culture and Society, Revised Edition.* New York: Oxford University Press.

Woodmansee, Martha. 1994. *The Author, Art, and the Market: Rereading the History of Aesthetics.* New York: Columbia University Press.

3 :: DESIRE

LAUREN BERLANT

In the study of gender and sexuality, one might expect work on desire and love to be about identity and intimacy, sexual object choice and erotic practice, the disparate dramas lived by various genders, and the central-ity of intimate inclinations, emotions, and acts to the assessment of a person's happiness. Ideally such a study would confirm what one already knows about desire and love, as there is nothing more alienating than having one's pleasures disputed by someone with a theory. Yet the ways in which we live sexuality and intimacy have been profoundly shaped by theories—especially psychoanalytic ones, which have helped to place sexuality and desire at the center of the modern story about what a per-son is and how her history should be read. At the same time, other modes of explanation have been offered by aesthetics, religion, and the fantasies of mass and popular culture, which are not usually realist but often claim to have distilled emotional truths about love's nature and force. In these domains, sexual desire is not deemed the core story of life; it is mixed up with romance, a particular version of the story of love.

In this volume, I engage desire and love in two separate essays. On the face of it, it makes sense to separate them, but the separation is heuristic, it never succeeds. Desire describes a state of attachment to something or someone, and the cloud of possibility that is generated by the gap be-tween an object's specificity and the needs and promises projected onto it. This gap produces a number of further convolutions. Desire visits you as an impact from the outside, and yet, inducing an encounter with your affects, makes you feel as though it comes from within you; this means that your objects are not objective, but things and scenes that you have invested attachment-value in, in a way that converts them into objects that prop up your world. So what seems objective and autonomous in them is partly what your desire has created and therefore is a mirage, a shaky anchor. Your style of addressing those objects gives shape to the drama with which they allow you to reencounter yourself. By contrast, love is the embracing dream in which desire is reciprocated: rather than being isolating, love provides an image of an expanded self, the normative version of which is the two-as-one intimacy of the couple form. (Parents and children are also idealized in love's relationality, but reciprocity is not necessary for that love to persist, and so it is a kind of love that always shadows what the couple can achieve.) In the idealized image of the couple's relation, desire will lead to love, which in turn will make a world for desire's endurance.

But there is a shadow around this image: who is to say whether a love relation is real or is really something else, a passing fancy or a trick someone plays (on herself, on another) in order to sustain a fantasy? This is a psychological question about the reliability of emotional knowledge, but it is also a political question about the ways norms produce attachments to living through certain fantasies. What does it mean about love that its expressions tend to be so *conventional*, so bound up in institutions like marriage and family, in property relations, in stock phrases and plots? This is a question about subjectivity too, therefore, but it is also about ideology. The difficulty of determining love's authenticity has generated a repository of signs, stories, and products dedicated to verifying that the "real thing" exists, both among people and in other relations—for example, between people and their nations, their Gods, their objects, or their pets. But these signs of love are not universal, and their conventionality suggests, in addition, that love can be at once genuine and counterfeit, shared and hoarded, apprehensible and enigmatic. Read together, this essay and the essay "Love" (chapter 11) therefore frame the relation between desire and love as a series of paradoxes that shift according to how the questions about attachment are phrased. Sometimes they refer to people who move within a wide range of genders and sexualities, but often they try to explain structures or conventions of identity and not the sociological or empirical experience of being in desire or having love.

In this essay, "desire" mainly describes the feeling one person has for something else: it is organized by psychoanalytic accounts of attachment and tells briefly the recent history of their importance in critical theory and practice. The second essay, on love, begins with an excursion into fantasy, moving away from the parent-child scene of psychoanalysis and looking instead at the centrality to desire of context, environment, or history: it examines ways that the theatrical or scenic structure of fantasy suggests its fundamentally social character, its importance as a site in which a person's relations to history, the present, the future, and herself are performed without necessarily being represented coherently or directly. Whether viewed psychoanalytically, institutionally, or ideologically, love is always deemed an outcome of fantasy. Without fantasy, there would be no attachment and no love. But fantasy will mean many incommensurate things, from unconscious investments in objects of all kinds to dreams inculcated in collective environments. The entry on love describes some workings of romance across personal life and commodity culture, the places where subjects learn to inhabit fantasy in the ordinary course of their actual lives.

We begin with the opening image from the film *Imitation of Life* (dir. John Stahl, 1934). As the introductory credits fade out, the camera cuts to a white bathtub full of water, where a small rubber duck floats. It would be more accurate to say that the duck bobs and weaves, that it is both fixed in the camera's gaze and unstable in the water. Off camera, we hear a little girl's plaintive voice say: "I want my quack quack!" The child's cry is responded to by what must be a mother's loving disciplinary voice, which replies, "Now, Jessie . . ." The camera remains all the while fixed on the bobbing duck. As the story develops and bodies become attached to voices, we discover that baby Jessie has a working mother, and that the child is being sent to day care so that the mother can go sell her wares. When the daughter resists being taken there she adopts the language of contract to remind her mother of what love obliges: "I love you and you love me and I don't want to go to the day nursery!" Soon the phone rings, and the mother, Bea Pullman, runs downstairs to answer it, leaving her child in the bathroom.

On the way to the phone Bea sees that breakfast is burning. She lowers the heat and takes the phone, where she does some business—she sells maple syrup, having taken over her late husband's sales route. Just then an African American woman comes to the door, mistakenly thinking that Bea has advertised for a maid; the woman, Delilah Johnson, is looking for a live-in situation for herself and Peola, her "light-skinned" little girl. Delilah offers Bea her services anyway. Bea resists the offer, for she has no money to pay wages; at that moment Jessie is overwhelmed by her desire for the "quack quack" and, imagining it within her reach, grabs for it and falls into the bathtub. The white mother runs to save her soaking daughter and the black mother reenters the house, saves the breakfast, and never leaves. The "quack quack" thus rescues them all from their chaotic and impossible domestic scenes.

The white daughter's desire for the duck that bobs and weaves and tempts but is always out of reach starts the plot that joins the two families' lives: for close to two decades the women and their daughters live together. Marketing a pancake recipe the African American woman provides, they all get wealthy. Yet the white family always takes economic and spatial precedence over its "partner," the black family, and everyone ends up wracked with longing for particular objects, which they fail painfully to secure. The world provides neither rest nor freedom for the African American women; the mother desires to "get off her feet" and educate her daughter, but does neither; the daughter wants to be "white, just like I look," and thereby free to inhabit any US space, but she too fails to realize that desire. Delilah and Peola, representing the perpetuity of racial, sexual, and economic hardship in the United States, exit the plot before the film finishes. For them, the question of desire can only be answered by transformations in the politically saturated conditions of sustenance that the material world does not offer them—changes that cannot be effected by individual will. *Imitation of Life* instead closes with the wealthy and beautiful white mother and daughter walking offscreen arm in arm, each secretly longing for a male lover she has renounced for the other's sake, while outwardly recalling the film's early moments of desire, chaos, poverty, and plenitude. As the final scene fades out, Bea recalls the day the four women met, saying to her daughter, "and you were saying 'I want my quack quack! I want my quack quack . . .'" It is an extremely bittersweet and defining closing moment, for it turns out that the child's initial utterance of desire prophesies something general about the traumatic destiny of desire in all of their lives.

So what does Jessie really want when she says she wants her "quack quack"—her unavailable working mother, her dead father, or something she senses but cannot name? Is it important that she calls her toy not a duck but what a duck is said to say, as though what she seeks is something too intimate to imitate, something that speaks desiringly to her and that she might come to possess through the exchange of language, and in particular, through being spoken to? Or does it suggest that desire is only secondarily about the relations among bodies, and primarily about voices and the intimate attachments they engender? And what of the daughter's desire for the duck? Would it be overreading to call it erotic? What is the relation between someone's objects of desire and her sexual "identity"? Does it mean something that, later on, Jessie falls in love with a man who studies fish for a living?

And what does the mother mean when she recalls the scene of her daughter's desire? If baby (duck) talk here is the pure language of desire, then perhaps Bea refers, in the end, to the ways one never seems to move beyond the logic of beginnings, of the film's and life's earliest moments. *Imitation of Life* frames these questions in the voice of infantile desire; yet the narrative develops another kind of idiom as well, which tells a story about the sexual, racial, and economic contexts in which African American and white women's fantasies of pleasure and freedom remain just that, intuitions of a world of fulfillment that does not yet exist for them. In any case, in ventriloquizing the plea for the apparitional "quack quack," Jessie's mother captions an entire film's image of pessimism, optimism, language, and desire: the object of desire, which has no proper name, but which in fantasy speaks passionately to you and frames your life, bobs and weaves and hits you more like a boxer than a duck when you reach out to possess it, only to discover that you can never duck in time, but must be dented by it, incidentally, weaving, recovering, and maybe reaching out again for it from within the relation that at once possesses and dispossesses you, forcing you to scavenge for survival while remembering that there is a better beyond to it. The impact of the object, and the impulse that involves the patterning of attachment, are the materials of sexuality and of the optimism (at least for affective relief) that must accompany taking up a position in it. An object gives you optimism, then rains on your parade—although that is never the end of the story.

+   +   +

Even in its most conventional form, as "love," desire produces paradox. It is a primary relay to individuated social identity, as in coupling, family, reproduction, and other sites of personal history; yet it is also the impulse that most destabilizes people, putting them into plots beyond their control as it joins diverse lives and makes situations. (Thus the painful genre "situation comedy" depends on the association of desire with disaster.) Central to the development of narratives that link personal life to larger histories, and to practices and institutions of intimacy, desire also measures fields of difference and distance. It both constructs and collapses distinctions between public and private: it reorganizes worlds (Berlant 1998, 281–88; Berlant and Warner 1998, 547–66). This is one reason why desire is so often represented as political: in bringing people into public or collective life, desire makes scenes where social conventions of power and value play themselves out in plots about obstacles to and opportunities for erotic fulfillment. (Think of *Romeo and Juliet*, *Tristan and Isolde*, *The Scarlet Letter*, *Gone with the Wind*, or *Titanic*.)

The first section of this essay will move through analyses of different ways that desire has been zoned by different kinds of human science. I use a language of zoning because desire tends to be associated with specific places (Berlant and Warner 1998). Partly this has to do with how desire materializes in incidents that become events, and sometimes memory. The disturbance desire makes is usually forgettable, and yet even the process of forgetting specifics can transform sites into scenes, spaces laden with affects and feelings that something significant has happened. But the zoning of desire is less personal, more normative, too. Consider, for example, erogenous zones, red light districts, master bedrooms, "private parts." Moreover, a relation of desire creates a "space" in which its trajectories and complexities are repeatedly experienced and represented; and as its movement creates tracks that we can follow on "the body" and in "the world," it creates an urge for mapping.

Both the theories and the profession of psychoanalysis have been crucial to the development of desire's modern conventions and forms—at least in the United States and Europe. A psychoanalytic model that locates the truth of a person in sexuality has been central to many of the modern narratives and norms that organize personal and institutional life. In addition, during the twentieth century in the United States a more general therapeutic or "self-help" culture developed, in which it is presumed that individuals both can and need to fix themselves. An industry of mental health experts has grown, focusing largely on a range of individual problems with intimacy: sexuality, family, and love are the main sites of stress and pedagogies of self-care, while concerns about food, alcohol, drug, or money addictions conventionally appear as symptoms of a person's damaged self or self-esteem. Many people now learn to believe or hope that they can purchase access to this expertise about surviving the destabilizing effects of desire, either by going into therapy or purchasing such commodities as books, diet foods, and over-the-counter medications, all means to supposedly enable mental health and/or happiness. Talk shows, advice columns, and even state agencies argue that solving problems with love and desire is the individual's responsibility.

In contrast, this essay presumes that individuation is a historical process through which people are constructed or made specific, and through which persons learn to identify particular aspects of themselves as their core traits. "Identity" might be defined as the kind of singularity that an individual is said to have: paradoxically, identity is also the individual's point of intersection with membership in particular populations or collectivities. Traditional psychoanalysis is a liberal discourse, insofar as its recourse to the individual requires a model of the abstract, universal, or structurally determined individual, who is inevitably organized and disorganized in a certain way by the encounter with desire. This presumption about structuration becomes too often attached to an image of happy normal individuals who adhere to measures of propriety in a prevailing social world. (Gilles Deleuze, from a different angle, calls this subject of data a "dividual," to emphasize that individuality itself is a cluster of qualities that don't express the totality of a person but rather her value as data to the reproduction of the normative world; Deleuze 1992, 3–7.) Thus, when we think about desire we will not think as much about the optimism and promise it usually expresses. Instead, we will think about sexuality as a structure of self-encounter and encounter with the world, about modern ideologies and institutions of intimacy that have installed sexuality as the truth of what a person is; that promote a narrowed version of heterosexuality as a proper cultural norm, and regulate deviations from it; and that nonetheless yield some carefully demarcated space to some kinds of nonnormative sexuality, such as gay and lesbian. We will then engage the ideologies of love marketed by the entertainment industries of Western mass culture, and ask how love became a way of imagining particular utopias of gender and sex. Throughout, we will be thinking about gender, identity, and desire, both as abstractions and as materialized in history. We will also be reflecting on kinds of longing that are not "normal" in that they are not confined to or well-described by any sexual identity form.

One more thing: as the tempting and elusive floating duck shows us, there is no way definitively to capture desire, in an object or in theory. This is why critical thought about what desire is almost inevitably becomes theoretical thought about thought itself: the minute an object comes under analytic scrutiny, it bobs and weaves, becomes unstable, mysterious, and recalcitrant, seeming more like a fantasy than the palpable object it had seemed to be when the thinker/lover first risked engagement. So, in order to explain some things about desire and love, these two essays will not even attempt to claim to understand their essential structure. Thinking about relations of desire and love as intensified zones of attachment, they will try to give you ways to identify their activity, track their movement, and map out the dents, incidents, accidents, and patterns of event they make on people and the world in which they circulate.

Psychoanalysis and the Formalism of Desire

Psychoanalysts do not agree on what the idea or entity "desire" is: conventionally associated with romantic concepts like love or lust, desire is also associated with the Freudian categories of "drive" and "libido," which refer to a flow of sexual energy that is said to put pressure on the individual (or "subject," someone with subjectivity) to move from sensual autonomy to a relation with the world. In this model, "desire" articulates the drives, or the infantile excitation that operates throughout the subject's life, with relation to objects: primary objects in the original caretaking environment, like the breast or the mother, and secondary ones through which the subject can repeat the experience of desiring in her adult life. In contrast, a Lacanian model would call desire less a drive that is organized by objects and more a drive that moves beyond its objects, always operating with them and in excess to them, with aims both to preserve and to destroy them. Different psychoanalytic schools offer many motives for this doubleness, all of which have to do with the inevitability of ambivalence, to which we shall later return.

These points about desire are crucial: desire is memorable only when it reaches toward something to which it can attach itself; and the scene of this aspiration must be in a relation of repetition to another scene. Repetition is what enables you to recognize, even unconsciously, your desire as a quality of yours. Desire's formalism—its drive to be embodied and reiterated—opens it up to anxiety, fantasy, and discipline.

It is important at this juncture, however, to distinguish between some kinds of anxiety and others. "Normal" pathways of desire expose people to different risks than do nonnormative desires (note the awkward wording: in most thesauruses, there are no eloquent value-neutral terms for the nonnormative, which is designated by words associated with the immoral or the monstrous). Heterosexual desire takes place in heteronormative culture—that is, a site where heterosexuality is presumed not only to be a kind of sexuality but the right and proper kind. For all of the instability, incoherence, and vulnerability heterosexuality engenders in the subjects who identify with it, the context in which it takes place not only supports it morally and organizes state, medical, educational, and commodity resources around it, but considers it the generic (the default, the natural) form of sexuality itself. An extraordinary amount of discipline, scrutiny, and threat keeps many heterosexuals behaving according to "the straight and narrow," but these institutional forces are also distributed in everyday life through informal policing—aggressive commentary, passive-aggressive judgmental murmuring asides and glances, and jokes, for example.

In contrast, gay, lesbian, transgendered, and even less standard sexualities have few generalized spaces or institutions of support; nowhere are they the taken-for-granted of the word "sexuality." This means that along with experiencing the vulnerability that comes to anyone who takes the risk of desiring the pleasures of intimacy, they bear the burden of experiencing a general devaluation of one's desires, which are generally considered antithetical to the project of social reproduction. Gays and lesbians, for example, are constantly exposed to a whole range of unpleasant consequences—from fear of familial rejection and social isolation to underemployment and physical brutality, simply because of their sexual identity. To the phobic—those who fear instabilities of privilege and embrace the social as a site of sameness, nonnormative sexualities threaten fantasies of the good life that are anchored to images of racial, religious, class, and national monoculture. This is why developing *spaces* of relative gay and lesbian saturation has been so important to building a less homophobic world; otherwise, nonnormative sexualities, during the twentieth century, mainly represented negative forms of social value, establishing a boundary through taboo and terror that has helped to prop up heterosexual culture so successfully that people are frequently surprised by their own normativity (Chauncy 1994; D'Emilio and Freeman 1998; Kennedy and Davis 1993; Newton 1993; Warner 1993). Moreover, if by the time you read this LGBTQ couples are an ordinary event in the everyday, this does not mean that heteronormativity has been vanquished. It might mean that one of its qualities—the couple or the family form, for example—is ruling the moral, legal, economic, and/or social roost in such a way that other-oriented practices might be held in contempt and/or illegalized. It might not, though! The incoherent relation of privileged fear and deference (within the ordinariness of social proximity) remains one of the great challenges to political and social analysis.

Freudian psychoanalytic theory popularized and drastically transformed how normative and nonnormative sexuality and sexual desires were being conceptualized and experienced at the beginning of the twentieth century. It would be imprudent to try here to summarize all of Freud's work on these subjects. (For a start, see Brennan 1992; Laplanche and Pontalis 1973; Minsky 1996; Rose 1982, 27–57.) What follows are some of the ways Freud thought about the *forms* desire takes. Questions about the designs of desire not only have consequences for the ways we think about intimate sexual practices, sexual identity, identification, and attachment; they also help us track sexuality in the political sphere and mass entertainment, since these public sites help to designate which forms of desire can be taken for granted as legitimate, in contrast to those modes of desiring that seem to deserve pity, fear, and antagonism.

It may seem far away from these social issues to turn to infantile sexuality, but it is here that psychoanalysis has historically developed its ways of describing the "normal" forms of activity, identification, and object-choice that organize the subject's primary experiences of pleasure, trauma, and desire. Right away we see that Freud's model not only revolutionized sexuality by locating the developmental origins of adult sexual practice in the acts and wishes of infants and children, but also that it produced an idea of eros that is far more complex and ambivalent than that which we find in popular notions of the Oedipal complex and romance ideology. These versions of love tend to disavow erotic ambivalence and install, in its place, a love plot—a temporal sequence in which erotic antagonism or anxiety are overcome by events that lead to fulfillment (Modleski 1982; Rabine 1985, 249–67; Radway 1984; Saunders 1995; Thompson 1995). But in Freud's model, the confirming and caring economy of love, involving both giving and receiving on the model of maternal plenitude, is all bound up with an economy of aggression. In this model, to love an object is to attempt to master it, to seek to destroy its alterity or Otherness. Here, aggression is not the opposite of love but is integral to it; one way to think about this is that in love, the lover hungers to have her object *right where she can love it*. This is why sadism, masochism, and perversion are not exceptions to the rule of desire in Freud's model but integral to human attachment. Love enables the pressure of desire's aggression to be discharged within a frame of propriety. In this view Freud is supported by other schools of psychoanalytic thought that, for all their differences, agree that the will to destroy the desired object (the death drive) and the will to preserve it (the pleasure principle) are two sides of the same process (for example, see Klein and Rivière 1964; Winnicott1958, 1971, 1986). Some post-Freudians, however, argue that Freud's model produces an image of sexuality as fundamentally masochistic (Bersani 1986; de Lauretis 1994; Freud 1949, 158–59; Freud 1957). This is because, regardless of how it is experienced by the desiring subject, desire can overwhelm thought, shatter intention, violate principles, and perturb identity. It is as though desire were a law of disturbance unto itself to which the subject must submit to become a subject of her own unbecoming.

There are intense debates in the psychoanalytic literature as to whether the primary form of infantile desire is *allosexual* (directed toward the other—in this case, the mother, the source of nourishment, her breast, her milk) or *autoerotic*. (I derive this usage of *allo-* and *auto-* from Sedgwick 1990, 59.) But without boundaries or the capacity to resist stimuli (the function of the ego, which the infant does not yet have), the infant might also be said to be unable to distinguish between her own body as erotogenic zone and the nourishment that seems to be organized around her bodily need.

At first the erotogenic zones are not organized genitally: the infant's whole body, the skin, and diffuse feelings of contact and movement provide the ongoing experience of pleasure. This is "polymorphous perversity." At the same time the infant's body is in a relation of exchange with its caretaking environment, and the sensuality of that environment begins to produce excitation on the infant's body, with its pulsating zones of repeated need, stimulation, and gratification. At some point the infant realizes that she is not continuous with the caretaking environment/mother/breast that she relies on for nurturance and pleasure. The infant's recognition of separateness produces a primary trauma, and this is the site at which reactive aggression and love become entwined in desiring activity. At this point, Jean Laplanche argues, the child develops strategies of autoeroticism, which is the only site of certain satisfaction once the mother is perceived to be Other. The infant also reroutes her self-pleasure back into the world, seeking substitutes for the lost breast/ mother so that, as Freud writes, "The finding of an object [of desire] is in fact a re-finding of it." But the infant (as child and adult) soon sees that even the gratifications of this refinding are mixed with anxiety, doubt, and disappointment, for the substitute object of desire is always more and less than the lost real thing (Freud 1949, 222; Laplanche 1976, 17–21).

The infant becomes motivated to sociability by her drive to reclaim an impossible attachment. She learns to give love as care, as manipulation, and as violence in order to get it. This is also the moment at which memory fragments of unfulfilled wishes generate the materials of the unconscious; the unconscious is caused by the repression of these traumas and wishes, which are later to become represented in symptoms, patterns, reiterations, and other forms that mark the half-remembered experience of lost love (Cixous 1983, 2–32; Phillips 1994, 22–38). *From this point of view, traumatic loss of continuity with the world is the core motive for the formation of subjectivity*. Freud's concept of melancholia might usefully clarify this: the melancholic is one who incorporates a lost object of desire into her ego, so that she never fully experiences the loss, since the loved one, even in absence, becomes merged with the self. This confusion of presence and absence leads to other-directed sadness and anger (I love them, why did they leave me, I am not myself without them, they cannot leave me) and to self-directed anger (I must not be worthy of love). After the traumatic separation from the mother, it is said, melancholia becomes integral to love itself, a form of masochism derived from the simultaneity of self-loss and the loss of the loved one (Bersani 1986, 81–96). Melancholia mirrors inversely the idealizing narratives about merged souls more happily associated with love. Indeed, Freud speculated that one's primary love affair is with one's ego, projected out onto the world and returned as difference. His complaint about homosexuality and hysterical femininity was that they were forms of narcissism without the necessary mediation of corporeal difference, and thus perhaps without the proper relation to primary trauma. Later in his career, the pervasiveness of homosexual desires in his patients returned to destabilize his early taxonomies.

On discovering her specific difference from the nurturing environment, the infant begins to construct forms that reproduce the predictable world of repeated affect that she initially experienced (for good or for ill: this is how we attach to relational modes that might also be threats to our well-being, associating those modes with what the world offers as love). This is also the function of Oedipal triangulation. Freud also holds that the child's entry into Oedipal relations secures the subject's sexual object-choice, organizes genitality in its proper sequence, and enables the formation of the superego, about which more below. At this stage Freud takes his model of desire from heterosexual masculinity. He describes a double process of attachment for the child: object-love between the child and his mother and identification between the child and his father. *Identification* with the same-sex parent is considered *metaphoric*, as a narcissistic relation of likeness produces a new sense of bodily continuity for the child; in contrast, the child's love for the mother now develops through the logic of difference that Freud calls *object-choice*, a *metonymic* relation that involves substituting like objects for the originary relation of plenitude—an adult desire for women's breasts, for example, substitutes for the infant's desire for milk. At the same time this relation is also called an *anaclitic* or *propping* relation, as the child's desire is structured by proximity, a relation of intimate difference, and a longing to overcome distance.

The Oedipal crisis occurs when the child realizes that, like all economies, the Oedipal economy involves scarcity: the father is his rival for the mother's love, a threat to its continuity in relation to the child. So the child endeavors to put himself in all of the places where desire might attach. Freud thus posits that each subject experiences a positive and a negative Oedipal process, the sexual ambivalence of which expresses the fundamental bisexuality of humans. The boy wants to vanquish the father; at the same time, because he identifies with the father, the son develops a masochistic relation to his own aggression, develops a virtually "feminine" attitude to protect his rival, and projects his own hostility onto the mother, who then figures as a threat to both men (Freud 1961a, 32; Deleuze 1971). But for "normal" masculine identity to develop, the Oedipal crisis must be resolved by an intensified identification with the father. Freud argues that this resolution is achieved by the boy's discovery of sexual difference—the shock of the mother's vagina, read as a traumatized site of penile "castration"—which has both catastrophic and productive effects on the boy. He identifies with and as the father or father-figure, as well as against him; he identifies with and against the mother, although not exactly "as."

One "healthy" effect of the discovery that the mother is castrated is the smashing of the Oedipus complex (Freud 1961b, 256–57). This development seems to resolve many sites and structures of shame in heterosexual development, not the least of which is the incest taboo. This enables the boy to desire as his father desires without hurting the father, because the son's desire now travels beyond the mother and outside of the family. At the same time he gets to keep the mother's attention. From this shift develops the superego, or ego-ideal, which tries to protect the boy from future trauma by disciplining his desire toward proper objects. Along with guaranteeing his heterosexual masculinity, this solution protects his primary relation to his mother: she remains the beloved original source of care and nourishment, but her frightening sexual difference requires that she be replaced by other women. Sexual attachments to new women provide an opportunity for the boy to perform successful masculinity by overcoming the now doubly posttraumatic ambivalence he has toward his mother (originating at the breast and the vagina).

Castration anxiety results in the more intensified homosocial identification that also constitutes normative masculinity. If one admits this speculative perspective, boys identify with the father and with men generally not only because they are the same gender; they develop solidarity because they have faced the same threats and feel the same strangeness of anxiety and ambivalence at the scene of their attachment to desire for women.

But sometimes the trauma of castration anxiety paralyzes the subject, freezing his sexuality at the point of crisis itself and endangering his successful accession to ordinary heteromasculinity. This is when perversions like *fetishism* develop. Freud's essays "Fetishism" and "Medusa's Head" suggest that the crisis of phallic fragility that binds men to each other and produces a polarized set of fascinations with women's bodily difference—aggressive/abject, idealized/disgusted—can also produce a formalism that repairs anxiety by covering it over, thus enabling the male to disavow his activated ambivalence toward women. The fetish is such a form.

A fetish is an erotically endowed object that someone can possess and control, yet, paradoxically, the fetish seems to control or possess the person who thinks she possesses it. It turns a story of masculine desire for women into a story of victimization by women that ends up in a scenario of heroic repair. Fetishism is fundamentally an aesthetic crisis: just as the Medusa petrifies whoever looks at her face, the boy, shocked at his mother's genital difference from him, displays his realization on his body. He becomes stiff (as in scared and as in erect); he visualizes pubic hair teeming with snakes (or penises) in the hair on his mother's head. In other words, the boy's body and sensorium produce representations of the mother's lost, castrated penis: the fetish is that which represents the object, its presence, and its absence. Its magic is that it protects the boy from experiencing absolute loss. Frequently, it is something the boy associates with the floor beneath his mother's dress or other surfaces associated with her (shoes, embroidery, fur). As such, the fetish enables desire to be controlled, to be manageable, to be comprehended, signified, and also screened out by the material form. Moreover, the fetish has no uniqueness or singularity, like the penis; it can always be possessed, re-produced, replaced, and collected. Thus it encompasses value and value-lessness, and construes desire through aggression and protectiveness. But the contradictions and complexities that motivate fetishism are hidden by the fetishized object. If the fetish originally marks a traumatic event, its availability for reproduction separates it from the event, de-contextualizes it into pure form, and enables the fetishist to become absorbed in an abstract present tense marked by repetition, fascination, and analytic distraction.

The sublimation of sexual desire into objects that replace the original one(s) also, paradoxically, protects the original object by protecting the child's attachment from any future destabilization. Indeed, in Freud's essays on the psychology of love, he suggests that men who have not successfully worked through Oedipal trauma will produce adult object choices that tend either toward overvaluation of the loved object or denigration of a series of inadequate women. (These are the two sides of fetishism in his analysis.) Here, as elsewhere, he suggests that antithetical relations of desire, like those of idealization and revulsion, can formally figure the same motive for desire's circulation. Frequently, he suggests that the fundamental ambivalence, bisexuality, and/or incoherence of human drives motivates the formalism of desire; but, he says, "civilization" requires their disavowal and sublimation to the good of hetero-sexual normalcy. "The final outcome of sexual development," he writes, "lies in what is known as the normal sexual life of the adult, in which the pursuit of pleasure comes under the sway of the reproductive function and in which the component instincts, under the primacy of a single ero-togenic zone, form a firm organization directed toward a sexual aim at-tached to some extraneous sexual object" (Freud 1949, 197). To the extent that this "extraneous sexual object" enables the desiring subject to deny his ambivalence on behalf of attaining sexual and intimate normalcy, his desire is fetishistic; that is, the fetish reproduces the general structure of desire, which is an activity that aims at repeating pleasure by finding substitutes for a lost or unstable object.

Freud's account of the accession of girls to heterosexual femininity through "reverse" Oedipalization has all the quality of a bad copy: some-times he argues that the process is simply transposed, such that the girl's identification with her mother and object-cathexis on her father come into crisis with the same conjoining of aggression and masochism as he finds in boys. He also argues that girls are not as motivated as boys to move through Oedipalization to discipline by the superego because girls are always already castrated, and thus unprovoked by its threat. This sug-gests to Freud that women therefore develop weaker superegos, a weaker sense of justice, a more contingent sense of self, and more easily disorganized and pathological desires. Other critics, as I will discuss below, will go on to say that this lack also gives women more freedom from compulsive normativity.

For Freud wrote many things during his career that do not quite cohere. On the subject of female masochism, for example, he offers a political analysis as well. He argues that women do possess a stream of threat-induced erotic aggressivity—just less intensively so than men—but that there is no socially sanctioned place for it, no drama in which female aggression accrues social value (Freud 1964, 132–35). Since desire always finds an object through which it can sustain itself, even at the cost of massive misrecognition, that aggression will then tend to return to its origin, the woman. This social explanation of "female masochism" contradicts the kinship-centric one we have been tracing, and marks an internal tension in Freud's work that continues in contemporary psychoanalysis. This incoherence does not necessarily delegitimate psychoanalysis as such; rather, it typifies a general problem that characterizes thought about power and subjectivity in modern capitalist/heteronormative contexts, in which "the individual" tends to be seen paradoxically: as a being driven by appetites and structures induced by the world, and as a sovereign, autonomous force relative to the constantly changing institutions of social life. But psychoanalysis also has shown that one's own incoherence-in-ambivalence meets up with the incoherence of social aims and demands in ways that either mirror each other or induce multiple fantasies of relief and repair. It has been suggested that the lack of fit is an unbridgeable space or aporia covered over by *ideology*, which so successfully produces subjects who see the world from the perspective of their own individual stories that other, more structural explanations of subjectivity seem themselves to violate the specificity and uniqueness of each individual's identity in the world (Žižek 1994b, 21; Žižek 1989). Critical theory's engagement with desire has also mobilized words like "excess," which refuses the "sense" that ideology makes out of explanations that do not cohere with an individualist model of sovereign desire, and which potentially enables more mutually structured transformations of subjects and worlds.

Needless to say, there has been much critical feminist work focusing on the benefit to men of concepts like penis envy and feminine lack that organize much of what Freud has to say about women's desire. But does this mean that Freud has no knowledge, after all, about what women want? Are his fictions of psychic order mainly symptoms of a more general turn-of-the-century misogynist malaise or a generically patriarchal imaginary? This position has been strenuously argued. But Freud's intuitions have also been remade into positive values by analysts like Nancy Chodorow, who suggest that women's identification with mothers makes women more flexible and less violent than men, rather than weaker or more masochistic. Jessica Benjamin, in contrast, argues that Freud's highly negative account of Otherness (traditionally the place of the Mother, the feminine) is both right and sadly lacking. Following Donald Winnicott, she argues that the fundamental ambivalence of desiring subjects toward their "objects" is just that, ambivalence; if one aspect of the subject's response to the violence of her originary traumatic separation is the experience of the enigmatic Otherness of the lover, the desiring subject nonetheless retains a desire to recognize her intimate as a person, a unique self. For even if, when someone desires, one motive is the mastery of the desired Other, it is also the case that people seek to recognize the Other as a subject, for only under these conditions can humans truly receive the recognition they crave. Benjamin's model of desire is, at root, far less organized by the antinomies of sexual difference than psychoanalytic models tend to be. Finally, Jacqueline Rose argues that Freud's work powerfully shows that sexual difference (heterosexualized gender identity) never achieves purity or stability. It always produces anxiety and lapses into incoherence. Or, as Freud himself contends, "pure masculinity and femininity remain uncertain theoretical constructions of uncertain content" (Freud 1961b, 258). No powerful umbrella theory has been invented to resolve these different articulations of gender, sexuality, and desire in psychoanalysis (Chodorow 1978; Benjamin 1995; Rose 1986).

One imputed result of women's weaker erotic organization—that is, of not having displaced and condensed the traumatized love of the mother onto a fragile and oversymbolized body part—is that women are deemed incapable of fetishism. Since fetishism has been shown to be a central structure of "normal" sexuality, women's lack of relation to it in traditional psychoanalysis has contributed to the sense that women are hysterical or narcissistically disordered with respect to the objects they desire. Teresa de Lauretis, Naomi Schor, Emily Apter, and others counter this implication. Schor argues that there is a feminine fetishism, and that it recognizes the play of presence and absence, aggression and idealization, trauma and plenitude, between the lover and the loved in the classic model of fetishistic desire: but because women's "castration" is a given, women can have an ironic relation to their erotic repetitions: they can admit them without disavowing or doing violence to them (Schor 1985, 301–10; Schor 1987; Apter and Pietz 1993, 92–100).

Teresa de Lauretis argues, instead, that there is a specificity to lesbian fetishism. If the fetish marks the traumatic loss of bodily totality for the lover who projects it onto the beloved's negatively valued corporeal difference, then lesbian desire has to create its own aesthetic markers of desired and threatening "difference," because the distinctions between female lovers cannot be mapped onto sexually "different" bodies. Castration, she argues, is therefore irrelevant to lesbians. As a result, intersubjective fantasy plays a bigger part in the production of lesbian love. In contrast to Freudian and heterosexual feminist theories of desire—which see love primarily as a fetishistic fantasy that obscures the very object of desire who animates it—de Lauretis's version of lesbian fetishism requires two lovers who fantasize together (de Lauretis 1994, 228–86). The erotic aesthetic they generate produces an intimate boundary, a space of bodily distinction and difference, that their desire crosses and recrosses—but not in order to destroy or make order from desire's unstable process. For de Lauretis, the fetishistic "perversion" of lesbian desire is productive, not destructive, of love.

+   +   +

In tracking the relation between Freudian theories of infantile desire and their posttraumatic repetition in adult life, we have seen that even if the libido is ungendered, each gender is associated with particular forms of representing and processing the ambivalent pressures of the drive's energy, whether generated by bisexuality or by traumas of infantile separation and castration. We have also seen that idealization, aggression, and melancholia, as well as "perversions" like masochism and fetishism, seem integral to the ordinary career of desire, as it struggles and fails continuously to find ideal objects on which it can rest. The formalism of desire thus both produces perversion and manifests itself in narratives that aim toward normalcy but, paradoxically, never reach completion: even "normal" desire operates incrementally, restlessly testing out its objects (Bersani 1986, 63–64; Silverman 1988, 1–41).

This might seem a melancholy conclusion, especially if your dream of desire is sustained by a particular combination of pleasure and satisfaction. Yet, as Eve Sedgwick argues, even if desire fails to find objects adequate to its aim, its errors can still produce pleasure; desire's fundamental ruthlessness is a source of creativity that produces new optimism, new narratives of possibility, even erotic experimentality (Sedgwick 1993, 206–11). Most people, however, do not experience consciously the benefits of the vicissitudes of their desires. This is in part because they frequently confuse their desire for the comfort and self-development of a reliable love with a desire for a degree of stability and nonambivalence that live intimacy can rarely sustain. Additionally, people are schooled to recognize as worthwhile only those desires that take shape within the institutions and narratives that bolster convention and traditions of propriety. They learn, further, to be afraid of the consequences when their desire attaches to too many objects or to objects deemed "bad": whether they find themselves longing for persons of an illegitimate or merely inconvenient-to-comfort sexuality, race, class, ethnicity, religion, or marital status.

Thus, even though the shapes desire takes can be infinite, one plot dominates scenes of proper fantasy and expectation. It is a plot in which the patterns of infantile desire develop into a love plot that will be sutured by the institutions of intimacy and the fantasy of familial continuity that links historical pasts to futures through kinship chains worked out in smooth ongoing relations. In the United States, this plot has been legally and aesthetically privileged, albeit widely adapted; as a dream of what life should provide, the desire for conventional love remains fairly strong across many fields of social difference. We have already seen that the public world of fixed gender identities organized by heterosexuality relies on the successful propagation of the belief that "normal" sexuality and desire are not only possible but imaginable, natural, and right. We have also seen that, for single or nonreproductive heterosexuals and for gays, lesbians, bisexuals, and transgendered subjects, the costs of not acceding to normatively sexualized life narratives are both ordinary and extreme, from shame to corporeal punishment by the carceral state and its citizens.

Psychoanalysis, Sex, and Revolution

The world of conventional intimate behavior came under vigorous attack during the radical upheavals of the 1960s; indeed, we would not be studying the category "desire" today had it not been a keyword in the anti-institutional political struggles of that period. The uses to which the category "desire" was put by European and US social radicals in and after 1968 presumed, as Freud presumed, that each person is a site of constantly flowing and explosive (and thus, potentially radicalizing) sexual energy. These radicals did not think, however, that the failure of desire to find appropriate objects was at all inevitable. Instead, they focused on rescuing sexuality from its deforming sublimation into alienated labor, social normalcy, and political quietism (Echols 1989; Marcuse 1964, 1969; Sayers et al. 1984, in which see esp. Stanley Aronowitz, "When the Left Was New," 11–43, and Ellen Willis, "Radical Feminism and Feminist Radicalism," 91–118). Desire was deemed to need rescue, as well, from its parodic form in advertising discourse, where it was so hyperbolized and banal that it was thought to enervate people, to make them paradoxically stimulated, bored, and complacent (Barthes 1975, 1976; Lipsitz 1990). This is why so much radical culture-building used Brechtian avant-garde tactics—to make strange and change the *forms* that desire was thought to take. See, for example, Laura Mulvey's demand in 1975 that the feminist avant-garde "destroy" the forms of visual pleasure, since their history is so saturated with misogyny: emancipation would only happen when the aesthetic of value animated by desire no longer valorized or reproduced the subordination of women (Mulvey 1989, 14–29). This is also why the "sexual revolution" placed the emancipation of "desire" or *jouissance* (the energy of the drives that is in excess to the rational ego, fixed identities, or normative institutions) at the center of many political upheavals—against the bourgeois family, conjugal sexuality, the relation of the state to citizens, exploitation, racism, and imperialism, the place of religion and education in social life, and the place of the body in politics. The feminist dictum "the personal is political" sought to reiterate the centrality of desire to life: the powerful forces of desublimated, freed, or rerouted desire were frequently imagined to have the power to topple unjust conventional intimacies and entire societies (Cixous 1981, 245–64).

Although its history as a champion of desire might have positioned psychoanalysis as a central tool in the radical reconceptualization of society, the profession at this time came under widespread critique for serving the interests of patriarchal, capitalist, imperialist, and racist state and social institutions, including the repressive and normalizing family that shapes the world of psychoanalytic epistemology. How could a science of the individual subject have such far-reaching adverse effects? The critiques take a variety of forms. First, psychoanalysis was charged with masking its normative distinctions—between men and women and between normal and abnormal sexuality—as natural ones. These naturalized "scientific" classifications were then deployed in arguments against the legitimacy of the sexually (appetitively) disordered—heterosexual women, gays, lesbians, the urban poor, and people of color. In addition, the hierarchies implied in these classifications were put to use in imperialist arguments (Chatterjee 1994; Kaplan 1996; McClintock 1995; Sommer 1984; Spivak 1992). The elevation of imperial "civilization" over the "barbarism" of the colonized was also thought to have had implications for political supremacy within national boundaries. The symbolic and material subordination of so-called degenerate groups—people of color, Jews, the impoverished, and women—seemed to require theories of psychological degeneracy, deficiency, or debility, and sexuality was a prime resource for those seeking "scientific" evidence (Gilman 1985; Haraway 1991).

Another side of this critique was also important to 1960s activists:

psychoanalysis was available for destructive appropriation because some versions of it relied on a confusion between a notion of the universal or abstract subject and the concept of the normal or "healthy" sexual subject. Freudian "ego psychology," a US variant said to encourage the unhappy subject's adaptation to normalcy, was the main target here. Wilhelm Reich, R. D. Laing, and other radical analysts of subjectivity were thought by some to offer more liberating, progressive, and nonnormative notions of "mental health" (Mitchell 1974). The hierarchies of value shielded by universalizing thought were a major target of radical philosophers and thinkers of the moment. The psychoanalytic profession was accordingly condemned for seeking to produce generic, universal, or "bourgeois" subjects, individuals who read the world only from the perspective of their own individuality; who learned to understand their lives solely in terms of family dynamics; and who were not enabled to see themselves as subjects marked by the impersonal as well as the personal contexts of history, intimacy, power, and desire. Universal notions of "man," central to modern philosophy and other disciplines, were held to have had materially damaging effects on subjectivity generally, especially for those who were considered unrepresentable in the idiom of the normal/universal (Irigaray 1985; Wittig 1992). In producing "scientific" knowledge that legitimated these norms of imperial personhood and species hierarchy, psychoanalysis was deemed no different than many of the human sciences and academic disciplines.

At the same time, other more ambivalent responses to the radical critique of psychoanalysis developed. Many critics, especially from the academic humanities, argued that psychoanalysis as an institution (and even Freud as a reader of his own work) actually misrepresented its own conclusions, as it produced two contradictory models of desire. One could be described by the aforementioned categories of oppressively traditional sexual difference and family role, Oedipal relations, and penis envy. The radical potential, in contrast, emanates from the model of the constantly bending, folding, and twisting incoherence of libidinal activity, all of which suggests (1) a model of the desiring subject who is decentered or unstable, with "identity" itself, whether sexual or gendered, therefore an always failed project, in that it is always aspirational and determined by multiple, diverse, and divergent aims (Brennan 1992; Butler 1990, 1993; de Lauretis 1994; Rose 1986), and (2) that the libidinal energies now routed into producing narrowed versions of normal/universal and individuated identity might be rerouted toward more expansive and generous sociabilities and worlds.

In the next few pages, we will follow up on the latter prospect: that the anxieties and instabilities of desire might be made to have socially transformative consequences, for good and ill. Many of the psychoanalytically informed theorists of desire who have pursued this line of thought rethink the ways suppressed and conventionally misrecognized desires destructively distort self- and social relations. "Identity" is, in this latter view, a mirage—a mirage of the ego that gives you an "I" and a name to protect you from being overwhelmed by the stimuli you encounter, and/or a mirage of the social order, which teaches you to renounce your desire's excess and ambivalence so that you can be intelligible under the discipline of the norms that make hierarchies of social value seem natural by rooting them in the pseudonatural structure of heterosexualized sexual difference.

This version of the mirage of stable identity has been most fully thought through by Jacques Lacan and social theorists who think with his work. Lacan defines "the subject" as an effect of the anxiety that is generated by the assumption of an identity within what he calls the symbolic order. From this point of view, the production of subjects with identities that particularize them is identical to the process of their shaping by ideology; this does not mean that there is no such thing as the enigma of personality but that persons find their form, their "selves," by way of fantasy, which includes the projection of impossible desires onto love objects that they hope will provide a bearable, durable sense of stability, alongside of the mediation of norms that make them socially intelligible. Identity is like a turtle shell out of which the subject keeps craning her or his neck to see if and where it might be possible to move: a way of locating, protecting, masking, and disciplining the person.

To make this argument, Lacan reinterprets the split in the scene of primary desire that we have already traced in Freud's work. Once the infant is forced to know her differentiation from the world, she experiences traumatic fragmentation, the instability of everything, abandonment, and loss of mastery; at the same time she misremembers her prior life as an experience of bodily wholeness or integrity. He suggests that she misremembers because, not only was the prior condition disorganized, appetitive, and libidinally unzoned, but the formation of a "memory" of that prior state, which was really just an affective sense and not anything we would typically understand as a memory, was not even possible before the event of the break. Thus her "memory" of this lost form is retroactively constituted, as is all desire and memory, via deferral, lag, displacement, and detour—what Freud calls *Nachträglichkeit*. Lacan calls the state of misremembered self-continuity and wholeness the *imaginary*, and defines the *symbolic* as the condition of traumatized fragmentation in which the subject—under threat of absolute loss/castration— must attempt to but never comfortably assume language and identity to manage her environment and speak her desire (for the mother, and then for the subsequent replacements).

The Lacanian *real*, which represents the unbearable and unsymbolizable limit that is sensed but always missed, puts pressure on the subject to disavow the anxiety of nonmeaning that nonetheless haunts her searching for foundations or anchors in objects. The real, one might say, exerts pressure on the drives to find objects to love, but those objects, bound to the symbolic, are always insufficient to the pressure of fantasy that keeps one driven toward them. But if the real is sensed, the imaginary and the symbolic seem bound to time, presence, and memory. The subject is said to experience these states as though they happened in chronological order—first, the imaginary, vaguely recalled as the time of complete security before the traumatic break, desire, and language set in; then the symbolic, the posttraumatic time of individual anxiety, desire, and speech, as well as the space of culture, ideology, hierarchy, and the abstraction of patriarchal Law. Lacan argues, however, that as the imaginary and the symbolic are simultaneous in the space of the subject's unconscious, but not identical to each other, their lack of fit produces the fluctuating and contradictory feelings of abjection, grandiosity, and ambivalence that the subject is fated to reconcile as "her" desire for the rest of her life (Burgin 1996, 179–275).

Lacan describes the symbolic as built around the abstract and all-powerful Name of the Father (think the Wizard of Oz, before he is revealed to be just an ordinary wizard). This paternal metaphor has a number of functions: in contrast to the perfect father the child thinks she actually has, the Name of the Father is that abstract authority that defines the Laws of cultural hierarchy through language, represses the forces that destabilize order, links social and individual privilege through masculinity, and organizes value fundamentally around sexual difference. Lacan's major work begins in the post–World War II era, and the Name of the Father can be read as a description of monumentalizing fascist technologies of desire, but Lacan's base of pedagogical influence was radically expanded in the era of the '68 "revolution," when a new generation of radicals adopted his ways of describing language, desire, and violence, despite the fact that this generation was countering a different moment in the practices of transnational capitalism. Here the definition of desire as a property of language is sutured to a view of desire as organized fundamentally through and experienced as a property of sexual difference and sexuality.

In contrast to Freud's literal description of castration anxiety at the center of sexual difference and heterosexual desire, Lacan focuses on the drama of symbolic castration in the production of identity and the desire that flows in excess of it. I have described the "Name of the Father" as the place of Law in the symbolic order of culture. It is signified by the phallus, which conjoins the separation of the sexes to the authority of abstract truth. Lacan takes up the symbolic and anatomical scenarios of castration through a distinction between the phallus and the penis, in which the symbolic term (phallus) signifies all of the relations of possession one can have to the object of desire: the penis (having it or not having it, being [bearing or symbolizing] it or not). But how abstract is the phallus? Many have argued that the phallus as the figure of the Law relies on the anatomical penis to give it form and prop it up (Gallop 1982). Yet in this version of sexual difference, it is not just women whose lack subordinates them to masculinist social regimes. Men are also subordinated to phallic masculinity. Even as there seems to be conventional referential continuity between the symbolic and the fleshly sign, masculinity is constantly threatened by the fragility of their linkage. In Oedipal terms, this ordeal is ceaseless, for the male child can never have the "mother" he has lost. He must possess substitute love objects and use the Law/language to master the anxiety created by his ambivalence, as that anxiety itself is the measure of his inadequacy at being well-gendered. For Lacan, therefore, sexual difference is organized around, not the penis and vagina, but the *gendering of anxiety*. Neither the male nor the female ever "possesses" the phallus: it can only represent loss and desire. In Lacanian terms, however, only the woman represents the *objet a*, the unattainable Other who always exceeds the phallic value she is supposed to represent. Men live wholly in the symbolic, insofar as they live the privilege and burden of identifying with/as the Law.

This suggests a painful contradiction within masculinity, for the very logic that authorizes the penis to be misrecognized as the phallus or Law sentences men to experience anxieties of adequacy and dramas of failure. The price of privilege is the instability at its foundation. How, then, does psychoanalysis help us to see the contingency that is disavowed in the domains of masculine privilege? Lacan argues that if the "unconscious is that chapter of my history that is marked by a blank [or] occupied by a falsehood," the censored material is written down in monuments like the symptoms that represent on the body, in archives of memory and seemingly impersonal traces that take on uncanny values, like childhood memories, in the presumptions of language and tradition, and in narrative norms (Lacan 1977, 46–50). Masculinity in particular involves creating the kind of mirage of identity an impostor or impersonator enacts. The solidity of the successful performance secures the aura of masculinity as a fixed and monumental presence (Copjec 1994, 234). Yet we also know that ambivalence, anxiety, and other forms of sexual surplus are never fully absorbed into the managerial economy of gender identity; in the symbolics of conventional masculinity, uncertainty and agitation are frequently projected onto women or "Woman," who becomes figured negatively as the origin of a *threat* to masculinity and positively as *temptation* and, more fetishistically, as *resolution* to ambivalence.

In contrast, Lacan argues that, in a woman's relation to the fetish object, what she becomes in ordinary masculine desire is a relation of masquerade: she must wear the mask to be intelligibly feminine, but because she is not fully absorbed by the symbolic, she can reveal more or less of the artificiality of her mask. This is a direct contrast to the impostor the male-identified man must be in order to obscure the difference between his penis and the phallus; because the impostor must seem natural in the identity he expresses, there can be little "play" in the expression of masculinity. But, Lacan argues, if women are subordinated by the threat that they represent to the authority of the phallus/penis, they are also the excess, the irreducible difference that cannot be managed by its regime. This exorbitant material, which is associated with "Woman" and exceeds the order of the symbolic, is also called *jouissance* and abjection: that sublime affect which shatters or overwhelms the subject's stability in language, in identity, and therefore also in society (Cixous 1983, 875–93; Kristeva 1982). In this conceptualization, women are positioned to generate a radically different kind of language, law, and desire (Lacan 1982, 162–71).

There has been a vast literature of feminist response to Lacan from within psychoanalysis, arguing that the abstraction "the Name of the Father" is really just the ideology of male supremacy in newly inscribed monumental form, or arguing that if a patriarchal identity form requires "Woman" to mirror it, then "Woman" is, after all, the holder of the Law (Rose 1982, 27–57; Žižek 1994a). In addition, the heterosexual presumptiveness of his model of desire has generated incisive critique (Roof 1991). Yet Lacan's theoretical sundering of the phallus from the penis has also productively informed feminist and LGBTQ work: since the cultural rules of intelligibility and value that overorganize desire into relations of identity are not considered invariably attached to particular bodies (e.g., the phallus does not equal the penis), as in Freud, and since masquerade and imposture seem to describe the relations of people to gender identity, it has been suggested that gender and sexuality are really the *effects* of identification or citation (Butler 1990, 1993; Edelman 1993; Bersani and Phillips 2008; Viego 2007). It has also been used to explain why live sexualities and sexually racialized nonnormative embodiments represent such a threat to powerful interests. Males adopt masculinity by citing the normative practices they see men do; the same goes for females; the same goes for heterosexuals who mobilize conventional gender classifications.

(For non-heteronormative patriarchial kinship, see Herdt 1997.) But inevitably, the sexual subject will always fail to be the generic one (Rose 1986). In this sense the linkage between conventional gendering and failure feels both melodramatic and mundane: what are the consequences if you try to "quote" the normal practices identified with your gender and you fail (think about *Superman*, *The House of Mirth*, *The Bluest Eye*, *Vertigo*, *Boys Don't Cry*)? What if you succeed in gendering yourself all too well, taking on your gendered identity as a fetish, a monumental substitute that tries to repress your anxiety about vulnerability, loss, and failure (think *Dracula*, *Madame Bovary*, *Blade Runner*)? The dramatic scenario of aspirational gender performance that I just outlined is ordinary life for many. Is not this scenario of gender and desire also the modern story of adolescent romance (as Thompson writes about in *Going All the Way* [1995])?

Judith Butler's antinormative view of sexuality, which follows from these kinds of questions, contends that if the laws of sexual and gender identity are collectively "misquoted" or redistorted by the abjected or marginalized subjects who refuse subordination to them, then the representational rules of those laws and norms can change (Butler 1993; Doane 1991). Indeed, the centrality of failure, negativity, and partial successes in the striving for gender to provide the foundation it promises but always fails to be is the condition for its symbolic and practical transformation. But a historical view of this optimistic scenario reminds us how much performative variation a dominant regime can absorb into its normative domain; for these citational changes on gender to reverberate as social critique of the law and for other subjects, a political context that amplifies them and links them to other transformative practices needs to exist. In addition, as suggested earlier, all men do not live the privilege of the patriarchalized "phallus" identically; nor does the fiction of "Woman" in the symbolic limit or mark all women in the same way: racism, colonialism, heteronormativity, class entitlement, and other forms of hierarchy interfere with the fantasy that sexual difference has a universal meaning (Abel, Christian, and Moglen 1997; Faderman 1991; Spillers 1987, 64–81; Spivak 1992; Steedman 1986). Despite their critical relation to the psychoanalytic tradition, thinkers in the Lacanian genealogy tend to work within its tendency to flatten out the differences in scale, intensity, and value of the effects different kinds of events have on the subject. In any case, we see here an important transformation in the history of the idea of subjectivity: the model of soulful universal rationality that defines the paradigmatic Enlightenment subject is supplanted by a model of the human who is destabilized not only by conflicting and powerful drives, but by the contradictory exigencies of identity as such. Sexual politics wagers that these contradictions can be made productive rather than paralyzing and repetitious—given the right material conditions for transformative consciousness and practice.

Another vital tradition of anti-psychoanalytic thought criticizes psychoanalysis in the name of desire's irregularity, excess, and incoherence, but this time the critique focuses on moving beyond notions of the bodily ego or identity entirely. Focusing on the *surface* or *topographical* trajectories of the *body*, Gilles Deleuze and Félix Guattari, Elizabeth Grosz, and others talk about the way the attachments that desire engenders constantly reorganize the body into a state, or states, of "becoming," which in turn radically reshapes the body as an erotic zone, a zone of meaning, value, and power (Deleuze and Guattari 1977; Grosz 1994; Griggers 1997; Probyn 1996). They use the language of "deterritorialization" and "reterritorialization" to describe the process by which desire undoes the zone of its identity and then remakes itself according to the mode in which it lands in a new space and "civilizes" it. In this view desire attaches itself to forms that, in turn, have an impact on the desiring subject, reorganizing its self-relation, changing the form and the spaces of its desire. The more attachments, the more transformation: the "rhizomatics" of desire produce a model of embodied affect constantly branching out. Genital sexuality in this view no longer has to organize the bodily senses, and both personal and political histories are therefore opened to practices beyond the violence of the "molar" (supposedly unified and bounded) identity form and institutional desire.

Capitalist dynamics of product and profit, which have intensified their organization and exploitation of the body during the last century, would also be overturned by this notion of the subject who becomes an entity outside of the triangulated Oedipal "Mommy–Daddy–Me" prison of psychoanalysis. This radical way of reading the subject's construction by her desire not only refuses the view that the subject is a traumatized infantile core knotted up by the compulsion to repeat a normative erotic organization, but also produces ways of reading sensation that has the subject's affect inevitably exceeding the normal and proper codes that try to organize her, as she moves through the world becoming impacted by and different within the event of her encounters. On the other hand, as we have seen, desire's restless drive toward finding spaces and shapes will always be met, if not overmatched, by the coercive and seductive forms of propriety, virtue, and discipline that organize societies, and individual will cannot dissolve these by force or by theory. What is the status of desire's excesses for the individual or social order, then? Can *anything* general be said about it?

Questions like this have brought under fire the concept of "desire" itself as a useful political or analytic tool. Critics like Michel Foucault and Gayle Rubin remove individual desire from the center of the analysis of sexuality. Instead, they focus on the practices of *populations* that are made socially visible in institutionally complex fields of power, like cities, prisons, clinics, and nations. In this view, "sexuality" is not what it often seems to be, the sum of the erotic desires and practices with which a person identifies, and which a person can express as if from the core of her being; nor is it the process of libidinization we have been tracking in the Freudian or Lacanian context. Sexuality does not emerge naturally from subjects, in Foucault's view. It is a field of normative bodily and affective practices with which subjects are taught to identify and about which they are taught to speak—to their families, their teachers, the church, the state, the medical profession, and especially psychoanalysts. It is produced by institutional and ideological relations between experience, knowledge, and power. A culture of individuating but institutionally inflected confession has grown up to engender "sexuality," which, Foucault says, is a form of discourse about "desire" and the genital practices that are said to express it; he argues that the main organs of modern sexuality are the mouth and the ear. From this perspective, the drives, desire, pleasures are underdescribed by the normative discourse called "sexuality."

But this does not mean that sexuality is merely an effect of implanted institutional domination. It is a historicizable and relational concept that can be traced to the emergence of modern classificatory institutions. Until relatively recently, sexual identity was not even an idea about desire's form, or a way of taxonomizing and disciplining people. For example, there may always have been people with same-sex desire and people who performed same-sex sex acts, but historians of sexuality tell us that the categories "homosexuality" and "heterosexuality" were invented in the 1890s as a part of a general movement to classify perverts or the non-normal in order to construct the terms of the modern, civilized individuality to which we have already referred. In other words, the unity of sexual desire, sexual identity, and sexual practice that "moderns" take as given in the late twentieth century has never been a "fact" of personhood at all (Chauncey 1994; Halley 1995, 24–38; Halperin 2002; also Burger 2003; Fradenburg 2002; Fradenburg and Creccero 1996; Goldberg and Menon 2005, 1608–17; Katz 1995; Lochrie 2005; Lochrie, McCracken, and Schultz 1997).

References

Abel, Elizabeth, Barbara Christian, and Helene Moglen, eds. 1997. *Female Subjects in Black and White: Race, Psychoanalysis, Feminism.* Berkeley: University of California Press.

Apter, Emily, and William Pietz, eds. 1993. *Fetishism as Cultural Discourse: Gender, Commodity, and Vision*. Ithaca, NY: Cornell University Press.

Barthes, Roland. 1975. *The Pleasure of the Text*. Trans. Richard Miller. New York: Hill and Wang.

———. 1976. *Sade, Fourier, Loyola*. Trans. Richard Miller. New York: Hill and Wang.

Benjamin, Jessica. 1995. *Like Subjects, Love Objects: Essays on Recognition and Sexual Difference*. New Haven, CT: Yale University Press.

Berlant, Lauren, ed. 1998. "Intimacy." Special issue of *Critical Inquiry* 24 (2).

Berlant, Lauren, and Michael Warner. 1998. "Sex in Public." *Critical Inquiry* 24 (2).

Bersani, Leo. 1986. *The Freudian Body: Psychoanalysis and Art*. New York: Columbia University Press.

Bersani, Leo, and Adam Phillips. 2008. *Intimacies*. Chicago: University of Chicago Press.

Brennan, Teresa. 1992. *The Interpretation of the Flesh: Freud and Femininity*. New York: Routledge.

Burger, Glenn. 2003. *Chaucer's Queer Nation*. Minneapolis: University of Minnesota Press.

Burgin, Victor. 1996. *In/different Spaces: Places and Memory in Visual Culture*. Berkeley: University of California Press.

Butler, Judith. 1990. *Gender Trouble: Feminism and the Subversion of Identity*. New York: Routledge.

———. 1993. *Bodies That Matter: On the Discursive Limits of "Sex."* New York: Routledge.

Chatterjee, Partha. 1994. *The Nation and Its Fragments: Colonial and Postcolonial Histories*. New York: Oxford University Press.

Chauncey, George. 1994. *Gay New York: Gender, Urban Culture, and the Makings of the Gay Male World, 1890–1940*. New York: Basic Books.

Chodorow, Nancy. 1978. *The Reproduction of Mothering: Psychoanalysis and the Sociology of Gender*. Berkeley: University of California Press.

Cixous, Hélène. 1981. "The Laugh of the Medusa" (1975). Trans. Keith Cohen and Paula Cohen. In *New French Feminisms*, ed. Elaine Marks and Isabelle de Courtivon. New York: Schocken Books.

———. 1983. "Portrait of Dora" (1976). Trans. Sarah Burd. *Diacritics* 13 (1).

Copjec, Joan. 1994. *Read My Desire: Lacan against the Historicists*. Cambridge, MA: MIT Press.

de Lauretis, Teresa. 1994. *The Practice of Love: Lesbian Sexuality and Perverse Desire*. Bloomington: Indiana University Press.

Deleuze, Gilles. 1971. *Masochism: An Interpretation of Coldness and Cruelty*. Trans. Jean McNeil. New York: George Brazilier.

———. 1992. "Postscript on the Societies of Control." *October* 59.

Deleuze, Gilles, and Félix Guattari. 1977. *Anti-Oedipus: Capitalism and Schizophrenia*. Trans. Robert Hurley, Mark Seem, and Helen Lane. New York: Viking.

D'Emilio, John, and Estelle B. Freedman. 1988. *Intimate Matters: A History of Sexuality in America*. New York: Harper & Row.

Doane, Mary Ann. 1991. *Femmes Fatales: Feminism, Film Theory, Psychoanalysis*. New York: Routledge.

Echols, Alice. 1989. *Daring to Be Bad: Radical Feminism in America, 1967–1975*. Minneapolis: University of Minnesota Press.

Edelman, Lee. 1994. *Homographesis: Essays in Gay Literary and Cultural Theory.* New York: Routledge.

Faderman, Lillian. 1991. *Odd Girls and Twilight Lovers: A History of Lesbian Life in Twentieth-Century America.* New York: Columbia University Press.

Fradenburg, L. O. Aranye. 2002. *Sacrifice Your Love: Psychoanalysis, Historicism, Chaucer.* Minneapolis: University of Minnesota Press.

Fradenburg, Louise, and Carla Freccero, eds. 1996. *Premodern Sexualities.* New York: Routledge.

Freud, Sigmund. 1949. *Three Essays on the Theory of Sexuality* (1905). In *The Standard Edition of the Complete Psychological Works of Sigmund Freud*, trans. and ed. James Strachey, vol. 7. London: Hogarth Press.

———. 1957. "The Economic Problem of Masochism" (1924). In *The Standard Edition of the Complete Psychological Works of Sigmund Freud*, trans. and ed. James Strachey, vol. 12. London: Hogarth Press.

———. 1961a. "The Ego and the Id" (1923). In *The Standard Edition of the Complete Psychological Works of Sigmund Freud*, trans. and ed. James Strachey, vol. 19. London: Hogarth Press.

———. 1961b. "Some Psychical Consequences of the Anatomical Distinction between the Sexes" (1925). In *The Standard Edition of the Complete Psychological Works of Sigmund Freud*, trans. and ed. James Strachey, vol. 19. London: Hogarth Press.

———. 1964. "Femininity" (1933). In *New Introductory Essays on Psychoanalysis*, in *The Complete Psychological Works of Sigmund Freud*, trans. and ed. James Strachey, vol. 22. London: Hogarth Press.

Gallop, Jane. 1982. *The Daughter's Seduction: Feminism and Psychoanalysis.* Ithaca, NY: Cornell University Press.

Gilman, Sander. 1985. *Difference and Pathology: Stereotypes of Sexuality, Race, and Madness.* Ithaca, NY: Cornell University Press.

Goldberg, Jonathan, and Madhavi Menon. 2005. "Queering History." *PMLA* 120 (5).

Griggers, Camilla. 1997. *Becoming-Woman.* Minneapolis: University of Minnesota Press.

Grosz, Elizabeth A. 1994. *Volatile Bodies: Toward a Corporeal Feminism.* Bloomington: Indiana University Press.

Halley, Janet. 1995. "The Politics of the Closet: Legal Articulation of Sexual Orientation Identity." In *After Identity: A Reader in Law and Culture*, ed. Dan Daniels and Karen Engle. New York: Routledge.

Halperin, David. 2002. *How to Do the History of Homosexuality.* Chicago: University of Chicago Press.

Haraway, Donna. 1991. *Simians, Cyborgs, and Women.* New York: Routledge.

Herdt, Gilbert H. 1997. *Same Sex, Different Cultures: Gays and Lesbians across Cultures.* Boulder: Westview Press.

Irigaray, Luce. 1985. *Speculum of the Other Woman.* Trans. Gillian Gill. Ithaca, NY: Cornell University Press.

Kaplan, Caren. 1996. *Questions of Travel: Postmodern Discourses of Displacement.* Durham, NC: Duke University Press.

Katz, Jonathan Ned. 1995. *The Invention of Heterosexuality.* New York: Dutton.

Kennedy, Elizabeth Lapovsky, and Madeline Davis. 1993. *Boots of Leather, Slippers of Gold: The History of a Lesbian Community.* New York: Routledge.

Klein, Melanie, and Joan Rivière. 1964. *Love, Hate, and Reparation*. New York: Norton.

Kristeva, Julia. 1982. *Powers of Horror: Essays in Abjection*. Trans. Leon S. Roudiez. New York: Columbia University Press.

Lacan, Jacques. 1977. *Ecrits*, trans. Alan Sheridan. New York: Norton.

———. 1982. *Feminine Sexuality: Jacques Lacan and the École Freudienne*, eds. Jacqueline Rose and Juliet Mitchell. New York: Norton.

Laplanche, Jean. 1976. *Life and Death in Psychoanalysis*. Trans. Jeffrey Mehlman. Baltimore: Johns Hopkins University Press.

Laplanche, Jean, and Jean-Bertrand Pontalis. 1973. *The Language of Psycho-Analysis*. Trans. Donald Nicholson-Smith London: Hogarth Press.

Lipsitz, George. 1990. *Time Passages*. Minneapolis: University of Minnesota Press.

Lochrie, Karma. 2005. *Heterosyncracies: Female Sexuality When Normal Wasn't*. Minneapolis: University of Minnesota Press.

Lochrie, Karma, Peggy McCracken, and James Schultz. 1997. *Constructing Medieval Sexuality*. Minneapolis: University of Minnesota Press.

Marcuse, Herbert. 1964. *One-Dimensional Man*. Boston: Beacon.

———. 1969. *An Essay on Liberation*. Boston: Beacon.

McClintock, Anne. 1995. *Imperial Leather: Race, Gender, and Sexuality in the Colonial Contest*. New York: Routledge.

Minsky, Rosalind, ed. 1996. *Psychoanalysis and Gender: An Introductory Reader*. New York: Routledge.

Mitchell, Juliet. 1974. *Psychoanalysis and Feminism*. New York: Random House.

Modleski, Tania. 1982. *Loving with a Vengeance: Mass-Produced Fantasies for Women*. Hamden, CT: Archon Books.

Mulvey, Laura. 1989. "Visual Pleasure and Narrative Cinema" (1975). In *Visual and Other Pleasures*. Bloomington: Indiana University Press.

Newton, Esther. 1993. *Cherry Grove Fire Island: Sixty Years in America's First Gay and Lesbian Town*. Boston: Beacon.

Phillips, Adam. 1994. "Freud and the Uses of Forgetting." In *On Flirtation: Psychoanalytic Essays on the Uncommitted Life*. London: Faber and Faber.

Probyn, Elspeth. 1996. *Outside Belongings*. New York: Routledge.

Rabine, Leslie W. 1985. "Romance in the Age of Electronics: Harlequin Enterprises." In *Feminist Criticism and Social Change: Sex, Class and Race in Literature and Culture*, ed. Judith Newton and Deborah Rosenfelt. New York: Methuen.

Radway, Janice A. 1984. *Reading the Romance: Women, Patriarchy, and Popular Literature*. Chapel Hill: University of North Carolina Press.

Roof, Judith. 1991. *A Lure of Knowledge: Lesbian Sexuality and Theory*. New York: Columbia University Press.

Rose, Jacqueline. 1982. "Introduction II." In Lacan 1982.

———. 1986. *Sexuality in the Field of Vision*. London: Verso.

Saunders, Jean. 1985. *The Craft of Writing Romance*. London: Allison and Busby.

Sayers, Sohnya, Anders Stephanson, Stanley Aronowitz, and Fredric Jameson, eds. 1984. "The 60s without Apology." Special issue of *Social Text* 9/10.

Schor, Naomi. 1985. "Female Fetishism: The Case of Georges Sand." *Poetics Today* 6.

———. 1987. *Reading in Detail: Aesthetics and the Feminine*. New York: Methuen.

———. 1993. "Fetishism and Its Ironies." In Apter and Pietz 1983.

Sedgwick, Eve Kosofsky. 1990. *Epistemology of the Closet*. Berkeley: University of California Press.

———. 1993. "A Poem Is Being Written." In *Tendencies*. Durham, NC: Duke University Press.

Silverman, Kaja. 1988. *The Acoustic Mirror: The Female Voice in Psychoanalysis and Cinema*. Bloomington: Indiana University Press.

Sommer, Doris. 1984. *Foundational Fictions: The National Romances of Latin America*. Berkeley: University of California Press.

Spillers, Hortense J. 1987. "Mama's Baby, Papa's Maybe: An American Grammar Book." *Diacritics* 17.

Spivak, Gayatri Chakravorty. 1992. "Acting Bits/Identity Talks." *Critical Inquiry* 18.

Steedman, Carolyn Kay. 1986. *Landscape for a Good Woman: A Story of Two Lives*. Newark: Rutgers University Press.

Thompson, Sharon. 1995. *Going All the Way: Teenage Girls' Tales of Sex, Romance, and Pregnancy*. New York: Hill and Wang.

Viego, Antonio. 2007. *Dead Subjects: Toward a Politics of Loss in Latino Studies*. Durham, NC: Duke University Press.

Warner, Michael. 1993. *Fear of a Queer Planet: Queer Politics and Social Theory*. Minneapolis: University of Minnesota Press.

Winnicott, D. W. 1958. *Collected Papers: Through Paediatrics to Psychoanalysis*. London: Hogarth Press.

———. 1971. *Playing and Reality*. London: Routledge.

———. 1986. *Home Is Where We Start From: Essays by a Psychoanalyist*. New York: Norton.

Wittig, Monique. 1992. *The Straight Mind and Other Essays*. Boston: Beacon.

Žižek, Slavoj. 1989. *The Sublime Object of Ideology*. London: Verso.

———. 1994a. *The Metastases of Enjoyment: Six Essays on Woman and Causality*. London: Verso.

———. 1994b. "The Spectre of Ideology." In *Mapping Ideology*, ed. Slavoj Žižek. London: Verso.

4 :: ETHNICITY ANNA SAMPAIO

Ethnicity is a fundamental form of social and political organization that serves as a tool for the construction of group and personal identity. Like gender, race, and class, it is a socially constructed marker that binds individuals to larger groups and associations by emphasizing a common past within a contemporary identity. While the precise definition of ethnicity has been contested, resulting in variations over time, today ethnicity typically refers to the shared customs, cultures, and traditions of a group of people, including such aspects as common language, religion, food, and music, as well as collective histories of discrimination and resistance to it.

Ethnicity as a concept gained popularity among academics during the great wave of immigration from Europe to the Americas at the beginning of the twentieth century. Between 1920 and 1950, social scientists increasingly turned to theories of ethnicity as an alternative to racist theories that suggested that one's status and position in society was strictly a function of biological heritage. Drawn by a desire better to understand the changing composition of the country brought on by a large wave of new immigrants to the United States from southern and eastern Europe, sociologists found concepts of ethnicity useful in analyzing and clarifying both the shared histories of these new Americans and the distinctions that kept them from becoming fully incorporated into the country. These groups came to be understood as ethnic minorities, namely, populations who shared a similar racial makeup with the dominant class of Anglo-Saxons and northern and western Europeans, but who held distinct customs, traditions, and even linguistic practices that set them apart and made them seem different. Ethnicity became a source of support and strength for immigrants as they faced both hostility and strong incentives to "assimilate"—to give up their unique cultural past in order to melt into the common definitions of Americanness and whiteness. Some members of ethnic minorities sought refuge among neighbors and

people who shared their cultural history, leading eventually to the formation of ethnic enclaves across the United States.

Despite the popularity of the term in describing cultural associations and forms of political organizing among European immigrants, its
salience when applied to racial minorities has been far more strained.
Efforts to categorize African Americans, Asian Americans, and American Indians simply as ethnic minorities, whose marginalization paralleled that of European immigrants, evaded the legacy of racial hierarchy
deeply embedded in American society and politics that privileged whites.
In the southwest specifically, "ethnicity theorists" often challenged the
pervasive and denigrating depictions of Mexican Americans, Latinos,
and other mestizos as biologically inferior, even as they proffered stereotypical notions of them as culturally backward. The application of these
theories in Americanization programs intended to assimilate Mexican
immigrants into an American identity revealed problematic tensions and
a tendency to view Mexicans and other nonwhites as culturally inferior.

Efforts by women of color to articulate intersectional identities, in
contradistinction to the privileging of gendered and racial norms emerging respectively from the women's liberation and civil rights movements,
introduced still other approaches to the study and embodiment of ethnicity. These new theories, framing identity as intersectional rather than
monolithic, recognized the simultaneous and often competing forms of
marginalization experienced by women of color, including those predicated on ethnicity, race, gender, class, and sexual preference. They again
redefined ethnicity both as a source of social and political organization
and a framework for analysis.

This essay explores the concept of ethnicity, looking specifically at the
historical formation and usage of the term in the twentieth century and
its popular application to the great wave of European immigrants. Implicit in this history is ethnicity's dual function both as a tool for social
scientists looking to explain the patterns of incorporation among some
groups and as a signifier for immigrants and minorities looking to form
social and political bonds with others who share a similar cultural past
in order to shield themselves from hostility and forms of discrimination.

In addition, the essay examines tensions in the application of ethnicity theories to racial minorities, particularly the manifestation of ethnic
theories in the lives of Mexican Americans and other Latinas and Latinos and the attending political projects of Americanization and assimilation, which privilege whiteness. One reason for highlighting the history
of Latinas and Latinos is the enduring attention to ethnicity, even as the
focus on race and racism in the United States becomes more pronounced
in their lives and that of other nonwhites. Ethnic divisions in the United

States remain a salient feature among Latinas and Latinos because the population straddles the line between definitions of race and ethnicity. Encompassing a broad array of national origin groups with complex colonial histories, Latinos don't easily conform to classic definitions of race (emphasizing phenotypical or ancestral uniformity) or ethnicity (emphasizing common customs and traditions). Feminist philosopher Linda Martin Alcoff notes that theories of ethnicity typically fail to capture the reality of most Latinos' lives, while simultaneously supplanting discussions of race and class inequalities (Alcoff 2000, 312–59). Ultimately, efforts by Mexican American women and Latinas generally demonstrate the work of women of color who reject, resist, and even reimagine definitions of ethnicity (as well as race and gender) to better explain their experiences in the United States. Paying attention to the applications of ethnicity in the lives of Mexican Americans and other Latinos thus reveals the complexities and limitations of historic definitions of ethnicity, especially when challenged to explain forms of racial and class inequality. Moreover, the experiences of Latinas and Latinos provide a platform for theorizing about ethnicity, race, class, and gender altogether.

Background: Ethnicity Theory and the Americanization Process

By the beginning of the twentieth century, the US had witnessed both an end to the formal institutions of slavery and a subsequent failure to address the enduring racial inequality and animosity aimed at nonwhites. Efforts to explain away the persistent marginalization of key segments of the country (particularly African Americans, American Indians/Native Americans, and women as a group) resulted in the popularity of theories of biological determinism, social Darwinism, and the accompanying eugenics movement. Until 1920 the prevailing view of social differences maintained that one's identity, temperament, intellect, and even character were encoded in biology, and as such social, political, and economic status was predetermined at birth. Biological determinists further explained differences between populations by focusing on skin color and concluding that white skin produced superior social characteristics, while darker skin imbued people with lesser social, cultural, and intellectual abilities that were impossible to alter (Omi and Winant 1994, 14; Rothenberg 1990, 44–47).

With regard to gender, theories of biological determinism were similarly invoked to argue that women lacked the mental, physical, or emotional capacity to fully participate in society and thus should be relegated to their own separate spheres. Already in the 1800s, when women pushed to gain access to institutions of higher education, some scientists had claimed that they could not be educated because they lacked sufficient cranial capacity. Others cautioned that diverting energy to women's brains in the course of academic study would result in the shrinking of their reproductive organs, leading eventually to problems of sterility. Overwhelmingly, women were characterized as weak, overemotional, and at the mercy of their hormones (Rothenberg 1990, 44–47).

Ultimately, the belief in the inherent inferiority of nonwhites, already institutionalized in laws restricting citizenship to white persons, became further ensconced in other laws and policies that attempted to limit the number of putatively unassimilable immigrants (namely, southern and eastern Europeans) from entering the United States, while simultaneously encouraging immigration from the British Isles, Scandanavian countries, and Germany (Daniels 2004).

Challenges to this view emerged from social scientists and progressives who emphasized ethnicity as the dominant social category that influenced identity and one that was suppressed by a system of discrimination. Sociologists Horace Kallen (1924) and Robert E. Park (Park and Miller 1921; Park, McKenzie, and Burgess 1925: Park 1928), whose work was extended in later years by Nathan Glazer (Glazer and Moynihan 1963, 1975; Glazer 1983) and Gunnar Myrdal (1962) put forth an alternative reading of humanity focused on "ethnicity" defined as a form of group identity predicated on one's shared culture (including religion, language, customs, nationality, and political identification) and descent (specifically heredity and a shared sense of ancestry). Park and the Chicago school of sociology maintained that race and the assertions of white privilege prevalent among biological determinists constituted a social category that was epiphenomenal—or secondary—to a larger framework of ethnicity that included elements of "culture" and "descent" (Park and Miller 1921).

Drawing their analysis from the then-contemporary great migration of Europeans, Park and the "ethnicity theorists" focused their analysis on conflicts experienced by this population, including the formation of distinct ethnic identities; struggles for incorporation among ethnic minorities; and the relationship of ethnicity to the prevailing political order. Central to this analysis was a push for immigrant incorporation and integration that revealed theoretical differences among those focused on ethnicity. Between 1930 and 1965, divisions arose between social scientists who believed European immigrants (and African Americans migrating north from the southern states) would assimilate into an American "melting pot," and those who believed they would gravitate toward a more pluralistic, albeit ethnically specific, form of civic participation. One significant distinction between these concepts relates to their interpretation of culture and inequality. While social scientists following the logic of an assimilationist model argued that ethnic groups shed their cultural baggage after arriving in the United States, cultural pluralists maintained that immigrants went through a transformation after their initial insertion into American life but would retain their distinct ethnic and cultural perspectives, if for no other reason than political gain (Omi and Winant 1994, 20–22). These ethnic and cultural differences included linguistic and religious practices, as well as family organization (such as the prevalence of extended family networks), gendered divisions of labor in the home, and culinary practices. In essence, advocates of assimilation favored an approach to culture and ethnicity that promoted conformance to standards tied to Anglo-Saxon traditions, customs, and values, which were themselves racialized and gendered but presented as quintessentially American.

Scholars favoring assimilation further argued that the American creed of democracy and equality would prevail in any ethnic conflict and undo problems of inequality and segregation. They viewed associations based on ethnicity (such as ethnic enclaves like "little Italy" in Boston or New York) as stages in a pattern of incorporation that would ultimately end in assimilation. As evidence, they pointed to the pattern of acculturation by which previous waves of European immigrants, such as German Americans, had been assimilated into American life (Glazer and Moynihan 1975; Myrdal 1962). On the other hand, scholars emphasizing cultural pluralism supported the elimination of formal barriers to civic participation, such as Jim Crow laws, while emphasizing equality of opportunity for individuals, as opposed to collective rights for entire racial and ethnic groups (Kallen 1924). Cultural pluralists subscribed to the belief that ethnic groups could and would retain forms of cultural difference while still integrating into an American context.

These distinct views on the degree to which ethnic populations should give up their customs, culture, and traditions and adopt an "American" identity were crystallized in the prominent metaphors used to illustrate their analysis. Assimilationists commonly invoked the "melting pot" image to capture the idea of immigrants melding into one giant American ideal, while cultural pluralists often retorted that the mix of individual ethnic groups was more like a "salad bowl," with different populations joined in a collective experience but without sacrificing essential differences or their integrity as separate entities.

As scholarship on ethnicity theory evolved, especially in the midst of civil rights movements that resulted in the repeal of various forms of de jure discrimination, both assimilationists and cultural pluralists increasingly turned to "culture of poverty" theories. These theories pointed to the internal cultural dynamics of ethnic minorities to explain enduring inequalities. Once formal obstacles to democratic participation were removed, they argued, immigrants would have to rely on their own resources (values, cultural logic, support networks, etc.) to propel them into successful positions. If ethnic minorities nonetheless remained in a state of inequality, then advocates of both assimilation and pluralism agreed that it was because of some failing within their own cultural environment. Thus, by midcentury, "ethnicity theorists" diverged from their more biologically deterministic predecessors by emphasizing culture over biology; however, they increasingly shared with the early racial theorists the presumption that problems of inequality or exclusion of ethnic groups were somehow related to the internal operations of those subordinate populations.

Extending Ethnicity to Nonwhites: "The Mexican Problem"

Studies of ethnic minorities took on distinctive manifestations in the discourse and popular culture of the American southwest. The application of ethnicity theories to Mexican Americans there paralleled the debates around other mixed-race and nonwhite populations in the United States, as well as research in Latin America, by simultaneously encouraging integration and overlooking enduring forms of racial and class inequality that prevented it. In particular, noted anthropologists such as Emory Bogardus (1934), Munro Edmunson (1957), Florence Kluckhohn (Kluckhohn and Strodbeck 1961), Lyle Saunders (1954), Ruth Tuck (1946), and William Madsen (1964) extended the "culture of poverty" thesis popular among ethnicity theorists to explain the persistent poverty, political disenfranchisement, and lack of education among Mexican Americans. Bogardus, for example, argued:

> The fundamental problem of second generation Mexicans is their lack of environmental stimuli.... They have not had the skilled leadership in organization work as the Japanese have had. Neither have they had popular speakers to challenge and arouse them, as the Negroes have had. The underlying community organization has been exceedingly simple. (Bogardus 1934, 277)

Researchers emphasizing an ethnicity model drawn from the experiences of European immigrants often presumed that Mexican Americans were largely bound by a "traditional culture"—one not fully familiar (and seemingly at odds) with the modernized customs, values, and skills of the Western world. This perception represented a variant of the "culture of poverty" thesis inasmuch as it not only concluded that culture was the ultimate drawback for Mexican Americans, but that this culture emanated from a nonrational, nonmodern, fatalistic set of practices that remained static over time. Thus, sociologist Ruth Tuck wrote:

> The Spanish-speaking person, by contrast (to Anglos), is likely to meet difficulties by adjusting to them rather than by attempting to overcome them.... In the collective recollection of village life there is only the remembrance of men and women who were born, resigned themselves to suffering and hardship and occasional joys, and died when their time came. (Tuck 1946, 129)

As a consequence of such representations, Mexican Americans were rarely seen as active subjects of history or as possessing a political consciousness comparable to that of Western populations. Instead, Mexican American men and women were situated as passive objects of social science inquiry and resigned participants in the sway of insurmountable tradition (Saunders 1954). Moreover, these views on Mexican culture were extended to gender dynamics, with Mexican men consistently described as traditional and unprogressive, and the entire Mexican community as steeped in *machismo* (Sanchez 1990).

Americanization and Mexican Americans in the Southwest

The push toward integration of ethnic minorities, a theme common to virtually all variants of the ethnicity theorists, was especially important in the experiences of Mexican Americans because of its manifestation both in academic debates and in social services that affected these communities on a daily basis. Nowhere was this more apparent than in the "Americanization" programs initiated by well-intentioned but ethnocentric Anglo school officials, church leaders, and youth organizations, which attempted to mold Mexican American children into "model citizens" and "capable workers" in the image of European immigrants of the previous generation (Ruiz 1993; Sanchez 1990, 1993; Vélez-Ibáñez 1996). As early as 1880, public educational institutions such as those in Tucson, Arizona, were encouraging Mexican American children to speak English, eliminate any discernable accents, and mirror the work habits, political practices, and religious rituals of their Anglo American counterparts (Vélez-Ibáñez 1996, 66). Children who failed to meet these standards were frequently ostracized, ridiculed, subjected to corporal punishment, and otherwise marginalized by teachers and administrators. Thus, this push toward Americanization fostered by ethnicity theorists (and fueled by the logic of assimilation) also carried with it a privileging of American "whiteness" by upholding the European immigrant experience as the quintessential model of integration (Ruiz 1993; Sanchez 1993).

This effort was not limited to educational institutions, but was equally reflected in the policies and practices of major employers, as well as in popular images emerging from a nascent Hollywood entertainment industry. Vicki Ruiz (1993) details how changes in clothing for young Mexican American women, who were entering the work force in record numbers by the 1940s, reverberated in various Mexican American households, where parents often perceived such changes as a challenge to their authority and to their own customs and traditions.

Mexican American women became frequent targets of Americanization programs because they were viewed as less resistant to authority and more willing to accept the proposition of conformity offered by state and local governments. Proponents of Americanization frequently subscribed to the notion of women as cultural caretakers within Latino communities, and thus believed they would be able to influence the traditions and cultural practices of other family members by securing the support of the women.[1] In fact, Sanchez (1990) discusses the origins of the Americanization movement among Progressive social reformers, many of whom were middle-class Anglo women who battled such "evils" as obscenity and the production and sale of alcohol. In California, the push toward Americanization took firm hold with the election of Progressive governor Hiram Johnson in 1910. Under Johnson's direction, the state passed legislation in 1913 that created the Commission of Immigration and Housing. This commission was charged with investigating the working and living conditions of all immigrants in the state and leading efforts to teach English to "foreigners" and involve them in Americanization programs (Sanchez 1990, 255).

The view of women as cultural caretakers and its relationship to the Americanization of Mexican Americans was prominent even in congressional hearings where legislators debated the formation of a guest-worker program for Mexican immigrants in the early half of the twentieth century. In testimony before the House Committee on Immigration and Naturalization, one expert argued:

> As the mother furnishes the stream of life to the babe at her breast, so will she shower dewdrops of knowledge on the plastic mind of her young child. Her ideals and aspirations will be breathed into its spirit, molding its character for all time. The child, in turn, will pass these rarer characteristics on to its descendants, thus developing the intellectual, physical, and spiritual qualities of the individual, which in mass are contributions to civilizations. (Quoted in Sanchez 1990, 255)

Ultimately, the push toward Americanization was adopted and championed by leaders within Mexican American and Latino communities, including high-profile organizations such as the YMCA, the Mexican Voice, the Mexican-American Movement Incorporated, and the League of United Latin American Citizens (Muñoz 1989). Mirroring the logic of ethnicity theorists, these organizations preached "character, good citizenship," and the teaching of "desirable values" to Mexican American youth, while advocating assimilation into American life as a means of improving their social welfare, and chastising those who failed to comply. Although many of these groups were cognizant of the conditions of poverty, segregation, and exclusion faced by Mexican American communities, they further echoed the concerns of ethnicity theorists by asserting that the essential problem with Mexican American youth in the United States was their relation to the traditions and attitudes of Mexican culture (Muñoz 1989, 33–36). Thus, Paul Coronel, president of the YMCA Mexican Youth Conference (a yearly summer youth program initiated for young Mexican American men in Los Angeles) said:

> We have concluded that our Mexican youth are not meeting the social and intellectual requirements of our highly progressive American civilization.... We are blaming no one but ourselves ... for our backward conditions. (Quoted in Muñoz 1989, 33)

For all the effort exhausted on achieving the illusive "American dream," programs such as the Americanization schools sponsored by the Los Angeles school district did little to affect the overall economic mobility of Mexican American children. Sanchez reports only minor improvements in income and occupational location between Mexican American parents and their children in this period. Instead, the schools acted as effective tools in binding Mexican American families to the state through the adoption of a "fictive ethnicity" that minimized ethnic difference and pacified Anglo anxieties in turbulent economic times, but which ultimately did little to further Mexican Americans' own social mobility (Sanchez 1993, 10–11). In addition, these programs normalized gendered constructions of motherhood that required Mexican American women be kept in the home and as permanent caretakers, as well as promoting a division of labor and norms of heterosexuality.

Mexican American activists, organizations, and intellectuals who emerged during this period often contributed to the process of Americanization. In doing so, they mirrored the logic and practices of their Anglo counterparts, frequently echoing the assertions of "ethnicity theorists" that Mexican culture created endemic and enduring shortcomings within Mexican American communities and that their successful incorporation could only be achieved by leaving behind their culture and heritage.

Challenging Ethnicity Theorists, Assimilation, and Americanization

By the late 1950s and early 1960s, the limits of ethnicity theory had become increasingly apparent, with challenges to historical discrimination, Americanization, and assimilation emerging from communities of racial minorities across the country. Activists and allies within communities of color resisted both the demeaning discourse of biological determinists and ethnicity theorists that privileged whiteness, and the institutionalization of these logics in state-sponsored initiatives. More importantly, a focus on race and racial inequality became a driving feature of critiques of previous generations and a basis for the construction of new forms of identity.

Among Mexican Americans, challenges both to the discourse driven by ethnicity theorists, which emphasized a culture of poverty among Mexican immigrants, and to service organizations that privileged Americanization and assimilation were integral to the birth of the Chicano movement. New studies emerged to explain the pervasive inequality experienced by Mexican American and other Latinos in the United States (particularly Puerto Ricans), producing theoretical challenges to the primacy of the ethnicity model. These theories included class-based critiques such as the internal colonial model, which maintained Chicanos and Latinos constituted a persistent economic and political underclass in the United States, as well as class-stratification research. However, nationalism—specifically a variant commonly referred to as cultural nationalism, and a concomitant embracing of Chicanismo and Chicano identity—became the most popular theoretical shift embodied in the movement (Acuña 1972).

Collectively, cultural nationalists reenvisioned Mexican Americans and other Latinos in the United States as minorities who shared comparable forms of historical discrimination, racism, cultural deprivation, and economic exploitation. By virtue of this shared past, they asserted that Latinos, like other minorities historically defined as nonwhite, constituted a racial group. In contrast to social theories emphasizing ethnicity as a primary source of collective association and identification, a focus on racial inequality and the assertion of a new racial subjectivity became important hallmarks of civil rights movements among African Americans, Asian Americans, and Chicanos and Latinos.

Among Mexican Americans and other Latinos, the theory of cultural nationalism drew particular attention to the long colonial relationship between the United States and Mexico (and often Puerto Rico) that left Mexican Americans economically and politically subordinate. Paying particular attention to the manifestations of white privilege in US territorial expansion into Mexico—ending with US control of the south-west and the takeover of Puerto Rico—cultural nationalists argued that Mexican Americans and Puerto Ricans had experienced similar his-tories of racist colonial oppression resulting in a collective disenfran-chisement.

Moreover, cultural nationalists critiqued the history of social research on these populations, which had devalued their existence with theories of biological inferiority (popularized among biological determinists, social Darwinists, and eugenicists) and cultural inferiority (especially among ethnicity theorists). They embraced instead an alternative interpretation of Mexican and Latin American culture that recaptured an indigenous past supplanted through colonization and spoke of liberation in the form of self-determination and cultural autonomy. Among movement activ-ists, Mexican American culture was embraced and held up as a testament to the communities' capacity for survival in the face of oppression—not as an obstacle to integration.

Among Chicano activists, this view was expressed clearly and force-fully in the work of artists such as the poet Alurista (1969), in manifestos and speeches by Rodolfo "Corky" Gonzalez, *El Plan Espiritual de Aztlán* and *El Plan de Santa Barbara*, and in the intellectual contributions of aca-demics such as Ernesto Galarza, Americo Paredes, and Octavio Romano and journals such as *El Grito*. Collectively, these writings outlined a phil-osophical guide for the Chicano movement as well as a specific course of action to empower Latino communities. The assertion of a new Chi-cano identity through these writings was coupled with the formation of a number of Chicano youth groups, most notably the Union of Mexican American Students (UMAS) and El Movimiento Estudiantil Chicano de Aztlán (MEChA), and supportive community-based organizations, such as the Crusade for Justice and the Brown Berets; and political organiza-tions (e.g., La Raza Unida Party), all of which helped to institutionalize the philosophy of Chicanismo. Finally, the promulgation of Chicano cul-tural nationalism and its future survival were ensured with the creation of Chicano studies programs at the high school, community college, and university level.

Ultimately, the Chicano and Puerto Rican movements compelled Latinos and other nonwhites to resist the process of Americanization preached by earlier generations and to construct their own identities, drawing on a reconstructed memory of their indigenous past and an em-bracing of their historical cultures and traditions. This movement pro-pelled many within the Mexican American and Puerto Rican communi-ties in the United States to resist the practice and logic of assimilation and Americanization and work toward an alternative identity, which in-

cluded a new definition of politics and political participation and emphasized cultural autonomy and self-determination.

Intersecting Gender, Race, and Ethnicity: Moving Beyond Ethnicity Theory and Nationalism

Challenges to previous discourses that denigrated Mexican American
and other Latino communities engendered additional conflicts as authors and activists in the Chicano movement privileged masculine rhetoric and subjectivities in their assertions of Chicano identity. Chicana
and Latina feminists critiqued the exclusion of women from key leadership positions, the lack of recognition to their work in service to the
movement, and the privileging of male agency pervasive in cultural nationalist discourse.

Chicana feminists who protested the gendered bias within "Chicanismo" were often met with hostility and backlash. As these feminists
frequently noted, the Chicano leadership belittled questions of gendered
stratification between Chicanos and Chicanas and relegated concerns
about gender, sexual harassment, or sexism to private conversation (García 1997, 5). Some Chicano leaders maintained that feminism was strictly
a middle-class white woman's movement with nothing to offer Chicanas
and that focusing on gender to the exclusion of "more pertinent" issues
of racism and class exploitation was politically subversive (Orozco 1986,
12). In the worst scenarios, Chicana and Latina feminists were ostracized
by both men and Chicana "loyalists" who waged personal and political attacks against them (*Las Hijas de Cuahtemoc* 1971, 2).

Following a tradition of African American feminists, Chicanas and Latinas theorized their own identities in a way that linked Chicana sexual
exploitation and gender discrimination to the movement's more familiar themes of racism and internal colonialism. Specifically, Chicana and
Latina feminists asserted their own identity as women of color simultaneously confronting forms of racial, ethnic, class, gender, and sexual
inequality. Caught between gendered movements for women's liberation that marginalized concerns of racial and ethnic discrimination and
the masculinized agency of the Chicano movement, which erased gendered divisions, Chicana and Latina feminism emerged as its own theory,
method, and political practice (García 1990, 1997; Orozco 1986; Pesquera
and Segura 1998).

By the 1970s Chicana and Latina feminists had formed supportive networks of academics and activists through a variety of publications: newsletters and newspapers such as *Las Hijas de Cuahtemoc, Comisíon Feminil
Mexicana Newsletter,* and *Chicana Service Action Center Newsletter* from

Los Angeles, *El Popo Femenil* from California State College, Northridge, and *La Razón Mestiza* from San Francisco, and journals such as *Encuentro Femenil* (García 1997). In 1983 these efforts were institutionalized in academic circles with the formation of the Chicana caucus of the National Association of Chicano Studies (NACS) and Mujeres Activas en Letras y Cambio Social (MALCS). Both organizations advanced the multilayered analysis of power and inequality advocated by Chicana feminists, as well as a new academic discourse centered on Chicana and Latina agency. The creation of these organizations was followed in 1984 by the first NACS conference ("Voces de la Mujer"), dedicated exclusively to examinations of gender within the discipline, and the inauguration of the Chicana/Latina summer research institute by MALCS in 1985.

Theoretically, Gloria Anzaldúa, Cherríe Moraga, and Norma Alarcón translated the movement for Chicana feminism into sophisticated scholarship that both reinvisioned mestiza history as a political, ethnic, gendered, *and* racialized process, and articulated a "new consciousness" and embodied subjectivity. Anzaldúa described this consciousness in her groundbreaking book *Borderlands/La Frontera*, transgressing academic and literary boundaries to assert a mestiza subjectivity as simultaneously heterogeneous, contradictory, dialectic, and engaged with the multiple forms of ethnic, racial, cultural, gendered, and sexual marginalizations:

> In a constant state of mental nepantilism, an Aztec word meaning torn between ways, *la mestiza* is a product of the transfer of the cultural and spiritual values of one group to another. Being tricultural, monolingual, bilingual, or multilingual, speaking a patois, and in a state of perpetual transition, the *mestiza* faces the dilemma of the mixed breed: which collectivity does the daughter of a dark-skinned mother listen to?... In attempting to work out a synthesis, the self has added a third element which is greater than the sum of its severed parts. That third element is a new consciousness—a mestiza consciousness—and though it is a source of intense pain, its energy comes from continual creative motion that keeps breaking down the unitary aspect of each new paradigm. (Anzaldúa 1987, 778–80)

Such challenges from Chicanas and Latinas to the limited constructions of race and gender prevalent in nationalist, civil rights, and women's liberations movements were mirrored within the United States in writings from American Indian, African American, and Asian American feminists. By the early 1980s, with the publication of anthologies such as *This Bridge Called My Back* (Moraga and Anzaldúa 1981), *The Third Woman* (Alarcón 1981b), and *All the Women Are White, All the Blacks Are Men, but Some of Us Are Brave* (Hull, Scott, and Smith 1982) and individual books such as bell hooks's *Ain't I a Woman: Black Women and Feminism* (1981) and *Feminist Theory from Margin to Center* (1984), a new discourse had emerged among women of color that confronted multiple intersecting forms of discrimination while simultaneously articulating a holistic identity, a new intersectional identity. Forming what Chela Sandoval (1991, 2000) calls a "U.S. Third World Feminism" rooted in an "oppositional consciousness" and a recognition of the intersections of ethnicity, race, class, gender, and sexual orientation, this discourse provoked debate, dissension, and even change across social movements and, once again, redefined writings and practice around ethnicity. (See also Alarcón 1981a; Beal 1970; Davis 1981; Dill 1983.)

While research and writing by and about women of color was by no means uniform, there were recurring critiques of the antiracist literature and practices emerging from the civil rights movements and from variations of mainstream feminism that excluded or marginalized the experiences of women of color. Feminists of color pointed to the tendencies among both movements to treat race, ethnicity, and gender as mutually exclusive categories of experience and analysis (Crenshaw 1991). In response, they asserted the saliency of ethnicity, race, and, by extension, the belief that movements toward "liberation" must be conducted in such a way as to affect change for all the members of their communities, including men (Davis 1981; Dill 1983; hooks 1981). Women of color also challenged variations of feminist scholarship and activism that emphasized individuality over collectivity and gender-based concerns over ethnicity, race, and class, noting that "sisterhood" often placed a premium on organizing as women, thus undermining the ethnic and racial identity of women of color (Morgan 1970).

In their efforts to bring political resolutions to these tensions, some feminists of color offered a cautious pluralism to the all-inclusive "sisterhood" and the all-encompassing cries of "Black Power" or "Chicano Power." This approach mirrored earlier responses by ethnicity theorists in challenging the assumption that women of color should simply give up their distinct ethnic, racial, and class backgrounds to forge a political identity that asserted gender above all else. Instead, efforts were made to bring different bodies of women together to "build coalitions around particular issues of shared interests," without the requirement that anyone subordinate their identity to the gendered, ethnic, racial, or class norms of another group (Dill 1983, 146).

Theoretically, the critiques of both antiracist literature and the limits of feminism provided a platform on which women of color could connect on a range of shared experiences: racial and ethnic discrimination, gender discrimination, heterosexism, domestic violence, health disparities, class stratification, and a host of other issues reflecting their daily struggles. In addition, these critiques established the groundwork for new approaches to questions of race, ethnicity, gender, class, and sexual orientation, including work in hybridity, mestizaje, intersectionality, and womanism. As these challenges evolved they produced both new approaches to notions of identity and incorporation, as well as more complex theoretical and epistemological tools to unlock enduring questions of inequality and justice. In short, this moment of both tension and renewal in the battle for social justice served as the genesis for a new turn on questions of ethnicity and race, one emphasizing the inextricable intersectionality of these concepts with other forms of inequality, especially gender, sexual orientation, and class (Collins 1998; Crenshaw 1991; Hancock 2007; Hawkesworth 2003; McCall 2005).

Conclusion

The concept of ethnicity evolved over the twentieth century, serving both as a tool for research and analysis and as a form of social and political organization for immigrants and advocates alike. Within social science research, ethnicity emerged as an important challenge to pervasive notions of biological inferiority that legitimated racial and gender segregation in post–Civil War America. Variations of ethnicity theory became important in the ongoing research into the wave of European immigrants who changed the cultural, social, and political makeup of the country in the early twentieth century.

Concepts of ethnic identity also proved significant for populations of immigrants who encountered discrimination and marginalization from an American identity predicated on narrow definitions of belonging and citizenship tethered to whiteness. Ethnic identity and ethnic enclaves supported immigrants, particularly those from southern and eastern Europe, as they battled efforts to exclude them from citizenship and becoming incorporated into America.

The historical grounding of ethnicity theory in the experiences of European immigrants became obvious as research in ethnic identity was extended to nonwhites, particularly African Americans migrating out of the southern states and Mexican Americans in the southwest. Tensions in the efforts to apply ethnicity theories to racial minorities, particularly in the push toward assimilation and Americanization of nonwhites, led to resistance and change among these populations in the emergence of civil rights movements. Especially interesting in the field of ethnic and racial studies were the ascent of nationalism and the privileging of masculinity and sexism that often accompanied it. Efforts to reject the scholarly denigration inherent in biological determinism and early forms of ethnicity theory, and to assert a more complex voice attuned to multiple dynamics of inequality in the face of antiracist and mainstream feminist literature, led to the genesis of intersectional scholarship. Grounded in the lived experiences of women of color, this scholarship once again redefined issues of ethnicity by linking questions of ethnicity and race to gender, sexual orientation, and forms of difference, and generated new tools for analyzing enduring questions of access, equality, and justice.

Note

1. Several of the Americanization programs targeting Mexican women in the southwest were modeled on social settlement programs aimed at Jewish and Italian immigrant women on the east coast prior to World War I (Ewen 1985; Friedman-Kasaba 2012). However, as Sanchez (1990) notes, there was a key difference in that programs targeting Mexicans lacked the earlier programs'belief in "immigrant gifts" or the presumption that immigrant culture could contribute to the larger society. Instead, Mexican culture was viewed by Americanists as an impediment to rapid and thorough integration into American society.

References

Acuña, Rodolfo. 1972. *Occupied America: The Chicano's Struggle toward Liberation*. San Francisco: Canfield Press.

Alarcón, Norma, ed. 1981a. "Chicanas' Feminist Literature: A Re-Vision through Malinntzin/ or Malintzin: Putting Flesh Back on the Object" (1981). In Moraga and Anzaldúa 1981.

———. 1981b. *The Third Woman*. Bloomington, IN: Third Woman Press.

Alcoff, Linda Martin. 2000. "Who's Afraid of Identity Politics?" In *Reclaiming Identity: Realist Theory and the Predicament of Postmodernism*, ed. Paula M. L. Moya and Michael R. Hames-Garcia. Berkeley: University of California Press.

Alurista. 1969. *El Plan Espiritual de Aztlán*. In *Aztlán: An Anthology of Mexican American Literature*, ed. Luis Valdez and Stan Steiner. New York: Random House.

Anzaldúa, Gloria. 1987. *Borderlands/La Frontera: The New Mestiza*. San Francisco: Spinsters/ Aunt Lute.

Beal, Francis. 1970. "Double Jeopardy: To Be Black and Female." In *Sisterhood Is Powerful: An Anthology of Writings from the Women's Liberation Movement*, ed. Robin Morgan. New York: Random House.

Bogardus, Emory. 1934. *The Mexican in the U.S.* Los Angeles: University of Southern California Press.

Collins, Patricia Hill. 1998. "It's All in the Family: Intersections of Gender, Race, and Nation." *Hypatia* 13:62–82.

Crenshaw, Kimberle Williams. 1991. "Demarginalizing the Intersection of Race and Sex: A Black Feminist Critique of Antidiscrimination Doctrine, Feminist Theory and Antiracist Politics." In *Feminist Legal Theory: Readings in Law and Gender*, ed. Katherine Barlett and Rose Kennedy, 23–41. San Francisco: Westview Press.

Daniels, Roger. 2004. *Guarding the Golden Door: American Immigration Policy and Immigrants since 1882*. New York: Hill and Wang.

Davis, Angela. 1981. *Women, Race, and Class*. New York: Random House.

Dill, Bonnie Thornton. 1983. "Race, Class, and Gender: Prospects for an All-Inclusive Sisterhood." *Feminist Studies* 9 (1).

Edmunson, Munro. 1957. *Los Manitos: A Study of Institutional Values*. New Orleans: Middle American Research Institute, Tulane University.

Ewen, Elizabeth. 1985. *Immigrant Women in the Land of Dollars: Life and Culture on the Lower East Side, 1890–1925*. New York: Monthly Review Press.

Friedman-Kasaba, Kathie. 2012. *Memories of Migration: Gender, Ethnicity, and Work in the Lives of Jewish and Italian Women in New York, 1870–1924*. New York: SUNY Press.

García, Alma. 1990. "The Development of Chicana Feminist Discourse, 1970–1980." In *Unequal Sisters: A Multicultural Reader in U.S. Women's History*, ed. Ellen Carol DuBois and Vicki L. Ruiz. New York: Routledge.

———. 1997. "Introduction." In *Chicana Feminist Thought: The Basic Historical Writings*, ed. Alma García. New York: Routledge.

Glazer, Nathan. 1983. "Blacks and Ethnic Groups: The Difference and the Political Difference it Makes" and "The Peoples of America." In *Ethnic Dilemmas, 1964–1982*, ed. Nathan Glazer. Cambridge, MA: Harvard University Press.

Glazer, Nathan and Daniel P. Moynihan. 1963. *Beyond the Melting Pot: The Negroes, Puerto Ricans, Jews, Italians, and Irish of New York City*. Cambridge, MA: MIT Press.

———. 1975. "Introduction" and "Concepts of Ethnicity." In *Ethnicity Theory and Experience*, ed. Nathan Glazer and Daniel P. Moynihan. Cambridge, MA: Harvard University Press.

Hancock, Ange-Marie. 2007. "When Multiplication Doesn't Equal Quick Addition: Examining Intersectionality as a Research Paradigm." *Perspectives on Politics* 5 (1): 63–79.

Hawkesworth, Mary. 2003. "Congressional Enactments of Race-Gender: Toward a Theory of Race-Gendered Institutions." *American Political Science Review* 97 (4): 529–50.

Hijas de Cuahtemoc, Las. 1971. Newsletter. Long Beach, CA.

hooks, bell. 1981. *Ain't I a Woman: Black Women and Feminism*. Boston: South End Press.

———. 1984. *Feminist Theory from Margin to Center*. Boston: South End Press.

Hull, Gloria, Patricia Bell Scott, and Barbara Smith, eds. 1982. *All the Women Are White, All the Blacks Are Men, but Some of Us Are Brave: Black Women's Studies*. New York: Feminist Press.

Kallen, Horace. 1924. *Culture and Democracy in the U.S.* New York: Boni and Liveright.

Kluckhohn, Florence Rockwood, and Fred L. Strodbeck. 1961. *Variations in Value Orientations*. New York: Row, Peterson, and Company.

Madsen, William. 1964. *Mexican-Americans of South Texas: Case Studies in Cultural Anthropology*. New York: Holt, Rinehart and Winston.

McCall, Leslie. 2005. "The Complexity of Intersectionality." *Signs* 30 (3): 1771–1800.

Moraga, Cherrie. 1981. "Between the Lines: On Culture, Class and Homophobia" and "La Guera." In Moraga and Anzaldúa 1981.

Moraga, Cherrie, and Gloria Anzaldúa, eds. 1981. *This Bridge Called My Back: Writings by Radical Women of Color*. Watertown, MA: Persephone Press.

Morgan, Robin. 1970. "Introduction." In Sisterhood is Powerful: An Anthology of Writings from the Women's Liberation Movement, ed. Robin Morgan. New York: Random House.

Muñoz, Carlos. 1989. *Youth, Identity, Power: The Chicano Movement*. New York: Verso.

Myrdal, Gunnar. 1962. *An American Dilemma: The Negro Problem and Modern Democracy*. New York: Harper & Row.

Omi, Michael, and Howard Winant. 1994. *Racial Formation in the United States: From the 1960s to the 1990s*. 2nd ed. New York: Routledge.

Orozco, Cynthia. 1986. "Sexism in Chicano Studies and the Community." In *Chicana Voices: Intersections of Class, Race, and Gender*, ed. Teresa Cordova. Alburquerque: University of New Mexico Press.

Park, Robert. 1928. Introduction to *The Ghetto* by Louis Wirth. Chicago: University of Chicago Press.

Park, Robert, and Herbert A. Miller. 1921. *Old World Traits Transplanted: The Early Sociology of Culture*. New York: Harper & Brothers.

Park, Robert, R. D. McKenzie, and Ernest Burgess. 1925. *The City: Suggestions for the Study of Human Nature in the Urban Environment*. Chicago: University of Chicago Press.

Pesquera, Beatrice, and Denise Segura. 1998. "Chicana Feminisms: Their Political Context and Contemporary Expressions." In *The Latino Studies Reader: Culture, Economy, and Society*, ed. Antonia Darder and Rodolfo D. Torres. Cambridge: Blackwell.

Rothenberg, Paula. 1990. "The Construction, Deconstruction, and Reconstruction of Difference." *Hypatia* 5 (1).

Ruiz, Vicki. 1993. "'Star Struck': Acculturation, Adolescence, and the Mexican American Woman, 1920–1950." In *Building with Our Hands: New Directions in Chicana Studies*, ed. Adela de la Torre and Beatríz M. Pesquera. Berkeley: University of California Press.

Sanchez, George J. 1990. "'Go After the Women': Americanization and the Mexican Immigrant Woman, 1915–1929." In *Unequal Sisters: A Multicultural Reader in U.S. Women's History*, ed. Ellen Carol DuBois and Vicki L. Ruiz. New York: Routledge.

———. 1993. *Becoming Mexican American: Ethnicity, Culture, and Identity in Chicano Los Angeles, 1900–1945*. New York: Oxford University Press.

Sandoval, Chela. 1991. "U.S. Third World Feminism: The Theory and Method of Oppositional Consciousness in the Postmodern World." *Genders* 10.

Sandoval, Chela. 2000. *Methodology of the Oppressed*. Minneapolis: University of Minnesota Press.

Saunders, Lyle. 1954. *Cultural Difference and Medical Care: The Case of the Spanish-Speaking People of the Southwest*. New York: Russell Sage Foundation.

Tuck, Ruth. 1946. *Not with the Fist*. New York: Harcourt, Brace and Company.

Vélez-Ibañez, Carlos G. 1996. *Border Visions: Mexican Cultures of the Southwest United States*. Tucson: University of Arizona Press.

5 :: GLOBALIZATION

CARLA FREEMAN

In the past twenty-five years, "globalization" has gone from being a specific structural-economic referent to trade and systems of production to a commonplace cultural and political gloss for everything from "McDonaldization" and the hybridization of world music to the growing force of electronic communication and financial systems. My goal is not to survey the burgeoning academic and popular literatures on globalization as an expression of late capitalism, or neoliberalism, but to highlight the curious manner in which these processes are implicitly and distinctively gendered. This character of globalization discourses might be summed up by the simple, if doubtful, analogous puzzle, "Is local to global as feminine is to masculine?"

Two convergent lines of concern inspire this question. The first is a feminist interrogation of "the gender of theory" (Lutz 1995, 249–66), and the second addresses what I see as some troubling epistemological trends in globalization discourse and scholarship. For the past twenty years, I have been teaching an anthropology and women's studies seminar called "Globalization and Culture" and have been consistently struck by the distinct categories into which the texts for the course tend to fit. One is comprised of dense and authoritative macroanalysis of the history, institutional structures, and economic forms of globalization. These have been seemingly bereft of gender analysis (see, for example, Harvey 1989, 2005; Appadurai 1990, 1–24; Featherstone 1990; Sklair 1991; Robertson 1992; Waters 2001; Hannerz 1990, 237–51). Even so, gender has been smuggled in. Not only has globalization theory been gendered masculine, but the macroprocesses defining globalization itself—the spatial reorganization of production across national borders, a vast acceleration in the global circulation of capital, technology, goods, labor, and ideas—are also ascribed masculine qualities. Meanwhile, there has been a parallel feminization of the local as defenseless terrain, weak and subject to the masculine powers, technologies, and authority of the global (Sassen 2003).

Another category of globalization scholarship includes ethnographic texts focusing on specific local contexts and yielding textured micro-analyses of people's (and especially women's) "insertion" into the global economy as workers and vulnerable inhabitants of third-world countries. Many such studies have highlighted the gendered configurations of global production and global consumption, and of patterns of transnational migration (e.g., Fernandez-Kelly 1983; Ong 1987, 1999; Wolf 1992; Parreñas 2001, 2005; Salzinger 2003; Thai 2005). Some newer work may be establishing a third category. Far-reaching, authoritative, and even polemical, this work engages gender directly, intertwining historical and local specificity with theory boldly (Gibson-Graham [1996] 2006; Ong 2006).

How might such alternative approaches give rise to new understandings of globalization? More generally, how does such work illuminate the fraught relationship between theory, ethnography, and cultural specificity/exceptionalism? As feminists have argued for some time, taking gender seriously not only adds to the analysis at hand but produces an altogether different and deeper one. In other words, a gendered dialectic of globalization entails not simply an accounting of differential *effects* of systems of global capitalism on women, as has so often been the case, but a critical investigation of the gendered discourses and practices that underpin these systems. By turning to the gendered qualities of globalization, this discussion proposes that we challenge the conceptual underpinnings that have implicitly construed global terrains and practices as masculine and local ones as feminine. When we question the hard lines of dichotomous concepts, as V. Spike Peterson has said, "not only does the boundary between them change but so does the meaning of the polar terms: they are not mutually exclusive but *in relation*, which permits more than the two possibilities posited in either-or constructions. Moreover, changing the meaning of the terms and bringing them into relation ... changes the theoretical frameworks within which they are embedded" (Peterson 1996, 18). Brought into relief are several powerful dichotomies that require dialectical engagement: global/local, masculine/feminine, economy/culture, production/consumption, formal/informal economies, and public/private life. The dialectic not only emphasizes the active production of new meanings and relations, but also challenges taken-for-granted causalities and disproportionate weightiness attached to one or another of these "spheres."

By taking up one empirical case, the example of Caribbean pink-collar workers *cum* "higglers" (or marketers) at the dawn of the new millennium, I hope to illustrate how globalization works economically and culturally in ways that resist such dichotomous thinking. The forms and meanings of globalization are shaped by large powerful forces and institutions as well as by less obvious agents engaged in a complex of activities. These are both embedded within and actively transforming practices of global capitalism. The particular group I am describing comprises women whose entry into transnational higglering was tied directly to their employment in the offshore informatics sector in Barbados, the focus of fieldwork I conducted between 1989 and 2000 (Freeman 2000). As contemporary transnational higglers and high-tech producers for foreign firms, these women, local small-scale actors, might be seen as the very fabric of globalization.

Reimagining the "Local"

I earlier outlined some of the competing orientations within the academic literature on globalization, some emphasizing global economics and others culture. In the economically inflected category, grand theorizing about globalization (works that attempt to trace both its roots and its current forms) has tended to equate contemporary globalization with "late" capitalism, the ever-expanding reach of which expresses itself in intensifying (and faceless) transnational flows of capital and labor and the reconfiguration of global markets (Harvey 1989; Sklair 1991; McMichael 1997). An emphasis on economics may either ignore gender or insert gender in its analysis. The culturally inflected category has focused on the spread of "global culture" through such media as television, the Internet, and the borderless, fast-paced dissemination and consumption of commodities and styles (Featherstone 1990; Waters 2001; Appadurai 1990, 1991:191–210; Hannerz 1990, 1996b; Robertson 1992). These two approaches have converged within specific accounts of local contexts in which new workers and consumers are imagined and actively created in the global marketplace.

Scholars from a number of disciplines—including sociology, anthropology, geography, and political science—have called for greater focus on the local contexts of globalization as a way of bringing home the lived realities of these mammoth forces. In addition to humanizing large-scale economic and social transformations, and thus providing means for both positive and negative readings of globalization on the ground, the most nuanced of local studies have made clear that the historical and structural underpinnings and contemporary forms of globalization are themselves deeply gendered and embedded in the particulars of culture. These works unearth specific ideological precepts about femininity and masculinity, as well as particular expectations for the roles of women and men. In selective labor recruitment along the global assembly line, modes of disciplining and controlling that labor, the marketing of goods and the creation of consumers, and patterns of migration within and across national borders, there are embedded (and sometimes quite explicit) expectations that rely deeply upon culturally specific ideologies and practices of gender.

Close, detailed ethnography has been an integral part of such local analyses. In order to register and interpret the dialectics of local/global processes and ideologies, it is crucial to have a sense of how, for example, money is made, relationships are fostered, politics are transacted, and goods and services are circulated in everyday life. Feminist critiques of globalization that are steeped in ethnographic research have yielded important insights into the effects of globalization upon women, men, specific ethnic and racial groups and classes, in different regional and national contexts. Such critiques have made it clear that macrostructural accounts are insufficient in describing the lived realities of globalization (Ong 1999, 2006; Freeman 2000; Salzinger 2003; Marchand and Runyan 2000). Interestingly, many of the patterns observed in the gendering of *theory* might also be seen in *methodological* approaches. In a sense, the masculine profile of globalization theory is counterposed not only to local fields but also, in particular, to the practice of ethnography. If, as Lutz (1995) has so provocatively argued, one of the very definitions of theory is signaled by the assumption that the writing reflects a wide variety of instances rather than a single case, and if most ethnographies, by design, focus on a single locality/case or at most "multisited" connections among two or among three, the implication is that ethnographic treatments of globalization are not generative of theory. But, as feminist critics have argued, if macroprocesses take shape only through the particular activities of particular people, then macro theory should, likewise, be grounded in the micro, in the particular (Abu-Lughod 1990, 7–27).

Unfortunately, while localizing analyses of globalization helps to answer one set of problems, it leaves another intact. This is especially evident where gender is concerned, for the turn to gender on local terrain has inadvertently been the slippery slope on which the equation between local and feminine is reinscribed. The assertion that we recast our view of the myriad contemporary processes we have labeled globalization through the study of the local cannot be a matter of subsuming one to the other, that is, a privileging of micro over macro. Rather, it should claim that understanding specific places, with their unique histories and dynamic economies and cultures vis-à-vis the intensification of global movements (of trade, travel, commodities, styles, ideologies, capital, etc.) helps us to grapple more effectively with the nature of these movements and their variable implications. Gendering globalization, then, does not mean turning our gaze on the local, but seeing how at every twist and turn—macro, micro, and in between—globalization is imagined and enacted in and through gendered ideologies, terms, and practices.

My goal here is not to assert the primacy of the local against a monolithic global. I seek, instead, to highlight the complex and often unexpected processes through which cultural and economic transformations are introduced, refashioned, embraced, and challenged in a rapidly changing world. In so doing, I suggest a framework in which such processes as travel, migration, labor, and consumption are analyzed at multiple levels, each mutually constitutive and gendered. Such a framework challenges the portrayal of the local as contained within, and thus defined fundamentally by, the global. In so doing, it decouples the link that has fused gender with the local and left the macro picture of globalization bereft of gender as a constitutive force. Understanding the specific dimensions of the contemporary Caribbean higgler's work *as global processes*, not as a result of them, prods us to think more flexibly about the relations between gender and globalization at large. As we will see, the transnational higgler challenges any notion that global spaces are necessarily gendered masculine and traversed by men, just as she disrupts familiar formulations in which "third world" or any group of "other" women is defined as either outside globalization or the naturally presumed back upon which global production depends.

The transnational higgler thus forces us to reckon with two intertwining problems that I have already sketched: the collapse of local specificity in macroanalyses of globalization and the equation between local and women/femininity that has effectively eclipsed gender from macroanalyses. A feminist reconceptualization of globalization understands local forms of globalization not merely as effects but also as constitutive ingredients in the changing shape of these movements themselves. Such a framework requires a stance toward globalization in which the arrows of change are imagined in more than one direction. Globalization is plural, malleable, and multidirectional. Its significance emerges not only via the movements of capital, labor, and information, but epistemologically, in the ways in which these are conceivable or analyzed. Globalization is gendered not only in the masculinization or feminization of systems of production, consumption, and exchange but also in the very models and analytical frameworks we bring to these processes.

Global Theory/Local Lives: Feminist Inroads

Let me examine in more detail how the new critical feminist scholarship works. One important way is to highlight how indeterminacy, and in particular the primacy of "flexibility" and various forms of "mobility," operates within the multiple dimensions of global processes. If neoliberal capitalism is predicated upon a free market and labor flexibility that allow companies to search for the most competitive supplies of labor and raw materials, thereby heightening individualism, feminist critics have described the ways in which such structural pressures create an increasing impetus for people to "retool" themselves to keep pace. Not only is there pressure on the individual to become an economic "entrepreneur" under globalization; the mandate for flexibility and mobility is mirrored in more private domains of life as well—in the constitution of intimacy and family life, and in the very ways in which health, bodies, and subjectivities are framed in public discourse (Stacey 1990; Martin 1994; Walkerdine 2003).

By examining flexibility—as a global force of both coercion and desire—feminist critiques have begun to undermine the ways in which, wittingly or not, masculinist macrostructural accounts of globalization have reproduced a model of locality and movement much like the older public/private formulation long debated within feminist social science. This model has depicted women and femininity as rooted, traditional, and charged with maintaining domestic continuity in the face of the flux and instability caused by powerful, masculinized global forces. Working between and across multiple levels of analysis (the individual, the family, the state, the region, and beyond), Aihwa Ong has argued that "while mobility and flexibility have long been part of the repertoire of human behavior" the logics of contemporary neoliberalism have given a new imperative and new meanings to these maneuverings: "Flexibility, migration, and relocations, instead of being coerced or resisted, have become practices to strive for rather than stability" (Ong 1999, 19).

Flexibility, then, disrupts gendered expectations in virtually all realms of life. These range from kinship systems that entrench mobility as masculine and domesticity/rootedness as feminine, to labor systems that increasingly enlist female migrant workers, and, while so doing, equate women's transnational labor movements with dutiful citizenship, motherhood, and care. In each case, men, women, and their families are increasingly faced with profound contradictions, structural rearrangements, and ambivalences. Where "traditional" femininity may have been associated with nonwaged, family-based labor, marriage, and motherhood, the contemporary global femininity demanded by transnational corporations emphasizes the primacy of women's wage-earning. Though enacted in the interest of the family, these may be enjoyed individually as well.

Such forays away from the family home are, in many parts of the world, considered anomalies wrought by neoliberal capitalism. Women's increasing physical independence often spawns suspicion and accusations of sexual promiscuity, and in many regions has been accompanied by increasing rates of sexual exploitation and violence against women. Chang and Ling (2000) and Lan (2006) have examined the lives of Filipina and Indonesian domestic workers in Hong Kong and Taiwan whose labor often involves a form of indentured servitude and sexual exploitation. However, these women also demonstrate resistance to such threats, enacting strategies to circumvent the surveillance placed on them by their employers. For example, some domestic workers adopt a homosexual identity they call "tomboyism" to combat harassment and accusations of promiscuity; others don "peasant" garb that reinscribes their "otherness" while hiding their figures and self-consciously perform a demure demeanor as sexually invisible members of the household. In so doing, they reinscribe their lowly feminine status in the private workplace, reserving their nicer clothes and "true" or aspirational selves for Sunday outings with friends (Lan 2006). These workers illustrate dramatically how gender and sexuality permeate, and are enacted through, globalization.

As an embodiment of worldliness, adventure, physical prowess, and cultural mastery, travel is still widely constructed as a masculine pursuit—though perhaps less so in the Caribbean than elsewhere. The growing circulation of women within the global arena—be they migrant domestic workers, nurses, factory workers for transnational corporations, "entertainment" workers, or new entrepreneurs—is thus viewed in many parts of the world as a recent and, for some, threatening challenge to the traditionally gendered configuration of space and motion. This is all the more notable as their remittances form the economic backbone of increasing numbers of "male-headed" households and developing economies. Meanwhile, globalization is being enacted in an ever widening array of forms via new communications technologies in which traditional geographical boundaries are upheld spatially (i.e., citizens remain in their own national territories) but transcended electronically (as with the burgeoning call centers in India). Whether by necessity or desire, people enacting flexibility and movement in all of these domains are developing new understandings of belonging, citizenship, intimacy, kinship, and personhood. Once again, discourses of globalization are only beginning to capture these complex evolutions.

Labor remains a primary lens in globalization studies, but the gendering of these work processes takes some unexpected twists and turns. In Mexican maquiladoras, for example, increasing numbers of men have been incorporated into assembly industries. The manner in which these jobs get defined along feminine/masculine lines comes to depend upon, not claims of a singularly defined feminine "nature" of the work, but a host of other factors, including opportunities for advancement and the possibility of earning a living wage (Salzinger 2003). The contours of gender and class and, indeed, our very understanding of what constitutes *labor* and *migration,* are being realigned in new, flexible experiments of "body-shopping" and "virtual migration" involving masculinized and highly skilled Indian computer programmers (Xiang 2007; Aneesh 2006). In addition to the factory, pink-collar, and white-collar spheres of global production is the "care-work" performed in the ever-growing feminized sphere of services, including new circulations of nurses (George 2005), nannies (Parreñas 2001), domestics (Lan 2006), and sex workers (Brennan 2004; Padilla et al. 2007; Altman 2002). Indeed, Sassen has called such phenomena globalization's "feminization of survival" (2003).

Within these arenas, scholars are beginning to explore an otherwise oddly hidden and potent medium of globalization—what we might call the *affective* economy. Whereas in feminist and critical theory (Ahmed 2004; Clough and Halley 2007), the "affective turn" has become a rich and growing field for some time, the dominance of macropolitical economic perspectives has kept these interventions relatively marginal to mainstream globalization analysis. However, the contributions of recent ethnographic accounts of globalization reveal that love, sex, affects, and emotion more generally are vital terrains of exploration in the contexts of transnational courtship and marriage (Hirsch 2003; Constable 2003), domestic work (Ehrenreich and Hochschild 2003; Lan 2006), motherhood (Hondagneu-Sotelo and Avila 1997, 548–71), and sexual intimacy and identity (Padilla et al. 2007; Bernstein 2007), as well as in the more familiar domains of factory labor (Pun 2005; Wright 2006) and transnational IT sevices (Mirchandani 2012). For, as Hochschild has shown in the experiences of migrant domestic workers, "feelings are distributive resources" of a very particular nature, distinct from other kinds of material resources, as they are not so much invested or withdrawn as redirected *unconsciously* (Hochschild 2003, 23). While others might be intent to distinguish between these, I use affect and emotion together to signal the embodied and the cultural, the social and the subjective economies of globalization.

Love, like labor, is neither uniform nor intrinsic but fashioned in the particularities of place, history, and culture. It is at once a resource, a medium of exchange, and a feeling. Filipina and Indonesian nannies recruited to nurture and love the children of their overseas employers, for instance, are expected to adopt and enact a particular emotional labor, just as the maquila worker is expected to embody a particular docile, dexterous femininity that makes her an "ideal" assembly line producer.

Far from the natural and universal qualities these are often assumed to be, the sentiments and temperaments of love and docility are required of and fashioned by these women in the contexts of their jobs. The implications of these emotional labors are complex and often full of ambivalences and paradoxes. They may entail alienation and pleasure. Indeed, the very manner in which public/private domains in which these labors are demarcated, experienced, and felt is in flux within these contexts of global production. When Southeast Asian migrant women work in the private sphere of employers' homes as nannies and domestics in Taiwan, for instance, their opportunities to express their individuality, their personal tastes and pleasures, and to forge friendships are curtailed in their domestic workspace. In this context, formerly "public" spaces (e.g., parks or train stations) become highly sought "private" venues in which to meet, dress up, and express themselves and their feelings (Lan 2006). As studies bring political-economic, psychoanalytic, and cultural readings to bear on the exchange of love and care, we see that globalization is forged and contested not in a faceless market but in complex exchanges of labor and emotion, discipline and desire—for capital takes many guises.

The turn toward affective dimensions of globalization has been fostered as well through a feminist refutation of the long-standing gendered opposition between production and consumption. This repudiation has deconstructed old stereotypes of the social actors involved in production and consumption (i.e., men produce, women shop/consume) and of the values ascribed to each set of activities (i.e., when women produce, they do so altruistically, for the family, and when men consume, they do so selfishly). The new literature on globalization has also begun to distinguish itself from earlier structural economic analyses by simultaneously engaging realms of culture and meaning, media, fashion, and performance to reveal the powerful hold of new modes of consumption and its capacity to reconfigure gender and class relations. In some cases, the new kinds of experiences and pleasures unleashed through consumption, or even just the dream of such experiences and pleasures, are seen to subsume, reframe, or further entrench an exploitative global labor entrapment. Others find in these practices and fantasies the emergence of new subjectivities and the possibilities for new paths of mobility. When taken together, globalizing modes of consumption and of production may have ironic and potentially transformative effects. By examining not only the practices of labor and consumption but also their subtle and powerful affective underpinnings, such efforts have the potential of opening up a critical new field of exploration.

Globalization across Formal and Informal Frontiers

I now turn to the figure of the transnational pink-collar worker/higgler. The higgler in the Caribbean context is a venerable figure, centuries old. Defined as a market intermediary, she is a buyer and seller, traditionally of produce and goods purchased from rural growers and sold in the town market and, in turn, making town commodities available in rural areas. The higgler has been a powerful figure in Afro-Caribbean history, a woman who has come to symbolize local economic ingenuity and female independence. Her importance has been multifaceted. From the days of slavery, the higgler was integral to establishing the internal marketing systems that have come to define much of the Caribbean region (Mintz 1955; Katzin 1959; Le Franc 1989; Freeman 2007). Her role under slavery was profound, both symbolically and practically. By transporting and making available a wide array of produce, herbs, and root crops grown by slaves during their "free" time on special provision grounds, and by providing dietary staples for slave and planter alike, she both subsidized and developed autonomy from the plantation system (Beckles 1989; Bush 1990). Over nearly two centuries, she also came to embody a figure of womanhood in which physical strength, travel, and business acumen were defining characteristics. In contrast to the white plantation mistress, whose life was circumscribed by the limits of domestic duty and propriety and who was expected to inhabit the interior spaces of home and church, the higgler operated in the rough and tumble public space of markets and in her travels to neighboring islands. She has been defined more by movement than by stasis, more by vivacity and grit than by a demure Victorian demeanor.

The country higgler was also a key bearer of news and gossip (Katzin 1959). Her style of banter and prowess in negotiation are well known and admired traits of West Indian womanhood that presented a powerful counterpoint to the more middle-class, European ideal denoted in the region's well-known concept of "respectability" (Wilson 1969; Besson 1993; Freeman 2007). Respectability, as a moral norm rooted in British colonial culture and powerfully associated with domesticity, order, and the Anglican church, operates for women of all races and classes. As an ideological yardstick, respectability works in contrast to "reputation," a behavioral norm primarily associated with masculinity and the lower classes. Reputation features aggressiveness, virility, performative display, and physical movement. If the calypsonian symbolizes reputation's cultural authenticity via lyrics of poltical critique, the higgler symbolizes reputation's economic independence in opposition to the hierarchy and institutional dominance of the plantation system. The colorful country higgler has been one of the most highly commodified images of West Indianness. Donning a head tie and printed skirt, confidently balancing her bountiful fruit tray atop her head or nestled beneath her generous bosom, she has become a synecdoche for both Caribbean womanhood and nationhood. She signifies a femininity that is both mother and worker, provider and consumer, toughness and economic agility; she symbolizes both locality and movement.

Today, a new form of higglering has expanded in the region, in which women travel on commercial airlines rather than trucks, buses, or banana boats, buying clothing and other consumer goods rather than mangoes or provision crops and reselling these in an active (and illegal) informal market at home. Otherwise called "suitcase traders" or "informal commercial importers," Caribbean higglers are a well known but little studied group (French 1988; Witter 1988; Ulysse 2007). The suitcase trade (named for the large bags carried abroad empty and packed full upon the higgler's return home) is an international phenomenon witnessed in many of today's major metropolitan areas, bustling cities within Africa, Latin America, and the Caribbean, and places outside of the circuits established centuries ago by colonialism.

Contemporary transnational higglers are both hailed for their ingenuity and bemoaned for the illegality of their trade by local governments and state development planners. On the one hand, the suitcase trade is an innovative enterprise concentrated in the hands of women, who represent the highest proportion of the nation's unemployed and underemployed; there can be little doubt that it contributes in significant ways by providing income to the formally unemployed and underemployed and by supplementing the low wages of many who work in free trade zones across the region. On the other hand, higglers' transactions elude taxation and duties and compete aggressively with local shopkeepers' sales, making them a source of great vexation in the eyes of the Barbadian state. Those higglers who travel regularly as a basis for their livelihoods are increasingly pressured by the local government to "regularize" their trade by selling in stalls in central markets in town. The Barbadian government has made attempts to monitor this trade by demarcating and licensing such market areas and, with them, insuring mechanisms for taxation.

The women whom I studied in the 1990s were then employed in one of the region's newest and fastest growing industries, offshore informatics, the outsourcing of back-office typing, coding, and data entry for primarily foreign companies. Many of these Barbadian women found themselves propelled into the additional pursuit of weekend higglering, and their lives, as such, became further enmeshed within and defined by globalization. Their experience highlights a number of hidden relations within processes of globalization. For most of these women, higglering was not an explicit identity or form of work. Instead, it represented an economic strategy for supplementing their low formal wages or, as many women told me, just a little extra way of "making do." Even more than the traditional, agriculturally based market woman, the informatics worker/higgler becomes multiply embedded in global processes, albeit in an unmistakably Caribbean form. As global producers, their historical roots are easily traced to their foreparents in the sugar industry. However, the high-tech nature of the work they produced (health insurance claims and other data transmitted in electronic form via satellite technology), together with their transnational shopping sojourns, place this group of higglers in a category of their own. Their practices suggest convergences across structural spheres (culture/economy, production/consumption, formal/informal sectors) that have otherwise been narrowly and separately portrayed. Each of these realms and their dynamic entanglements demonstrate the subtle enactments of local/global gendered subjectivities and processes.

Like globalization scholarship more broadly, most of the past two decades' research on globalization in the Caribbean region has centered on economic development and, specifically, upon three related phenomena: (1) the neoliberal emphasis on the expansion of export production (not just primary exports like sugar and bananas and manufactured goods like garments and electronics, but also a growing array of information, financial, and tourism-related services, including sex tourism); (2) the proliferation of the informal sector in these societies; and (3) the central participation of women within both of these arenas. The expansion of the informal sector has often been described as a by-product of export-oriented industrialization, with patterns of labor migration linked to the specific configurations of these spheres. Recognition has grown of the interconnections between these two sectors, not only institutionally (Portes and Walton 1981; Harvey 1989; Castells, and Benton 1989) but at the level of the individual. Increasing numbers of people are simultaneously engaged in formal export industrial labor and informal economic activities (St. Cyr 1990; Freeman 1997; Quiñones 1997). In my fieldwork among informatics workers in Barbados, I quickly discovered that, as demanding as these jobs were in terms of sheer discipline, the rigor of the labor process, and expectations for overtime, most of the women operators simultaneously engaged in one or more forms of informal income-generating activity "on the side." They baked and decorated cakes for special occasions; they styled hair in their kitchen "salons"; and they bought and sold clothing and accessories for networks of kin, friends, and workmates. This last form of informal work, what I am calling "transnational higglering," is tied in intriguing ways to women's formal jobs in informatics.

In the 1990s offshore informatics was a new expression of global industrialization, referring simply to the transnational movement of information-based work for US, British, and other corporations outside of metropolitan centers and into developing countries, where it is now performed by new, low-wage labor forces. These Barbadian experiments in the off-shore processing of "office work" and other back-office services set the stage for the burgeoning call centers, IT help desks, software development sites, and other service industries now located in India, the Philippines, and other developing economies. As with other outsourcing ventures, the draw of Barbados for off-shore informatics was quite simple: comparatively lower wages, a well-educated, "disciplined," and English-speaking labor force (thanks to the legacy of British colonialism), and various tax and infrastructure inducements provided by the Barbadian government.

Like many other labor-intensive industries along the global assembly line (e.g., garments, textiles, electronics), informatics was quickly defined as a feminine arena. Nearly every computer cubicle of the dozen or so informatics "open offices" that operated in Barbados was occupied by a woman between the ages of eighteen and thirty-five, who diligently entered electronic data from airline ticket stubs, insurance claims forms, or legal briefs as she attempted to meet the stringent quotas set by managers. Even a cursory glance at these women and their officelike production floors revealed their thorough entrenchment in global processes. Operators committed to memory the place-names and data codes associated with the various North American cities to which they are electronically linked; they participated in American management practices such as "total quality management," taught to their Barbadian managers by British business consultants; they bought imported accessories displaying the logos of designers from Europe and the United States (jewelry, underwear, handbags, and the like); they rented pirated videos of movies taped from US cable channels from mobile stalls parked outside their industrial zones during break times and between shifts; and many, on their vacation time or long holiday weekends, engaged in transnational higglering trips to purchase the very goods (clothing, shoes, and accessories) that would demarcate them visually from their sisters and neighbors working in a range of factories nearby.

Informatics employers directly fostered these trips in a fascinating matrix involving corporate prescriptions for "professional" and disciplined workers; a reward structure in which credits for exceptional levels of productivity and commitment could be exchanged for airline tickets; the women workers' desire for new and reasonable fashions to further their workplace "professionalism" and after-work wardrobe; and, finally, the opportunity to earn money through travel abroad. For example, Barbados's largest informatics employer (with over a thousand women employees) offered its workers "thank-you cards," or productivity rewards, in the form of travel vouchers on American Airlines, which was owned by the same parent company. These coupons enabled many of the women in this company to travel abroad for the first time in their lives. Again reflective of the youthful and feminine profile corporate managers held of their employees, these awards included companion tickets for a female family member to serve as chaperone. Women's destinations were influenced in part by networks of kin and friends living overseas, as well as by the limits of their coupons (e.g., two were required for a trip to San Juan, then American Airlines' regional hub, and three for New York).

A number of other factors influenced employees' participation in the suitcase trade in a more indirect way. I have argued elsewhere that company dress codes and the emphasis on "professionalism" generated both discipline among the workers and a determination to distinguish themselves from "ordinary" factory workers through particular modes of adornment and style. Women went to great lengths to make, commission, and purchase new clothes and accessories, and the suitcase trade offered one of their major sources for distinctive fashions. In this case, the demand for new styles and new consumer goods was integrally tied to the particular formation of a "pink-collar" worker within the informatics sector, a process configured by a complex set of factors including foreign and local modes of discipline and surveillance, gender ideologies, and aesthetics (Freeman 2000).

The fact that these high-tech working women juggled work in the formal and informal sectors is not in itself remarkable in the history of Barbados or the region more generally (Comitas 1964; Carnegie 1987; Senior 1991). "Cutting and contriving" to make do is a well known and highly valued Caribbean tradition. However, the particular linkages, both structural and symbolic, between the formal transnational export sector and the emergent trade in consumer goods by suitcase traders has only begun to be explored as a dimension of simultaneous processes of globalization, local culture and development, and identity (Ulysse 2007).

Gendering Globalization across Production/Consumption Frontiers

In her challenge to the separation between production and consumption practices, the informatics worker/higgler is a particularly intriguing figure, since her labor has become deeply bound up in changing desires and expectations for consumption—for herself, her family, her community of customers, and potentially the nation at large. More than the average consumer, she comes to epitomize the argument that consumption is itself a form of economic activity equal in importance and integrally connected to that of production. The pink-collar worker in the off-shore informatics industry in Barbados takes her wage (and her corporate thank-you card) and invests it in the purchase of goods abroad, with the eventual goal of reselling them in informal networks back home. The challenge to a singular script of globalization cannot be made solely in the economic bases of production but requires turning as well to the realm of consumption and, more generally, to the cultural and affective dimensions of these processes. Because the contemporary higgler's primary goal is the provision of consumer goods to such markets back home, she faces the task on her sojourns of translating tastes and desires between "home" and "host" cultures, as well as managing her own relationships and movements on foreign territory, to a large extent through modes of consumption. In this sense, her consumption becomes a personal performance carried out abroad and as an entrepreneur back home, as well as a social practice that effects the circulation of goods and, potentially, their gendered meanings more broadly.

How Barbadian women's higglering practices help us think differently about the gendered relations of production/consumption and locality/globalization may be read in part through Danielle's story. Danielle was employed in one of the largest informatics firms in Barbados when I first met her in 1989. She was open about her simultaneous pride in—and boredom with—her job as a "materials controller." Her day was spent on slippered feet, handing out pages of text to sedentary keyers whose job it was to enter them electronically for foreign publishers. This job involved keeping track of who had which pages, and which pages needed to be double-keyed, all the while not keeping any of the typists waiting, as their pay depended upon fast and accurate data entry. Likewise, Danielle was on call to assist the supervisors and shift managers. While she complained about the boredom and frustration of being squeezed between keyers' and supervisors' demands, she enjoyed the security of a regular paycheck.

Her informatics workplace, like that of others, was a feminine space not only by virtue of being staffed by predominantly women workers but also through the forms of discipline and training utilized in the labor process. Young men were typically located in special work areas designated appropriate because they required either physical strength (lifting heavy bags of airline tickets, for instance) or higher skills (computer programming). Even without higher levels of education or skills, the few men employed as data-entry operators were quickly promoted out of the data-processing floors into special and less visible areas in which they were trained to perform specific jobs. In some of the same ways as the women workers, the men adopted aspects of respectability and professionalism that were coded as feminine in the Barbadian context. Their dress was conservative: button-down "collared" shirts, usually white and unembellished; tailored slacks; optional ties; and "hard" shoes. Their hair was worn short. The discourse of the workplace as a whole was geared toward a particular set of prescriptions for femininity and emphasized dress, comportment, and professionalism through talent shows and workshops and demonstrations about makeup, dress, and office demeanor. Femininity was also inscribed in the ordinary, highly disciplined labor process, which required precision, punctuality, and high levels of surveillance. Masculinity in its "reputational" forms were largely written out. As I describe at length elsewhere (Freeman 2000), young women's competitive sartorial display was a source of pride as well as profound tension for the industry managers and the women themselves; official newsletters and dress codes thus emphasized more conservative, understated, and "respectable" modes of attire and comportment.

Even in the early days of our meeting, Danielle let on that her real ambition was to open a business and "be my own boss." During those months, she was perfecting her sewing and making skirt-suits for herself and her workmates on commission. Having learned how to cut her own patterns by hand, she could turn out a simple suit in a matter of an hour or two.

As a result, Danielle could supplement her formal wage in informatics with fairly regular income earned informally as a seamstress. The relation between her sewing and her formal job was tied closely to the conventions of professional dress and comportment for office workers in a transnational firm. In addition to sewing, transnational higglering trips had become a widespread practice among Danielle's workmates, and she and several friends arranged a long weekend together in San Juan over an Easter holiday. As was typical, Danielle arranged a package ticket with a local travel agency, including ground transportation to a reasonable motel (costing roughly fifty-five dollars a night for a double room). On this and similar trips, she traveled with her friend and previous workmate Marcelle, who had worked her way up in the informatics industry to a managerial position in a new firm. While their husbands and other female relations watched their children (two each), Danielle and Marcelle undertook these long-weekend trips with the dual goals of profit-seeking work and pleasure-seeking escapade. Departing from Barbados, Danielle checked two large empty suitcases, carrying with her ticket a wish list of orders to fill for herself, her family, and her customers.

The imperative for Danielle's new image as an informatics worker was articulated both from above (management) and below (fellow work-mates). This image reflected not only corporate demands but also the desirability of a new pink-collar identity, which she and her coworkers struggled hard to create and maintain. So now, on buying trips, the purchase of clothing and accessories was not only an act of consumption but also of production—of still newer images, modes of comportment, and subjectivities in a transnational symbolic order. This production of self, both symbolic and material, has an economic value as well as a cultural and subjective one, as it became a vital dimension of the successful marketing of her goods back home.

Through these complex practices, Danielle became simultaneously imbricated in a dialectic of shop-floor production (albeit in an officelike setting), the consumption of clothing and style, and the symbolic and material production of a new feminine and classed self. At each node of this imbrication, there is a clear and salient exchange of economic as well as symbolic value, and a complex emotional matrix of pleasure, desire, and exhaustion. Significantly, in this process Danielle was transformed from being primarily *instrumental* in the forces of globalization (as an employee of a multinational corporation) to becoming *agentive,* an actor who is paid by others for her privileged knowledge and attractive goods. Disciplined and remade in the formal workplace of informatics, she further embellished this new sense of self on her buying trips, through which she became a new agent of globalization.

On one trip to St. Lucia, Danielle and Marcelle were met by Danielle's cousin, who lived and worked in the capital, Castries. Their four-day trip included a busy combination of shopping for jeans, children's clothes, and casual leather shoes; an excursion to see the famous Pitons and dramatic waterfalls; and evenings out at popular nightclubs. The women spoke about the excitement and exhilaration they felt being out on their own at night, for these were activities they seldom enjoyed at home. In the shops, Danielle straddled the roles of consumer and eventual broker, and balanced the requests on her list against prices, availability, and the new styles she ventured her customers would like. They enjoyed trying on "sexy styles" and modeling clothes for each other that they thought friends and coworkers would like. Looking at her display of snapshots, which followed the familiar convention of posed portraits in front of national sites as well as playful candids inside the stores, one would be hard pressed to decipher this higglering journey as anything but a long-weekend tourist excursion.

The particular meanings of Danielle's trips are significant precisely in their multiplicity, for they presented opportunities not only for generating income but equally for seeing new sites, enjoying herself, feeling fashionable and adept at finding "good deals," and constructing forms of femininity that defy some traditional class and gender boundaries. Danielle and Marcelle were both married women, mothers, and working women—one held a position of responsibility in a high-prestige industry; the other, having quit her job in informatics, now enjoyed the entrepreneurial autonomy of running a bar/convenience store out of her home. They went to church with some regularity (not the formal Anglican church of their upbringing, but a livelier new Pentecostal church they and growing numbers of Barbadians have come to enjoy), and they could generally be described as straddling the upper-working/lower-middle classes. They move easily between the "respectable" feminine etiquette of middle-class family life and work, facilitated by the new modes of consumption they now enjoyed, and the "reputation"-like practices of independent travel, nightclubbing, bold bodily display, and self-fashioning often associated with masculinity and lower-class culture (Wilson 1969). The special combination of economic goals (profit making and cost saving) with pleasure-seeking desires gives these trips a dimension of both credibility and suspicion in the eyes of the women's husbands and boyfriends. Women are known to capitalize on the former to allay the latter.

In short, the transnational higglers challenge the traditional regional gender dichotomy of masculine reputation/feminine respectability by simultaneously enacting behaviors previously imagined to be the preserve of *either* men or women, middle or lower classes, white or black. For herself and her family, the transnational higgler may be primarily involved in the pursuit of income and her own self-fashioning; but at the same time she becomes an arbiter of both local and transnational styles, taste, and bodies of knowledge for the customers she supplies with goods. Her own embodiment of femininity—the particular ways in which she occupies and traverses spaces, her adoption of new styles, modes of comportment, and articulation of "professionalism"—is conveyed through goods and her own expressions of self to her customer networks and to the globally inflected community at large. These practices, in turn, present possibilities for redrawing conventional trajectories of upward mobility and the gendered boundaries of class and race (Freeman 2007). Through new modes of dress and travel tied simultaneously to their roles as producer (higgler/informatics worker) and consumer, they enact global processes that are also locally distinct. Their incorporation into the global labor market resembles that of women factory workers in other developing countries but also foreshadows that of the call-center operators who have since replaced them in the endless twists of global restructuring.

Conclusion

The case of the informatics worker/higgler helps to illustrate how, through changing modes of production and consumption, these social actors have become multiply territorialized across a global arena and, in the process, have become *agents* of globalization. They are local subjects living within a globalized terrain, both in Barbados, as informatics workers and as consumers in contact with global goods and culture, and on their higglering sojourns abroad, as consumers and marketers of goods and as "tourists" engaged in the consumption of other languages, people, cuisine, and cultures. They are rooted in Barbados, and their Barbadianness is increasingly defined and sharpened through new modes of production, consumption, and travel in ways that link their country with numerous other sites across the world. Their subjectivities—as members of the working/middle classes, and as Barbadian, West Indian, Caribbean, and black women—become, not surprisingly, increasingly defined in relation to new experiences and to others they encounter through their travel as higglers. Higglering, then, as a form of labor and consumption and the nexus of new social, cultural, economic, and intersubjective relationships, constitutes a realm in which identities (national, regional, class, racial, gender, and sexual) and ways of feeling become articulated and redefined.

The activities of the Caribbean pink-collar worker/higgler might transgress gender norms in many parts of the world and even other parts of the region, but for Barbadian women, these travels are quintessentially feminine. First, travel and physical mobility in general have never been off limits to women, and second, their purchases worked both to reinforce and to challenge notions of traditional or respectable femininity. These new consumption practices were most often directed toward the feminine body (clothing/fashion), children's needs (clothing and toys), and domestic space (curtains, sheets, small kitchen appliances, and clothes)—all reinforcing women's roles (including those of their female customers) as mothers and homemakers. Thus, if some of the fashions and materials they purchased transgressed respectable femininity at home in Barbados, others became the very foundation upon which conformity to codes of professional style were constructed.

As a female producer/consumer, the informatics worker/higgler represents an intriguing dimension of neoliberalism in which participants within the informal sector and in global factories come to enact new modes of globalization. They are not merely its effects. It is precisely their evolving sense of agency, their mutually reinforcing engagements across formal and informal economies and across the transnational spaces in which they produce and consume, that both the macro models of globalization and some of the early local accounts fail to illuminate fully. These engagements in production and consumption as they are configured across space and time have taken shape in ways that both deeply depend upon and redefine femininity and masculinity. The powerful force of gender in processes of globalization is plain. So are the limitations of interpreting such movements solely within the framework of implicitly but resolutely masculinist models of capitalist expansion.

The informatics worker *cum* higgler can be seen as embedded within processes of globalization in myriad and multidimensional ways. She demonstrates that local actors are resilient in *responding* to the demands of global capitalism. They cope with low wages and a highly disciplined labor process while redefining transnational prescriptions for "ideal" labor in the light of local historical traditions of women's simultaneous expectations for wage work and motherhood. The informatics worker/higgler also makes clear that women are involved in *crafting* multiple modes of global capitalism. Ironically, perhaps, she signifies not a *resistance* to globalization, as critics might be inclined to hope, but the intensification of its reach and, in some sense, the democratization of its rewards. She gives new shape to a long-standing female tradition of Caribbean marketing, and yet she continues its renowned expression of femininity, in which movement, sharp wits, and tough business acumen are vital ingredients. She capitalizes upon her formal wage-earning (and often exploited) status in the global informatics industry by turning productivity inducements (travel-voucher rewards) into profit-making ventures and by utilizing her networks of workmates as a market for her imported wares.

In what way might we derive generalizable lessons from the story of a transnational higgler such as Danielle? She is distinct from Caribbean transnational higglers or suitcase traders who make their entire livelihood from this informal trade, as well as from agriculturally based higglers who continue to peddle their produce in the local marketplaces. In an effort to challenge the tendency within globalization literatures to overlook local actors and their particular interventions in or initiations of global practices, one can run the risk of romanticizing as well as overplaying their significance. The disappearance of the informatics firms in Barbados, and the current scramble to woo higher value-added IT firms to this developing nation, are clear indications of the dramatic tides of globalization beyond these women's control. No one would claim that transnational higglers influence the direction or form of global production or consumption in the same ways or on the same scale as do corporate global actors (e.g., finance capitalists or heads of multinationals). Yet, the women's roles as transnational informatics workers and independent marketers (travelers/tourists, consumers, producers, and arbiters of taste and styles between local and foreign sites) represent forms of global action on local stages whose significance is expressed directly in the ways they and their customers choose to live and define themselves. The women illustrate that globalization works in multiple and changing ways that are steeped in history, culture, and gender and that operate in local contexts in relations that are inherently dialectical and always in flux. Danielle pushes us to challenge not only the dualisms of local/global, private/public, and ethnography/theory, but also the implicit gendered categories within them—local/ethnography as feminine (i.e., static, traditional, homebound, private, informal, and consumption-oriented) and global/theory as masculine (mobile, modern, cosmopolitan, public, formal, and production-oriented).

The task before us, then, is not to disregard Danielle as exceptional to the mainstream of global effects, nor to ignore the ways in which globalization denies agency to many in its wake, but to attune our critical gaze to the range of actors and practices on the global stage and, thereby, to rethink the very concept of globalization itself—its roots, its forms, and its myriad entailments and implications. In so doing, it will become more and more clear that theorizing the macrostructural without account of such incursions and articulations offers limited explanatory power. Returning to my initial question, we can see that while much of the early globalization literature cast the local as feminine and the global as masculine, an individual such as Danielle invites a more complex reading. She reminds us that gender, labor, subjectivity, and economy are dynamic processes enacted in and through the forces of history and culture. Interacting with each other, these forces and processes inevitably change each other, manifesting themselves in new forms, expressions, and subjective experiences. In turn, these transformations invite equally supple and responsive tools of observation, inquiry, and analysis.

References

Abu-Lughod, Lila. 1990. "Can There Be a Feminist Ethnography?" *Women and Performance: A Journal of Feminist Theory* 5.

Ahmed, Sara. 2004. *The Cultural Politics of Emotion.* Edinburgh: Edinburgh University Press.

Altman, Denis. 2002. *Global Sex.* Chicago: University of Chicago Press.

Aneesh, A. 2006. *Virtual Migration: The Programming of Globalization.* Durham, NC: Duke University Press.

Appadurai, Arjun. 1990. "Disjuncture and Difference in the Global Cultural Economy." *Public Culture* 2 (3).

———. 1991. "Global Ethnoscapes: Notes and Queries for a Transnational Anthropology." In

Recapturing Anthropology: Working in the Present, ed. Richard Fox. Santa Fe, NM: School of American Research Press.

Beckles, Hilary McD. 1989. *Natural Rebels: A Social History of Enslaved Black Women in Barbados.* New Brunswick, NJ: Rutgers University Press.

Bernstein, Elizabeth. 2007. *Temporarily Yours: Intimacy, Autenticity, and the Commerce of Sex.* Chicago: University of Chicago Press.

Besson, Jean. 1993. "Reputation and Respectability Reconsidered: A New Perspective on Afro-Caribbean Peasant Women." In *Women and Change in the Caribbean,* ed. Janet Momsen, 15–37. Bloomington: Indiana University Press.

Brennan, Denise. 2004. *What's Love Got to Do with It? Transnational Desires and Sex Tourism in the Dominican Republic.* Durham, NC: Duke University Press.

Bush, Barbara. 1990. *Slave Women in Caribbean Society, 1650–1838.* Bloomington: Indiana University Press.

Carnegie, Charles V. 1987. "A Social Psychology of Caribbean Migrations: Strategic Flexibility in the West Indies." In *The Caribbean Exodus,* ed. Barry B. Levine, 32–43. New York: Praeger.

Chang, Kimberly A., and L. H. M. Ling. 2000. "Globalization and Its Intimate Other: Filipina Domestic Workers in Hong Kong." In *Gender and Global Restructuring: Sightings, Sites and Resistances,* ed. Marianne H. Marchand and Anne Sisson Runyan, 27–43. New York: Routledge.

Clough, Patricia Ticineto, and Jean O'Malley Halley, eds. 2007. *The Affective Turn: Theorizing the Social.* Durham, NC: Duke University Press.

Comitas, Lambros. 1964. "Occupational Multiplicity in Rural Jamaica." In *Work and Family Life: West Indian Perspectives,* ed. Lambros Comitas and David Lowenthal, 157–73. New York: Anchor.

Constable, Nicole. 2003. *Romance on a Global Stage: Pen Pals, Virtual Ethnography, and "Mail Order" Marriages.* Berkeley: University of California Press.

Ehrenreich, Barbara, and Arlie Russell Hochschild, eds. 2003. *Global Woman: Nannies, Maids, and Sex Workers in the New Economy.* New York: Metropolitan Books.

Featherstone, Mike, ed. 1990. *Global Culture: Nationalism, Globalization and Modernity: A Theory, Culture and Society Special Issue.* Newbury Park, CA: Sage.

Fernández-Kelly, María Patricia. 1983. *For We are Sold, I and My People: Women and Industry in Mexico's Frontier.* Albany: SUNY Press.

Freeman, Carla. 1997. "Reinventing Higglering in Transnational Zones: Barbadian Women Juggle the Triple Shift." In *Daughters of Caliban: Caribbean Women in the Twentieth Century,* ed. Consuelo Lopez-Springfield, 68–95. Bloomington: Indiana University Press.

———. 2000. *High Tech and High Heels in the Global Economy: Women, Work, and Pink Collar Identities in the Caribbean.* Durham, NC: Duke University Press.

———. 2007. "The 'Reputation' of Neo-liberalism." *American Ethnologist* 34:252–67.

French, Joan. 1988. "It Nice." In *Higgerling/Sidewalk Vending/Informal Commercial Trading in the Jamaican Economy,* ed. Michael Witter. Occasional Paper Series no. 4. Mona, Jamaica: Department of Economics, University of the West Indies.

Gibson-Graham, J. K. (1999) 2006. *The End of Capitalism as We Knew It.* 2nd ed. Minneapolis: University of Minnesota Press.

George, Sheba Mariam. 2005. *When Women Come First: Gender and Class in Transnational Migration.* Berkeley: University of California Press.

Hannerz, Ulf. 1990. "Cosmopolitans and Locals in World Culture." *Theory, Culture, and Society* 7: 237–51.

———. 1996. *Transnational Connections: Culture, People, Places*. New York: Routledge.

Harvey, David. 1989. *The Conditions of Postmodernity*. Oxford: Blackwell.

———. 2005. *A Brief History of Neoliberalism*. Oxford: Oxford University Press.

Hirsch, Jennifer. 2003. *A Courtship after Marriage: Love in Mexcian Transnational Families*. Berkeley: University of California Press.

Hirsch, Jennifer S., and Holly Wardlow, eds. 2006. *Modern Loves: The Anthropology of Romantic Courtship and Companionate Marriage*. Ann Arbor: University of Michigan Press.

Hochschild, Arlie Russell. 2003. "Love and Gold." In Ehrenreich and Hochschild 2003.

Hondagneu-Sotelo, Pierrette, and Ernestine Avila. 1997. "'I'm Here but I'm There': The Meanings of Latina Transnational Motherhood." *Gender and Society* 11 (5).

Katzin, Margaret. 1959. "The Jamaican Country Higgler." *Social and Economic Studies* 8 (4): 421–40.

Lan, Pei-Chia. 2006. *Global Cinderellas: Migrant Domestics and Newly Rich Employers in Taiwan*. Durham, NC: Duke University Press.

Le Franc, Elsie. 1989. "Petty Trading and Labour Mobility: Higglers in the Kingston Metropolitan Area. In *Women and the Sexual Division of Labour in the Caribbean*, ed. Keith Hart, 99–123. Mona, Jamaica: Consortium Graduate School of Social Sciences, University of the West Indies.

Lutz, Catherine. 1995. "The Gender of Theory." In *Women Writing Culture*, ed. Ruth Behar and Deborah A. Gordon. Berkeley: University of California Press.

Marchand, Marianne H., and Anne Sisson Runyan, eds. 2000. *Gender and Global Restructuring: Sightings, Sites and Resistances*. New York: Routledge.

Martin, Emily. 1994. *Flexible Bodies: Tracking Immunity in American Culture from the Days of Polio to the Age of AIDS*. Boston: Beacon.

McMichael, Philip. 1997. *Development and Social Change: A Global Perspective*. Thousand Oaks, CA: Pine Forge Press.

Mintz, Sidney W. 1955. "The Jamaican Internal Marketing Pattern: Some Notes and Hypotheses." *Social and Economic Studies* 4:95–103.

Mirchandani, Kiran. 2012. *Phone Clones: Authenticity Work in the Transnational Service Economy*. Ithaca, NY: Cornell University Press.

Ong, Aihwa. 1987. *Spirits of Resistance and Capitalist Discipline: Factory Women in Malaysia*. Albany: SUNY Press.

———. 1999. *Flexible Citizenship: The Cultural Logics of Transnationality*. Durham, NC: Duke University Press.

———. 2006. *Neoliberalism as Exception: Mutations in Citizenship and Sovereignty*. Durham, NC: Duke University Press.

Padilla, Mark, Jennifer S. Hirsch, Miguel Monoz-Laboy, Robert Sember, and Richard G. Parker, eds. 2007. *Love and Globalization: Transformations of Intimacy in the Contemporary World*. Nashville, TN: Vanderbilt University Press.

Parreñas, Rhacel Salazar. 2001. *Servants of Globalization: Women, Migration, and Domestic Work*. Palo Alto, CA: Stanford University Press.

———. 2005. *Children of Global Migration: Transnational Families and Gendered Woes*. Stanford, CA: Stanford University Press.

Peterson, V. Spike. 1996. "Shifting Ground(s): Epistemological and Territorial Remapping in the Context of Globalization(s)." In *Globalization: Theory and Practice*, ed. Eleonore Kofman and Gillian Youngs. London: Continuum International Publishing Group.

Portes, Alejandro, and John Walton. 1981. *Labor, Class, and the International System*. New York: Academic Press.

Portes, Alejandro, Manuel Castells, and Lauren A. Benton, eds. 1989. *The Informal Economy: Studies in Advanced and Less Developed Countries*. Baltimore: Johns Hopkins University Press.

Pun, Ngai. 2005. *Made in China: Women Factory Workers in a Global Workplace*. Durham, NC: Duke University Press.

Quiñones, Maria. 1997. "Looking Smart: Consumption, Cultural History and Identity among Barbadian Suitcase Traders." *Research in Economic Anthropology* 18:167–82.

Robertson, Roland. 1992. *Globalization: Social Theory and Global Culture*. Newbury Park, CA: Sage.

Salzinger, Leslie. 2003. *Genders in Production: Making Workers in Mexico's Global Factories*. Berkeley: University of California Press.

Sassen, Saskia. 2003. "Global Cities and Survival Circuits." In Ehrenreich and Hochschild 2003, 254–74.

Senior, Olive. 1991. *Working Miracles: Women's Lives in the English Speaking Caribbean*. Bloomington: Indiana University Press.

Sklair, Leslie. 1991. *Sociology of the Global System*. New York: Harvester Wheatsheaf.

St. Cyr, Joaquin. 1990. "Participation of Women in Caribbean Development: Inter-Island Trading and Export Processing Zones." In *Economic Commission for Latin America and the Caribbean*. Caribbean Development and Co-Operation Committee.

Stacey, Judith. 1990. *Brave New Families: Domestic Upheaval in Late-Twentieth-Century America*. New York: Basic Books.

Thai, Hung Cam. 2005. "Globalization as a Gender Strategy: Respectability, Masculinity, and Convertibility across the Vietnamese Diaspora." In *Critical Globalization Studies*, ed. Richard P. Appelbaum and William I. Robinson, 313–23. New York: Routledge.

Ulysse, Gina A. 2007. *Downtown Ladies: Informal Commercial Importers, a Haitian Anthropologist, and Self-Making in Jamaica*. Chicago: University of Chicago Press.

Walkerdine, Valerie. 2003. "Reclassifying Upward Mobility: Femininity and the Neo-liberal Subject." *Gender and Education* 15:237–48.

Waters, Malcolm. 2001. *Globalization*. 2nd ed. New York: Routledge.

Wilson, Peter J. 1969. "Reputation and Respectability: A Suggestion for Caribbean Ethnology." *Man*, n.s., 4 (1): 70–84.

Witter, Michael, ed. 1988. *Higglering/SidewalkVending/Informal Commercial Trading in the Jamaican Economy*. Occasional Paper Series no. 4. Mona, Jamaica: Department of Economics, University of the West Indies.

Wolf, Diane L. 1992. *Factory Daughters: Gender, Household Dynamics, and Rural Industrialization in Java*. Berkeley: University of California Press.

Wright, Melissa W. 2006. *Disposable Women and Other Myths of Global Capitalism*. New York: Routledge.

Xiang, Biao. 2007. *Global "Body Shopping": An Indian Labor System in the Information Technology Industry*. Princeton, NJ: Princeton University Press.

6 :: HUMAN RIGHTS

ELIZABETH SWANSON GOLDBERG

The Fourth United Nations Conference on Women, held in early September 1995 in Beijing, brought together delegates from UN member countries "determined to advance the goals of equality, development, and peace for all women everywhere in the interest of all humanity" (Beijing Declaration 2). The conference resulted in the Beijing Declaration and Platform for Action, which continues to be "the global community's most comprehensive policy document for the empowerment of women and gender equality." As the website of UNIFEM, the UN Development Fund for Women, recalls, "The Declaration famously stated that 'women's rights are human rights.'"

These words became the mantra of the global women's human rights movement as it gained momentum in the 1990s. They make the point that it is neither redundant nor a statement of the obvious to proclaim that women's rights are, in fact, human rights. At its heart is a fundamental assertion, one that has never been taken for granted: that the category "human" is inclusive of women. To examine human rights through the framework of gender is to explore a history of gaps and exclusions, rather than to trace a history of progressive implementation over time.

While the Beijing Declaration and Platform for Action, ratified by sixty-nine countries, provides the latest globally recognized framework within which to advance women's human rights, it is less widely known that the United Nations and the delegates who produced this document were challenged three days before they sat down at the negotiating table by judges who presided over the Global Tribunal on Accountability for Women's Human Rights, convened by Rutgers University's Center for Women's Global Leadership and cosponsored by several major nongovernmental organizations. The tribunal presented testimony from twenty-two women from around the world addressing four topics: violence against women; economic discrimination and exploitation; violations of health and bodily integrity; and political persecution. The premise of the tribunal was twofold: first, that neither national governments nor the United Nations had done enough to ensure that women were protected under existing international human rights conventions; second, and more importantly, that the rights violations most consequential to women's lived experience were not addressed by existing international human rights conventions. As Noeleen Heyzer, director of UNIFEM, stated at the tribunal, "We are not waiting for permission to have our human rights recognized, but rather are stating that issues like female infanticide, illiteracy, violence against women, female sexual slavery, and the feminization of poverty are all fundamental human rights issues and must be addressed as cornerstones of all human development agendas" (quoted in Reilly 1996, 18). Two thousand participants witnessed this testimony, wondering along with convener Charlotte Bunch whether the UN would "rise to fulfill the vision of its original statement of purpose as a defender of the human rights of all people," or whether women would have to "go elsewhere to find a way to promote and protect" their human rights (Reilly 1996, 21).

The Global Tribunal on Accountability for Women's Human Rights was one manifestation of that "elsewhere" referenced by Bunch, an extrajudicial forum for women to be recognized with regard not only to their experiences of rights violations but also to their aspirations for the fulfillment of their human rights. Indeed, women's human rights were born and raised outside the institutional frameworks of human rights in the West; how could it be otherwise given that contemporary human rights are a product of the patriarchal governments, societies, and cultures that initially conceived the ideas of democracy and "rights"? As recently as 1995, with the Fourth UN Conference on Women, women from all over the world still gathered as individuals, collectives, and nongovernmental organizations outside the rooms holding the official delegation to fight for full incorporation into the customary international law that comprises the human rights regime. What is true for human rights in a broad sense, then, is also true for the women's human rights movement: it is a hydra-headed formation moving on multiple limbs at varying rates in various contexts, gaining and losing ground all at once in the spheres of law, government, culture, and economics. The long-standing tension between the institutionalized regime of human rights law and the creation of cultures of human rights from the bottom up is not incidental to human rights in the twenty-first century. Rather, it is constitutive of the global human rights movement, necessary for its health, since claiming rights—no matter who the claimant and what the regime—has always been a radical project.

Considering human rights in terms of gender requires two lines of inquiry, related yet distinct. The first takes up where the Global Tribunal in 1995 left off: documenting the struggle for the inclusion of women in human rights law, which also depends upon the recognition of violations, and therefore the construction of rights, unique to women. This search for inclusion closely parallels movements for women's civil rights and is vulnerable to the postmodern critique of the rational, unified subject, upon which the conception of the "human" in human rights is based— a critique that also challenges the idea of gender as a stable, unified category upon which to build a politics of inclusion. The second inquiry, grounded in this critique of gender as a category, pursues human rights claims for sex and gender identities and identifications that fall between or outside the culturally manifested biological binary of man/woman. This latter direction has demanded of human rights that it account for and embrace the range of gender identifications and sexualities embodied in the designations gay, lesbian, bisexual, transgender, intersex, and queer (GLBTIQ). Both inquiries remain rooted, essentially, in a politics of recognition, and indeed must remain so until the seeming universality of violence against women and GLBTIQ people is overtaken by the creation of cultures and policies of human rights that reach more substantively toward their own universal applications.

Historical Exclusions

Human rights do not originate in one historical moment, geographical location, or cultural tradition. On the contrary, multiple genealogies may be constructed to trace the ideas and practices that comprise contemporary human rights to a range of philosophical, religious, and cultural sources. Contrary to a general sense that human rights originated in the West and are, therefore, in their modern and contemporary forms an imperialist imposition upon non-Western cultures and peoples, scholarship has revealed principles and practices that fall under the heading "human rights" (that is, respect for human dignity and bodily autonomy) in early oral and written texts from virtually every culture on earth. Most scholars, however, acknowledge the Babylonian Code of Hammurabi (1770s BCE), a set of principles regarding treatment of different members of society articulated with the force of law, as the earliest expression of what we have come to know as human rights, indicating that while human rights embody sociocultural aspects of human interaction, they are in fact primarily a matter of recognition before the law.

For the purposes of this essay, the term "human rights" refers to the contemporary human rights movement, accompanied by its body of customary international law, that came into being with the United Nations

Universal Declaration of Human Rights (UDHR) of 1948. Aligned with the United States' Declaration of Independence and the French Declaration of the Rights of Man and of the Citizen, human rights as articulated in the UDHR are "rights held by individuals simply because they are part of the human species" (Ishay 1997, 3). This contemporary formulation eliminates two external authorities previously called upon as sources of and anchors for rights: nature—as in natural law, or those transcendent qualities of human nature and the natural world that inform morality and the proper treatment of others; and God—the divine originator and guarantor of rights for humans because humans were created by the Creator. As many scholars have pointed out, this contemporary formulation of rights is tautological and thereby fundamentally unstable: *human rights are rights possessed by humans*. For Joseph Slaughter, "Tautology is the emphatic form of saying what everyone already knows and feels—of common sense, or the formal manifestation of a hegemonic will to common sense" (Slaughter 2007, 77). The problem with grounding contemporary human rights in the rhetorical figure of the tautology is that the category *human* is decidedly not commonsensical, neither biologically determined nor obvious. Instead, it is a culturally constructed, historically and, more significantly, politically determined category that changes over time at the behest of hegemonic forces, precisely the ones most likely to violate the rights of certain (non)humans when it is expedient or profitable to do so. And while Article 2 of the UDHR asserts that "everyone is entitled to all the rights and freedoms set forth in this Declaration, without distinction of any kind, such as race, colour, sex, language, religion, political or other opinion, national or social origin, property, birth or other status," it codifies at the same time the inequalities of imperialism in its assertion that "no distinction shall be made on the basis of the political, jurisdictional or international status of the country or territory to which a person belongs, whether it be independent, trust, non-self-governing, or under any other limitation of sovereignty." In other words, the declaration claiming equality for all peoples was signed and ratified by governments that were actively engaged in oppressing others through the mechanisms of colonization and imperialism, and that created and enforced racist and sexist laws, policies, and practices. Not surprisingly, governments continue to manipulate the law precisely in order to position individuals and groups beyond its reach.

The contemporary human rights movement inaugurated by the UDHR has been, then, expansive and constrained, aspirational and corrupt. Its triumph lies in its provision of a framework flexible enough to accommodate individuals and groups struggling to claim recognition over time and across cultures, even as its architecture will always remain subject to social and political forces resistant to such claims. Among many cases in point—and relevant to this essay—has been the resistance to the Convention on the Elimination of All Forms of Discrimination against Women, which, while signed by the United States in 1979, has yet to be ratified, meaning that the US is not bound by its principles. This is but one in a sea of examples demonstrating how governments may selectively endorse or actively resist the progress of human rights through developments in international law. Inasmuch as they are grounded in the human desire for recognition situated within such broader fields of sociopolitical conflicts and exclusions, then, human rights claims will never be final or complete—which is not to say that they are a failure. On the contrary, they provide vehicle and fuel for the recognition of human similarities and differences that forms the basis for protection from and redress for violations.

Aside from the ordinary historical struggle for recognition and inclusion, the deeper constraint of human rights lies in the gap between the "human being," who is mentioned only once in the UDHR preamble, and the legal "person" who is the subject of each of the declaration's articles. This space between the human and the person follows from the world's configuration according to the nation-state, which in turn recognizes individuals as citizens rather than as humans. It is, after all, the "person" who has the right to recognition before the law (Article 6), although, as many human rights scholars have argued, the idea of the person is largely a "fiction"—that of the rational, moral individual capable of bearing the rights and duties of membership in a state. The legal category of personhood derives from the Enlightenment vision of citizens consenting to the social contracts of democratic nation-states, which differs sharply from the "bare" human, stripped of citizenship and stateless. The paradigmatic modern case of the bare human is the Nazi holocaust survivor, and it is this displaced person to whom Hannah Arendt referred in 1946 at the time the UDHR was being drafted, as the exemplar of the paradox at the heart of human rights:

> The conception of human rights, based upon the assumed existence of a human being as such, broke down at the very moment when those who professed to believe in it were for the first time confronted with people who had indeed lost all other qualities and specific relationships—except that they were still human. The world found nothing sacred in the abstract nakedness of being human. (1976, 299)

This paradox has solidified in the contemporary moment, persistently revealed in the experiences of stateless people, including those who are internally displaced or who are nomads, refugees, or asylum seekers; those like the Kurdish and Palestinian peoples, whose territories have not been recognized as states; and those who have been removed to locations beyond the legal jurisdiction of any state and the reach of the UDHR's putative protections, such as prisoners at Camp Delta in Guantánamo Bay Prison. The paradox that human rights are unavailable to people who, being "nothing but human," are the most vulnerable and in need of such protections derives from the fact that the international human rights apparatus recognizes *persons* who gain status as members—citizens—of discrete states, as opposed to *humans* who are inherently members of a global cosmopolitan human community. Historically, women have been the objects of a double exclusion from the human rights project: as humans and as persons or citizens. Let us begin with the former.

The UDHR does not so much define as describe a human, which is partly what makes its tautological construction so problematic: human beings are "born free and equal in dignity and rights" (in other words, human rights accrue to human beings who are born with rights). Human beings are "endowed with reason and conscience," and human beings "should act towards one another in a spirit of brotherhood" (Article 1). The most concrete characteristics of a human, according to the UDHR, are dignity, reason, and conscience, and these characteristics determine our interactions, which should, it follows, be undertaken "in a spirit of brotherhood." Even if we follow contemporary convention and take "brotherhood" to be inclusive of all human people, the *Oxford English Dictionary (OED)* definition of the word helps to situate it historically in the exclusionary patriarchy from which both definitions of humans and of rights were born: "an association of brothers; a fraternity, guild, society, association of equals for mutual help, support, protection, or action." In both substantive definition and historical origin, the language of "brotherhood" that defines the human in the UDHR refers to spaces and social formations from which women were forcefully excluded. The same is true of the qualities attributed to the human—reason and conscience. Notwithstanding Article 2's inclusion of "sex" as a protected category, women have a tenuous hold on the classification human, another paradox at the heart of the human rights system. This time the paradox can be attributed to the division of space into public and private spheres.

While the split between public and private spheres is not culturally universal, the division of labor upon which it is based in the Western context certainly is. Societies have always organized themselves around roles designed by those in power to ensure survival and to maximize strength and prosperity of the group or tribe in relation to others. In most cultures on earth, these roles originated in the body; for women, this boiled down to their reproductive capacities. Women's social roles, biologically determined by their function as childbearers, were limited to wife and mother. In this way, women's traits and qualities were bound to their bodies such that they were understood to be weak, nurturing, and emotional, lacking the physical strength and intellectual capacity of men. Of course, neither this construction of weakness nor the division of space into public and private accrued to all women, as Western societies depended on the physical labor of African slaves and other indentured workers. This exclusion of African women not only from the category "human" but also from the category "woman," particularly in the moment that women were agitating to undo the limits of the public/private divide and to claim their rights, was precisely the problem addressed by Sojourner Truth in 1851 at the Women's Rights Convention in Akron, Ohio, when she famously demanded, "Ain't I a Woman?"

As Truth's speech intimates, one of the synergies between the women's movement and the abolition movement in the United States in the nineteenth century emerged from the idea that both (white) women and slaves were property. In the Western context (and in many other societies around the world), women were the property of the father until they were given in the contract of marriage to the husband. Relegated to the private sphere of the home, they were expected to bear children (preferably sons) and to manage the domestic work. Of course, women's roles differed according to class status, with enslaved women or women of lower classes joining in agricultural work or, later, wage labor in cleaning, cooking, nursing, or other service. Still, the primary value for all women was first as sexual object and second as reproductive vessel. Within this patriarchal construct, women were more chattel than human, considering that they were excluded from the developing "brotherhood" that included some early forms of mobility through access to education, through status within the formal structures of the church, through the acquisition of labor and crafts skills, and through the political life of their communities.

While traces of what we now know as human rights can be found in the earliest religious texts and in classical Greco-Roman philosophies, their realization as a matter of policy and practice was essentially coterminous with the emergence of democracy; hence, the focus on the legal "person," the citizen, in the UDHR. Excluded from the category "human," women fared no better with the category "citizen," as men began to formulate and fight for a shift from feudal monarchies to egalitarian nation-states. This shift, which took place over the course of three centuries, was underwritten by the social-contract theories of men such as Thomas Hobbes, John Locke, and Jean-Jacques Rousseau, who argued for a natural political movement from the vertical organization of monarchical societies to the horizontal order of brotherhood, and, with it, freedom from tyranny and oppression. As feminist political theorists have shown, the division of space into public and private informed the exclusion of women from this new political order. Even as men claimed their freedom by rejecting the patriarchal location of authority in the father-king, they retained conjugal rights over women as the source of their own power. Contract theorists were able to avoid the question of women's rights by constructing men's sexual right to women as *natural*, rather than political, and thereby to incorporate it as a feature into the new egalitarian societies they sought to create. As Carole Pateman has shown, women in the early democracies were subjugated to men as an irrevocable function of the warlike state of nature that the establishment of a political democracy sought to mitigate:

> The fraternal social contract creates a new, modern patriarchal order that is presented as divided into two spheres: civil society or the universal sphere of freedom, equality, individualism, reason, contract and impartial law—the realm of men or "individuals"; and the private world of particularity, natural subjection, ties of blood, emotion, love and sexual passion—the world of women, in which men also rule. (Pateman 1988, 43)

The conception of man's birthright to equality, freedom, and "rights" that emerged with the struggle for democracy did not extend to women, in part because they were never so much person as property, neither human nor, when it became possible, citizen. As a result, the fight to claim women's human rights has paralleled the fight for women's rights more generally, their claims to recognition and participation in the public sphere less a matter of incorporation into the category human than a matter of claiming the rights of citizenship.

These struggles roughly parallel the work of the first and second waves of feminism, to gain the right to vote (political participation) and rights to education and work (opportunity). While at the time of this writing, women in the United States still earn an average of 77 cents to men's dollar, it is a matter of law in most places on earth that women can vote, and in some places that women can participate in the political lives of their communities and cannot be discriminated against on the basis of gender or sex for any job or other opportunity (Fitzpatrick 2010). It may seem counterintuitive that the rights struggle did not progress from recognition of the basic human to the more complex and particular recognition of the citizen; however, the women's human rights movement emerged only in the latter half of the twentieth century, after particular civil rights had been gained. In some ways, the great civil and women's rights movements of the 1960s and 1970s in the United States share in common this focus upon legal and political recognition as the path to freedom and equality, a path that has led to the sad realization that simply codifying discrimination as illegal is not enough to undo the deeper social, cultural, and familial biases that ground ongoing violations of rights.

To get at these subterranean issues requires a closer examination of the term *recognition* and what it entails in a human rights context. The idea of recognition has profound implications not only for the treatment of individuals and groups within larger social and political settings, but also for the formation of the self, the individual upon whom the very idea of human rights is built. The conception of the bounded, stable individual, endowed with reason and conscience and accepted as such into the human family, has been largely discredited, not only by the many practical exclusions and oppressions of individuals in different places and times, but also because the very existence of that stable individual has been called into question in the postmodern moment. The individual imagined by Enlightenment thinkers such as Kant and Descartes as a discrete subject formed through his ability to think, and therefore to understand and to act upon the world around him, has been critiqued as an abstraction, a symptom of the will to power revealed as such, and as a fiction, in that the individual is continuously made and remade through the ever-shifting performance of identity and negotiation of power relations within specific social contexts and histories. There is some irony in the critique of the Enlightenment subject as hegemonic, given that the discourse of the Enlightenment individual originated with those same political discourses of freedom and equality responsible for the birth of human rights. Indeed, those first egalitarian discourses had to find a way to undo the earlier communitarian configurations of the subject, to replace recognition of *classes* of people hierarchically and immovably linked in the "great chain of being" with recognition of *individuals* equally subject to the force of the law and free to move up or down the ladder of social hierarchies. Still, when one compares the putatively universal figure of the individual upon which the nation-state and the human rights regime have been based with the actual individual historically recognized before the law—white, male, Christian, heterosexual, propertied—the ironies of that epistemological foundation (along with the merits of its deconstruction) become more clear.

More subtle is the Hegelian notion of recognition as part of the construction of the self. Hegel reacted to Kant's idea of the individual fully formed as an atomistic subject existing in relation to the world-as-object by theorizing a subject that is only constituted through its interactions with others. These interactions occur constantly (hence, the changeability of the subject) and begin with the primal level of desire. For Hegel, the subject acknowledges its own lack through its desire for others, its dependence upon the external world and upon acceptance from others in that world. The struggle for recognition is the foundation for all relations, whether interpersonal or sociopolitical in scale. Indeed, as Costas Douzinas has shown, the Hegelian conception of self is crucial to the understanding of how human rights impacts individuals, given that "rights formalize and stabilize identities by recognizing and enforcing one type of reciprocal recognition" (Douzinas 2002, 404). For Douzinas, "rights claims are the result of defective or inadequate recognition," which produces a gap between an individual's sense of herself and her understanding of her social identity, which may lessen her sense of dignity and self-respect (2002, 391). In this way, the dialogue between individuals and their social contexts in terms of the recognition of their human rights is constitutive of ongoing identity formation, with potentially damaging effects. The consequences of inadequate recognition are far-reaching in the case of women, who continue to struggle to insert themselves as embodied subjects whose rights are both recognized and protected by the human rights regime. They are even more injurious for those identities that fall so far outside its field of vision as to be largely unimaginable. Among these identities are sex and gender minorities.

Toward Inclusivity

The drafters of the UDHR walked a precarious line between universal and particular in constructing their international bill of rights. On the one hand, they were charged with creating a document characterized by language embracing all of humanity in universal terms; on the other, delegates to the United Nations Commission on Human Rights fought for recognition of difference, particularly national, cultural, and religious difference. The same tension between similarity and difference marks the drive to include women within human rights protections: women want to be recognized and protected as individuals within the universal definition of the human, and women want to be recognized and protected in all their particularity as women.

The two most relevant areas of particularity for women are the body and the home/family, or the private sphere. Just as women's options and experiences have historically been defined by their bodies, so too many of the violations they have suffered have been abuses against their (differentiated) bodies. And just as women were (and in many ways and places still are) confined within the private sphere of the home and family, so too most of the violations they have experienced have taken place within that space, and have therefore been neither visible to nor recognized by the law. Rape and domestic violence are primary examples.

Major achievements for the women's human rights movement in the last twenty years include the 1998 inclusion of rape as an "act of genocide" in the International Criminal Tribunal for Rwanda and the 2008 acknowledgment of rape as a crime against humanity by the UN Security Council. Before that time, rape had not been prosecutable as a crime against humanity but was conceived of as a kind of collateral damage of war, a personal or domestic problem rather than a human rights problem. Even when it was recognized and prohibited, as, for instance, in the Geneva Conventions, there were literally no cases in which it had been prosecuted on human rights grounds until the women's human rights movement of the 1990s began exerting pressure. Crucially, women's human rights activists have fought for recognition of rape not only as a crime of war but also as a crime against humanity on the basis of gender, refusing to accept an encompassing distinction between rape that happens in time of war for political or ethnic reasons and rape that happens in the home or community and is based solely on gender. As legal scholar Rhonda Copelon argues, "The understanding that rape in war is a crime against humanity has to have an impact on the treatment of gender violence as a human rights violation and on how we see other violence against women in everyday life" (Copelon 1995, 67). Such advocacy is of crucial importance in achieving recognition of the kinds of violations that happen to women because of their embodied nature, and that happen to women in the private sphere, long neglected by a human rights apparatus that formally acknowledges only abuses that take place in the public sphere and are committed by a public official or someone acting on behalf of a public official.

Similarly, until very recently, gender-based persecution was not recognized as legitimate grounds for gaining asylum in the United States or western European countries.[1] The 1952 Geneva Convention on the Status of Refugees authorizes that asylum may be granted to people who have a "well-founded fear of being persecuted for reasons of race, religion, membership of a particular social group or political opinion." To this day, gender-based persecution, such as female genital mutilation (FGM)[2] or domestic violence, has only been recognized as grounds for asylum when lawyers have performed the semantic gymnastics of arguing for asylum based upon women's "membership in a particular social group"—that is, that women are members in the particular group "women."

If it remains this difficult to recognize the unique violations that women experience based upon their embodied and sociocultural identities, how can we begin to account for the human rights of gender and sexual minorities? This question unfurls the staging ground for the next wave of gender-based advocacy. In keeping with the postmodern critique of the stability of identity and identity categories such as gender, advocates in this arena argue for an "undoing," to borrow from Judith Butler, of rigid readings of gender that cannot account for the range of gender and sex identities and identifications and of sexual orientations. Movements to recognize the rights of gay and lesbian people were a less visible part of the freedom movements that began in the 1960s, and some inroads have been made in the West toward recognition under the law, as well as through cultural representations that seek to normalize the presence of gay and lesbian people by increasing their depictions in a wide range of media outlets. In a global context, same-sex desire is still a crime punishable in some places by imprisonment or even death—and the extrajudicial murder of GLBTIQ people, often disavowed as an identity-related crime by local police, is rampant globally. In spite of the intensity and pervasiveness of such violence, the predominant site of struggle for the rights of sexual minorities remains the legalization of same-sex marriage. While clearly an important form of legal recognition, limiting advocacy to this form of inclusion bears the unintended consequence of constraining queer sexualities within the structure of heteronormative legal relationships, excluding sexual and interpersonal relations that do not follow the traditional marriage structure sanctioned by the state, if not by religion.

Advocacy for the rights of sexual and gender minorities provides the greatest challenge to date to the identity-based understanding of civil and human rights in its push to acknowledge that which is socially and biologically uncategorizable and has therefore purposefully been rendered invisible, while also being subjected to the most rigorous forms of social and medical control. This challenge is not solely about recognition of same-sex desire and relationships, or of bisexual, questioning, or queer desires and relationships, although these issues remain unsettled in terms of human rights. Rather, the challenge posed by the struggle for the rights of transsexual, transgender, and intersex people also calls into question the basic anatomical contours of what constitutes the *human* in human rights. Defying categorization according to social, cultural, familial, political, and especially medical norms, transsexual and transgender people are individuals whose gender identifications do not coincide with their biological sex, while intersex refers to individuals who are born with "a reproductive or sexual anatomy that doesn't seem to fit the typical definitions of female or male" ("What Is Intersex?" n.d.). If biological sex with corresponding gender assignment is taken as one of the fundamental givens of human existence, then recognition for trans and intersex people constitutes a profound provocation to dominant sociocultural, political, and legal orders.

Indeed, resistance to and bias against people occupying these sex and gender identities is so deeply engrained that the very idea of recognition as a basis for human rights is called into question. As Butler points out:

> There are advantages to remaining less than intelligible, if intelligibility is understood as that which is produced as a consequence of recognition according to prevailing social norms. Indeed, if my options are loathsome, if I have no desire to be recognized within a certain set of norms, then it follows that my sense of survival depends upon escaping the clutch of those norms by which recognition is conferred. (Butler 2004, 3)

That recognition is awarded or withheld to the degree that identity matches institutionalized norms profoundly affects personal identity construction, as evidenced by elevated suicide rates for GLBTIQ youth, for instance. It also affects one's ability to live authentically *into* one's self and to move openly in the world *as* one's self, given the omnipresent threat of violence against gender and sexual minorities. This is arguably the most urgent work of human rights in the context of gender: to expand the limits of recognition until mandated recognition is no longer necessary to preserve and protect differentiated human lives.

Let us see how this might work. Beginning with recognition as the ethical condition of the constitution of self in social context, we find that acknowledgment or validation supplied through the act of (positive) recognition is an acknowledgment of the *worth* of something or someone. Worth, in turn, is the substance of the *dignity* that is the wellspring of both humanity and human rights. The irreducible quality of dignity, according to the Kantian formulation, calls us to recognize all humans as ends in themselves, rather than as means to an end, meaning that we cannot use or misuse other humans as tools for our own purposes but, rather, must respect their inherent value even in their radical otherness. From this respect for dignity come *rights*, which can only expand to encompass all humans to the extent that societies are able to decouple recognition from hierarchical norms that devalue or revile certain identities.

It is important to note that the earliest usage of *recognition* meant acknowledgment of a debt, and that the notion of dignity is substantiated in the "worth" of a human, another name for which is "value," which is, not incidentally, "worth or quality as measured by a standard of equivalence" (*OED* online). While the human rights project aspires to transcend any standards of measure for human dignity, pronouncing instead its unquantifiable, intrinsic nature, such an aspiration returns us to the wobbly foundations of the tautology of human rights: human rights are the rights of humans. The challenge for human rights has been to proclaim the equal dignity of all humans while addressing the unequal valuation of human lives in social contexts. The lives of women and girls all over the world are devalued in relation to the "standard of equivalence" that is male life, and this near-universal devaluation is the nut that human rights must crack in order to live up to its own aspirations in terms of gender and other vulnerable identities.

The devaluation of girls and women, as well as of sexual and gender minorities, is manifested most painfully and prominently in the normalization of gender violence. Although the major human rights documents include sex as a protected category, girls and women are under threat at every stage of the life cycle. To illustrate the pervasiveness of this devaluation and to give concrete name to some of the dangers and violences that it brings into being, I invite you to join me at the happy occasion of a multiple wedding.

This wedding took place in January 2012, at a shelter home near Mumbai, India. There were five couples seated in thrones on a dais and surrounded by hundreds of well-wishers and piles of gifts. The brides, dressed in richly embroidered wedding dresses with hennaed hands and jeweled faces, were all survivors of brothel slavery. The girls had been trafficked from villages in Maharashtra state into brothels in Mumbai, and had spent between two and four years there before being rescued and relocated to the shelter home, where they received medical treatment and counseling services.

What are the opportunities for remaking a life for a survivor of sex trafficking? If she can find a way back to her home, she will likely be the subject of profound stigma based on the time spent in the brothel; such stigma will be exacerbated if she is HIV-positive. If she is in her teens, she will probably not have the opportunity to return to school, nor will she feel comfortable doing so. Prospects for marriage in the traditional way will be remote because of her history, yet for many survivors, especially those coming from more traditional settings, marriage may still seem the best path to reintegration into the community after the trauma of having been sold for sex.

Fortunately for these survivors, the waiting list for brides from the shelter home is extraordinarily long: over two thousand men have applied to be matched with a wife at this shelter alone. But is this really a "fortunate" circumstance? Given the social stigma attached to trafficked girls, what could be driving this demand? A simple answer is that if a man is not married by the time he has passed marriageable age, his chances of finding a wife in his village drop radically. But why would so many men be passing their marriageable age without finding suitable brides? Where are all the marriageable women?

The more substantive answer points again to the devaluation of the lives of women and girls: the shortage of girls can be explained by what demographers call "the missing millions," the gender imbalance resulting from practices of sex-selective abortion, infanticide, and neglect (such practices are most prevalent in India and China but happen elsewhere as well—and the underlying devaluation of girls and women is global in nature). While the facts of sex-selective abortion and female infanticide are particularly spectacular, more common and just as dangerous is the uneven distribution of care and resources among boy and girl children. In a family with limited resources operating within a larger cultural context in which girls and women are devalued, it is likely that boys will be prioritized in the distribution of food. Should a girl child fall ill, it is more likely that she will be treated at home and less likely that she will receive medication, attention from a doctor, or hospitalization.

The violence (and rights violations) resulting from the devaluation of girls is, then, systemic, threatening girls and women at all stages of the life cycle. The negative value placed on a girl child's life results in a shortage of girls of marriageable age. The reduction of a girl to a commodity enslaved and sold for sex results in a surplus of girls and women located outside of the social structures and life cycles of their communities. This perfect storm has created an entirely new marriage market in which men contract to marry girls rescued from slavery—women vulnerable, devalued, and still constructed in relation to their sexual and reproductive functions.

Lest readers come away with the sense that such devaluation of women and its accompanying violence is a "third-world" phenomenon, keep in mind: the putative equality of women in Western cultures has not brought full recognition of women's rights as human rights, as this essay has been at pains to show. It has also not undone the deep sociocultural reduction of women's value to their bodies and reproductive functions, nor has it disrupted the pervasive representational structures that inform these value judgments. Violence against women remains rampant in Western cultures, in the form of rape, domestic violence, and other more spectacular cases such as serial killing, in which the perpetrators are male 95 percent of the time and their victims female 73 percent of the time (Arndt and Heitpas 2004, 124). Consider cases such as the targeting of schoolgirls in an Amish schoolhouse in Nickel Mines, Pennsylvania, and in a public school in Bailey, Colorado, in 2006. In both cases, male gunmen entered the school buildings and selected girls as their targets, allowing boys to leave (in the Colorado case, the killer was even more specific, targeting only blonde girls). In both cases, sexual violence was part of the attack. Violence against GLBTIQ people is also higher in comparison to their heterosexual counterparts in populations where such statistics are tracked, and of course such crimes are most likely underreported, given the complexities of visibility for many GLBTIQ people.

At the Global Tribunal on Accountability for Women's Human Rights, convener Charlotte Bunch called the audience's attention to the pervasiveness of violence against women everywhere. She drew attention to the ways in which citizens of the United States often assign the term "culture" to other spaces, constructing places in Africa and Asia as having rich cultural traditions by comparison with the US, which is perceived to be without unified or meaningful cultural traditions (the cultureless norm against which other, less economically and technologically advanced societies are measured). And then she rejoined that, indeed, the United States *does* have a deep and powerful cultural tradition, and that tradition is *violence*. She supported her provocative claim by describing the pervasiveness of violence across US media, entertainment, and material life, arguing that the particular prominence of violence against women is so much the essence of US culture as to be nearly invisible. Bunch was speaking, in 1995, from the early edge of the organized women's human rights movement, and clearly a great deal of progress has been made since then. Still, advocates of gender and human rights must continue to expand the range of gender identities for which recognition by the global human rights apparatus is applicable until mandating recognition becomes superfluous, until power is no longer violently asserted upon differentiated humans, and until hegemonic norms are sufficiently disrupted that human rights protections can be mobilized for exceptional rather than everyday discrimination.

Notes

1. Directive 2004/83/EC, a 2004 document meant to define asylum standards for the European Union, explicitly recognizes persecution by nonstate actors and gender-based persecution, an extremely encouraging sign.

2. Terminology for this practice is deeply contested based upon one's perspective: for those who oppose the practice on human rights grounds, it is referred to as FGM; the term used to describe FGM as an acceptable cultural practice is female circumcision, and a word used by those who wish to remain neutral is female cutting. I use FGM here to recognize the context of asylum and human rights.

References

Arendt, Hannah. 1976. "The Decline of the Nation-State and the End of the Rights of Man" (1946). In *The Origins of Totalitarianism*. New York: Harcourt.

Arndt, W. B., and T. Heitpas. 2004. "Critical Characteristics of Male Serial Murderers." *American Journal of Criminal Justice* 29 (1).

Beijing Declaration and Platform for Action. http://www.un.org/womenwatch/daw/beijing /pdf/BDPfA%20E.pdf (accessed February 24, 2013).

Butler, Judith. 2004. *Undoing Gender*. New York: Routledge.

Copelon, Rhonda. 1995. "Women and War Crimes." *St. John's Law Review* 69 (1).

Douzinas, Costas. 2002. "Identity, Recognition, Rights or What Can Hegel Teach Us about Human Rights?" *Journal of Law and Society* 29 (3).

Fitzpatrick, Laura. 2010. "Why Do Women Still Earn Less Than Men?" *Time,* April 20. http://www.time.com/time/nation/article/0,8599,1983185,00.html (acccessed May 1, 2012).

Ishay, Micheline. 1997. *The Human Rights Reader: Major Political Essays, Speeches and Documents from Ancient Times to the Present*. New York: Routledge.

Pateman, Carole. 1988. *The Sexual Contract*. Stanford, CA: Stanford University Press.

Reilly, Naimh, ed. 1996. *Without Reservation: The Beijing Tribunal on Accountability for Women's Human Rights*. Center for Women's Global Leadership, Rutgers University. http://www.cwgl.rutgers.edu/globalcenter/publications/without.html (accessed April 6, 2012).

Slaughter, Joseph R. 2007. *Human Rights, Inc.: The World Novel, Narrative Form, and International Law.* New York: Fordham University Press.

UN General Assembly. 1948. *Universal Declaration of Human Rights*. Resolution 271 A(III), adopted December 10, 1948. http://www.unhcr.org/refworld/docid/3ae6b3712c.html (accessed May 24, 2012).

"What Is Intersex?" N.d. Intersex Society of North America (http://www.isna.org/faq/what_is_intersex; accessed 15 May 2012).

7 :: IDENTITY

RAEWYN CONNELL

"Identity" is one of the key words of contemporary culture, a way of answering the questions "Who am I?" and "Who are we?" The specific idea of "gender identity" is now very widespread, answering these questions in terms of masculinity or femininity. But the concept is not as simple as it seems. In fact, over the course of centuries, the word *identity* has almost completely reversed its meaning. As we shall see, the apparently straightforward idea of gender identity runs into serious conceptual and political problems, and it is debatable how far, and in what sense, it should be used in gender analysis.

When the word was taken over from late Latin into English in the sixteenth and seventeenth centuries, *identity* meant exact agreement, sameness, having-the-one-substance. It was used when a writer mentioned a thing or person remaining the same over time or in different circumstances, as the philosopher John Locke did in his famous *Essay concerning Human Understanding* (1690). In this sense, "identity" was sometimes contrasted with "diversity" or "variety."

Initially, then, the concept was one of a family of philosophical and religious terms that expressed the theme of unity. This theme has been powerful in many (though not all) of the world's great traditions of thought. The Athenian philosopher Plato expressed it in his theory of forms. Beneath the shifting, transitory, imperfect, and chaotic world of our experience, his dialogue *The Republic* argues, there must exist a deeper reality where we find the pure and unchanging forms of things.

The idea of a stable, deeper reality, of which everyday life provides only distorted copies or imperfect imitations, has been immensely influential in European thought ever since. It runs through philosophy and art, religion, and natural science (where mathematics can represent the hidden reality), and eventually appears in psychology and social science. The theme of unity has not only been powerful in Europe. The unity of God is more strongly stressed in Islam than in trinitarian Christianity.

The Islamic concept of "Tawheed," referring to the indivisibility of God and the unity of the cosmos, is the basis of arguments about the indivisibility of knowledge, the connection between religion and science, and the unity of the human and natural. These themes have been important in modern Islamic responses to economic and cultural domination by the West (Ghamari-Tabrizi 1996, 317–30).

By the nineteenth century, the term *identity* had become thoroughly naturalized in English, and was used in literature as well as philosophy and mathematics. It generally still meant "sameness," though sometimes in the sense of personal existence, as the poet Byron used it in *Don Juan* (1819–1824). The word could emphasize "Who I am" as against "Whom I am not."

By the late nineteenth century, the question of "Who I am" had become more and more of a problem for the speakers of European languages. The feudal social order was dead, replaced by a restless capitalism, gigantic new cities, enormous labor migrations, and turbulent working classes. A radical workers' movement gave new impetus to the theme of unity, challenging class division in the name of human equality. One of its leading thinkers, Karl Marx, created a powerful synthesis of socialist ideas that saw class struggle as the driving force of history, leading toward a future of classless unity.

However, even as Marx's vision of an ultimate oneness was gaining power, cultural and political developments were producing deeper social division. Global empires brought Europeans and North American settler populations face-to-face with radically different cultures, and urgently posed the question of human sameness and difference. Was the Cheyenne or the Zulu the white man's brother? Was the Australian Aboriginal, or the Bengali, on the same plane as the British conqueror? Some said yes, but more and more voices among the conquerors said no. A new language of "race" emerged during the nineteenth century to deny human unity.

Simultaneously, and intertwined with the new language of race, a change was occurring in conceptions of gender. Men and women had long been thought of as the same kind of being, although the male was a more perfect and powerful version of it than the female. European intellectual culture in the eighteenth and nineteenth centuries increasingly rejected this view and defined men and women as different in nature, even opposites (Laqueur 1990). Men and women were irrevocably assigned to "separate spheres" suited to their different natures. There was a material basis for this: fascinating archaeological research has traced the physical separation of workplace from domestic life, and the gradual segregation of cities like New York on gender as well as class lines (Wall 1994).

Entrenched in the very stones of the city, the belief in separate spheres became so powerful that it was accepted even by most nineteenth-century feminists.

Thus, in the later nineteenth century, European and North American bourgeois culture—by then the dominant culture in the world—contained a powerful ideology of innate differences. These were supposed to be differences of character as well as physical type, and were reflected in hierarchies of class, race, and gender. Such beliefs have deeply affected twentieth- and twenty-first-century cultures, influencing popular thinking as well as intellectual formulations about every kind of difference and inequality.

Yet this view of human nature was challenged almost as soon as it was established in bourgeois culture, often by appealing to an older view of human identity. The belief in invidious human differences was challenged from without, for example by anticolonial intellectuals. In 1927 Mohandas K. Gandhi, the most influential leader of the Indian independence movement, said:

> In my opinion there is no such thing as inherited or acquired superiority.... I believe that all men are born equal. All—whether born in India or in England or in America or in any circumstances whatsoever—have the same soul as any other. And it is because I believe in this inherent equality of all men that I fight the doctrine of superiority which many of our rulers arrogate to themselves. I have fought this doctrine of superiority in South Africa inch by inch, and it is because of that inherent belief that I delight in calling myself a scavenger, a spinner, a weaver, a farmer and a labourer. (Gandhi 1993, 207)

Gandhi also contested the idea of fixed hierarchies *within* a given society. He was a noted defender of the "untouchables" in India; indeed, the passage just quoted comes from a critique of Brahmin upper-caste arrogance in relation to other castes. He even came, in the later part of his life, to doubt the hierarchy of gender he had formerly accepted. Some of Gandhi's moral and political successors who carried forward his doctrine of nonviolence, such as Martin Luther King Jr., were centrally concerned with domestic racism.

The ideology of fixed differences was also challenged from within European culture. Indeed, it was in the capital of one of the oldest European empires, Vienna, that a revolution in psychology began. Sigmund Freud has had so broad an influence on modern thought that it is hard to realize how radical his psychology was. It has had a profound impact on gender studies, most of all because it questioned the idea of fixed, homogenous character types for men and women. Freud's clinical practice, as a pioneering psychiatrist, showed how men's and women's personalities in adulthood were the product of a long, conflict-ridden process of emotional development.

Freud argued that the flux and confusion of everyday thought could only be understood by reference to a deeper mental reality, an unconscious level where desires were inaccessible to ordinary thought because they had been repressed. Repression is not a given condition but happens at particular moments in the course of one's life. One such passage is the "Oedipal" crisis in childhood, where primitive sexual desires addressed to one's parents meet social prohibitions. Freud came to see adult personalities as being *by necessity* internally divided and full of conflict, and the patterns of adult mental life—including femininity and masculinity, heterosexuality and homosexuality—as the outcomes of particular life histories, of specific courses of events.

Freud did not himself use the term *identity*, except casually. He did, however, give increasing importance to the process of "identification" (Laplanche and Pontalis 1973). In identification, one incorporates the characteristics of another person, with whom one has emotional ties, into one's own personality. An example is provided by one of Freud's most famous case histories, of the "Rat Man," a reserve officer in the Austro-Hungarian army at the time of his treatment (Freud 1955, 151–318). The young man found his life severely disrupted by various obsessions, including one involving rats. Freud traced the sources of these troubles back through his family and sexual history to his childhood relationship with his father. Underneath the apparently friendly and admiring attitude of the son was a mass of fear and rivalry. The internal conflict about obedience to the father, a professional soldier in his youth, was formative for the boy and broke out afresh in early adulthood, when the young man was going on military maneuvers.

Identification therefore need not be conscious, and it need not be harmonious. On the contrary, one can have conflicting identifications—with a father, with a mother, with other figures. Unity with the object of emotion does not imply unity within the self.

The idea of pathology growing out of a life history became the central idea of modern clinical psychology and the basis of a vast range of therapies in which people comb their childhoods for the sources of their current troubles. The idea was developed in varying ways by Freud's argumentative followers. One of the first, Alfred Adler, made the most important addition—the social dimension. A socialist doctor in Vienna, Adler was concerned with the health of the working class and was also influenced by the women's movement of the day. Both socialism and feminism led him to the view that one's social location, especially one's degree of social power, was a crucial determinant of personal histories and psychological conflicts. The ultimate answer to the neuroses produced by a divided society, Adler ([1927] 1992) came to believe, was to develop a unifying sense of social responsibility and mutual obligation.

This insight about society and power was developed in varying ways by psychoanalysts and social observers. In the hands of a writer who was both, Erik Erikson, Adler's insight became the basis of the twentieth century's most influential statement about "identity." Erikson's *Childhood and Society* offered an interpretation of modern personal, social, and political problems as difficulties in achieving identity: "The study of identity, then, becomes as strategic in our time as the study of sexuality was in Freud's time" (Erikson [1950] 1965, 242). Erikson also offered a highly conservative view of differences between the genders, based on the idea that a woman's psychology was determined by her reproductive capacities and "inner spaces." But this was entirely separate from his concept of identity.

The key terms in long, complex books often have some ambiguity, and this is true of *Childhood and Society*. Erikson's concept of "identity" has two significantly different meanings. The first is a concept of personal identity. Following Freud's theoretical insights and clinical method, Erikson saw adult personality as formed by a long, conflict-ridden process of growth. Also following Freud, he distinguished several agencies within the mind, marked by conflicting impulses and repressions.

But where Freud's work focused on conflicts involving the unconscious agencies (the "id" and the "superego"), Erikson emphasized issues involving the "ego," the mental agency where the conscious sense of self is located and which functions as our negotiator with the outside world. Personal identity, in Erikson's thought, meant the integration of the ego. It meant the coherence and interconnection among the psychological mechanisms by which the ego handles the pressures imposed on it from both the unconscious agencies and the outside world. This feat of balance, if successful, is registered in a stable sense of self. Thus the question "Who am I?" is answered by the ego's success in mastering the trials and tribulations of psychological development.

Erikson made a striking suggestion about the timing of this process. He picked up the Freudian idea that there are different stages in a child's psychosexual development and elaborated it into a model of the whole life cycle. Each of the eight stages Erikson named has its characteristic psychological conflict, which has to be resolved before moving on to the next. In one of these stages—the stage of adolescence—conflict around "identity" is central. Erikson's first book was followed by writings focused on adolescence, such as *Identity, Youth and Crisis* (1968).

The idea that adolescence is a time of "identity crisis" became immensely influential, not only in youth studies but also in popular culture. This era in the United States saw the rise of rock and roll, a self-conscious youth subculture, and the politicized youth movements of the 1960s. These trends were widely interpreted as a "search for identity" by youth.

The second meaning of Erikson's concept of identity concerns culture and society. Erikson adapted the Adlerian theme of social context but read the present in the way Adler read the future. That is, he ignored contemporary social divisions in favor of focusing on traits or self-conceptions shared by all the members of a given society. This led him to write of culture in a manner closely paralleling his writing about the individual person, suggesting that the different courses of development in the United States, Germany, and Russia led to different national identities. In this highly speculative part of Erikson's work, the question of "identity" became a question of *membership* in a particular community. The community in question was the nation-state (or the tribe, when Erikson wrote about a non-Western context). In this usage, the concept of identity still referred to unity or oneness, but at the level of society rather than the individual.

The main impact of Erikson's work was in psychology and youth studies. The concepts of personal identity and conflicts about identity became key terms in popular psychology at a time when psychotherapy was expanding from a small, specialized branch of medicine to a large industry, especially in the United States. Around the professions of psychiatry, counseling, family therapy, and so on spreads a wide range of self-help movements and popular psychology books with self-help themes and titillating snippets of "case histories." Though most of the writings from this movement are intellectually empty, they have popularized the ideas for both women and men that (a) identity is achieved, not given, and (b) identity is problematic, under threat, somehow in crisis—and in need of "work."

While these developments were occurring in psychology, the main form of progressive politics in the countries of the global North was provided by the labor movement and socialist parties. Mainstream socialist thought understood the exploitation of the working class to be the central form of oppression and saw militant workers as the main agents of social change. Turn-of-the-century socialists often supported other movements for social change: women's emancipation, freedom for colonies, race equality, and what we now call human rights. Yet these were always thought to be subsidiary to the class struggle. Socialism saw itself as the expression of the unity of humanity and the working class as the bearer of the common good. In orthodox Marxism, this belief became dogma. In the communist parties, which overwhelmed most other forms of socialism during the twentieth century, no political priorities other than the "class line" were permitted.

In the worldwide social ferment of the 1960s and early 1970s, especially in the political cauldron of the rich countries' New Left, this priority was dramatically challenged. In the United States, the civil rights struggle of African Americans was the most prominent mass movement for change. The peace movement, which challenged the war in Vietnam, was more often opposed than supported by "hard-hat" manual workers and their organizations. In Europe, Marxist parties were baffled by the student movement, which seemed to follow no assignable class logic. Conversely, left-wing parties were regarded by the new feminism as part of the patriarchal establishment. Far from supporting the new gay liberation movement, orthodox Marxists regarded homosexuality as a sign of the decadence and corruption of capitalist society.

In due course, progressive alliances of the older kind were reestablished. Labor parties proved more hospitable to feminism and to civil rights movements than their conservative opponents, as conservative parties increasingly exploited racial antagonism and homophobia. Yet the 1960s and 1970s were a watershed in the radical politics of the rich countries. The priority of class struggle was lost, and "new social movements," increasingly transnational in scope, became critically important. In the course of this change, a new form of political mobilization became prominent, which in the United States in the 1980s was called "identity politics." This included, but has not been limited to, gender politics.

Identity politics involves social movements—as does environmental politics—but social movements of a special kind. They are built around membership in a specific group and assert the distinctiveness, dignity, and distinctive needs of that group. Identity politics can take place within a nation or transcend national boundaries. Familiar examples are the Black Power movements, women's liberation, indigenous people's movements, and gay liberation. Ethnonationalisms (for example, Serbian and Croatian in the former Yugoslavia) and religious-political movements (for example, political Protestantism versus Catholicism in the United Kingdom and United States, Hindu nationalism in India, and classical Zionism in Israel) have some of the same features.

In contrast to the universalist aims of socialism or of liberalism, identity politics makes no claim to represent humanity in general or the common interest. At its center is what is distinctive about a particular group. This *may* be the group's material disadvantage. African Americans in the United States, for instance, are poorer than white Americans as a group, especially in terms of property ownership. Indigenous people such as Australian Aborigines or the native peoples of the Americas, except where they have land rights, have very low incomes and are seriously underresourced in terms of educational, medical, and other services. Women, who historically have been collectively much poorer than men, have long been excluded from most positions of power and authority and are still massively underrepresented in both state and corporate leadership (Inter-Parliamentary Union 2013; and see *Fortune* magazine June 19, 2013).

To traditional claims for political equality and social justice, identity politics adds another: the claim for respect, or what Nancy Fraser (1995) calls "struggles for recognition." In structures of inequality such as race and gender, the group at the bottom has not only been materially deprived but has usually been blamed and discredited into the bargain. For instance, a great deal of our dominant culture, from the classics to the moderns, condemn women as brainless, feeble creatures deeply in need of guidance from their fathers and husbands. As Katherine in Shakespeare's *The Taming of the Shrew* puts it:

I am asham'd that women are so simple,
To offer warre, where they should kneele for peace:
Or seeke for rule, supremacie, and sway,
When they are bound to serve, love, and obay.
Why are our bodies soft, and weake, and smooth,
Unapt to toyle and trouble in the world,
But that our soft conditions, and our harts,
Should well agree with our externall parts? (V.ii.177–84)

Nineteenth-century imperialism, like slavery in the United States, left an equally toxic legacy of racial hatred and vilification, in which oppressed races were defined as incorrigibly stupid, violent, or bestial. Homosexual people, as soon as they were identified as a distinct category, were defined as degenerate, perverted, criminal, or sick. The poor have long been blamed for poverty.

In the face of such cultural abuse, identity politics has asserted the dignity of the oppressed group, insisting that there is an identity worth claiming, an identity in which one can take pride. Hence black pride, gay pride, red pride movements, and the search for women's culture and foremothers. Hence the celebration of distinctive customs, religions, or languages—the black church, or the Irish language (a cause now lost), or local dress (also mostly lost).

"Identity" in identity politics is both social and personal, both the name of a group and a sense of self, linked by the idea of membership. One engages in identity politics because one is a member of such and such a group, and because being a member of that group is central to the person one is. These connections are not static, and identity politics may not just "express" identity but actually reshape the group. The remaking of urban gay communities by the gay liberation movement in the 1970s (Altman 1982) is a well-known example. So is the worldwide growth of indigenous peoples' movements (Brecher, Childs, and Cutler 1993). For instance, the number of people identifying themselves as "Aboriginal and Torres Strait Islander" in Australian censuses and surveys increased markedly after the growth of identity politics among this massively disadvantaged people.

The construction of a shared identity through identity politics takes several forms. First, an oppressed group can take the very material of oppression and turn it on its head. The Black Power movement in the US rejected euphemisms like "colored" (as in the National Association for the Advancement of Colored People, or NAACP), embraced the blunt and then derogatory "black," and turned the language of stigma into the language of pride. Rap groups have now pushed the process further, using the term *nigger* to assert identity.

Next, constructing an identity may involve the creation of new cultural forms. This was the focus of an important strand of feminism in the 1970s and 1980s, which sought to define women's culture and find a new vocabulary and style for women's writing. More often, however, defining an identity involves a rediscovery and celebration of what was formerly despised, marginalized, or forgotten. The last few decades have seen the celebration of forms as diverse as Central Desert paintings in Australia, women's science, underground sexual cultures, and African styles of clothing.

Identity politics has thus been a significant force for cultural diversity. The unity or wholeness of each of these identities is necessarily defined against other unities—it does not embrace or include them. If I am black or brown or yellow, I am not white. If I am a man, I am not a woman. Accordingly, "identity politics" has become a term designating plurality and especially the acceptance of *difference* as a political principle. The language of difference self-consciously displaces the universalist language of socialism.

Discussing difference and identity in a Latin American context, Sonia Montecino draws on a history very different from that of the global metropole: the colonial remaking of culture across Latin America and the ideology of "marianismo" that came out of it (Montecino 2001). This cultural formation constructs women's identity on the model of the sacrificial mother, especially the mother of sons. Montecino argues that in a society influenced by a powerful ideology of homogeneity it is difficult to draw out differences. But differences do emerge, in acts of resistance and reappropriation, and there are in fact multiple feminine identities. The subject is in process, not fixed. The incorporation of paid work in women's lives—which happened earlier in the working class than in the middle class—ruptures the ideology of marianismo. Women's emergence into the public realm sharpens issues about subordination, so the form of gender politics shifts. Among the privileged, where housework and child care are handed off to working-class women, an older pattern of feminine labor allows the modernization of gender relations among the elite.

In a broader perspective, Montecino argues, gender identities in Latin America are formed in the same way as class identities—within projects of social change. This contrasts with the individualism of most "identity" discourse in the global North. It is important, then, to see the *collective* identities being formed in women's movements in countries such as Chile. Feminist movements, from the time of suffrage struggles on, have emphasized equality and sex differences. Survival movements among indigenous women assume the existing gender division of labor that feminist movements contest. Mothers' movements struggle for sons' lives, for human rights, or for "the family." While feminist movements struggle for change in identities and for women to move into men's spheres of action, mothers' movements use the cultural legitimacy afforded by old identities—and have sometimes opposed radical change.

In Montecino's view, real changes in women's position have occurred, notably better education, smaller families, and more paid employment. But public politics is still dominated by men on the assumption that women are domestic. A "conservative modernity," she suggests, is well expressed in the realm of gender identity.

Two troubling paradoxes emerge around identity politics. First, the identities celebrated in identity politics were originally those of oppressed groups. Identity politics thus appears to be a renaming, with an emphasis on culture and psychology, of what used to be called "liberation struggles." But there is a logical difference: a dominant group can also define and celebrate its identity, and thus engage in identity politics. Indeed, this is historically quite common. Race politics in the world created by Western imperialism has generally involved a celebration of the "white" race and its virtues. Hitler, with his vague belief in the Aryan and his not at all vague hatred of Jews, was at the violent end of a very wide spectrum. The White Australia policy, as official policy, persisted up to the 1960s, and the apartheid regime in South Africa persisted to the end of the 1980s. Research and debate have shown the persistence (and also the complexities) of "white" self-images in the United States as well (Fine et al. 1997).

A similar point applies to gender. The solidarity of men against the encroachments of women is asserted in many settings: upper-crust clubs, working-class unions, sports broadcasts, academic treatises, pubs, bars, armies, boardrooms, churches, mosques, and temples. Research such as Morrell's (2001) study of elite boys' schools in colonial South Africa shows how segregated institutions (such as boarding schools) simultaneously reinforce gender hierarchy and create a particular shared definition of masculinity.

In an ironic twist, with the right-wing attack on "political correctness," dominant groups such as men, whites, and heterosexuals have been redefined as *victims* of discrimination caused by affirmative action programs and disadvantaged groups asking for "special rights." Attempts to start social movements among the privileged using the rhetoric of disadvantage have had limited appeal, though the claim that gay marriage tramples on the "religious freedom" of conservative church groups has had some purchase in the United States. The mobilization of upper-caste youth against affirmative action for disadvantaged castes in India is even more striking. Generally, however, the interests of the privileged are better articulated through institutions such as corporations, the state, and the church. Mainstream Christianity and mainstream Islam are reliable supports for the authority of men over women, and almost every government in the world supports the wealthy against the challenges of the poor.

The second paradox concerns the basis of the identities that groups are claiming. Freud and Erikson argued that personal identity is constructed through a long and complex process. The intellectuals of liberation movements took the same view of the collective identities of the oppressed. For instance, the Martiniquan Frantz Fanon, in *Black Skin, White Masks* (1952) and *The Wretched of the Earth* (1961), showed how the identities of the colonized grew out of a history of domination. Creating a new culture required a massive effort to come to terms with that history and its toxic consequences; indeed, it required decolonizing violence. Similarly, 1970s feminism in the affluent countries put a lot of effort into showing how girls and women acquired feminine identity by internalizing a socially defined "sex role." Gay theorists talked about the "self-oppression" resulting from the absorption of homophobic attitudes from straight society.

However, as Steven Epstein (1987) has shown, a theory that identities are socially constructed and imposed by a dominant culture is a two-edged tool. It provides a critique of that dominant culture, but it cannot account for patterns of desire as people actually experience them. Social constructionism can be both unsatisfying and risky. There is a power to Sojourner Truth's "Ain't I a Woman?" that is somehow lacking from "Ain't I a bearer of socially constructed feminine stereotypes?" For lesbians and gay men to emphasize the socially constructed nature of homosexuality is to lay them open—in a homophobic society—to attempts to abolish homosexuality. What is socially created can be socially destroyed or abandoned. The religious right has avidly picked up this theme, defining homosexuality as a "lifestyle" and attempting with great vigor to ban, discredit, or harass it.

In the face of such threats, identity politics has been liable to retreat into essentialism. This means claiming that identities such as "women," "gay," or "black" are based on *natural* categories and express unchangeable characteristics. In a famous essay, Gayatri Spivak (1988) suggests that subaltern groups might adopt a "strategic essentialism," a kind of provisional *as-if* identity politics that build solidarity for struggle. This idea became popular in academic feminism as a way of combining a social-constructionist understanding of gender with the need for political mobilization by women. Unfortunately, there is not much strategy but a lot of essentialism in most identity appeals. Identity politics has led into strange byways, such as gay enthusiasm for the search for a "gay gene." Dubious biology aside, the problem here is that a claim to identity, far from being a liberatory act, may be buying into a system of social control.

In popular speech, the term *identity* probably occurs most often in the phrase "identity card" or "identity document." Bars, banks, gas stations, insurance firms, websites, employers, buildings, and transportation centers such as airports all ask for "ID"—as do the police. The identity card, now often a "photo ID," is a document issued by an authority, identifying the bearer for a purpose under the authority's legal control—but once issued, is available for other purposes too. The procedures for getting certain identity documents, especially passports and visas, are now elaborate, so that the authority can satisfy itself that it is not issuing two documents to one person and that the subject really is who she or he claims to be. These concerns have been sharpened by the current unceasing agitation about "security" risks, and by anxiety about "identity fraud," a kind of crime that trades on the assumption that identity is individual and unique.

"Identity" as defined by an ID creates even more pluralism than "identity" in identity politics. Here, "identity" distinguishes one particular person from everyone else in the world. That is to say, there are over seven billion identities in the world just now, with the number growing every day.

This use of the term retains the old sense of the continuity of personal existence. Indeed, a key reason for having IDs is to make an *inescapable* link between the-person-now and the-person-that-was. The ID nails you to your past: your national origin, your gender, your birth date, your qualifications, your marriages, and also your traffic accident history and your police record. With the growth of corporate databanks, and requirements to use ID in all sorts of transactions, you are also nailed to your credit history, your financial record, and (increasingly, via online systems such as Google) your past patterns of consumption.

"Identity," then, can be a matter of surveillance and regulation. This goes far beyond identity documents. Modern society has many ways of classifying and labeling people: in terms of medical and mental syndromes ("asthmatic" or "psychotic"), life-history stages ("adolescent" or "geriatric"), economic status ("unemployed" or "DINK"), conformity to rules or norms ("delinquent" or "hyperactive"), and so on. A famous example is the American Psychiatric Association's *Diagnostic and Statistical Manual* (*DSM*), which classifies mental disorders and has, at various times, classified and then declassified homosexuality and "gender identity disorder" as mental illnesses. The *DSM* is now in its fifth edition, and each revision has been accompanied by fierce professional and lay debate. The debate occurs because such systems of classification—a very important basis of the human sciences—are not innocent. They are typically connected with institutions or social techniques that need to classify people into large groups in order to administer them: to separate the criminal from the law-abiding, the sick from the healthy, the ignorant from the educated—and the men from the women.

These systems of knowledge, and the institutions that use and even embody them (such as schools, hospitals, jails, or welfare offices), do more than recognize previously existing identities. They also *impute* identities to people by locating them in particular classifications. The power of this process has been made clear by sociological research on "labeling." Once you are labeled a juvenile delinquent, for instance, your imputed identity is likely to become the basis for other people's reactions to you, regardless of what you yourself are now doing. Even more broadly, as gender studies demonstrates again and again, once a person is labeled a "woman" or a "man," that person's sense of self and relationships with others will be heavily preordained by that label. As studies in ethnomethodology show, one is held accountable in terms of the categorization (Fenstermaker and West 2002).

The creation of a "homosexual identity," which itself is part of the creation of the modern European-American gender system, illustrates these themes. Sexuality is an integral dimension of the overall structure of gender relations, and classifications of sexual behavior have been important in defining what is acceptable as gender performance, for instance, what is "masculine" or what is "a good wife." But these judgments change over time.

In medieval and early modern European societies, specific homosexual acts were often defined as shameful or as criminal, lumped together with other disruptions of religious or social order, and sometimes punished very brutally. Enforcement, however, was erratic (Greenberg 1988). In the late nineteenth century, laws changed. They criminalized homosexual behavior generally, which led to regular police surveillance and arrests, especially for homosexual men. At about the same time, homosexuality was defined as a medical condition, a syndrome. This was part of an extension of medical classifications to include sexual behavior, marked by the Austrian doctor Richard von Krafft-Ebing's famous book *Psychopathia Sexualis* (1886). Historians debate to what extent a sexual subculture had already created some kind of "homosexual identity," but as Jeffrey Weeks (1977) has shown, there can be little doubt that legal and medical discourse helped to shape the modern category of "the homosexual," and to define "the heterosexual," by contrast, as normality. In brief, a person no longer simply did homosexual things, such as sodomy. One *was* a homosexual, and seen by others as such. The interactionist sociology of Kenneth Plummer (1975) in Britain confirmed the point: "societal reaction" to sexual difference is a powerful determinant of the personal identity that emerges. Guy Hocquenghem made the point more radically: "The homosexual exists first of all in the normal person's paranoia; the judge knows him to be guilty, just as the doctor knows him to be sick" (Hocquenghem 1978, 75).

So labeled, "the homosexual" confronts a dilemma in sexual politics. To assert a homosexual identity is *both* liberating and regulative. It cannot fail to be both. To mobilize politically and culturally around one's sexual identity as a homosexual may be freeing, but it unavoidably appeals to the same classification system that generates the concept of homosexuality as deviance. On the other hand, to reject the classification altogether, to walk away from identity as homosexual, is to abandon the ideas and social support that may be vital in fighting oppression. A lone individual may attempt to evade classification but cannot contest it.

Yet collective action *might* disrupt the classification system. This is the reasoning behind forms of sexual politics, now often called "queer" politics, that refuse a conventional, and conventionally stigmatized, homosexual identity but also refuse to go back in the closet. An aggressive assertion of difference, and a multiplication of differences *within* that difference, is meant to create trouble for the strategies of social control that rely on putting people into boxes. In the United States, an initial focus was put on differences within lesbian and gay communities—on the distinction of black from white, young from old, S&M from vanilla. Even the good old butch/femme distinction among lesbians was brought out of the cupboard and celebrated.

Queer politics is not "identity politics" in the older sense; indeed, it is a kind of anti-identity politics. And it has certainly had a cultural impact. Queer rekindled a radicalism in sexual politics that had been hard to sustain through the AIDS/HIV pandemic, and emphasized diversity within lesbian and gay communities (Reynolds 2002). How much the overall categorizations have been disrupted is another matter. "We're queer, we're here" still implies an identifiable *we*. One unintended effect of queer is, perhaps, to bring out finer classifications, to replace a "homosexual identity" with an array of more tightly defined homosexual identities—white middle-aged leather dyke, black male drag queen, and so on. Another effect is to shift the basis of classification. The category "queer" is now often used to link homosexual groups with groups who consider themselves heterosexual but whose lives also involve disruptions of gender boundaries or conventions: cross-dressers, transgender people, effeminate men, and masculine women. Among these groups, the familiar boundaries of the gender order are most profoundly in question.

The strategy of disrupting boundaries and identities draws support from postmodern intellectual developments that suggest classification systems might be inherently unstable. When identity politics have posited a deep, stable, prelinguistic source of identity for a group—for example, essentialist concepts of race or gender—it has been difficult to accept the shifts in philosophy and cultural analysis associated with postmodernism. Models of stable, unified identity are notably undermined by the work of the French philosopher Jacques Derrida. In the enormously influential book *Of Grammatology* (1976), Derrida contests the idea that language simply maps the self-identity of beings in nature, and that the terms of our language can thus have unitary meanings. Rather, he presents the spectacle of a restless play of language in which the relation between a sign and its referent can never be fixed, where meaning is always provisional. The concepts that are supposed to be represented by language can have neither stability nor logical simplicity.

Though the philosophical procedures of deconstruction are not widely understood (for an excellent introduction, see Norris 1987), the general idea that the boundaries of categories are shifting and permeable has circulated very widely indeed. From this has come a pervasive sense that identities are unstable.

To say that boundaries and identities are unstable is logically different from saying that classification systems and identities are plural. It is one thing to say, "My identity is provisional and open to change," and quite another thing to say, "I have multiple identities." Since the 1970s and 1980s, when feminists from the global South challenged the global North's definition of gender politics, and feminists of color in the United States challenged monolithic notions of "woman" and of "the lesbian," the idea of multiple identities has been a leading theme in women's studies and gender studies. It has led to a widely held view that identities as women or men are interwoven with identities derived from bodily abilities or disabilities, sexuality, ethnicity, race, class, education, religion, nation, or region, and from other shaping forces. As the Australian sociologist Gillian Bottomley wrote:

> Analyses based on static notions about the maintenance of traditions or the separation of sets of relations labeled ethnic—or gender or class or religious or linguistic—cannot convey the constant interweaving of processes of transformation and cross-referencing in heterogeneous societies. (Bottomley 1992, 121)

This "constant interweaving" is traced with great subtlety in Bottomley's studies of changing gender identities in migrant communities. But the issue is much broader; this interweaving or intersection is a general feature of social life in the contemporary world. Writing about lesbians in India and South Africa, Amanda Lock Swarr and Richa Nagar extend such conclusions:

> We build on the growing body of feminist scholarship that recognizes the imperative of positing identity categories such as race, class, gender, sex, and sexuality as essentially interrelated and simultaneously experienced. It is now agreed that one cannot speak about any one of these identities in isolation because of their "complex relationality." (Swarr and Nagar 2003, 495–96)

The intellectual climate that has supported the growing political concern with diversity has thus led research toward an interest in plural and shifting gender forms and an equally plural and shifting set of connections between gender and sexuality. This trend has strongly affected the recent growth of research and debate on masculinity. In contrast to discussion of "*the* male sex role" in the 1970s, and to populist discourse about "true masculinity," researchers have come to speak of "masculinities" in the plural. Research has shown great diversity among cultures in their constructions of gender for men (Cornwall and Lindisfarne 1994). Other research has documented multiple masculinities within the same culture, and even more fine-grained distinctions within the same institution, peer group, or workplace (Connell 2005).

So there has been a strong trend toward recognizing multiple gender identities. But this requires us to reconsider what is meant by "identity" in the new usage. The discourse has shifted ground significantly. Erikson's concept of identity referred to the integration of the ego *as a whole*. Philosophical and literary writing about identity also long referred to the continuity of selfhood for the person as a whole. In current discussions of "gender identities," "sexual identities," "ethnic identities," and the like, we are referring each time just to *one aspect* of a person—her or his involvement in gender relations, sexual practices, ethnic structures, and so on.

To Robert Stoller, the American psychiatrist who popularized the concept of "gender identity," the shift did not matter very much because he assumed that the integration of the personality as a whole *was* largely focused on the sense of being male or female. This was what he called "core gender identity" (Stoller 1968), in an argument that has had great influence, for instance on the medical treatment of transsexual women and men, who are presumed by Stoller to have established the wrong core gender identity very early in life.

But others could speak equally meaningfully of "race identity," "class identity," or, with Erikson, "national identity." Indeed, nationalism, a dominant political form in modern history, makes national identity the crucible of personal identity. The study of women, men, and gender has often asked about the relations between gender and national identity (e.g., Nagel 1998). If we acknowledge the "constant interweaving" of which Bottomley writes, we *must* attend to these different forms of identity in order to understand any one, such as gender identity.

Common speech and journalism take even further the locating of identity in one activity or condition. Media reports refer to one's identity as a teenager, as a mother, as a fundamentalist Christian, as a fanatical stamp collector, as a unionist, or as a corporate executive. Practically any social activity, it seems, can be the basis of an "identity."

Even the well-researched "identities" of gender and sexuality, on close examination, prove less solid than we usually think. For instance, Arne Nilsson's (1998) beautifully crafted study of homosexual history in a Swedish city identifies three ways of being homosexual: "so," commonly a bit effeminate; "real men," often working-class youth; and "fjollor," flamboyant queens. Three distinct identities, we might think. But Nilsson also shows how the patterns of homosexual life grew out of the structure of an industrial and maritime city, with crowded housing, a sharp gender division of labor, a high density of men in public spaces, a non-respectable working-class street life, connections to other cities via the shipping trade, certain patterns of policing, and many poor young men, who might enter homosexual relationships for a period and then move on. The distinctive forms of homosexual practice changed as these conditions changed in the 1950s, with rising affluence, suburban working-class housing, the growth of the welfare state, and moral panics about the seduction of youth. A sharper cultural distinction between heterosexual and homosexual people followed the increasing privacy of sexual conduct itself. This case study shows in fine detail how the configurations of sexual and social practice, which might easily be read as identities, were dependent on historically transitory social conditions, and for many participants were only a limited part of a sexual life history.

In conclusion, given the changes in meaning, and alternative ways of understanding the issues, is "identity" still a worthwhile concept? Certainly, the word has been immensely overused. It often serves merely as a pretentious synonym for self, reputation, or social standing, slapdash uses that have hindered, not helped, our understanding of gender and sexuality.

Even worse, there are cases where to use the term *identity* for a configuration of gender or sexual practice is actively misleading and conceals important dimensions of reality. Guy Hocquenghem, whose acid formulation of the social origin of homosexual identity was quoted above, went on to argue that homosexual desire is *in principle* inchoate, anarchic, an impersonal flux and not a personal unity. It is desire that escapes being "oedipalized," that is, organized and formulated by the patriarchal social order. Homosexuality, it would follow, is not an identity at all, but the opposite of an identity, being desire and practice that *cannot* be welded into a unity.

Hocquenghem's argument misses the evidence that homosexual desire is to some extent structured by gay communities themselves. Yet we could also argue that it does not go far enough. A great deal of *heterosexual* desire also fails to be "oedipalized." Heterosexual desire, too, is often perverse, impersonal, transitory, unbounded. Heterosexual desire often evades, or pushes against, the social authority that constructs fixed positions and bounded identities in a heterosexual order. As Lynne Segal puts it in *Straight Sex*:

> Sexual relations are perhaps the most fraught and troubling of all social relations precisely because, especially when heterosexual, they so often *threaten* rather than confirm gender polarity. (Segal 1994, 254–55)

With heterosexual practice, too, we must ask whether an identity has been constructed and is being sustained (often aggressively, because it is too fragile to be taken for granted); we cannot take heterosexual "identity" for granted.

We may also question Erikson's conviction that it is *desirable* to have a unified identity. Erikson saw that as a task to be accomplished in the course of growing up. Most other people who have written about identities have likewise assumed that everybody ought to have one. But is this really so desirable? Some identities I can think of are pretty revolting, in their consequences for other people. To weld one's personality into a united whole is to refuse internal diversity and openness. It may also be to refuse change. Reform in gender relations, for instance, may require a destructuring of the self, an experience of gender vertigo, as part of the process. I have documented this for one group of men in the environmental movement who were trying to change traditional masculinity (Connell 2005, chap. 5). The American sociologist Barbara Risman (1998) found a similar pattern of transition in "fair families" in the United States. Living with contradictions, rather than trying to erase them, may be more valuable.

We may, however, save the concept of identity if we are prepared to use it in a more specific and precise way. There are two main options. In the first option, we can still use "identity" in an Eriksonian way, to mean the integration of the self, or the person, as a whole—provided we also acknowledge how provisional and imperfect this integration will be. Sartre's ([1960] 1968) concept of personhood as a "project," a *unification* accomplished by a person's actions through time, is a better base for the concept than any static model of personality. With this approach, we can still speak of "gender identity," *but only when it is specifically the case* that for such and such a person or group, gender actually *is* the basis of the integration and structuring of personality. In other words, some people might have a gender(-based) identity, and other people might not. The project of "identity politics," at the personal level, can then be seen as the project of *structuring personal life in a particular way*, that is, around the membership (e.g., man, black, British, lesbian) at issue in a particular social movement.

In the second option, we can use "identity" to name *the kind of person one is designated to be* by a system of classification and control. Here, the model is the identity document and the selfhood assigned by social authority, or by informal but powerful ways of naming and categorizing people. This conception of identity, too, must be modified by recent thinking—especially by recognizing that systems of classification change historically. This is dramatically shown by the recategorizing of homosexual conduct in non-Western societies under the impact of international gay culture, mass media, and the HIV/AIDS crisis. In Thailand, for instance, existing sex/gender categories for males, mainly "phu-chai" (man, mainly heterosexual) and "kathoey" (effeminate or cross-gender, receptive homosexual) have had a series of additions: "bai" (bisexual), "gay-king" (homosexual, preferring to be insertor), "gay-queen" (usually effeminate, preferring to be receptive), and "gay-quing" (masculine or effeminate, and sexually versatile) (Jackson 1996). Dennis Altman in *Global Sex* (2001) shows that this powerful process of cultural interaction takes different shapes in different parts of the world. In cases like Thailand, local patterns persist—here, the indigenous categories are maintained and added to. In other countries, a rupture occurs, and local sexual culture is more extensively colonized. But even when claims to a US-style "gay" identity are made, they are likely to involve some synthesis, some hybridization, between local and imported ways of being and acting.

With either of these two concepts of identity, it is essential to recognize that people are active in shaping their own lives, and that systems of classification are never received passively. The groups subjected to categorization interact with the categories, sometimes contesting them and sometimes putting them to new uses. Seen in this light, the concept of identity points not to fixed locations, but to arenas of psychological and cultural struggle. "Becoming somebody," as Philip Wexler (1992) put it in his splendid study of American high schools, is not easy in a culture riddled with alienation, whose institutions try to reduce every aspect of life to the level of a commodity. As identity politics movements have often had to recognize, "identity" may be more an ambition than a fact. The questions "Who am I?" and "Who are we?" may never have reliable answers.

References

Adler, Alfred. (1927) 1992. *Understanding Human Nature*. Trans. C. Brett. Oxford: Oneworld.

Altman, Dennis. 1982. *The Homosexualization of America, the Americanization of the Homosexual*. New York: St. Martin's Press.

———. 2001. *Global Sex*. Chicago: University of Chicago Press.

Bottomley, Gillian. 1992. *From Another Place: Migration and the Politics of Culture*. Cambridge: Cambridge University Press.

Brecher, Jeremy, John Brown Childs, and Jill Cutler. 1993. *Global Visions: Beyond the New World Order*. Boston: South End Press.

Connell, Raewyn. 2005. *Masculinities*. 2nd ed. Berkeley: University of California Press.

Cornwall, Andrea, and Nancy Lindisfarne, eds. 1994. *Dislocating Masculinity: Comparative Ethnographies*. London: Routledge.

Derrida, Jacques. 1976. *Of Grammatology*. Baltimore: Johns Hopkins University Press.

Epstein, Steven. 1987. "Gay Politics, Ethnic Identity: The Limits of Social Constructionism." *Socialist Review* 93/94:9–54.

Erikson, Erik H. (1950) 1965. *Childhood and Society*. Harmondsworth: Penguin.

——. 1968. *Identity, Youth and Crisis*. New York: Norton.

Fanon, Frantz. (1952) 1967. *Black Skin, White Masks*. Trans. C. Markmann. New York: Grove Press.

——. (1961) 1968. *The Wretched of the Earth*. Trans. C. Farrington. New York: Grove Press.

Fenstermaker, Sarah, and Candace West, eds. 2002. *Doing Gender, Doing Difference: Inequality, Power, and Institutional Change*. New York: Routledge.

Fine, Michelle, Lois Weis, Linda C. Powell, and L. Mun Wong, eds. 1997. *Off White: Readings on Race, Power, and Society*. New York: Routledge.

Fraser, Nancy. 1995. "From Redistribution to Recognition? Dilemmas of Justice in a 'Post-Socialist' Age." *New Left Review* 212:68–93.

Freud, Sigmund. 1955. *Notes upon a Case of Obsessional Neurosis* (1909). In *The Standard Edition of the Complete Psychological Works of Sigmund Freud*, trans. and ed. James Strachey, vol. 10. London: Hogarth Press.

Gandhi, Mohandas K. 1993. *The Penguin Gandhi Reader*. Ed. Rudrangshu Mukherjee. New Delhi: Penguin Books India.

Ghamari-Tabrizi, Behrooz. 1996. "Is Islamic Science Possible?" *Social Epistemology* 10 (3–4).

Greenberg, David F. 1988. *The Construction of Homosexuality*. Chicago: University of Chicago Press.

Hocquenghem, Guy. 1978. *Homosexual Desire*. Trans. D. Dangoor. London: Allison and Busby.

Inter-Parliamentary Union. 2013. "Women in National Parliaments." http://www.ipu.org/wmn-e/world.htm.

Jackson, Peter A. 1996. "The Persistence of Gender: From Ancient Indian *Pandakas* to Modern Thai *Gay-Quings*." *Meanjin Quarterly* 55 (1): 110–20.

Krafft-Ebing, R. von. (1886) 1965. *Psychopathia Sexualis*. New York: Paperback Library.

Laplanche, Jean, and Jean-Bertrand Pontalis. 1973. *The Language of Psycho-Analysis*. Trans. Donald Nicholson-Smith. London: Hogarth Press.

Laqueur, Thomas. 1990. *Making Sex: Body and Gender from the Greeks to Freud*. Cambridge, MA: Harvard University Press.

Montecino, Sonia. 2001. "Identidades y diversidades en Chile." In *Cultura y desarollo en Chile*, ed. Manuel Antonio Garretón, 65–98. Santiago: Andres Bello.

Morrell, Robert. 2001. *From Boys to Gentlemen: Settler Masculinity in Colonial Natal 1880–1920*. Pretoria: University of South Africa.

Nagel, Joane. 1998. "Masculinity and Nationalism: Gender and Sexuality in the Making of Nations." *Ethnic and Racial Studies* 21 (2): 242–69.

Nilsson, Arne. 1998. "Creating Their Own Private and Public: The Male Homosexual Life Space in a Nordic City during High Modernity." *Journal of Homosexuality* 35 (3–4): 81–116.

Norris, Christopher. 1987. *Derrida*. London: Fontana.

Plummer, Kenneth. 1975. *Sexual Stigma: An Interactionist Account*. London: Routledge and Kegan Paul.

Reynolds, Robert. 2002. *From Camp to Queer: Remaking the Australian Homosexual*. Melbourne: Melbourne University Press.

Risman, Barbara. 1998. *Gender Vertigo: American Families in Transition*. New Haven, CT: Yale University Press.

Sartre, Jean-Paul. (1960) 1968. *Search for a Method*. New York: Vintage.

Segal, Lynne. 1994. *Straight Sex: Rethinking the Politics of Pleasure*. Berkeley: University of California Press.

Spivak, Gayatri Chakravorty. 1988. *In Other Worlds: Essays in Cultural Politics*. New York: Routledge.

Stoller, Robert. 1968. *Sex and Gender: On the Development of Masculinity and Femininity*. New York: Science House.

Swarr, Amanda Lock, and Richa Nagar. 2003. "Dismantling Assumptions: Interrogating 'Lesbian' Struggles for Identity and Survival in India and South Africa." *Signs* 29 (2): 492–516.

Wall, Diana diZerega. 1994. *The Archaeology of Gender: Separating the Spheres in Urban America*. New York: Plenum Press.

Weeks, Jeffrey. 1977. *Coming Out: Homosexual Politics in Britain, from the Nineteenth Century to the Present*. London: Quartet.

Wexler, Philip. 1992. *Becoming Somebody: Toward a Social Psychology of School*. London: Falmer Press.

8 :: JUSTICE JANE MANSBRIDGE

When a group has relatively little power, its political success often depends on an appeal to "justice." Women, gay men, lesbians, transgendered people, and queers, like other marginalized groups, have had to make this appeal often. Whether in the debates over women's suffrage in the US Congress in the early twentieth century, debates over women's rights in South Africa's African National Congress in the late twentieth century, or debates over gay marriage in the first decade of the twenty-first century, considerations of justice have affected the decisions of powerholders in ways that power—the threat of sanction or the use of force—could never have done.

Yet the meaning of justice is now, always has been, and always will be heavily contested. One thin, formal, and relatively empty meaning—treating the similarly situated in a similar manner—probably applies in every culture. In practice, social evolution and struggle must fill in that meaning: *Who* are similarly situated? *What* counts as similar treatment? In all societies—but in some more than others—competing meanings of justice weave and contend together to produce a conceptual field filled with internal contradictions and both dominant and challenging meanings.

That conceptual field also produces different understandings of justice for different domains. I may consider it just to reward my children each according to their needs, my kindergarten students each according to their efforts, and my employees each according to the price their product will fetch in the market. Each context and its role in the larger culture influences in greater or lesser ways the meanings of justice in the other contexts. The way I treat my children may influence the way I treat my kindergartners, and so forth. In a market society, the way I treat my employees is likely to influence the way I treat my children and kindergartners more heavily than in a peasant society. Barriers between contexts serve to reduce this kind of cross-context influence. A strong social, political, and economic barrier between "private" and "public" realms makes me less likely to treat my kindergartners the way I treat my children, and vice versa.

In these contested contexts, it is a mistake to see justice as an understood goal that is simply "there," to be reached or even pursued. Politically, disadvantaged groups can often benefit from a justice portrayed as unproblematic and simply there, a beacon lighting the way to right behavior. Yet they can also be shortchanged by prevailing understandings of justice that rule out challenges over which people are similarly situated and what counts as similar treatment. The members of any disadvantaged group thus have two political tasks. First, they must try to preserve consensus on conceptions of justice that sustain attacks on the institutions that harm them. Second, they must achieve sufficient analytic distance to criticize the conceptions of justice that marginalize or exclude them. In the ensuing struggle over what justice mandates, subordinate groups must draw for justification on the existing dominant conceptual apparatus, on countercultural idea systems, and on their own experiences, for which they must often search to find new words.

In the midst of battle, political actors often become impatient with the need to persuade others (including more powerful others) on the basis of justice. Tactics based on persuasion come to seem weak, soft, or even based in resentment or envy, especially in contrast to the exercise of power, which broadcasts autonomy, defiance, and self-reliance. In fact, however, women, lesbians, gay men, bisexuals, transgendered individuals, and others deeply marginalized by dominant systems of sexuality, gender, and power usually do not have sufficient access to force or threats of sanction to coerce dominant groups into action. Terrorism and other highly targeted shows of strength may have some impact, but that impact often comes at great cost in other values, including justice (e.g., to the innocent) and the loss of external support. In addition, force and the threat of sanction are often surprisingly weak as tactics, as they must be maintained constantly. Successful expressions of power by less powerful groups in a society have therefore almost always been linked to claims of justice, in spite of the problems inherent in making a justice claim. Because appeals to justice are so critical to the politics of ending subordination, it is worth sorting out their weaknesses and their strengths by examining some of the ways that concepts of justice have supported, and will always support, prevailing systems of domination and subordination, as well as the ways that concepts of justice can be used to diminish or bring an end to domination.

Formal Justice

The ideal of formal justice has the great strength of having equality at its core and the great weakness of not specifying equality of what. When Aristotle approached the study of justice the way he approached his study of botany—first reporting and classifying what he saw in the social and political worlds—he found, and could not ignore, the much-cited popular formulation: "Justice is equality." Because, with his aristocratic sympathies, he did not want simply to accept the implication that in politics justice required an equal role in the state for every citizen, he argued that the equality in that formula should mean "proportional equality"—to each according to his contributions, a concept recently developed by Pythagoras—not "quantitative equality"—exactly the same amount for everyone (Aristotle, *Nichomachean Ethics* V.iii.4–17, *Politics* 1280 a 8–10; Plato, *Laws* 757a-d).

The ancient Greeks, who had evolved the saying "justice is equality," and Aristotle, who wanted to revise that phrase in an inegalitarian direction, both had a point. Justice does require equality, in the sense of relevantly similar treatment, among equals. But who are the equals? Those in Aristotle's audience who were convinced by his reasoning would have concluded that citizens who contributed the same amounts *to* the state were the equals who should be rewarded by the same amount of influence *in* the state. His opponents, hewing to the original proverb, would have concluded that roles in the state should be distributed equally among all the citizens. No one at the time would have argued that justice required considering "foreigners," even those born in Athens, as members of the group within which Aristotle and his opponents contested the distribution of rewards. Nor would most Athenians consider for a minute that children, women, or slaves could be among those to whom justice might assign a political role—equal or proportional—in governing the state. These groups did not come within the purview of the distributive rule as contemporaries contested it. They came instead under an unspoken rule that excluded them from discussion.

Formal justice thus demonstrably has one huge weakness. As S. I. Benn and R. S. Peters have formulated the concept, "To act justly ... is to treat all [individuals] alike except where there are relevant differences between them" (1959, 128). Formal justice says nothing substantive about what differences should be considered relevant. Substantive justice, by contrast, concerns the question of what differences should be considered relevant. A system can thus be formally just, treating individuals within categories alike, but substantively unjust, because the reasons for the category definitions are unjust.

Nevertheless, Benn and Peters point out, even purely formal justice produces an implicit rule: "Presume equality until there is reason to presume otherwise" (1959, 128). In making this point, they rely on an earlier analysis by Isaiah Berlin (1955–1956), who had uncovered this potentially disruptive, somewhat radical underside to an otherwise formal and empty definition of justice. The argument for the default pressure of equality in formal justice has three steps. The first is to recognize that every society has rules. Indeed, one might say that without some sort of informal rules, or norms, there can be no society, only an unassociated collection of individuals. Rules are coextensive with society itself. The second step is to recognize that within the categories of any rule all units are equal. That is, if the rule is that "Xs get Y," all Xs must get Y—or a relevant reason must be given for the difference in treatment. Such a relevant reason, however, effectively changes the rule to mean "All Xs with relevant characteristic Z get Y." This means no more than "All Zs get Y," a formulation that provides that within each category of the rule, whatever that rule is, the units are equal and must be treated equally.

Berlin's contribution was to recognize that this fact, inherent in the very meaning of a rule, puts the burden on the defenders of the status quo to justify the boundaries of any existing category. The third step of the argument points out that whenever boundaries fall and two categories collapse into each other, then all of the units within the new larger boundaries are equal. The default category is equality.

In a society based on tradition, the justification of existing categories may be relatively easy, as having always been so. The society will, of course, sometimes struggle over whether particular individuals belong to a particular category. In struggles over inheritance, for instance, claims from one side may be held to be stronger than claims from the other, or old agreements waiving certain claims may be remembered differently by different parties. People may disagree over which of several possibly applicable rules in fact applies. Many judgments will be delegated to a wise man or men, or some form of village court, to make a decision appropriate to the contingencies of the particular situation. Through a series of particularistic decisions, the categories implicit in the social rules may gradually change.

In more modern societies, with written rules designed to apply universalistically and without adaptation to everyone—rather than particularistically, as adapted by a wise individual or group to discrete situations—the categories delineated in rules can more easily come under explicit challenge. When changing material conditions, the evolution of ideals, or the mutual encounter of cultures open the possibility for change, the excluded can look for ways to attack as arbitrary the boundary that excludes them and demand reasons for their exclusion.

The debates in the US Congress over suffrage for women (as well as for Black men and people between the ages of eighteen and twenty-one), to the extent that they dealt with the issue substantively, took exactly this form—a struggle over category boundaries. When proponents of extended suffrage did more than refer vaguely to "rights" or "consent," they attacked each reason opponents gave for placing men inside the boundary of full citizenship and women outside (or White men inside and Black men outside), arguing that the reasons relevant to the category of citizenship applied equally to each group.[1] More recently, proponents of gay marriage have attacked each reason opponents give for excluding same-sex couples from the category of those allowed to marry and argued that the reasons for marriage—including the desire to make a public commitment of each to the other—apply equally to same-sex and to heterosexual couples (Metz 2010).

The same logic prevails in everyday struggles for justice. In 1994 in Chicago, a low-income White woman in her late thirties told a focus group of women about a dispute she had had with some boys in school:

> They'd be like, "Sit down!"—you know, in elementary school—"You're not supposed to be playing football!" And I'm like, "Why?" "Well, because you're a girl." And I'm like, "You have to come up with some better reason than that!"[2]

This argument is based on the logic of formal justice. Whenever, as in this case, relevant reasons for different treatment cannot be given, formal justice exerts an underlying pressure toward equality. This structural feature of formal justice does not depend on any transcendent foundation. It applies in the social world as well as in the institutions of government and the law. It can be a powerful weapon in the hands of the less powerful.

But formal justice—the concept that all should be treated alike except when there are relevant differences—is only one strand among the many meanings clustered under the name of justice. Although I stress its uses here, I do not want to suggest that other meanings of justice, such as compensation, balance, righteousness, and appropriate decision, have a lesser status. The word *justice* is an umbrella term, covering many uses, loosely linked and sometimes contradictory—as with almost all concepts that human beings evolve and use in their languages. A cluster of meanings loosely thought of as "justice" could contain elements, such as mercy, that are used as antonyms to a more restricted meaning of "justice." When I speak of "justice," I mean the larger and analytically inclusive umbrella. When I speak of "formal justice," I mean the single strand expressed in the formula "Treat similar cases similarly."

Justice in Different Domains

Struggles over the boundaries of categories are heavily influenced by how people define the domain within which a rule applies. In Jennifer Hochschild's (1981) interviews with residents of New Haven, Connecticut, for example, both rich and poor supported a more egalitarian form of justice in their homes and in politics, and a more "differentiated" or inegalitarian form of justice in the economic domain. Michael Walzer has argued more broadly that the concepts of justice appropriate to one "sphere" of human life—such as community membership, the exercise of power, the receipt of honor, the making of money, or the exchange of love—are not necessarily appropriate to other spheres. He concludes that "there has never been a single criterion, or a single set of interconnected criteria, for all distribution" (Walzer 1983, 4). For Walzer, quoting Pascal, "Tyranny is the wish to obtain by one means what can only be had by another" (1983, 18). Money, for example, should not buy love, honor, or power. Just distributions in any of these spheres involve logics internal to those spheres.

More problematically, Walzer also argues that the kinds of justice appropriate to each sphere derive from social meanings, and that "social meanings are historical in character; and so distributions, and just and unjust distributions, change over time" (1983, 9). Feminist theorist Susan Moller Okin (1989) has seized upon this formulation to point out that the "shared understandings" that create the social meaning of justice at any historical moment are not themselves the product of an egalitarian deliberative process. Those meanings are heavily influenced by the dominant classes in the society, including their understandings of what social arrangements are natural, inevitable, or God-given. Women, gay men, lesbians, and members of all marginalized groups hoping to benefit from an appeal to justice must therefore look not only to arguments derived from logics internal to a particular sphere but also to more transcendent logics that may link or encompass several spheres. Although both logics derive ultimately from social understandings, each of the social understandings in turn responds, and can be made to respond, to arguments from internal consistency, analogy to other spheres, and relevant reasons.

Barriers between spheres in Western culture—and particularly the barrier between the public and private spheres—have often disadvantaged women. The public/private barrier long relegated women to the sphere of the domestic, excluding them from public decision-making. It also placed many concerns of women, such as spousal and child abuse, outside the scope of political decisions. The reigning theory for centuries was either that a different system of justice ought to apply in the intimate realm of the family or that within the family "justice" ought not to apply at all. Yet, as Okin argues, the dynamics of unequal family power, the inevitable shaping of family structures by societal and governmental regulation, the family's position in developing its younger members' ideas of justice, and the effect of the family division of labor on life chances outside the family all make it crucial to recognize and to try to correct existing injustices within families.

The concept of different spheres can have a deeply conservative effect. Yet the boundaries between spheres themselves can be destroyed or redrawn on grounds of justice. In the civil rights movement, African Americans attacked public regulations, private contracts, and social interaction all at once. In the feminist movement, women attacked their exclusion from legislatures, from higher-paid employment, and from household power all at once. In the gay rights movement, activists demanded, and knew that their success depended on, same-sex marriage equality in both the public and private spheres.

Struggles over "Justice" in the United States

The primary weakness in any appeal to justice is that dominant groups often set the accepted meaning of justice, at least for a while. In early American thought, for example, "justice" meant primarily the rule of law.[3] The word did not signal concern for the redistribution of income and wealth, except when these writers worried that majorities would unjustly undermine the rights of private property (Madison, Hamilton, and Jay [1788] 1987, 10, 44, 51; "Note to the speech on the right of suffrage," *Records of the Federal Convention of 1787*, 3:450). For the landowners and merchants from whose number the framers of the Constitution were drawn, the new nation's viability required maintaining justice as sanctity of contract. Radical populist movements in these early days of the commonwealth repeatedly challenged the justice of particular institutions, such as the banking system, free trade, or monetary policy, but their challenges had little impact on the formal political thought of the time.

It was not until the late nineteenth century that the American Progressives began to question systematically the justice of existing patterns in the distribution of wealth and income. This questioning drew on the new Social Gospel, socialist thought in Europe, Fabian thought in Britain, the ferment of ideas that immigrants had brought to the cities, and the misery engendered by industrialization. While in earlier contexts, "justice" had the conservative cast of meaning primarily the protection of existing property rights, by the turn of the century the new concept of *social* justice, which made its way from the margins to mainstream political thought, was fueling an egalitarian critique of existing systems of production and distribution. John Dewey ([1932] 1985) pointed out in explanation that as the isolated farm passed into history, and as public parks, lighting, waterworks, libraries, and schools gradually came to replace the private provision of these goods, questions of justice were bound to arise regarding their distribution.

Even in this progressive critique, however, justice belonged to the public realm and not to the private. It was the Black struggles for justice that first posed a challenge to this restriction, with "justice" appearing often in the titles of pamphlets on abolition and the evils of slavery, which extended to the private realm. In the context of slavery, unlike the context of property, the term was almost always oppositional. By the 1960s, the civil rights movement brought this oppositional usage sharply to the fore in the demands of Martin Luther King Jr. for "justice and equality," "justice, goodwill, and brotherhood," and "freedom and justice"—demands that in practice crossed the boundaries between public and private.

When, in the aftermath of the activism of the 1960s, a few American philosophers turned from the previously dominant analytic and linguistic concerns of their profession to normative theory and explicitly tackled the problem of just distribution, they ignored both the intimate realm in general and gender in particular. Consider John Rawls's magisterial *A Theory of Justice* (1971), which tried to construct a universally applicable theory of distributive justice on liberal premises. His intuitive idea follows the example of a parent with two children and one cookie who lets one child divide the cookie and the other have first choice. Realizing that he or she will get the smaller piece, the cutter will try to divide the cookie as equally as possible. Rawls thus asks us to participate in a thought experiment in which individuals hypothetically agree upon a distribution of "primary" goods (such as rights and liberties, income and wealth, and even self-respect) while imagining that they might end up on the bottom (getting the smallest piece of the cookie) in the world created by the distribution to which they agree. He advances this thought experiment as a procedure for determining what institutions are just: if one would agree to an institution knowing that one might find oneself in one of the lowest positions within that institution, it is just.[4]

As a member of a dominant class, however, Rawls had predictable blind spots. Susan Okin (1989) saw immediately that he had neglected to apply his theory to the family. He had simply omitted gender from the potential future characteristics of which one would be ignorant in hypothetically agreeing to the fundamental institutions of society. Yet if one might end up a woman, one would not design family institutions that make women politically, socially, and economically vulnerable. Any family design that puts women at a disadvantage is thus, by Rawls's logic, unjust.

Okin also confronted the primary critic of Rawls's theory of justice, the libertarian Robert Nozick (1974). Nozick's work challenged Rawls's theory on the grounds that, like utilitarianism, it took into account only the "pattern" of any given distribution of goods at a particular time (as a snapshot might), and not the history of how that distribution came about. Goods do not arrive as manna from heaven, he argued, but are produced by individuals who have rights in what they have produced. Nozick considered "just" any distribution in which individuals keep whatever goods they can accumulate through just production and just transfers. Nozick thus assumed a right to everything one produces. Okin argued to the contrary that "possession" is socially constructed; it does not follow automatically from "production." In her clinching example, women produce children through hard labor, but do not and cannot thereby conclude that they have property rights in their product. Justice cannot therefore be defined by production leading to possession. Like Rawls, Nozick had failed to take women's experiences into account.

These examples reveal both the weaknesses and the strengths of justice as a political and philosophical weapon. The weaknesses lie in the dominant classes' power to define the concept at any given moment. The strengths lie in the possibility that outsiders—from the high school–educated woman in a Chicago focus group to the feminist academic Susan Okin—can use logic and experience to claim their due. Some such challenges are successful. Rawls, for one, later adopted Okin's analysis.

Justice as a Political Weapon

The availability of justice as a political weapon depends heavily on the cultural context. All cultures seem to employ a concept of justice in the most formal sense, and almost all cultures have a god or spirit that avenges injustice in some way. Yet cultures at different times vary dramatically in the degree to which justice is a central value to their cosmos. Gods, goddesses, and spirits are also at different times and in different places associated with different aspects of justice—some with omniscience and retribution, some with law, order, and right conduct, some with truth, some with guaranteeing contracts and oaths, some with the wise settlement of disputes, and some with mixtures of many themes. The gods of justice may be as active as the Yoruban god Shango, the "slayer of liars," or as abstract as the Indian Dharma, who represents order, righteousness, and the way, a beneficent aspect of Yama (Leach 1992). Undoubtedly, rulers have often relied on these gods to keep order, just as challengers to the established order have invoked them in their causes.

The longest-lived tradition of using justice to resist oppression derives from the biblical story of Exodus, which describes the founding of the land of Israel and the establishment of Jewish law. Today, the *Encyclopedia Judaica* considers justice "the moral value which singularly characterizes Judaism both conceptually and historically." God's commandments to men, and especially to Israel, are, in this view, "essentially for the purpose of the establishment of justice in the world." The story of Exodus does not explicitly mention justice; it focuses, rather, on oppression. It tells of the "affliction" of the Jewish people in Egypt, whose lives were made "bitter with hard bondage" (Exodus 6:9), so that the Lord said, "The cry of the children of Israel is come unto me: and I have also seen the oppression wherewith the Egyptians oppress them" (Exodus 3:9). The word that is translated here as "oppress" connotes a pressing down, with superior power, unjustly, to extract some benefit for the oppressor. In much of the biblical usage, the words for oppression seem also—with great implications later for women, colonial peoples, and many others—to embody a structural and group-based analysis. The concept applies when one group of people, having greater power than another, uses its power to extract unjust benefits from the weaker group.

In the story of Exodus, the Lord several times tells the Jewish people to memorialize the event in the Passover ceremony, which would become the most important ceremony of the Jewish calendar, next to keeping the Sabbath. After giving the Ten Commandments to Moses, the Lord lays down in more detail the outlines of the law, including two specific mentions of oppression: "Thou shalt neither vex a stranger, nor oppress him: for ye were strangers in the land of Egypt" (Exodus 21:21) and "Thou shalt not oppress a stranger, for ye know the heart of a stranger, seeing ye were strangers in the land of Egypt" (Exodus 23:9). The second passage implies, unusually for that era and importantly for future political persuasion, that empathy should dissuade the powerful from using their power to take advantage of others. The rest of the Judaic Bible elaborates, specifying that one should not oppress a neighbor (Leviticus 6:2, 19:13); a hired servant, hireling, or workers (Deuteronomy 24:24; Malachi 3:5; Isaiah 58:3); a stranger or alien (Jeremiah 7:6; Ezekiel 22:29); the poor (Psalms 12:5; Ecclesiastes 5:8; Proverbs 14:31, 22:16, 28:3; Amos 4:1; Ezekiel 18:12); a widow (Jeremiah 7:6; Zechariah 7:10); or the fatherless (Zechariah 7:10). Except for the neighbor, these are all groups whose members are comparatively weak and therefore vulnerable. The Psalms add that "the Lord also will be a refuge for the oppressed, a refuge in times of trouble" (9:9), and "the Lord executeth righteousness and judgment for all that are oppressed" (103:6, 146:7). Indeed, the Hebrew language seems to have had several separate words, with different roots, for the concept that translates into English as "oppressed," "oppression," and "oppressor" (based on citations in Young [1880] 1955). The Judaic concern for oppression, once securely lodged in the Old Testament of the Christian Bible, became an ideological powder keg within Western culture, waiting for each generation to reinterpret it, fashion it into a political weapon, and ignite it.

Other religious and political traditions, particularly around the Mediterranean, also mandate justice as a central theme, but usually without the specific Judaic stress on oppression. Ancient Greek philosophy, for example, examined in some detail the norms inherent in what we now call distributive justice and retributive justice. Justice played a significant role in both Greek and Roman thought, but the concept of oppression was far less prevalent. The New Testament of the Christian Bible stresses justice as much as the Old Testament does but has fewer than twenty references to oppression (some of which refer back to Old Testament events), compared to more than a hundred in the Old Testament.

The Qur'an, too, speaks often of the mandate to do justice, as do subsequent Islamic scholars, such as Ibn Khaldûn ([1377] 1980). "Social justice" is the rallying cry of most of today's Islamic movements. Yet the Qur'an, like the Christian New Testament, places relatively little stress on oppression. The Qur'an once mentions not oppressing the orphan (93:9) and once concern for oppressed children (94:127). In thirteen additional places, it uses the telling term *istad'afa*, which means to "esteem another as weak" and, more tellingly, "to take advantage of one's weakness," although even here the term is often translated "to abase" rather than "to oppress" (Kassis 1983, 402). As a general rule, the Qur'an simply prescribes being just and "doing good" to orphans, the needy, and the wayfarer by giving them food, wealth, or what one has acquired in war (e.g., 2:83; 76:8, 2:177, 2:215, 8:41, 59:7). The stress is on charity, not on refraining from the use of one's strength to extract benefits from a structurally vulnerable group.

Many other religions make justice central without a developed concept of oppression. For the Ibibio people of Nigeria, for example, "God evens things out" (Okure 1983, 38). God executes judgments with justice and impartiality, and the more a human judgment approximates the justice of God, the more it is just (1983, 39). Among the minor gods or spirits, Eka-Abasi is the guardian of morals and law, the bringer of fertility, and the master of the ancestral spirits. One invokes her when one wants to show one is speaking the truth or seeking justice (1983, 42). The ancestral spirits, who are intermediaries between God and man, "rule because they are just and ... are just because of their closeness to God" (1983, 45). The Ibibio are "very conscious of justice and try to be just in their dealings.... Punishment for wrongdoing is not administered just to make the wrongdoer suffer, or to teach him he has done wrong; instead, it is regarded as medicinal and always aims at restoring the proper social order by bringing the wrongdoer back into proper relationship with the community and the spirits—reconciliation" (1983, 46).[5] For the Ibibio, justice embraces many other virtues, preeminently truth. Their proverbs say, "A truthful person is a righteous [just, upright] person," "Sincerity [uprightness, straightness] is the soul of business," and "A sincere man is the rock of justice and peace" (1983, 62–63).

Justice does not play this kind of central social role in Hindu, Buddhist, Taoist, or even Confucian philosophy. In the Hindu religion or way of life, Yama, the lord of death, dispenses justice, arranging different punishments for wrongdoers after death. Because in Hinduism (as in some forms of Buddhism) just and unjust acts affect one's subsequent life, justice is deeply implicated in one's continuing *karma*. But the "pure devotee" of Krishna fulfills the law of the universe in a way that does not depend on worldly wrongdoing and justice. He attains dispassion, enabled through the grace of Krishna, to reach "the eternal, imperishable abode" (see, e.g., *Bhagavad Gita* 18:52, 56). In Buddhism, right action, as part of the eightfold path, prescribes selflessness, compassion, and charity. The relatively modern concept of "engaged" Buddhism draws on mindfulness and other core Buddhist values to promote peace and ecological sustainability (Hanh 1993; Tucker and Williams 1997). But Buddhism does not produce a strong mandate to fight injustice as such (Conze 1959; Burtt 1955; Suzuki 1956).

Taoism takes its practitioners beyond justice to the "way," or *Tao*. As Lao Tzu wrote, suggesting a hierarchy in which justice lies near the bottom, "When the way is lost, goodness may still remain. When goodness is lost, kindness may still remain. When kindness is lost, justice may still remain. When justice is lost, ritual may still remain. But when ritual is all, that may be the beginning of confusion" (*Tao Teh Ching*, chap. 38). The sage ruler acts without contriving, governs naturally with virtue, is thus "fair to all" and "the people do not feel oppressed" (65, 66). Justice is here far from the ultimate good, but still better than chaos.

In Confucianism, the *Chun Zu*, or gentleman, never parts company with goodness, tries to discover and range himself beside the right (*Analects* 4:5, 10, 16), and acts justly by bringing his own internal character in line with the right (*The Great Learning*). If the rulers have an upright character and therefore act justly, the commoners will support them. Confucians thus emphasize cultivating a good individual character rather than making the pursuit of justice itself a central good.

In Western culture, by contrast, the religious and political tradition derived in part from Judaism makes the very existence of injustice and oppression a thorn in the side of God. The simple identification of a practice as unjust or oppressive thus becomes a resource for social and political change, for God himself can be said to command the oppressed to rise against injustice. At the time of the American Revolution, Thomas Paine wrote that "every spot of the Old World is overrun with oppression" ([1776] 1922, 37), Thomas Jefferson linked oppression and tyranny ([1816] 1904, 491), and the Anti-Federalists protested the potential oppression of the proposed national government (see Patrick Henry in the "Federal Convention of 1787," and "Brutus" and Melancton Smith in the "Anti-Federalist Papers," both in Ketchum 1986). The abolitionists, drawing explicitly and implicitly on the Old Testament, protested the oppression of the American slaves. William Lloyd Garrison trumpeted, "Let southern oppressors tremble" (1831, 1), while Abraham Lincoln, in a letter to a friend, called himself "one who abhors the oppression of Negroes" ([1855] 1907, 218). Twenty-four years after emancipation, Frederick Douglass could still argue persuasively that "where any one class is made to feel that society is an organized conspiracy to oppress, rob and degrade them, neither persons nor property will be safe" ([1886] 1992, 229). Women thus had a powerful tradition on which to draw when they claimed, in the Seneca Falls Resolution, that mankind had "oppressed [women] on all sides" and concluded that women were "aggrieved, oppressed, and fraudulently deprived of their most sacred rights."

These speakers' claims on the received values of their own time and culture pulled, from a complex and contested field, themes that resonated with their hearers. Within this cultural tradition, political activists could reach back into a history structured partly by religion, partly by political evolution, and partly by the logic of formal justice. Once their hearers had begun to doubt the reasons formerly adduced as relevant for treating the colonies differently from England, Blacks differently from Whites, women differently from men, or gay men and lesbians differently from heterosexuals, first the colonies, then Black men, then women, and then gay men and lesbians could demand equality and consider it "oppression" when the more powerful took advantage of their group's vulnerabilities. When material changes and sustained attacks on traditional reasons undermined the validity of the reasons for different treatment, the logic of formal justice provided the logic on which claims for equal treatment could be based, while at the same time the cultural heritage of appeals to justice against oppression provided accessible language, images, and frames for making the claims.

Appeals to justice and against oppression are not necessary for social change. Economic evolution might eventually have undermined plantation slavery. Stronger organizations might have developed to facilitate slave revolt. Compassion, love for all living beings, the renunciation of violence, a commitment to harmlessness—these Buddhist values, and many other values, both religious and secular—might eventually have affected the lives and freedom of the slaves. Women's increasing education, encouraged by economic imperatives, would probably have combined with values other than justice to one day bring them the vote. A modernizing world would probably eventually have brought with it an acceptance of a variety of sexual orientations. In addition, no appeal to justice can produce results without interacting with historically specific institutions, traditions, material circumstances, and constellations of power and motive. Nevertheless, in a society with strong traditions of invoking justice, subordinate groups can excavate and appropriate aspects of those traditions, even when the sources, as in the case of religion, also perpetuate existing systems of domination and subordination. The pivotal moment in the creation of oppositional consciousness comes today when subordinate groups recognize and claim injustice in their relations with dominant groups (see Mansbridge 2001 and citations therein).

Challenges to the Normative Claims of "Justice"

The Western tradition has not only generated a cultural pattern of deriving resistance to oppression from an underlying concept of justice; it has also produced deep intellectual challenges to that pattern. Two important challenges to "justice" derive from Marxism and feminism.

For Karl Marx and Friedrich Engels, justice under capitalism meant "bourgeois justice," and would continue to mean only that until the economic and political triumph of the proletariat. When that triumph produced different and better material circumstances, the term would evolve to mean something different, which Marx and Engels did not and would not predict. Perhaps in the second stage of communism, when all the wellsprings of productivity had been released and scarcity abolished, justice too, in its distributive incarnation, would disappear, for each would receive according to need (Marx [1875] 1938; Buchanan 1982). Both Marx and Engels often mocked the highfalutin and, they believed, deceptive claims to universal "justice" and "truth" implicit in the writings of the socialists and anarchists of their era as well as in the writings of the bourgeoisie.[6]

Marx's strictures on the meaninglessness of "justice" have negatively affected its political use, particularly in Europe. Left-leaning writers criticizing present social arrangements have preferred to use the concept of oppression, seeing this as only a descriptive term, rather than the concept of injustice, seeing this as a prescriptive, morally based term. Yet Marx's own use of the concepts of oppression and exploitation depends on the normative conclusion that these acts are morally wrong. Marx's labor theory of value and his larger idea of exploitation embody the idea that the workers' labor is forced and unpaid, and that these features incorporate injustice (Buchanan 1982, 44, 97).[7]

Marx and Engels were right in arguing that the reigning ideas of justice in any era will be deeply affected by the interests of the era's most powerful groups. They may also have been right in suggesting that changes in concepts of justice will tend to be caused by, rather than to cause, deep changes in the modes of production. They were wrong, I believe, to the degree that, believing only dominant economic groups could influence the meaning of justice, they neglected the potential influence of subordinate economic groups, as well as subordinate gender, sexual, racial, religious, and national groups, on that meaning. They were also wrong to the degree that they denied any independent causal effect, beyond material forces, from the concept of justice itself.

The feminist critique of justice has two prongs. The first, like the Marxist critique, recognizes that the ruling class of any era will establish—not necessarily with intent—an understanding of justice and "impartiality" that implicitly makes its own stance synonymous with neutral impartiality (Young 1990, 115–16). In response to the traditional concept of impartiality, feminist theorists suggest either focusing on eliminating particular, identifiable sources of bias (Friedman 1991), substituting a deliberative political process designed to encourage the participation of those who are usually marginalized (Young 1990, 112), or enlarging the concept by stressing the differences among humans and the need to try to understand the other's reality (Benhabib 1987, 81; Minow 1987, esp. 75–76).

In a similar attack on false stances of neutrality, Black feminist theorists have pointed out that the primarily White and middle-class women whose writings and leadership greatly affected the early second wave of the women's movement in the United States often universalized, as "women's," experiences that were relatively class-, race-, and nation-specific—experiences such as being "put on a pedestal," having a "problem with no name," or feeling the "click" of feminist revelation. Seemingly neutral reforms intended to improve the conditions of "women's" work excluded domestic work, in which until 1960 a majority of Black women were employed. In US law, one could bring a discrimination case as either a Black (under legal precedents sometimes tailored for men) or a woman (under legal precedents sometimes tailored for White women), but not as an individual at the intersection of the two (Crenshaw 1989, 139–67). Although race plays such a deeply structuring role that few women's experiences escape being affected by it, early feminist thinking made white women the seemingly neutral norm (Harris 1990; Collins 1990; Smith and Smith 1981; Wallace 1990; Spelman 1988).

The feminist critique of justice that warns of the power of the ruling class has a strong basis. If formal justice requires equality within categories, and if some struggles over formal justice involve expanding membership in the category to which a rule applies, toppling the boundaries between categories tends to admit new members to a category that remains defined by the characteristics of its previous members. Women, for example, are accepted into the categories to which an "impartial" justice applies to the degree that they already have or adopt the (assumed to be relevant) characteristics of men. Wanting to be "in" makes normative that which is already in. If a new group is granted suffrage on the grounds of an equal "capacity to reason," the very argument that provided a battering ram against the category's boundary can become grounds for subtle or not so subtle disadvantage within the category—as when "reason" becomes defined as the ability to interpret the US Constitution to the satisfaction of a southern registrar or as a capacity held to its highest degree by Whites and men. Radical experimentation with or performance of gender thus requires poking, prodding, contesting, and challenging the meanings and connotations of past and present categories, while at the same time accepting and even reveling in some of those meanings and connotations.

The second prong of the feminist critique of justice responds to the historical fact that in Western philosophy, written almost entirely by men, justice—and particularly abstract, universalist, "rational" justice—has often been identified with maleness, and a contrasting characteristic—whether attunement to family relations, nurturance, care, particularistic relationships, sympathy, mercy, or simply emotion itself—with femaleness. This dichotomy has been reinforced by the social and political roles of women and men, including, until this century, the exclusion of women from formal legal and judicial systems.

In the 1960s and 1970s, the psychologist Lawrence Kohlberg (1981) devised a series of moral dilemmas that he used to establish "stages" of moral growth. He placed in the highest stage responses to the dilemmas that expressed an abstract, universalistic understanding of justice. Highly educated American or European males most often achieved this stage. The psychologist Carol Gilligan contested Kohlberg's ordering. She showed that in response to his dilemmas many women define themselves "in a context of human relationship" and judge themselves according to their ability to care (Gilligan 1982, 17). This stance, she argued, was not a "lower" stage of moral development than one focused on justice, but rather a different, equally worthy, approach.

Gilligan's work released a torrent of supportive analyses, rehabilitating the "female" virtues of care and connection. Long before Gilligan, both feminists and antifeminists had valorized the link between femaleness and nurturance. Feminists in the "first wave" of the women's movement in the United States had argued that women's special capacity for maternal nurturance could ideally produce a politics of loving cooperation (Gilman [1915] 1979). Arguments for women's suffrage had stressed not only women's "sameness" with men, to break down the category boundary, but also their "difference" from men, in their ability to bring to the polity particular virtues drawn from their experiences as wives and mothers (Cott 1986). "Maternalist" imagery and thought has continued to affect women's political action throughout the world (Nelson and Chowdhury 1994; Elshtain 1994).

Early in the "second wave" of the feminist movement in the United States, feminists also argued that "women's culture" was more caring and less rapacious than that of men. Some attributed women's special skills of "intuition" and "empathy" to their relative powerlessness (Dixon 1970, 8), some to the actual or culturally expected experience of motherhood (Alpert 1973, 6). Later, the psychologists Dorothy Dinnerstein (1977) and Nancy Chodorow (1978) ascribed what Chodorow called "women's relatedness and men's denial of relation" to the male child's need to differentiate himself from his mother and create a separate, oppositional entity. "The basic feminine sense of self," Chodorow concluded, "is connected to the world, the basic masculine sense of self is separate" (1978, 181, 169). Gilligan adopted much of Chodorow's analysis, arguing that "masculinity is defined through separation while femininity is defined through attachment" (1982, 8; but see Gilligan 1986, 29 for a criticism of Chodorow).

At the same moment that Dinnerstein and Chodorow were developing their theories, other feminist theorists were beginning to excavate the explicit gender-coding of the dichotomy of male-justice-reason versus female-care-sympathy that prevailed in Europe at the time of Immanuel Kant, who greatly influenced Kohlberg. In a key passage on the dichotomy of reason versus sympathy, Kant had maintained that only actions done from duty, not sympathy, had "true moral worth." While conceding that some minds are "so sympathetically constituted" that "they find pleasure in spreading joy around them, and can take delight in the satisfaction of others," he concluded that "action of this kind, however proper, however amiable it may be, has nevertheless no true moral worth, but is on a level with other inclinations." If a sympathetic inclination is "happily directed to that which is in fact of public utility and accordant with duty," then it "deserves praise and encouragement, but not esteem" (Kant [1785] 1949, 15–16). Feminist theorists have now demonstrated that more than twenty years before he penned these central passages, Kant had revealed how his crucial distinction between duty and sympathy mapped onto his characterizations of men and women: "Women will avoid the wicked not because it is unright, but only because it is ugly.... Nothing of duty, nothing of compulsion, nothing of obligation!... They do something only because it pleases them.... I hardly believe that the fair sex is capable of principles" (Kant [1763] 1960, 81). Hegel also associated female gender with an incapacity for universality, which in his larger schema played a central role (Hegel [1821] 1952, 123). As he put it, "Women regulate their actions not by the demands of universality but by arbitrary inclinations and opinions" ([1821] 1952, 264).[8]

"Male = justice, women = care," is thus deeply encoded in Western philosophy. Yet if men and women in the current Western world do differ on a dimension of justice (and universality) versus care (and particularity), those differences are probably not large. Kohlberg and Gilligan's findings of gender difference in the United States appear primarily among the highly educated, because it is primarily in this class that men distinctively adopt a "rights" or "justice" orientation, to which the women's "care" or "relationships" orientation can be compared (Baumrind 1986). And even within this highly educated group, most studies cannot find a difference between men and women on this dimension.[9] Moreover, even the stereotypes are not invariant across cultures. People in the United States are more likely than people in other countries to consider women "emotional" and men "rational."[10]

Wherever the stereotypes exist, they often feed upon themselves. When women see themselves and are seen as more attuned to emotion, empathy, and intimate connection, concrete practices both draw from and reinforce that connection. Women allow themselves to demonstrate their emotions openly. Girls and women look more for emotion and expression in their friendships, centering their conversations with friends more on discussions of relationships, while men develop more instrumental or goal-oriented friendships based on shared activities (Markus and Oyserman 1989). These gender-coded practices then have effects on the way both genders view the economic, political, and social worlds. Mentally healthy people usually like themselves. When the larger social world indulges in "gratuitous gendering," that is, creating and accentuating dichotomies based on gender (Mansbridge 1993), one would expect women to value "their" side of the equation (e.g., the "care" versus the "justice" side) and to defend it against the male devaluing they perceive around them.

Philosophically, most theorists contend that the two constructs of "care" and "justice" are not entirely separate (Flanagan and Jackson 1987; Sher 1987; Tronto 1989; Okin 1990). Indeed, in one study of the interpretation of moral fables by a student of Gilligan, even though a majority of American male students chose a justice interpretation and a majority of female students an interpretation focusing on care, every student was eventually able to adopt the other orientation—about half spontaneously, after being asked simply, "Is there another way to think about this problem?" and the rest after prompting (Johnston 1988). Yet the gender-coding of the concepts remains. Both men and women in the United States tend to rate the care orientation as more feminine and the rights orientation as more masculine (Ford and Lowery 1986). If Western publics in the late twentieth century coded "caring" as female and "justice" as male, and if philosophical ideas associated with women were devalued as compared to the ideas associated with men, one would expect at least some feminist theorists rightly to defend the value of the "female" ideals of connection and care.[11] Human beings often think in terms of oppositions. Moreover, we tend to line up pairs of opposites and implicitly connect them, contrasting all of the values aligned on one side to all of the values on the other. Because male versus female is a pervasive binary opposition, when philosophical ideas are conceived in a binary, oppositional structure, they too tend to become gender-coded. Not surprisingly, the female side of the opposition is usually comparatively devalued. The feminist debates that pit "justice" against "care" thus draw attention to the restrictive elision of the dichotomies reason/emotion, justice/care, and male/female.

Feminist theorists of care are right to point out that in the late twentieth-century West, perhaps particularly in the United States, abstract universalistic justice is already coded as male, while care, connection, and relationships are coded as female. They are right to point out that this oppositional coding has had a long history in the West, perhaps as long as the history of written philosophy itself. They are also right to argue that we should give more weight to human ideals, such as care and connection, that have been forced into opposition with "justice," stressing that these understandings have probably been devalued in part simply through their association with women. They are wrong, I believe, to the degree that they claim to have found in care and connection "women's" essential or authentic voice. Women's voices are plural. The very meaning of "woman" is flexible and a site of contest (Butler 1990). We cannot know what the voices of people with female physiognomies would say if the effects of male dominance were removed. As Catharine MacKinnon put it, "Take your foot off our necks, then we will hear in what tongue women speak" (MacKinnon 1987, 45; also 1989, 49–59, 106–54).

The Normative Resources of the Relatively Powerless

Every word we speak, and every ideal we can imagine, comes infused with the effects of millennia of power, through which members of the dominant gender, class, race, sexual preference, and other group have made their own state normative and others deviant. To take perhaps a trivial example, my writing in English in a volume that may have international circulation reinforces infinitesimally the growing dominance of that language as a medium of global intellectual communication. The population of the globe coming to communicate in one language might greatly promote human learning. But the language that emerges as dominant will not be neutral. Similarly, languages that make male and female nouns and gender agreement central to their syntax reinforce the idea that gendered meanings underlie all creation. Gendered pronouns make it hard to identify a human actor without reference to her or his gender.

As Foucault so persuasively pointed out, no situation is or can be "free" from power. Each of us is constituted by power and exercises power in every interaction. Indeed, much of the power that confronts any movement for change is "dispersed, heteromorphous, localized, [and] accompanied by numerous phenomena of inertia, displacement and resistance; hence one should not assume a massive and primal condition of domination, a binary structure with 'dominators' on one side and 'dominated' on the other, but rather a multiform production of relations of domination" (Foucault [1977] 1980, 142).

In appealing to any ideal, therefore, subordinate groups always risk the possibility, usually amounting to certainty, that the very ideal to which they appeal will embody elements that further subordinate them. For women in early twenty-first-century Western nations, "liberty" will often subtly connote a liberty unfettered by human connection. "Equality" will often subtly connote taking on the characteristics of men. "Fraternity" implies with no subtlety that community and politics are the province of men. "Justice" will often connote cold reason and impersonality, in implicit contrast to care, sympathy, and mercy. Received understandings of justice, in practice, will also always reinforce existing distributions of goods and ways of thinking that benefit the dominant classes.

Nevertheless, forces for change almost always need normative resources, among them preeminently the appeal to justice. Even when a subordinate group outnumbers the dominant one, the attempt to exercise power based only on self-interest will usually fail. Groups that can draw on normative appeals (or, better still, a mixture of material and normative rewards) can coordinate cooperation better. The revolution that can tell its activists, "Give your lives for the group because it is just," will succeed more easily than the revolution that can say only, "Give your lives for the group because it will benefit you in the long run."

Similarly, all dominant groups seem to justify their dominance with reasons. Words combating those reasons do more than just rally the morale of the oppressed; they also weaken the will of the oppressors. These arguments do not have to rely on Reason, that is, a single absolute truth that would inevitably emerge over time from any enlightened discussion. They can simply rely on reasons, that is, any set of considerations meaningful to both speakers and listeners. Such reasons are always culture specific in that they make sense or not in the light of the experience of those who use them.

James Scott recounts the gossip that peasants circulated against the most voracious landowners in a Malaysian village, describing this "ideological work" as aiming "to control by convincing" (Scott 1985, 23). Breaches of what was thought to be fair—for example, the peasants' belief that in distributing building materials "equal shares are fair"(1985, 227)—provoked indignation over the perceived injustice, discomfiture among decision-makers who could not find convincing justifications for their decisions, and future noncooperation by the aggrieved. The conceptual structure of formal justice, with its persistent underlying pressure toward equality when no relevant reasons can be given for doing otherwise, helps explain the sense of injustice in the small village studied by Scott.

Without having to rely on foundations such as God, Reason, or Natural Law, the formal philosophical structure of justice thus becomes a major weapon for the weak. So too do other elements of the cluster of concepts gathered under the name of "justice," such as appropriate compensation and retribution. Like the words *free*, *equal*, and *dignity*, the word *just* does not accidentally have a positive valence. Although contested, the concept responds to important, probably universal, human needs and modes of thinking. Claims to justice, like claims to freedom, equality, and dignity, cannot have been conceived without experiencing their loss. But everyone has experienced some form of those losses at one point or another. It is precisely because both dominant and subordinate classes in any hierarchy value these goods, while often disputing their meaning and application, that they can become persuasive weapons for the weak.

Dominant traditions, oppositional traditions, and current experience provide the persuasive material with which subordinate groups must work. Traditional practices and beliefs, although deeply permeated by meanings and connotations that serve to maintain existing structures of domination and subordination, also hold for subordinate groups resources that vary by historical context and contingency. Oppositional cultures, often loosely structured and full of contradictions, also offer meaningful fragments (e.g., "men are dogs," "white folks can't be trusted") that in the right historical and institutional context can be tied to justice and woven into a more cohesive fabric. Experience, usually interpreted through lenses ground by habit, generates new situations that in turn need "new words" (Hurston [1937] 1990), such as *racism, sexism, male chauvinism*, and *homophobia*. Old words, like *oppression* in the Old Testament, nurtured in the culture and practices of subordinate groups ("oppressed so hard they could not stand"), take on new life in the context of a new social or political movement.

No one of these sources—tradition, oppositional culture, or experience—is reliable. Any tradition, such as Old Testament resistance to oppression, also smuggles in concepts, such as "the chosen people," that can reinforce attempts at dominance. Oppositional cultures themselves problematically derive from and usually reinstate to some degree practices that reinforce subordination. Oppositional movements have their own dynamics that strengthen them politically but shape the message they disseminate, sometimes to the long-run detriment of their followers. Even "gut" experience sometimes derives from our mammalian or ancestral human heritage, and no longer serves well in our changed circumstances. Formal justice, as we have seen, often reinforces existing categories of "same" and "different." Other components of justice, such as the search for appropriate restitution, can similarly ossify and reinforce reigning conceptions of the status quo.

Nevertheless, the idea of justice is powerful. It can make members of dominant groups question their own legitimacy. It can ignite in subordinates a righteous fury that makes the selfish more selfless and fills the fearful with almost superhuman courage. It is not surprising that ideas of justice play such a large role in the formation of oppositional consciousness. All the components of justice prepare the tinder, ready for the spark of political action.

Notes

1. Contests over justice and suffrage have been primarily struggles over boundaries, as the category of those who could vote has gradually expanded to include first non–tax-paying and non–property-owning White males, then Black males, then women, then people aged eighteen through twenty. Few in the United States have yet proposed giving resident noncitizens voting rights, on the model of Sweden and some other European countries.

2. The focus group, drawn from a representative Chicago sample, was made up of White English-speaking women who had said in an earlier survey both that they had less than a college education and that they considered themselves "feminist."

3. It is conventional to distinguish between "procedural" justice, meaning just procedures or equal treatment under the law; "compensatory" or (in punishment) "retributive" justice, meaning the attempt to approximate the restoration of an purportedly just former status quo through some form of balance (e.g., in punishment, "an eye for an eye"); and "distributive justice," meaning justice in distributing valued goods, such as income and wealth or influence in the state. Yet these categories are not all mutually exclusive. Rawls (1971) has devised criteria for *distributive* justice that are *procedural*, in that they derive from a hypothetical procedure. The free market has sometimes been considered a matter of *procedural* justice in that under appropriate laws it requires only equal treatment under the law; others consider it a form of *compensatory* justice, in that in free exchange losses are compensated justly by gains determined by the market. The criterion of formal justice can apply in any of these realms.

4. As Rawls himself later recognized, this conception of procedural justice is not universal but rooted in the liberal tradition. It assumes at the outset that the hypothetical individuals making choices are free and equal. It also argues, somewhat implausibly, that such individuals, choosing an economic, social, and political system without knowing where they will end up, would decide to make liberty (particularly liberty of conscience and of citizenship) "lexically" (absolutely) prior to all other goods. I find it useful to think of what Rawls explicitly called a "theory" of justice as one element in a discursive struggle over the applied meaning of justice in any specific context. If all parties agree on some basic assumptions of freedom and equality, Rawls's thought experiment may move the participants from the stage of mere mutually contradictory assertion ("This is just" versus "It is not") to asking on what distribution all would agree if they thought they might end up in the least advantaged position.

5. The Ibibio word *ufik*, based on the root *fik*, meaning "press down," can be translated "oppressed," but more frequently means crooked, bent, or wrong, the opposite of physical straightness or uprightness (Okure 1983, 61).

6. Against bourgeois writers, Marx and Engels argued that "your jurisprudence is but the will of your class made into a law for all" (Marx and Engels 1976, 501). To the objection that "there are, besides, eternal truths, such as Freedom, Justice, etc., that are common to all states of society," they answered that justice, as a construction of the ruling class in each era and as a response to exploitation by that class, must be understood differently in each historical context (1976, 504). Engels ridiculed the socialist and anarchist writers for their subjective, individually differing interpretations of "absolute truth, reason and justice," which created a "mish-mash allowing of the most manifold shades of opinion," in contrast to the "science" of their own enterprise, which was "placed on a real basis" (Engels 1989, 297). Marx mockingly assimilated the socialist Proudhon's "eternal justice" to the church fathers' "eternal grace" and "eternal faith" (Marx [1867] 1977, 178–79 n2), while Engels compared it to phlogiston, the imaginary substance that, before the understanding of the role of oxygen, was invoked to explain combustion (Engels 1969: 362–66). As Engels expressed the "materialist conception of history" against the "utopian socialists" of his generation, "the final causes of all social changes and political revolutions are to be sought, not in men's brains, not in men's better insights into 'eternal truth and justice,' but in changes in the modes of production and exchange. They are to be sought, not in the *philosophy*, but in the *economics* of each particular epoch. The growing perception that existing social institutions are unreasonable and unjust ... is only proof that in the modes of production and exchange changes have silently taken place with which the social order, adapted to earlier economic conditions, is no longer in keeping" (Engels 1989, 306; emphasis in original). Engels also wrote that although history results from many individual wills, partly motivated by "ideal motives," such as "enthusiasm for truth and justice," the motives are of only secondary importance. The real "driving forces ... behind these motives" are the conflicts between class interests—the interests of the aristocracy, the bourgeoisie, and the proletariat (Engels [1888] 1941, 49–51). Against the anarchist Bakunin's claim that national boundaries should be "drawn in accordance with justice and democracy," Engels insisted that "such fantastic abstraction from the conditions actually prevailing," such "ethical categories" as "'justice,' 'humanity,' 'freedom,' 'equality,' ... sound very fine, it is true, but *prove absolutely nothing* in historical and political questions." These "pious wishes and beautiful dreams are of no avail against the iron reality" (Engels 1977, 363–65; emphasis in original).

7. For the controversy over the role of the concept of justice in Marx, see Cohen, Nagel, and Scanlon 1980; Wood 1980; Buchanan 1982; Lukes 1985. Both in its original biblical incarnation and in the contexts in which Marx used it, the English word *oppression* connotes moral wrong. See *Oxford English Dictionary*, definition 4. Two early English examples occur in Shakespeare: "For who would bear ... the oppressor's wrong" (*Hamlet* III.i) and "I am ... oppressed with wrongs" (*King John* III.i).

8. For the feminist retrieval of philosophical gender-coding in Kant, Hegel, and others, see Gould (1976, 18); Blum (1982); Lloyd (1983); Grimshaw (1986, 42–44). For feminist arguments that support sympathy as a moral virtue worthy of esteem, in contrast to Kant's emphasis on duty, see Blum (1980; 1988, 472–91); Baier (1986); Held (1987); and Sher (1987). For the Kantian rejoinder, see Herman (1993). For a non–gender-coded valorization of universalistic justice and "rational" legal systems, in contrast to particularistic justice in non-European cultures and the "emotional demands of those underprivileged classes which clamor for substantive justice," see Weber ([1922] 1968, 845ff, esp. 892).

9. See Mansbridge 1993. Studies of empathy, a characteristic related to "care," reveal that gender differences appear primarily when the study gives the individuals interviewed cues as to what is being measured. It is unclear how much of which gender differences are biological and how much due to social learning. Some biologically based differences, for example, in the tendency to physical aggression, have been well established (Maccoby 1974).

A biological basis for a tendency does not, however, necessarily generate a normative imperative for human beings collectively or individually to support that tendency. Presumably because of our primate heritage, human beings are more likely to defecate spontaneously than are most nesting mammals. (It is far harder to toilet train a human baby than a cat or even a dog.) But all human societies discourage this natural biological tendency, usually to the point of almost eradicating it among competent adults.

10. In a study of twenty-eight countries, with college students in each country coding a list of three hundred adjectives as "male" or "female," students in the United States showed the greatest consensus in coding "rational" as male and "emotional" as female. The English-speaking Commonwealth countries tended to follow, then many of the European countries. Pakistani students coded the adjective "emotional" as male as often as female, presumably because the word in that language connotes martial valor, and coded "rational" as female almost as often as male (calculated from evidence in Williams and Best [1982], app. 2). The data are not available to compare cross-culturally the gender codings of justice and care, but commenting on Gilligan's work, Patricia Hill Collins suggests that an ethics of "connection" and "caring" may typify the behavior and norms not only of women in the United States, but also both men and women in Africa (Collins 1990, 206 ff.; also Harding 1987). On the other hand, the anthropologist Ronald Cohen (1972, 39–57) suggests that "empathy" is "not a proper way to behave" in some African tribal societies and argues that the Anglo-European focus on empathy may result historically from many generations of small, inwardly focused nuclear families with a relatively low instance of infant death. To make sense of these relationships would require distinguishing different forms of connection, care, and empathy, then parsing in specific cultural contexts the relations of these somewhat different values with different forms of justice.

11. Feminist theorists have revealed, for example, that traditional Western understandings of property, autonomy, contract, and obligation have been heavily influenced by masculinely coded commitments to separation and pure voluntarism, in contrast to connection (Nedelsky 1989, 2011; Held 1990; Hirschmann 1989).

References

Alpert, Jane. 1973. "Mother Right: A New Feminist Theory." *Off Our Backs* 3 (May 8).

Baier, Annette. 1986. "Hume: The Women's Moral Theorist?" In *Women and Moral Theory*, ed. Eva Kittay and Diana Meyers. Totowa, NJ: Rowman & Littlefield.

Baumrind, Diana. 1986. "Sex Differences in Moral Reasoning: Response to Walker's (1984) Conclusion That There Are None." *Child Development* 57:511–21.

Benhabib, Seyla. 1987. "The Generalized and Concrete Other." In *Feminism as Critique*, ed. Seyla Benhabib and Drucilla Cornells. Minneapolis: University of Minnesota Press.

Benn, S. I., and R. S. Peters. 1959. *The Principles of Political Thought*. New York: Free Press.

Berlin, Isaiah. 1955–1956. "Equality." *Proceedings of the Aristotelian Society* 56:301–26.

Blum, Laurence A. 1980. *Friendship, Altruism and Morality.* London: Routledge and Kegan Paul.

———. 1982. "Kant and Hegel's Moral Rationalism: A Feminist Perspective." *Canadian Journal of Philosophy* 12:287–302.

———. 1988. "Gilligan and Kohlberg: Implications for Moral Theory." *Ethics* 98.

Buchanan, Allen E. 1982. *Marx and Justice: The Radical Critique of Liberalism*. Totowa, NJ: Rowman & Allanheld.

Burtt, Edwin A. 1955. *The Teachings of the Compassionate Buddha*. New York: New American Library.

Butler, Judith. 1990. *Gender Trouble: Feminism and the Subversion of Identity*. New York: Routledge.

Chodorow, Nancy. 1978. *The Reproduction of Mothering: Psychoanalysis and the Sociology of Gender*. Berkeley: University of California Press.

Cohen, Marshall, Thomas Nagel, and Thomas Scanlon, eds. 1980. *Marx, Justice and History*. Princeton, NJ: Princeton University Press.

Cohen, Ronald. 1972. "Altruism: Human, Cultural, or What?" *Journal of Social Issues* 28.

Collins, Patricia Hill. 1990. *Black Feminist Thought*. London: Allen and Unwin.

Conze, Edward. 1959. *Buddhism: Its Essence and Development*. New York: Harper.

Cott, Nancy. 1987. *The Grounding of Modern Feminism*. New Haven, CT: Yale University Press.

Crenshaw, Kimberle. 1989. "Demarginalizing the Intersection of Race and Sex." *University of Chicago Legal Forum*.

Dewey, John. (1932) 1985. *Ethics*. In *John Dewey: The Later Works*, vol. 7. Ed. Jo Ann Boydston and Barbara Levine. Carbondale: Southern Illinois University Press.

Dinnerstein, Dorothy. 1977. *The Mermaid and the Minotaur: Sexual Arrangements and Human Malaise*. New York: Harper Colophon.

Dixon, Marlene. 1970. In *It Ain't Me Babe* (April 7).

Douglass, Frederick. (1886) 1992. "Strong to suffer, and yet strong to strive." Address delivered on the twenty-fourth anniversary of emancipation, Washington, DC, April 16. In *The Frederick Douglass Papers*, vol. 5. Ed. John W. Blassingame and John R. McKivigan. New Haven, CT: Yale University Press.

Elshtain, Jean. 1994. "The Mothers of the Disappeared." In *Representations of Motherhood*, ed. Donna Bassin, Margaret Honey, and Meryle Mahrer Kaplan. New Haven, CT: Yale University Press.

Engels, Friedrich. (1888) 1941. *Ludwig Feuerbach and the Outcome of Classical German Philosophy*. New York: International Publishers.

——. 1969. *The Housing Question*. 2nd ed. (1873). In *Selected Works*, vol. 2. Moscow: Progress Publishers.

——. 1977. "Democratic Pan-Slavism," *Neue Rheinische Zeitung* (February 11, 1849). In *Works*, vol. 8. London: Lawrence and Wishart.

——. 1989. *Socialism: Utopian and Scientific* (1880). In *Works*, vol. 24. London: Lawrence and Wishart.

Flanagan, Owen, and Kathryn Jackson. 1987. "Justice, Care and Gender: The Kohlberg-Gilligan Debate Revisited." *Ethics* 97:622–37.

Ford, Maureen R., and Carol R. Lowery. 1986. "Gender Differences in Moral Reasoning: A Comparison of the Use of Justice and Care Orientations." *Journal of Personality and Social Psychology* 50:777–83.

Foucault, Michel. 1980. "Powers and Strategies" (1977). In *Power/Knowledge: Selected Interviews and Other Writings, 1972–1977*. Ed. Colin Gordon. Trans. Colin Cordon et al. New York: Pantheon.

Friedman, Marilyn. 1991. "The Practice of Partiality." *Ethics* 101:818–35.

Garrison, William Lloyd. 1831. *The Liberator* 1 (1) (January 1).

Gilligan, Carol. 1982. *In a Different Voice*. Cambridge, MA: Harvard University Press.

———. 1986. "Moral Orientation and Moral Development." In *Women and Moral Theory*, ed. Eva Kittay and Diana Meyers. Totowa, NJ: Rowman & Littlefield.

Gilman, Charlotte Perkins. (1915) 1979. *Herland*. New York: Pantheon.

Gould, Carol C. 1976. "Philosophy of Liberation and Liberation of Philosophy." In *Women and Philosophy*, ed. Carol C. Gould and Marx W. Wartofsky. New York: Capricorn/G. P. Putnam.

Grimshaw, Jean. 1986. *Philosophy and Feminist Thinking*. Minneapolis: University of Minnesota Press.

Hahn, Thich Nhat. 1993. *For a Future to Be Possible: Commentary on the Five Wonderful Precepts*. Berkeley: Parallax Press.

Harding, Sandra. 1987. "The Curious Coincidence of Feminine and African Moralities." In *Women and Moral Theory*, ed. Eva Kittay and Diana Meyers. Totowa, NJ: Rowman & Littlefield.

Harris, Angela. 1990. "Race and Essentialism in Legal Theory." *Stanford Law Review* 42: 581–616.

Hegel, Georg Wilhelm Friedrich. (1821) 1952. *The Philosophy of Right*. Oxford: Oxford University Press.

Held, Virginia. 1987. "Feminism and Moral Theory." In *Women and Moral Theory*, ed. Eva Kittay and Diana Meyers. Totowa, NJ: Rowman & Littlefield.

———. 1990. "Mothering versus Contract." In *Beyond Self-Interest*, ed. Jane Mansbridge. Chicago: University of Chicago Press.

Herman, Barbara. 1993. *The Practice of Moral Judgment*. Cambridge, MA: Harvard University Press.

Hirschmann, Nancy J. 1989. "Freedom, Recognition and Obligation: A Feminist Approach to Political Theory." *American Political Science Review* 83:1227–44.

Hochschild, Jennifer. 1981. *What's Fair? American Beliefs about Distributive Justice*. Cambridge, MA: Harvard University Press.

Hurston, Zora Neale. (1937) 1990. *Their Eyes Were Watching God*. New York: Harper & Row.

Ibn Khaldûn. (1377) 1980. *The Muquddimah: An Introduction to History*, trans. Franz Rosenthal. Bollingen Series 43. Princeton, NJ: Princeton University Press.

Jefferson, Thomas (l816) 1904. "Letter to Du Pont de Nemours." In *The Writings of Thomas Jefferson*, vol. 14. Ed. Andrew A. Lipscomb. Washington, DC: Thomas Jefferson Memorial Association.

Johnston, D. Kay. 1988. "Adolescents' Solutions to Dilemmas in Fables." In *Mapping the Moral Domain*, ed. Carol Gilligan, J. Victoria Ward, and Jill McLean Taylor. Cambridge, MA: Harvard University Press.

Kant, Immanuel. (l763) 1960. *Observations on the Feeling of the Beautiful and the Sublime*. Trans. John Goldthwait. Berkeley: University of California Press.

———. (1785) 1949. *Fundamental Principles of the Metaphysic of Morals*. Trans. Thomas K. Abbott. Indianapolis: Bobbs-Merrill.

Kassis, Hanna E. 1983. *A Concordance of the Qur'an*. Berkeley: University of California Press.

Ketchum, Ralph, ed. 1986. *The Anti-Federalist Papers and the Constitutional Convention Debates*. New York: Penguin/Mentor.

Kohlberg, Lawrence. 1981. *Essays on Moral Development*. San Francisco: Harper & Row.

Leach, Marjorie. 1992. *Guide to the Gods*. Ed. Michael Owen Jones and Frances Cattermole-Tally. Santa Barbara, CA: ABC-CLIO.

Lincoln, Abraham. 1907. "Letter to Joshua F. Speed" (1855). In *Abraham Lincoln: Collected Works*, vol. 1. Ed. John G. Nicolay and John Hay. New York: Century.

Lloyd, Genevieve. 1983. "Reason, Gender and Morality in the History of Philosophy." *Social Research* 50:491–513.

Lukes Steven. 1985. *Marxism and Morality*. Oxford: Oxford University Press.

Maccoby, Eleanor Emmons, and Carol Nagy Jacklin. 1974. *The Psychology of Sex Differences*. Palo Alto, CA: Stanford University Press.

MacKinnon, Catharine A. 1987. *Feminism Unmodified*. Cambridge, MA: Harvard University Press.

———. 1989. *Toward a Feminist Theory of the State*. Cambridge, MA: Harvard University Press.

Madison, James, Alexander Hamilton, and John Jay. (1788) 1987. *The Federalist Papers*. Ed. Isaac Kramnick. New York: Penguin.

Mansbridge, Jane. 1993. "Feminism and Democratic Community." In *Democratic Community: NOMOS XXXV*, ed. John W. Chapman and Ian Shapiro. New York: New York University Press.

———. 2001. "Complicating Oppositional Consciousness." In *Oppositional Consciousness*, ed. Jane Mansbridge and Aldon Morris. Chicago: University of Chicago Press.

Markus, Hazel, and Daphna Oyserman.1989. "Gender and Thought: The Role of Self-Concept." In *Gender and Thought: Psychological Perspectives*, ed. Mary Crawford and Margaret Gentry. New York: Springer-Verlag.

Marx, Karl. (1867) 1977. *Capital*. Vol. 1. New York: Vintage/Random House.

———. (1875) 1938. *Critique of the Gotha Program*. New York: International Publishers.

Marx, Karl, and Friedrich Engels. 1976. *The Communist Manifesto* (1848). In *Works*, vol. 6. London: Lawrence and Wishart.

Metz, Tamara. 2010. *Untying the Knot: Marriage, the State, and the Case for Their Divorce*. Princeton, NJ: Princeton University Press.

Minow, Martha. 1987. "Justice Engendered: A Feminist Foreword to the Supreme Court 1986 Term." *Harvard Law Review* 101:10–95.

Nedelsky, Jennifer. 1989. "Reconceiving Autonomy." *Yale Journal of Law and Feminism* 1:7–36.

———. 2011. *Laws Relations: A Relational Theory of Self, Autonomy, and Law*. Oxford: Oxford University Press.

Nelson, Barbara, and Najma Chowdhury. 1994. *Women and Politics Worldwide*. New Haven, CT: Yale University Press.

Nozick, Robert. 1974. *Anarchy, State and Utopia*. New York: Basic Books.

Okin, Susan Moller. 1989. *Justice, Gender and the Family*. New York: Basic Books.

———. 1990. "Thinking Like a Woman." In *Theoretical Perspectives on Sexual Difference*, ed. Deborah L. Rhode. New Haven, CT: Yale University Press.

Okure, Patrick Akaninyene Basil. 1983. *The Notion of Justice among the Ibibio People*. Rome: Pontificia Universitats Lateranensis, Academic Alfoniana, Institutum Superius Theologiae Moralis.

Paine, Thomas. (1776) 1922. *Common Sense*. New York: Peter Eckler Publishing.

Rawls, John. 1971. *A Theory of Justice*. Cambridge, MA: Harvard University Press.

Records of the Federal Convention of 1787. (1911) 1966. Ed. M. Farrand. 4 vols. New Haven, CT: Yale University Press.

Scott, James C. 1985. *Weapons of the Weak: Everyday Forms of Peasant Resistance.* New Haven, CT: Yale University Press.

Sher, George. 1987. "Other Voices, Other Rooms? Women's Psychology and Moral Theory." In *Women and Moral Theory*, ed. Eva Kittay and Diana Meyers. Totowa, NJ: Rowman & Littlefield.

Smith, Barbara, and Beverly Smith. 1981. "Across the Kitchen Table: A Sister-to-Sister Dialogue." In *This Bridge Called My Back*, ed. Cherrie Moraga and Gloria Anzaldúa. Watertown, MA: Persephone Press.

Spelman, Elizabeth V. 1988. *Inessential Woman: Problems of Exclusion in Feminist Thought.* Boston: Beacon.

Suzuki, Daisetz Teitaro. 1956. *Zen Buddhism: Selected Writings.* Garden City, NY: Doubleday.

Tronto, Joan C. 1989. "Women and Caring: What Can Feminists Learn about Morality from Caring?" In *Gender/Body/Knowledge*, ed. Alison M. Jaggar and Susan R. Bordo. New Brunswick, NJ: Rutgers University Press.

Tucker, Mary Evelyn, and Duncan Ryuken Williams, eds. 1997. *Buddhism and Ecology: The Interconnection of Dharma and Deeds.* Cambridge, MA: Harvard University Press.

Wallace, Michele. 1990. "A Black Feminist's Search for Sisterhood." In *Invisibility Blues.* New York: Verso.

Walzer, Michael. 1983. *Spheres of Justice.* New York: Basic Books.

Weber, Max. (1922) 1968. *Economy and Society.* Ed. Guenther Roth and Claus Wittich. New York: Bedminister Press.

Williams, John E., and Deborah L. Best. 1982. *Measuring Sex Stereotypes.* Beverly Hills, CA: Sage.

Wood, Allen W. 1980. "The Marxian Critique of Justice" (1972). In Cohen, Nagel, and Scanlon 1980.

Young, Iris Marion. 1990. *Justice and the Politics of Difference.* Princeton, NJ: Princeton University Press.

Young, Robert. (1880) 1955. *Analytical Concordance to the Bible.* New York: Funk and Wagnalls.

9 :: KINSHIP

JANET CARSTEN

The *Oxford Dictionary of English Etymology* entry for "kin" begins "family, race; class, kind," and goes on to list words that share *kin*'s Indo-European base:

> agnate, cognate; benign, malign; nation, nature; genus, general; generate; generous; degenerate, regenerate; genius, ingenious; ingenuous, ingenue; indigenous; kind; progeny; -gen, gono-; gentile; genital, genitive, germ, germinate, germane. (Onions 1966, 505)

Nation and nature; generous and malign; gentile and germ—all derive from the same root. It takes little reflection to see that they are all potentially part of our experience of being kin. Yet the study of kinship has often seemed to rest on peculiarly narrow assumptions about what kinship is. These assumptions have in turn inspired some exceptionally dry and abstruse academic debates between proponents of rival theories of kinship, debates that have touched on issues of gender in a number of striking ways. The knotty relation between kinship and gender makes the omission of "gender" from the *ODEE* list seem less odd than it might appear, although the dictionary does mention that the sense "gender, sex" was present in Old English and early Middle English.

From the beginning of the twentieth century, the comparative study of kinship within the social sciences became the specialty of the emerging discipline of social or cultural anthropology. Anthropologists made the description and analysis of local kinship systems (whether in Africa, Polynesia, Melanesia, or Asia) central to their studies. Conversely, until the last quarter of the twentieth century, scholars who wished to make a mark in the discipline were more or less expected to include kinship as a central part of their ethnographic work.

While kinship became the *locus classicus* of anthropological scholarship, what was meant by "kinship" was itself an artifact of a particular set of academic assumptions that—implicitly at least—had gender at their core. As kinship became in the mid-twentieth century an increasingly technical field of study, it was often difficult to see how the mathematical models of kinship systems that anthropologists produced, or their dense analysis of kin terms, actually connected to the everyday, familiar lived experience of being kin. These models were largely put together and argued over by men. This might be seen as paradoxical, since women held a relatively high profile in the institutionalization of anthropology in British and North American universities. Yet those who made a mark in the field of kinship studies were the leading male anthropologists of their day: Bronislaw Malinowski, A. R. Radcliffe-Brown, George Peter Murdock, Edward Evans-Pritchard, Meyer Fortes, and Claude Lévi-Strauss.

For several generations of anthropology students, kinship was also the subject everyone loved to hate—notoriously dry and difficult, remote from the interests of "real" people—including students. It now seems banal to observe that this was a corollary of the particular way kinship had come to be defined. The kinship of midcentury studies seemed increasingly abstract and removed from the practice of actual lived relations and the powerful emotions that they engendered.

It was no coincidence that this kind of kinship was in many respects quite removed from the lives of women. Anthropologists held that the importance of kinship in so-called primitive societies largely resided in its political and religious aspects. Economics and politics were considered to be embedded in kinship relations, and were often described as being dominated by men. In advanced industrialized societies, by contrast, sociological studies tended to assume that kinship was not a central feature of social organization but was relatively isolated from other aspects of economic and political life, constituting a private, domestic domain. Here kinship was considered to be the female domain par excellence but was of minor sociological interest.

These understandings shaped the process of data collection. A popular myth of the discipline held that many of the pioneering figures among women anthropologists were themselves accepted as "honorary men" in the societies in which they undertook fieldwork. Having high status as colonial outsiders, they could talk to high-ranking men as equals (at the very least), rather than be relegated to the low-status world of women. Until surprisingly recently, female graduate students were commonly encouraged by their teachers to adopt this "method" in the field.

The dominance of this kind of kinship study in anthropology was undermined in the 1970s by second-wave feminism as a political movement, and by feminist scholarship in the academy. A new generation of women anthropologists produced a raft of studies that focused on the lives of women, at the same time demonstrating the extent to which previous ethnographic accounts had excluded the everyday significance of domesticity, foregrounding instead male concerns in terms of politics and religion. Gradually, the study of women's lives as a subject of interest was superseded by a more theoretical concern with the way gender itself was symbolically constructed in different societies. To some extent, this new body of work displaced the central importance of kinship within anthropology. It also provoked an important discussion about the relation between kinship and gender, and how these terms were defined. The displacement of kinship studies within anthropology can be partly attributed to the new prominence of gender as a field of academic interest beginning in the 1970s and continuing through the 1980s, but it also resulted from broader theoretical shifts within the field of anthropology and beyond to other disciplines. The theoretical and methodological paradigms of the discipline at midcentury were challenged by the rise of postcolonial studies, a shift to a more historically informed anthropology, and a move from a concern with structure to one of practice and process. The previously self-evident divisions of anthropology into the domains of religion, kinship, politics, and economics could no longer be taken for granted. And in this reconfiguration, kinship emerged in a rather different guise.

Evolutionism

In retrospect, it seems clear that even the earliest attempts at a comparative study of kinship institutions undertaken by nineteenth-century social evolutionary theorists like Sir Henry Maine, John Ferguson McLellan, and Lewis Henry Morgan had gender issues at their core. Broadly, these studies attempted to trace the historical evolution of family forms from some chaotic state of "primitive promiscuity," in which sex and marriage were entirely unregulated (or, in Maine's theory, from a state of "patriarchal despotism"), to that high point of civilization occupied by the well-ordered family form of nineteenth-century European and North American society: the patriarchal, monogamous family set in the wider context of a territorial state and the institution of private property. Between the primitive and the civilized came a varying number and sequence of stages, including group marriage, exogamy, matriarchy, polyandry, and polygamy (see Kuper 1988).

Modern anthropology has long since abandoned an explicitly evolutionary agenda, and it is clear that the sequences of kinship forms proposed by nineteenth-century evolutionary anthropologists were not based on any evidence that would be accepted today. Notions that all human societies had progressed from a stage where sex and marriage were utterly unregulated (primitive promiscuity) or women were dominant over men (primitive matriarchy) were simply projections, the outcome of a particular nineteenth-century social theory, and were quite speculative in nature. Nevertheless, partly because some of Morgan's work was later taken up by Karl Marx and Friedrich Engels, and partly because of the central place of relations between the sexes in ideas about the evolution of family forms, which became a focus for twentieth-century feminist scholarship, these theories have retained a historical significance in anthropology and in the study of gender.

The idea that all societies had progressed from a state in which sex and marriage were unregulated, in which anyone could have sex with anyone else, arose from the comparative analysis of kin terms collected by philologists, as well as the study of historical legal institutions. Morgan (1871) argued that there was a fundamental distinction between terminological systems that made a distinction between Father and Father's Brother or Mother and Mother's Sister, and those that did not. He called the former type of system "descriptive," the latter, "classificatory." In a descriptive system, the distinction between Father and Uncle, or Mother and Aunt, not only conforms to known biological connections, it also underlies categorical differences in the appropriate way of behaving toward these relatives. The suggested link between kin terms and behavior was crucial. Morgan did not argue that, where classificatory terminologies were found, people simply failed to make a distinction between Mother and Mother's Sister or between Father and Father's Brother, but that the *origin* of this kind of classificatory terminology lay in an earlier period in which such distinctions were either not made or had no social significance. In other words, at some earlier time, the kinship system entailed groups of brothers marrying their sisters—that is, group marriage. From this already hypothetical early stage, there was no difficulty in positing an even earlier time, when sex and marriage were unregulated by incest taboos or marriage rules of any kind. It was clear that motherhood was different from fatherhood in that pregnancy and birth made a mother recognizable even if her identity was not socially significant, whereas a father's identity was ascribed by marriage. This difference in the recognizability of motherhood and fatherhood was the subject of an important area of later anthropological debate in the examination of beliefs about procreation in different cultures, and in more recent discussions about the social significance of reproductive technologies (see below).

The study of kin terminology and the suggested relation between language and behavior are topics that have also remained on the anthropological agenda, even though the evolutionary sequences proposed by Morgan and other nineteenth-century theorists have long been dis-

placed. The other area of Morgan's work that had a particularly enduring influence on modern anthropology and on gender studies was his attempt to establish a causal mechanism for the evolution of family forms.
In *Ancient Society* (1877), Morgan suggested that as society developed
from very simple technological stages, in which subsistence was based on
hunting, fishing, and gathering, to more developed systems of pastoralism and then settled agriculture, there was an increasing input of labor,
and with it the ownership of property became more important. As property was no longer held in common, men sought to control their investment in labor and safeguard their estates through rules of inheritance.
Along with these developments in technology and property-holding, it
became more important to know who your children were and to pass on
property within a small family group. And so, Morgan proposed an evolutionary scheme of technological development, in various stages from
hunting to pastoralism to settled agriculture, which propelled a parallel
evolution of kinship institutions, also in a number of stages, from primitive promiscuity, matriarchy, and group marriage to patriarchy, polygamy, and monogamy.

As already mentioned, part of the wider impact of Morgan's work was
due to the way it was taken up by Marx and Engels. Engels's *Origin of the
Family, Private Property and the State*, originally published in 1884, was
closely based on Morgan's theories. But whereas Morgan's work was intended as an academic treatise, Engels's had a directly political agenda.
In demonstrating how an increased technological sophistication had led
to the development of different institutions of property ownership and
inheritance, and to successive changes in marriage and family forms, Engels was also showing that the institution of private property was the
historic outcome of a sequence of changes—it was neither inevitable
nor necessarily permanent. Similarly, rather than suggesting that the
Victorian patriarchal, monogamous family was the most civilized of kinship institutions (as was implied by most anthropological theories of the
time), Engels was highly critical of this institution and the oppression of
women it entailed. Taking it as one possible form of family that accompanied a capitalist economic system, he not only showed that other systems of kinship had existed historically but that in the future this family
form might give way to a different kinship arrangement in which relations between the sexes were based on a much greater degree of equality.

To varying degrees, the anthropological study of kinship has retained
this political possibility of offering alternative examples of kinship arrangements from those found in Western societies. It is very clear that
feminist work in the 1970s, which examined women's lives, as well as
different labor arrangements, systems of property ownership, and re-

lations between the sexes—particularly in societies where hunting and gathering was the main means of subsistence—owed much to the kind of suggestions set out by Morgan and Engels. The kind of evolutionary development proposed by these writers remained on the agenda in other contexts too. For obvious reasons, Soviet and Chinese anthropology retained an evolutionary agenda for much of the twentieth century.

Synchronic Studies of Kinship

Kinship remained central to the discipline of social and cultural anthropology during most of the twentieth century, but anthropologists generally distanced themselves from any evolutionary overtones to their cross-cultural depictions of kinship arrangements. For early and mid-twentieth-century anthropologists like Malinowski, Radcliffe-Brown, Evans-Pritchard, Murdock, and Fortes, the interest of kinship systems was derived from the fact that in the societies they studied, political organization operated through the institutions of kinship. In the absence of modern state structures or institutions of government, the political functioning of society was maintained by a system of elders and chiefs who were linked to the rest of the population through kinship ties, and whose authority was vested in their position in a wider kinship group, which operated through ties of descent. Succession to office was determined by kinship. Often, religion too operated in an idiom of kinship and was intrinsic to the legitimation of political authority. Thus Fortes (1961, 1983) described how, among the Tallensi of West Africa, the duty of filial piety and ritual obligation of juniors to elders was part of a religious system of ancestor worship, but it was also simultaneously intrinsic to a hierarchy of political authority of elders over juniors that was based in the descent group. In this way, religion and politics (as well as economics) were inextricably based in kinship.

It was the fact that politics operated through kinship that made the study of kinship institutions essential to grasping how such societies worked—their stable political functioning and their cohesive order. In this sense, what was meant by kinship was not so much the everyday world of domesticity, or close family life, but the wider "political" structure of nested descent groups, lineages, tribes, and clans. For the mid-century school of British social anthropology, in particular, it was difficult to see how political stability could be achieved in the absence of the unilineal descent group—a kinship unit based on the descent of its members from a common ancestor in either the male or the female line. The lineage functioned as a corporate group, owning property in common, and conceiving of itself as a jural unit. The descent system could operate through the female line to a uterine ancestor, or through agnatic principles in the male line. Whether the descent system was matrilineal or patrilineal, however, had no necessary correlation with political authority—even in matrilineal systems it was men who held positions of political authority. Here anthropologists made a clear distinction between matriliny as a principle of descent, and matriarchy as a system in which women had political dominance over men. In fact, although matriarchy had been a prominent feature in some nineteenth-century evolutionary schemas (most notably in Johannes Bachofen's work), anthropologists did not find evidence of matriarchal systems in the contemporary societies they studied.

There were, however, different social implications inherent to matrilineal and patrilineal descent systems. Anthropologists described now matrilineal kinship created tensions for men in terms of affiliation and residence and the cohesiveness of the group. Descent groups were exogamous—the members of one lineage took their spouses from a different lineage. If men married out and lived with their in-laws (or affines) after marriage, then the political group of men in authority would be geographically dispersed. If it was women who moved to their husband's group after marriage, then the children belonging to the matrilineal group (as well as their mothers) would be dispersed, creating problems in terms of the continuity of the descent group. Either way, men were caught between their affiliation to their wife's groups and to their own natal lineage. Anthropologists described a number of possible residential solutions within a nexus of rules governing marriage and succession to what was termed the "matrilineal puzzle" (Richards 1950). But, of course, it was also the case that a patrilineal system involved similar issues of affiliation, only here it was women who were somehow betwixt and between—caught between affiliation to their father's group and that of their husband. No doubt it was significant that it was the position of men in a matrilineal system that anthropologists regarded as a subject worthy of close analytical attention.

We can see how anthropologists' analytical understandings of kinship were founded on implicit distinctions involving gender. In the work of both Malinowski and Fortes, and other midcentury anthropologists, the family was seen as a universal social institution, necessary to provide the needs of care and socialization of infants. The public world of men's political action was prioritized over the more intimate social relations of the house involving women and children. Fortes (1969) made an explicit distinction between what he called the "domestic domain" and the "politico-jural domain" of kinship. What was primarily of interest to anthropologists was how kinship functioned in the politico-jural domain. This was what gave continuity and stability to the social structure. The domestic domain was important in linking the person to the wider descent group and to the politico-jural domain, and in providing the source of the moral force of kinship—what Fortes called the "axiom of amity." It was within the domestic domain that children first learned the moral imperative of kinship relations, which was then extended to the wider descent group. It now seems intriguing that although Fortes was the source of an analytic distinction between the domestic and the political that would later be subjected to strong feminist critique—for assuming what should have been made the subject of examination—his own work contains detailed descriptions of domestic life and mother-child relations in the societies he studied. But the kind of rhetorical use that Engels, and later feminist scholars, made of kinship institutions in other cultures—explicitly to imagine the possibility of a society in which relations between women and men were based on equality—was absent.

One might say there was a kind of intrinsic conservatism to the functionalist and structural functionalist kinship studies of the mid-twentieth century. Partly because most of these studies were intentionally ahistorical, giving a kind of snapshot of a society at a particular moment, there was little sense of how institutions changed and transformed themselves over time, or how they might be the outcome of particular historical processes. In fact, later studies have shown how the systems of descent groups described in immaculate detail by Africanist anthropologists of this era were often quite idealized in form. The unproblematic boundedness of tribal groups was very much the outcome of policies and impositions of colonial governments. On a more local level, it was clear (e.g., in the work of Evans-Pritchard) that whatever the analytic prominence given to such institutions as the lineage, the actual participants in such systems might be rather more hazy about which descent group they actually belonged to (see Kuper 1988; McKinnon 2000).

Alliance Theory

In contrast to mid-twentieth-century British anthropological studies of kinship, which focused on descent as an organizing principle, in France the highly influential work of Claude Lévi-Strauss took marriage or alliance as the central feature of kinship. Lévi-Strauss's massive comparative study, *The Elementary Structures of Kinship*, was published in French in 1949 and in English translation in 1969. But the versions of kinship put forward by what became two opposing schools of anthropological thought were quite different kinds of beast. Lévi-Strauss's intellectual project was a much more general one than that of his British counterparts. Whereas Anglophone scholars were engaged in describing and analyzing how particular societies worked—what kinds of kinship rules existed, how people actually behaved—Lévi-Strauss was concerned with understanding the operations of the human mind in a general sense.

Kinship was of interest to Lévi-Strauss principally as revealing the principles that govern all human mental activity. And this is why in his later work he turned to the study of Amazonian myth, which could be seen as a "purer" realm of thought, undisturbed by the material and practical factors in which kinship is necessarily embroiled. For Lévi-Strauss, the most fundamental principle of human activity was exchange. Here he was influenced by the work of Marcel Mauss ([1925] 1990) on the importance of the gift in primitive society, and the reliance of all systems of gift-giving on the principle of reciprocity. Women were the most valuable of all gifts, Lévi-Strauss argued, because they ensured the continuity of the group through reproduction. Therefore the only possible return for the gift of a woman in marriage was another woman. When one group of men give away their sisters to another group in marriage, they institute a system of marital exchange.

In stressing exchange as the central feature of human sociality, Lévi-Strauss also emphasized the importance of relations *between* social entities rather than the *content* of the entities themselves. His analysis proceeds from the idea that to understand humankind as inherently social, we have to understand the relations between the units of social life (whether these are myths or kinship groups) rather than the nature of these units themselves. Thus, a structural analysis of a myth begins by dividing the myth into various elements, which can then be related to each other in a system of structural opposition: hot/cold, wet/dry, male/female, and so on.

Lévi-Strauss suggested that the centrality of exchange is also the origin of the incest taboo. Incest taboos are a common feature of all human culture, and for Lévi-Strauss they mark a transition from the animal world of nature to the human world of culture. The effect of incest taboos is, in Lévi-Strauss's terms, to force men to exchange their sisters in marriage rather than keeping them for themselves. In this way, he explains how although the content of incest prohibitions varies from culture to culture, their origin and effects are always the same—to enjoin exogamy, marriage outside the group. In *The Elementary Structures of Kinship*, Lévi-Strauss gives a detailed structural analysis of different marriage systems in which people are supposed to marry a particular category of kin. The rules may be extremely complex—sometimes involving reciprocity between groups that not only continues from one generation to another, but may involve a large number of groups and considerable lapses of time. Without going into the details of Lévi-Strauss's schema, it is possible to see that the implications of his analysis were very radical. Although his book was a study of what he called "elementary systems"—systems in which explicit rules positively enjoined people to marry certain categories of kin—he argued that the same principles of exchange and reciprocity were at work, albeit masked by other factors, including class, in "complex systems" where no such positive rules existed.

By placing exchange and marriage at the center of his analysis, Lévi-Strauss focuses on the relations between kin groups rather than relations within them. Similarly, rather than suggest the nuclear family as a universal institution of kinship, Lévi-Strauss proposes a universal "atom of kinship" composed of mother, father, child, and mother's brother. These four elements were necessary to place exchange—between a mother's brother and a woman's husband—at the center of the most basic unit of kinship.

Whether one saw descent or marriage as central to kinship clearly had important implications for the study of kinship and human culture more generally. Structuralism was in its ascendancy in the 1960s and 1970s, and one enduring mark that this kind of analysis left on kinship studies in anthropology was to highlight the fundamental significance of exchange and marriage. Marriage was henceforth understood by anthropologists, whatever their stripe, as an enduring set of relations between groups, involving a whole nexus of goods and prestations. This was particularly important when anthropologists turned their attention away from Africa, where descent systems predominated, to the study of kinship in other regions (for example, New Guinea and Amazonia) where exchange proved a key principle of social life.

But there were also important criticisms to be made of Lévi-Strauss's theories. The tendency of structural analysis to see elements of social life in terms of opposed principles sometimes had the effect of reducing complex social phenomena to rather simpleminded two-column lists. Today, the atom of kinship—and particularly Lévi-Strauss's lack of hesitation in assigning a simple positive or negative sign to relations within it—is no longer taken very seriously. More fundamentally, feminist scholars took exception to Lévi-Strauss's assertion that it was always men who exchanged women in marriage, and the consequent implication that women were mere objects of exchange. Apart from objecting to the androcentric premises on which Lévi-Strauss's argument was built (see, for example, Rubin 1975; McKinnon 2001), when feminist scholarship in anthropology began to foreground a more focused attention to women's lives, it became clear that women often played a very active role in marital negotiations, and marriage could not simply be understood as the exchange of women by men.

Although in the 1960s and 1970s the debate between the proponents of alliance and descent theories seemed to dominate kinship studies in anthropology, and to mark a fundamental theoretical divide, today the commonalities between these two schools are more obvious. Both kinds of analysis had a tendency to omit any discussion of historical transformation. Both were highly normative in spirit, allowing for little variation in what being a husband, or a father, wife, or mother, might involve in a particular society. And both tended to see men as the principal actors in social and political life, and to take for granted that the everyday intimacies of domestic life were not a subject of great interest for anthropologists.

The Culturalist Critique

I have already mentioned that studies of kinship in Western societies by sociologists, historians, and anthropologists tended to assume that kinship was a relatively minor aspect of social organization. Here kinship was seen as divorced from political, economic, and religious life, and more or less reduced to the nuclear family. Although the degree of control women exerted over the household and family was recognized as quite variable, the family constituted an isolated, private, domestic, and above all "female" domain. Where social scientists or historians investigated kinship in Europe, they tended to view its instrumental aspects—in property relations, inheritance patterns, and economic exchanges—as paramount.

This understanding of kinship in the West was undermined from several different directions that, increasingly, reinforced each other. One was the feminist critique of the analytical status of the "domestic domain" as a haven from the world of work and harsh economic imperatives, which I discuss in the following section. Another came from the culturalist critique of kinship within anthropology that was launched in the United States by David Schneider. Schneider's *American Kinship* was first published in 1968, with a second edition printed in 1980. It presented a way of doing kinship studies that was radically different from either the British functionalist school or French structuralism. Schneider himself was strongly based in a Weberian tradition in anthropology and sociology, and influenced too by Talcott Parsons. His starting point was to see kinship, like religious or nationalist ideology, as a system of meaning, and to understand the ideas and symbols it embodied as a belief system for participants in American culture.

Schneider described sexual procreation as the core symbol of American kinship, which was itself divided into two orders—the order of nature and the order of law. Ties of consanguineal kinship were seen as natural in American culture and based in shared biogenetic substance; relations of marriage were governed by a "code for conduct" that was enshrined in law. The sexual union of two partners in marriage united the order of nature and that of law, substance, and code. Kinship ties were described by Schneider as embodying "diffuse, enduring solidarity," and this was central to the ideological and moral force of kinship.

Today, *American Kinship* remains a classic study, although one might suspect this is more because of the openings it provided for a new way of doing kinship than for its actual description of kinship in urban Chicago (where the fieldwork on which it was based was carried out) or in American culture more generally. In a quite slim volume, Schneider, as his later critics argued (and he himself conceded), had reduced American kinship to a remarkably homogenized set of principles that ignored differences of age, sex, class, and locality, as well as the significance of ethnicity. How different contexts, different backgrounds, or personal histories might shape different understandings of kinship was not discussed. It is all the more striking, therefore, that some of the most innovative work in the anthropology of kinship in the late twentieth century and beyond has been carried out by students of Schneider and others for whom his work was clearly influential but who were among his most forceful critics. What these studies have in common is the idea that, like more overtly political or religious ideologies, kinship operates as an ideological system, and alongside its more practical aspects this constitutes part of its significance.

Gender, Property, and the Demise of Kinship

The study of kinship, like much else in anthropology and the wider academy, underwent profound changes in the 1970s and 1980s. To a great extent, these intellectual shifts were inspired by political movements for change outside the academy—notably, the transformative effects of anticolonialism and the feminist movement. For anthropology, both of these had serious implications. It became clear that the synchronic study of social structure, which ignored the determining effects of colonial history and the political significance of anticolonial movements in the polities of many of the societies that anthropologists studied, was neither intellectually tenable nor politically acceptable. A more historically based and politically aware anthropology began to take shape.

At the same time, the inadequacies of highly normative accounts of politics, religion, and kinship, which had tended to dominate midcentury studies of non-Western societies by anthropologists, became obvious. Anthropologists became more concerned with documenting the experiences and voices of different actors in a given social context—women as well as men, the young and the old, the politically disadvantaged as well as leaders and chiefs. A focus on previously muted voices and on modes of resistance to politically and economically repressive regimes of governance began to take center stage. Initially, much of this work was part of a Marxist turn in the 1970s; subsequently, it was greatly influenced by the writings of Michel Foucault.

Within kinship studies, the influence of a Marxist critique in the 1960s and 1970s highlighted the way kinship functioned as a form of property relations. Drawing inspiration from the writings of Marx, Engels, and Morgan, these studies examined how kinship might mask the existence of social hierarchies of class or property, and how kinship relations might also function as relations of production. Work in this vein was also concerned with the transition from precapitalist relations to capitalism, and often took a social evolutionary or historical perspective. A concern with the economics of kinship—with marriage, dowry, inheritance, the ownership of land and livestock by kin groups—was an important theme in the work of Jack Goody (1983, 1990) and other historians and anthropologists concerned with comparing the development of the family and capitalism in Europe with kinship and economic systems in Asia or Africa.

The more instrumental effects of kinship have remained an important theme in the study of kinship. The work of Pierre Bourdieu (1977) has been influential in highlighting the significance of the social uses of kinship. This "practice-based" anthropology seeks to demonstrate the way in which people may retrospectively attribute their behavior to the existence of kinship rules, rather than the rules directly producing certain forms of behavior. It has thus opened an avenue for a less reductive way to acknowledge the instrumental significance of kinship than was allowed for in some of the earlier Marxist studies.

Within anthropology more generally, however, the centrality of kinship was undermined, partly because the ways kinship had been defined in much midcentury anthropology—either as an essential part of the stable political functioning of stateless societies, or as revealing the deep structures of human thought—were themselves displaced. The increasingly technical and abstract arguments among kinship theorists were either difficult to grasp or politically irrelevant to many students in this era. To some extent, the kinds of topics that had previously fallen within the rubric of kinship became the subject of the new interest in gender relations. In the 1970s a number of important works in anthropology appeared that documented the lives of women and examined the nature of relations between women and men (see, for example, Rosaldo and Lamphere 1974; Reiter 1975). These studies were clearly inspired by the feminist movement outside the academy. Implicitly or explicitly, they were often attempts to answer a set of questions about the possibility of more equal relations between women and men than those that prevailed in the capitalist West. If anthropologists could find counterexamples to the gender hierarchy and family relations of the modern West in contemporary non-Western cultures, this would be of political as well as academic interest. For this reason, many of these studies, which were influenced by the Marxist turn in the early 1970s, focused on labor processes and the division of labor between women and men in production and reproduction.

From the late 1970s on, feminist scholarship increasingly turned from the description of women's lives in other cultures to the symbolization of gender. What was at issue were fundamental questions that a previous generation of anthropologists had either ignored or to which answers were assumed within their analytical constructs. What did it mean to be a woman or a man in a particular society? What precisely did the roles of wife or mother, daughter or sister, husband, father, son, or brother involve? How was gender constructed? No longer could the straightforward division between the "public," "political" world of men and the "private," "domestic" domain of women be taken for granted (Yanagisako 1979). Were such distinctions universally valid? How was the domestic or the political constituted in a particular society? The critical examination of what the domestic involved in both Western and non-Western contexts challenged the idea of the family and home as a realm of security from the world of work and productive labor in capitalist society. It also undermined the notion that apparently nonnormative familial forms, such as female-headed, or "matrifocal," households, were dysfunctional, seeing them instead as the outcome of historically embedded economic and political forces (see Stack 1974; Smith 1987). Such work also eroded the distinction that anthropologists had taken for granted between the West and the non-West—the idea that while kinship was central to the organization of noncapitalist societies, in the West it was reduced to something of peripheral sociological significance.

These questions dominated the study of gender in anthropology, but they also had a profound effect on the study of kinship. Relations between men and women, the nature of the domestic, the household, the gendered division of labor, marriage, procreation—all were topics that came under new analytic scrutiny in the anthropology of gender. But they could also legitimately be considered as part of the study of kinship. The relation between kinship and gender was clearly in question: which had logical priority? were they separate analytic domains, or were they, as Collier and Yanagisako (1987) argued, "mutually constituted" fields? To a considerable extent, what had previously been seen as kinship was displaced by the new interest in gender, and the study of kinship itself seemed to be in decline.

As an analytic construct, gender itself was premised on a distinction between the physical and the social—it was defined in relation to sex but focused on the way male or female attributes were the subject of social processes. The distinction between sex and gender was an analytic device that enabled anthropologists or sociologists to escape from the physical determinism that seemed to dog analyses of the relations between women and men. Where anthropologists found evidence of inequalities between the sexes, it seemed difficult to avoid explaining these without returning to the physical facts of procreation, pregnancy, and childbirth (see, for example, Ortner 1974; Errington 1990; Butler 1993). A focus on the social construction of gender and on cross-cultural variations in how procreation was understood was the basis for important analytic strategies in showing that what were taken to be physical "facts" could be interpreted in a highly variable manner.

The deconstruction—or denaturalization—of what had been taken to be "natural facts" became a central theme in the study of gender in anthropology (see Yanagisako and Delaney 1995), and has also had a crucial impact on kinship studies. The physical facts of procreation had, of course, been a topic of interest to analysts of kinship as far back as the nineteenth century. Malinowski (1929) had made famous the fact that the Trobriand islanders he studied at the beginning of the twentieth century apparently did not recognize the role of fathers in sexual procreation. Debates on this topic were part of the standard fare of kinship studies. In the 1980s David Schneider argued that anthropologists' definitions of kinship were premised on the centrality of sexual procreation in Western kinship. But if sexual procreation was not regarded as the basis of kinship, or was understood quite differently in some of the cultures that anthropologists studied, then this placed the whole analytic status of kinship in question. The comparative study of kinship assumed that what was being studied—kinship—was everywhere defined in the same way. In his *Critique of the Study of Kinship* (1984), Schneider argued that this was manifestly not the case. Anthropologists had imported their own ethnocentric assumptions into their analyses, and this invalidated the comparative exercise.

For Schneider, as for many others in the early 1980s, the conclusion seemed inescapable. There was no justification for maintaining "kinship" as a discrete domain in anthropological analysis. The way forward would involve a thorough dismantling of the artificial divisions between politics, religion, kinship, and economics on which holistic ethnography had been based.

Constructing Relatedness: The Malay Case

To graduate students of this era, kinship was the least attractive of subjects. It combined theoretical complexity with political irrelevance, and particularly after Schneider's wholesale demolition job, students readily assigned it to the past of the discipline rather than its future. But this left many practitioners of anthropology in something of a quandary when they undertook fieldwork.

Imagine for a moment doing fieldwork on the lives of women in a Malay island fishing village as I did in the early 1980s: living with a Malay family in a two-room house; documenting and being part of the many everyday occurrences for the young women living there; being left to look after a small baby during the daytime; taking a midday meal of rice and fish on the floor of the kitchen with family; being sent to make the coffee when unexpected visitors arrived; enjoying the quiet, easy familiarity of the evenings when friends and neighbors dropped by for a chat and a betel quid. Imagine the joking, storytelling, and affection between women of one house and their immediate neighbors while they attended to household tasks and, as well, their unpleasant quarrels and recriminations (see Carsten 1997).

The most striking realization, as I tried to make sense of my first chaotic impressions of the world in which I found myself suddenly immersed, was, paradoxically enough, of the central importance of kinship. After years of struggling to understand theoretical arguments about kinship, and their relevance to an analysis of everyday life, I was suddenly and inescapably confronted with the lived reality of kinship. I had expected to spend much of my time observing and participating in the lives of Malay women. I had not expected this to involve a long endeavor to grapple with the problem of what "being kin" meant to the Malay people I lived with.

The process of learning what Malay relatedness was about began for me with simply living together with a family in the enforced intimacy of their house. In the first weeks of fieldwork, I often found myself spending long hours inside houses—both the one I was living in and those of neighbors close by. Together with my foster mother, and more gradually by myself, I visited other houses in the village, both formally and informally. Much of this time was spent with women and with small children, men being mostly absent from the house during the day. I began to reflect on the importance of the house itself to Malay notions of kinship. The house is in fact strongly associated with women. Not only do women spend much of their time in houses, in contrast to men, but a proper house must have a female household head, and it also has a "house spirit" who is female. When villagers go to marriage feasts or funerals, they go as representatives of their house. Usually, this means that the eldest married couple of the house attends village functions. One might say that houses have a private, internal aspect that is strongly associated with women, and a more public face that is both male and female and associated with married couples.

One of the things I learned very early on in my fieldwork was the importance of feeding in the lives of those who share one house. Not only was the food delicious, cooked with care and attention, but it was invested with great symbolic importance. As a visitor to many houses, I knew only too well how difficult it was to refuse an offer of food. Indeed, I often felt that a kind of bodily transformation was being worked on me, as I was persuaded to consume far more food than I would normally eat. Malay houses have only one hearth, and this is in many ways the symbolic focus of the house. It would be unthinkable for different members of the house not to share cooking and eating arrangements. The most important constituent of the diet in the Malay view is rice. To "eat a meal" in Malay can only be rendered as "to eat rice"; this is the main part of what constitutes a proper meal. More than all other types of food, rice is associated with bodily well-being. This is because, as I was often told, within the body it is transformed into blood.

I had many months, and many meals, in which to ponder the significance of the shared consumption of rice in ideas about relatedness. In the process, I learned that houses have another crucial aspect. As well as being associated with women, they are also strongly linked to the sibling sets born there. When a couple marry, they initially live with either the wife's or the husband's parents. Eventually, after they have one or two children, they establish a new house. And so houses are associated with the birth of brothers and sisters, or sibling sets, which are the reason for their coming into existence.

Siblingship is central to Malay ideas about relatedness, in many ways more important than the ties between parents and their children. Ties between brothers and sisters are regarded as very close, and people think of themselves as connected through these ties rather than those of descent. When I asked, as I often did, how a certain person was related to someone else, I was always given a series of connections that would finish with "so-and-so and so-and-so were two siblings." Similarly, as I tried to make sense of who lived in the different houses of the village and their interconnections in the first months of fieldwork, I came to understand the patterns of residence through tracing particular sibling sets. Often neighboring houses of one compound were occupied by adult members of a sibling group or their descendants. I also came to understand how siblingship is the idiom for much more diffuse ties of kinship. Cousins are addressed using sibling terms, and there was a sense in which the villagers thought of the many kinship links that existed between them as being derived from siblingship.

Very gradually, I came to understand that for the Malay people I lived with, relatedness was not simply derived from ties of procreation. The emphasis on siblingship in any case suggested that filiation (ties between parents and children) might not provide the key to kinship. My own intense experience of being fostered in a Malay family, sharing their house and food, made me realize that one could become kin through living and eating together. For the Malays I lived with, kinship means sharing bodily substance, particularly blood. Blood itself is derived principally from the mother during the period when the fetus is nourished in her womb, and to a lesser extent from the father. It is also derived from the full rice meals that household members eat together. The frequency with which children are fostered either with relatives or with non-kin demonstrated that my own experience was by no means unique. The ties that come to exist between children and their foster families are thought to be particularly strong, and this is expressed both emotionally and physically. If they stay long enough, foster children are thought to come to physically resemble their foster parents in the same way as birth children. Indeed, people would often comment on changes to my physical appearance while I stayed in the village with obvious interest and approval, noting that my skin was becoming darker or that I was putting on weight.

My own understanding of the ideas I have described here was arrived at in the most gradual way. This involved, first of all, learning to look for kinship where it was made—in houses, by women. For it was women who were most heavily involved in the processes of kinship: in the labor activities that reproduce the house, cooking and feeding, having and nurturing children and foster children, arranging marriages, visiting other houses, and fulfilling responsibilities toward grandchildren. I had to learn that much of what I had been taught about "kinship" was of limited relevance to the Malay ideas I encountered.

But there was also clearly a sense in which making kinship was absolutely central to the lives of those I was living with. In order to highlight these indigenous ideas and to distinguish them from analytic debates about kinship, I found it helpful to think in terms of "relatedness" rather than kinship, and then to try to build up a picture of what this relatedness constituted from elementary principles. As I have made clear, the starting point for this endeavor was the neglected perspective of women and the "domestic," and its importance for kinship in general. Together with other late twentieth-century studies of kinship, this work can be positioned intellectually as, broadly, in a culturalist and post-Schneiderian tradition that is informed by current theoretical and ethnographic work on gender.

The Phoenix Rises from the Ashes

For a while, in the early 1980s, theoretical interest in kinship, as well as good studies of it, seemed very much on the decline. And yet, in spite of the iconoclastic tone of Schneider's critique and the impact it had, the contours of the discipline today seem in many ways remarkably unchanged. Students on the whole still learn their politics, religion, economics, and kinship in separate courses. It is true that in many cases kinship has been replaced by "kinship and gender," in deference to the idea that the domains of gender and kinship can no longer be considered in isolation from each other. But why has kinship remained on the agenda at all? One part of the answer is surely historical. Kinship has for so long been central to the discipline of anthropology that it seems impossible to teach the history of the subject without a specially devoted course. Another part of the answer can be related to the actual practice of ethnography.

The Malay case demonstrates how, whatever the intellectual baggage of particular fieldworkers, the course fieldwork takes is dictated as much by the preoccupations of those who are being studied as by those who are doing the studying. Many fieldworkers find themselves caught up in events and issues in quite unanticipated ways. It is also an obvious truth that in most—if not all—cultures, relationships between people considered to be close are of immense concern. In a larger sense, thinking about relatedness provides an indigenous idiom for theorizing about what holds people together in a given society. In this sense, relatedness is the everyday subject and object of much creative energy. As many have discovered, doing kinship is more or less unavoidable for the fieldworker.

There is a further reason for the fact that kinship has "phoenix-like . . . risen from its ashes," as Schneider put it in an interview published shortly before his death (Schneider and Handler 1995, 193). This once again relates to nonacademic concerns. In both America and Europe, the last decades of the twentieth century and the beginning of the twenty-first witnessed an intense and highly politicized debate about the nature of the family. Rising divorce rates and increasing numbers of women in full- or part-time employment have made the roles of mothers and fathers a subject of deep social concern. Abortion, adoption, homosexual rights, reproductive technologies, and child abuse have all become political issues, intensifying the debate about what the modern Western family should look and be like. It was paradoxical that the family should have been so much a matter of public concern at a time when anthropologists who might have been considered to have some expertise on matters of kinship were turning away from the subject. On the whole, sociologists and psychologists have taken a more prominent part in discussions on the ills afflicting the modern family than anthropologists.

Nevertheless, from the 1990s on, there were signs of a renaissance in the anthropological study of kinship. Incest, child abuse, abortion, gay kinship—all have been the subject of anthropological work. Debates on the ethical problems arising from the new reproductive technologies have focused on a number of issues, such as rights to knowledge of paternity and the nature of motherhood—does it reside in a genetic connection, in bearing and giving birth to a child, or in bringing up the child? Motherhood and fatherhood have ceased to be unitary or even given principles in Western kinship. These issues have reminded anthropologists that the difference between mothers and fathers, what being a mother or father consists of, and the "facts" of procreation have all been subjects of anthropological scrutiny since the nineteenth century (see Strathern 1992a; Edwards et al. 1999).

Recent studies of kinship in the West have been very much culturalist accounts. They have been influenced by Schneider, while painting a much more nuanced picture of how different people understand kinship in different ways than those represented in his study of American kinship. They have in turn enabled a further reflection on the nature of kinship in non-Western cultures in a fruitful comparative spirit—the hallmark of anthropology.

The Future of Kinship

Although Schneider's critique seemed to many to be the final nail in the coffin for the anthropological study of kinship, by the 1990s a resurgence was apparently under way. Paradoxically, it is clear that Schneider's work—however flawed one might consider it—has been part of the inspiration for this renaissance, as has the analytic concern with gender. The culturalist and feminist critiques made necessary—and also enabled—a reexamination of many anthropological assumptions about how kinship had been defined, and focused attention on indigenous understandings of kinship, including those of contemporary Western societies. New topics and themes in kinship studies have emerged alongside gender, and many of these have involved a more sustained examination of everyday life and the importance of women and children in practices of kinship. Notions of the person, bodily substance, the house, emotions, and feeding are very much on the agenda in the comparative study of kinship.

Anthropologists have increasingly turned their attention to the forms of kinship in the West. The old division between sociological studies of the family in the West and the anthropology of kinship in non-Western societies has, to a considerable extent, been eroded. Part of the reason for this is the heightened political debate about the nature of the family in the West that I referred to above. But the momentum for such studies has also been reinforced by fundamental changes in the global economy, and in labor relations. Recent work has thus sought to show the persistent significance of kinship *within* capitalist and postcapitalist relations of modernity (see, for example, McKinnon and Cannell 2013; Yanagisako 2002). Such work necessarily deconstructs the myth of a domain of the family insulated from the relations of production under capitalism, but it also attends to the counterpart of this myth—the largely unexamined premise that capitalist production itself was sealed off from the world of kinship. It thus builds on earlier feminist scholarship on the family, kinship, and labor.

Another significant impetus in recent research has been provided by innovations in medical technology in the fields of reproduction, organ transplantation, and genomics. Anthropologists have been able to show the relevance of their discipline to the emerging ethical and definitional issues that these technologies highlight. In examining technologically assisted aspects of procreation, anthropologists have drawn on an older comparative literature, but they have also illuminated some newer concerns.

One important theme in this new work has been the relation between the "biological" and the "social." Schneider's assertion that sexual procreation was not always and everywhere seen as the source of kinship ties disrupted this analytic distinction. Anthropologists had generally maintained that kinship studies began with the social recognition of kinship ties, and that actual biological ties were not their concern. Schneider and others highlighted the tensions involved in this distinction—what exactly was seen as biology, or where the distinction between biological and social was made might not be the same in all cultures. The "denaturalization" of presumed biological facts was also a prominent theme in feminist scholarship and in studies of gender.

It is not necessarily obvious what meaning a distinction between biological and social aspects of kinship would have in particular non-

Western contexts. In the Malay example I discussed above, kinship may be derived from procreative ties, but it can also be brought into being through living and eating together in one house. Nor is it immediately apparent which of these processes should be labeled "social" and which "biological"—or precisely what importance this distinction would have for those involved. In the West, too, detailed ethnographic studies of gay kinship (Weston 1991), or of the effects of prenatal diagnostic screening (Rapp 1999), show how the social, cultural, or technological may interfere with the presumed foundational significance of biology.

The work of Marilyn Strathern (1992a; 1992b) and others highlighted how advances in medical technology mean that what had previously been considered "natural" has been increasingly technologized and made a matter of consumer choice. Nature itself can no longer be taken for granted as a realm of the given rather than the made. And this has profound implications for the assumed givenness of kinship. Thus, not only procreation but also the division between the social and the biological, which is central to Western ideas about kinship and to scientific knowledge more generally, are likely to remain the subject of close examination in the years to come. New technological advances in biomedicine will continue to provide an important impetus for kinship studies, as will the persistent political salience of debates about the changing forms of family life in the West in the face of profound transformations to the global economy. As a recent work by Marshall Sahlins (2013) attests, biology is likely to remain on the agenda both for those who consider themselves social constructionists and relativists, and for those who advocate a new kind of universalistic agenda for kinship studies through evolutionary or cognitive psychology. While not all of this work necessarily makes explicit reference to gender, much of it has been fundamentally shaped by the feminist project of denaturalization of the so-called facts of life and of familial relations. Continued interest in all of these topics is likely to reinforce the value of a sustained anthropological commitment to the comparative study of kinship.

References

Bourdieu, Pierre. 1977. *Outline of a Theory of Practice*. Cambridge: Cambridge University Press.

Butler, Judith. 1993. *Bodies That Matter: On the Discursive Limits of "Sex."* New York: Routledge.

Carsten, Janet. 1997. *The Heat of the Hearth: The Process of Kinship in a Malay Fishing Community*. Oxford: Clarendon Press.

———. 2004. *After Kinship*. Cambridge: Cambridge University Press.

Collier, Jane Fishburne, and Sylvia Junko Yanagisako.1987. "Toward a Unified Analaysis of Gender and Kinship." In *Gender and Kinship: Essays toward a Unified Analysis*, eds. Jane Fishburne and Sylvia Junko Yanagisako, 14–50. Stanford, CA: Stanford University Press.

Edwards, Jeanette, Sarah Franklin, Eric Hirsch, Frances Price, and Marilyn Strathern. 1999. *Technologies of Procreation: Kinship in the Age of Assisted Conception.* 2nd ed. London: Routledge.

Engels, Frederick. (1884) 1972. *The Origin of the Family, Private Property and the State.* London: Lawrence and Wishart.

Errington, Shelly. 1990. "Recasting Sex, Gender and Power: A Theoretical and Regional Overview." In *Power and Difference: Gender in Island Southeast Asia*, ed. Jane Atkinson and Shelly Errington. Stanford, CA: Stanford University Press.

Fortes, Meyer. 1961. "Pietas in Ancestor Worship." *Journal of the Royal Anthropological Institute* 91:166–91.

———. 1969. *Kinship and the Social Order.* Chicago: Aldine.

———. 1983. *Oedipus and Job in West African Religion.* Cambridge: Cambridge University Press.

Goody, Jack. 1983. *The Development of the Family and Marriage in Europe.* Cambridge: Cambridge University Press.

———. 1990. *The Oriental, the Ancient and the Primitive: Systems of Marriage and the Family in Preindustrial Societies of Eurasia.* New York: Cambridge University Press.

Kuper, Adam. 1988. *The Invention of Primitive Society.* London: Routledge.

Lévi-Strauss, Claude. (1949) 1969. *The Elementary Structures of Kinship.* Rev. ed. Trans. James Harle Bell, John Richard von Sturmer, and Rodney Needham. Boston: Beacon.

Malinowski, Bronislaw. 1929. *The Sexual Life of Savages.* New York: Harcourt, Brace and World.

Mauss, Marcel. (1925) 1990. *The Gift: The Form and Reason for Exchange in Archaic Societies.* Trans. W. D. Halls. London: Routledge.

McKinnon, Susan. 2000. "Domestic Exceptions: Evans-Pritchard and the Creation of Nuer Patrilineality and Equality." *Cultural Anthropology* 15 (1): 35–83.

———. 2001. "The Economies in Kinship and the Paternity of Culture: Origin Stories in Kinship Theory." In *Relative Values: Reconfiguring Kinship Studies*, ed. Sarah Franklin and Susan McKinnon, 277–301. Durham, NC: Duke University Press.

McKinnon, Susan, and Fenella Cannell, eds. 2013. *Vital Relations: Modernity and the Persistent Life of Kinship.* Santa Fe, NM: School for Advanced Research Press.

Morgan, Lewis Henry. 1871. *Systems of Consanguinity and Affinity of the Human Family.* Washington, DC: Smithsonian Institution.

———. 1877. *Ancient Society: Researches in the Lines of Human Progress from Savagery through Barbarism to Civilization.* New York: Holt.

Onions, C. T., ed. 1966. *Oxford Dictionary of English Etymology.* Oxford: Oxford University Press.

Ortner, Sherry B. 1974. "Is Female to Male as Nature Is to Culture?" In *Woman, Culture and Society*, ed. Michelle Rosaldo and Louise Lamphere. Stanford, CA: Stanford University Press.

Rapp, Rayna. 1999. *Testing Women, Testing the Fetus: The Social Impact of Amniocentesis in America.* New York: Routledge.

Reiter, Rayna R., ed. 1975. *Towards an Anthropology of Women.* New York: Monthly Review Press.

Richards, A. I. 1950. "Some Types of Family Structure amongst the Central Bantu." In *African Systems of Kinship and Marriage,* ed. A. R. Radcliffe-Brown and Daryll Forde, 207–51. London: Oxford University Press.

Rosaldo, Michelle, and Louise Lamphere, eds. 1974. *Woman, Culture and Society.* Stanford, CA: Stanford University Press.

Rubin, Gayle. 1975. "The Traffic in Women: Notes on the 'Political Economy' of Sex." In Reiter 1975.

Sahlins, Marshall. 2013. *What Kinship Is—and Is Not.* Chicago: University of Chicago Press.

Schneider, David. M. 1980. *American Kinship: A Cultural Account.* 2nd ed. Chicago: University of Chicago Press.

———. 1984. *A Critique of the Study of Kinship.* Ann Arbor: University of Michigan Press.

Schneider, David M., and Richard R. Handler. 1995. *Schneider on Schneider: The Conversion of the Jews and Other Anthropological Stories.* Durham, NC: Duke University Press.

Smith, Raymond T. 1987. "Hierarchy and the Dual Marriage System in West Indian Society." In *Gender and Kinship: Essays toward a Unified Analysis* Collier, ed. Jane Fishburne and Sylvia Junko Yanagisako, 163–96. Stanford, CA: Stanford University Press.

Stack, Carol. 1974. *All Our Kin: Strategies for Survival in a Black Community.* New York: Harper & Row.

Strathern, Marilyn. 1992a. *Reproducing the Future: Essays on Anthropology, Kinship and the New Reproductive Technologies.* Manchester: Manchester University Press.

———. 1992b. *After Nature: English Kinship in the Late Twentieth Century.* Cambridge: Cambridge University Press.

Weston, Kath. 1991. *Families We Choose: Lesbians, Gays, Kinship.* New York: Columbia University Press.

Yanagisako, Sylvia Junko. 1979. "Family and Household: The Analysis of Domestic Groups." *Annual Review of Anthropology* 8:161–205.

———. 2002. *Producing Culture and Capital: Family Firms in Italy.* Princeton, NJ: Princeton University Press.

Yanagisako, Sylvia, and Carol Delaney, eds. 1995. *Nauralizing Power: Essays in Feminist Cultural Analaysis.* New York: Routledge.

10 :: LANGUAGE DEBORAH CAMERON

"Language" is not, on the face of things, an abstruse technical term, nor does gender studies have a special claim to "own" it. Its apparent simplicity and generality are deceptive, however, for in fact it is among the most confusing and controversial terms with which contemporary students of gender have to grapple.

Anyone who examines a random sample of the copious literature on language and gender produced since the 1970s will soon encounter statements that appear to be using the word *language* in radically different senses. In the literature of sociolinguistics, our hypothetical reader may encounter assertions like "women tend to lead in linguistic change"; in the writings of feminists influenced by Lacanian psychoanalysis, by contrast, she may come across the claim that "women are excluded from symbolic language." Are these statements talking about the same *language*?

In a word, no. For the linguist who makes the first statement, "language" refers to the kind of structural entity we name "English," "Japanese," or "Xhosa." From this perspective, to study language and gender means to investigate the ways in which the resources of particular languages like English or Japanese or Xhosa are used by their speakers to represent, display, construct, or perform gender identity and difference. For the Lacanian, by contrast, "language" is a more abstract concept. Saussure's idealized *langue,* for instance, is a system of meaningful contrasts through the acquisition of which human subjects are brought to take up their place in culture. In this model, we do not "speak language" (or *languages,* plural); language "speaks us."

The differences between the linguist and the Lacanian are sufficiently profound to make dialogue between them difficult; what one assumes as obvious, the other may regard as alien or even unintelligible. A sociolinguist who specializes in the microanalysis of women's talk, for example, will find claims that women are "excluded" from language not so much disputable as meaningless—comprehensible, if at all, only in metaphorical terms. A Lacanian critic, conversely, will hardly be persuaded to relinquish her claim just because someone plays her a recording of women talking. The Lacanian has not only a different notion of language from the linguist but a different notion of subjectivity and a different epistemology (theory of how we can know things and what counts as evidence for a given claim).

The linguist and the Lacanian critic stand here for broader intellectual tendencies. Linguistics (here, sociolinguistics) belongs to the tradition of empirical social science, Lacan to the tradition of what is loosely called "critical theory" or "poststructuralism." One of the main differences between these traditions precisely concerns the significance accorded to language. Poststructuralist thinking is marked by what is often described as a "linguistic turn." This "turn" is most easily understood as a turn away from seeing language as merely reflecting or naming preexisting states of affairs, and toward seeing it as *constitutive* of reality. From that perspective, "the way things are" is not independent of the way we speak and write about them; on the contrary, it is through speech and writing that we produce the categories that organize our world.

Yet although the study of language and gender as carried on by social scientists (not only linguists but also anthropologists, sociologists, and psychologists) remains "empirical"—in the sense of being grounded in detailed observations of language use in particular social contexts—it has not been unaffected by the "linguistic turn." Above, for instance, I suggested that sociolinguists were concerned with the way speakers "use" the resources of their languages to produce gender identity and difference. This formulation could be (and has been) criticized. It suggests that the speakers preexist the languages they "use," and that they exercise a high degree of agency in this use of linguistic resources. But one might raise questions about the degree of control speakers have over language: how far do they determine their own ways of speaking, and how far do already-established ways of speaking, as it were, determine them? In addition, I described the things speakers do with linguistic resources variously as *representing, displaying, constructing*, and *performing* gender. But it is evident that the choice of verb here makes a difference in our understanding of what is going on. Something "displayed" already exists, whereas something "constructed" is thereby brought into being. Largely because of the influence of critical theory and its linguistic turn on feminist scholarship in general, issues about the constitutive role of language, the agency of language users, and the way we understand their linguistic behavior (i.e., does it display, construct, or perform gender?) have come to be debated not only by critical theorists, but also among sociolinguists who study language and gender empirically.

Is Language "Sexist"?

For many people, what the conjunction of "language" and "gender" most readily calls to mind is the much-debated issue of "sexist language." Since at least the 1970s, feminists have advanced the argument that institutionalized conventions for writing and speaking systematically represent the sexes as different and not equal. (It should be noted that the concept of "language" underlying this claim is the linguist's concept mentioned above: it is "English" or "Japanese" or "Xhosa" that is said to be sexist.)

Discussions of sexism in language(s) have focused on two patterns in particular. One is androcentrism (male-centeredness). In English, for example, feminists point to the generic use of masculine personal pronouns ("the artist must be true to *his* vision") and the use of *man* to name the human species or as a suffix in occupational titles (chair*man,* sports*man*). The other salient pattern is the sexualization and derogation of terms that refer to women. *Mistress* has a sexual meaning that *master* does not; *spinster* is derogatory where *bachelor* is not. These two patterns are found in some form across a wide range of European and non-European languages. What they symbolize—and reproduce—is an implicit assumption that men are the universal human norm, whereas women are, in the eighteenth-century phrase, "the sex." Feminists have acted on this analysis of sexism in language by promoting a kind of linguistic reform or "language planning" that seeks to eliminate sexist conventions, replacing them either with gender-neutral alternatives (*athlete* instead of *sportsman,* say), or with paired terms intended to make women "visible" (sports*women* and sports*men.*) The first institutional guidelines on "nonsexist language" were issued by the publisher McGraw-Hill in 1973, and similar guidelines are now commonplace (which is not to say they are always fully complied with). Feminist language reform has typically been a practical rather than a purely academic concern, but it has also and inevitably raised theoretical issues about how language works, who (if anyone) controls it, and what relation it has to extralinguistic reality. Those issues have caused contention, not only between feminists and others but also among feminists themselves.

One theoretical argument turns on whether sexist conventions arise "naturally" in the course of language change (which is often figured as an "organic" process, like evolution), or whether they—like the feminist reforms that now oppose them—are conscious, ideologically motivated inventions. In the case of the English generic *man,* for instance, opponents of feminist language reform are fond of observing that it is the reflex of a genuine generic meaning "person," which contrasted in Old English with two sex-specific terms, *wæpman* (man) and *wifman* (woman).

The generic and the masculine forms have simply fallen together by an accident of language history. Analogous arguments have been advanced about *he* as a generic, but in this case an alternative explanation can be documented in some detail, since the English generic masculine was promoted assiduously by prescriptive grammarians. In many cases, they justified their selection on grounds not of its linguistic naturalness, but explicitly and specifically of its ideological appropriateness: the masculine, they argued, was "the worthier gender" in reality, and that should be reflected in language use.

At bottom, the argument here is about whether language is a phenomenon of nature or of culture: those who subscribe to the "nature" view regard it as futile or even sacrilegious to meddle in matters linguistic. Applied to the specific issue of sexist language, this argument acquires a particular resonance because of its homology with the familiar argument that sexual difference and inequality are themselves part of the "natural" order, as opposed to being mutable products of culture. Feminists are portrayed by these opponents as misguidedly attempting to change two things that are not amenable to their intervention and should not be subjected to it: the essential nature of men and women, and the language in which that essential nature is expressed or represented.

Other critics of feminist linguistic reform are cultural conservatives who base their opposition to change on the argument that languages are precious repositories of cultural tradition; deliberately departing from that tradition, then, is like desecrating an ancient monument. Yet other critics are (in the strict theoretical sense of the term) liberals, whose objection is not to the idea of language change as such, but rather to the idea of change being imposed for political ends by ideological zealots. Like George Orwell, who is often invoked in their writings, liberal critics worry that the real aim of politically motivated linguistic reform is not merely to change usage but to control or police thought.

In 1991 the *New York Times* took exception to a section on nonsexist language in a new edition of *Webster's Collegiate Dictionary*, which included among other items the term *waitron*, a gender-neutral alternative to *waiter/waitress*. The *Times* editorialized: "Such jarring usages ... confuse symptom and cause.... Words will change, without strain or contrivance, when attitudes change, in the minds of waitrons and patrons alike." This is a hybrid of the "natural" and the liberal positions, and it begs a number of questions. If it is "words" that change (rather than speakers who "contrive" to change them), the implication is that language has its own natural dynamic; but at the same time, language change is forecast to be a response to a cultural development, namely, a change in speakers' attitudes concerning gender relations. The position taken by the *Times* could be summed up in the proposition that language evolves (naturally) to meet the (cultural) needs of its speakers. But how exactly "language" does this is not explained.

The problem here is that commonplace phrases like "language change" and, indeed, "sexist language" tend to reify and mystify the phenomenon they refer to by obscuring the fact that what actually changes, or is sexist, is not "language," which has no independent agency, but the behavior of language users. It follows that waiting for a language to change itself, as the *Times* appears to recommend, is as pointless as waiting for a light bulb to change itself. One can argue about whether the bulb really needs replacing and who should put in the replacement, but if it is ever to be changed, there will have to be some active human intervention, or, as the *Times* would have it, "contrivance."

The *Times*'s charge that feminist language reformers "confuse symptom and cause" raises another vexed theoretical issue: is sexist language merely the expression of more fundamental sexist attitudes, or is it a key instrument whereby those attitudes are created and reproduced? In the 1970s and early 1980s, some feminist writers (notably Dale Spender, whose book *Man Made Language* first appeared in 1980) pursued the second line of argument, invoking the ideas of the mid-twentieth-century American linguists Edward Sapir and Benjamin Lee Whorf in support of it. The suggestion that what a community takes to be reality is "relative" to the categories provided by the grammar of its native language is known as the "Sapir-Whorf hypothesis of linguistic relativity." Sapir and Whorf used the idea to explore what struck them as sharp differences of perception between speakers of "standard average European" languages and indigenous American languages. After the Chomskyan revolution in linguistics, which placed emphasis on the universal properties of all natural languages, Whorfian ideas fell into disrepute; when feminists revived them it was in the service of an argument rather different from Whorf's. Spender's claim was not that men and women perceive reality differently because they speak different languages, but that both sexes inherit a "man-made language"; women are thus compelled to view the world through the lens of grammatical and semantic androcentrism.

This selective revival of Whorfian ideas for feminist purposes can be seen as one reflex of the linguistic turn in feminist scholarship—a tendency that in general looks more toward "continental" (that is, European, and especially French) poststructuralist thought. Whorfianism, like poststructuralism, gives language a constitutive role in the production of social reality and licenses the view that there is no "neutral" language. In the hands of a writer like Spender, or the linguist and science fiction novelist Suzette Haden Elgin (who went so far as to invent a "women's language"), Whorfianism also has a utopian element. Against the present dystopic situation, in which women are alienated in and by language, is set the possibility of eutopia, a language in which women's reality can finally be expressed. A similarly utopian tendency is readily discernible in feminist poststructuralist thinking. Theorists such as Luce Irigaray offer a view of women's present relation to language at least as dystopian as Spender's: language is not just imperfectly adapted to women, it excludes and denies them (e.g., Irigaray 1987). For some poststructuralist feminists, the eutopian alternative is *écriture féminine*, with its injunction to "write the [female] body."

The view that no language is neutral with regard to gender has exerted a powerful influence even on those feminists who reject utopian theorizing (e.g., Black and Coward 1998). It has not escaped their notice, either, that the nonneutrality argument can be deployed not only to indict the sexism of conventional usage but to criticize those feminist reform efforts whose goal is to substitute supposedly neutral terms for androcentric and sexist ones. Over time, feminists representing a range of theoretical and political positions have expressed increasing dissatisfaction with approaches that promote "gender neutral" terminology as a solution to the problem of sexism in language. As Anne Pauwels (1998) points out, the commonest strategy adopted has been "form replacement"; that is, a specific form (word, phrase, or morphological marker like the English suffix *-man*) is identified as "sexist" and is replaced in all contexts by an alternative deemed "nonsexist" or "neutral." This, however, overlooks the fact that formally neutral terms can be deployed in sexist ways. Let me give but one example. Following the US invasion of Panama in 1989, the then–US president George H. W. Bush was reported as saying, "We cannot tolerate attacks on the wife of an American citizen." He said nothing to indicate that the woman he referred to was not herself an American citizen, though no formal property of the word *citizen* excludes women from the category. In the terminology of nonsexist guidelines, *citizen* contrasts with, say, *serviceman* in being a "neutral" term. Yet Bush could construct a perfectly intelligible utterance in which he used *citizen* as if it referred only to men.

Conversely, an advertisement placed in newspapers by the pro-choice organization National Abortion and Reproductive Rights Action League (NARAL) described the choice to continue or terminate a pregnancy as "the most personal decision an American can make." Since men do not get pregnant, *American* here plainly means "American woman." By flouting the expectation that generic terms like *American* will be used either inclusively or androcentrically, but not exclusively in relation to women, NARAL made the point that women too are "Americans" and deserve the same legal rights and protections that other Americans—men—take for granted. This rhetorical strategy works only because readers understand that the formally gender-neutral word *American* can be used, and often has been used, in ways that exclude female referents.

Utterances like Bush's and NARAL's suggest that sexism might be better conceived not as a property of some finite set of linguistic forms but as an effect of the way linguistic forms are deployed in *discourse* (which may be glossed for my purposes here as "language used in some context for some purpose"). The usual targets for reform, such as generic *he* and *man,* are cases in which a sexist meaning has become fossilized. In the same way that frequently used metaphors may in time become formulaic clichés, so certain habits of language use may become institutionalized as invariant grammatical conventions. But just as not all metaphors are dead metaphors, not all sexist utterances involve the use of words or grammatical rules that are categorically sexist. The word *citizen,* for example, does not invariably have the meaning "male citizen"; and there would be nothing anomalous about my announcing that "Claire and John are both American citizens," whereas "Claire and John are both chairmen of their departments" is anomalous and "Claire and John are both men" even more so. An illuminating analysis of sexist language cannot begin and end with the "fossil" cases any more than an illuminating analysis of metaphor can deal exclusively with clichés.

The point that we must look at sexist *discourse* if we wish to shed light on the narrower phenomenon of "sexist language" has also been belabored by feminists who see the apparent failure of certain reforms to work as they were supposed to. For example, English-speaking feminists proposed to replace the two female titles *Miss* and *Mrs.* with a single title, *Ms.,* which would be unmarked for marital status and thus symmetrical with the single male title *Mr.* The proposal has succeeded in the sense that *Ms.* is widely used, but it has failed in the sense that many people still do not use it in the way the reformers intended. Some speakers use it for all women, others not at all, but in the middle is a significant group of speakers who seem to have replaced the binary married/unmarried opposition with a three-way distinction in which *Ms.* denotes "anomalous" categories: older unmarried women, divorced women, lesbians, and militant feminists who reject conventional marital relations. The intention was to get rid of marital status distinctions, but the effect has been to create more of them.

As this example demonstrates, the meanings of terms are determined neither by the intentions of their originators nor by what it says in dictionaries and guidelines on correct usage: meaning is ongoingly constructed in *discourse,* the communicative behavior of real people in real social situations. If a certain semantic distinction or category remains salient in the worldview of real people, attempts to get rid of it by erasing its formal linguistic trace will fail. The system will be reconstructed in discourse using the linguistic material to hand. This suggests, *contra* Whorf and his feminist enthusiasts, that there are limits on the potential for language change in and of itself to alter the way language users categorize reality. To that extent, the *New York Times* editorial discussed earlier has a valid point: speakers' attitudes do affect the uptake of a proposed change. But the success or failure of any given reform still depends on what speakers *do* with language: they, not "the language," are the arbiters of meaning and the agents of change.

The theorizing that underpins nonsexist language guidelines and the utopianism of Lacanian or Whorfian ideas may appear very different, but from the perspective adopted by some feminist linguists they have something important, and problematic, in common. Both tend to treat language too much as a free-floating abstract system, paying too little attention to the matrix of social activities and relationships in which language use and language learning are always in fact embedded. Language is either taken to reflect something more fundamental (as in the *Times* editorial) or elevated to the position of the most fundamental "cause" of women's subordination. The alternative would be to argue that our habits of language use emerge alongside (not prior to, nor after) our habits of thought and action; these habits are constantly and mutually shaping one another. Planned change is most likely to produce politically consequential effects when it works on all of them simultaneously—when, for example, institutional nonsexist language guidelines are promulgated not in isolation *from* but in tandem *with* initiatives to change women's position in other ways.

Though ways of speaking and writing (and of thinking and behaving) do preexist individual language users—we are never in the position of inventing our language from scratch—this does not necessarily license the very strong claims of linguistic determinism implied by the formula that language "speaks us." More exactly, though language does in one sense "speak us," we also speak it: the relation is dialectical. Meanings are neither fixed for all time nor so plastic that anyone can change them by fiat; rather, they are contested, and struggled over in countless exchanges among individuals (see, e.g., McConnell-Ginet 2011). Individuals do not, of course, have untrammeled power (the production of meaning cannot be a purely private and subjective process), but such agency as we acknowledge in relation to language change should certainly be attributed to speakers and not to "the language itself."

What Is It to Speak as a Woman or as a Man?

Debates on "sexist language" focus on our ways of speaking and writing *about* women and men. But in societies that categorize persons by sex/gender, we are also obliged to speak or write *as* women and men. Language use is one of the activities in which we gender ourselves and one another, and a great deal of discussion of "language" in gender studies has revolved around alternative ways of understanding that process. What does it mean to speak as a woman or as a man? Is it possible to speak as neither, or as both?

The observation that women and men in various societies have characteristically different ways of speaking goes back a long way. It occurs, for example, in writings produced by European travelers to the New World from the sixteenth century on, who were struck by the marked linguistic gender differentiation they observed among "savage" peoples. It was recognized that analogous differences existed in European societies too, though these seemed to European observers less extreme. Well before the emergence of feminist research on language, some linguistic scholars attempted to analyze male-female speech differences as a general phenomenon. Probably the best-remembered of the prefeminist commentators is Otto Jespersen, who included in his 1922 book *Language: Its Nature, Development and Origin* a now notorious chapter titled "The Woman" (reprinted in Cameron 1998). This is an odd compendium of personal observations, recycled travelers' tales, and sweeping generalizations about women's "instinctive" shrinking from coarse language and their distinctive "periods" (i.e., sentences), which Jespersen compares to a string of pearls joined together with "and"; men, by contrast, are credited with the ability to form subordinate clauses. But while Jespersen may have been a male chauvinist, he was not a biological determinist. The main conclusion of his chapter is that male-female differences in the use of language reflect the sexual division of labor and other role differentiations within a given culture.

The first sustained analysis of gendered language use written from a feminist perspective, Robin Lakoff's *Language and Woman's Place* (1975), has continuities with Jespersen's "The Woman." Lakoff proposed the existence, alongside what she called "neutral language," of a "women's language" (WL) whose use connoted femininity (or in men, effeminacy). Among the characteristics of WL, Lakoff listed superpoliteness, the use of mild expletives (and the avoidance of strong ones), empty and trivial lexical elaboration (an extensive vocabulary of color terms, for instance), tag questions of the "It's a nice day, isn't it?" variety, and rising intonation on declarative sentences. These were not random choices: Lakoff argued that all had the function of making a speaker sound deferential, weak, and unsure of herself—in short, powerless. Nor was it unreflective androcentrism on Lakoff's part to counterpoise "women's language" to "neutral language" rather than "men's language." She was, precisely, asserting that women's language is "marked"—a deviation from the norm—and that this reflects the status, in male-dominated societies, of men as the default category of persons while women are "the sex." She argued that women are faced with a painful choice: to use neutral language and be perceived as unfeminine, or to use women's language and be perceived as, in important respects, less than human.

Lakoff's essay prompted a rush to empirical investigation of the "women's language" hypothesis (*Language and Woman's Place* was an "armchair" work, based on Lakoff's intuitions about usage in her own social milieu). The results, often inconclusive or contradictory, could be summed up by saying that not all women speakers use WL and not all speakers who use WL are women. It is evident, moreover, that Lakoff had in mind a particular group of women (white, straight, monolingual, belonging to the professional class), whereas femininities come in many other varieties. But criticisms of Lakoff based on the empirical inadequacy of her proposals arguably miss an important point: "women's language" is not necessarily best understood as "the language actually used by women" (or even "by *some* women"). It might better be understood as a *symbolic* category, a cluster of linguistic features invested with culturally recognizable meanings that real speakers may draw on in order to "index" femininity.

These speakers need not be "real" (in the sense of anatomical/genetic) women. Interestingly, it seems that male-to-female (MTF) transgendered individuals are avid consumers of advice on how to inhabit their chosen gender linguistically that is based on Lakoff's delineation of WL (see Cameron and Kulick 2003). Another group of people whose behavior in certain contexts conforms unusually closely to Lakoff's description are the telephone sex workers studied by the linguist Kira Hall (1995). Their job is to produce, using only the resources of language and voice, a version of femininity whose erotic charms male customers are willing to pay for, and they find something like WL particularly appropriate for the purpose. One of the skilled performers interviewed by Hall was a man, and many others were women whose "real" identities did not match the white, Anglo, middle-class, heterosexual femininity of which WL is most obviously symbolic. What is going on in these cases is not the linguistic expression of some preexisting, authentic self, but a calculated performance. Furthermore, what the performance involves is not a faithful imitation of an empirically observed model (the "average" woman does not talk in the way the telephone sex workers do), but rather an appropriation and recirculation of culturally salient meanings. Analogizing it to a drag act, Hall calls this "cross-expressing."

Hall's study of sex workers belongs to a recent current in sociolinguistics and linguistic anthropology that is influenced by Judith Butler's notion of gender as "performative"—not a pregiven identity that is merely reflected or expressed in our behavior, but something that has to be accomplished in repeated acts of self-stylization (Butler 1991). Sociolinguists who adopt this view are apt to point out that the term "performative" comes in the first place from the study of language (specifically, from the philosophical writing on language of J. L. Austin). The prototypical performative act is a speech act, an utterance like "I apologize" or "I hereby declare this meeting closed" that does something *in* the world as opposed to just saying something *about* the world. It therefore seems appropriate to consider speaking as one of the most fundamental activities in which people constantly and repeatedly perform gender (that is, bring it into existence, accomplishing it). The applicability of this account is most obvious when we consider the conscious performances of the sex workers, or of people who are trying to "pass," but in principle it is also applicable to more "ordinary" cases.

Butler's work represents a variant of queer theory, and one of the possibilities opened up by that paradigm is that decoupling gender from sex might pave the way for a culture that recognizes a multiplicity of genders rather than just two. Applied to language, this proposal would imply that "speaking as a woman" and "speaking as a man" are not the only alternatives. Recently, some linguists have looked for evidence of other possible speaking positions in the linguistic self-styling practices of gay, lesbian, and transgendered speakers. However, they have tended to find either attempts to adopt as fully as possible the speaking position associated with the "target" gender (a strategy recommended to MTF transsexuals in particular, as noted above) or performances that mix "feminine" and "masculine" elements. This produces a distinctive style but without radically disturbing the binary gender system, since the ingredients of the style have been coded within that system and retain their gendered meaning.

Cases of "mixed" performance often occur where people do not identify with one gender exclusively and mobilize linguistic resources (such as personal pronouns and gender markers on adjectives or verbs) to switch between masculine and feminine self-stylizations. Their performance of gender is not consistent over time, but at any given moment they are indexing either masculinity or femininity and not something else entirely. (An example of this phenomenon is provided by Hindi-speaking Indian hijras—eunuchs, locally regarded as a "third sex"—on whom, see Hall and O'Donovan 1996.) A different strategy is described by Robin Queen (1997) in her analysis of the characteristic style of North American lesbian comic books, where characters' lesbian identities are indexed by juxtaposing maximally incongruous stereotypical gender markers: cursing (masculine, working class) may be combined with hedging and rising intonation (feminine, middle class) in the same chunk of dialogue. Like the hijras' use of grammatical gender markers, this strategy depends for its effect on our recognition that X is "feminine" and Y is "masculine." There is no third option, Z, that is not already coded within the binary gender system.

That, of course, is not surprising, given that, as I remarked before, we are never in a position to invent an entirely new language. It does, however, raise a question of some import for feminists. Queer theory has a tendency to celebrate the crossing of gender boundaries and the mixing of gendered messages as both individually liberating and politically subversive. But feminists might object that the gender codes in play here are invested with meanings not merely of masculinity and femininity but of dominance and subordination. Femininity is not constituted in language by some arbitrary collection of linguistic features, but by a cluster of features that connote *powerlessness*. If that point is granted, individuals may be in some sense "liberated" by their use of "women's language"—Kira Hall's telephone sex workers, for instance, make what they consider a good living out of it—but it is more difficult to argue that their performance subverts the established power structure. Indeed, one could argue that the sex workers are actively reproducing that structure, and individually advantaging themselves, therefore, at the expense of women as a class.

Against this, the argument for cross-expressing as subversion is that *citations* of existing cultural codes—for example, stereotypically feminine speech produced by a trans-woman—do not just reproduce what is being cited without alteration. The context (time, place, occasion, speaker) is novel, and the meaning of a linguistic act is always context-dependent. Citation of a stereotype does reproduce that stereotype but, by placing it in a different frame, potentially makes evident that it *is* a stereotype, and so tends to undermine conventional belief in the naturalness of gendered behavior. The denaturalization of gender (and in particular its uncoupling from biological sex) is a goal shared by feminists and queer theorists, but arguably for rather different reasons, which suggests a potential tension between queer and feminist language politics. The ultimate target of feminist critique is not ideologies of natural difference per se; rather, it is the power relations those ideologies help to maintain. Denaturalizing gender is therefore a means to an end rather than an end in itself; the end, moreover, is not to free up masculinity and femininity so that anyone regardless of sex can identify with either position, or both. If you believe that gender is actually produced (like class) by one group's exploitation of another, then the end of exploitation entails the destruction of gender as we know it—in which case no citation of existing gender norms can be sufficiently radical.

The relation between language and power has been a contentious issue in gender studies. Early feminist work, following on from Lakoff, emphasized that the observed differences between women's and men's ways of speaking were not just there to distinguish the two genders but also to facilitate the domination of one by the other. For instance, research on heterosexual couples' domestic conversation showed that women asked more questions aimed at eliciting talk from men and provided more backchannel cues for their interlocutors to go on talking (Fishman 1983). This difference does not seem arbitrary: there is an obvious and compelling link with the broader social pattern whereby women provide all kinds of domestic and personal services to men rather than vice versa. If the function of male-female differences in linguistic behavior were simply to distinguish men from women, if we were dealing with something like the way men's coats button in the opposite direction from women's (the only point of which is to announce the gender of the garment's intended owner), then we would expect to find at least some differences that could not be explained in terms of male privilege and female subordination. Many feminists have argued, however, that this is not, in fact, what we do find; the evidence points to a link between difference and dominance.

A challenge to this position came from feminists who proposed in the 1980s that gender differences in language use should be approached in the same way as ethnic or national differences, and talk between men and women treated as a form of "intercultural" communication, which is liable to go wrong less because of inequality between the parties (though that may exacerbate other difficulties) than because of conflicting expectations that lead to misunderstanding. (This approach was popularized through the writing of the interactional linguist Deborah Tannen, whose book *You Just Don't Understand* was a best-seller in the early 1990s.) It is argued that men and women acquire their ways of speaking as children, and largely through interaction in single-sex peer groups. Boys' peer groups are larger than girls', are organized more hierarchically, and require their members to compete for status. Girls' groups operate with a more egalitarian ethos that emphasizes intimacy and connection. Girls and boys thus develop quite different notions of what conversation is for and what norms apply to it. When later they begin to form significant relations with one another, the gendered understandings they bring to interaction come into conflict. A man will assume that a woman's utterance means what he would mean by it, and that she expects the kind of answer he would expect, and vice versa. The result is that men and women often talk at cross-purposes, having misread each other's intentions. Tannen (1994) suggests that those feminists who explain men's linguistic behavior as a form of dominance are making a similar error of interpretation, imputing to men the intention to dominate women when in fact their behavior with women just replicates what is normal among their equals, other men. Just as one would not argue that, say, Japanese interactional norms are preferable to Israeli ones, but would tend to advocate a policy of mutual understanding and tolerance, so one should not criticize either men or women for ways of speaking that are part of their identities—and in Tannen's view only minimally susceptible to change.

One objection to the "gender difference is cultural difference" thesis turns on the point I mentioned above, that the differences under discussion cannot convincingly be represented as arbitrary in terms of their symbolic meaning and real-world effects. Even if we accepted the generalizations made about male and female speech patterns by the "cultural difference" theorists—many of which have, in fact, been challenged by more recent empirical research (e.g., Goodwin 2006 on girls; Way 2011 on boys)—we would surely have to ask if it is a random coincidence that boys' peer groups produce competitive or status-oriented speakers while girls' peer groups produce cooperative, connection-oriented ones. Could the opposite as easily have been the case? Or does the *content* of this difference have something to do with traditional expectations of men and women, that they will exert influence in the public and the domestic sphere, respectively? If so, the analogy between gender and ethnicity or nationality is misleading. Japanese and Israelis differ from one another, but their habitual ways of behaving have not been designed specifically to *complement* one another within a social order and an institution (marriage) that is premised on hierarchy as well as difference.

Another objection, ironically, is that the "culture" approach is insufficiently sensitive to cultural differences. Who are these "men" and "women" it talks about? What language(s) do they speak, what country do they live in, what class and ethnic group do they belong to? Are they all heterosexual? Are they all exactly the same? Overall, the large body of research literature whose subject is the speech of men and women is vulnerable to the criticism that most of what it has to tell us concretely applies to an extremely narrow segment of the groups it purports to discuss. The ethnographic literature provides some striking counterexamples to the thesis that men compete and women cooperate, and indeed to every other general thesis proposed about men's and women's language since 1975. If the notion of "speaking as a woman" or "as a man" is meaningful at all, it surely cannot refer to some timeless, universal, socially undifferentiated category of womanhood/manhood. Even within one cultural milieu, no one speaks only "as a woman" or "as a man": gender inflects and is inflected by other categories of identity.

Jespersen's "The Woman" introduces the reader to men and women from widely disparate cultures and historical periods: here are hunter-gatherers in Africa, there Caribs in the Lesser Antilles in the 1600s, while over there Copenhagen housewives rub shoulders with female characters from nineteenth-century English novels. From this mass (or mess) of data, Jespersen set out to extract some coherent account of what it was to speak as a woman and, to a lesser extent, as a man. His impulse was to generalize, synthesize, and universalize—or as today's scholars, influenced by poststructuralist and postmodernist theory might put it, to homogenize, totalize, and essentialize. With few exceptions, linguists who study gender today have given up on Jespersen's project, preferring to investigate particular women and men speaking in particular contexts on particular occasions. Grand narratives about women's and men's language do persist, but nowadays their home is on the popular psychology shelf and not in the academic library.

Gender, Language, and Silence

The account I have given of the debate on sexist language and of ideas about what it is to speak as a woman or man might suggest that the history of the term *language* in gender studies is one of increasing complication. I will end this essay by illustrating the point through a brief examination of feminist approaches to a phenomenon that has attracted much discussion among language and gender scholars: *silence.*

A common perception among post-1968 feminists has been that silence is in some sense *the opposite of* language, that it denotes the absence of speech or, more generally, of communication. As such, it is also associated with the subaltern position of women and with the feminine ideal that epitomizes that subalternity, that is, that denial of access to language is an important aspect of women's oppression, and the silence—or silencing—of women symbolizes that denial. As evidence, feminists have adduced the tradition of folk-wisdom that complains of women's loquacity, the regularity with which conduct books and other literature for the guidance of women warned them to be silent, and such canonical statements as Saint Paul's "The woman should be silent in church." Early travel writing and modern anthropological literature are likewise full of examples of women's speech being forbidden in certain situations (outside their own houses, say, or in public gatherings or on ritual occasions), while as late as the early nineteenth century in America it was scandalous for a woman to speak publicly in front of a mixed audience (Bean 2006). Feminist consciousness-raising, writing, and political action have regularly been figured as "breaking the silence." Not surprisingly, then, an early concern of language and gender studies was to investigate the ways in which women were silent or silenced. Proposals ranged from the highly theoretical, for example, Cora Kaplan's (1986) Lacanian account of women's internalizing a prohibition on rhetorical or "high" language, to the claims made by researchers like Candace West and Don Zimmerman (1983) and Pamela Fishman (1983) that women were frequently reduced to silence when men interrupted them or failed to listen to them. This discourse was organized around a series of simple oppositions and parallels: speech/silence, men/women, power/powerlessness, good/bad.

But views of silence have since been complicated in ways that are characteristic of scholarly discourse on language and gender more generally. It is acknowledged, for instance, that the simple opposition between speech and silence is flawed; silence, too, communicates, and in that sense is part of language. Like any communicative act, however, silence has the potential to mean many things, not just the one feminists initially focused on, namely, submission. Silence may indicate submission, but it can also betoken resistance. To remain silent under torture, to refuse to speak in the confessional, to withhold words of love or cries of pain from someone whose desire for them oppresses you—these are strategies of resistance, of power more than powerlessness. The meaning and value of silence, moreover, is variable across cultures and contexts. The silence of a boring seminar is different from the silence of a Quaker meeting. The silence of a worker or servant being scolded by a boss or master may communicate a mixture of deference and contempt—enough contempt, say, to make the master uncomfortable, but not enough that the master can criticize his subordinate's demeanor as contemptuous rather than deferential.

The general point here concerns the complexity of meaning, and the difficulty of maintaining any kind of analysis that is not sensitive to that complexity. The way "language" was understood by feminists in early critiques of sexism and early accounts of women's speech posited simple and unitary correspondences of form and meaning: some words were "sexist," others "neutral"; women's use of a particular linguistic feature, like the tag question, could be read as expressing a single invariant trait, like insecurity. Acknowledging that language is not a fixed code makes the interpretation of linguistic data more dependent on an understanding of the whole context in which people are speaking (or being silent). It shifts the focus of investigation away from global generalizations about language and gender, and foregrounds questions about the processes through which meaning is locally constructed—which are also, from many current theoretical perspectives, the processes through which gender is constructed. It encourages scholars to be more reflexive about our own meaning-making and gendering processes: to ask, for instance, how we came to construct silence as meaning femininity and powerlessness. The point is not to deny that it *does* mean those things—among others— but to understand meaning as an effect of cultural processes, including our own theorizing.

The linguistic anthropologist Susan Gal (1991) has suggested that the silence so often attributed to women, especially non-Western women, may in many cases be not their own silence so much as the silence of Western scholarship *about* them. When an investigator describes the women of community X as silent, the investigator might mean no more than "they did not talk to me." Another linguistic anthropologist, Don Kulick, observes that women can be "rendered mute by the types of talk we choose to analyze" (1993, 512). Kulick is discussing the literature on conflict talk across cultures, which has tended to concentrate on forums in which conflicts are resolved, and from which women are often excluded. His own article concerns women (in New Guinea) who belie the stereotype that women avoid conflict; such women challenge Western preconceptions about language and gender, but Western scholars' preference for studying conflict *resolution* has often prevented them from noticing that.

I choose this example because the irony is so obvious: belief in women's silence may lead scholars to act in ways that actually silence women; belief in women's distaste for open conflict may be maintained because the investigators themselves find conflict distasteful. But the example illustrates a much more general point. Here we might recall the feminist argument against generic uses of *man*: they conceal difference and make one group of people (men) the prototype for all. Trinh Minh-ha (1998) extends the same argument to uses of *woman* in feminist discourse: it purports to be inclusive but prototypically refers only to "first-world" women. And the argument could also be extended to *language*, an English word whose meaning is both abstract/generic and concrete/specific (cf. "the human language faculty," "the Japanese language," "the language you and I are using right now"). In the study of language and gender, the danger of thinking about "language" in abstract and generic terms is that we will, indeed, render many speakers "mute," not because they do not speak, but because their ways of speaking and meaning are not intelligible within the framework of our implicit prototype.

Feminists today are careful to speak of "women," not "woman," of "femininities and masculinities" in the plural, of gender itself as a nonunitary phenomenon. This pluralizing and particularizing has been encouraged by, among other developments, the linguistic turn of poststructuralism and postmodemism. And yet there is a sense in which this "turn" has had the *opposite* effect in relation to "language." Theorists warn against "totalizing fictions," but their abstract, all-encompassing (and invariably singular) notion of language looks remarkably like one. In the same way that gender has come to be seen as a process rather than a fixed state, we need to shift our focus away from the mythical, unitary "language" and toward ways of speaking/signing/writing, conceived also as processes. That will enable us to ask not "How do women/men speak?" or "How does language speak [of] women and men?" but something more like "How, in a given context, do these two processes, gender and language using, interrelate to produce 'women' and 'men'?"

To be sure, this line of inquiry will not produce user-friendly conceptual categories like "sexist language" and "women's language," let alone such popular rallying cries as "Men are from Mars, Women are from Venus." But perhaps it is ultimately more enlightening to put language under a microscope than to squint at it through a telescope.

References

Bean, Judith Mattson. 2006. "Gaining a Public Voice: An Historical Perspective on American Women's Public Speaking." In *Speaking Out: The Female Voice in Public Contexts*, ed. Judith Baxter. Houndmills, Basingstoke: Palgrave-Macmillan.

Black, Maria, and Rosalind Coward. 1998. "Language, Social and Sexual Relations" (1981). In *The Feminist Critique of Language: A Reader*, 2nd ed., ed. Deborah Cameron. New York: Routledge.

Butler, Judith. 1991. *Gender Trouble: Feminism and the Subversion of Identity*. New York: Routledge.

Cameron, Deborah, ed. 1998. *The Feminist Critique of Language: A Reader*. 2nd ed. New York: Routledge.

Cameron, Deborah, and Don Kulick. 2003. *Language and Sexuality*. Cambridge: Cambridge University Press.

Fishman, Pamela. 1983. "Interaction: The Work Women Do." In *Language, Gender and Society*, ed. Barrie Thorne, Cheris Kramarae, and Nancy Henley. Rowley, MA: Newbury House.

Gal, Susan. 1991. "Between Speech and Silence: The Problematics of Research on Language and Gender." In *Gender at the Crossroads of Knowledge*, ed. Micaela di Leonardo. Berkeley: University of California Press.

Goodwin, Marjorie Harness. 2006. *The Hidden Life of Girls: Games of Stance, Status and Exclusion*. Malden, MA: Blackwell.

Hall, Kira. 1995. "Lip Service on the Fantasy Lines." In *Gender Articulated: Language and the Socially Constructed Self,* ed. Kira Hall and Mary Bucholtz. New York: Routledge.

Hall, Kira, and Veronica O'Donovan. 1996. "Shifting Gender Positions among Hindi-speaking Hijras." In *Rethinking Language and Gender Research,* ed. Victoria Bergvall, Janet Bing, and Alice Freed. London: Longman.

Irigaray, Luce. 1987. "L'ordre sexuel du discours." *Langages,* no. 85: *Le sexe linguistique.*

Kaplan, Cora. 1986. "High Language and Women's Silence." In *Sea Changes: Culture and Feminism.* London: Verso.

Kulick, Don. 1993. "Speaking as a Woman: Structure and Gender in Domestic Arguments in a New Guinea Village." *Cultural Anthropology* 8 (4): 510–41.

Lakoff, Robin. 1975. *Language and Woman's Place.* New York: Harper & Row.

McConnell-Ginet, Sally. 2011. *Gender, Sexuality and Meaning.* New York: Oxford University Press.

Pauwels, Anne. 1998. *Women Changing Language.* London: Longman.

Queen, Robin. 1997. "'I Don't Speak Spritch': Locating Lesbian Language." In *Queerly Phrased: Language, Gender and Sexuality,* ed. Anna Livia and Kira Hall. New York: Oxford University Press.

Spender, Dale. 1980. *Man Made Language.* London: Routledge and Kegan Paul.

Tannen, Deborah. 1990. *You Just Don't Understand.* New York: Morrow.

———. 1994. *Gender and Discourse.* New York: Oxford University Press.

Trinh Minh-ha. 1998. "Difference: A Special Third World Women's Issue." In Cameron 1998.

Way, Niobe. 2011. *Deep Secrets: Boys' Friendships and the Crisis of Connection.* Cambridge, MA: Harvard University Press.

West, Candace, and Don Zimmerman. 1983. "Small Insults: A Study of Interruptions in Cross-Sex Conversations between Unacquainted Persons." In *Language, Gender and Society,* ed. Barrie Thome, Cheris Kramarae, and Nancy Henley. Rowley, MA: Newbury House.

11 :: LOVE

My essay on desire (chapter 3) mainly focuses on the organization of
the drives into object-anchored desires, orientations, and styles of relating. Explanations of desire are organized by various psychoanalytic
accounts of attachment, identity, and affect, and the recent history of
their importance in critical theory and practice is briefly recounted. This
entry, on love, begins with an excursion into fantasy, moving away from
the familial scene of psychoanalysis and examining the encounter of unconscious fantasy with the theatrical or scenic structure of normative
fantasy. Whether viewed psychoanalytically, institutionally, or ideologically, in this essay love is deemed always an outcome of fantasy. Without
fantasy, there would be no love. There would be no way to move through
the uneven field of our ambivalent attachments to our sustaining objects, which possess us and thereby dispossess us of our capacity to idealize ourselves or them as consistent and benign simplicities. Without
repairing the cleavages, fantasy makes it possible not to be destroyed by
all that.

We will pursue different notions of love by way of some of the workings of romance in personal life and commodity culture, the places where
subjects learn to populate fantasy with foundational material for building worlds and lives.

Fantasy

Foucault's vision of a noninstitutionalized mode of pleasure untethered
to symbolization or norms brings us to a final form desire is said to take
in psychoanalytic theory. This is the concept of *fantasy*. What Freudians
and Lacanians mean by fantasy is not what one might expect. In popular
culture, fantasy is a dreamy narrative that brackets realism and, without entirely departing from it, connects up a desiring subject with her
ideal or nightmare object. In Freudian psychoanalysis, by contrast, fan-

tasy takes the shape of unconscious wishes that invest images with the force of their ordering impulse and, in certain instances, converts them into objects and symptoms. Jean Laplanche and Jean-Bertrand Pontalis (1973) then move through Lacan to call fantasy the *setting* for desire's enactment, a setting in which desire gets caught up in sequences of image and action that are not the same thing as their manifest representation (de Lauretis 1994; Kaplan 1986).

To comprehend fantasy, then, we need to move between unconscious structurations of desire and the conventions meant to sanitize them into an intention. After all, the fundamental gift-message of modern popular culture—"You are not alone—pretends that this fact is a simple relief. Yet we know that this gift is overwhelming and often at odds with itself. It at once valorizes the subject's uniqueness and her general qualities, it asserts that she is deserving of a kind of pleasure that feels like recognition and transformation, and it distributes a sense that she is sovereign yet dependent on her objects to achieve that aim, among other things. The whole cluster of tendencies is fulfilled in all sorts of action films, whether the tenor of survival is at a large or small scale. If we think of romance as a genre of action film in which the need to survive is played out through a series of dramatic pursuits, actions, and pacifications, then the romance plot's setting for fantasy can be seen as less merely conventional and more about the plotting of intensities that hold up a world that the unconscious deems worth living in.

Take, for example, the work marketed as "the greatest love story of all time," Margaret Mitchell's *Gone with the Wind*. Readers of this novel (1936) and viewers of its film adaptation (1939) typically see the relation of Scarlett O'Hara and Rhett Butler as the perfection of romantic fantasy because each meets a passionate match in the other and because, even though their great love fails, it *is* a great love that stands the test of time and marks the lovers permanently (Taylor 1989). It does not matter that the man understands the woman entirely, while the woman has no clue about herself or him: indeed, Rhett is a better man *and* woman than Scarlett. *Gone with the Wind* may stretch gender norms in the characters' pursuit of economic and romantic aims, but the novel maintains throughout the romantic rule that gives license to the man, who wears it as physical and psychological superiority. (This pattern of the representing the women as a chaotic life force requiring education and the discipline of men who know both themselves and women better than they do continues into the present as a feminist impasse in the television series *Girls* [2012–present] and the Richard Linklater trilogy *Before Sunrise* [1995], *Before Sunset* [2004], and *Before Midnight* [2013].)

But a scene- and sense-oriented reading of the fantasy at play in *Gone with the Wind* might suggest that desire is played out in a *compulsion to repeat* variations on a fantasy tableau: a tableau of mutual love at first sight that always leads to a circuit of passionate battle, seduction, disappointment, and desire (in this case, because whenever one lover feels love the other feels hard or defensive). The elaboration of this core in a spectacular epic tale of romance, devastation, and survival set against the backdrop of the American Civil War, and especially Sherman's scorched-earth march through the South, then mirrors the personal plot in the political one. All of this suggests that in *Gone with the Wind* heterosexual romance and sovereign nationality require fantasy to work its magic on subjects, generating an optimism that both plays out ambivalence and disavows complexity. The story narrates the compulsion to repeat as a relation between a sensual utopia (here, the Confederacy, romantic intimacy) and a jumble of obstacles that must be narratively mastered so that the utopia might be approached once again. *The scene of desire and the obstacles to it become eroticized, rather than the love that seems to motor it.* "Tomorrow is another day," the text's famous platitude, converts the fantasy scene of love for persons and worlds into a scene of the love of cliché, of repetition itself.

This kind of interpretive shift, from couple-oriented desire to the erotics of a scene of encounter with the fantasy, requires repositioning the desiring subject as a *spectator* as well as a participant in her scene of desire, and suggests a kind of doubleness the subject must have in her relation to pursuing her pleasure. John Berger (1972) has suggested one version of this relation of doubleness: because women are the primary objects of sexualization in heterosexual culture, they learn to identify both as desiring subjects and as objects of desire. Berger illustrates this split with the tableau of a woman who walks across a room and imagines, as she does so, being watched navigating the space. But the psychoanalytic claim about the subject as spectator to her desire is even more mobile and divided than Berger would allow. The centrality of repetition to pleasure and of deferral to desire indeed places the desiring subject *in* her story and also makes her a reader *of* her story. These two forms, acting and interpretation, enable the desiring subject to reinhabit her own plot from a number of imaginary vantage points simultaneously.

Laplanche and Pontalis's "Fantasy and the Origins of Sexuality" has been especially influential in establishing this view of the specificity of fantasy-work in the production of desire (1986). They argue that fantasies are scenes into which the subject unconsciously translates herself in order to experience, in multiple ways, the desire released by the originary sexual trauma and the paradoxical, ambivalent attachments it generates. Fantasy donates a sense of affective coherence to what is incoherent and contradictory in the subject; provides a sense of reliable continuity amid the flux of intensities and attachments; and allows out-of-sync-ness and unevenness of being in the ordinary world at once to generate a secure psychotic enclave and to maintain the subject's openness to the ordinary disturbances of experience.

To think this way about the manifestations of fantasy is to change how we have been defining the sexual and desiring subject. We are no longer solely negotiating a passage of desire between the infant and her mother, or the adult and the sexual objects that later come to substitute for the traumatically lost mother. We are focusing now on the space of desire, in a field of scenes, tableaux, episodes, and events. Fantasy is the place where the subject encounters herself already negotiating the social. The origin of fantasy may still be the trauma of infantile separation—that's one theory. However we account for its origins, though, it's clear that the subjectivity desire makes is fundamentally incited by *external* stimuli that make a dent on the subject. The affective disturbance can reassemble one's usual form in any number of shapes or elaborations: in personal styles of seduction, anxious or confident attachment, confusion, shame, dread, optimism, or self- or other-directed pleasure, for example. Or in stories about who one is and what one wants, stories to which one clings so as to be able to reencounter oneself as solid and in proximity to being idealizable.

It is often said therefore that the desiring subject is well served by the formalism of desire; although desire is anarchic and restless, the objects to which it becomes attached stabilize the subject and enable her to as-sume a reliable-enough identity. In this model, a person is someone who is retroactively created: you know who you "are" only by interpreting where your desire has already taken you. But we have already seen that your desire does not take you to its predestined object, the thing that will repair the trauma (of maternal separation, of sexual difference) that set you on your voyage in the first place. Desire is practical; it takes what it can get. It has bad eyesight, as it were: remember, the object is not a thing but a cluster of phantasmic investments in a scene that represents itself as offering some traction, not a solution to the irreparable contradictions of desire. On your behalf, in an effort to release you from abandonment to autoeroticism—or, more precisely, to restore your autoeroticism to sociability—your desire *misrecognizes* a given object as that which will restore you to something that you sense effectively as a hole in you. Your object, then, does not express transparently who you "are" but says *some-thing* about what it takes for you to anchor yourself in space and time. Meanwhile, the story of your life becomes the story of the detours your desire takes (see Sedgwick 1993).

Freud's "A Child Is Being Beaten," the master text for this line of thought, proposes that when the subject fantasizes scenes of desire she takes multiple positions in those scenes; in this case, a patient says she hears a young boy being beaten in the next room and identifies as the beater, the beaten, the spectator, and the eavesdropper. Each of the positions in the scene of fantasy connects to a different aspect of the desiring subject's senses and sense of power; the grandiosity of the fantasy enables the subject to saturate mentally all experience and all feeling. Earlier I described the ways in which romance narrative turns erotic ambivalence into serial experience by spacing out desire, obstacle, and romantic overcoming in the intervals of narrative time. The post-Freudian model of fantasy as the scene of desire provides another way of representing ambivalence without its internal tensions: rather than tracking conflicting aims among the various kinds of attachment the subject feels, the scenic form of fantasy enables the desiring subject to produce a series of interpretations that do not have to cohere as a narrative but that nonetheless make up the scene. This model of the subject demands reading the way a photograph, or a hieroglyph, does: it requires multiple strands of causal narration. This is what Freud meant by "overdetermination": to be overdetermined is to see oneself and one's objects of interest as the point of convergence of many forces. This model of a thing's multiple causation explains how, despite our wild affects and thoughts, we retain a phantasmic sense of reliability and solidity; it explains how we can maintain conflicting ideas of who we and what our objects are without collapsing or becoming psychotic.

Take, for example, the scene of intimate ambivalence par excellence: infidelity. In the real life of normative intimacy, the different relationships brought into competitive proximity in infidelity are frequently revealed via tableaux or scenicness. Someone walks into a room at the wrong time, or someone cannot get out of her mind the image of the adulterous sex; someone cannot forget the way the room looked when she came into the unhappy knowledge. The cheating lover may occupy multiple positions in the scene: the lover, the beloved, the guilty one, the injurer, the agent, the victim. If the adulterer opines that she is cheating because her primary relationship has failed her miserably, she is using the logic of romance narrative to split apart the scene of ambivalence: distressed couple, happy infidelity. But if the caught or confessing wanderer insists to her partner and her lover that neither relationship has anything to do with the other, she is arguing from the logic of fantasy, protecting all positions as sites of her own desire. Her explanation cannot be called *false* if the sexual wanderer experiences the scene this way: neither is it true in the sense of adequately explaining the tangle of motives and impulses that produced her acts. This is why fantasy and romantic narrative generally are best described as structures of *psychical reality*, neither true nor false where facts are concerned, but affectively true insofar as the compulsion to repeat that organizes it is the reality through which the subject projects desire and processes experience (Laplanche and Pontalis 1973; Kaplan 1986).

As with all animating forms, this model of fantasy implies a theory of the subject. But it repudiates completely the model of the subject whose desire is the truth of her identity and whose actions are the expressions of her desire. The subject (of fantasy) might be read instead as the place where the fragmentation of the subject produced by primal trauma is expressed through repetition: this is the Freudian view, and it directs our attention to the drama of small differences through which the subject attempts to master her "normal" and her "perverse" inclinations. But the scene of fantasy can also be said to reveal the fundamental noncoherence of the subject, to which violence is done by the demands of the identity form, and which may well play out a competition between the subject's desire to be recognized by her object and her desire to destroy the object she desires (Klein and Rivière 1964). Either of these models (mastery, destructive/reparative impulses) can be seen in the ways that the subject takes up patterning with respect to her objects. In any case, because people are distinguished to themselves, their intimates, and in history by their particular structures and styles of repetition, the subject becomes coherent and inhabits her identity only as she repeats an attachment to a scene that features her self-performance. But how do we understand this in more political or social terms? Foucault argues that ideologies of the *normal* turn certain subjects into a "population" by way of the taxonomic state, the corporealized hierarchies of capitalism, and medical, legal, educational, and religious practices. Subjects who become intelligible within these regimes of normativity are trained to repeat identification with particular fantasy forms, which is to say they are incited to identify with some repetitions and styles over other repetitions and styles. In this sense, the promise of social belonging recasts Enlightenment ideologies of happiness, individual autonomy and uniqueness, and freedom in terms of normative conventionality. As a result, some critics argue that even normalized or conventional social relationships can be perverse, in that their fulfillment can entail implicit or underdeveloped fantasies of bucking social convention; in this Marxist/psychoanalytic tradition of thought, conventions themselves are placeholders for desired political, as well as personal, transformation beyond the horizon of the ordinary appearances and immediate sensations of belonging (Berlant 1994; Berlant 1997; Jameson 1979; Negt and Kluge 1993).

Desire, Narrative, Commodity, Therapy

Alfred Hitchcock's *Marnie* (1964) tells the story of a woman who appears to hate men but who uses her competence and her beauty in a way that has the structure of a seduction. Efficient in the office and icily striking, she so bewitches her bosses that, vulnerable with desire, they relax their managerial rules around her. And once they manifest this double vulnerability, she absconds with their money. This is the backstory of the film's first scene: we enter as the police interview a Mr. Strutt, who has been both aroused and embezzled by Marnie (played by Tippi Hedren). Here is the first thing he, or anyone, says about her: "That little witch. I'll have her put away for twenty years. I knew she was too good to be true. Always so eager to work overtime, never made a mistake, always pulling her skirt down over her knees as though they were a national treasure."

You would call Marnie a plain seductress, were it not that her confidence game always bleeds beyond the scene of the crime to other disturbed places, spaces of antithetical power and abjection. Each time she steals she changes identity, takes a brief vacation to ride her prized horse, brings gifts and funds to her mother, who thinks that she has triumphed legitimately in the financial world.

What to make of this pattern, this woman? At the start, we think Marnie might be a sociopath: in the five opening minutes, before the film shows her face, it shows her body remaking its feminine style and choosing from among several legal identities. That femininity is the scene of her disruption is figured in the way she hides fraudulent Social Security cards in the secret compartment of a gold reticule. But we soon see that Marnie has been subject to trauma, and that her repeated routine is a circuitous way of seducing, not men, but her mother—to love her, protect her, accept her, repair her blockages to manifesting maternal love. It turns out that Marnie killed a man when she was young, a drunk and menacing client of her prostitute mother, and that her mother took the rap for it; the memory, half-repressed by Marnie's traumatic amnesia and her mother's cold and protective silence about the event, is figured constantly by symptoms such as panic attacks, nightmares, and sexual frigidity, which, unlike Marnie herself, never seem to lie.

But Marnie meets up with a man who is her match. Along with running a business, Mark Rutland (played by Sean Connery) studies animal instincts (zoology, entomology, and marine biology) and specializes in engendering "trust." He falls for Marnie during the first panic attack he sees, and as he learns of the criminal ways in which she has made men "pay" for the sex they never had, he pays back the debts her robberies have incurred. Then Mark focuses on fixing her sexual problem: he exploits her fear of prison to trap her into marriage and eventually rapes her in their honeymoon bedroom. Then, hastily acquiring some psychoanalytic expertise through books like *Sexual Aberrations of the Criminal Female*, *Frigidity in Women*, and *The Psychopathic Delinquent and Criminal*, he compels Marnie to renounce her aversion to intimacy and to beg him for help; in turn, Mark enables Marnie's "real" story to come out in the open and accomplishes healing through the narrative conversion of trauma to love.

Marnie's closing lines in the film—"I don't want to go to jail, Mark. I want to stay with you"—confirm both parodically and sincerely the husband's sense that romance and the psychological sciences use much the same contract to aid the impaired subject, the one who desires but cannot achieve entry into a love plot. In this contract, a masterful subject tells a more vulnerable one that he will enable her to assume a full and sustaining identity if she devotes herself entirely to inhabiting the intimate scene he prepares for her. At first, Marnie refuses the terms of this exchange, designating them as tools that use money and institutional power to advance the sexual entitlement of men. As she remarks mockingly, "You Freud, Me Jane." But *Marnie* also suggests that, to be healthy, the woman must conclude that consent to the normative contract of intimacy is indeed the condition of her happiness, and that the terms of her earlier protests were a part of her mental illness. Marnie does this by coming to believe that Mark's judgment and love will produce for her a clean break with the past, and thus a return to her "own" story. This fantasy of narrative repair suggests that psychoanalysis is the science of desire's shattering and traumatic history, while romance involves magical thinking about desire's future. It matters not that Hitchcock might have seen all of this resolution ironically or that he might have sadistically identified with both protagonists. What matters is that this transfer from the epistemology of symptom to that of repair through love's genre is conventional, and does not read as avant-garde or unintelligible.

Marnie's gendered distribution of therapeutic modes suggests that the conventional narratives and institutions of romance share with psychoanalysis many social and socializing functions. As sites for theorizing and imaging desire, they manage ambivalence; designate the individual as the unit of social transformation; reduce the overwhelming world to an intensified space of personal relations; establish dramas of love, sexuality, and reproduction as the dramas central to living; and install the institutions of intimacy (most explicitly the married couple and the intergenerational family) as the proper sites for providing the life plot in which a subject has "a life" and a future. That these forms are conventions whose imaginary propriety serves a variety of religious and capitalist institutions does not mean that the desire for romantic love is an ignorant or false desire: indeed, these conventions express important needs to feel unconflicted and to possess some zone where intimacy can flourish. But in the modern United States and, to different degrees, the places its media forms influence, the fantasy world of romance is used normatively—as a rule that legislates the boundary between a legitimate and valuable mode of living/loving and all of the others. The reduction of life's legitimate possibility to one plot is the source of romantic love's terrorizing, coercive, shaming, manipulative, or just diminishing effects—on the imagination as well as on practice.

+ + +

Most important to this essay is addressing the ways that fantasies of romantic love and of therapy posit norms of gender and sexuality as threats to people's flourishing and yet themselves are part of the problem for which they offer themselves as a solution. It's not just that psychoanalysis has tended to organize the world around a scene that privileges modes of embodiment, anxiety, and authority that serve straight men's interests in maintaining (even a contingent) privilege; at the same time, popular romance, pretending no science, arranges the world around heterofeminine experiences and desires for intimacy. In each discourse, the sexual other is deemed, a priori, to be emotionally inadequate. Of course, people of any gender rarely or barely inhabit these ideals fully or unambivalently, but these ideals nonetheless mark the horizons of fantasy and fulfilled identity by which people come to measure their lives or process their confusions (Sedgwick 1990). The institutions and ideologies of romantic/familial love declare woman/women to be the arbiters, sources, managers, agents, and victims of intimacy: the love plots that saturate the public sphere are central vehicles for reproducing normative or "generic" femininity. In this next segment of our investigation of desire/fantasy, we will focus on its romantic commodities: first, on some of its popular narrative forms and, second, on three related kinds of popular culture that organize the conventional meanings of desire, gender, and sexuality—therapy culture, commodity culture, and liberal political culture.

+ + +

So far in this essay, desire has appeared as an ambivalent energy organized by processes of attachment. It manifests an enormously optimistic drive to generate sustained intimate contact. But its typical forms are also said to be motivated by psychic trauma, associated with perversion and melancholic masochism and structured by dramas of incest, castration, shame, and guilt. In the popular culture of romance such instability and ambivalence are always managed by the girdle of love. These dramas are always formed in relation to a fantasy that desire, in the form of love, will make life simpler, not crazier. Boy meets girl, boy loses girl, boy gets girl: this generic sequence structures countless narratives both high and low, sometimes with the genders reversed (take, for example, the 1938 film *Boy Meets Girl*, directed by Lloyd Bacon, a tale about the representational conventions and effects of Hollywood's obsession with romance).

The fantasy forms that structure popular love discourse constantly express the desire for love to simplify living. The content of these narratives is, in a sense, just a surface variation on a narrowly constructed theme: love's clarifying wash is expressed positively, in bright-eyed love stories, and negatively, in narratives that track failure at intimacy in the funereal tones of tragedy or the biting tones of cynical realism. Even when ambivalence organizes a narrative, keeping desire and negativity in close quarters, love is often named as the disappointing thing that ought to have stabilized these antithetical drives. Thus, in the wish for romance, love plots insist on a law for desire. But the law is, as usual, contradictory. In the popular rhetoric of romance, love is a most fragile thing, a supposed selflessness in a world full of self; its plots also represent the compulsion to repeat scenes of transgression, ruthlessness, and control, as well as their resolution into something transcendent, or at least consoling, still, stabilized—at least for a moment.

The pseudoclarities of sexual difference play a large part in conventionalizing this relation of risk and fantasy. Love plots are marked by a longing for love to have the power to make the loved one transparent, and therefore a safe site on which to place one's own desire without fear of its usual unsettling effects. The trope of "love at first sight" expresses this wish as well: when I saw you, it was as though I had lived my whole life in a moment—I knew, then, my fate. The best-selling book *The Bridges of Madison County* by Robert James Waller expresses this set of desires, but not because they are conventional: the fictive author's frame narrative marks the story as a revolutionary repudiation of a culture that has hardened to love's transformative and self-realizing potential. Its protagonists, Robert Kincaid and Francesca Johnson, do not experience love at first sight but feel so inexorably drawn toward each other that they soon "know" that all of human history has worked to bring them together and given them instant mutual knowledge. To express the feeling that love has finally brought them what love is supposed to bring everyone, the book uses a language of ghostliness and haunting, for the feeling of love that they both cherished and relinquished as they grew older and disappointed now returns like a ghost, a transparent body that haunts *them*, infuses *their* lives with a spirit. When they make love, which they do for just a few long days before Francesca's husband returns, all of material life dissolves into "shape and sound and shadow"; their language breaks down into elemental "small, unintelligible sounds" (Waller 1992, 108). The perfect asociality of their intimacy means that when Robert leaves Francesca they can experience their love for the rest of their lives as a perfect object, an animating ghost that was true to their desire.

The wish this novella expresses—that a man would come to a woman and understand her without aggressive probing, that he would be critical of masculinity without being ashamed of it or of himself, that he would be capable of both hardness and softness, and that this would provide a context for the woman to experience herself as freely as he does—is the structural stuff of popular romance. The story that love is invulnerable to the instabilities of narrative or history, a beautifully shaped web of lyrical mutuality, is at the ideological core of modern heterosexuality. It enables heterosexuality to be construed as a relation of desire that expresses people's true feelings. It says nothing of the institutions and ideologies that police it (in *Bridges* the local community has a sharp nose for adultery). To the degree that a love story pits lyrical feelings about intimacy against the narrative traumas engendered in ordinary or public life, it participates in the genre of romance: the love plot provides a seemingly nonideological resolution to the fractures and contradictions of history. The mix of utopianism and amnesia this suggests is, as we have previously said, the fetish-effect of fantasy.

But what about the many times when love fails to sustain a concrete life context and the identities shaped within it? What about the times when the intimate other remains opaque to the desiring subject? Why are the transparency and simultaneity promised by love not automatically considered a mirage and a fraud, given the frequency with which this wish is disconfirmed by experience? It should not be surprising to learn that narratives of romantic failure are dedicated, frequently and paradoxically, to reanimating the belief in love's promise to structure both conventional life and the magical life of intimate mutuality across distance and difference. Toni Morrison's *Sula* frames two such moments, in each of which the fetish of a transparent, transcendent experience of desire is marked by an extreme, absorbing, death-driven melancholia.

Most famously, *Sula* has been called a lesbian novel, for the relations between Sula and her friend Nel organize everything good about their lives. (Not much is good about their lives except their friendship, really: they live in the United States between World War I and World War II, a period of severe economic distress and racial subordination.) Because there are no institutions or ideologies to give them sustaining language and contexts for their intimacy, and because heterosexuality names the structure of living for them, Sula dies before Nel realizes that Sula was her most intimate partner all along. Nel then releases an elemental howl (much like the murmuring sounds in *Bridges*) that figures the transparent truth of their mutual love, a love that can only be lived as the memory of something that did not happen, after history has reached its limit.

In contrast, Sula experiences this desire for transparency in the real time of love—but not with Nel. It is with her lover Ajax, the man with whom, as an adolescent, she first experienced sexual excitement. Later in life, they become lovers. To Sula this means wanting to know everything about him, which is the same as wanting him to be transparent. But Ajax's body is an obstacle to this, so during sex Sula fantasizes tearing off his skin, dissecting him layer by layer until she reaches the being beneath: rubbing his skin until the black disappears, taking a nail file or old paring knife to scrape at the layer of gold beneath, using a chisel to crack open what's left until the body is broken down to its earthly elements (Morrison [1973] 1982, 130–31). As she experiences this her body goes weak with a spreading orgasm; it ejects her from personhood, swallowed by the violent unboundedness of sex.

Directly after this event, Sula becomes the most conventional beribboned feminine lover imaginable. Ajax sees this, and he flees her; she declines and dies of a broken heart. Once again, love's promise violently fails, and once again it is women who experience the impossibility of optimism (and of femininity) in the overwhelming face of its failure. Yet one might also say that *Sula* signals a different horizon of possibility for desire, a form of intimacy made of sights and smells and inchoate intensities, more than sounds, identity, or language. This form of desire disregards the conventional institutions and ideologies of intimacy, including conventional heterosexuality and the reproductive family, which seem in the book to ravage the very desires they uphold and societies they structure.

+ + +

This desire for love to reach beyond the known world of law and language enables us to consider the idea that romantic love might sometimes serve as a placeholder for a less eloquent or institutionally proper longing. A love plot would, then, represent a desire for a life of unconflictedness, where the aggression inherent in intimacy is not lived as violence and submission to the discipline of institutional propriety or as the disavowals of true love, but as something less congealed into an identity or a promise, perhaps a mix of curiosity, attachment, and passion. But as long as the normative narrative and institutionalized forms of sexual life organize identity for people, these longings mainly get lived as a desire for love to obliterate the wildness of the unconscious, to confirm the futurity of a known self, to dissolve the enigmas that marks one's lovers.

The formalism of Sula's desire, apparent throughout the novel, finds its most visible evidence in her will to destroy the object she loves in order to understand it. This opens up another way to address the logic of romantic love. If, on the one hand, the desire for transparency in love is associated with producing a deep internal calm about identity, on the other hand, desire frequently seeks out and occupies the extremes of feeling. Sula does not think she is having a violent fantasy about Ajax; she thinks that she is loving him, and that love means the emancipation from self, here figured in the materiality of his body. Yet Sula's desire to dissect her lover raises questions about the relation between romance and pornography: What if her fantasy were written as a man's desire for a woman, expressed, during sex, as his desire to slice away at her body? How would you read this if it were a gay or queer fantasy? Does an explanation that uses a paradigm of masculine sexual privilege to explain Sula's "confusion" of desire with fantasies of violence "solve" these questions of fantasy, power, ethics, otherness, and the effects of gendering?

Sharon Thompson (1995) and others argue that there is effectively no difference between pornographic representations of sex and romance conventions. Both are said to involve the overcoming of people by desires, and both fantasize scenes of sexuality using realist modes of representation. It has been suggested that women use romantic fantasy to experience the rush of these extremes the way men tend to use pornography, that fantasizing about intensified feeling can be a way of imagining the thrill of sexual or political control or its loss—or, conversely, a way of overwhelming one's sexual ambivalence or insecurity with a frenzy of representation. It can also be a way of experiencing one's perverse impulses without taking on the identity "pervert." It is true that romance approaches the extremes of feeling and desire by way of a discourse of love, but love can be thought of as a way of managing the sheer ambiguity of romantic language and expectation. These suggestions give narrative shape to our previous discussion of the psychoanalytic model of fantasy. In that context as well as here, these alternative possibilities for reading the sexual genres of fantasy express tensions internal to sexuality, and heterosexuality in particular. But insofar as heterosexuality has become the primary site that organizes self-knowledge and self-development, gay, lesbian, and bisexual narratives of desire must be in dialogue with the utopian expectations of conventional love, and its different motives for fantasy.

+ + +

I have been using fiction to give us a sense of love's narrative conventions. Fiction provides models of the relation between love's utopian prospects and its lived experience, and modern women's fiction in particular seeks to create subjects who identify with love's capacity to overcome the troubles of everyday life. Romantic narrative conventions argue for continuing to believe that femininity is defined through an unambivalent faith in the love plot while also developing a critical distance on that belief, as it measures the costs of women's submission to men (who are said to have less skill and investment in the project of intimacy).

This latter, critical, discourse has its own space outside of the novel: therapy culture. Since about 1910, love talk has been associated with therapeutic rhetoric in US popular culture. Advice columns, self-help pedagogy, didactic short stories, moral exhortations, autobiographies, and case studies have popularized psychoanalysis, muted its discussions of the pervasiveness of perversion, and sought to help people, especially women, adjust their desires and their self-relations to the norms and forms of everyday life. (The gay and lesbian public sphere proliferates with self-help and advice literatures too; these scenes of representation and advice help nonnormative sexual subjects trade information about the specificity of their practices of love and sex, which overlap without reproducing entirely the norms of heterosexual culture.)

Self-help discourse has tended to reproduce the split in romance ideology that we have been developing; valorizing the promise of love and the mutual obligations of lovers, it presumes that problems in love must be solved by way of internal adjustment, to make certain that its conventional forms can remain and keep sustaining the signs of utopian intimacy. Individuals are told that the normative ideologies and institutions of intimacy can work for them, although men and women are different species who will never experience the intimate other's desire in the same language or with the same intensity; that there are "rules" of seduction and for the maintenance of the intimate other that should be followed, but about which it is bad to be explicit; that romantic intimacy is an addiction that stimulates weakness and stunts growth, and yet is central to maturity; that sex should be central, but not too central, to love; that the norms of propriety and responsibility that organize conventional lives are right, decent, and possible, but also boring, violent, and incomplete; and that, within reason, anyone should get what she wants. This includes conventional norms about sexual practice itself; as discussions about sex have become more publicly available, it would seem that more varied practices have been normalized over the course of the twentieth century. Yet remaining remarkably stable has been the ideology that sex must seem natural: heterosexuality seems to require that any pedagogy between lovers must take place away from the sex itself, so that the image of the sex act as an expressive act of an unambivalent or whole individual can be preserved. This form of hypocrisy is, currently, conventional to sex. Generally, this ideology is addressed to women, who are deemed responsible for maintaining the emotional comfort of everyone in their sphere, but the unstated presumption in much self-help culture is that heterosexual intimacy is constantly in crisis and that its survival is crucial for the survival of life as we know it (a claim that is not false, but which, of course, does not tell the whole story of how desires are served by the reproduction of heterosexuality as a norm that gets called Nature).

When people whose sexual lives do not assimilate to the norms organized by this pedagogy adapt the logics of romantic love to themselves, they too can adapt their lives to the ways its institutions and moral codes have historically steadied and screened out the threatening instability of desire. But since, as we have suggested, gay men and lesbians have had, historically, few institutions to enable the kinds of stability and disavowal available to heterosexuals, a greater degree of public explicitness has characterized nonnormative forms of intimacy. This threatens traditional sexual subjects. David Sedaris, for example, confirms this in the opening of his autobiographical tale "Ashes": "The moment I realized I would be a homosexual for the rest of my life, I forced my brother and sisters to sign a contract swearing they'd never get married. There was a clause allowing them to live with anyone of their choice, just so long as they never made it official" (Sedaris 1997, 235). But these kinds of rhetorical and practical improvisations on the "normal" life of lived desire does not mean that queer sexual subjects do not fantasize about love and its rich stabilizing promises the way straights do. The couple in love is a seductive desire, a fantasy of being emancipated into form's holding environment, but like all fantasies that might be lived, it requires a world that can sustain it, a context of law and norm that is only now emerging for gays and lesbians, just as it did not exist for women generally until the middle of the twentieth century.

Self-help consumers are exhorted to adjust themselves to these norms as though everyone, or at least all women, has the same, generic desires. Their failure to find a life to sustain their desires is the subject daily of interminable talk shows on television and radio, in gossip columns and fan magazines, on the Internet, and in the political public sphere. Yet that failure is considered evidence, not of the impossibility of these theoretical statements about love, but only of individual failure. As a result, an entire industry produces ever more therapeutic commodities offering strategies for surviving desire. Romance aesthetics is part of this strategy to link consumption to emotional survival. The huge industry of *things* that sustains itself on the reproduction of romantic fantasy (*Bridges*, for example, generated at least one film, two CDs, seven books, and numerous reading groups worldwide) simultaneously deisolates subjects who are suffering from desire, and yet names them as both the source of and the solution to their problems. (When was the last Marxist self-help book?) This emphasis pushes people to think of their private lives as the only material over which they might have any control (despite all evidence to the contrary). As love and its intimate contexts come to bear the burden of establishing personal value generally, and especially for women, popular culture initiates a contradictory image set for establishing emancipatory agency: love induces stuckness and freedom; love and its absence induce mental/emotional illness or *amour fou;* love is therapy for what ails you; love is the cause of what ails you. In this context, psychotherapy appears as that which can exacerbate or help you cure lovesickness, but popular culture genres offering wise conventionalities can cause and help you cure lovesickness as well as or even better than psychotherapy.

Take, for example, the fantasy of romance as therapy that shapes the 2012 feminist "indie" art film *Ruby Sparks* (dir. Jonathan Dayton and Valerie Faris). In it, Calvin (Paul Dano), a pale, white male writer in the J. D. Salinger tradition of ficto-autobiography, has a massive writing block. He has no life, and he cannot write. His therapist suggests that, to cure his blockage both to fantasy and to living, Calvin write about a person who can see what is lovable in his scruffy, drooly, gender-confused dog (a male dog that urinates in a bitch-squat style). Calvin does not find this suggestion comic, which it is. Instead, he dreams about a young woman named Ruby Sparks giving that kind of kind attention to the abject dog, then writes her into existence as his own lover to love and accept him completely. After being briefly disturbed by the psychotic implications of bringing her to life (and unaware of aesthetic precedents from Galatea on), he becomes a happy man living in a bubble with his ideal girl.

But as time passes, Calvin finds Ruby (Zoe Kazan) insufferable. He writes her as strong and artistic but cannot tolerate her autonomy when she develops her own story; he rewrites her as a slavishly loving doormat but is turned off by her subordination when she now wants only him. As he revises her according to the specifications of his wish, he both desires and loathes her, feeling in and out of control: does this mean that he is a bad writer or an ordinary lover? He can't bear any revision, any version of *what he fantasizes that he wants.*

Finally, in a climactic *Tales of Hoffman*–like scene, Calvin reveals Ruby to herself as an automaton, a nonhuman under his power. Then, converting from mad scientist/slave master to sentimental revolutionary, he writes a final page of the novel that ends it all, but not exactly by killing her—or himself. In his closing sentences, he proclaims that "history" hereby releases Ruby to herself, and he delivers her unto "freedom." This freedom from history and from Calvin's control turns out, in the end, to amount to *her amnesia about his control of her*. Calvin, however, though he loses Ruby, retains control over the memory of her. (See, in contrast, the similar plot of the 2004 Charlie Kaufman film *Eternal Sunshine of the Spotless Mind*, where the nebbish man and the dream woman both erase their memories.)

As if to admit that Ruby was nothing but a placeholder for his projections, Calvin then writes a successful "fiction" about this "real" woman, called, generically, *A Girlfriend,* and this seems to be a hit. He then demands that his psychotherapist accept *his* fantasy of hetero-romance as real— that is, accept that Ruby was flesh-and-blood real. This combination— pretending to release control when he is exerting the most control; demanding that the judging world, in the person of his therapist, relinquish its control over the real and defer to the patient's personal fantasy; and holding his control over everyone and everything as his enduring precious secret—is deemed a successful end of Calvin's therapy *and* the condition under which powerful art and love emerge.

Calvin's fantasy of an impossible love (whose structure is incoherent— contingent, contradictory, aggressive, passive, tender, and dissociated) occupies what Laplanche has called "a psychotic enclave" (Laplanche 1989). This separateness and misrecognition is just the condition of ordinary love, given the enabling structure of fantasy. What makes this particular film so revealing for our purposes is that popular therapeutic culture offers a form for seeming to repair the intractable fractures within and between people by way of the demand for the very love that also intensifies these cleavages. But the film does not fall down once tied in these knots. Instead, in its habitation of the romantic comedy genre, the injuries of love are healed not by paying attention to the details of constancy and inconstancy that love generates, and not by agreeing to try to live in love's awkward synchrony, but rather by insisting on the sovereignty of fantasy: accept *my* fantasy of love as *our* realism. This is like the conclusion *Marnie* reached, but if in Hitchcock's film Marnie is the criminal/patient-as-lover who must accept Mark's fantasy or march off to prison, here the solution is deemed more just and satisfying for Ruby, because she has her "freedom"—from Calvin, from memory, and from consciousness.

What is the difference between Calvin's version of the lover's demand and a stalker's insistence that she is in a relationship with her unwilling object? The fantasy, which is at the heart both of popular culture and Lacanian psychoanalysis, is that love is the misrecognition you like, can bear, and will try to keep consenting to. If the other will accept your fantasy/

realism as the condition of their encounter with their own lovability, and if you will agree to accept theirs, the couple (it could be any relation) has a fighting chance not to be destroyed by the aggressive presence of ambivalence, with its jumble of memory, aggressive projection, and blind experimentation. This is not a cynical bargain but the bargain that fantasy enables for any subject to take up a position in a sustained relation. At the same time, though, *Ruby Sparks* also calls on popular romance comedy genres to defang the violence and discomfort that inevitably ensue when the scene of love seeks out but never quite finds its resting form.

The couple meets again in the film's final scene. When we meet Ruby at the beginning of the film, she is an unblocked painter who is untrained but has a lot of confidence in her art—and therefore is all of the things that Calvin is not. At the end of the film, Ruby has no distinguishing talent. We encounter her lounging in the park, happily reading *A Girlfriend*, the book that is both her own story and a story that her amnesia bars her from recognizing as her own. She asks Calvin not to ruin the ending; he promises not to foretell and foreclose the ending, this time. Their agreement, to keep a secret and not to ask what it is, is the foundation of their love. The secret is the secret of their judgment of each other. But also he knows a story she will now never know. To not tell the ending is to not tell the beginning. It is a "happy ending" for the film, as amnesia and the closet are the conditions under which the lovers will take up positions as mutual fantasizers.

The film's attempt to use romantic comedy to heal the tragedy of what's unbearable in love is predicted by its staging of their first real date, at a zombie movie, which is followed by a scene in which Calvin eats a dip that looks a lot like brains. This joke about the conditions for normative happiness sees the romance as more likely to revitalize the zombie fantasy of heterosexual romance—to dip into it *after* it's dead—than is the psychotherapy that Calvin undergoes throughout the film. Psychotherapy admits that fantasy is unconscious; popular culture thinks it is all gesture, style, story, and mood. If experience and memory dent love, it argues, let's try to retain its new car smell by foreclosing incidents that could become disturbing events. So if popular culture does dip into the scenarios of psychic fantasy that enable the subject to bear the disturbed relation between what Eve Sedgwick calls the reparative and destructive gestures of attachment to one's objects (persons and worlds), it also refuses any story that does not affirm love's fundamentally healing properties.

+ + +

The use of the logic of romantic desire to neutralize, at least symbolically, the violence and attraction at play in hierarchical social relations implicitly suggests that structures and institutions of power can always be overcome by personal feelings and personal choices. It is not surprising, then, that the commodity form has a central place in the valorization of conventional or "normal" desire (see Illouz 1997; Peiss 1986). The interactions of capitalism and desire, as we have already seen, are extremely complicated and contested. Capitalism could not thrive without an attention to and constant stimulation of desire, which means that the centrality of romance and sex to its persuasive strategies creates subjects simultaneously primed for conventional intimacy and for profit-generating relations to consumption and labor.

Marx classically notes that the magical autonomy of the commodity form obscures the economic, social, and ideological relations that animate it in the process of its production: so, too, the mass-cultural discourse of romance obscures, the way a fetish does, the relations between the hegemonic processes of collective life and what people typically imagine as love. People learn to identify with love the way they identify with commodities; the notions of personal autonomy, consent, choice, and fulfillment so powerful in love discourse seem to be the same as those promised by national capitalism. At the same time, romance is a vehicle for marketing heterosexuality as the very form of fantasy and also the normal context in which fantasy can be lived, but not in a generic way: the heteronormative love plot is at its most ideological when it produces subjects who believe that their love story expresses their true, nuanced, and unique feelings, their own personal destiny.

This idealistic and commodified aspect of romance has also inspired some ways of relating dominant and subordinate peoples to each other across fields of difference and ambivalence. As we described earlier, liberal political culture posits individual autonomy and self-development at the center of value in social life. Romance ideology participates in this project by depicting sentiment or *feeling* as the essential and universal truth of persons. Feeling is what people have in common despite their apparent differences. Thus liberals have long responded to antagonism between dominant and subordinate peoples by saying to the dominant culture: the people you think of as other only *appear* to threaten your stability and value by their difference; they have feelings too; they suffer too; therefore you are essentially alike. You desire the same thing "they" do, to feel unconflicted, to have intimacy. If you feel ambivalent, or in some relation of antagonism and fascination to the members of the population from which you feel intensely estranged, you can understand your unease the way you understand sexual difference under heterosexuality, as something that can be overcome by *desire* and cultivated *identification*. Many people argue that love of the other is a powerful tool for bringing marginalized groups into the dominant social world; on the other hand, sentimental identification with suffering created by national, racial, economic, and religious privilege has long coexisted with laws that discriminate among particular forms of difference, privileging some against others (laws against interracial, interreligious, or gay marriage, for instance).

Conclusion

What are the relations among the world-building drives of love, the critical and utopian fantasies contained there, the project of psychoanalysis (the science), and self-help (its popular culture)? How does the constant return of the subject to adjusting herself and her intimate others at the scene of her conflicted desire enable and disable the difficult and risky parts of self- and social transformation? What is the relation between the aggressivity of desire and its need to protect and sustain its objects while also exposing them to fantasy's projections, delegations, idealizations, its inevitable play of distortion? Apart from creating jealousy, threat, or moral superiority, what might it do to people to reveal to themselves and each other that their particular desires are unbearable in their contradictions, unknown in their potential contours, and yet demand reliable and confirming recognitions? How might it become bearable to face the ways visceral responses combine convention and something else, perhaps inarticulate or illegitimate desires? What does it mean that, unreliable in desire, we nonetheless demand the other to be perfectly attuned to what's out of tune? How can we be honest about the conflicting motives of aggression? Where are the social infrastructures through which people can reimagine their relation to intimacy and the life building organized around it in ways that are as yet uninevitable or unimaginable?

+ + +

My two essays in this volume have tried to say some things about desire and love: that there are no master explanations of them; that they destabilize and threaten the very things (like identity and life) that they are disciplined to organize and ameliorate; that there is a long history of gendering the anxieties love induces even in its optimistic subjects; that love's abstractions and institutions have long been used to enforce signs and sites of propriety, such that the generic subjects imagined in a love plot tend to be white, Western, heterosexual, and schooled to the protocols of "bourgeois" privacy; that these tacit proprieties have been used to justify the economic and physical domination of nations, races, religions, gay men, lesbians, and women. Yet here the story must return to the happy ending in which desire melds with the love that speaks its conventional name. Even now, despite everything, desire/love continues to exert a utopian promise to discover a form that is elastic enough to manage what living throws at lovers. In telling the story of some things that have been touched by the intensities of desire, fantasy, and love, the project of these essays is also to reopen the utopian to more promises than have yet been imagined and sustained.

References

Berger, John. 1972. *Ways of Seeing*. London: Penguin.

Berlant, Lauren. 1994. "'68, or Something." *Critical Inquiry* 21:124–55.

———. 1997. *The Queen of America Goes to Washington City: Essays on Sex and Citizenship*. Durham, NC: Duke University Press.

de Lauretis, Teresa. 1994. *The Practice of Love: Lesbian Sexuality and Perverse Desire*. Bloomington: Indiana University Press.

Illouz, Eva. 1997. *Consuming the Romantic Utopia: Love and the Cultural Contradictions of Capitalism*. Berkeley: University of California Press.

Jameson, Fredric. 1979. "Reification and Utopia in Mass Culture." *Social Text* 1:130–48.

Kaplan, Cora. 1986. "*The Thorn Birds*: Fiction, Fantasy, Femininity." In *Formations of Fantasy*, ed. Victor Burgin, James Donald, and Cora Kaplan, 142–66. London: Methuen.

Klein, Melanie, and Joan Rivière. 1964. *Love, Hate, and Reparation*. New York: Norton.

Laplanche, Jean. 1989. *New Foundations for Psychoanalysis*. Trans. David Macey. London: Basil Blackwell.

Laplanche, Jean, and Jean-Bertrand Pontalis. 1973. *The Language of Psycho-Analysis*. Trans. Donald Nicholson-Smith. London: Hogarth Press.

———. 1986. "Fantasy and the Origins of Sexuality" (1964). In *Formations of Fantasy*, ed. Victor Burgin, James Donald, and Cora Kaplan, 5–64. London: Methuen.

Morrison, Toni. (1973) 1982. *Sula*. New York: Penguin.

Negt, Oskar, and Alexander Kluge.1993. *Public Sphere and Experience: Toward an Analysis of the Bourgeois and Proletarian Public Sphere*. Minneapolis: University of Minnesota Press.

Peiss, Kathy Lee. 1986. *Cheap Amusements: Working Women in Turn-of-the-Century New York*. Philadelphia: Temple University Press.

Sedaris, David. 1997. *Naked*. Boston: Little, Brown.

Sedgwick, Eve Kosofsky. 1990. *Epistemology of the Closet*. Berkeley: University of California Press.

———. 1993. "A Poem Is Being Written." In *Tendencies*. Durham, NC: Duke University Press.

Taylor, Helen. 1989. *Scarlett's Women: Gone with the Wind and Its Female Fans*. New Brunswick, NJ: Rutgers University Press.

Thompson, Sharon. 1995. *Going All the Way: Teenage Girls' Tales of Sex, Romance, and Pregnancy*. New York: Hill and Wang.

Waller, Robert James. 1992. *The Bridges of Madison County*. New York: Warner Books.

12 :: MYTH

WENDY DONIGER

Gender and Myth

In this essay, I will argue that the study of myths from long ago and from countries (if not galaxies) far away has a great deal to contribute to our contemporary understanding of gender in America. By "myths" I mean stories, but not just any stories; all myths are stories, but not all stories are myths. Let me begin by saying what a myth is *not*: a myth is not a lie, or a false statement to be contrasted with truth or reality or fact or history, though this is perhaps its most common meaning in casual popular talk today. But in the history of religion, as well as in the history of the history of religions (that is, the academic discipline that studies religions in a comparative context), the term *myth* has far more often been used to mean "truth." In these two traditions, what a myth *is* is a story that is sacred to and shared by a group of people who find their most important meanings in it; a story believed to have been composed in the past about an event in the past or, more rarely, in the future, an event that continues to have meaning in the present because it is remembered; a story that is part of a larger group of stories (O'Flaherty 1988, 25–33).

Plato used the word in both senses, as lie and as truth. On the one hand, Plato was the first great demythologizer, as the great historian of religions, Mircea Eliade (1969), pointed out long ago. Most famously in the *Republic*, but also in the *Timaeus*, the *Laws*, and *Philebus*, Plato attacked mythmaking poets like Homer and Hesiod, contrasting the fabricated myth with the true history (Detienne 1986, 86–87). But on the other hand, since he believed that people feel that they need myths, Plato was willing to construct new ones for them. And so he transformed ancient mythic themes to make the myth of Eros in the *Symposium* and the myth of the creation of the universe in the *Statesman* and the *Timaeus*, and he actually applied the word *myth* (which he called *mythos*, since he spoke ancient Greek) to the story of the world that he created in the *Phaedo* and to the myth of the transmigration of Er that he created at the end of the *Republic*. Thus Plato regarded the myths that he didn't like as lies and the myths that he *did* like, that he created himself, as truths.

Myth continues to speak with this forked tongue to the present day. For one of the defining characteristics of a myth, in contrast with other sorts of narratives (such as novels), and the greatest of myth's survival tactics, is its ability to stand on its head, to hunt with the hounds of truth and run with the hare of antitruth. This is what allows a myth, more than other forms of narrative, to be shared by a group of people (who have various points of view) and to survive through time (through different generations with yet more points of view). For a myth is a neutral structure that allows paradoxical meanings to be held in a charged tension, that remains transparent to a variety of constructions of meaning (Doniger 1999). The Italian mythologist Roberto Calasso has argued that myths, unlike other stories, "are made up of actions that include their opposites within themselves. The hero kills the monster, but even as he does so we perceive that the opposite is also true: the monster kills the hero" (Calasso 1993, 280). And the novelist Salman Rushdie has argued that "*for every story there is an anti-story* ... every story ... has a *shadow self*, and if you pour this anti-story into the story, the two cancel each other out, and bingo! End of story" (Rushdie 1990, 160). This is what is meant by the so-called multivocality of myths, their ability to express simultaneously a number of different voices, different points of view.

And it is this ability to express two apparently opposed truths at once, to express a paradox that can never be resolved, as the great French structural anthropologist Claude Lévi-Strauss noted (1963, 229; 1966, 22), that makes myths so useful in deconstructing polarized ideas. The chameleon quality of myth works in opposition to the more monolithic and dogmatic aspects of religions; where myth encourages a wide range of beliefs, dogma would narrow that range. The Jewish theologian Martin Buber made this point very well:

> All positive religion rests on an enormous simplification of the manifold and wildly engulfing forces that invade us: it is the subduing of the fullness of existence. All myth, in contrast, is the expression of the fullness of existence, its image, its sign; it drinks incessantly from the gushing fountains of life. Hence religion fights myth where it cannot absorb and incorporate it.... It is strange and wonderful to observe how in this battle religion ever again wins the apparent victory, myth ever again wins the real one. (Buber 1955, xi)

What Buber says about religion, I would limit to dogma. With that corrective, his statement is a marvelous testimony to the ability of myth to keep open the doors of the imagination within the most constricting dogmatic frameworks. It is also generally true, I think, that where the dogmatic aspects of religions concern themselves primarily with sexuality, myths tell us stories about gender.

But the Janus quality of myths means that these open doors let in (and out) both constricting and liberating gender paradigms, both sustaining and challenging bipolar concepts of gender. For example, traditional religions generally recognize only two genders and regard sexuality as, overwhelmingly, heterosexuality. What homosexual themes there are in traditional myths are seldom overt, because such myths almost always have, as a latent agenda, the biological and spiritual survival of a particular race, in both senses of the word: race as contest ("whoever gets there first, wins") and race as species (the "outnumber-them" agenda: "be fruitful and multiply"). Such myths regard homosexual acts as potentially subversive of this agenda (or at the very least, irrelevant to it, perhaps not part of the problem, but certainly not part of the solution). The ascetic aspects of Hinduism and Christianity, among other religions, create a violent dichotomy between heterosexual marriage, in which sexuality is tolerated for the sake of children, and the renunciate priesthood, in which asceticism is idealized and sexuality entirely rejected, or at least recycled. Traditional religious texts regard homosexual union not, like heterosexual marriage, as a compromise between two goals in tension (procreation and asceticism) but as a mutually polluting combination of the worst of both worlds (sterility and lust).

In this taxonomy, homosexual love represents what the structural anthropologist Mary Douglas (1966) has taught us to recognize as a major category error, something that doesn't fit into any existing conceptual cubbyhole, "matter out of place"—in a word, dirt. (Here we may do well to recall the ways in which homophobic language often employs "dirt" symbolism.) Gender issues may or may not be intrinsically religious, but religious ideas are certainly intrinsically gendered, because gender plays a central role in the wider religious concern with order. Broadly speaking, a structuralist might say that, in religious thinking, gender/sexuality = culture/nature. Religious communities and dogmas tend to disqualify the pieces that don't fit their paradigm; if the paradigm is defined as male (as it usually is), they discard or devalue the female (or the homosexual, or the bisexual). Thus, women (and, sometimes, eunuchs or bisexuals) are cast as the villains in many founding myths dealing with such central religious topics as death, evil, and disease. And traditional myths seldom explicitly depict homosexual unions at all, let alone sympathetically.

Yet there are myths that do challenge the dominant polarized heterosexual paradigm. The more or less rigorous strictures that traditional societies place upon human gender and sexuality have, as their flip side, myths in which gods violate all of those strictures. And, as we will see below, myths of transsexuality challenge the very categories in which myths of conventional sexuality and gender are cast.

The Psychology and Theology of Myths

Compounding the multivocality of the myths themselves is the multivocality of interpretations of myth. Psychological and political interpretations of myths about gender see them as addressing real human problems, what the historian of religions Bruce Lincoln (1986) calls sociogonic problems, ideas about the origins of society: How did the human race begin? How did men come to be different from women? Theological interpretations of the myths see them as addressing cosmological and cosmogonic problems: How did death and evil enter the world? Why are we here? For a psychologist, the human concerns of the myths provide a logical and psychological warp on which the theological versions are woven, but for a theologian, the philosophical problem is the warp, the psychosexual problem of the weft woven onto it.

If we view the human concerns as the logical and psychological base from which the theological versions were derived, we are following in the footsteps of the ancient school of interpretation that we call Euhemerism (named after an ancient Sicilian named Euhemerus, who demythologized the Greek gods), the belief that myths are not only based upon true stories about real people, but that they were originally *told* as stories about specific real people: from a "rational" core of legend about human heroes there developed an "irrational" overlay about gods. By attempting to unravel this unfortunate process, the Euhemerists (re)rationalized the myths: that is, they took stories ostensibly about the gods and made them (back, as they saw it) into stories about humans. The ancient Greek historian Herodotus was arguing in this way when he said (at 2.54–57) that the myth of black doves coming from Egypt and prophesying with a human voice was derived from the true story of a (presumably black?) slave woman who came from Egypt and was first thought to speak like a bird (that is, like a "barbarian"), until she learned Greek (and thus gained a "human voice").

Friedrich Max Müller, the German-born Oxford professor regarded as the founder of the discipline of Indo-European mythology, argued in several highly influential works (*Comparative Mythology*, 1856; *Lectures on the Science of Language*, 1869) that mythology was nothing but a "disease of language," created when ancient philosophers mistook (rational) statements about natural phenomena (particularly connected with the

sun) for (irrational) statements about deities. Sigmund Freud may be regarded as a latter-day Euhemerist when he argues, as in *Totem and Taboo*
(1913), that stories that appear to be about god are really about your father. The interpretive process of rationalization (regarding the supernatural as derived from the natural) argues that the myth itself has *irratio-
nalized*, turning what is rational (observable human behavior) into what
is irrational (unobservable divine behavior).

Irrationalization occurs in mythology when ideas about women and
men are transformed into myths about gods and goddesses, when stories
about human women and men become inextricably entangled in the toils
of human sexual tragedy and take flight in the illusion provided by myth.
But the opposite process, rationalization, is equally common and important, when ideas about gods and goddesses are translated into myths
about men and women, as insoluble theological problems take on flesh
and seek their solutions, always in vain, on the human stage. That is,
theological questions are posed, and in the attempt to answer these questions, human images and concerns are projected into myths about the
divine world. The meanings of these myths must be sought not merely
in the superficial anthropomorphic forms and quasi-human events that
people myths, but also in the darker theological questions that lie behind
them. For the royal road that connects myth and experience is a two-way
stretch; the myth is a bridge between actual human experience and the
fantasy that grows out of that experience and, in turn, transfigures it.
Some variants narrow the gap by rendering the fantasy in almost realistic terms; but the gap, however small, remains nevertheless.

Superficially, secular texts are often driven by the religious archetypes
of a myth and may contain profound religious insights, just as religious
texts may also contain secular insights. Clearly the two realms are inextricably tangled together, and the psychological and theological concerns of the myth stand as metaphors for one another, like the Escher
drawing of the hand drawing the hand drawing the hand. Thus many religions answer the theological question "How did death and evil come into
the world?" by linking it with the sociogonic question "How did women
come to be different from men?" (Answer: Women brought death and
evil, which made them different; don't ask who brought women). So, too,
many stories about gods turn out to be largely about human problems,
and, contrariwise, many stories about human beings raise truly theological questions. After all, humans often ask theological questions, and
gods are often all too human. Psychological, political, and theological
questions may be asked of the same myth; it is not the case that one can
ask psychological and/or political questions only of "realistic" myths and

theological questions only of "fantastic" myths. As the social anthropologist Ernest Gellner has remarked:

> As in a well-run kosher kitchen, separate pots were used for the milk of the noumenal and the meat of the empirical.... But the whole point is that mankind in general is seldom if ever conceptually kosher. The transcendent is *not* neatly and conscientiously separated off from the empirical. Most traditions are appallingly unfastidious about their conceptual crockery. (Gellner 1985, 180)

And so, once we look for it, we will find ideologies of gender encoded in texts that are ostensibly concerned with theological issues and theologies expressed through stories that seem to be about human gender. In the rest of this essay, I will attempt to excavate the gender issues in several different sorts of texts and traditions, from the contemporary feminist spirituality movement to the enormous, often surprising range of gender identities posited in Hindu myths (with occasional comparative glances at the Greeks and other Others).

The Myth of Matriarchy

Gender has become a highly topical theme in one particular branch of cross-cultural mythology, the reconstruction of the mythology of goddesses by the Goddess-worshipping wing of the women's movement known as feminist spirituality, a group that I will call, for convenience, the Goddess-feminists. Their myth turns out to be not just a wrongheaded myth, but the flip side of an earlier wrongheaded myth, the wrongheaded myth of male origins and male supremacy. Here is the Cliff Notes version of the Goddess-feminist version of the male chauvinist myth of origins:

> God, male, made the world. Men, with God's help, created culture; in the beginning, there was patriarchy. Men ruled over women and suppressed them, for women (nature) posed a threat to (male) culture.

And here is the alternative, Goddess-feminist myth:

> God, female, made the world. Women, with Her help, created culture, and ruled; in the beginning, there was matriarchy. When women ruled, the earth was a far better, kinder, gentler, more nurturing place. Male gods overthrew the Goddess; men took over culture, and ruled; and patriarchy has prevailed ever since. Male rule has led to the mistreatment of women and to the rape of the earth. (For Ecofeminism assumes that, from the beginning, Earth was a woman, Gaia.) If God is once again recognized as

female, women will rule again, and the earth will again be a gentle, nurturing place.

But, as every mythologist knows, there is always more than one version of a myth, and I have my own alternative version of the Goddess-feminists' version:

> In the beginning was Bachofen, the dragon of primeval matriarchy. Along came Marija Gimbutas, the primeval Goddess riding on her white mare. Would that she had slain the matriarchal dragon! But alas, O best beloved, it was not to be. The two mated, and their monstrous offspring was the matriarchal Goddess.

And here is my commentary on this alternative telling:

The myth of matriarchs and patriarchs (or the mommas and the papas), which began with J. J. Bachofen's *Myth, Religion and Mother Right* (1859), was further developed by Friedrich Engels in *The Origin of the Family, Private Property, and the State* (1884) and revived by Elizabeth Gould Davis in *The First Sex* (1971). Under a hail of furious attacks, many Goddess-feminists backed down, but only far enough to invent alternative words for alternatives to patriarchy. Riane Eisler, in *The Chalice and the Blade* (1987), coined the term *gylany* for a society in which there is equality between females (from the Greek *gyne*) and males (from the Greek *aner*). But it is the concept, not the word, that is at fault: we simply do not know *what* there was before there was patriarchy, and there is no point in further obfuscating this lacuna by inventing new terms for our ignorance.

The belief in a primeval Goddess has inspired many writers, including Jessie Weston (*From Ritual to Romance*), Carl Gustav Jung (*Four Archetypes*), Erich Neumann (*The Great Mother*), Robert Graves (*The White Goddess*), Adrienne Rich (*Of Woman Born*), and Mary Daly (*Beyond God the Father* and *Gyn-ecology*). Merlin Stone began her famous book, *When God Was a Woman* (1976) with the myth: "In the beginning God was a woman. Do you remember?" But she had forgotten, and Marija Gimbutas reminded her, in one of the most influential books about the primeval Goddess: *The Goddesses and Gods of Old Europe 7000–3000 BC: Myths, Legends and Cults* (1974). The solidity and originality of Gimbutas's archeological research were in no way diminished by her own increasingly ideological interpretations, but those leanings did contribute to her Deafication by Goddess-feminist acolytes who have trivialized Gimbutas's ideas through repetition, sloppiness, and exaggeration; the Goddess is now drowning in a sea of books in which thealogy masquerades as scholarship. Even Gimbutas herself, in her introduction to *The Language of the*

Goddess (1989), opens the door to the Goddess-feminist reinterpretation: "Old Europe and Anatolia, as well as Minoan Crete, were a *gylany*. A balanced, non-patriarchal, and non-matriarchal social system is reflected by religion, mythologies, and folklore, by studies of the social structure of Old European and Minoan cultures, and is supported by the continuity of the elements of a matrilineal system in ancient Greece, Etruria, Rome, the Basque, and other countries of Europe." In her last book, published shortly before her death (*The Civilization of the Goddess,* 1991), Gimbutas traced this Goddess religion from the Paleolithic through the Bronze Age.

Gimbutas's interpretation of the evidence has been challenged by subsequent scholarship. Cynthia Eller (1993, 150–51) wisely assesses the myth of matriarchy supplanted by patriarchy, Goddess by gods: "The rhythm of this story is unmistakable, moving in a great wave pattern across human history. Respect for the female surges, then ebbs; perhaps it will surge again.... With apologies to Mircea Eliade, I call this story the movement's 'sacred history.'" Sarah B. Pomeroy (1975), too, confesses that she has come increasingly to view the "possibility of a prehistoric society in the Greek world in which women enjoyed a higher status than men, or were equal to them ... as a myth." It is interesting to note that both of these scholars use the word *myth* (and the phrase that Eliade used as a synonym for "myth," "sacred history") primarily in its pejorative sense of "lie" (in the sense of a false history), but with overtones of something more positive, something more like "a story that carries true meaning." As statements about prehistory, the two myths of origins (male chauvinist and feminist) are equally unfalsifiable and equally shackled by the old habit, now long abandoned by historians of religions, of equating origins with essences. But many Goddess-feminists continue to cling to their myth, and it is not hard to see why. After all, as a thealogical speculation, the Goddess-feminist credo has much more to offer than the chauvinist. To say that matriarchy preceded patriarchy is to make a statement on the same order as "God created the world in seven days." Such statements do have very real uses, even when archaeology and other forms of evidence prevent them from being accepted as historically accurate. As Eller rightly remarks, "Spiritual feminists have not tarried in bringing together these diverse sources to germinate a myth that is both historically plausible and religiously useful" (Eller 1993, 152). And Pomeroy concurs: "Modern feminists find the theory of female dominance in religion as well as in other areas of prehistoric culture attractive, as though what had happened in the past could be repeated in the future. This popular view is understandable, since, if women were not subordinate in the past, we have *ipso facto* proof that they are not so by nature" (Pomeroy 1975, 12).

But it is important to separate, and to judge separately, the belief in primeval matriarchy, for which there is no reliable evidence, and the belief in the widespread prehistoric worship of goddesses, for which there is considerable evidence, much of it marshaled skillfully and persuasively by Marija Gimbutas. Pomeroy is skeptical about the "attempt to connect a hypothetical earth mother of prehistory to mother goddesses of classical mythology," but she is more sanguine about classical Greece, for which "the mother goddess theory provides a convenient, if unprovable, explanation of the following puzzles: Why are there more than four times as many neolithic female figurines as male ones? . . . Why does Hesiod describe earlier generations of divinities as female-dominated, while the last generation, the Olympian, is male-dominated?" (Pomeroy 1975, 13, 15) And, I might add, why does the ancient Greek tragedian Aeschylus, in the *Eumenides* (1–7), argue that Phoebus Apollo was preceded at Delphi by a goddess, Phoebe, and his male priest by her priestess? As I have argued elsewhere (O'Flaherty 1980), the hypothesis, however speculative, of a proto-Indo-European horse goddess (that white mare on which I seated Marija Gimbutas in the Goddess-feminist myth) untangles a number of tangles in our extant Indo-European mythologies.

But it is not possible to defend the hypothesis of primeval matriarchy with any sort of academic rigor, and Gresham's Law comes into play: bad books drive out good. Vicki Noble's *Motherpeace: A Way to the Goddess through Myth, Art, and Tarot* boasts, like McDonald's, "More than 100,000 copies sold." The old habit of seeking origins casts its distorting shadow on scholarship in this area, for it is not necessary to argue from the dubious visual data of the prehistoric evidence; if all we want to do is show that it is possible to worship goddesses, why bother to do prehistory badly, looking backward, when we can look sideways at examples of explicit texts in the historic and contemporary periods? Looking sideways, however, involves us in a new set of problems, for the utility of most extant texts for the construction of possibilities of feminist worship is seriously impeded by the fact that most of them were written by men and hence are biased against a positive feminist interpretation.

Realizing that Freud is Bad For Women, and ignoring, for the most part, the useful revisions of Freud by feminists like Julia Kristeva (1986), most Goddess-feminists flee to the depth psychologist C. G. Jung (who was to Freud what Trotsky was to Lenin), but this is a movement from the frying pan to the fire. For the static nature of Jung's archetypes—universal images embedded in what he called the "collective unconscious" (1954)—tends to erase all the significant differences between goddesses in favor of a single Goddess, consigning them all to a murky Jungian limbo in which all goddesses look alike in the dark. This eliminates precisely those details that are most likely to reflect the particular circumstances of the lives of real women, and indeed ignores the social construction of gender altogether (O'Flaherty 1988, chap. 2).

Goddesses and Women: The Clytaemnestra Scenario

The reduction of all goddesses to one too easily leads to the reduction of all aspects of women to what Mary Lefkowitz, in a devastating critique felicitously entitled "The Twilight of the Goddess," calls "a genital identity." As Lefkowitz puts it:

> The first reduction could not have been accomplished without the second. What, after all, could women in wildly different societies, and the representations of women in wildly different traditions, have in common with each other, except for the most rudimentary biological characteristics? (Lefkowitz 1993)

And she points out that such a reduction "will surely harm women, by simplifying and demoting them to creatures of mere sexuality." Several excellent collections of essays have combatted this trend by emphasizing the striking differences between goddesses in different cultures (Kinsley 1989; Motz 1997; Preston 1982).

But there are other reasons why goddesses are Bad For Feminists, or, to put it differently, why what's good for goddesses is bad for women. What we know about cults of the goddess from historic texts and the evidence of contemporary society indicates that, where goddesses are worshipped, women are mistreated even more than usual. The same play by Aeschylus that tells us that goddesses preceded gods and priestesses preceded priests concludes by putting Apollo and Athena on record as arguing that women play no role in the production of children (they merely keep the sperm warm and safe for nine months) and hence that powerful women like Clytaemnestra (of whom the very first thing we learn, in the first play of the Aeschylus trilogy, is that she has "the mind of a man") have no recourse against matricide, and no vote in Athens. The logic of what I would call the Clytaemnestra Syndrome seems to be that the more intrinsically powerful, and hence dangerous, goddesses are perceived to be, the more intrinsically powerful, and hence dangerous, human women are perceived to be, and hence the greater the need to keep human women far away from the actual use of any power in the world. The fates of the devotees of Athena, Inanna, and Kali should discourage Goddess-feminists from following this track any farther. If the history of the worship of goddesses teaches us anything at all about the empowerment of women, it is that spiritual power may very well flow from heaven to earth, but political power flows from earth to heaven.

Shari L. Thurer, in of *The Myths of Motherhood*, does not want to admit this: "While we cannot assume that there is a fixed relation between the status of women and the worship of a goddess in all cultures—in contemporary India, for example, the widespread oppression of women exists alongside the worship of a female divinity, the Hindu Devi—in many civilizations where the Goddess held sway, women did too, to a certain extent" (Thurer 1994, 10). I think not, not to any *useful* extent; and the Hindu example should be chilling enough. Pomeroy extends the caveat to Christianity, too: "To use the mother goddess theory to draw any conclusions regarding the high status of human females of the time would be foolhardy. Later religions, in particular Christianity, have demonstrated that the mother may be worshiped in societies where male dominance and even misogyny are rampant" (Pomeroy 1975, 20).

The feminist historian of Judaism Tikva Frymer-Kensky (1992) extends the caveat yet further to the goddesses of Sumeria and Akkadia. Noting the many different sorts of powers, not limited to fertility, that these goddesses had, she argues that although these polytheistic systems did give females a certain separate status, they subordinated women, marginalized them, and limited them to roles of fertility, sexuality, nurturance, and wisdom. In contrast, she argues, women were actually regarded as more equal partners under patriarchal Judaism, despite their subordinate social position. I am more convinced by Frymer-Kensky's argument that women were treated badly in prebiblical, goddess cultures than by her argument that they were treated better in biblical times. I think it was a matter of heads (polytheistic goddess-worship) women lose, and tails (monotheistic worship of a male god) women lose. But Frymer-Kensky's primary argument about the disadvantages of prebiblical goddesses constitutes a brilliant feminist corrective to the Goddess-feminist myth of matriarchy.

Lefkowitz, singling out Frymer-Kensky alone for praise, nevertheless defends the Greeks and the varied powers of their goddesses, arguing that polytheistic systems, whether of male or female divinities, were "mercifully without an ideal of exclusiveness" and that "multiplicity and diversity were defining features of the divine" (Lefkowitz 1992). True, but there is no evidence that these admirable features were extended to human women, as Lefkowitz, too, implicitly acknowledges. Pomeroy reached a conclusion closer to Frymer-Kensky's (and my own) about the negative aspects of polytheism, though she argues from very different premises:

The distribution of desirable characteristics among a number of females rather than their concentration in one being is appropriate to a patriarchal society.... Unable to cope with a multiplicity of powers united in one female, men from antiquity to the present have envisioned women in "either-or" roles. As a corollary of this anxiety, virginal females are considered helpful, while sexually mature women like Hera are destructive and evil. (Pomeroy 1975, 8)

I would agree with Pomeroy that both polytheism and monotheism fragment women, though I would add that they divide them into different sorts of fragments (Doniger 2013a).

Several scholars have suggested that the myth of matriarchy is a Golden Age myth (Talalay 1994, 179; Ashe 1992). But given the rather discouraging track record of the worship of goddesses in the past and the present, it might be best to argue, as Teilhard de Chardin (2002) argued about the Golden Age, that the myth of matriarchy is about the future, something that we might look forward to. There is no reason *not* to believe that there might be matriarchies in the future and that they might clean up some of the mess that the men have made. This is not a historical argument but a hope, one that is supported by numerous isolated images of multivalent goddesses found throughout the world, goddesses far less fragmented and polarized than the images of women (and of gods) that prevail in the dominant cultures of Europe and America today. Yet most of the goddesses that I know eat their children, castrate their consorts, drink blood, and generally behave in ways that may well provide appropriate role models for many of us but which do not inspire confidence in a more gentle, nurturing matriarchal world. Goddess-feminists tend to ignore the actual character of the goddesses that they look to for inspiration.

In the final analysis, for all the effort by Goddess-feminists to subvert dominant paradigms, they have so far failed to imagine gender identies as fluid and truly transgressive. Perhaps the most serious shortcoming of the myth of matriarchy as a charter for human women is that it enshrines rather than challenges the polarization of gender.

Myths of Transsexuality

Serious gender scholarship in the field of religion has therefore, in recent years, turned away from the issue of matriarchy to focus instead upon mythologies that transgress the polar circles of male and female, in order to investigate the possibilities of transsexuality and bisexuality offered in various religions. The field of Indology, in particular, has illuminated and challenged Western ideas about gender. For example, Hindu men in ritual situations may cross-dress for either of two apparently opposed reasons: in devotion to Krishna, men position themselves as female worshippers who are the lovers of Krishna, cross-dressing and even mimicking menstruation. On the other hand, in devotion to the Goddess, men adopt a strategy not of intercourse but of imitation, dressing like women to be like her; the Hijras, in particular, cross-dress and sometimes even castrate themselves in her service (Nanda 1990). Traditional Hinduism is generally starkly homophobic, but the second-century CE *Kamasutra* speaks, entirely nonpejoratively, of a "third nature" (*tritiya prakriti*, a term that first appears a few centuries earlier, in the *Mahabharata*) or perhaps a "third sexuality" in the sense of sexual behavior. Such a person is born male but cross-dresses, takes on aspects of stereotyped female-gendered behavior ("chatter, grace, emotions, delicacy, timidity, innocence, frailty and bashfulness"), and "gets her sexual pleasure and erotic arousal as well as her livelihood" from living as a courtesan with male partners (*Kamasutra* 2.9.1–5; Doniger 2013b).

But non-Western mythologies of gender are not necessarily open to more liberal constructions of gender than our own; some of them are simply open to *different* constructions than ours. As we noted above, myths can be traditional, subversive, or both at once. Myths of the origin of sexual differentiation generally affirm social boundaries; myths of transsexuality may subvert them but do not always do so. Many myths involve the transformation of someone into a person of the other biological sex, with different physical sexual organs, and this is what, in this context, I would call transsexuality (Doniger 2013c, 2013d). Transsexuality more broadly refers to the subjective perception that one has been given the wrong body, that the sex of the mind/soul/personality/gender does not correspond to the sex of the body. In this sense, transsexuality is a dilemma for which myths of transsexual transformation imagine a solution. But in the context of the mythology of gender, I would restrict the term to the narrower meaning of transsexual transformation.

Transsexual transformation is easily achieved by gods (through magic), more painfully by mortals (through surgery). Far more common are stories of transformation of gender, changes in the superficial, social trappings of sex, dressing as someone of the other sex, which I would call transvestism. The considerable literature on transsexuality in ancient India (O'Flaherty 1980; Goldman 1993; Doniger 2013c, 2013d) might make the reader wonder whether Hindu mythology regards sex and gender as intrinsic parts of human identity. At first glance, it does not seem so; after all, these stories were composed within a world in which you probably were recently, and would soon be again, a member of another species. Yet the texts of Hindu religious law (*dharma*) very seldom speak of rebirth into another sex and gender. Gender is relatively easily sloughed off in some texts in which a male is entirely transformed into a female, with a female mentality and memory (aspects of gender rather than sex). Yet many texts, probably reflecting the dramatic, even grotesque, asymmetry between the status and treatment of people of different genders in actual life in ancient India, seem to reflect the very opposite view, a view of gender as astonishingly durable: the male merely assumes the outer form of the female, retaining his male essence, his male memory and mentality. Even the Vedantic theory of illusion, which disparages the body in favor of the soul, implies that you may very well remain a male in some essential way even when you happen to take on a female body; even when memory is transformed, the male almost always reverts to his maleness in the end. This is the dominant pattern of narratives of illusion from the medieval period, dating from about 1000 to 1500 CE (O'Flaherty 1984, 81–89), which tell, for instance, of the sage Narada, who became a woman and lived a full life, taking on the mind of the person whose form he assumed; she forgot that she had been Narada, and the man she married assumed that she had always been a woman, yet Narada eventually returned to his life as a man (*Devibhagavata Purana* 6.28–29). Thus, in myths of transsexual transformation, we must distinguish between the sexual transformation of the body and the gendered transformation of the mind, memory, and personality; sometimes both change, but sometimes sex changes while gender remains unchanged.

Many of the males in Hindu myths who are magically transformed into women but change only their superficial physical genitalia, retaining a male memory, undergo the transformation in order to kill a male enemy. This happens most dramatically in the myth, recorded in a number of medieval Sanskrit texts, in which the demon Adi takes the form of Parvati, the wife of the god Shiva, in an attempt to kill Shiva with teeth inside his/her (Adi's) vagina; Shiva, fooled at first, has intercourse with Adi but then realizes the deception and kills Adi with a razor placed on the tip of his penis (*Padma Purana* 1.46–47; O'Flaherty 1975, 251–61). Less gruesome, but equally deadly and more successful, is the transsexual masquerade of the god Vishnu as Mohini ("the Deluder"), told in a number of ancient Sanskrit texts:

> When the demons stole the plant and elixir of immortality from the gods, Vishnu took the form of Mohini, a beautiful enchantress, seduced the demons, and returned the elixir to the gods. Then Shiva and Parvati came to Vishnu, and Shiva asked him to show him the form of Mohini. Vishnu did so, but when Shiva saw Mohini, he was overcome by lust and immedi-

ately ran after her, abandoning Parvati who stood with her head lowered in shame. Shiva raped Mohini, and his seed fell upon the ground. Mohini disappeared, and Shiva returned to Parvati. (*Brahmanda Purana* 4.10.41–77; O'Flaherty 1973, 228–29)

Vishnu uses sex to destroy a demonic enemy and steal back the elixir, just as the Greek god Zeus creates and sends Pandora to punish Prometheus and mankind for the theft of fire, the Greek equivalent of the Indian elixir (Hesiod, *Works and Days*). But where the male Hindu trickster, Vishnu, himself masquerades as Mohini, a woman, the male Greek god, Zeus, merely creates a woman, Pandora, the "deceiving female form," a "false woman" who is "not a man disguised but woman herself" (Loraux 1991, 390–94).

In the myth of Mohini, Vishnu takes on merely the outer form of the woman and resumes his own form after returning the elixir to the gods; only at Shiva's express request does Vishnu, on a second occasion, resume his Mohini form. Vishnu seems to retain his male consciousness even in other variants of this myth in which he goes so far as to produce a child with Shiva, whose seed—shed on the ground, with no reference to a male or female partner—gives birth to a child, regarded as the child not of Mohini and Shiva but of Vishnu and Shiva (Hari-Hara-Putra, "Son of Hari and Hara," where Hari is a name of Vishnu and and Hara a name of Shiva) (*Bhagavata Purana* 10.88.14–36; *Shiva Purana* 3.20.3–7). Since Vishnu retains his male memory when he becomes Mohini, he can be regarded as having male homosexual relations, playing first the active role with the demons and then the passive role with Shiva, an inadvertent masquerade in which Mohini is the victim rather than the aggressor. From Shiva's standpoint, however, it is a heterosexual act, except in one interesting Telugu variant of the story, in which, when Shiva makes love to Mohini, in the middle of the act Mohini turns back into Vishnu, and Shiva goes on with it—a very rare instance of a consummated, explicit male homosexual act in Hindu mythology (personal communication from Velcheru Narayana Rao, March, 1995). Is this, and indeed the corpus of Mohini stories as a whole, a coded description of male rape?

But sometimes the transformation goes even deeper than mere physical transformation, such that male memory, too, is transformed into female memory, with female desires; the resulting creature makes love *and* babies. This is the case in the myth of Ila told in the great Sanskrit epic the *Ramayana* of Valmiki (7.87–90), dating from about 200 BCE, and in the story of Narada, to which I have alluded above. This pattern of male-to-female (MTF) transformations reaffirms gender stereotypes: males (or females with male memories) kill, while females (with female memories) make babies. Female-to-male (FTM) transformations also reinforce this pattern: when they are deep, the new male memory kills. Thus, in the other great Sanskrit epic, the *Mahabharata* (5.170–87, 189–93; 6.103–14; 8.59–60; O'Flaherty 1980, 307), dating from about 300 BCE, the abducted and abandoned Amba becomes reincarnate as a woman, Shikhandini, who is then magically transformed into the male Shikhandin to avenge Amba's abduction by killing the man responsible for it. Shikhandin remembers that he was born as Shikhandini, but not that he was Amba in a previous birth, and this loss of memory makes it possible for him to kill the man who done him/her wrong, a man (Bhishma) who knows that Shikhandin/i is the reincarnation of Amba, even though Amba does not. Thus Bhishma knows the justice of his death at the hands of "one who used to be a woman," as he himself puts it, referring to Shikhandin's origin not as Amba but as Shikhandini. But Amba is deprived of her agency; she cannot enjoy her revenge, for she must become a man, and lose her female consciousness, in order to take on the killer instinct needed to carry it out.

The Asymmetry of Gender

Contrasts such as these, between MTF and FTM transformations, suggest that, when the same stories are told about men and about women, the plot takes a different turn, for the same acts have different consequences when men and women engage in them; a story about a transsexual woman cannot be simply transformed into a tale of a transsexual man. There are a number of related asymmetries that characterize all myths of gender, not merely transsexual myths.

Where men are usually cursed to become women, women often choose to be men—a not surprising asymmetry, since the culture regards male status as higher than female. The male body is regarded as the norm, and so it is both rare (because disadvantageous) and weakening (for the same reason) to go from male to female. FTM transvestites are regarded as sexy and powerful, while MTF transvestites are funny. While the men in these stories who are magically transformed into women may be ashamed, or disenfranchised, they do not usually kill anyone; but when men merely *pretend* to become women, they often become vicious killers. When Draupadi (the heroine of the *Mahabharata*) is forced to go to bed with Kichaka, a womanizer who has power over her, her husband Bhima takes her place in the bed and beats Kichaka to a pulp, a ball of flesh so mutilated that the people who find the corpse ask, "Where is his neck? His arms? His hands? His head?" (*Mahabharata* 4.21.1–67). The sexist assumption is that every woman is lethal (the poison damsel) and every woman is a fake (the Pandora scenario). But why is this fear of women not averted when the partner is imagined, on some level, as male? Instead, the homophobic paradigm of the murderous transvestite goes on to argue that a fake woman (that is, a man pretending to be a woman—like Bhima with Kichaka—or, less often, a woman transformed into a man, with a man's mind—Shikhandin) is doubly lethal. Any woman corrupts; a transvestite woman corrupts absolutely.

MTF transsexuals are usually said to experience greater sexual pleasure as women than they had as men. The Greek sage Teiresias, who became a woman for a while and then a man again (MTFTM), asserted that women had greater pleasure from love than men did (Apollodorus 3.6.7; Ovid 3.315–40), and in a parallel Hindu story about a man magically transformed into a female, the MTFTM (named Bhangashvana) insists not only that as a woman did s/he have greater pleasure in sex, but that she preferred the children she produced as a woman to those she produced as a man (*Mahabharata* 13.12.1–49; O'Flaherty 1980, 305–6). (In other texts, it is said that a woman has eight times more pleasure than a man—or, sometimes, eight times as much desire, which, to the misogynist mind, is even more threatening; *Garuda Purana* 109.33). But the FTM Amba/Shikhandin, who is elaborately and explicitly denied any sexual pleasure at all, becomes predictably murderous. It would certainly be simplistic to overlook the misogynist implications of the argument that women enjoy sex more than men do. Moreover, to do so would also be to fall, tautologically, into the very gender stereotypes that these myths are forging right under our eyes: males kill, women enjoy sex.

The Hindu myths I have cited provide evidence that cross-dressing is often motivated by politics (hence killing) rather than, or in addition to, sexuality, and this is a pattern that seems to obtain in European mythology as well. Marjorie Garber (1992) is certainly right in asserting that cross-dressing always has a sexual subtext, but there are meaningful surface texts, too. Often, for instance, women will cross-dress to avoid being raped, and to the extent that rape is sexual (in distinction from other forms of violence and domination), this is a sexual reason to cross-dress. Finally, cross-dressing (or transsexual transformation) in order to murder a *sexual* enemy (as Amba avenges her own abduction), whether or not the killing involves a sexual act, might also be construed as a sexual motive. When it does involve a sexual act (as in the killing of Kichaka), there can be no doubt that it has a sexual motive; the "sweet death" or "little death" of the orgasm or the romantic *Liebestod* becomes a bitter, full-sized, and most real death.

The Other Side of Androgyny

Some myths about transsexuality perceive sex as so dangerous that they attempt to eliminate not only the woman but the other partner altogether, to produce the only truly safe sex—when you are alone (as in Woody Allen's joke about masturbation: you meet such nice people that way). This is the case in a genre that the Indologist A. K. Ramanujan collected and called "The Prince Who Married his Own Left Side": a prince refused to marry any woman; instead, he commanded that his own body be cut in half; the right half healed and became the full prince, while the left half became a woman, whom he married. But the prince still feared the woman, kept her distant from himself, and ultimately drove her to be unfaithful to him and (in some variants) to kill him (Ramanujan 1986). Here again we glimpse the darker psychological implications of the theme of sexual transformation: the man who will marry only the woman within him hates her and may be killed by her. The prince who rejects women by limiting the field of possible suitors to himself is directly descended from the androgyne, the original male who splits off from half of his body a woman to be his mate, first described, in India, in the Upanishads (*Brihadaranyaka Upanishad* 1.4.3), in the sixth century BCE. The Tantric yogi, too, copulates with the female principle inside his own body (the Kundalini), thus becoming his own sexual partner—a neat but, as we have seen, not a unique trick (O'Flaherty 1980, 295–96).

The world title in this sort of narcissism surely belongs to the Hindu saint Chaitanya (1486–1533), in whom Krishna and Radha became simultaneously incarnate; this happened because Krishna wished to become his lover, Radha, so that he could know what it was like to love him(self) (*Chaitanya Charitamrita* of Krishnadasa Kaviraja). The seeds of that transformation lie in earlier texts that describe the transformations of Krishna himself, and his worshippers, the cowherd women or, in some cases, cowherd men: several of the cowherd women, abandoned by the teasing Krishna, fantasize that they themselves are Krishna (*Bhagavata Purana* 10.30), while the cowherd men wish to become women (and, as we have noted, the male worshippers of Krishna sometimes dress as women) in order to make love with Krishna. Similarly, it is said that the men who saw Rama, the hero of the *Ramayana,* wanted to become women to make love with him (Govindaraja on *Ramayana* 2.3.39), and the women who saw Draupadi, the heroine of the *Mahabharata,* wanted to become men to make love with her (Goldman 1993, 383). And, to close the circle, it is said that the men who saw Rama and wanted to become women to make love with him became reincarnate as the cowherd women and made love with him when he had taken the form of another incarnation of Vishnu, Krishna (*Padma Purana* 6.272.165–67).

In the same vein, the Buddhist monk Soreyya was so taken by the beauty of the elder Mahakaccayana, whom he glimpsed at the bath, that he wished to marry him, and his genitals were instantaneously transformed from male to female; like Bhangashvana, Soreyya has children both as a male and as a female and prefers the children of his female persona (*Dhammatthakatha* 3.9; on *Dhammapada* 43; cited in Goldman 1993). No one seems to have dared to ask him which way the sex was better. A Greek and Roman parallel to the Hindu story of the man who married his own left side is the tale of Narcissus, as told by Ovid: Narcissus was born when the river god Cephisus raped the blue nymph Leiriope. The seer Teiresias (himself, as we have seen, a sometimes transsexual) told Leiriope, "Narcissus will live a long time, as long as he does not know himself." He was so beautiful that many people fell in love with him, but he rejected them all, for he was too proud of his own beauty. One person who fell in love with him was the nymph Echo, who could use her voice only to repeat what someone else said. When Echo tried to embrace Narcissus he repelled her, and she spent the rest of her life pining for him until only her voice remained. Finally, Artemis caused Narcissus to fall in love with his own reflection in a clear spring. Unable to possess the image, he lay gazing helplessly into the pool. Echo stayed beside him and echoed his cries as he plunged a dagger into his breast and died. Out of his blood there grew the narcissus plant (Ovid 3.341–510) (and, we may add, the name of a psychological syndrome). Pausanias rationalized the story in the Euhemerist manner by arguing that Narcissus had an identical twin sister who died; Narcissus was inconsolable until he saw his own reflection (Pausanias 9.31.6). The Latin myth demonstrates the devastating reflexivity of perverse erotic love, an all-too-human weakness that makes necessary the creation of empty reflections of sound and sight (Doniger 1993, 31–58).

There are other Western stories about this sort of reflexive androgyny, such as the myth related by Aristophanes in Plato's *Symposium* (189E–191E), roughly contemporaneous with the myth of the androgyne in the Upanishads: an original circular creature, half male, half female (or, in other cases, with two male or two female halves), was split in two and condemned to spend its life trying to reunite with its own other half. This image of wholeness and completion is globular, sated, self-contained; it represents an extreme of self-love, purely physical, that depicts human sexuality in terms of excess (the male-female pairs become adulterers and adultresses; the male-male pairs, pederasts; and the female-female pairs, man-hating lesbians). So, too, in the *Malleus Maleficarum* (1971, 1.3:26), the textbook used to persecute witches in seventeenth-century Europe, the devil is said to become first a succubus (to take the sperm from the man "she" sleeps with) and then an incubus (to place that sperm in the woman that "he" sleeps with), in order to impregnate himself, as it were, because he is sterile. And the myth of Narcissus, or the man who married his left half, lives on in Robert Louis Stevenson's *Strange Case of Dr. Jekyll and Mr. Hyde,* the story (I think) of a man who has a homosexual affair with a creature that he splits off from himself.

But if these myths of androgyny are inspired by the hope of avoiding death at the hands of a sexual partner of any gender, they do not succeed: many of these episodes result in death. By and large, these are not happy stories, nor charters for the affirmation of a polymorphous, Jungian androgny. But some do give us more positive paradigms. For example, one Buddhist text expresses a total disregard for gender:

> A bodhisattva should regard all living beings as a wise man regards the reflection of the moon in water or as magicians regard men created by magic … like the track of a bird in the sky; like the erection of a eunuch; like the pregnancy of a barren woman. …
>
> The goddess employed her magic power to cause the elder Sariputra to appear in her form and to cause herself to appear in his form. Then the goddess, transformed into Sariputra, said to Sariputra, transformed into a goddess, "Reverend Sariputra, what prevents you from transforming yourself out of your female state?" And Sariputra, transformed into the goddess, replied, "I no longer appear in the form of a male! My body has changed into the body of a woman! I do not know what to transform!" The goddess continued, "If the elder could again change out of the female state, then all women could also change out of their female state. All women appear in the form of women in just the same way as the elder appears in the form of a woman. While they are not women in reality, they appear in the form of women. With this in mind, the Buddha said, 'In all things, there is neither male nor female.'" Then the goddess released her magical power and each returned to his or her ordinary form. She then said to him, "Reverend Sariputra, what have you done with your female form?" Sariputra: "I neither made it nor did I change it." Goddess: "Just so, all things are neither made nor changed, and that they are not made and not changed, that is the teaching of the Buddha." (Vimalakirti 1976, 56, 61–62)

This is the ultimate philosophical support for the fluidity of gender—it is an argument that, in the sacred realm, or with the understanding that we might hope to obtain from the sacred realm, gender is nothing but an arbitrary social construct, devoid of ontological meaning. But this is, as we have seen, just one half of the argument. For these texts remind us of two truths in tension, a paradox: one view of gender makes it as easy to slough off as a pair of pants (or a dress); but this view is often challenged by myths in which skin is more than skin deep, in which the mind and the memory, too, are gendered, an intrinsic part of the mortal coil that is not quite so easily shuffled off.

Finally, these texts teach us that gender is itself a myth, in both of the double-edged senses of the word with which I began this essay: it is a lie, since it positions as natural, "given," and inevitable what is primarily cultural, learned, and transformable; but it is true, since it is, like any myth, deeply imbedded in our linguistic and narrative assumptions, "given" by culture if not by nature, and thus a powerfully compelling force that we ignore to our peril.

References

Apollodorus. 1921. *The Library*. 2 vols. Text and trans. J. G. Frazer. Cambridge, MA: Loeb Classical Library.

Ashe, Geoffrey. 1992. *Dawn behind the Dawn: A Search for the Earthly Paradise.* New York: Henry Holt.

Bhagavata Purana. 1972. With the commentary of Shridhara. Benares: Pandita Pustakalaya.

Brahmanda Purana. 1857. Bombay: Venkatesvara Steam Press.

Brihadaranyaka Upanishad. 1913. In *One Hundred and Eight Upanishads.* Bombay: Nirnaya Sagara Press.

Buber, Martin. 1955. *The Legend of the Baal-Shem Tov.* New York: Harper.

Caitanya Caritamrta of Krsnadasa Kaviraja: A Translation and Commentary. 2000. Trans. Edward Cameron Dimock Jr. Harvard Oriental Series 56. Cambridge, MA: Department of Sanskrit and Indian Studies, Harvard University.

Calasso, Roberto. 1993. *The Marriage of Cadmus and Harmony.* New York: Knopf.

de Chardin, Teilhard. 2002. *Christianity and Evolution.* New York: Harvest Books.

Detienne, Marcel. 1986. *The Creation of Mythology.* Chicago: University of Chicago Press.

Devibhagavata Purana. 1960. Benares: Pandita Pustakalaya.

Doniger, Wendy. 1993. "Echoes of the *Mahabharata:* The Parrot as Narrator of the *Bhagavata Purana.*" In *Purana Perennis: Reciprocity and Transformation in Hindu and Jaina Texts,* ed. Wendy Doniger. Albany: SUNY Press.

———. 1999. *The Implied Spider: Politics and Theology in Myth*. New York: Columbia University Press. 2nd rev. ed., 2010.

———. 2013a. "Are Hindus Monotheists or Polytheists?" In Doniger 2013e.

———. 2013b. "The Third Nature: Gender Inversions in the *Kamasutra*." In Doniger 2013e.

———. 2013c. "Bisexuality and Transsexuality among the Hindu Gods." In Doniger 2013e.

———. 2013d. "Transsexual Transformations of Subjectivity and Memory in Hindu Mythology." In Doniger 2013e.

———. 2013e. *On Hinduism.* Delhi: Aleph Book Company; New York: Oxford University Press, 2014.

Douglas, Mary. 1966. *Purity and Danger.* London: Routledge.

Eliade, Mircea. 1969. *The Quest.* New York: Harper.

Eller, Cynthia. 1993. *Living in the Lap of the Goddess: The Feminist Spirituality Movement in America.* New York: Crossroads.

Frymer-Kensky, Tikva. 1992. *In the Wake of the Goddesses: Women, Culture, and the Biblical Transformation of Pagan Myth.* New York: Free Press, 1992.

Garber, Marjorie. 1997. *Vested Interests: Cross-Dressing and Cultural Anxiety.* New York: Routledge.

Garuda Purana. 1969. Benares: Pandita Pustakaya.

Gellner, Ernest. 1985. *The Psychoanalytic Movement, or, The Cunning of Unreason.* London: Paladin Grafton Books.

Gimbutas, Marija. 1974. *The Goddesses and Gods of Old Europe 7000–3000 BC: Myths, Legends and Cults.* Berkeley: University of California Press.

———. 1989. *The Language of the Goddess.* San Francisco: Harper.

———. 1991. *The Civilization of the Goddess.* San Francisco: Harper.

Goldman, Robert P. 1993. "Transsexualism, Gender, and Anxiety in Traditional India." *Journal of the American Oriental Society* 113 (3): 374–401.

Herodotus. 1987. *The History.* Trans. David Grene. Chicago: University of Chicago Press.

Hesiod. 1914. *Works and Days.* Trans. Hugh G. Evelyn-White. Cambridge, MA: Loeb Classical Library.

Jung, Carl Gustav. 1954. *The Archetypes and the Collective Unconscious.* Trans. R. F. C. Hull. New York: Pantheon.

Kinsley, David. 1989. *The Goddesses' Mirror.* Albany: SUNY Press.

Kristeva, Julia. 1986. *The Kristeva Reader.* Ed. Toril Moi. New York: Columbia University Press.

Lefkowitz, Mary. 1992. "The Twilight of the Goddess." *New Republic* (August 3).

Lévi-Strauss, Claude. 1963. *Structural Anthropology.* Trans. Claire Jacobson and Brooke Grundfest Schoepf. Harmondsworth: Penguin.

———. 1966. *The Savage Mind.* Chicago: University of Chicago Press.

Lincoln, Bruce. 1986. *Myth, Cosmos, and Society.* Cambridge, MA: Harvard University Press.

Loraux, Nicole. 1991. "Origins of Mankind in Greek Myths." In Yves Bonnefoy, *Mythologies* (a restructured translation of Yves Bonnefoy's *Dictionnaire des Mythologies,* prepared under the direction of Wendy Doniger). Chicago: University of Chicago Press.

Mahabharata. 1933–1969. Poona: Bhandarkar Oriental Research Institute.

Malleus Maleficarum of Heinrich Kramer and James Sprenger. 1971. Trans. Montague Summers. New York: Dover.

Motz, Lotte. 1997. *The Faces of the Goddess.* New York: Oxford University Press.

Nanda, Serena. 1990. *Neither Man nor Woman: The Hijras of India.* Belmont, CA: Wadsworth.

Noble, Vicki. (1983) 1994. *Motherpeace: A Way to the Goddess through Myth, Art, and Tarot.* San Francisco: Harper.

O'Flaherty, Wendy Doniger. 1973. *Siva, the Erotic Ascetic.* London: Oxford University Press.

———. 1975. *Hindu Myths.* Harmondsworth: Penguin.

———. 1980. *Women, Androgynes, and Other Mythical Beasts.* Chicago: University of Chicago Press.

———. 1984. *Dreams, Illusion, and Other Realities.* Chicago: University of Chicago Press.

————. 1988. *Other Peoples' Myths: The Cave of Echoes*. New York: Macmillan. (Reprint, Chicago: University of Chicago Press, 1995.)

O'Flaherty, Wendy Doniger, and David Grene. 1988. *Oresteia*. A New Translation for the Court Theatre Production of 1986. Chicago: University of Chicago Press.

Ovid. *Metamorphoses*. 1977. Trans. Frank Justus Miller. Cambridge, MA: Loeb Classical Library.

Padma Purana. 1893. Poona: Anandasrama Sanskrit Series 131.

Pausanias. 1918–1935. *Description of Greece*. Trans. W. H. S. Jones. Cambridge, MA: Loeb Classical Library.

Pomeroy, Sarah B. 1975. *Goddesses, Whores, Wives and Slaves: Women in Classical Antiquity*. New York: Schocken Books. Reprinted, with new preface, 1994.

Preston, James, ed. 1982. *Mother Worship: Themes and Variation*. Chapel Hill: University of North Carolina Press.

Ramanujan, A. K. 1986. "The Prince Who Married his Own Left Side." In *Aspects of India: Essays in Honor of Edward Cameron Dimock,* ed. Margaret Case and N. Gerald Barrier, 1–16. New Delhi: American Institute of Indian Studies and Manohar.

Ramayana of Valmiki. 1960–1975. Baroda: Oriental Institute.

Rushdie, Salman. 1990. *Haroun and the Sea of Stories*. New York: Grant Books.

Shiva Purana. 1964. Benares: Pandita Pustakalaya.

Stone, Merlin. 1976. *When God Was a Woman*. New York: Dial Press.

Talalay, Lauren E. 1994. "A Feminist Boomerang: The Great Goddess of Greek Prehistory." In *Gender and History* 6 (2): 165–83.

Thurer, Shari L. 1994. *The Myths of Motherhood: How Culture Reinvents the Good Mother*. Boston: Houghton Mifflin.

Vimalakirti. 1976. *The Holy Teachings of Vimalakirti*. Trans. Robert A. F. Thurman. University Park: Pennsylvania State University Press.

13 :: NATURE　ANNE FAUSTO-STERLING

My dreams sometimes conjure up the woods and stream visible from the living room window of my childhood home. The images are vivid, in color and gender-specific. The pheasant I watch is not merely a bird but, with ornithological precision, a brilliantly colored male with long, magnificent tail feathers, or a brown, well-camouflaged, short-tailed female; the ducks are either mottled brown mallard mothers with ducklings in tow, or the bright green-headed male. The state of nature in my reverie is serene and safe. When danger enters, it is always human or monstrous, a thing capable of destroying my natural haven. In my childhood, danger did, indeed, come from without, from humans who did not care for Communists or Jews, or smart, intellectual, independent adolescent girls. Safety and solace lay in the woods. Those youthful sensations of safety and danger still lie so strongly within me that I can barely suppress my alarm when interacting with students who may never have seen a live frog or even a living cow, and who find natural objects such as worms and snakes neither comforting nor awe-inspiring but repellant.

Clearly, my relation to and understanding of that thing we call nature differs from those of my students. Indeed, over the centuries humans have devised varied accounts of the natural world and their relation to it. But there is nothing natural about nature. The pheasants that wandered through my family's woodland symbolized my safe haven, but the bird did not arrive on US shores until 1866 (Palmer 1899), imported by bird lovers anxious to establish Eurasian species on American soil. Its arrival followed almost three centuries in which European immigrants both redefined and reshaped the nature (note here a second usage of the word, referring to the inherent character of a thing or person) of the American continent. My dream nature is that of the nineteenth-century romantic, not of the seventeenth-century Native American.

In the Euro-American lexicon, nature has been the eye of the needle through which stories about race and gender have been threaded. The

North American continent "discovered" by Europeans was a vast wilderness, often described by explorers as uninhabited, rich, savage, and wild. It seemed to represent primeval nature, unsullied by human touch. Contemporary historical work (e.g., Cronon 1983; Merchant 1989; Silver 1990) offers a different analysis. Seventeenth-century New England had a population of at least sixty-five thousand Native Americans organized into villages, tribes, and nations. They survived well, maintaining their population at a steady level by combining hunting, gathering, and agriculture. Native Americans had divided, but fairly flexible, gender roles, a fact that confused the more role-rigid colonizing Europeans. Women gathered and farmed (including the heavy physical labor of clearing land and carrying up to twenty-four hundred pounds of fish yearly to fertilize the crops). Men hunted, fished, and helped with heavy labor.

The native inhabitants had their own elaborate understandings of the nature of nature and of human relations to the physical world. Nature and its inhabitants were live actors. Spirits, such as the Corn Mother, wielded great power, but so did those belonging to animals and even inanimate objects, such as trees and rocks. Given nature's agency, humans had to treat her and all of the earth's inhabitants with great respect. The reciprocity between humans and nature can be seen in the Cherokee legend of Little Deer (Awiakta 1993). Once upon a time, the story goes, human hunters began to kill too many animals, threatening the continued existence of life itself. When the animals met in council, the deer's chief, Awi Usdi (also known as Little Deer), proposed that humans agree to hunt only when the need was real and that they show respect for the animals whose lives they took. In ceremonial preparation for the kill, humans were to ask Little Deer for permission, and afterward they were to respectfully beg the dead animal spirit's pardon. If the hunters failed to keep their end of the bargain, Little Deer promised to track them down and cripple their limbs.

Early European settlers and explorers, however, could not "see" the complexity of these unfamiliar human lifeways. They attributed the open, parklike physiognomy of the southern New England woodlands, and the sparse underbrush and the ease with which one could ride or walk for miles within the forests, to the constitutive nature of the region. Learning the truth, that Native Americans regularly used fire to clear the forest underbrush so that they could more easily hunt and reduce the number of hiding places for vermin, did not change their opinion. To the European, the native people were themselves a part of nature, also savage, wild, and uncivilized.

In her nonfiction book *Seedtime in the Cumberland*, novelist Harriet Arnow describes the Cumberland River of Kentucky during the late eighteenth century. European travelers considered the land to be uninhabited, except by occasional natives, but the "empty" forest was filled with buffalo, elk, and deer: "Red-billed parakeets ... red and gray squirrels, raccoons, opossums, foxes, great droves of wolves, panthers ... and in the river hundred-pound catfish and twenty-pound perch ... many beaver ... swans, wild geese ... were plentiful" (Arnow 1960, 57). In Arnow's descriptions, the woodlands seem to be empty of humans. But early descriptions of the Kentucky woodland as "park-like" and so devoid of undergrowth that "a traveler could see a deer at 150 paces" (1960, 56) strongly suggests that Native Americans lived in the area and actively managed the forests, deliberately burning the underbrush to enable easy passage and improve hunting conditions.

The notion that Europeans "discovered" vast empty forests teeming with animal life and timber was rapidly reinforced by the decimation of native populations. In the early 1600s, not long after the Europeans had arrived, epidemics of the plague and smallpox, previously unknown on the American continent, swept through the native populations. Within fifty years the indigenous populations of New England had dwindled from more than sixty thousand to only ten thousand. By 1800 the Cherokee, Choctaw, and Chickasaw living in Arnow's seemingly empty woodland had experienced similarly drastic population declines. And by the time Europeans had begun to colonize in earnest, they really did see a "virgin continent" almost devoid of human habitation—and thus available for the taking.

As much as any, Charles Mann's work had given the lie to a notion of the Americas as untamed wilderness. As he writes in *1491*, there may have been more people living in the Americas than in Europe. Native Americans had managed and shaped the land, built huge monuments, cultivated sophisticated water management projects, and more (Mann 2005). Furthermore, the European invasion reshaped American nature in surprising ways: earthworms, mosquitoes, cockroaches, honeybees, varieties of rats, and more arrived with Europeans and changed what we call nature in the Americas (Mann 2011).

Not all visions of newly discovered lands evoked the unspoiled Garden of Eden. Amerigo Vespucci, whose feminized first name became that of the New World, wrote that native women went about "naked and libidinous; yet they have bodies which are tolerably beautiful" (Tiffany and Adams 1985, 64). Vespucci's innocents lived to be 150 years old, and giving birth caused them no inconvenience. Despite being so at one with nature, however, Vespucci found Native American women to be immoral. He believed them to have special knowledge of how to enlarge their lover's sex organs, induce miscarriages, and control their own fertility. The early explorers linked the metaphor of the innocent virgin (both the women and the virgin land) with that of the wildly libidinous female. The descriptions oscillated between the "blissfully ignorant, pure, and welcoming savage" at one with a nurturing, mothering nature and the unmanageable, wild native. Here we see the ineluctable intertwining of race, gender, and nature. Mother earth offered bounty and livelihood but also uncontrollable, destructive force. William Bradford, for example, landing on Cape Cod in 1620, described a "hideous and desolate wilderness, full of wild beasts and wild men" (Merchant 1989, 101).

Carolyn Merchant correlates particular understandings of nature with specific modes of economic production. And since nature is often personified as a female, differing views of gender also emerge. In contrast to the true New England natives, for example, the first European settlers constructed a geographically fixed, preindustrial agricultural system of subsistence farming and trading within isolated and more or less self-sufficient local communities. These settlers conceptualized nature as the active, deputized agent of God. She was, paradoxically, a virgin and a mother, while animals and minerals lost agency and were transformed into passive objects and commodities. Men's and women's production spaces were more sharply divided than in Native American society, and, in contrast to the more gender-integrated and communal social life of tribal villages, the social world of eighteenth-century Euro-Americans revolved around the family farm. Increasing the labor force to enable farm expansion became essential. Here the farmer tamed the wild land, producing food by serving "as midwife to nature," while the wife became "midwife to humans" (Merchant 1989, 25).

By the nineteenth century in New England, manufacturing and commerce had taken hold. Agriculture transformed from subsistence to market production, and money took over from barter as the means of economic exchange. Males dominated the use of machines for production. Nineteenth-century New Englanders represented nature as a passive female who taught mechanical laws to those who studied her. The earth's contents, animal and mineral alike, became natural resources and potential objects of scientific investigation. The nineteenth century witnessed vast changes in population distribution and growth and the creation of what historians have called the "spermatic economy"—that is, the "sublimation of sexuality into economic production" (Merchant 1989, 25). Socially, a truly public sphere, the province of men, separated itself clearly from the private, nuclear household—the domain of women (see also Ulrich 1990).

Changes in reproduction, social organization, and economic production also affect both our understandings of nature as that external something that science seeks to understand and know, and the very nature of knowledge itself. Symbolically, the Native American used animism to represent nature. In their mythology, humans could take on animal form and vice versa. Humans and animals could alter their fates through reciprocal interaction. Eighteenth-century Euro-Americans rejected animism, living with a fatalistic view that God had organized the universe according to some predetermined organic whole. Fate lay in the stars and the heavens, and humans had but to accept their lot. But nineteenth-century capitalism brought with it the hope of controlling destiny. Europeans saw nature in mechanistic terms, as a clock that could be dismantled, reassembled, and dominated. Merchant (1980) has described similar transformations in worldview on the European continent during an earlier period (see also Merchant 2003).

Race, Gender, Science

Such different symbolic understandings of nature led, in turn, to different ways of knowing. Native animism entailed a unity of spirit and mind. One obtained knowledge through direct, one-on-one communication. (To find out why the deer hunt fared poorly, one might hope to communicate directly with the deer.) In contrast, preindustrial, agrarian Euro-Americans used analogy to understand the world. They tried to understand the ways in which nature, also created by God, might be in sympathy with or harbor antipathy toward particular events. A visual awareness of the signs and symbols that nature used to communicate her wishes dominated their world. Members of societies dominated by technology, however, struggle to control nature rather than resignedly submitting to her control. As part of this effort, which in Europe reaches back at least to the sixteenth century, an analytic consciousness developed that separated mind from body. The mind became associated with reason and masculinity, the body with an irrational, and at times uncontrollable, female nature. All modes of thought became dualistic, subject separated from object, mind from body, male from female, nature from nurture, savage from civilized, black from white (Plumwood 1993).

One important consequence of this construction of nature was the association of masculinity with reason and science. In the industrial era, the only legitimate knowledge comes from scientific analysis; the whole is rendered comprehensible by breaking it down into its parts, a task that only (white) masculine reason could accomplish. Thus science became an illegitimate place for women and people of color, since only by detaching oneself from nature, banning the feminine irrational from one's mind, could one seek to understand and master her. As Evelyn Fox Keller has so poignantly written:

> In a science constructed around the naming of … nature as female and the parallel naming of … mind as male, any scientist who happens to be a woman is confronted with an *a priori* contradiction in terms. This poses a critical problem of identity: any scientist who is not a [white, European] man walks a path bounded on one side by inauthenticity and on the other by subversion. (Keller 1985, 174)

Historians are not alone in linking understandings of nature, colonialism, and racial and gender ideology. Contemporary ecofeminists include both political activists and scholars concerned about the destruction of the nonhuman world of living beings. The word *ecofeminism* codes for a diverse set of practices and viewpoints. As a social movement, it emerged from the feminist, peace, and ecology movements of the 1970s and crystallized in a 1980 conference entitled "Women and Life on Earth." Merchant offers a taxonomy, sketched below, of four major ecofeminist strains of thought and how they differ in the ways they connect race, gender, and colonial and economic domination to domination over the natural world (Merchant 1992; for other taxonomies of ecofeminism, see Warren 2000; Mies and Shiva 1993).

The first, *liberal feminism*, accepts the idea that nature is a passive outsider subject to scientific and engineering attempts to manipulate and control it. Better environmental management can be attained through more insightful applications of the scientific method and through use of the established legal system to regulate human activity. Liberal feminists suggest that discrimination against women has prevented them from taking an active role in the scientific and legal regulation of nature. They point with pride to the environmental activist groups founded and motored by women, and suggest that fighting to bring more women into the ranks of scientists and politicians will ultimately translate into improvements in environmental science and laws. Liberal feminists view nature as inanimate and accept the idea that humans, acting as rational individuals, ought to dominate the earth.

Next, *Marxist feminists* see the domination or control of nature as the pathway to human freedom, since nature provides the material basis (food, raw materials, and so on) upon which we build human life. Human nature is not fixed or "natural," but historically specific, produced by the economic and social relations of a particular culture. The destruction of the environment results from capitalist modes of production—where greed and the accumulation of wealth take precedence over concerns for environmental protection. In a Marxist feminist future, men and women would both work equally in the environmental sciences; production would be to satisfy human needs only, rather than to accumulate surplus and wealth; and the "rational" human, now acting collectively rather than individually, would find a way to live on earth without further polluting and destroying the environment.

Third, to the *cultural feminist*, Merchant suggests, nature is both spiritual and personal. Conventional science and technology, with its emphasis on domination and control, is the cause rather than the cure for environmental problems. For such thinkers, biology (especially reproduction) lies at the heart of human nature. Cultural feminists argue that the male-dominated environmental movement pays too little attention to environmental threats to female reproduction, and they celebrate a perceived connection between women and nature.

Finally, like the Marxists, *socialist feminists* find in nature the material basis of all life. But they understand that the concept of nature is socially and historically constructed, and that both production and reproduction have transformed the environment. Human nature is created through the interactions of biology and the historical practices that define a variety of human divisions (especially race, gender, class, and age). Socialist feminists complain that the traditional environmental movement fails to recognize nature itself as an active participant, while also omitting women's reproductive roles and the concept of reproduction from their worldview. Socialist feminists envision a partnership between humans and the natural world. They examine the effects of colonial domination on women, nature, and indigenous inhabitants, while also analyzing the effects of technological interventions (especially the many aspects of the new reproductive technologies) on more traditional modes of reproduction.

Many third-world women whose lives have been deeply affected by colonialism and its sequelae have become environmental activists. India's Chipko movement provides an example. In India, women have traditionally used forests as an intricate ecological resource providing fuel, medicinal plants, soil stability, water, and fodder. Women utilized complex forest habitats as a sustainable resource. But international economic interests encouraged the Indian government to promote the use of large-scale agriculture to produce crops for export. This resulted in the cutting down of forests and extensive monoculture, which in turn destroyed watersheds, produced killing floods, and lessened the amount and diversity of locally available food. This sequence of events impoverished economically marginal women who lost the forests as their source of sustenance.

The women, however, drawing on a lengthy tradition, fought back. In ancient Indian cultures, people worshipped tree goddesses and saw the forest as sacred. For more than three hundred years, women had periodically defended the forest against destruction by employing nonviolent direct action, hugging the trees and sometimes chaining themselves to them. In the 1970s women revived these strategies in order to save the forests for multiple uses and the valleys from the flooding that resulted from hillside logging. The Chipko women saved areas from deforestation through mass actions, obtaining the support of local men and defying lumberjacks and police (Shiva 1988, 1999, 2012). Today in India, women continue to organize around and study the relations between women, food, traditional women's knowledge, biodiversity, and sustainable living (Shiva 2012).

The Chipko women are not alone. Throughout the third world, women engage in local activist movements to preserve their environment and livelihoods. For example, professor (and future Nobel Prize winner) Wangari Maathai of Kenya responded to rural women's complaints that they lacked firewood, clean water, and nutritious food by teaching them how to plant trees. Since Maathai established what came to be known as the Green Belt Movement (in 1977), hundreds of thousands of women and men have planted over forty-seven million trees, restoring downgraded environments and improving the lives of poor women and men. Maathai found that to plant trees and maintain the environment, she and her followers had to engage with broader political questions. With tree-planting, she linked social and economic change to an environmental agenda, and in the process developed a vision for Africa's future (Maathai 2010).

Postcolonial Science and Technology Studies and/versus Feminist Philosophies of Science

As I have suggested thus far, colonialists and imperialists persistently describe nature in racialized and gendered terms, while at the same time using gender to depict colonial relations. Two fields of scholarly inquiry, so-called postcolonial science and technology studies (STS) and feminist philosophies of science, have picked at different ends of this interweaving of race, gender, nature, and science but have yet to join their voices in a full-throated analytical effort. The following comments are based on an essay by Sandra Harding (2009, 401–21; see also Harding 2008).

Over the past thirty or so years, Euro-American analysts of gender and science have pursued several important themes. They began by asking (first) where all the women scientists were. Their approach has been twofold—searching for hidden women, scientists whose contributions and careers did not make it onto the pages of mainstream history books, and examining current barriers to scientific careers for women (Rossiter

1982, 1995, 2012; Schiebinger 1993). The ideas underlying these inquiries included the simple concept of equity, as well as the sometimes inchoate notion that a more diverse scientific workforce would produce better science. A second project examined how and why some fields of science had taken on the task of "proving scientifically" that women are biologically inferior (Fausto-Sterling 1993; Hubbard 1990; Bleier 1984; Fine 2010; Bluhm and Jacobson 2012). Third, scholars asked how scientists nonconsciously wove cultural concepts of gender into the production of scientific and technological knowledge (e.g., Fausto-Sterling 2000; Wajcman 1991).

There are both parallels and differences between the analysis of gender and science and projects to analyze the relationships between colonialism, imperialism, science, and technology. Chief among these are what Harding calls "counter-histories" (2009). Just as feminist critics have written new histories of science that include women, postcolonial science projects have rewritten stories about the achievements of Western science, demonstrating how these have often required particular kinds of exploitation of indigenous goods and knowledge. This point of view connects to a second theme—a critical reevaluation of the importance of traditional knowledge. Lastly, postcolonial STS efforts have been aimed at the possibility of developing non-Western, local science and technology projects.

Harding (2009) charts some of the conflicts between the gender and science and the postcolonial science movements. For this essay, however, I want to focus on their intersections, on where approaches to the study of nature itself are both gendered *and* racialized. Consider, for example, efforts to chart the effects of gender relations on science and technology in colonialist and imperialist regimes. Historically, indigenous women have often provided knowledge about and identification of indigenous pharmacologies "discovered" by colonialists and exported as new medicine to the colonizing countries. Seventeenth-century naturalist Maria Sybylla Merian's reliance on her indigenous female servants in Suriname for information on local plants and insects (Schiebinger 2007) and Joseph-François Lafitau's 1716 "discovery" of Canadian ginseng (he asked a Mohawk medicine woman) are two well-documented examples (S. J. Harris 2005). Simultaneous with such knowledge extraction, Western scientists such as Linnaeus were categorizing nature in gendered terms (Schiebinger 1993; Browne 1989), and, in another twist of the mind, racial distinctions were often gendered in ways that helped the imperial order to claim legitimacy (Stepan, 1998; Russett 1989; Harrison 2005).

Moving into the modern period, discussions of modernization theory and of gender and development have led to some critical conclusions.

First, development projects that rely heavily on modern (Western) science often have bad consequences for women. Those women and men positioned on the outskirts of modernity are frequently lost during modernization efforts. Second, traditionalists who resist modern science may be represented as irrational, lacking in the "manliness" required to pursue rational, scientific approaches to development. To break out of this trap requires not only that gender dominance applied to women be addressed, but also that the meanings of masculinity be reformulated. In the process, the story of who can know about science and nature and how knowledge is put to use for the benefits of developing nations can be rewritten.

Reproducing

The concept of reproduction, which can be applied to both the biological and social aspects of human life and the natural world, links the various strands of ecofeminism. At one level, it seems as if biological reproduction "couldn't be more natural." Yet, as we have developed the technological capabilities to choose when to reproduce, and to manipulate the events of fertilization, implantation, and child birth, these natural processes have become "denatured," that is, subject to increasingly complex levels of technological intervention. The intercession of medical and reproductive science in the processes of human reproduction provides a node for intense argument about the nature of gender. Again, not all feminists use the same theoretical models to frame the debate.

During the first forty years of the twentieth century, women activists fought to make safe, effective birth control widely available. In the face of legal restrictions on the dissemination of birth control information, activists such as Emma Goldman and Margaret Sanger went to jail to promote their goals (Gordon 1976). These early birth control activists held complex and often contradictory visions of female nature. On the one hand, they found the unregulated production of large numbers of children to be detrimental to a woman's health and to the health of the family. They did not, in other words, feel that it was a natural good for women to produce the largest number of children possible. They advocated the use of artificial birth control technology—primarily barrier methods and spermicides. On the other hand, they often used the ideal of natural motherhood in their arguments. Having too many children could interfere with women's mothering instincts, especially if a family was too poor to support all of the children or repeated birthing made the woman too ill to cope with her brood. Thus artificial intervention to control the frequency of (natural) reproduction would allow the flourishing of women's maternal instinct.

Large sectors of the birth control movement used distinctly classist and racist arguments as part of their struggle. They took up eugenicist claims that the poorer classes—including darker-skinned immigrants to the United States—would overproduce and thus overwhelm the white middle and upper classes. Birth control and sterilization of the "unfit" became essential to stopping this natural tendency of the poor to have so many children. Sanger made it short and sweet: "More children from the fit—less from the unfit. That is the chief issue of birth control" (quoted in Paul 1995, 20). Conservatives who opposed birth control technology and education for women, however, argued that both would lower the birthrate among middle-class women, thus allowing the lower classes to overgrow middle- and upper-class society.

In the first half of the twentieth century, then, feminists concerned with the technology of birth control had two motives: first, to make life better for all women and, second, to control the birthrate of poor, immigrant women and women of color (especially in comparison to that of middle- and upper-class women). Members of the modern women's liberation movement, which burst onto the stage in the late 1960s, also confronted questions of reproductive technology. But they framed the issues somewhat differently. This generation of women did not necessarily see science and technology as a friend providing a pathway to reproductive freedom.

Instead, modern feminists confronted what they defined as the paradox of the body and technology. On the one hand, women's "nature" seemed inextricably tied to their reproductive biology; on the other, their biology provided an argument against equal social and political rights. Should women turn to technology to avoid becoming slaves to their bodies, even though in doing so they detached themselves from a potential source of power—their close connection to reproduction? Or should they declare their oneness with nature and draw special value and prestige from their unique abilities to bear children? Taking the latter path would leave women vulnerable to biologically based arguments against full social, political, and economic equality. (These were the years when the official physician of US vice president Hubert Humphrey confidently declared that it would be dangerous for a woman to become president because, in a menopausal fit, she might lack the judgment and steady hand to steer a safe course through some perilous world crisis.)

One important "declaration of independence" from the body's tyranny was a book entitled *The Dialectic of Sex: The Case for the Feminist Revolution* by Shulamith Firestone (1970). Firestone proposed a radical denaturing of reproduction. Arguing that childbirth and the traditional family provided the fertile soil out of which grew women's oppression, she suggested a technological fix. "Pregnancy," she wrote, "is barbaric ... and, moreover, childbirth hurts" (226). Rather than return to a demedicalized "natural" childbirth, Firestone believed that "the cult of natural childbirth itself tells us how far we've come from true oneness with nature" (227). Her solution: develop the technology for completely artificial reproduction—babies in a test tube, development in an incubator. Feminist fiction from this period, such as Marge Piercy's *Woman on the Edge of Time* (1979), explored the same themes.

While the technological capabilities for complete development outside the womb are closer to being within our grasp today than in 1970, there is still no agreement among feminists (or anyone else) that it would be good to use such scientific knowledge. Firestone believed that artificial reproduction could make men and women equally responsible for reproduction—thus setting them on a more equal footing. Rather than being inherently dehumanizing, the possibility of in vitro reproduction would "make possible an honest reexamination of the ancient value of motherhood" (227). Indeed, the use and abuse of reproductive technology provides a large slate upon which feminists sketch out arguments with one another and with a broader constituency about the nature of reproduction and mothering.

Like many others, feminists of several stripes have raised the specter of a dystopic future. What if it were to become the norm to choose fetal sex, hair color, or skin color? What level of disability would warrant selective abortion? Would we develop a culture in which the spectrum of human variability became uncomfortably narrow? Would women live under a new tyranny—the injunction to give birth only to physically and mentally "perfect" children? And how would we define perfection?

At least into the start of the twenty-first century, it has been helpful to use the categories of cultural feminism, liberal feminism, and socialist feminism to understand the debates about reproductive technology. Cultural feminists share a widespread distaste for most reproductive technology. They value the experience of childbirth and reproduction and see most medical interventions in the process as artificial and unnatural. Their political analyses blame the patriarchal nature of science and technology itself. One visible spokesperson for the anti–reproductive technology movement identified such technological research as morally reprehensible (Corea 1979). The call of international groups, such as the Feminist International Network on the New Reproductive Technologies, to monitor and attempt to control new scientific developments is not unwarranted, especially if one does not trust scientific institutions to work in women's best interests.

But at least some women feel it is in their best interest to avail themselves of the new technology. Liberal feminists analyze questions of reproductive technology in terms of choice. Women, operating as free and independent individuals, ought to have a full range of available options, with birth control devices tailored to individual needs and differences; the choice to give birth "naturally" in a hospital or at home; the choice, should all modes of birth control fail, to abort a fetus; and the choice, should nature fail to "take its course," to seek medical help in becoming pregnant or to hire another woman to bear a child on their behalf.

Using the autonomous individual able to make free choices as a model, however, runs liberal feminists into some pretty dark alleys. With the sequencing of the human genome, more and more tests designed to identify possible birth defects become available and the "choices" offered pregnant women become immense. Already amniocentesis, ultrasound, or the removal of cells from the protective membranes surrounding the fetus can identify hundreds of possible problems with a developing fetus. Individual women are faced with impossible choices. A test that reveals a fetus to have spina bifida or Down syndrome, for example, will say nothing about the severity of the defect. Will the child be only mildly inconvenienced or profoundly retarded? And what does the birth of a profoundly disabled child do to a family in a culture with no effective social support system for chronic disability? Anthropologist Rayna Rapp wrestled with just such a choice (1984, 97–100; 2000) when she learned she was carrying a Down syndrome fetus. On the one hand, she could envision devoting her life to the child and fighting to improve the lot of the disabled. On the other hand, she noted that such acts of love bore serious consequences. Neither she nor her husband had younger relatives who might care for the child in the event of their own deaths. "In a society where the state provides virtually no decent, humane services for the mentally retarded," Rapp writes, "how could we take responsibility for the future of our dependent Down's syndrome child?" (1984, 98; see also Landsman 1998, 69–99).

Socialist feminists criticize both cultural and liberal feminists. Their general starting point is that pregnancy, birth, and motherhood cannot be properly understood through appeals to nature or the natural. Instead, social, cultural, historical, and economic conditions always define the terms and logic of the debate. In this view, the body and its functions are never "natural," that is, attributable to some pure state of nature, but always socially embedded and contingent upon cultural discourse and practice. Furthermore, the entire notion of individuals choosing as free agents becomes suspect if one looks carefully at the divisions among women. Madonna and a woman on welfare do not have the same ability to choose options within a given medical care system.

Sociologist Michelle Stanworth (1987) discusses several critical problems with both cultural and liberal feminist analyses. First, the definitions and functions of motherhood have changed. In the past, women spent more time in pregnancy and childbirth, but children grew up and left home at earlier ages. In modern Euro-American cultures, motherhood focuses more on child-rearing than on childbirth. Thus, while it may be important to analyze, monitor, and intervene in the development of new reproductive technologies, such intercessions should not cause us to lose sight of the far greater social arena occupied by questions of gender and child-rearing.

Second, it is important to analyze reproductive technology in the context of the health care system in general. Reproduction is but one arena of many in which women may receive inadequate or inappropriate health care. Third, women are themselves stratified by age, race, class, and ethnicity, and each of these factors affects the quality and quantity of available health care. These same differences among women also influence what kinds of "choice" are available and what attitudes individual women take toward particular reproductive options (Rapp 1990). In pointing out such differences, socialist feminists challenge the natural status of the central symbols "womanhood" and "motherhood."

Now, in the second decade of the twenty-first century, however, widespread use of reproductive technologies has become a quotidian fact, to be analyzed in current practice rather than with an eye toward prevention. Ethnographer and STS scholar Charis Thompson (2005), for example, studied the daily events of assisted reproductive technology (ART) as they played out in a clinic. She watched and recorded as the threads of science, nature, kinship, gender, race, and sexuality interwove in a world-producing dance within the clinic setting. She found that the reproduced world was essentially conservative, recreating through science a view of nature as the central arbiter of gender, class, and race relations.

Empirical studies of the egg- and sperm-donation markets in the United States confirms this naturalization using prevailing "Western" social and cultural narratives of the meaning of having and raising children in a race-, class-, and gender-stratified society. Dorothy Roberts (2009) uses the term "reprogenetics" to describe how reproductive technologies shift the promotion of well-being from the hands of government to the lives of individual women. With this shift has come a marketing of reproductive services to women of color as well as to white women. While at one level this can be seen as a good thing, the ART clinics have layered on a special set of raced-based genetic testing that Roberts argues further ensconces the idea of race as primarily a biological category, something which Daniels and Heidt-Forsythe (2012) convincingly document.

There seem to be two broad approaches to the current state of affairs for reproductive technology markets. One is to let the markets, unregulated, do their thing; the other would be to establish formal government regulations for reproductive technology markets, at either the state or the federal level. For feminists and antiracists, what might be the pros and cons of each approach? As Jesudason writes, "the stakes are high: reproductive autonomy for women ... the geneticization of race and difference, access to the technologies" and the possibility that in a government regulated market certain births would be considered "unacceptable" (Jesudason 2009, 903). Comprehensive government regulation of ART and especially of genetic embryo selection reopens the possibility of a population-level neo-eugenics—of great concern to feminists, people of color, and people with disabilities. The alternative, having all selection decisions made privately and individually, might seem at first to avoid the problem. But as Roberts writes, "Genetic selection procedures are increasingly treated as social responsibilities reinforced not only by cultural expectations but also by legal penalties and incentives" (Roberts 2009, 797).

At this historical moment, there seem to be two possible visions for the future. In a dystopic future, genetic science would reinforce a biological definition of race that in turn would reinforce racial and economic divisions through the kinds of genetic testing available to differently defined groups. Roberts (2009) and Jesudason (2009), however, can also imagine a utopic future spearheaded by radical feminists who resist the use of genetic screening via alliances with antiracist, disability rights, and economic justice movements.

What's "Natural" about the Body?

As is "natural" in a capitalist society, the language of production permeates discussions of reproduction. Scientists speak of zygotes—what you get when you join the sperm and egg to produce a growing embryo—as "the products of conception." The products come with varying price tags, depending upon to whose womb they are transferred. "Genetic counseling, screening and testing of fetuses serves the function of 'quality control' on the assembly line of the products of conception, separating out those products we wish to develop from those we wish to discontinue" (Rothman 1989, 21). Such language has the power to transform. As babies become products, pregnant women become unskilled assembly line workers. Again, we see that there is nothing natural about having babies. As social, cultural, and economic interactions change, so too do our understandings of gender and the body.

If there is nothing "natural" about pregnancy, childbirth, and mother-hood, what, then, *can* nature tell us about the experience and potential of being born female? Does nature inevitably dictate the future capabili-ties and lifestyles of children with two X chromosomes? Or is it only the experiences and opportunities we have as we grow up that dictate our potentials? For centuries, these alternatives have been posed as a ques-tion of nature versus nurture—the so-called nature/nurture problem. A lot rests on the outcome. The idea that woman's nature accounts for her role in life while explaining her inferior political and economic status is ancient. It seems that no matter what new office a woman aspires to, she will be greeted by naysayers who claim that her nature renders futile her aspirations.

At the turn of the twentieth century, some doctors argued that wom-en's biological natures made it impossible for them to endure, without bodily harm, the rigors of higher education. Today, some argue that women are, by nature, less mathematical, less aggressive, and more nur-turing than men. Their arguments emphasize the nature variable in the equation:

NATURE (physical sex) + nurture (socialization and experience) = gender

If they are right, certain inevitable conclusions follow: that fewer women can and will become successful scientists, that women are less likely to rise to the very top of the field in almost any profession or business, and that family care, after all, is best done by the ladies. Meanwhile, others stress the importance of nurture:

nature (physical sex) + NURTURE (socialization and experience) = gender

This of course points to other conclusions.

The argument about nature, nurture, and education has not gone away. Today some parties argue that boys and girls are naturally so differ-ent that it does them a *disservice* to educate them in the same classroom. As a result of a national campaign based on this premise, over five hun-dred public schools in the United States have established single-sex aca-demic classes (Eliot 2009). There are two points to be made here. First, the evidence that single-sex classrooms are better is loudly disputed (see http://lives.clas.asu.edu/acces/ v. http://www.singlesexschools.org/). Recently, a group of psychologists reported single-sex education to be ineffective at best and harmful (because it increases gender stereotyping and diverts funding from proven educational methods) at worst (Lewin 2011; Halpern et al. 2011:1706–7).

Biology-based arguments about sex and education recur century after century because we continue to work with the wrong theories of human development (Keller 2010). The body is not a mosaic of natural parts and nurtured parts, but rather a dynamic system that responds to social input by developing in new ways. In the case of human behavior, differential nurturing and socialization undoubtedly shape individual brain development. This shaping is continuous and builds upon what is already present. So individual life history is part of the body's story (Taylor 2009; Thelen and Smith, 1994). The terms of the debate—NATURE or nurture, NURTURE or nature—are simply not right. Unless we change them, we will spin our wheels for yet another century (Spencer et al. 2006).

Two overlapping arenas of thought—dynamic systems theory and developmental systems—provide a promising framework for breaking out of the nature-nurture dilemma. In an article memorializing Esther Thelen's work, Spencer et al. (2006) identify four critical dynamic systems concepts: (1) A new emphasis on *timing* and (2) the concept that behaviors are *softly assembled* (A. Harris 2005). A softly assembled behavior is temporarily stable and provides a platform for individual experimentation and future development. (3) *Embodiment.* The body integrates perception, action, and cognition. Thelen and her colleagues and students have demonstrated with great elegance that experience shapes embodiment (e.g., Corbetta and Thelen 2002; Newell, Liu, and Mayer-Kress 2003). (4) A new respect for *individual development.* Most sex differences present a conundrum. On the one hand, we can make verifiable claims about statistically significant group differences; on the other, the differences are usually small enough that we are reluctant to apply policies or specify health care based on group characteristics to any particular individual. Women and men may, on average, have different symptoms for heart attacks, but we would not want to ignore a "male typical" symptom because a woman is exhibiting it. Thelen's insistence on studying individual patterns of development is thus highly relevant to the study of sex-related differences, in which we see initial differentiation that barely rises to the level of group difference diverge by age three into a few larger reliable group differences. Emphasizing individual developmental variability enables us to reframe the basic question of difference: How do larger group differences emerge with time from a starting point of large individual variability but small group differences?

Clearly, there are some aggregate physical differences between men and women. For instance, men are on average taller and stronger. But because male and female are such diverse categories, a bare statement such as this is almost meaningless. Age, amount of physical training, ethnicity, nutrition, and numerous other factors that contribute to the nurture portion of the equation matter in assessing claims of physical difference. A healthy, athletically trained twenty-year-old female might be stronger than a sedentary male classmate. A Watusi woman will almost certainly be taller than a pygmy man. Even for what many view as obvious natural differences between men and women, nature is diverse, and nurture battles its way into the equation. Is there any aspect of gender that one might claim results purely from nature? Probably not. Nevertheless, some argue that nature often predominates. One contemporary focus for such views is observed differences in gendered behavior and social roles. A major voice on the side of nature comes from a group of scholars who call themselves evolutionary psychologists.

Evolutionary psychologists argue that sex differences in behavior evolved in response to natural and sexual selection during an early period of human evolution (Cosmides, Tooby, and Barkow 1992). Modern sexual selectionists believe that selection acts on individual males and females. Each individual pursues a life strategy aimed at optimizing his or her reproductive fitness (defined as the number of offspring that live long enough to themselves reproduce). Such thinkers contend that because of their different contributions to reproduction (mammalian females devote energy to maintaining a fetus inside their bodies, while males simply start things rolling with a shot of sperm), males and females are likely to have evolved different approaches to courting, mating, and infant care. (For overviews and critiques of these varied positions see Zuk 2002; Gowaty 1997; Travis 2003; Bolhuis and Wynne 2009; Brown, Laland, and Mulder 2009; Alonzo 2009. For a Darwinian feminist discussion of motherhood and mothering see Hrdy 1999.)

Although fully believing in the existence of evolution and natural selection, other scientists question the theoretical basis upon which modern accounts of sexual selection stand; yet another school of thought, Darwinian feminists, use the framework of sexual selection to provide a starting point from which to seek out additional information about male and female behavior. Darwinian feminists focus on variability—as did Darwin himself. They argue that a key feature of human evolution has been the expansion of the trait of developmental flexibility, leading to the ability to adapt behavior to context. As Darwinian evolutionist Jane Lancaster writes, "There is no single evolved pattern to be found in the human life-course.... Rather, evolutionary processes have favored ... a pattern of ... plasticity and behavioral variation" (Lancaster 1991, 7). In illustration, Lancaster considers the question of teenage pregnancy. While the idea of young (and often poor) women having babies alarms politicians and social workers, such behavior may make more than a little sense to the teenage parent. For members of the middle class, delaying parenthood opens up educational and earning opportunities that increase their access to resources needed for rearing children. The result: increased fertility and low rates of infant mortality. In contrast, the health and fertility of lower-class women deteriorates more rapidly, their rates of infant survival peaking nearly five years earlier than do those of middle-class mothers. With no prospect for joining the middle class, according to some analysts, "underclass women make the best of a very bad lot by reproducing as single parents while still in their teens," before their health begins to suffer and while they still have the support system offered by an extended family network (Lancaster 1991, 9). This evolutionary account does two things. First, it suggests that for women without economic or social prospects, teenage pregnancy is a positive choice, not a pathology. Second, it offers a political solution. If, as a society, Americans wish to decrease the frequency of single-parent teen pregnancy, they must provide lower-class young women with a path out of poverty and its accompanying poor health and inadequate education. Only then will it be in poor young women's reproductive self-interest to postpone pregnancy.

Yet another Darwinian feminist, Barbara Smuts (1992), agrees that an evolutionary account of human variation can lead to radical political conclusions. She considers a different flash-point topic: male violence against women. Men, she says, use aggression to control women, but that doesn't mean that males are inherently aggressive or females inherently submissive. Rather, men use aggression as a tool to enhance their reproductive opportunities: if the threat or use of violence inhibits female infidelity or if a man can have sex with his partner whenever he wishes, even if he must rape her to do so, he increases the likelihood of fathering her children. Aggression of this sort is not, however, inevitable. It will only persist under conditions in which it pays off. As Smuts proposes, aggression against women may further a male's reproductive interest, but it may harm that of his mate—who could perhaps do better by mating with a wider variety of males. Among humans, Smuts hypothesizes (with support from a rich variety of anthropological data) that male violence against women is greatest when female alliances are weak, when women lack the support of their families of origin, in cultures in which male alliances are especially important and highly developed, in cultures which lack sexual equality, and in situations in which males have greater control of resources. If Smuts is right, then a clear political agenda in the battle against spousal abuse emerges. In addition to the already highly developed shelter movement (female-female alliances), a continued redistribution of resources (pay equity and equal job opportunity, for example) and continued efforts to encourage social equality will all help.

For several centuries, feminist thinkers have disputed the claim that women's bodies account for their lesser economic and political worth.

Modern feminists made an analytical breakthrough when they postulated a separation between sex—the physical composition of the body—and gender—the social and cultural roles "assigned" to sexually different bodies. Cross-cultural studies have shown gender to be highly malleable—what count as masculine activities in one part of the world might be the province of femininity in another. This being the case, feminists have argued that gender has little to do with the nature of the body, and everything to do with how the body becomes socialized and acculturated into a gender-divided society.

As time passes, however, a model of gender construction in which culture acts upon an apparently passive or inert nature has felt increasingly problematic to feminist theorists. The sex/gender separation has led some, for example, to downplay differences between bodies. If gender accounts for all differences, then what to do with things only women do—for example, becoming pregnant? The solution dictated by the sex/gender, nature/nurture divide has been to treat pregnancy and childbirth as disabilities—just as one would a sports injury. This is, however, a strange option. Treating pregnancy and birth as illness or injury denies their essential place in the human life cycle and suggests that they are, in some sense, abnormal. In capitalist cultures generally, nature is configured as passive and feminine, a thing without agency upon which culture, science, or some other agent imbued with masculine power acts. Is it possible that the very fruitful sex/gender distinction, which initially enabled a host of changes in the social and political structures of gender in Europe and America, nevertheless mirrors the same old masculine/feminine oppositions? To disassemble this sex/gender opposition, feminist theorists have begun to attend to the nature of sex in the body itself.

A strong new theory of the body must offer an account of how the material body both acts upon and is acted upon by culture. Critical theorist Elizabeth Grosz acknowledges that sexual differences are bodily differences, but these material differences are, nevertheless, fundamentally social and cultural. "The body," she writes, "must be reconceived, not in opposition to the culture, but as its preeminent object" (Grosz 1995, 32). Elsewhere, she invokes the image of the Möbius strip, a three-dimensional loop formed from a strip of material that is given a half twist, then joined end to end. The two faces of the original material—culture and some prior natural body, in this analogy—now flow endlessly into one another: topologically, the Möbius strip has only one side (Grosz 1994).

The practices of contemporary medical science animate the Möbius-like blending of body and culture. For example, about one in a hundred infants is born without a consistent body sex. Such infants may be chromosomally female but genitally male. Or may have ovaries and two

X-chromosomes but also a scrotum and enlarged clitoris. Or be a completely intact male with an unusually small penis. Clinical manuals are quite specific about how to "treat" such children. Any clitoris deemed "too large" for a female body (usually one half to one centimeter) is surgically cut down to size. A microphallus child (defined as having a penis of less than 2.5 centimeters, or 2 times the standard deviation for newborn penis size) is surgically converted to a female; that is, he is castrated, his penis, even if perfectly formed, is reduced to the size of a clitoris, and a vagina is surgically created. In this example, we see that medical scientists literally create sex, while at the same time policing the boundaries of the sexed body—using measurements and standard deviations to decide what can count as a male or as a female body (Fausto-Sterling 1993, 2000).

Since the rise of the Intersex Society of North America (since replaced by the Accord Alliance), there have been ongoing efforts to obtain medical interventions that make sense for the individual, rather than for some preformed notion of sex/gender. Many now use the term Disorder of Sexual Development, rather than Intersex (http://www.accordalliance .org). Debates continue apace about gender, natural bodies, normal bodies, and ways in which both medical and legal interventions redound on our very conceptions of the natural, making it clear, in the end, that there is nothing natural about sex/gender (Morland et al. 2009; Greenberg 2012; Karkazis 2008).

Grosz notes the many additional interactions that sculpt our bodies. In medicine, we get new parts and have old ones renewed; sometimes the replacements are plastic or electronic. We decorate our bodies with tattoos and jewelry, sculpt them through diet and exercise. We incorporate categories into our very physiological interior. We *produce* our bodies as signs to be read by others. Our bodies, she writes, "become intextuated, narrativized; simultaneously, social codes, laws, norms, and ideals become incarnated" (Grosz 1995, 35). In a similar vein, Donna Haraway introduces the concept of the cyborg—a composite creature, part technological, part biological. We are, she suggests, all cyborgs to one degree or another. Indeed, the cyborg has become a staple of much speculative writing about changes in our understanding of the relations between culture/nature and human/machine (Haraway 1991; see also Martins 2003).

Psychologist and feminist theorist Elizabeth Wilson expands importantly on Grosz's work, calling on feminists to embrace biological knowledge as a tool that can enrich our understandings of "women's place" in the world. She uses iconic discussions of the history of hysteria to make her point. "We may," Wilson writes, "be well equipped to answer why hysterics convert, but we appear to be collectively mute in response to the question of how they convert" (Wilson 2004, Kindle locations 84–85). Indeed, the task of understanding the biology of embodiment has begun in earnest, and a new era of feminist analysis of the body is under way (Fausto-Sterling 2005, 2008; Cheslak-Postava and Jordan-Young 2012).

Perhaps ironically, newer biological understandings that the nervous system *requires* environmental input to help shape and refine the quantity and quality of connections between cells within the brain and with the peripheral nervous system strongly support a Möbius strip concept of the brain and behavior. Again, neither the body nor experience is prior, but each acts continuously upon the other as individual patterns of behavior and of neuronal connections appear. Consider sight: specific nervous connections between light receptors in the eye and translators in brain are not *programmed* by some genetic blueprint; rather, genetic activity guides development by responding to external signals reaching specific cells at specific times. Early in embryonic development, these signals come from other cells; later, signals include spontaneous electrical activity generated by developing nervous tissue and, still later, light entering through the newborn and infant eye. A functional system emerges from a context-bound system in which seemingly random activity—spontaneous nerve firings and visual input—gives rise to a more highly structured form and function. Thus brain development, in utero and for many years after birth, exhibits considerable plasticity and can be understood as a response to worldly experience. The nerve cells in a kitten's eye require the stimulation of light to develop properly. The brain connections in a rat raised in a complex, stimulating environment are more luxuriant and complex than those of a rodent confined to a small cage. The human is born with an undeveloped brain that acquires its abilities as its owner acts in the world and responds to physical and emotional stimuli. Even cells in the adult brain can retool or sometimes divide, making new connections if they lose their original contacts (Fausto-Sterling 2003; Hua and Smith 2004).

Nature, then, is neither static nor obvious. It has a history that reflects human relations both to other humans and to the production of food and shelter. It has often been conceptualized as female and set in opposition to masculine reason and rationality. Scientists, exerting such reason, seek to know and control the natural world. Yet to the extent that we attribute agency and activity to nature, science can never gain complete control of its actions. Similarly, both nature and nurture account for the creation of gender. The body is neither a pliable vessel shaped by culture's whimsy nor a rigid vase to be filled with socially available knowledge. From before birth until after death, it is more like wet clay turning continuously on a potter's wheel. The amount of water, speed of the wheel, and use of marking tools and hands form and reshape it. But the mineral content of the clay confers properties of its own on the mix, influencing how hard it will fire and how dry it can get without crumbling into bits.

References

Alonzo, Suzanne, H. 2009. "Social and Coevolutionary Feedbacks between Mating and Parental Investment." *Trends in Ecology and Evolution* 9:99–108.

Arnow, Harriet. 1960. *Seedtime in the Cumberland.* Lexington: University of Kentucky Press.

Awiakta, Marilou. 1993. *Selu: Seeking the Corn-Mother's Wisdom.* Golden, CO: Fulcrum.

Bleier, Ruth. 1984. *Science and Gender: A Critique of Biology and Its Theories on Women.* New York: Pergamon.

Bluhm, Robyn, and Anne Jaap Jacobson. 2012. *Neurofeminism: Issues at the Intersection of Feminist Theory and Cognitive Science.* Palgrave Macmillan Monographs. Kindle edition.

Bolhuis, J. J., and C. D. Wynne. 2009. "Can Evolution Explain How Minds Work?" *Nature* 458 (7240): 832–33.

Brown, G. R., K. N. Laland, and M. B. Mulder. 2009. "Bateman's Principles and Human Sex Roles." *Trends in Ecology and Evolution* 24 (6): 297–304.

Browne, Janet. 1989. "Botany for Gentlemen: Erasmus Darwin and 'The Loves of Plants.'" *Isis* 80 (304): 593–621.

Cheslack-Postava, K., and R. M. Jordan-Young. 2012. "Autism Spectrum Disorders: Toward a Gendered Embodiment Model." *Social Science and Medicine* 74 (11): 1667–74.

Corbetta, D., and E. Thelen. 2002. "Behavioral Fluctuations and the Development of Manual Asymmetries in Infancy: Contributions of the Dynamic Systems Approach." In *Handbook of Neuropsychology*, 2nd ed. (vol. 8, pt. 1), ed. S. J. Segalowitz and I. Rapin. New York: Elsevier Science.

Corea, Gena. 1979. *The Mother Machine: Reproductive Technologies from Artificial Insemination to Artificial Wombs.* New York: Harper & Row.

Cosmides, Leda, John Tooby, and Jerome H. Barkow. 1992. "Introduction: Evolutionary Psychology and Conceptual Integration." In *The Adapted Mind: Evolutionary Psychology and the Generation of Culture*, ed. Jerome J. Barkow, Leda Cosmides, and John Tooby. Oxford: Oxford University Press.

Cronon, William. 1983. *Changes in the Land: Indians, Colonists and the Ecology of New England.* New York: Hill and Wang.

Daniels, Cynthia, and Erin Heidt-Forsythe. 2012. "Gendered Eugenics and the Problematic of Free Market Reproductive Technologies: Sperm and Egg Donation in the United States." *Signs* 37:719–47.

Eliot, Lise. 2009. *Pink Brain, Blue Brain: How Small Differences Grow into Troublesome Gaps—and What We Can Do about It.* Boston: Houghton Mifflin Harcourt.

Fausto-Sterling, Anne. 1992. *Myths of Gender: Biological Theories about Women and Men.* 2nd ed. New York: Basic Books.

———. 1993. "The Five Sexes." *Sciences* (March/April).

———. 2000. *Sexing the Body: Gender Politics and the Construction of Sexuality.* New York: Basic Books.

——. 2003. "The Problem with Sex/Gender and Nature/Nurture." In *Debating Biology: Sociological Reflections on Health, Medicine and Society*, ed. Simon J. Williams, Lynda Birke, and Gillian A. Bendelow, 123–32. London: Routledge.

——. 2005. "The Bare Bones of Sex, Part I: Sex and Gender." *Signs* 30 (2).

——. 2008. "The Bare Bones of Race." *Social Studies of Science* 38 (5).

——. 2012. *Sex/Gender: Biology in a Social World*. London: Routledge.

Fine, C. 2010. *Delusions of Gender*. New York: Norton.

Firestone, Shulamith. 1970. *The Dialectic of Sex: The Case for Feminist Revolution*. New York: William Morrow.

Gordon, Linda. 1976. *Woman's Body, Woman's Right: Birth Control in America*. New York: Grossman.

Gowaty, Patricia Adair, ed. 1997. *Feminism and Evolutionary Biology*. New York: Chapman Hall.

Greenberg, J.A. 2012. *Intersexuality and the Law: Why Sex Matters*. New York: New York University Press.

Grosz, Elizabeth. 1994. *Volatile Bodies: Toward a Corporeal Feminism*. Bloomington: Indiana University Press.

——. 1995. *Space, Time, Perversion*. New York: Routledge.

Halpern, D.F., L. Eliot, R.S. Bigler, R.A. Fabes, L.D. Hanish, J. Hyde, et al. 2011. "Education: The Pseudoscience of Single-Sex Schooling." *Science* 333 (6050).

Haraway, Donna. 1991. *Simians, Cyborgs and Women: The Reinvention of Nature*. New York: Routledge.

Harding, S. 2008. *Sciences from Below: Feminisms, Postcolonialities and Modernities*. Durham, NC: Duke University Press.

——. 2009. "Postcolonial and Feminist Philosophies of Science and Technology: Convergences and Dissonances." *Postcolonial Studies* 12 (4).

Harris, A. 2005. *Gender as Soft Assembly*. Hillsdale: Analytic Press.

Harris, Stephen J. 2005. "Jesuit Scientific Activity in the Overseas Missions, 1540–1773." *Isis* 95:71–79.

Harrison, Mark. 2005. "Science and the British Empire." *Isis* 96:56–63.

Hrdy, Sarah Blaffer. 1999. *Mother Nature: A History of Mothers, Infants, and Natural Selection*. New York: Pantheon.

Hua, Jackie Yuanyuan, and Stephen J. Smith. 2004. "Neural Activity and the Dynamics of Central Nervous System Development." *Nature Neuroscience* 7 (4): 327–32.

Hubbard, Ruth. 1990. *The Politics of Women's Biology*. New Brunswick, NJ: Rutgers University Press.

Jacobson, Anne Jaap. 2012. "Seeing as a Social Phenomenon: Feminist Theory and the Cognitive Sciences." In Bluhm and Jacobson. *New York:* Palgrave Macmillan.

Jesudason, Sujatha Anbuselvi. 2009. "In the Hot Tub: The Praxis of Building New Alliances for Reprogenetics." *Signs* 34 (4): 901–24.

Karkazis, K. 2008. *Fixing Sex: Intersex, Medical Authority and Lived Experience*. Durham, NC: Duke University Press.

Keller, Evelyn Fox. 1985. *Reflections on Gender and Science*. New Haven, CT: Yale University Press.

——. 2010. *The Mirage of a Space between Nature and Nurture*. Durham, NC: Duke University Press.

Lancaster, Jane. 1991. "A Feminist and Evolutionary Biologist Looks at Women." *Yearbook of Physical Anthropology* 34:1–11.

Landsman, Gail H. 1998. "Reconstructing Motherhood in the Age of 'Perfect' Babies: Mothers of Infants and Toddlers with Disabilities." *Signs* 24 (1).

Lewin, Tamar. 2011. "Single-Sex Education Is Assailed in Report." *New York Times*, September 23, A19. http://www.nytimes.com/2011/09/23/education/23.

Maathai, Wangari. 2010. *Replenishing the Earth: Spiritual Values for Healing Ourselves and the World.* New York: Doubleday.

Mann, Charles C. 2005. *1491: New Revelations of the Americas before Columbus.* New York: Knopf.

——. 2011. *1493: Uncovering the New World Columbus Created.* New York: Knopf.

Martins, Susana S. 2003. "Imagining the High-Tech in Contemporary American Culture." PhD thesis, Department of English, Boston College.

Merchant, Carolyn. 1980. *The Death of Nature: Women, Ecology and the Scientific Revolution.* New York: Harper & Row.

——. 1989. *Ecological Revolutions: Nature, Gender, and Science in New England.* Chapel Hill: University of North Carolina Press.

——. 1992. *Radical Ecology: The Search for a Livable World.* New York: Routledge.

——. 2003. *Reinventing Eden: the Fate of Nature in Western Culture.* New York: Routledge.

Mies, Maria, and Vandana Shiva. 1993. *Ecofeminism.* London: Zed Books.

Morland, I., A. Dreger, S. M. Creighton, and E. K. Feder, eds. 2009. *Intersex and After.* Durham, NC: Duke University Press.

Newell, K. M., Y.-T. Liu, and G. Mayer-Kress. 2003. "A Dynamical Systems Interpretation of Epigenetic Landscapes for Infant Motor Development." *Infant Behavior and Development* 26:449–72.

Palmer, T. S. 1899. "A Review of Economic Ornithology in the United States." *Yearbook of the United States Department of Agriculture*, 258–92.

Paul, Diane. 1995. *Controlling Human Heredity: 1865 to the Present.* Atlantic Highlands, NJ: Humanities Press.

Piercy, Marge. 1976. *Woman on the Edge of Time.* New York: Knopf.

Plumwood, Val. 1993. *Feminism and the Mastery of Nature.* New York: Routledge.

Rapp, Rayna. 1984. "The Ethics of Choice." *Ms.* (April).

——. 1990. "Constructing Amniocentesis: Maternal and Medical Discourses." In *Uncertain Terms: Negotiating Gender in American Culture*, ed. Faye Ginsburg and Anna Lowenhaupt Tsing, 28–42. Boston: Beacon.

——. 2000. *Testing Women, Testing the Fetus: The Social Impact of Amniocentesis in America.* New York: Routledge.

Roberts, Dorothy. 2009. "Race, Gender, and Genetic Technologies: A New Reproductive Dystopia?" *Signs* 34:783–804.

Rossiter, M. W. 1982. *Women Scientists in America: Struggles and Strategies to 1940.* Baltimore: Johns Hopkins University Press.

——. 1995. *Women Scientists in America: Before Affirmative Action.* Baltimore: Johns Hopkins University Press.

——. 2012. *Women Scientists in America: Forging a New World since 1972.* Baltimore: Johns Hopkins University Press.

Rothman, Barbara Katz. 1989. *Recreating Motherhood: Ideology and Technology in a Patriarchal Society*. New York: Norton.

Russett, C. E. 1989. *Sexual Science: The Victorian Construction of Womanhood*. Cambridge, MA: Harvard University Press.

Schiebinger, Londa. 1993. *Nature's Body: Gender in the Making of Modern Science*. Boston: Beacon.

———. 2007. *Plants and Empire: Colonial Bioprospecting in the Atlantic World*. Cambridge, MA: Harvard University Press.

Shiva, Vandana. 1988. *Staying Alive: Women, Ecology and Development*. London: Zed.

———. 1999. *Stolen Harvest: The Hijacking of the Global Food Supply*. Boston: South End Press.

———. 2012. "Global Visionary Solutions for a Secure and Sustainable Energy and Food Future." http://www.vandanashiva.org (accessed March 26, 2012).

Silver, Timothy. 1990. *A New Face on the Countryside: Indians, Colonists, and Slaves in South Atlantic Forests, 1500–1800*. Cambridge: Cambridge University Press.

Smuts, Barbara. 1992. "Male Aggression against Women: An Evolutionary Perspective." *Human Nature* 3:1–44.

Spencer, J. P., M. Clearfield, D. Corbetta, B. Ulrich, P. Buchanan, and G. Schoner. 2006. "Moving toward a Grand Theory of Development: In Memory of Esther Thelen." *Child Development* 77(6): 1521–38.

Stanworth, Michelle. 1987. "Reproductive Technologies and the Deconstruction of Motherhood." In *Reproductive Technologies: Gender, Motherhood and Medicine*, ed. Michelle Stanworth. Minneapolis: University of Minnesota Press.

Stepan, N. 1998. "Race, Gender, Science and Citizenship." *Gender and History* 10 (1): 26–52.

Taylor, P. J. 2009. "Infrastructure and Scaffolding: Interpretation and Change of Research Involving Human Genetic Information." *Science as Culture* 18 (4): 435–59.

Thelen, E., and L. B. Smith. 1994. *A Dynamic Systems Approach to the Development of Cognition and Action*. Cambridge, MA: MIT Press.

Thompson, Charis. 2005. *Making Parents: The Ontological Choreography of Reproductive Technologies*. Cambridge, MA: MIT Press.

Tiffany, Sharon W., and Kathleen J. Adams. 1985. *The Wild Woman: An Inquiry into the Anthropology of an Idea*. Cambridge, MA: Schenkman.

Travis, C. B., ed. 2003. *Evolution, Gender and Rape*. Cambridge, MA: MIT Press.

Ulrich, Laurel. 1990. *A Midwife's Tale: The Life of Martha Ballard, Based on Her Diary, 1785–1812*. New York: Knopf.

Wajcman, Judy. 1991. *Feminism Confronts Technology*. University Park: Pennsylvania State University Press.

Warren, K. 2000. *Ecofeminist Philosophy*. Lanham, MD: Rowman & Littlefield.

Wilson, Elizabeth A. 2004. *Psychosomatic: Feminism and the Neurological Body*. Kindle edition.

Zuk, Marlene. 2002. *Sexual Selections: What We Can and Can't Learn about Sex from Animals*. Berkeley: University of California Press.

14 :: POSTHUMAN RUTH A. MILLER

Stelarc walks the Posthumanist talk.   William Gibson (2012)

Stelarc is a performance artist best known for swallowing, weaving, piercing, or otherwise introducing into his body mechanical, robotic, or bio-engineered parts. William Gibson is a science fiction writer best known for coining the term *cyberspace* in the early 1980s. Neither has a great deal to do with gender studies. But Gibson's comment on Stelarc's art is nonetheless a comment on what the posthuman is doing in gender studies. The posthuman has altered both gender's talk and gender's walk—reconfiguring both the problem of gendered speech and the problem of the gendered body. Moreover, the posthuman has complicated one of the basic goals of gender-based activism—namely, the search for agency. And finally, the posthuman has raised the specter, or the promise, of a postgender, as well as posthuman, world. When Gibson comments on Stelarc's walking talk, therefore, he is pointing to the radical rearticulation, if not the potential dissolution, of gender-conscious ways of thinking, doing, being, and living.

A History of the Posthuman

A neologism, the posthuman is an ambivalent term. It is ethically and politically up for grabs—and gender studies scholars have used it to express approval as well as uneasiness. For some, it represents a promising new approach to well-established problems in the study of gender. For others, the challenges it poses to the field's conventions are politically paralyzing.

The term's meaning and influence, however, have also changed over time. The posthuman, as a concept, came into common use at the end of the twentieth century, alongside futuristic, utopian scenarios in which, for instance, Gibson's (or misreadings of Gibson's) "cyberspace" would replace physical space and immortal, infinite, digitized minds would transcend mortal, finite, material bodies. In these technophilic fantasies, the virtual or digital posthuman was opposed, and superior, to the (merely) embodied human. Today, these late twentieth-century stories seem hopelessly dated. As much as they continue to lurk behind the term, they have little influence in posthuman studies of gender.

Instead, and perhaps unexpectedly, the posthuman has become a key concept in *histories* of gender. Neologism though it may be, the posthuman has been mobilized most effectively when gender studies scholars have searched for antecedents to ongoing rhetorics that link gendered existence to apparently nonhuman things—to machines, to nature, or to environments—to anything *but* the disembodied, virtual, or digital human intellect. The posthuman has been mobilized most effectively, in other words, when scholars have sought to explain why gendered existence has *historically* evoked nonhuman organic, mechanical, or environmental material.

As much as the virtual or the digital is present in the work that calls itself posthuman, then, it is the concept's invocation of physical matter that makes it relevant to gender studies today. After all, when Stelarc suspends himself from hooks embedded in his flesh as a posthuman statement, this performance is hardly virtual or disembodied. Nor is the posthuman as it operates in the field of gender studies. Indeed, there are distinct affinities between the scholarship that draws on posthuman analytic categories and recent scholarship that describes itself explicitly as "materialist" or "new materialist." As Diana Coole and Samantha Frost have written in a volume introducing the latter concept, "Unprecedented things are currently being done with and to matter, nature, life, production, and reproduction. It is in this contemporary context that theorists are compelled to rediscover older materialist traditions while pushing them in novel, and sometimes experimental, directions" (Coole and Frost 2010, 4). Just as the posthuman looks to a past physical world in order to challenge many of the conventions underpinning gender studies today, "new materialists" look to older, sometimes forgotten, materialist traditions for answers to contemporary political problems.

When searching for a gender-relevant history of the posthuman, it is thus perhaps better to turn away from disembodied human minds and toward a second trend in late twentieth-century cybernetic writing. This second trend runs in nearly complete opposition to the 1980s-era technophilic genre with its utopian dreams of incorruptible, dematerialized minds that could not die. Drawing on the figure of the cyborg—the "cybernetic organism"—it emphasized instead the physical, material, and finite qualities of posthuman existence. As Donna Haraway wrote in her influential feminist work, the "Cyborg Manifesto," the cyborg held out the possibility of a politics that recognized the "partial" and "contradictory" aspects of both individual and collective life (Haraway 1990, 157). This variation on the posthuman was thus not only squarely situated in the physical world; it was also an invention of gender studies scholars. This interpretation of the posthuman, in fact, was in many ways a response to a perceived crisis in feminist writing.

This crisis had appeared by the 1980s, when a great deal of work in gender studies had come under attack. Committed as this late twentieth-century writing was to overcoming, subverting, or appropriating for ostensibly more noble purposes such binaries as subject/object, active/passive, culture/nature, mind/body, or indeed inclusion/exclusion, it seemed nonetheless to reaffirm, rather than dissolve, oppressive power relations. As long as the rational, speaking, human subject remained the norm of gender studies, and as long as the mute, nonhuman (or dehumanized) object remained its cautionary tale, achieving an active subject position seemed always to involve objectifying some other, passive not-quite-subject. As long as gender studies scholars developed theories of inclusive identity and inclusive subjectivity with these human-centered binaries in mind, that is to say, exclusion seemed, paradoxically, to be the endpoint of inclusion.

Haraway proposed the cyborg as a theoretical tool for addressing these problems. In particular, the cyborg represented a move away from the self-contained, embodied, speaking human—this human whose existence always demanded oppositions between subject and object—and toward hybrid-human, or nonhuman, things. Taking the cyborg as an intellectual starting point, in other words, helped scholars to question the historical, political, and methodological validity of the binaries and oppositions that continued to undermine so much work in gender studies. The cyborg encouraged scholars to set aside these binaries rather than accept them as a necessary—if also necessarily contestable—framework of inquiry.

Historically, for example, the posthuman figure of the cyborg suggested that the oppositions listed above were not as salient as they appeared to be. Politically, this figure challenged scholars to consider an alternative feminist ethics predicated on the simultaneity of subjecthood and objecthood. And finally, methodologically, the cyborg helped to chart a path through the ethical morass that had resulted from traditional feminist attempts to replace passive, mute dehumanized objects with active, speaking human subjects.

If the quest to extend the sphere of human subjectivity seemed always to end in further objectification, the cyborg seemed to hint that gender studies scholars should abandon this quest in favor of less totalizing projects. Perhaps, as Haraway wrote, feminists should dream less of speaking a "common language ... of a perfectly faithful naming of experience" and more of "learn[ing] from our fusions with animals and machines how not to be Man, the embodiment of Western logos" (Haraway 1990, 173). In short, Haraway's cyborg suggested a feminist existence predicated on simultaneity and synthesis. And it suggested a move away from feminisms aimed at producing, above all, speaking, active, human subjects divorced or dissociated from mute, passive objects.

Indeed, throughout the late twentieth century, the key quality of this posthuman figure was its hybridity. As, again, a "cybernetic organism," it was simultaneously mechanical, virtual, and organic. It was both subject and object, both active and passive, both culture and nature. The cyborg was also best described with reference to *process* rather than *identity*. This posthuman figure thus not only dismantled the dichotomies, oppositions, and binaries on which much of gender studies scholarship had relied. It also led scholars away from the problem of being and toward the problem of doing. The cyborg helped scholars to theorize gender as an ongoing, material, and mutable activity rather than as a variation on existence. Put differently, the cyborg questioned the practicality as well as the ethics of endlessly extending active, political identities to an ever-expanding field of potential human subjects. As Kristin Asdal has put it, "Haraway's point is not that we need new representations, but rather new forms of *practice*" (Asdal 2003, 71).

But the cyborg was only the first of many posthuman formulations. By the turn of the twenty-first century, what had been a focus largely on hybridity—hybrid humans, hybrid organisms, hybrid bodies—had generalized into a discussion of human as well as nonhuman systems, networks, and environments. As a result, the communicative speech and embodied subjects that had remained key categories even of posthumanist gender studies analysis began to give way to alternative, dispersed, and distributed norms.

Moreover, when these noncommunicative material systems—say, networked machines, decomposing waste, or natural environments—replaced the cyborg as the starting point for posthumanist gender studies scholarship, a new question took center stage: if gendered existence and gendered performance have historically been associated with these and other environments, systems, fields, and accumulations of matter, then might these nonhuman entities be said to have (or do) gender? Put differently, can we describe gender as a distributed or dispersed phenomenon?

Posthuman Speech

Addressing this question requires reconceptualizing two key concepts in gender studies scholarship: speech and the body. The idea that speech is a purely human quality—that the defining characteristic of the human is its capacity for embodied speech (and that the defining characteristic of speech is that it produces human subjects)—is very old. This old idea has played out in a number of political and philosophical contexts. Politically, for example, the *right* to speak has been understood to separate human citizens from their mute, not quite political, and—to their detriment— not quite human, counterparts. Philosophically, speech has been defined *as* speech only to the extent that it constitutes a field of discourse within which embodied human subjects might be formed or dissolved.

In both cases, when speech is detached from human communication, human bodies, or human subjectivity, it becomes not-speech. Nonhuman and noncommunicative, such speech is nothing more than noise— with little relevance to scholarship that seeks to describe or theorize gender. Indeed, as long as speech is defined narrowly as an embodied human phenomenon, dispersed or distributed gender is an impossibility. If gender is linguistic, and if language is embodied and human, then gender must likewise be embodied and human.

But what if speech is not a purely human quality? What if we detach speech not only from human subjectivity but also from human bodies? What if speech is not about humans communicating but about systems operating—about, say, networked machines running code? What, in other words, if speech is posthuman rather than human?

There are three consequences to accepting the validity of these premises. First, speech begins to manifest itself not through bodies but through systems. Instead of crafting bodies, speech begins to constitute material environments. Second, and related, speech becomes speech in these scenarios when it *acts*, and not (necessarily) when it *communicates*. Speech becomes performative because it is a physical activity that may, secondarily, involve communication, rather than because it is a communicative activity that may, secondarily, become physical. And finally, when gender is theorized with this type of speech as a reference point, gender can indeed be characterized as a dispersed or distributed phenomenon. When posthuman speech happens, executes, or operates, gender can very well be performed across material systems as well as discrete bodies.

The idea that speech or language might be best described as a distributed system, rather than as a tool for creating content or meaning, is, of course, not unique to posthumanist writing. A number of thinkers in the field of semiotics have privileged language as a system over language as content, without necessarily turning to hybrid, posthuman, or nonhuman examples. By the turn of the twentieth century, for instance, Ferdinand de Saussure was already positing the relational, as opposed to objective, quality of speech as a problem for language theory (Hayles 1990, 178).

The specifically posthuman contribution to this way of thinking about language has been to emphasize, first, the *material potential* and, second, the *empirical validity* of this systemic or distributed speech. Whereas human-centered theories of language systems discuss the relations between abstract signs and abstract referents, posthuman theories describe the play of language as, specifically, a play of physical matter—as, for instance, the switching of a computational bit from 1 to 0 and back again. Whereas human-centered advocates of disassociating language from content have highlighted the ethical, political, or aesthetic problems with defining speech as nothing more than a tool of communication, posthumanist advocates have argued that, empirically, speech cannot be described in such a way.

An example might help to clarify these two qualities of distributed speech. The modern scientific laboratory, according to many writers invested in posthuman language theory, is an arena in which speech operates in a material and systemic manner. Within the scientific laboratory, they posit, any line between speaking subject and mute object disappears—indeed, the very purpose of the laboratory is to foster the speech of nonhuman matter. As Bruno Latour, a writer often cited in these contexts, has put it, the laboratory is the place where "galaxies, neurons, cells, viruses, plants, and glaciers" speak together with scientists in order to participate in "collective life" (Latour 2004, 68). Key to responsible scientific inquiry, he continues, is scientists' ability to relinquish their belief in their own, unique linguistic experience and existence.

If human scientists do have a role in the laboratory, therefore, it is not to speak *for* nonhumans. It is not to extend human speech metaphorically to the nonhuman, to grant honorary human status to nonhuman things, or to incorporate more and more bodies into the sphere of human identity or agency (Latour 2004, 70). Rather, in the laboratory, humans participate alongside the nonhuman in a collective speech activity that constitutes a material environment—an environment in which divisions between subject and object, between politics or culture and nature, or between activity and passivity cannot be maintained. Humans speak neither for, nor against the backdrop of, things or environments. Their speech, melded into nonhuman speech, is itself material and environmental. It is dispersed because the laboratory is a public space that is by definition given over to the horizontal, rather than hierarchical, participation of human and nonhuman things, environments, and behaviors.

Here, then, is an example of distributed speech in action. But is this speech also physically or materially performative? And is it physically performative without necessarily being communicative? A second, differently distributed case of nonhuman speech might help to answer these questions. Computational speech, like speech in the laboratory, is environmental rather than subjective. Like speech in the laboratory, computational speech produces and works through fields or systems. It does not constitute subjects or discrete bodies, and it has little to do with the identity of those (machines) that speak it.

More to the point, machine code is also characterized by physical operation rather than by communication. Code executes—and it executes via electrical circuits. Only secondarily might it transmit meaning. As N. Katherine Hayles has written, "Whereas in ["natural" or human] performative utterances *saying is doing* because the action performed is symbolic in nature and does not require physical action in the world, at the basic level of computation *doing is saying* because physical actions also have a symbolic dimension that corresponds directly with computation" (Hayles 1999, 275).

Unlike the conventional human speech act, in other words, computational speech activity is performative, not because its symbolic or communicative qualities *become* physical, but because physical execution, rather than symbolic communication, is its defining characteristic. Indeed, the information theory upon which computational code rests assumes, first, a separation of "information from meaning" (Hayles 1990, 6) and, second, that the fundamental problem of information is a problem of storage rather than of the communication (Hayles 1990, 55). This theory, that is to say, assumes speech to be a series of linguistic performances that are hyperbolically physical but that do not, necessarily, transmit meaning.

As a result, machine code is indeed like speech in the laboratory: distributed, performative, and material without being communicative. It, alongside other variations on posthuman speech, thus in turn suggests the possibility, at least, of a theory of gender that highlights gender's distributed, material, and environmental qualities. Or, put differently, if performative speech *is* gendered, then arguably the machine running code and the laboratory's material-linguistic environment are equally so. If performative speech is a key problem or issue for gender studies, then so too are systems, networks, and environments.

Posthuman Bodies

As much as these theories of posthuman speech gesture toward exciting new interpretations of the physical play of gendered language, however, they also pose potentially fatal conceptual challenges to the gendered body. Therefore, the second key concept that writing on distributed, dispersed, and posthuman gender demands we revisit is the body. Scholars have disagreed on how much posthuman theories of gender have minimized, or should minimize, the body as a conceptual category. Some, for example, have attempted to absolve the posthuman of its apparent responsibility for marginalizing—or dissolving—the body as a category of feminist analysis. Others, such as Annette Burfoot, have condemned the posthuman for its seemingly relentless attack on this key feminist concept (2003, 47–71, 68).

Of the major critiques of posthuman disembodiment, the most prevalent might be best characterized as the "nothing more than" critique. If the materiality of posthuman speech is environmental, systemic, or computational, this critique begins—if posthuman speech eludes bodies, or worse, transforms bodies into environments, systems, or networks—then embodied humans become likewise nothing more than environments, spaces, instruments, or things. If the performance, execution, or operation of posthuman speech replaces the human body with dispersed matter, then the body is reduced to worse than nothing. It becomes a passive object or an empty environment.

Scholars who read DNA as a variation on distributed, material, or posthuman language, for instance, have been extensively criticized for transforming the body into nothing more than code—in this case genetic code. Once transformed, such bodies become, first, environments—platforms for the replication of DNA. Second, they become tools—the means by which DNA replicates, rather than the end goal of DNA. Finally—and arguably most importantly for gender studies scholarship—these bodies become collections of codified parts (organs, cells, immunological responses), objects that can be detached, decontextualized, bought, sold, or patented (Thacker 2003, 72–97, 87).

Here, then, posthuman speech inverts the usual story of bodies constituted by and through language. When DNA is read as a type of performative material-linguistic system, speech dissolves bodies into both mere information (nothing) and mere things (something)—into spaces and environments as well as tools or objects. Indeed, posthuman speech is responsible in this narrative for nothing less than the transformation of the formerly inviolate human body into an object and space of consumer desire. The implications for gender studies scholarship are obvious.

Another variation on this "nothing more than" theme appears in the dystopian science fiction that has been taken up by many scholars of posthuman language and embodiment. This genre of writing has described, for instance, bodies distributed across virtual and mechanical infrastructures—bodies, once again, indistinguishable from the computational or mechanical network that is their ostensible tool. It has also described computational code or a computer virus as a bodily, biological, or organic illness. It has thus posited, essentially, information turned into plague, with the body as the contagious vessel of this plague (Hayles 2005, 227).

Once again, the implications for gender studies scholarship are clear. It is difficult to find a variation on feminist theory that does not, in some form or another, repudiate the transformation of human bodies into environments, tools, or vessels. And yet here speech is turning the body into exactly those things—spaces, instruments, and inert objects. Posthuman theories of speech and matter thus seem to undermine one of the most crucial political, ethical, and intellectual bases of gender studies scholarship. If accepted, these posthuman theories would seem to bolster the very worst kinds of gendered violence and oppression, to celebrate the transformation of the body into a thing that not only can, but should, be consumed, violated, and instrumentalized.

But the "nothing more than" critique is itself vulnerable to critique. Indeed, if the moral problems with being nothing more than an environment, system, thing, or tool are bracketed, it becomes possible to develop an *alternative* ethics of gendered matter. Instead of criticizing posthuman speech for turning bodies into things that might be bought or sold, for instance, it becomes possible to criticize a legal framework whose reliance on divisions between human bodies and nonhuman matter unproblematically exposes all nonhuman things to commerce and consumption. Similarly, instead of criticizing posthuman speech for replacing the active body with the passive environment or tool, it becomes possible to criticize a political discourse that reifies the distinctions between active and passive, user and tool—and then places the environment squarely in the realm of the latter.

The scholarship that accepts posthuman speech and posthuman materialism as valid categories for gender analysis, in other words, mimics an ethical and political move that is familiar to many in the field of gender studies. An earlier generation of scholars tackled the fear of being "nothing more than" a body—the fear of losing even the ambivalent status of disembodied, not-quite-equal citizen in a patriarchal constitutional structure. Scholars who draw on posthuman theories of language in their efforts to address ongoing gender-based violence or oppression tackle a similar fear of being "nothing more than" a material environment—the fear of losing even the ambivalent status of embodied subject. They ask whether it might not be liberating or empowering to question the value of the body in the same way that it was liberating or empowering to question the value of disembodied, liberal, rights-based citizenship. They ask whether jettisoning embodiment might be just as politically, ethically, and intellectually valuable as jettisoning Aristotelian theories of political engagement or Cartesian theories of subjectivity.

But of course, this acceptance of posthuman speech as a disembodied, but still material, phenomenon leads, in turn, to a second major criticism that scholars have addressed to posthuman language theory. These scholars are motivated less by a sentimental attachment to the body and more by a very specific political and ethical concern: if posthuman speech dissolves the body, a third term—agency—seems also to lose its coherence. As a generation of gender studies scholarship has shown, it is impossible to describe agency without reference to embodied speech. When posthuman speech is described as performative and material but *not* embodied, therefore, it appears to destabilize the basic foundations of most theories of agency. Dismantling the nexus between body and speech on which critical, gender-conscious stories of agency rest, posthuman language theory seems to leave agency adrift.

The concern that the posthuman might paralyze gender studies scholarship, broadly defined, is thus not unfounded. As much as some have argued that agency can be redone—that we can seek a distributed agency, or an agency that operates across material and linguistic systems, in the same way that we can seek a distributed gender—others have used the opportunity proffered by the posthuman to question the value of agency altogether. This latter set of scholars has begun to theorize gender postagency. But is postagency really just another term for postgender?

Postagency

One of the traditional goals of gender-conscious scholarship on agency has been to challenge or revise nineteenth-century writing that attributed agency only to active, political, disembodied, and usually male, subjects. Nineteenth-century writers were by no means unaware of the body's political existence, or of the complex relationship among the body, speech, and agency. For the most part, however, they understood the body to be the inert property—and speech to be the likewise inert tool—of the agent. Rational, liberal subjects used speech and owned their bodies. Indeed, agency manifested itself specifically in the rational subject's ability to use language as a tool and to manipulate, as John Locke had earlier put it, the body as property within the confines of a liberal social contract (Hyde 1997, 54–55).

Gender studies scholars criticized this interpretation of speech, embodiment, and agency for both political and philosophical reasons. Politically, this interpretation left gendered subjects—subjects defined more often than not as those who could only partially own their bodies or who had only partial control over their speech—as necessarily partial agents. Philosophically, this definition of agency failed to account for the active work that both speech and bodies do. Scholars who accepted this theory of speech and agency seemed to ignore the ways in which the subject was as much an instrument of language as language was an instrument of the subject. As Judith Butler influentially argued, these scholars ignored the mutually constitutive character of bodies and speech (1997, 5, 159). And, as a result, they missed the gendered, situated, and material foundations of agency as a political, ethical, and cultural force.

Gender-conscious scholarship thus began to redefine agency by, first of all, taking embodied speech seriously. This scholarship situated agency at the intersection of discourse and embodiment. Writers in this genre challenged the notion that agency must be associated with active subjects who wielded language as a tool—with subjects who directed a passive, inert speech. Understanding the subject, the subject's body, and speech to be mutually productive—each vulnerable to the other—this writing redefined agency as a set of bodily and linguistic interactions (Butler 1997, 26–27). Agents were defined not by their ability to use language and to own their bodies but by their ability to find new modes of embodiment within an always preexisting field of discourse. Speech was not a tool but a field, within which the agent operated and to which the agent was linked but not chained. The agent was the subject who could repeatedly recontextualize and resignify a body within a historic discursive field (Butler 1997, 99).

This theory of agency remains influential in much gender studies writing. It not only challenged the nineteenth-century definition of agency as a thing that subjects had—and a thing, moreover, that allowed those subjects to use bodies and words as tools. It also offered a convincing alternative story of speech, bodies, and gender. Defining agency as an activity or process helped scholars both to reintroduce gender into political, ethical, and scholarly conversations and to recognize the material, as well as political, work that words and bodies do. Defining agency as a process, for instance, allowed scholars and activists to respond to "words that wound" with the recognition that these "words might, through time, become disjoined from their power to injure and recontextualized in more affirmative modes." Situating agency at the intersection of language and body, that is to say, made it possible to deactivate linguistic violence rather than simply redirecting it—as "the relentless search for legal remedy" to, say, hate speech would have us do (Butler 1997, 15).

But the posthuman disrupts this interpretation of agency and denies these affirmative modes of speaking. By emphasizing the distributed rather than singular character of physical existence, and the operative rather than communicative character of language, the posthuman removes both the subject and the body from the equation. Inhabiting not only a discursive field but also a material field, the posthuman demands that agency, too, be distributed. When matter is physical but disembodied, and language is operative but not communicative, embodied subjects become tangential or even irrelevant to theories of agency. If agency does exist, it must be dispersed. It cannot be embodied.

Gender studies scholars have criticized these posthuman theories of distributed agency from a variety of directions. Some have suggested, for example, that the notion of disembodied yet material agency is necessarily contradictory. Pinpointing ever smaller sites of agency within a distributed linguistic-material system does not by any means do away with the body, they argue. It simply miniaturizes the body, occludes and decontextualizes the relationships among human as well as nonhuman bodies, and thereby risks a return to the Cartesian mind-body dualities that posthuman theories of distributed agency ostensibly seek to undermine (Hayles 2005, 173–74). Distributed agency, according to these critics, involves miniaturizing the body until the body is small enough to ignore—a move that would have appealed to the nineteenth-century liberal writers whose theories of agency sought to neutralize the activities of both bodies and matter.

At the same time, however, these scholars argue that nonhuman things remain very much relevant to the agency of embodied, communicating human subjects. Indeed, interpretations of agency that start with the embodied human subject, they state, can easily, ethically, and productively be extended to nonhumans as persons (if not as humans). The agency theorized already by gender studies scholars, in other words— contingent, careful, and fragile as it is—*is* an agency that nonhumans might enact (Hayles 2005, 177). A *purely* posthuman agency is impossible. But a human agency that extends to nonhumans—nonhumans as diverse as litter, worms, electrical grids, food, and stem cells (Bennett 2010, xiii)—might be very much worth exploring.

Other scholars, however, argue that any extension of agency to nonhuman things—even if it is an agency that takes the human as a norm— is politically dangerous. Not only does such an extension recklessly lump human bodies in with other matter, exposing them to objectification and consumption; it also neutralizes agency as a tool for dismantling racist, sexist, and classicist social structures. Elaborating posthuman theories of agency thus involves, in this literature, playing an intellectual game that draws attention away from the political goals that have traditionally motivated gender studies scholars (Burfoot 2003, 68–69). Posthuman theories of agency are nothing more than a trivial academic pastime that weakens the activism that gender studies scholarship is supposed to encourage and foster. To the extent that gender studies is concerned with agency, this second group of authors insists, it must be concerned only with humans.

Finally, a third set of writers has also dissociated agency from the nonhuman, but it has then questioned the usefulness of agency as a term in gender studies scholarship. These scholars have recognized that, indeed, agency is wed to communicative (rather than operational) language, that invocations of agency are necessarily invocations of embodied human subjectivity, and that diluting agency through dispersal or distribution *does* confuse, perhaps to an unacceptable degree, human-centered, gender-conscious activism. This writing thus seeks to bracket agency. Rather than challenging or attempting to reconfigure agency, scholars writing in this genre try to describe gender without agency (Allen 2003:6–24, 18). They try to imagine a noncommunicative, operational speech that, nonetheless, does not lose gender. And they try to imagine a disembodied materiality that also keeps gender at the forefront of the conversation.

The point of this last trend in the writing on posthuman gender and agency is not that agency is unethical or that human-centered gender studies scholarship is incorrect. It is that gender may operate beyond the purely human realm—that distributed systems of, say, machines, litter, electricity, or organic matter may also have or do gender. And if gender does operate in such ways, then it may be better, for methodological reasons alone, to ignore agency for the moment. Instead of trying, somehow, to make existing critical theories of agency—where agency involves embodied human subjects repeatedly resituating themselves within fields of discourse—work for those without bodies and those without subjectivity, this writing tries to conceptualize a nonhuman gender without agency.

Conclusion: Postgender?

But this move brings us back to the question at the heart of the posthuman as a critical term in the study of gender: can a system, network, or environment characterized by distributed speech, distributed matter, and distributed (or no) agency have or do gender? Some argue that agency is too crucial to gender studies to bracket or to lose. Without agency, there is no gender (Butler 1997, 49–50). And if this is the case, then the posthuman challenge to gender studies must either be ignored (the human remaining the sole concern of gender studies scholarship), or it must be embraced (gender studies somehow remaining relevant in a world without gender).

Another approach to this question, however, is to remember that more often than not the term *posthuman* evokes the *past* in gender studies scholarship. Among gender studies scholars, the posthuman is, again, a *historical* concept. It is a way of thinking about why, in the past, gendered existence and gendered activities have so often been attributed to non-human things, spaces, environments, machines, or systems. The posthuman, in other words, has helped scholars to think in new ways about how and why gender has *already* been dispersed or distributed throughout material systems. If the posthuman does spell the end of gender, then gender has long since met its end.

But obviously, there was no end to gender. And in the same way that the *post-* in the posthuman is necessarily incomplete, so too is any ongoing posthuman assault on gendered ways of thinking, doing, being, and living—as, in fact, is this introduction to the term *posthuman*. In part, this introduction to the posthuman is incomplete because the term is amorphous and its meaning continues to be contested. More so, though, it is incomplete because the posthuman exists in a state of temporal flux. The story told here is an unabashed progress narrative—moving from misguided 1980s-era technophiles, to late twentieth-century gender studies scholars discovering the value of the cyborg, to more recent writers taking posthuman matter more seriously. But it is a progress narrative very much at odds with the nonlinear temporal frameworks within which the posthuman operates. The posthuman, after all, is obsolete when it is mobilized to describe the (1980s-era sci-fi) future. And its potential for future application is situated squarely in references to the past. The "after" that it describes never happened.

But perhaps this temporal instability—this obsolete, disembodied future that continues to taint the posthuman—is what makes the term most useful for gender studies scholars. This smear of Cartesian dualism—of digitized minds living forever beyond matter, in "cyberspace"—after all, reminds scholars that the material must always be taken seriously. If it is not taken seriously, then the endpoint to inclusive studies of speech and bodies is indeed absurd and a bit embarrassing.

Or, to get at this idea from a different direction, the posthuman is an impure term. It does raise questions about gendered speech, gendered matter, gendered existence, and gendered activity—perhaps troubling questions. But it cannot serve as a basis for the sort of political projects— these repeated and doomed attempts to incorporate more and more people into ostensibly empowering identity categories—for which so much twentieth-century feminist activism has been criticized. Fragile, mutable, and unstable, the posthuman opens up for scholars a safe place to think about gender as an intellectual category. It does not lend itself to activism—to scholarship that seeks a better future.

Indeed, as Gibson writes with reference to Stelarc's posthuman body, this body "has never seemed 'futuristic.'" Rather, it is the stuff of "circuses, freak shows, medical museums, the passions of solitary inventors . . . Victorian schemes for electroplating the dead" (Gibson 2012, 188–89). Although Gibson and Stelarc have little to do with gender, therefore—and nothing to do with gender-based activism—their interpretation of the posthuman resonates. This is a term whose politics rests precisely in its temporal, material, and indeed ethical mutability. It conjures, provocatively, the specter of a postgender world. But then it places this specter in the salons of Victorian spiritualists rather than in the manifestos (despite the cyborg) of contemporary theorists.

References

Allen, Dennis W. 2003. "Viral Activism and the Meaning of 'Post-Identity.'" *Journal of the Midwest Modern Language Association* 36.

Asdal, Kristin. 2003. "The Problematic Nature of Nature: The Post-Constructivist Challenge to Environmental History." *History and Theory* 42:60–74.

Bennett, Jane. 2010. *Vibrant Matter: A Political Ecology of Things*. Durham, NC: Duke University Press.

Burfoot, Annette. 2003. "Human Remains: Identity Politics in the Face of Biotechnology." *Cultural Critique* 53.

Butler, Judith. 1997. *Excitable Speech: A Politics of the Performative*. New York and London: Routledge.

Coole, Diana, and Samantha Frost, eds. 2010. *New Materialisms: Ontology, Agency, and Politics*. Durham, NC: Duke University Press.

Gibson, William. 2012. *Distrust That Particular Flavor*. New York: G. P. Putnam.

Haraway, Donna. 1990. *Simians, Cyborgs, and Women: The Reinvention of Nature*. London: Routledge.

Hayles, N. Katherine. 1990. *Chaos Bound: Orderly Disorder in Contemporary Literature and Science*. Ithaca, NY: Cornell University Press.

———. 1999. *How We Became Posthuman: Virtual Bodies in Cybernetics, Literature, and Informatics*. Chicago: University of Chicago Press.

———. 2005. *My Mother Was a Computer: Digital Subjects and Literary Texts*. Chicago: University of Chicago Press.

Hyde, Alan. 1997. *Bodies of Law*. Princeton, NJ: Princeton University Press.

Latour, Bruno. 2004. *Politics of Nature: How to Bring the Sciences into Democracy*. Trans. Catherine Porter. Cambridge, MA: Harvard University Press.

Thacker, Eugene. 2003. "Data Made Flesh: Biotechnology and the Discourse of the Posthuman." *Cultural Critique* 53.

15 :: POWER

WENDY BROWN AND JOAN W. SCOTT

In the explosion of theory that accompanied the "second wave" of the women's movement in the 1960s and 1970s, "power" was at once central, conceptually underdeveloped, and contradictorily deployed. For the most part, power was conceived as that which men wielded over women: practices of legal and familial restrictions on women's lives, rape and domestic violence, the dismissal or silencing of women's intellectual and artistic capacity, and forced maternity and responsibility for children. Given this rough equation of power with violence, oppression, deprivation, and illegitimate authority, and given as well the tacit equation of power with masculinity and its privileges, powerful women were cast as "male identified" and relations of power between women were considered either a remnant of male dominance or oxymoronic. Feminist theory thus foundered on a paradox in which power was only and always oppressive and repressive even as "sisterhood was powerful" and women's "empowerment" was the aim of consciousness-raising and feminist organizing. Feminist visions of emancipation and equality, then, simultaneously required power, reviled power, and projected a world in which power was radically reduced if not eliminated.

Part of the difficulty emerged from the fact that early second-wave feminists employed a standard modernist grammar of power, treating power as an attribute of a closed social system, as something held by one group of people over another or exercised by one person upon another, or stored in institutions themselves designed to serve the powerful and reproduce privilege. As long as feminists conceived of power only as a tangible and objective substance that some individuals have and others lack, and that men wield directly over women or through "male" institutions such as law or family, feminist theorizing about gender and power remained wedded to an equation of power with rule backed by force. Within the terms of this equation, feminists were unable to explain the presence of male dominance where both rule and force were absent. Equally important, they were unable to explain the production and reproduction of gender itself.

In *The Second Sex*, Simone de Beauvoir wrote of the complex social and psychological process of becoming a woman: "The delights of passivity are made to seem desirable to the young girl by parents and educators, books and myths, women and men; she is taught to enjoy them from earliest childhood; the temptation becomes more and more insidious; and she is the more fatally bound to yield to those delights as the flight of her transcendence is dashed against harsher obstacles." (de Beauvoir 1953, 335). The creation of feminine subjectivity, Beauvoir pointed out, is most often achieved without recourse to violence, and yet it is a linch-pin in the edifice of male domination. Put in other terms, gender is an achievement of power, but of a power that does not necessarily depend on the overt exercise of force or the presence of a ruler. It is precisely this kind of power—understood to create gender rather than to operate on preexisting women and men—that modernist grammars of power do not address. Feminists deploying these grammars thus found it difficult to theorize the very object of feminism—the production of gender—in terms of power, and in this regard could not realize the aim of radically denaturalizing and historicizing women's subordination and providing the terms for women's emancipation. In short, without theories of power adequate to explaining the making of gender, gender itself remained an undeconstructed entity or essence. Notwithstanding Beauvoir's insis-tence that "one is not born but rather becomes a woman," women were seen as positioned but not produced by power.

A brief consideration of liberalism and Marxism, the two prevalent models of social and political power inherited by second-wave feminists, will make clear their inadequacies for feminism. Classical and contempo-rary liberalism renders power in terms of the capacity to enact a design of the will (Hobbes [1651] 1996). Power in this view assumes sovereignty, in the state, on one side, and in sovereign individuals, on the other. That is, both the state and the individual are presumed to have the capac-ity to enact their wills, and power is the expression of this capacity. For a feminism that employs this view, the power that secures male domi-nance resides in laws that privilege men, as well as in family structures and ideology that anoint fathers and husbands as rulers. "Patriarchy," on this model, is defined as a *system of rule*. Within these terms, the politi-cal agenda for liberal feminists inevitably centers upon reforming sexist laws, producing feminist public policy, and challenging male rule in the family. While a wealth of empirical research and important legal and po-litical reforms have taken place under this agenda, this formulation of power leaves liberal feminists unable to explain why and how male dominance persists when women have secured legal equality and when men no longer rule (or are not present) in the household (Mede 1998, 53, 91–95). When women have civil and political rights equal to those of men and are no longer governed by a patriarchal head of household, how and in what ways are women still subordinated as women?

For Karl Marx, power is generated by labor, congealed as capital, institutionalized in structures of class, and dissimulated through an ideology that denies the significance of relations of production to social inequality and domination. Feminists drawing on this view of power either formulated "patriarchy" in terms of the relation between women's unremunerated labor in the household and second-class status in the workforce, or analogized gender to class by considering what might be *like* labor in producing the material basis for women's oppression. The former was expressed in theories of "capitalist patriarchy" and other formulations showing how women's subordination and exploitation is required by class-stratified societies.[1] The latter reached its most comprehensive expression in the work of Catharine MacKinnon, who argued explicitly that "sexuality is to feminism as work is to Marxism" (MacKinnon 1982, 515). In both cases, male dominance was defined as a *system of stratification* in which one or more material activities—reproduction, housework, consumption, or sexuality—were understood as the currency of a closed system of social subordination.

If the liberal feminist formulation of power, in its concentration on rule, inevitably sustains the invisibility of the social, psychological, and economic dominions of power's operation, the Marxist feminist frame posits a monological analysis that treats all dimensions of male dominance as converging in a single source and operation of power. (It is worthy of note that MacKinnon begins her work on the analogy between class and gender, labor and sexuality, by noting that feminism is frequently dismissed as politically insignificant by Marxists precisely because it is thought not to devolve upon a single cause or mechanism [MacKinnon 1982, 528].) "Patriarchy" in both cases suggests the existence of a system, and of a systematic quality to power, that can neither account for the variety of ways in which gender is lived, enacted, regulated, and enforced within a particular culture, nor for the variety of its expressions and injuries across time and place. Neither approach to power can account for the highly differentiated production of gender itself—the making of diverse gendered bodies, activities, and domains. And neither approach can account for the production and organization of gender through language (including discourses of biology), through nonstate institutions, through everyday practices, and through the organization of the psyche. Both elide power in these domains, indeed conceive of power as lying elsewhere. Both also treat power as uniform and comprehensive, organizing all aspects of human relations in the same way. Consequently, these theories could not comprehend or articulate differences among women except by referring to other powers of stratification, such as race and class. Feminist theory could not articulate, analyze, or explain difference *within* gender. Thus the charge that early feminist theory was essentialist and universalist, and, more particularly, heteronormative, middle-class, and white, is partly explicable through the inadequacies of the conceptions of power with which feminist theorists were operating.

In the 1980s the notion of social construction and its new conceptions of the subject brought the problem of power squarely to the center of feminist concerns. But it is the combination of poststructuralist thought and critical encounters with psychoanalytic theory that did most to reconceive power in this period. In what follows, we offer two instances of this reconceptualization: one centered on Michel Foucault, the other derived from Sigmund Freud and Freudian psychoanalysis. Respectively, these two approaches have facilitated feminism's grasp of the *constitution* of gender and of gendered orders. Foucault's emphasis on power's capacity to produce, position, and regulate the subject, and psychoanalytic attention to the production and ordering of subjectivity, together offer insights into gender production and organization that radically rework and complicate a feminist, political, psychological, and social agenda. Foucault and Freud, however, are neither the only important contemporary theorists of power for feminism (that portfolio would have to include Louis Althusser, Jacques Derrida, and Gilles Deleuze, among others), nor are they easily rendered compatible. While Foucault offers incisive techniques for understanding the making of subjects and social orders through historically variable discourses and institutions, with the exception of almost inadvertent and poetic asides, he largely eschews symbolic or unconscious orders of power. Conversely, the attention of psychoanalysis to the production of individual subjectivity in symbolic and unconscious registers rests uneasily with historically and culturally specific analyses of power, even though Freud himself clearly took historical and cultural specificities into account when analyzing individual psychic behavior. While there have been some attempts from feminists and others (e.g., Butler 1997) to combine Freudian and Foucauldian analyses, in the discussion that follows we treat Foucault and psychoanalysis as two relatively distinct instances of the reconceptualization of power in feminist efforts to theorize both the production of male dominance and feminist resistance.

Foucault

Michel Foucault is well known for his insistence that power is ubiquitous, but it is a mistake to understand this formulation as suggesting that power equally and indiscriminately touches all elements of the social fabric, belongs to everyone, or is irrelevant to domination or oppression. What Foucault's insistence on the "everywhereness" of power displaces is a formulation of power as emerging only in explicit scenes of domination or rule-giving. Instead, it construes the subject as simultaneously brought into being and subjected by power—a process Foucault calls "subjectivization"—and thus detects power in domains, elements, discourses, and organizations of space conventionally conceived of as free of power. This can be grasped most easily by reviewing Foucault's critique of existing models of power.

Foucault's challenges to modernist conceptions of power involve a critique of sovereignty, the commodity model of power, and what he calls the "repressive hypothesis" (Foucault 1978, 1980). In place of these conventional formulations, Foucault offers what he calls an "analytics" of power that centers on an appreciation of power's productive, regulatory, and dispersed character. In his insistence that subjects are the effects of power, rather than the a priori of power, he also calls attention to the variety of modalities in which power emerges. The signature power in modernity, for example, is "the administration of bodies and the calculated management of *life*" ("biopower"), as opposed to "the ancient right of *death* ... a power whose highest function was ... to kill" (Foucault 1978, 138–40). Power in modernity functions most extensively through the disciplines, what Foucault terms "an anatomo-politics of the human body," rather than through monarchical or juridical forces external to bodies.

The sovereign model of power is the most common *political* notion of power, the notion that casts the problem of power in terms of ruling and being ruled, or, in Lenin's formulation, "who does what to whom." Power, in this view, is held by and in individuals, and is exercised over others. The conception of power as operating through sovereignty serves as the very premise of liberal democracy, in which power/rule is understood to rest in the people rather than a monarch or sovereign group, and in which the enactment of legislation or law is taken to be the sign of power. We are presumed to be sovereign subjects when we are self-legislating, which is to say that we are presumed to will for ourselves as sovereign subjects when there is no sovereign to whom we owe obedience, when another is not giving rules to us, not ruling over us. Foucault challenges the sovereign model of power by problematizing the notion of sovereignty itself, insisting that the conditions of sovereignty or imagined sovereignty are themselves suffused with power. Thus, sovereignty is revealed as an effect or emblem of power rather than its source, a move that transmogrifies sovereignty from a universal wellspring of state formation and individuality to a historically specific expression and dissimulation of power relations.

The commodity model of power is the most common *economic* notion of power, although it has substantial relevance to popular understandings of political domination and oppression as well. Here, power is conceived as a transferable or circulating good, and as thoroughly material. Although Foucault does not resolutely hold Marx to this model (indeed, Marx's move to derive all social power from labor anticipates Foucault's insistence on the productive character of power), the Marxist notion of labor power as extractable and commodifiable, as constituting the basis of capital, and hence the power of capitalism, inevitably partakes of the understanding of power as a commodity, even if this commodity circulates according to the rules of a structure or system rather than according to individual will. The notion of sovereignty also relies on a notion of power as commodifiable. The very possibility of transferring sovereignty from the people to a king, or divesting the king of sovereignty and distributing it to the people, and the understanding of these acts as transfers or divestments of power, entails a conception of power as a commodity.

The commodity model of power also undergirds social analyses that treat some groups as having power and others as lacking it, analyses that treat powerlessness as the necessary corollary of power, or analyses that refer to power as equivalent to privileges that can either be exercised or surrendered, depending on the moral standing of the subject in question. Foucault's challenge to this model of power is a challenge to the very formulation of power as an object, a transferable substance, as external to and hence potentially alienable from the subject who is said to hold it. Foucault insists that power is constitutive of subjects, not simply wielded by them, that it operates in the form of relations between subjects and is never merely held by them, and that it is dispersed and often weblike in nature, rather than an objectifiable entity or even relation. While we might quarrel with Foucault's attribution of the commodity model of power to Marx, who at least on a structuralist reading would seem to share Foucault's view of power as subject-constituting, relational, and circulating through a system rather than being "held" by particular individuals, Foucault's stakes in this attribution are also worth noting. Foucault aims to underscore the economism in the Marxist account of power, along with power's assumed transferability and its relative externality to subjects. That is, Foucault's objection to the "science" of Marxism pertains precisely to its location of power in "systems" or structures, within which subjects are positioned (rather than produced), and which, as systems, can be overthrown and replaced simply by changing the nature of the ownership and relations of production.

The repressive model of power is the most common psychological notion of power, although, like the commodity model, it is also part of what the notion of sovereign power draws upon. What Foucault names the "repressive hypothesis" in his *History of Sexuality* (1978) signals an understanding of power as always repressive or restrictive—a "negative" view of power in Foucault's account. The repressive hypothesis implies that power's purpose as well as power's action is the containment of desire (Freud), of the natural passions and lawlessness of the body politic (Hobbes), or of individual freedom (Mill). (Most liberal political theory regards power as repressive and liberty as its antithesis. The liberal argument for the minimal state thus aims to limit power in order to promote liberty.) The trade-off between uncivilized freedom and civilized repression presented in Freud's *Civilization and Its Discontents* (1930, SE 21), like arguments over First Amendment limitations about whether ugly or hurtful speech is a price of free speech, are centered in a formulation of power as repressive, and a formulation of freedom as unchaining subjects from such power. So also are claims, reaching from Mary Wollstonecraft (1792) and J. S. Mill (1879) to Luce Irigaray (1985), that woman's true nature is repressed by male dominant regimes, and will emerge when she is emancipated from this dominance. Foucault's challenge to the repressive hypothesis is threefold: (1) power is productive rather than simply repressive, that is, power creates meanings, subjects, and social orders; (2) power and freedom are not opposites insofar as there is no subject, and hence no freedom, outside of power; and (3) repressive models of power tacitly posit a human subject untouched by power underneath power's repressive action.

Foucault does not claim that power is without qualities of sovereignty, commodification, or repression but rather that power—especially its contemporary modalities—will, when conceived in such terms, misconstrue its most salient characteristics and movements. With regard to sovereignty, Foucault argues in his genealogical works that power does not just rule but regulates and normalizes—it does not simply give commands but also installs its imperatives in discourses that mask them as norms and detach them from any commanding agent. He opposes too the view of power as a commodity, an understanding of power as circulating through the social fabric, as irrigating that fabric, and as relatively intangible except in its effects. The commodity model of power is also undone by the emphasis Foucault places on knowledge as a domain and instrument of power, about which more shortly. Foucault opposes the repressive model of power most directly with the contention that power is productive, by which he does not mean "positive" or affirmative, but rather that it produces subjects, knowledges, events, and social formations, that it brings them into being and does not simply repress them. Even where power does appear repressive, Foucault insists that such repression never acts simply as a lid or damper, but rather acts to produce particular kinds of subjects through the discursive norms established by repressive regimes. Thus, bodies, sexualities, and genders are not simply the physical material on which power works, but are themselves *effects* of power, effects that emerge through particular regimes of knowledge and power.

The conventional models of power that Foucault opposes together express a commitment to power as a tangible, empirical thing—present in a rule, an order, a person, or an institution. They also cast power as independent of truth and knowledge, and in so doing attempt to distinguish power from the mechanisms of its legitimation. While Foucault is careful not to equate power and knowledge, but rather to pose their relationship as a problem to be explored, he nevertheless establishes knowledge as a significant field of power, especially in modalities of power that operate microphysically on the subject and through regulatory norms (see Judith Butler's essay "Regulation" in this volume). For these claims, Foucault builds on Nietzsche's insistence that the human will to power expresses itself in part through a will to knowledge. He also extends Max Weber's (1978) recognition that power, authority, and legitimation are intertwined with one another such that orders of legitimation must be understood not simply as justifications of power but as modalities of power.

It is in the power/knowledge relation, and the recognition of the extent to which power operates as a field or regime of truth, that the importance of Foucault's notion of the concept of discourse emerges. Different from mere language or speech, discourse, for Foucault, embraces a relatively bounded field of terms, categories, and beliefs expressed though statements that are commonsensical within the discourse. As an ensemble of speech practices that carries values, classifications, and meanings, discourse simultaneously constitutes a truth about subjects and constitutes subjects in terms of a truth regime. For Foucault, discourse never merely describes but also constructs, represents, and positions subjects. It creates relationships and channels of authority through the articulation of norms and degrees of deviation from those norms. Thus, for example, discourses of femininity simultaneously represent what a woman is, construct and position women in terms of that representation, and exclude "unfeminine" subjects (male or female) from the category "woman." Insofar as discourse simultaneously constructs, positions, and represents subjects in terms of norms and deviations posited by the discourse, representation itself comes to be seen as constitutive of subjects and the world in which they operate. But Foucault's understanding of discursive constitution also challenges the notion of independent modalities of social power that result in a closed or total system of domination (e.g., the labor theory of value or "patriarchy"). He replaces such notions with a depiction of the unsystematic interplay of discourses that converge as well as conflict with one another. Thus, for example, contemporary norms of mothering that establish the good mother as well as its monstrous counterpart derive not from pure discourses of gender but from discourses regulating other modalities of social power. What establishes the "welfare mother," the "single mother," the "lesbian mother," or the "crack mother" as deviating from normative motherhood are discourses of class, race, and sexuality, not only gender, and yet gender is also suddenly made to appear as comprised of these discourses, as inherently impure, local, spliced, polyglot.

Foucault's challenge to conventional models of power thus disrupts the notion of social *systems* of rule and replaces it with an understanding of the multiplicitous, infinitely detailed, and above all incomplete or haphazard content of particular regimes of truth governing and constituting subjects. His insistence on the relentlessly historical nature of particular formations of power, and even particular styles or "technologies" of power, replaces an image of power governing a social totality with an image of power suffusing the present via an array of historical discourses that do not harmonize or resolve in a coherent, closed system. However, this does not mean that institutions such as the state cannot be spoken about or theorized, for example, as vehicles of male domination. While a Foucauldian approach requires that the state not be conceived as an entity or unity, as historically transcendent or metaphysically unified in meaning and function, or as itself the source of masculinist political domination, it is possible to undertake a Foucauldian genealogy to trace the ways in which particular discourses of masculinist power circulate through laws, policies, and knowledges constitutive of what is commonly conceived as the power of the state (Brown 1995).

Foucault's formulation of discourse poses a fundamental challenge to Marx's view of power as material and of ideology as a distorted account of that materiality (Marx and Engels 1970). Indeed, Foucault challenges the very coherence of the notion of ideology as a false representation of a putative material reality. If discourses establish truth, and construct and position subjects in terms of that truth, then power is *inside* a discourse or truth regime rather than external to it. What a prevailing discourse says female and male are is a great deal of what fashions us as women and men, just as the naturalization and superordination of heterosexuality is achieved through discourses of family, sexuality, gender difference, reproduction, and nature rather than prior to or outside those discourses. The significance of this for feminism is that the fight over "truth," which is to say, the fight over discursive productions of truth, becomes a central terrain of political struggle. Thus, for example, the past twenty-five years of feminist efforts to change the way rape and rape victims are talked about and treated in police stations, emergency rooms, and courtrooms has not simply reformed speech and manners in those settings but has fundamentally transformed the meaning of sexual violence in its relation to gender. Discourses that naturalize or trivialize such violence or that blame the victim construct gender differently from discourses that cast sexual violence as an intolerable assault on women's personhood.

Taken together, the implications of Foucault's critiques of conventional understandings of power, combined with his elaboration of the concept of discourse as a conduit of power, are far-reaching for feminist conceptualizations of gender, oppression, resistance, and transformation. What feminism surrenders consequent to Foucault's critique is the idea that women's subordination is the consequence of power held in straightforward fashion by men or the state, wielded in commands or laws, and operating to repress women's innate strength or true nature. It sacrifices the notion of patriarchy as a total system, rooted in a single cause and operating through a coherent machinery. It also gives up the conceit of a clear enemy embodied in particular people (men) or institutions (laws), although Foucault's critique may enable a more precise formulation of the powers constituting and circulating through men and laws. In Foucault's insistence that "power relations are both intentional and nonsubjective," he challenges feminists to reckon with the strategic effects of an order of dominance that has no "headquarters presiding over its rationality" and consequently "no soul of revolt," no "pure law of the revolutionary" that will once and for all bring down the regime (Foucault 1978, 94–96). Thus, a feminism derived in part from Foucault's analytics of power surrenders not only the fiction of power's residence in particular subjects and institutions, but also a formulation of resistance that imagines seizing power or imagines finding a place "outside power," a strategy of resistance independent of the powers that constituted it.

What feminism stands to gain from Foucault is a way of understanding women's subordination as achieved in discourse, through regulatory norms, and as operating through, on, and by women themselves—"the individual which power has constituted is at the same time its vehicle."[2] Feminism gains as well an understanding of power as inhering in the very making of gender and, importantly, as producing gendered bodies rather than being based on them. The body, on a Foucauldian understanding, would not be the source or a priori of gender but part of what is constructed by discourses of gender. Feminism gains, too, the capacity to discern gender power in putatively nongendered sites and discourses. If, as Foucault writes, "power is never localized here or there, never in anybody's hands, never appropriated as a commodity or a piece of wealth," then it is also the case that gender is never simply a subject or an object, never a pure instance of itself, but rather a murky manifestation in the circulation of powers (1980, 98). Thus, rather than conceiving patriarchy as a coherent system, the powers that produce male dominance are articulated as having multiple sources and operating along multiple historical trajectories, coursing through a variety of social relations, and imbricated with historically specific discourses productive of sexuality, race, class, and other markers of subjectivity. Gender, understood as the effect of power, thus sacrifices the analytic independence of gender from other modes of subject production but gains the capacity for analyzing the historical production of gender through and alongside other modalities of social power. Gender is never only or purely gender, and thus, paradoxically, disperses at the very moment that Foucault's formulations of power bring its constitutive elements clearly into view.

Psychoanalysis

While "power" as a social phenomenon is at the center of Foucault's work, neither power nor the realm of "the social" is the direct object of psychoanalytic theorizing. Rather, it is the psychic and symbolic processes at work in the formation of individuals as sexed subjects that preoccupies psychoanalysis. For this reason, some feminists have turned to psychoanalytic theory for explanations of the persistence of gender inequalities in the face of momentous social, political, and economic changes. They have found in the work of Sigmund Freud, Jacques Lacan, and their many critics and followers, ways of linking theories about individual psyches to explanations of social phenomena, particularly what seem to be enduring structures of male dominance. The publication of Juliet Mitchell's *Psychoanalysis and Feminism* in 1974 made it possible to set aside caricatures of Freud's biological determinism ("anatomy is destiny" was not Freud's prescription, she argued, but his description of deeply rooted Western beliefs) and to use psychoanalytic theory instead as a critique of biological determinism—a notion that not only informed commonsense thinking about gender but also a good deal of feminist theorizing. (Thus Kathleen Barry [1979, 164–65]: "Sex-is-power is the foundation of patriarchy.... Institutionalized sexism and misogyny—from discrimination in employment, to exploitation through the welfare system, to dehumanization in pornography—stem from the primary sexual domination of women in one-to-one situations." And Shulamith Firestone [1970, 8]: "Unlike economic class, sex class sprang directly from a biological reality: men and women were created different, and not equally privileged.... The biological family is an inherently unequal power distribution.")

In 1914 Freud had dismissed as "monstrous" Alfred Adler's suggestion that "the strongest motive force in the sexual act is the man's intention of showing himself master of the woman—of being 'on top'" (SE 16:53). This kind of reductionism, Freud thought, misunderstood the complexity and the force of sexuality (sex, according to Adler's logic, became an instrument of aggression or the expression of an innate masculine "will to power"), its place in the formation of gendered identities (masculine and feminine were mistakenly taken to correspond inevitably to the physical bodies male and female), and the role of the unconscious in the determination of object choice. Freud insisted that the psyche could neither be reduced to physiology nor entirely separated from it. The operations of the psyche, moreover, were not transparent, since they were influenced by unconscious processes that did not work according to rationalist models. The science of psychoanalysis, as Freud articulated it, was to provide systematic ways of reading the unconscious through its representations, whether these took the form of images, words, behaviors, or physical symptoms. Although aimed specifically at the treatment of individual neurotics, psychoanalysis inevitably addressed the relationship between individuals and society, the personal and the cultural. It was in the effects of the individual's negotiation with the rules and requirements of collective life, as articulated in the norms of "culture," that one could track the unconscious. For Freud, the central pivot of this negotiation was sexuality.

Since it addresses sexuality and sexual difference, psychoanalysis has proven useful for thinking about gender and power. This usage falls, roughly, into two different approaches, one of which takes power to be an established system, gender to be a fixed relationship of inequality, and sexual difference to be the determinant of sexual identity. It finds in psychoanalysis a key to the reproduction of ideology through the internalization of norms. It takes theories of the Oedipus complex and the myth of castration to explain the mechanisms of the maintenance and reproduction of patriarchy in the course of Western history. And it interprets manifestations of male dominance (in the work force, the family, and politics) as effects of the Oedipal stage of psychic development, which establishes sexual difference as the "law of the father" and the foundation of social order. This approach has many of the limits of the models of power Foucault criticized; in addition, it fails to account for the evident variations in gendered subjectivity (the range of "masculine" and "feminine" behaviors, the refusal or inability to accept normative roles, the emergence of queer and trans) and for change.

The feminist use of psychoanalytic theory that parallels the Foucauldian critique of established models of power challenges the sense of inevitability and immutability associated with the idea that social order and psychic health are determined by unconscious adherence to the father's law. Instead of fixed structures of gender (patriarchy, male domination), this body of work formulates subjectivity as a process at once more fluid and fraught. This approach veers between utopian idealization of the revolutionary potential of the unconscious and a more sober assessment of the persistence of unresolvable tensions between the unconscious and the conscious (or the ego, the superego, and the id). Those who insist on these tensions stress the variable and indeterminate relationship between the individual and the social. They emphasize that the process of becoming a woman or man (to return to Beauvoir's formulation) is not the same for all individuals. Masculinity and femininity are not predictable attributes that correlate neatly with the physical traits of male and female or with social prescriptions for gender roles, as Freud pointed out repeatedly:

> Sex is a biological fact which, although it is of extraordinary importance in mental life, is hard to grasp psychologically. We are accustomed to say that every human being displays both male and female instinctual impulses, needs and attributes; but though anatomy, it is true, can point out the characteristic of maleness and femaleness, psychology cannot. For psychology the contrast between the sexes fades away into one between activity and passivity, in which we far too readily identify activity with maleness and passivity with femaleness.... However this may be, if we assume it as a fact that each individual seeks to satisfy both male and female wishes in his sexual life, we are prepared for the possibility that those [two sets of] demands are not fulfilled by that same object, and that they interfere with each other unless they can be kept apart and each impulse guided into a particular channel that is suited to it. (*Civilization and Its Discontents, SE* 21:105–6)

Feminists have developed this idea using formal psychoanalytic notions such as fantasy or the drive to explain the existence of a broad range of possible sexual identities and behaviors and a variety of possible social formations. Their arguments suggest that the relationship between social reproduction and individual psyches is one to be explored rather than assumed, and that the Oedipus myth is not foundational but rather a particular historical/cultural organization of the drive.

The Oedipus Complex

Feminist appropriations of Freud have used his discussions of the Oedipus complex to explain the psychic foundations of patriarchy. Freud conceived of the Oedipus complex as a universal process that established the terms of sexual difference, the directions of human desire, and the rule of law. It is important to note that the Oedipus complex was a theoretical construct; not every child goes through the exact process Freud described. It is a hypothetical frame, a lens through which individual psychic formation might be understood. In the course of a child's development (usually between the ages of three and five), Freud posited, he unconsciously grasps that his desire for the mother (the desire to become one with her again) is not only unrealizable but prohibited by the father's desire for and previous claim to her. The father's power to enforce his claim is taken to be the power of castration, which the child imagines is the reason for the difference between men and women: since the child assumes that all people have the same genitals, he concludes that women have lost the penis, and that men can lose it too. "The assumption that all human beings have the same (male) form of genital," writes Freud, "is the first of many remarkable and momentous theories of children. It is of little use to a child that the science of biology justifies his prejudice and has been obliged to recognize the female clitoris as a true substitute for the penis" ([1905] 1962, 61).

Boys and girls deal with this fantasy differently: boys fear castration as the ultimate punishment for their sexual activity, but sexual activity (as well as other forms of masculine domination) also becomes a demonstration of the fact that they have not been castrated; girls (whose developmental process is more complex) resent and seek to compensate for their presumed loss, ultimately by symbolically equating a baby with a penis: "Her Oedipus complex culminates in a desire, which is long retained, to receive a baby from her father as a gift—to bear him a child" (1924, *SE* 19:178–79). For those working with the theories of the French psychoanalyst and philosopher Jacques Lacan, castration has a more complicated meaning. According to Lacan, the child's desire for the mother involves its wish to satisfy her desire; the realization that this is impossible consists of a double castration. The mother is imagined as castrated, as having a lack that must be supplied by someone else. The child is castrated because s/he cannot fill the lack. In this imagined scene, only the father can provide what is lacking; only he possesses the phallus.

These references to castration do not describe an actual situation, nor a set of consciously reasoned processes, but rather a shared cultural fantasy about the origin of sexual difference whose "efficacity" (as the French analysts Jean Laplanche and Jean-Bertrand Pontalis define it) is that "it brings into play a proscriptive agency (the prohibition against incest) which bars the way to a naturally sought satisfaction and forms an indissoluble link between wish and law" (1974, 286). The link is dialectical: not only does law impose boundaries on desire, it also incites the very desire it forbids. (For comparison, the relation between law and desire works in much the way Foucault portrays the relation between power and resistance. Law does not repress but rather incites desire.) It is in this way that castration anxiety can be understood to have become generalized and so the basis for moral and social regulation (and its transgression). The law here functions as a symbolic power; "real" social rules rest on and derive their legitimacy from cultural myths and collective fantasies.

The Oedipus complex, the myth of castration, and the law of the father all revolve around the phallus, the ancient symbol of masculine power. And although the phallus is a symbol and not an actual organ (the signifier of all signifiers for Lacan), some writers suggest that it has been conflated with the penis in the Western cultural imagination. The illusion that phallus and penis are one establishes sexual difference as an asymmetrical relationship between men and women (one has the power that the other lacks), but the fact that it is an illusion also means that there is uncertainty about the reality of possession. The desire of an Other is required to "prove" that a subject has the phallus, and even this does not constitute definitive proof.[3] Masculinity (and femininity) thus becomes a matter of repeated enactments of a subject's relation to the phallus. They are, moreover, "positions" taken, not functions determined by biology. The lawgiver need not be a real father, nor even a man, but someone who symbolically occupies the position of regulating or thwarting desire. Relations of power between women can, then, also be analyzed in these terms.

In the illusory equation of phallus and penis lie both the rationale for male dominance and the (unconscious) motor of its perpetuation. Since possession of a real penis does not in fact guarantee the enjoyment of the symbolic power of the phallus,[4] all kinds of social institutions and practices are devised to put it into effect. It is here that symbolic power can be seen to translate into a quest for and implementation of social power with material effects. Historically, this has included kinship structures based on exchanges of women (see Janet Carsten's essay "Kinship" in this volume), patrilineal transmission of property (and the literal affixing of the father's name to his offspring and heirs), the restriction of kingship to men, the definition of democratic citizenship and political participation as a male right, the designation of certain crafts and professions as exclusively masculine, the representation of nationalist, revolutionary, and counterrevolutionary movements as fulfillments of masculinity, and the exclusion of women from church hierarchies and educational institutions. The instances can be multiplied and diversified—and they have been by scholars who appropriate psychoanalytic theory to discern the unconscious appeals to and consolidations of sexual identity in historically specific contexts. (These examples are, obviously, restricted to the realm of gender and sexual identity and do not pretend to explain other sorts of exclusions based on race, religion, or economic status.)

A good example of this kind of use of psychoanalysis is Neil Hertz's essay "Medusa's Head: Male Hysteria under Political Pressure." The article considers a number of texts (by Edmund Burke, Victor Hugo, Alexis de Tocqueville, and Maxime Du Camp) that recount disturbing experiences in (French) revolutionary circumstances (in 1789, 1848, and 1871) and that use the same trope—the author sees or is confronted by an ugly, threatening, Medusa-like woman—to convey the horror. Linking unconscious fear of castration to political anxiety, Hertz takes the monstrous woman to represent the authors' fear of the possibility of their castration. "At the barricades, the women's—or the revolutionaries'—lack of 'property' betokens the soldiers'—or society's—risk" (Hertz 1983, 30). Fear of revolution is converted in some cases to political conservatism. The psychic charge that seeks to defend against castration invokes the symbolic, all-powerful phallus; Freud refers to the "apotropaic effect" created by the display of the erect male organ. The equation of phallus and property in this situation intensifies the political commitment and the behavior of the opponents of revolution. Hertz cites Freud's essay "Fetishism" to make the connection explicit:

> For if a woman had been castrated, then his own possession of a penis was in danger; and against that there rose in rebellion the portion of his narcissism which Nature has, as a precaution, attached to that particular organ. In later life a grown man may perhaps experience a similar panic when the cry goes up that Throne and Altar are in danger, and similar illogical consequences will ensue. (Freud *SE* 21:153)

The point is not only that masculinity is imbricated with politics, but that power often seeks its legitimacy—and does so successfully—by associating the phallus with whatever cause is at stake. (For other examples, see Muel-Dreyfus 1996; Moreau 1982; Salecl 1994; Scott 1996; Theweleit 1987.) This helps explain the great disappointments experienced by feminists at the failure of certain "democratic" political and social movements to grant women full equality or even to place such equality on the agenda. If power is equated with the phallus, then its articulation, consolidation, or defense gets expressed by literally excluding women, by cordoning their influence into specialized, "separate spheres," or maintaining them in (or returning them to) a subordinate status.

For those who appropriate psychoanalytic theory to analyze gender and power, particular social and political arrangements are less important than the symbolic structures that undergird them and which they inscribe. Thus, patriarchy would be defined not simply as a system in which rulership is modeled on hierarchical family structures that give children their father's names and transmit property through the paternal line. Still less would the actual presence of fathers in households guarantee the continuity of patriarchal law. Rather, from the perspective of symbolic representation, it is the signifying power of the phallus that is passed from one generation to the next through unconsciously acquired processes. (For Lacan, these are linguistic processes: castration and the differentiation of the sexes marked by castration that come with the subject's entry into language.) These processes establish the conceptual basis for sexed subject positions and social relationships that equate masculinity with men's power over women. (For a sociologist's attempt to link social and psychological processes, see Connell 1987.) The important point here is that power does not inhere in a structure, nor is it a possession; rather, it is something that is signified symbolically, understood phantasmatically, and enacted according to these terms. Relations of power find their legitimation by referring to or invoking unconscious belief in the centrality of the phallus.

Of course, there are feminists who have offered critiques of theories that assume the primacy of the phallus in the articulation of the differences between the sexes. Drawing on the work of Melanie Klein (Whitford 1992), feminists Jessica Benjamin (1988), Nancy Chodorow (1978 and 1989), and Dorothy Dinnerstein (1977) have argued for the greater importance of the mother (and the greater symbolic importance of the breast) in the child's psychic formation. But their work does not offer an alternative explanation for what others point to as the persistent signifying power of the phallus. This power does not seem to have been diminished over time by changes in household organization, legal inheritance patterns, or citizenship qualifications. In fact, it is at the collective (social, economic, and political) level, where normative rules are articulated and enforced through appeals to symbolic structures, that "patriarchy" (that is, the symbolic law of the father) seems most starkly evident, despite variations in the sexed identities of individual subjects. (Again, see Butler's essay "Regulation," chapter 18.)

The feminist philosopher Luce Irigaray (1985) maintains that patriarchy must be understood as a symbolic structure but one susceptible to change. She argues that feminist interventions, addressed to reformulating unconscious representations, are not only possible but necessary (see also Whitford 1991, 1992). If the symbolic power of the phallus is to be dislodged, Irigaray insists, intervention must take place where this power is enshrined or represented and in its terms: the symbolic terms of the unconscious. For Irigaray, the project of feminist theorizing is the articulation of a feminine symbolic divorced from its Oedipal moorings.

The Drive

For those seeking ways to think about change within the terms of psychoanalytic theory, the "drive" seems an alternative to the seemingly intractable Oedipus complex. If the phallus is the symbolic representative of the law in psychoanalytic theory, the drive is that which, operating at the law's limit, cannot be represented in symbolic terms. The drive is neither a possession nor an attribute of the subject; rather, it is a constitutive force of individual subjectivity. The drive is a "border concept," neither entirely psychic nor entirely somatic. It has its source in unconscious representations that become libidinally located in various regions of the body. The drive is experienced as a quest for a satisfaction that can never be fulfilled. The infant sucks at its mother's breast to satisfy hunger, but sucking becomes inextricably associated with pleasure apart from the need for food. The infant will suck its fingers or other objects, hallucinating and thereby seeking to reproduce its pleasure. In the process, the breast may become an object of libidinal desire and the mouth and fingers erotogenic zones of the body.

Laplanche (1992) attributes the drive to the child's reaction to "enigmatic signifiers," unconscious libidinal messages from adults that the child cannot fully interpret, cannot symbolize, and which it represses. This "primal repression" becomes the source of the associations and mental representations that establish the relations between parts of the body and objects of desire. It also is the source of symptoms and suffering, the "malfunctioning" of the subject within the terms of normative social regulation. The mental representations are individually variable and a source of constant internal stimulation. As such, they motivate action—they are a force that expresses the individuality of a subject (by identifying parts of the body and objects that are phantasmatically associated with pleasure) and establishes some of the terms of his/her relationships with others.

Although the example of the nursing infant sucking at the breast suggests a direct line between experience, the drive, and its objects, this is, in fact, not always the case. Freud described four "vicissitudes" of the drive—displacement, reversal, repression, and sublimation—and three polarities—subject/object, pleasure/unpleasure, and active/passive. Thus, the drive sometimes reverses its aim (instead of looking at an object, the subject wants to be seen) or inverts its content (love becomes hate). The drive sometimes transposes its object so that, for example, instead of wanting to inflict pain on another, the subject finds pleasure in being hurt. The alternation between active and passive (giving/receiving pain, pleasure, love; seeing/being seen/making oneself visible to another) is also characteristic of the drive and is only mistakenly (according to Freud and Lacan) correlated with male and female. The operations of the drive are not differentiated by sex (Freud insisted that "there is only one libido," although libido is sometimes used synonymously with drive), and they don't follow normative rules; neither do they conform to developmental models that correlate adult sexual satisfaction with genital activity and heterosexual object choice. It is for this reason that Lacan asserted that "there is no such thing as a sexual relation," by which he meant that there was no natural, unmediated relation between woman and man and that sexual relations did not involve two whole subjects but rather a subject and a "part-object," that is, a representation of a fantasized source of pleasure. (For more on this, see Evans 1996; Shepherdson 1997. We are grateful to Charles Shepherdson, Emily Zakin, Elizabeth Weed, and Debra Keates for help in thinking through these questions about the drive.)

Thus the drive works unpredictably, evading normative prescriptions or investing them with alternative meanings. Erotic significance can be attached to any part of the body; many different objects can be taken as potential sources of sexual pleasure, since the notion that desire can be satisfied by any object is a fantasy (Collins 1997). Here lies a potential for conceiving a kind of power that not only resists social power (the power that rests on the law of the father), but also one that could be collectively mobilized (Žižek 1997, 147–52). Charles Shepherdson (personal communication, 1998) characterizes this way of thinking about the drive in these terms:

> It seems to me that if Power in Foucault gives us both subjection and subjectification (becoming a "subject" if not an agent in the classical sense), so also Lacan gives us a Law that brings with it this curious "outside" which is sexuality, drive, not (symbolic) meaning but a sort of force or act (like Foucault's desire to make things different, without necessarily knowing where he is going ahead of time), a force or act that is, at first,

just symptom, just suffering, just death drive, but then bears the possibility of a kind of freedom. (e-mail correspondence)

For Elizabeth Grosz, the point is not to locate the drive outside the law, in opposition to it, but to imagine social relations of power as effects—as forms of organization of the drive. If the drive can be organized in Oedipal terms, presumably it can be reorganized along other lines. As she writes: "The concept of the drive is one which problematizes the binary oppositions between mind and body, nature and culture, for it entails both terms. The drive may thus prove a strategically vital term in various feminist challenges to the governing concepts and methods within the history of Western thought" (Grosz 1990, 1994).

Conclusion

The instances we have offered of alternatives to modernist conceptions of power represent two divergent, often conflicting bodies of theory. Recent feminist scholarship using each tends to adopt one theoretical frame or the other, rather than intertwining them or allowing them to supplement or challenge one another. Varying degrees of exception to this can be found in the work of, among others, Jessica Benjamin, Wendy Brown, Judith Butler, Rey Chow, Elizabeth Grosz, Ranjana Khanna, Mandy Merck, Jacqueline Rose, Joan W. Scott, Ann Laura Stoler, and Lynne Segal, each of whom has blended Foucauldian and Freudian insights into power differently and for different purposes. Khanna, for example, is concerned with postcolonial feminist critique while Segal's focus is primarily on Euro-Atlantic feminist discourses of sexuality.

We conclude, however, not with specific recipes for combining these two theoretical approaches to power but by underscoring their productivity for feminist thinking. Both Foucault and Freud formulate power not as a commodity to be possessed or lost but as constituting and animating subjects, including gendered subjects. Both understand power as that which produces rather than only positions subjects, and also as that which produces the contents of subjectivity rather than simply repressing them. And both treat power as something incessantly and permanently negotiated by subjects; neither imagines a world without power or a condition in which the problematic of power has been overcome. Thus, the lines of convergence in these two approaches to power are at once conceptual—power is taken neither as an entity nor a totality but as something enacted and circulated—and methodological—the analysis asks how certain mechanisms of power work as specific forms of knowledge, social practice, and psychic/subjective processes. Instead of taking the difference of sexed bodies as a starting point for the analysis of gender and power, these approaches ask how, under what conditions, and in what terms—in the history of individuals and societies—differences of sex are produced as relations of power. Together, these approaches might be said to constitute elements in a feminist "analytics of power."

Notes

The authors are grateful to William Callison for his work in improving and correcting this essay.

1. "Capitalist patriarchy" was a widely used and widely debated term in the 1970s. For a general introduction, see Zillah Eisenstein (1979).The "housework debates" concerned the question of how women's unremunerated domestic labor might be understood to contribute to capitalist profits as well as women's subordination, and centered as well on what the best political forms for illuminating and resisting this exploitation might be. The debates were extensive and appeared in many different venues, but for an introduction see Dalla Costa and James (1972) and Seccombe (1974, 1975).

2. The longer passage from which this statement is drawn may be useful: "The individual is not to be conceived as a sort of elementary nucleus ... a multiple and inert material on which power comes to fasten or against which it happens to strike, and in so doing subdues or crushes individuals. In fact, it is already one of the prime effects of power that certain bodies, certain gestures, certain discourses, certain desires, come to be identified and constituted as individuals. The individual, that is, is not the vis-à-vis of power; it is, I believe, one of its prime effects. The individual is an effect of power, and at the same time, or precisely to the extent to which it is that effect, it is in the element of its articulation. The individual which power has constituted is at the same time its vehicle" (Foucault 1980, 98).

3. As Lacan says: "The demand for love can only suffer from a desire whose signifier is alien to it. If the desire of the mother is the phallus, then the child wishes to be the phallus so as to satisfy this desire. Thus the division immanent to desire already makes itself felt in the desire of the Other, since it stops the subject from being satisfied with presenting to the Other anything real it might *have* which corresponds to this phallus—what he has being worth no more than what he does not have as far as his demand for love is concerned, which requires that he *be* the phallus" (Lacan [1958] 1982, 83).

4. C. Laurin: "In this distant period, the erect phallus symbolized sovereign power, magically or supernaturally transcendent virility as opposed to the purely priapic variety of male power, the hope of resurrection and the force that can bring it about, the luminous principle that brooks neither shadows nor multiplicity and maintains the eternal springs of being. The ithyphallic gods Hennes and Osiris are the incarnation of this essential inspiration" (cited in Laplanche and Pontalis 1974, 313).

References

Barry, Kathleen. 1979. *Female Sexual Slavery*. New York: New York University Press.
Benjamin, Jessica. 1988. *Bonds of Love*. New York: Pantheon.

Brown, Wendy. 1995. *States of Injury: Power and Freedom in Late Modernity*. Princeton, NJ: Princeton University Press.

Butler, Judith. 1997. *The Psychic Life of Power: Theories in Subjection*. Palo Alto, CA: Stanford University Press.

Chodorow, Nancy. 1978. *The Reproduction of Mothering: Psychoanalysis and the Sociology of Gender*. Berkeley: University of California Press.

———. 1989. *Feminism and Psychoanalytic Theory*. New Haven, CT: Yale University Press.

Collins, Daniel G., ed. 1997. *UMBR(a): On the Drive* 1.

Connell, R. W. 1987. *Gender and Power: Society, the Person, and Sexual Politics*. Palo Alto, CA: Stanford University Press.

Dalla Costa, Mariarosa, and Selma James. 1972. *The Power of Women and the Subversion of the Community*. London: Butler and Tanner.

de Beauvoir, Simone. 1953. *The Second Sex*. Trans. H. M. Parshley. New York: Knopf.

Dinnerstein, Dorothy. 1977. *The Mermaid and the Minotaur: Sexual Arrangements and Human Malaise*. New York: Harper & Row.

Eisenstein, Zillah, ed. 1979. *Capitalist Patriarchy and the Case for Socialist Feminism*. New York: Monthly Review Press.

Evans, Dylan. 1996. *An Introductory Dictionary of Lacanian Terms*. New York: Routledge.

Firestone, Shulamith. 1970. *The Dialectic of Sex: The Case for Feminist Revolution*. New York: Morrow.

Foucault, Michel. 1978. *The History of Sexuality*. Vol. 1, *An Introduction*, trans. Robert Hurley. New York: Vintage.

———. 1980. "Two Lectures," trans. Alessandro Fontana and Pasquale Pasquino. In *Power/Knowledge: Selected Interviews and Other Writings, 1972–1977*, ed. Colin Gordon. New York: Pantheon.

Freud, Sigmund. 1953–1974. *The Standard Edition of the Complete Psychological Works of Sigmund Freud [SE]*. Ed. and trans. James Strachey. 24 vols. London: Hogarth.

———. [1905] 1962. *Three Essays on the Theory of Sexuality*. Ed. and trans. James Strachey. New York: Basic Books.

Grosz, Elizabeth. 1990. *Jacques Lacan: A Feminist Introduction*. London: Routledge.

———. 1994. *Volatile Bodies: Toward a Corporeal Feminism*. London: Routledge.

Hertz, Neil. 1983. "Medusa's Head: Male Hysteria under Political Pressure." *Representations* 4 (Fall): 27–54.

Hobbes, Thomas. [1651] 1996. *Leviathan*. Ed. Richard Tuck. Cambridge: Cambridge University Press.

Irigaray, Luce. 1985. "Any Theory of the Subject Has Already Been Appropriated by the Masculine." In *Speculum of the Other Woman*. Trans. G. Gill. Ithaca, NY: Cornell University Press.

Lacan, Jacques. [1958] 1982. *Feminine Sexuality*. Trans. Jacqueline Rose. Ed. Juliet Mitchell and Jacqueline Rose. New York: Norton.

Laplanche, Jean. 1992. *Jean Laplanche: Seduction, Translation, Drives*. Ed. John Fletcher and Martin Stanton. London: Psychoanalytic Forum, Institute of Contemporary Arts.

Laplanche, Jean, and Jean-Bertrand Pontalis. 1974. *The Language of Psycho-Analysis*. Trans. Donald Nicholson-Smith. New York: Norton.

MacKinnon, Catharine A. 1982. "Feminism, Marxism, Method, and the State: An Agenda for Theory." *Signs* 7 (3).

Marx, Karl, and Friedrich Engels. 1970. *The German Ideology*. Ed .C. J. Arthur. New York: International Publishers.

Mede, Theresa. 1998. "'What Comes after Patriarchy?': Introduction" and "Persistent Patriarchy: Ghost or Reality?" with Pamela Haag. *Radical History Review* 71 (Spring).

Mill, John Stuart. 1879. *On Liberty; The Subjection of Women*. New York: Holt.

Mitchell, Juliet. 1974. *Psychoanalysis and Feminism*. New York: Vintage.

Moreau, Thérèse. 1982. *Le Sang de l'histoire: Michelet, l'histoire et l'idée de la femme au XIXe siècle*. Paris: Flammarion.

Muel-Dreyfus, Francine. 1996. *Vichy et l'éternel féminin: Contribution à une sociologie politique de l'ordre des corps*. Paris: Editions du Seuil.

Salecl, Renata. 1994. *The Spoils of Freedom: Psychoanalysis and Feminism after the Fall of Socialism*. London: Routledge.

Scott, Joan W. 1996. *Only Paradoxes to Offer: French Feminists and the Rights of Man*. Cambridge, MA: Harvard University Press.

Seccombe, Wally. 1974. "The Housewife and Her Labour under Capitalism." *New Left Review* I/83 (January–February): 3–24.

———. 1975. "Domestic Labour: Reply to Critics." *New Left Review* I/94 (November-December): 85–96.

Shepherdson, Charles. 1997. "A Pound of Flesh: Lacan's Reading of *The Visible and the Invisible*." *Diacritics* 27 (4): 70–86.

Theweleit, Klaus. 1987. *Male Fantasies*. Minneapolis: University of Minnesota Press.

Weber, Max. 1978. *Economy and Society: An Outline of Interpretive Sociology*. Ed. Guenther Roth and Claus Wittich. Berkeley: University of California Press.

Whitford, Margaret. 1991. *Luce Irigaray: Philosophy in the Feminine*. London: Routledge.

———, ed. 1992. *The Irigaray Reader*. Malden, MA: Blackwell Publishers.

Wollstonecraft, Mary. 1792. *A Vindication of the Rights of Woman: With Strictures on Political and Moral Subjects*. Vol. 1. 2nd ed. London: Printed for J. Johnson, No. 72, St. Paul's Church Yard.

Žižek, Slavoj. 1997. "Desire: Drive = Truth: Knowledge." *UMBR(a): On the Drive* 1.

16 :: PUBLIC/PRIVATE

MICHAEL WARNER

What kind of world would make the values of both publicness and privacy equally accessible to all? This question has often been taken up in modern political philosophy. But that apparently simple question raises, and is made complicated by, another one: How would the experience of gender and sexuality have to be different in such a world?

The link between these two subjects has been noticed for millennia. The story is told of the Greek philosopher Diogenes that whenever he felt a sexual need he walked into the central marketplace and masturbated. According to a later Greek commentator, he was in the habit of "doing everything in public, the works of Demeter and Aphrodite alike" (Diogenes Laertius, quoted in Foucault 1985, 54). This was not usual in Athens in the fourth century BCE. Diogenes provoked disgust. His behavior was a kind of "performance criticism," as Foucault has called it, a way of calling attention to the visceral force behind the moral ideas of public and private (Foucault 1985, 54). Diogenes was attempting, to a degree that has scarcely been rivaled since, to do without the distinction entirely. He evidently regarded it as artificial, contrary to nature, the false morality of a corruption that mistook itself for civilization.

More than two thousand years later, a different challenge to the morality of public and private created an equally queasy sensation. In the late 1820s, the Scottish-born Frances Wright toured America, lecturing against slavery and for women's rights, birth control, and workers' rights. She provoked nearly universal attack for her public appearances, leading the American Catharine Beecher in *Letters on the Difficulty of Religion* (1836) to write:

> Who can look without disgust and abhorrence upon such an one as Fanny Wright, with her great masculine person, her loud voice, her untasteful attire, going about unprotected, and feeling no need of protection, mingling

with men in stormy debate, and standing up with bare-faced impudence, to lecture to a public assembly.... I cannot conceive any thing in the shape of a woman, more intolerably offensive and disgusting. (Beecher quoted in Grimké 1989:138. On Beecher, see Sklar 1973; Boydston, Kelley, and Margolis 1988)

Beecher is offended, eloquently so, by a woman in public. To her, this kind of public behavior—mingling with men, lecturing before audiences, going around with no escort, offering ideas in debate—should be left to men. So deep is this conviction for Beecher that Wright's behavior makes her seem masculine. In fact, the abusiveness in this passage is not so much about Wright's ideas or her acts as about her being: her person is masculine, her voice loud, her attire out of taste; she stands up and is seen. Like her sister Harriet Beecher Stowe, Catharine Beecher did more than simply turn away in disgust. She went on to write several books that articulated, more explicitly than ever before, the theory of separate spheres—that women's place was the home and that women's influence on the world should be moral rather than political. Ironically, in doing so, she became one of the most public women of her day.

In both of these examples, the distinction between public and private comes under an explicit challenge. In both cases, it is not just a distinction but a hierarchy, in which the space of the market or the assembly is given a special importance. In both cases, being in public is a privilege that requires filtering or repressing something that is seen as private. In both cases, too, the transgression is experienced not as merely theoretical, but as a violation of deep instincts about sex and gender. Who can look at it, in Beecher's words, "without disgust and abhorrence"? It is not hard to see, then, why the terms *public* and *private* have often seemed to present a difficulty. The terms are complex enough and shifting enough to allow for profound change; yet in practice they often do not seem theoretical at all. They seem to be preconceptual, almost instinctual, rooted in the orientations of the body and common speech.

The critical literature on public and private is immense, but very seldom does it do justice to the visceral force that the distinction has in these examples. Often, the impression seems to be that public and private are abstract categories for thinking about law, politics, and economics. And so they are. But their power, as feminism and queer theory have had to insist, goes much deeper. A child's earliest education in shame, deportment, and cleaning is an initiation into the prevailing meaning of public and private, as when he or she locates his or her "privates" or is trained to visit the "privy." (The word *public* also records this bodily association: it derives from the Latin *poplicus*, for people, but evolved to *publicus* in connection with *pubes*, in the sense of adult men, linking public membership to pubic maturity.) Clothing is a language of publicity, folding the body in what is felt as the body's own privacy. Some bodily sensations—of pleasure and pain, shame and display, appetite and purgation—come to be felt, in the same way, as privacy. Like those of gender, the orientations of public and private are rooted in what anthropologists call habitus: the conventions by which we experience, as though naturally, our own bodies and movement in the space of the world. Public and private are learned along with such terms as "active" and "passive," "front" and "back," and "top" and "bottom." They can seem quasi-natural, visceral, fraught with perils of abjection and degradation, or, alternatively, of cleanliness and self-mastery. They are the very scene of selfhood and scarcely distinguishable from the experience of gender and sexuality.

That makes them hard to challenge. In the case of gender, public and private are not just formal rules about how men and women should behave. They are bound up with meanings of masculinity and femininity. Masculinity, at least in Western cultures, is felt partly in a way of occupying public space; femininity, in a language of private feeling. When Diogenes masturbates in the market, the public display of private need may appear disturbing or shameful, but it is not said to throw doubt on his masculinity. His blunt, bold simplicity can be seen as virile integrity, in part because it is so very public. When Frances Wright lectures in public, Catharine Beecher perceives her as mannish, even monstrously so. Women, accustomed to being the spectacle displayed to male desire, often experience the visibility of public space as a kind of intimate vulnerability. Men, by contrast, often feel their masculinity challenged when their bodies are on display as objects of erotic desire (see Deutsche 1990, 21–23).

In the case of sexuality, too, not all sexualities are public or private in the same way. Same-sex persons kissing, embracing, or holding hands in public view commonly excite disgust even to the point of violence, whereas mixed-sex persons doing the same things are invisibly ordinary, even applauded. Nelly boys are said to be "flaunting" their sexuality, just by swishing or lisping. They are told to keep it to themselves, even though the "it" in question is their relation to their own bodies. Butch men, meanwhile, can swagger aggressively without being accused of flaunting anything. Just as feminists since Fanny Wright have found that to challenge male domination in public is to change both femininity and the norms of public behavior, lesbians and gay men have found that to challenge the norms of straight culture in public is to disturb deep and unwritten rules about the kinds of behavior and eroticism that are appropriate to the public.

Public and private are bound up with elementary relations to language as well as to the body. The acquisition of language is an education into public and private speech genres and their different social contexts, which are commonly contexts of gender. In one sense, much emphasized by Ludwig Wittgenstein, all language and all thought are public, a feature of the language games that make intelligibility possible. Yet there are degrees of formality in speech and writing that create a continuum of publicness. In many languages, these are sharply divided and lexically distinct, as with the French *tutoyer* and *vouvoyer*. Among the Xavante studied by Laura Graham (1993), the public speech of the morning and evening adult-male convocations is marked by singing styles, polyphonic discourse, and special protocols of pronoun usage and verb conjugation, as well as body posture. In many societies, including the Xavante, classical Athens, and the antebellum United States, these differences are frankly avowed as differences of status and gender: men can speak in public concourse, women cannot. The difference between genres of private and public speech anchors the sense of home and intimacy, on the one hand, and social personality, on the other.

The different senses of self and membership mediated by these contexts can seem scarcely comparable. Parents, lovers, strangers, or peers may appear in one context but not the other. In modern culture, where there are so many different genres of speech and writing, each with a different context for one's personality, the felt gap between public selves or roles and private ones has given rise to a Romantic longing for unity—at least among those with the privilege of being public. (The most famous example is Rousseau's *Confessions*, a kind of modern successor to Diogenes.) That longing for unity can also be seen in modes of collective public intimacy such as ecstatic spirituality. Inevitably, identity politics itself magnetizes such longings, affirming private identity though public politics and promising to heal divisions of the political world by anchoring them in the authentically personal realm and its solidarity. In the ideals of ethnic identity, or sisterhood, or gay pride, to take the most common examples, an assertive and affirmative concept of identity seems to achieve a correspondence between public existence and private self. Identity politics in this sense seems to many people a way of overcoming both the denial of public existence that is so often the form of domination and the incoherence of the experience that domination creates, an experience that often feels more like invisibility than like the kind of privacy you value.

Definitions and Contexts

Throughout the Western tradition, private and public have been commonly and sensibly understood as distinct zones. The boundary between bedroom and market, home and meetinghouse, can be challenged or violated, but it is at least clear enough to be spatially distinct. Moving from one to another is experienced as crossing a barrier or making a transition—like going from the privacy of one's bedroom to the public room of a convention hall. In medieval thought (which inherited a notion of the *res publica* from Roman law), the public was almost solely a spatial concept, meaning anything open, such as the outside wall of a house. Modern culture has redrawn the spatial distinction, adding new layers of meaning to the term *public*, but preserving the idea of physical boundaries. Nineteenth- and twentieth-century middle-class architecture, for example, separates parlors or "living rooms" from family quarters or "withdrawing rooms," trying to erect literal walls between public and private functions even within the home. (Catharine Beecher specialized in this new style of home economics.) Modern American law frequently defines privacy as a zone of noninterference drawn around the home. So strong is this association that courts have sometimes refused to recognize a right to privacy in other spaces.

But this ideology and its architecture represent an ideal or extreme type. Public and private are not always simple enough that one could code them on a map with different colors—pink for private and blue for public. The terms also describe social contexts, kinds of feeling, and genres of language. So although public and private seem so clearly opposed that their violation can produce a sharp feeling of revulsion, the terms have many different meanings that often go unnoticed. However disgusting Catharine Beecher found the idea of a woman lecturing in public, for example, her own writings on the subject were profoundly public: they were published (that is, printed and marketed); they addressed the powerful ideal of public opinion; and they established Beecher as a figure of public fame and authority. Despite the self-evident clarity of the distinction, different senses of public or private typically intermingle in this way. A private conversation can take place in a public forum; a kitchen can become a public gathering place; a private bedroom can be public and commercial space, as in a hotel; a radio can bring public discussion into a bathroom; and so on. American courts, too, have developed other ways of defining public and private in which the terms refer to relationships rather than places. The right to privacy, for example, can be linked to marriage or the right to form intimate associations. Or it can be defined by ideals of autonomy and self-determination, as in the notion of reproductive freedom. In some of these conceptions, publicness and privacy belong to different places; in other conceptions, they belong to different relationships; in still others, to persons. These differences can have conflicting implications in law as in theory (on these rival paradigms, see Thomas 1992, esp. 1444–47).

In law as in theory, moreover, public and private can sometimes be used as descriptive, value-neutral terms, simply as a way to make sense of observed practice. At other times, they are used as normative, evaluative terms, naming and invoking ideals that are *not* always observed. And they can have one application outside a context, as analytic or quasi-objective categories, while having quite another inside a context, orienting people to different poles in their own experience: people's private conversations, for example, can be regarded by a third party as public opinion.

To confuse matters further, the terms often seem to be defined against each other, with normative preference for one term; but this is not always the case. The private (from *privatus*, deprived) was originally conceived as the negation or privation of public value. It had no value in its own right. But in the modern period, this has changed, and privacy has taken on a distinctive value of its own, in several different registers: as freedom, individuality, inwardness, authenticity, and so on. Public and private sometimes compete, sometimes complement each other, and sometimes are merely parts of a larger series of classifications that includes, say, local, domestic, personal, political, economic, or intimate. Almost every major cultural change—from Christianity to printing to psychoanalysis—has left a new sedimentary layer in the meaning of the public and the private. (Print culture gave us publication; psychoanalysis, a new sense of the private person.) In modern contexts, the terms have been used in many different and overlapping senses, combining legacies from classical thought and law with modern forms of social organization.

It is no wonder, then, that so many thinkers have sought to sort out the terms, to bring to them a kind of clarity that usage seldom provides, one that might do justice to the visceral conviction that there ought to be a clear distinction. Some thinkers have done so energetically enough that their accounts have become part of the terms' symbolic weight; examples discussed here are Immanuel Kant, Hannah Arendt, and Jürgen Habermas. Yet attempts to frame public and private as a sharp distinction or antinomy have invariably come to grief, while attempts to collapse or do without them have proven equally unsatisfying.

It might be useful, therefore, to consider the range of the often conflicting meanings of public and private. The relations of public to private can take any of the following forms at least:

	PUBLIC	PRIVATE
1	open to everyone	restricted to someone
2	accessible for money	closed even to those who could pay
3	state-related; now often called public sector	nonstate, belonging to civil society; now often called private sector
4	political	nonpolitical
5	official	nonofficial
6	common	special
7	impersonal	personal
8	national or popular	of a group, class, or locale
9	international or universal	particular or finite
10	in physical view of others	concealed
11	outside the home	domestic
12	circulated in print or electronic	circulated orally or in manuscript media
13	know widely	known to initiates
14	acknowledged and explicit	tacit and implicit

15. "the world itself, in so far as it is common to all of us and distinguished from our privately owned place in it" (Arendt 1958: 52).

This list amplifies remarks by Nancy Fraser (1992). Matters are further complicated by several senses of private that have no corresponding sense of public, including

16. related to the individual, especially to inwardness, subjective experience, and the incommunicable
17. discretely or properly comported, in the sense of the French *pudeur* (grasped in English only through its opposite, impudence, as when Beecher accuses Fanny Wright of "bare-faced impudence")
18. genital or sexual.

There are also a variety of legal contexts, from constitutional law to property law, each with its own inflection of privacy. In the tradition of *Griswold v. Connecticut* and *Bowers v. Hardwick*, for example, heterosexual marriage is defined as a "zone of privacy" with special protections against state incursion (see Thomas 1992; Halley 1994; Halley 1999, 145–204).

Public, too, is an exceedingly complex noun, and what is meant by "the public" or "a public" or "the public sphere" will require a good deal of explanation (for more, see Warner 2002:65–124). Publicity, too, is a distinct concept, meaning not merely publicness or openness but the use of media, an instrumental publicness associated most with advertising and public relations. None of these terms has a sense that is exactly parallel to or opposite of private. None are simple oppositions, or binaries. Because the contexts overlap, most things are private in one sense and public in the other. Books can be published privately; a public theater can be a private enterprise; a private life can be discussed publicly; and so on. Marriage, too, is thought of in modern culture as the ultimate private relation, but every marriage involves the state if it is to carry the force of law. It will be seen below that the public sphere in Habermas's influential account *is* private in several crucial senses. And much work on gender and sexuality in cultural studies has shown that publics in various ways enable privacy, providing resources for interiority and contexts for self-elaboration. *Public* and *private* are crucial terms for understanding these examples. But in each case, the terms need to be understood in more than one context and with some attention to their history.

Although many forms of the public/private distinction have been challenged in feminism and in queer theory, we should not forget that a challenge to one form of the distinction may not necessarily have the same implications for others. None of the versions of public and private listed above can be dismissed as merely archaic, since they are immanent to a host of norms and institutions of modern life and may in many respects be desirable. It remains as difficult now as it was for Diogenes's fellow citizens to imagine a world with neither public nor private.

Public and Private in Feminist Theory

Any organized attempt to transform gender or sexuality is a public questioning of private life, and thus the critical study of gender and sexuality entails a problem of public and private in its own practice. Both the contemporary women's movement and gay liberation took shape as social movements in the 1960s, when counterculture had begun to imagine a politics that would transform personal life across the board, giving public relevance to the most private matters. Other social movements—temperance, abolition, labor, suffrage, antiracism—had also challenged prevailing norms of public and private. A leading defense of racial segregation in the American south, for example, was that private owners of property or businesses had the right to admit whom they chose, just because it was private property. To fight such arguments, it was necessary to advance a strong vision of the public relevance of private life, a vision expressed in the phrase "civil rights." Even more, though, the women's and gay movements represented groups who were by definition linked to a conventional understanding of private life—gender roles, sexuality, the home and family. They were public movements contesting the most private and intimate matters. Their very entry into public politics seemed scandalous or inappropriate. An understanding of public and private was implied not just in their theories and policy platforms, but also in their very existence as movements.

In second-wave feminism at the height of identity politics, many took a fairly radical—even draconian—solution to the problem of public and private. They argued that the distinction was virtually synonymous with patriarchy. Male was to public as female was to private. In an essay titled "Woman, Culture, and Society: A Theoretical Overview," Michelle Zimbalist Rosaldo claimed that the gendering of public and private helped to explain the subordination of women cross-culturally. In this context, private meant domestic spaces and functions, and public referred to contexts in which men spoke and made decisions for the community (Rosaldo 1974).

There has been much debate about how widely this pattern holds. The women's rights movement had come into being against an especially rigid version of this spatialized and gendered scheme, the separate-sphere ideology of the nineteenth century. But Rosaldo's theory laid it at the origins of masculinist culture. Jean Bethke Elshtain, concerned with the normative development of terms in Western thought, was critical of the oversimplifications in this argument. Yet she traced the endurance of a gendered opposition of public and private from Plato and Aristotle to modern thought (Elshtain 1981). Either way, the scale of the problem was enormous. Carol Pateman was able to claim that "the dichotomy between the private and the public is central to almost two centuries of feminist writing and political struggle; it is, ultimately, what the feminist movement is about" (Pateman 1989, 118).

One consequence was to see domestic and private matters, normally outside the public view, as now being a legitimate area of common concern. In practice, this meant not just public opinion but also state intervention in things like marital rape, spousal abuse, divorce, prostitution, and abortion rights. Encountering male domination mainly in the spaces usually called private, notably the home, women could only struggle against that domination by seeing it as a kind of politics. In the words of Catharine MacKinnon:

For women the measure of intimacy has been the measure of the oppression. This is why feminism has had to explode the private. This is why feminism has seen the personal as the political. The private is the public for those for whom the personal is the political. In this sense, there is no private, either normatively or empirically. (MacKinnon 1987, 100)

This is a fairly extreme formulation, and to some degree a contradictory one, since one meaning of privacy is bodily autonomy and its protection from violence; MacKinnon draws on this normative ideal even as she claims to "explode" privacy. She does so because she is writing in the context of *Roe v. Wade*, criticizing what she sees as the inadequate liberal logic by which abortion is legitimated only as a private privilege rather than as a public right.

Other feminists put a different emphasis on the critique of public and private. Pateman argued that the practical consequence of the feminist critique would be much broader than women entering public areas reserved for men, the way Fanny Wright tried to do in the 1820s; rather, it would be an entire transformation of gender roles, for men as well as women, leading to a world in which the differences between women and men would be systematically uncoupled from the divisions between home and public, individual and collective life, personal and political. Most immediately, "If women are to participate fully, as equals, in social life, men have to share equally in child-rearing and other domestic tasks." More generally, "Equal parenting and equal participation in other activities of domestic life presuppose some radical changes in the public sphere, in the organization of production, in what we mean by 'work' and in the practice of citizenship" (Pateman 1989, 135).

These arguments in feminist scholarship are related to the political strategy declared in the famous slogan "The personal is political" (for the context, see Echols 1989). This slogan can be taken to mean many different things. The most basic is that the social arrangements structuring private life, domestic households, intimacy, gender, and sexuality are neither neutral nor immutable, that they can be seen as relations of power and as subject to transformation. The implications of this insight, I hardly need to add, are still unfolding. In the words of one scholar, it is the "unique and world historical achievement" of the women's movement to have laid bare "the social nature of the family, the 'public' nature of the 'private,' the internal connections that exist between the family and the economy" (Zaretsky 1994, 206).

For others, "the personal is political" means not that personal life could be transformed by political action, but that politics should be personalized; that is, everyone's political views should be read as expressing his or her particular, subjective interests—identities of race, class, gender, and sexuality inevitably color everyone's perspective. This second interpretation of "the personal is political" leads to a sometimes disabling skepticism about any claim to transcendence or any appeal to universal ideals or the common good. Both of these views—the political critique of personal life and the identitarian critique of political life—are often described, confusingly enough, as identity politics.

The very success of the feminist critique of public and private has led to new questions. If the personal is political, is a distinction between public and private always to be rejected, or exploded, as MacKinnon puts it? The slogan requires a relatively broad sense of "political," to mean contested or shaped by domination; it leaves vague the question whether inequities in "personal life" are to be redressed through private action, nonstate public action, or state intervention, all of which can be political in this broad sense. For many, it has been understood to mean that these distinctions should no longer matter.

Perhaps rhetorically, Joan Wallach Scott claimed in *Gender and the Politics of History* that the politics of gender "dissolves distinction between public and private" (Scott 1988, 26). Such rhetoric lumps together the enormous range of meanings of public and private, and it has therefore been blamed for everything from the rise of confessional memoirs to political correctness and the totalitarian tendencies of some legislative reform programs (hate-speech laws, antipornography statues, and such). MacKinnon's legal programs, in particular, have been seen as justifying an authoritarian style of state regulation in the way they lead to the criminalization of pornography and sex rather than of domination or harassment per se. Should nothing be private? Or, on the other hand, should everything be privatized? Should the state intervene to transform gender relations in the workplace and household?[1]

The answers to these questions have consequences for matters of equity, affirmative action, abortion, birth control, rape, adoption, divorce and child support, palimony, sexual harassment, welfare, health care, day care, segregated education, and so on. In many of these areas, feminism encouraged an activist state to assert the public relevance of private life. Yet the effect was not, as some feminists had hoped (and others feared), to eliminate or "dissolve" the boundary between public and private. Often state action was justified in the name of private right. Ironically, in the United States, it was largely in the contexts of feminist agitation—especially over birth control and reproductive freedom— that privacy came to be fully recognized as a domain of constitutional law. Some distinctions have eroded, or changed; at the very least, these initiatives of the women's movement, and the understanding of public and private implied by them, enabled a significant expansion of the liberal welfare state into new areas of social life.[2]

Nancy Fraser, for one, has pointed out that some feminists' insistence on an oversimplified distinction between public and private blinded them to these consequences. By using "the public" or "the public sphere" to mean everything outside the home, they blurred together official politics, the state, the market, and other forms of association. Making these distinctions among different meanings of public and private has practical advantages, Fraser writes, "when, for example, agitational campaigns against misogynist cultural representations are confounded with programs for state censorship or when struggles to deprivatize housework and child care are equated with their commodification" (Fraser 1992, 110). In other words, while the personal is "political" in a broad sense, state regulation may not always be appropriate. And while the private realm of the home should often be a matter of public care and concern, the market—like the state and like the majoritarian public of mass media—has its own destructive tendencies and may be a bad model of "the public."

Scholars have also argued that public and private have always been more than a dichotomy. Some feminist scholars have shown that women have been involved in both public and private realms in most historical periods, often to a surprising degree (for example, Ryan 1990). Women's networks—of gossip, kinship, affect, and countereconomies—have had important public aspects even at the height of Victorian ideology. We have seen, for example, that while Catharine Beecher was criticizing Fanny Wright for violating a boundary between public and private, Beecher was herself pursuing an active and innovative career in the public sphere. Recent versions of feminism, stressing the diversity of women's positions in different contexts of class, race, religion, or locale, have emphasized that the dominant dichotomies often fail to account for these variations. Other feminists, elaborating deconstructive readings of gender categories that emphasize their uneven deployment or internal incoherence, have tried to conceive public and private in less spatializing, hypostatized ways (on this history within feminism, see the excellent account in Dietz 1995).

It may be doubted whether any group, even in the most restrictive contexts of power, has been able to monopolize all dimensions of publicness or all dimensions of privacy in the way MacKinnon suggests men have done. At any rate, the distinction is never drawn solely in one way or solely as an antinomy. The gendered division of labor, for example, is a classic and seemingly clear instance of the ideological distinction between public and private—in this case, between public work and private labor. In this system, as many feminists have noted, gender, labor, and publicness are so closely aligned that they seem synonymous. Public work is paid, is performed outside the home, and has long been the realm of men. Private labor is unpaid, is usually done at home, and has long been women's work. Far from being symmetrical or complementary, this sexual division of labor (and division of sexual labor) is unequal. Public work, for example, is understood to be productive, forming vocational identity, and fulfilling men as individuals; private labor is understood as the general reproduction of society, lacking the vocational distinction of a trade or a profession, and displaying women's selflessness. This gendered difference in callings persists, with its unequal mapping of public and private, though the entry of women into trades and professions has weakened it somewhat.

Yet the same separation of spheres has always had other, more complex meanings of public and private besides this direct correlation in gender domination and economic systems. Even the most extreme separation of spheres turns the home and its adjunct spaces into a functional public for women—spaces that can be filled with talk and with the formation of a shared world. There are normative countercurrents as well. In capitalism, paid work came to be understood as private economic life. The workplace lost some of the publicness that had been the hallmark of the guilds and trades. So while men were marking their workplace off more sharply from the increasingly female domestic space, they were also marking it off from the public. Professionalism recuperated some of that publicness for its highly trained classes in a new rhetoric of expertise—but not for wage labor. Male workers, in other words, underwent a loss of public life as artisanal household economies yielded to new, more modern separations of workplace and home life (this history is traced for an American context in Wilentz 1984; Johnson 1978; and Zaretsky 1986). The domestic and reproductive functions of the family, meanwhile, acquired ever greater public significance as reform movements made them the objects of so much discourse and as nationalism came to be symbolized through them. Many women, like Catharine Beecher and her sister Harriet, found an entry into public life exactly through these discourses about privacy in reform, in nationalism, in evangelical Christianty, and in antislavery. They could do so in large part because private markets for print linked women as readers and writers (see esp. Kelley 1984 in the large and growing literature on this topic). Women in many places also elaborated parallel or informal economies—private, but public in the sense that they lay beyond the home. These developments were simultaneous with the rise of separate-sphere ideology, not simply later reactions against it.

The economic separation of the male public from the female private, in short, was never a static system. It was one normative strand among others in the elaboration of public and private. To say this is not to minimize its power or to underestimate the degree of male domination that it represented. In fact, because the interweaving of gender, labor, and publicness was indirect rather than definitional, it could often go unrecognized—and still does. To see this might help us to understand why inequality persists despite the apparent breakdown of the most static forms of the gendered division of labor—why, for instance, so many of the publics of women's culture continue not to recognize themselves as publics because they think of their authenticity and their femininity as rooted necessarily in private feeling and domestic relations; or why so many men failed to understand the privatization of economic life as a loss because they thought of their work as having an extradomestic, vocational publicness.

The Liberal Tradition

Given these complexities, how did the notion of public and private come to be imagined as a binary in need of demolition? The answer lies in the way a whole set of distinctions were powerfully aligned in the liberal tradition, reaching back at least to John Locke, but widely institutionalized in politics and law by the nineteenth century. This tradition began as a critique of patriarchy, and one of its unintended consequences was the development of modern feminist thought in the eighteenth century. But by the time of second-wave feminism in the 1960s, this liberal tradition had come to pose serious limitations to both feminist and gay movements.

In liberal thought, private persons, no longer defined by privation or powerlessness, had become the proper site of humanity. They possessed publicly relevant rights by virtue of being private persons. Rights meant no longer the privileges that went with various public legal statuses— fief owner, copyholder, husband, lord of the manor, chief eunuch, citizen, princess—but rather claims that all persons could make on the basis of private humanity. The public, no longer understood as the audience or subjects of the ruler, became a community with independent existence, even sovereign claims and the ability to resist or change rulers. Both public and private were redefined, and both gained enormously in significance following the conception of state power as limited and rights as vested in private persons (Skinner 1978; Macpherson 1962).

This language for politics also gained in forcefulness from the use of similar terms in arguments for capitalism (Hirschman 1977). The motto of Bernard Mandeville's *Fable of the Bees* (1714) is a famous example: "Private vices, public benefits." According to Mandeville, the competitive pursuit of self-interest ("private vices") could be counted on to yield good effects ("public benefits"), counteracting mere selfishness through the interactions of the market. Such thinking, as later developed by Adam Smith and others, lent powerful support to the idea that economic life, as a realm of private society, should be kept free from state or public interference. In time, capitalist culture would give this distinction between public power and private economy an additional dimension, remapping social life into distinct arenas of work and "personal life," including the intensified privacies of intimacy, friendship, and the domestic (see the multivolume history edited by Philippe Ariès and Georges Duby, esp. vol. 3, Chartier 1989).

Meanwhile, the state was evolving into a modern bureaucracy, with its normative distinction between the public function of office and the private person of the officeholder. And as private persons came to be seen as driven by self-interest, the public came to be defined as disinterested. Those aspects of people's lives that particularize their interests came to be seen as inappropriate to public discussion. To be properly public required that one rise above, or set aside, one's private interests and expressive nature. This notion of a separation between public voice and private selfhood is often called "bracketing"; a closely related idea in John Rawls's liberal legal theory is called the "veil of ignorance" (on "bracketing," see Fraser 1992; on the "veil of ignorance," see Rawls 1989).

All of these characteristically modern developments made possible a vision of freedom as negative liberty, inherent in private persons, and a vision of political life as the restraint of power by a critical public. In these respects, they lent great resources to the development of a critique of gender and sexuality. Early feminism, in writers such as Mary Astell, Mary Wollstonecraft, Judith Sargent Murray, and the Grimké sisters, was articulated through the normative language of the liberal tradition. They were especially enabled by its vision of the rights-bearing private person, its role for a critical public, its principled skepticism about power (Scott 1996). Sarah Grimké, for example, in *Letters on the Equality of the Sexes and the Condition of Woman* (1837), was able to take the universal self of reason as an argument for women's access: "When human beings are regarded as *moral* beings, *sex*, instead of being enthroned upon the summit, administering upon rights and responsibilities, sinks into insignificance and nothingness." Having bracketed sex in this way, Grimké goes on to argue for a thorough degendering of social relations: "We approach each other, and mingle with each other, under the constant pressure of a feeling that we are of different sexes; and, instead of regarding each other only in the light of immortal creatures, the mind is fettered by the idea which is early and industriously infused into it, that we must never forget the distinction between male and female" (Grimké and Grimké 1989, 217). Grimké longs to transcend sex, and in order to do so she declares it irrelevant, something "infused" into the individual, something to "forget." The ideal of the universal voice of reason has allowed her a kind of public participation. But the price she pays is that differences of sex have been ruled out of consideration as merely private.

In this respect, the same liberal tradition that enabled the first wave of the feminist movement also posed immediate obstacles to it as a movement, as it would later to the gay movement. Women such as Wollstonecraft and Grimké argued that their rights as individuals needed new respect. In doing so, they appealed to the ideal of a disinterested, abstract, universal public—just the kind of public in which particularized views and the gendered body would always seem matter out of place, like Fanny Wright's mannish impudence or Diogenes's masturbation. This tension was felt subjectively by many women, including Sarah Grimké's sister, Angelina, who braved the denunciation of relatives, friends, and strangers, as well as the occasional violent mob, in her willingness to appeal to "the irresistible torrent of rectified public opinion," but whose scandalous appearances in public caused her, as she confessed to her diary, great shame and self-doubt. When she married abolitionist Theodore Weld, her public speaking tours ended (Grimké and Grimké 1989, 217).

This subjective anxiety over the public display of the body and the gendered norms of comportment also has a direct equivalent in liberal notions of what is appropriate for public discussion and political action. Because the home was the very realm of private freedom that liberalism had wanted to protect from state intervention, it was off-limits to politics. And the rights of women, seen as an issue internal to the home, were therefore best left to the private judgment of each family. They were inappropriate to politics. Women would have to deal with men in the privacy of their own families, not in public. But of course the private context of the family was just where men were thought naturally to rule. As Eli Zaretsky puts it, "The separation between public and private occluded the perpetuation of relations of domination—those beyond legitimate authority—into modern society. It did this politically by rendering those relations 'private'" (Zaretsky 1994, 201). The curbing of the state, in the name of private liberty, had entailed a curb on politics as well, freezing in place all those for whom the private was the place of domination rather than liberty.

This side of the liberal tradition continues to limit the transformative ambitions of feminism, and the gay movement as well. For example, the gay writer Andrew Sullivan ends his book *Virtually Normal* with an appeal to the liberal distinction between public and private, arguing for a politics based on "a simple and limited principle":

that all *public* (as opposed to private) discrimination against homosexuals be ended and that every right and responsibility that heterosexuals enjoy as public citizens be extended to those who grow up and find themselves emotionally different. *And that is all.* No cures or re-educations, no wrenching private litigation, no political imposition of tolerance; merely a political attempt to enshrine formal public equality, whatever happens in the culture and society at large. (Sullivan 1995, 171)

Everything else, "whatever happens in the culture and society at large," is private, and therefore off-limits to politics. But that includes almost the entirety of homophobia and sexism and the countless daily relations of privilege and domination they entail. Any political attempt to change those conditions is seen, in Sullivan's scheme, as an illegitimate attempt to get government involved in private life, a "political imposition of tolerance." Although this conception of politics is often called neoconservatism, its core ideas derive from the heyday of nineteenth-century liberal thought. (For the vicissitudes of this political tradition, and the ironies by which its central ideas have migrated from right to left and vice versa in twentieth-century politics, see Brinkley 1998.)

In fact, the liberal distinction between public authority and private freedom has always been in tension with other views, notably with civic humanism since Machiavelli. The indispensible reference here is J. G. A. Pocock (1975), who has been criticized by many historians for overstating the incompatibility of republican and liberal traditions (for recent treatments and somewhat different views, see Appleby 1992 and Kramnick 1990). Liberalism still has powerful contemporary exponents, such as Rawls (1989, 1996). But most of the major figures of our time on the subject of public and private have reacted against the liberal tradition. Feminist such as Pateman and MacKinnon, for example, point out that the liberal protection of the private from public interference simply blocked from view those kinds of domination that structure private life through the institutions of the family, the household, gender, and sexuality. Arendt tried to show how many of the strongest conceptions of humanity had been lost or forgotten when freedom was identified with the protection of private life rather than with the give-and-take of public activity. Habermas showed that modern society is fundamentally structured by a public sphere, including the critical consciousness of private people, but that these public ideals and norms are betrayed by modern social organization. And Michel Foucault rendered a strong challenge to the liberal tradition almost without using the terms *public* and *private,* by showing in great detail how its key terms and immanent values—public, state, private, freedom, autonomy—fail to account for power relations.

The Public Sphere

A rather different face of liberalism's distinction between public and private can be seen in Kant's celebrated 1784 essay "What Is Enlightenment?" "The *public* use of reason," Kant writes, "must at all times be free, and it alone can bring about enlightenment among men; the *private* use of reason, however, may often be very narrowly restricted without the progress of enlightenment being particularly hindered." Kant's has been called a "two hats" theory; he imagines men (not women) moving constantly between these two contexts, having different freedoms and different relations to power in each (Laursen 1996). But the surprising turn comes in his definition of public and private uses of reason: "I understand, however, under the public use of his own reason, that use which anyone makes of it *as a scholar* [*Gelehrter*] before the entire public of the *reading world*. The private use I designate as that use which one makes of his reason in a certain *civil post* or office which is entrusted to him" (Kant 1996).

To most readers, this will seem counterintuitive. The holder of a civil post would in most senses be a public figure—paid by the state, working for the common good, accountable to the community, acting in full view. The scholar or writer would commonly be thought of as private—unofficial, not supported by the state, speaking on behalf of no one but himself, perhaps unknown except through this writings. Yet to Kant the telling fact is that the holder of a civil post cannot simply follow his own will; he must obey rules established by his role. He may disagree with something he is required to say, but his thoughts remain private, whether he agrees or not. The scholar or writer makes his views known as widely as possible. He is not limited to his role but speaks "as a member of the entire commonwealth, or even of cosmopolitan society." He can freely criticize church or state. Kant makes it clear that this reasoning takes place in a print public, "the entire public of the *reading world*," and that it is more than national; but a clergyman speaking officially to his congregation addresses "only a domestic assembly, no matter how large it is; and in this respect he is not and cannot be free, as a priest, because he conforms to the orders of another" (Kant 1996). (For a useful discussion of this passage, see Chartier 1991, 20–37.)

A striking feature of this account is Kant's emphasis on the different publics to which thought can be relevant, ranging from inner freedom to domestic assemblies, commonwealths, cosmopolitan society, the transnational public of scholars, and even "the entire public of the *reading world*." Some publics are more public than others. They give greater scope to criticism and exchange of views. But by the same token, they may be less directly political, perhaps not anchored in a state or locality.

With this conception, Kant articulates a key distinction—though one that continues to be confused or overlooked even in sophisticated theoretical accounts—between public and political. These are often thought to be synonymous. They are very nearly so, for example, in Arendt, where the model of the public is clearly the polis (the Greek city-state), and equally (or oppositely) in the slogan "the personal is political." What belongs to the polity is by definition of public relevance. But Kant recognizes that there are publics, such as the reading world, that do not correspond to any kind of polity. They enable a way of being public through critical discourse that is not limited by the duties and constraints of office or by loyalties to a commonwealth or nation. These critical publics may, however, be political in another or higher sense. They may set a higher standard of reason, opinion, and freedom—hence the subversive potential in his picture of enlightenment. In later years, Kant was forced to hedge on this implication; as he ran afoul of the censors, he narrowed the definition of *Gelehrter* to the scholar per se rather than the reader in general (Laursen 1996, 258–61). Locke, too, had recognized the existence of a critical public not limited to the official politics of the state and having all the freedom from authority of private right. But in Locke this public tends to be imagined as the national people, endowed with the sovereign ability to change rulers. It is in this sense a back-projection from the state. Kant's publics, though less literally revolutionary, range more widely, at least in print.

The difference between the public and the political has been taken up, closer to our own day, by Habermas in *The Structural Transformation of the Public Sphere* (Habermas [1962] 1989; see also Habermas 1974). Subtitled "An Inquiry into a Category of Bourgeois Society," the book reflects the Frankfurt School tradition of "immanent critique"; Habermas does not set out to invent or celebrate a putatively lost idea of the public (though he has sometimes been read this way); he wishes to show that bourgeois society has always been structured by a set of ideals that were contradicted by its own organization and compromised by its own ideology. These ideals, however, contained an emancipatory potential, Habermas thinks, and modern culture should be held accountable to them. But far from moving toward a more radical realization in practice, modern culture has compromised the ideals further. "Tendencies pointing to the collapse of the public sphere are unmistakable," Habermas declares at the beginning of the book, "for while its scope is expanding impressively, its function has become progressively insignificant" ([1962] 1989, 4).

The main structural transformation of the title is the historic shift that Habermas assigns to the late seventeenth and eighteenth centuries. Habermas begins with an aristocratic or monarchical model that he calls the "representative public sphere," in which power is displayed before a public (and in which Louis XIV was able to say "L'état, c'est moi"). The publicity of the court was embodied and authoritative. The monarch's presence was always public, and courtliness always had an audience. This kind of publicity yielded to a newer model of publicness in which the public is composed of private persons exercising rational-critical discourse in relation to the state and power. (The "sphere" of the title is a misleading effect of English translation: the German *Öffentlichkeit* lacks the spatializing metaphor and suggests something more like "openness" or "publicness." The French translation, *L'espace public*, is worse.)

This shift came about, Habermas claims, through a wide range of cultural and social conditions that developed in the seventeenth and eighteenth centuries, including the rise of newspapers, novels, and other private forms of print; coffeehouses, salons, and related private contexts of sociability in which argument and discussion could take place; the rise of critical discussion of art, music, and literature; the reorientation of domestic architecture; the development of an idea of the family and intimate life as the proper seat of humanity, from which persons could come together to form a public; and the development of a notion of the economy, beyond the household, as a realm of civic society that could be taken as the object of discussion and debate. Through these developments, a public that "from the outset was a reading public," became "the abstract counterpart of public authority" and "came into an awareness of itself as the latter's opponent, that is, as the public of the now *emerging public sphere of civil society*" ([1962] 1989, 23).

The public in this new sense, in short, was no longer opposed to the private. It *was* private. As the self-consciousness of civil society, it was opposed to the state:

> The bourgeois public sphere may be conceived above all as the sphere of the private people come together as a public; they soon claimed the public sphere regulated from above against the public authorities themselves, to engage them in a debate over the general rules governing relations in the basically privatized but publicly relevant sphere of commodity exchange and social labor. The medium of this political confrontation was peculiar and without historical precedent: people's public use of their reason. (Habermas [1962] 1989, 27)

The public sphere in this sense is "a category of bourgeois society," as the subtitle maintains, not just because its members are mostly bourgeois but also because the reorganization of society around the institutions of public criticism was one of the means by which bourgeois society came into being, conscious of itself as "society." Habermas cites Kant's "What Is Enlightenment?" and its ideal of a private citizen as a scholar "whose writings speak to his public, the world." This "world" is both broad, stretching notions of cosmopolitanism and world progress to include "the communication of rational beings," and particularized, being grounded in "the world of a critically debating reading public that at the time was just evolving within the broader bourgeois strata. It was the world of the men of letters but also that of the *salons* in which 'mixed companies' engaged in critical discussion; here, in the bourgeois homes, the public sphere was established" (Habermas [1962] 1989, 106).

As Craig Calhoun points out in his introduction to *Habermas and the Public Sphere*, a radical reversal has taken place between the bourgeois conception traced by Habermas and the Greek conception of public freedom: "Unlike the Greek conception, individuals are here understood to be formed primarily in the private realm, including the family. Moreover, the private realm is understood as one of freedom that has to be defended against the dominion of the state" (Calhoun 1992, 7).

Habermas shows that this understanding of the public sphere had its early critics. Chief among these was the young Karl Marx, who objected to the nature of this new private freedom leading "every man to see in other men, not the *realization*, but rather the *limitation* of his own liberty" (quoted in Habermas [1962] 1989, 125). Noting the contradiction between the universal claims of public reason and its particular basis in bourgeois society, Marx wanted to imagine "the social conditions for the possibility of its utterly unbourgeois realization" (Habermas [1962] 1989, 128). Indeed, workers and excluded groups of many kinds were beginning to grasp this possibility, as the explosion of nineteenth-century social movements makes clear. Labor, Chartism, temperance, and other movements were enabled by the new conditions of the public sphere. But liberal critics, such as Alexis de Tocqueville and John Stuart Mill, saw this expansion of critical discussion as a threat to the public sphere and began to treat the public as a force of unreason. Habermas thinks that at this juncture liberal thought began to betray its own best ideals:

> The liberalist interpretation of the bourgeois constitutional state was reactionary: it reacted to the power of the idea of a critically debating public's self-determination, initially included in its institutions, as soon as this public was subverted by the propertyless and uneducated masses. (Habermas [1962] 1989, 136)

Habermas does not here mention the playing out of the same contradiction regarding gender, an omission for which he has been taken to task by feminist critics and which he has since acknowledged.[3] The important point for him is that the emancipatory potential of the public sphere was abandoned rather than radicalized and that changing conditions have now made its realization more difficult than ever. Habermas stresses especially two such conditions: the asymmetrical nature of mass culture, which makes it easier for those with capital or power to distribute their views but harder for marginal voices to talk back, and the growing interpenetration of the state and civil society, which makes it harder to conceive of the private public sphere as a limitation on state power. These tendencies amount to what Habermas calls a "refeudalization" of the public sphere—in effect, a second "structural transformation." They produce a public that is appealed to not for criticism but for benign acclamation. Public opinion comes less to generate ideas and hold power accountable and more simply to register approval or disapproval in the form of opinion polls and occasional elections. "Publicity once meant the exposure of political domination before the public use of reason; publicity now adds up the reactions of an uncommitted friendly disposition," Habermas writes. "In the measure that is shaped by public relations, the public sphere of civil society again takes on feudal features" (Habermas [1962] 1989, 195). Even the bourgeois conjugal family, which had in theory served as the basis of private humanity (an appearance that, according to Habermas, had always been contradicted by its real functions), now finds most of its functions taken over by mass culture and by other institutions such as schools. As a result, it "has started to dissolve into a sphere of pseudo-privacy" (Habermas [1962] 1989, 157).

Habermas's analysis has been the subject of a voluminous debate, much of it marred by reductive summaries and naïve confidence that highly capitalized mass media can be defended and celebrated as "popular culture." Three themes from this debate are important enough to warrant some comment here. First, the public-sphere environment Habermas describes can be seen as the context of modern social movements, including identity politics. Social movements take shape in civil society, often with an agenda of demands vis-à-vis the state. They seek to change policy by appealing to public opinion. They arise from contexts of critical discussion, many of them print-mediated. The question for debate, then, is to what extent the environment for critical social movements is becoming more undemocratic, "refeudalized," or colonized by changing relations among the state, mass media, and the market. This is not a simple issue. It has to do with the increasingly transnational nature of publics, of civil-society structures such as corporations or nongovernmental organization, and of interstate regulatory apparatuses (see Negt and Kluge 1993, esp. the introduction by Miriam Hansen; Berlant and

Warner 1994). It has to do as well with the apparently conflicting trends of an every higher capitalization of media, which are increasingly controlled by a small number of transnational companies, and the apparent decentralization of new media.

Second, movements around gender and sexuality do not always conform to the bourgeois model of "rational-critical debate," especially as that model has been subsequently elaborated by Habermas. In *The Structural Transformation of the Public Sphere*, Habermas speaks of "people's public use of their reason." But what counts as a use of reason? In later works, he put forward a highly idealized account of argumentative dialogue (for a critique of this turn, see Lee 1992). But movements around gender and sexuality seek to transform fundamental styles of embodiment, identity, and social relations—including their unconscious manifestations, the vision of the good life embedded in them, and the habitus by which people continue to understand their selves or bodies as public or private. Because this is the field that people want to transform, it is not possible to assume the habitus according to which rational-critical debate is a neutral, relatively disembodied procedure for addressing common concerns, while embodied life is assumed to be private, local, or merely affective and expressive. The styles by which people assume public relevance are themselves contested. The ability to bracket one's embodiment and status is not simply what Habermas calls making public use of one's reason; it is a strategy of distinction, profoundly linked to education and to dominant forms of masculinity.

Just as the gendered division of public and private kept women from challenging their role in any way that might have been political, public interactions are saturated with protocols of gender and sexual identity. Just as Diogenes's masturbating in the market will be seen by some as philosophy, by others as filth, the critically relevant styles of publicness in gay male sexual culture are seldom recognized as such but are typically denounced as sleaze and as crime. For modern gay men and lesbians, the possibilities of public or private speech are distorted by what we call the closet. "The closet" is a misleading spatial metaphor. As Eve Kosofsky Sedgwick has shown so well, it is a name for a set of assumptions in everyday life as well as in expert knowledge: assumptions about what goes without saying; what can be said without a breach of decorum; who shares the onus of disclosure; what can be known about a person's real nature through telltale signs, without his or her own awareness; and who will bear the consequences of speech and silence (Sedgwick 1990). Speech is everywhere regulated unequally. Yet ironically, common mythology understands the closet as an individual's lie about him- or herself. We blame people for being closeted. But the closet is better understood as the culture's problem, not the individual's. No one ever created a closet for him- or herself. People find themselves in its oppressive conditions before they know it, willy-nilly. It is experienced by lesbians and gay men as a private, individual problem of shame and deception. But it is produced by the heteronormative assumptions of everyday talk. It feels private. But in an important sense it is publicly constructed.

In such a regime of sexual domination, publicness will feel like exposure, and privacy will feel like the closet. The closet may seem to be a kind of protection. Indeed, the feeling of protection is one of the hallmarks of modern privacy. But in fact the closet is riddled with fear and shame. So is publicity under the conditions of the closet. Being publicly known as a homosexual is never the same as being publicly known as a heterosexual; the latter always goes without saying and troubles nothing, whereas the former carries echoes of pathologized visibility. It is perfectly meaningless to "come out" as a heterosexual. So it is not true, as common wisdom would have it, that homosexuals live private lives without a secure public identity. They have neither privacy *nor* publicness, in these normative senses of the terms. In the United States, the judiciary, along with the military and its supporters in Congress and the White House, has gone to great lengths to make sure that they will have neither (Halley 1999). It is this deformation of public and private that identity politics—and the performative ritual known as coming out—tries to transform.

In some ways, a more daunting version of the same problem faces the transgendered, who do not always wish to appeal in the same way to a private identity as the basis for a public revaluation. Often, it is the most private, intimate dimension of sex assignment and self-understanding that must be managed at the same time with the public and social presentations, though these may move at different rates and to different degrees. The task of managing stigma may often present itself as being like the closet, and it may display a similar inequality in claims to knowledge. The epistemological leverage of medical experts, for example, appears as a very public kind of knowledge and authority, objective and neutral where the patient's claims are understood to be subjective and interested, perhaps even pathological. Transgendered people typically have to struggle against that superior claim to know what's good for them or what their true nature is, even while they are dependent on those same experts for assistance, care, and public legitimacy. But of course, a sex transition is not something that can be managed privately, and because it is a transition rather than a newly revealed prior condition, "coming out" is not an entirely helpful analogy.

A notion of privacy as a right of self-determination may prove in many contexts to be extremely valuable to the transgendered. A merely naturalized privacy, on the other hand, might block access to the health services and other kinds of publicly available assistance that self-determination might require. The private facilities of public institutions—locker rooms, bathrooms, and such—can be the most public of battlegrounds, especially for female-to-male individuals. And the transgendered routinely have to cope with the public, institutional, and state dimensions of such otherwise "personal" and private issues as naming, sex classification, health, and intimate associations. Transgender activism continually points to the public underpinnings of privacy, and probably nowhere more so than in its own practice, which seeks to put into circulation a new publicly available language for self-understanding.

As these examples illustrate, the meaning of gender and sexuality in dominant culture is only partly determined in domestic or familial life. It is also constantly being shaped across the range of social relations, and perhaps especially in the mass media, with their visual language of incorporation and desire. The public sphere as an environment, then, is not a place where one could rationally debate a set of gender or sexual relations that can in turn be equated with private life; the public sphere is a principal instance of the forms of embodiment and social relations that are themselves at issue.

This is a reason for skepticism about the reigning protocols of what counts as rational-critical debate, including the idea that one needs to bracket one's private self in order to engage in public discussion. But the same reciprocity between public and private is also an advantage to public-sphere analysis in relation to some other critical methods, notably psychoanalysis. Psychoanalysis as a cultural phenomenon, as Zaretsky points out, has contributed profoundly to the twentieth-century revaluation of personal and private life. But as a method, psychoanalysis has been limited in its ability to deal with issues of public and private. Most psychoanalytic analyses of gender and sexuality focus on intrasubjective dynamics and familial relations, generalizing from these to abstract levels of culture, such as the Symbolic and the law of the father. In so doing, they methodically embed the equation of gender and sexuality with the realm of the family and the individual—blocking from view the mediation of publics and the multiple social, historical, and political frames of privacy. Freud himself struggled to overcome this limitation in *group psychology*, and some later reconstructions of psychoanalytic method, from Frantz Fanon to feminist film theory, have further revised his vocabulary with the aim of incorporating social contexts of domination into our understanding of psychic life, and vice versa. Yet the distance between psychoanalytic generality and the complex histories of public and private remains great (Zaretsky 1994; Brenkman 1993).

Finally, there is some tension between the publics of gender or sexuality and the public sphere as an ideal. On this point, there has been some confusion; critics commonly accuse Habermas of having adopted a false ideal of a unitary public.[4] But Habermas does not imagine a public unified in reality, as a constituency or a single media context. "Nonpublic opinions," he writes, "are at work in great numbers, and 'the' public opinion is indeed a fiction" (Habermas [1962] 1989, 244). From the beginning, his account stressed many different kinds of public discourse, from tavern conversation to art criticism. The ideal of unity of the public sphere is best understood as an imaginary convergence point that is the backdrop of critical discourse in each of these contexts and publics— an implied but abstract point that is often referred to as "the public" or "public opinion" and by virtue of that fact endowed with legitimacy and the ability to dissolve power. A "public" in this context is a special kind of virtual social object, enabling a special mode of address. As we saw in Kant's "What Is Enlightenment?" it is modeled on a reading public. In modern societies, a public is by definition an indefinite audience rather than a social constituency that could be numbered or named (Warner 1990). *The Structural Transformation of the Public Sphere* can be read as a history of the construction of this virtual object and its mode of address, where a key development is the fiction of "public opinion" as the ideal background of all possible publics. Habermas did not describe it in these terms, and in later work on communicative rationality he increasingly collapsed public reason into the model of face-to-face argumentative dialogue—thus making the special context of publics disappear from the analysis. But there is no necessary conflict between the public sphere and the idea of multiple publics.

Counterpublics

The stronger modification of Habermas's analysis—one in which he has shown little interest, though it is clearly of major significance in the critical analysis of gender and sexuality—is that some publics are defined by their tension with a larger public. Their participants are marked off from persons or citizens in general. Discussion within such a public is understood to contravene the rules obtaining in the world at large, being structured by alternative dispositions or protocols, making different assumptions about what can be said or what goes without saying. This kind of public is, in effect, a counterpublic: it maintains at some level, conscious or not, an awareness of its subordinate status. The sexual cultures of gay men or of lesbians would be one kind of example, but so would camp discourse or the media of women's culture. A counterpublic in this sense is usually related to a subculture, but there are important differences between these concepts. A counterpublic, against the background of the public sphere, enables a horizon of opinion and exchange; its exchanges remain distinct from authority and can have a critical relation to power; its extent is in principle indefinite, because it is not based on a precise demography but mediated by print, theater, diffuse networks of talk, commerce, and the like. Counterpublics are often called "subaltern counterpublics," but it is not clear that all counterpublics are composed of people *otherwise* dominated as subalterns. Some youth-culture publics or artistic publics, for example, operate as counterpublics, even though many who participate in them are "subalterns" in no other sense. At any rate, even as a subaltern counterpublic, this subordinate status does not simply reflect identities formed elsewhere; participation in such a public is one of the ways by which its members' identities are formed and transformed.

Habermas's rich historical account of the norms and practices of publicness in modernity can thus reopen the relations between the personal and the political. A public, or counterpublic, can do more than represent the interests of gendered or sexualized persons in a public sphere. It can mediate the most private and intimate meanings of gender and sexuality. It can work to elaborate new worlds of culture and social relations in which gender and sexuality can be lived, including forms of intimate association, vocabularies of affect, styles of embodiment, erotic practices, and relations of care and pedagogy. It can therefore make possible new forms of gendered or sexual citizenship—meaning active participation in collective world making through publics of sex and gender.

Such a model of citizenship or public personhood would be very different indeed from the bourgeois public sphere, though deeply indebted to it as a background set of conditions. The bourgeois public sphere consists of private persons whose identity is formed in the privacy of the conjugal domestic family and who enter into rational-critical debate around matters common to all by bracketing their embodiment and status. Counterpublics of sexuality and gender, on the other hand, are scenes of association and identity that transform the private lives they mediate. Homosexuals can exist in isolation, but gay people or queers exist by virtue of the world they elaborate together, and gay or queer identity is always fundamentally inflected by the nature of that world. The same could be said of women's counterpublics, or those of race or youth culture. These public contexts necessarily entail and bring into being realms of subjectivity outside the conjugal domestic family. Their protocols of discourse and debate remain open to affective and expressive dimensions of language. And their members make their embodiment and status at least partly relevant in a public way by their very participation (Warner 2002:159–186; Berlant and Warner 1994).

It is in part to capture the profound difference between the conception of citizenship made possible in such counterpublics and the one prevailing in the bourgeois public sphere that so many critics in gender and sexuality studies have recently turned to the long-unfashionable work of Hannah Arendt. Arendt was especially unfashionable in second-wave feminism. Far from "dissolving the distinction between public and private," Arendt insists on it. For many feminist readers, what stood out was that "when Hannah Arendt defines politics in terms of the pursuit of public happiness or the taste for public freedom, she is employing a terminology almost opposite to that adopted within the contemporary women's movement" (Anne Phillips, quoted in Dietz 1995, 18). Both Adrienne Rich, in *On Lies, Secrets, and Silence*, and Mary O'Brien, in *The Politics of Reproduction*, interpreted Arendt as embracing the system in which male is to public as female is to private. They dismissed her as an essentially masculinist thinker. Lately, however, an impressive range of feminists and other thinkers have begun a reconsideration. They argue that for Arendt public and private refer less to the norms of gender than to the different conditions for action that define humanity. For those who think that gender and sexuality are defined through action in relation to others, and that they can be made subject to transformation for that reason, Arendt can be read as prescribing what Bonnie Honig calls "an agonistic politics of performativity" (Honig 1995, 135–66).

In *The Human Condition*, Arendt tries to reconstruct dimensions of humanity put at risk by the world alienation of the modern age. Against the current of her time, in which privacy and personal life came to be viewed as the realm of individuality and freedom, Arendt sees both freedom and individuality in the world-making public activity of the polis, because it is a common framework of interaction that is needed to allow both a shared world of equals and the disclosure of unique agency. The private, by contrast, is the realm of necessity and the merged viewpoints of family life. Arendt believes that the necessities of private life are inappropriate to politics. But she does not say this out of a prudish morality; her ideal of political life is a creative fashioning of a common world, and she understands the word *private* to refer to those conditions—including love, pain, and need in general—that she thinks of as not being defined or transformed by such creative fashioning. As Mary Dietz emphasizes, both public and private in this usage are existential categories, not social description. They are different contexts for personhood. The public that Arendt values so much is the scene of world making and self-disclosure; it is therefore to be distinguished both from the prevailing system of politics and from any universalist notion of rational debate. It is a political scene, necessarily local because the self and the shared world disclosed through it emerge in interaction with others.[5]

Arendt sees at least three great ruptures separating our own time from the classical culture in which the world-making dimension of public action was understood. The first is Christianity, with its eternal private person and devaluation of the public world; the second, Romantic individualism, which leads us to see the private not as the privation of publicness but as an originary value in its own right; and the third, what she calls the rise of the social. By "the social" Arendt means the modern way of understanding human relations, not as the medium of action and speech but as behavior and regulation. Fundamental human capacities of world making are restricted in scope and consequence by mass society, administration, and instrumentality.

In the context of the Cold War (*The Human Condition* was published in 1958), this was a bold argument, fundamentally criticizing both totalitarianism and liberalism. Because Arendt's public is an action context for speech and an agonistic scene of interaction, it is the realm of rhetoric, not command; there is an implicit contrast here to the totalitarianism that Arendt had treated in her previous book, as well as to juridical models of power generally (Arendt 1958, 27–28; on the relation between *The Human Condition* and *The Origins of Totalitarianism*, see Zaretsky 1997). But Arendt also offers her description of public and private as a contrast to the distinction between the state and the society with which it is often made synonymous, especially in liberalism.[6]

The difference between Arendt's pragmatic sense of the public and the liberal universalist sense is sharp. It also occasions unforeseen tensions in Arendt's own thought, and thus opportunities for reading her against the grain. The women's movement and queer culture would represent model cases of public world making, and for the same reason that they are generally understood to be opposed to "family values":

> Being seen and being heard by others derive their significance from the fact that everybody sees and hears from a different position. This is the meaning of public life, compared to which even the richest and most satisfying family life can offer only the prolongation or multiplication of one's own position with its attending aspects and perspectives. The subjectivity of privacy can be prolonged and multiplied in a family, it can even become so strong that its weight is felt in the public realm; but this family "world" can never replace the reality rising out of the sum total of aspects presented by one object to a multitude of spectators. (Arendt 1958, 57)

Familialist conceptions of national or public membership come in for such withering remarks in part because Arendt has in mind the background of fascism; but this analysis has not lost its relevance in the post–Cold War period. Arendt writes that in mass society "people suddenly behave as though they were members of one family, each multiplying and prolonging the perspective of his neighbor" (1958, 58). While mass society might seem to be, in many respects, the opposite of the family, the commodity-ridden waste against which the intimacy of the hearth is usually contrasted, for Arendt these two models of social space share a basic limitation on action and speech. (The point might be illustrated through the mid-1990s phenomenon of the Promise Keepers movement, or "family values" rhetoric generally.) Of course, some feminists (especially in what is called "difference feminism") and some queer theorists might take a more expansive view of the family. Arendt clearly has in mind a classic middle-class family life, with its ideals of property interest, ethnic subjectivity, primary allegiance, and undisputed will.

Much of the energy currently being derived from Arendt's work by feminist and queer thought lies in the possibility of reading the slogan "the personal is political" with an Arendtian understanding of the political. This entails the working assumption that the conditions of gender and sexuality can be treated not simply as the given necessities of the laboring body, but also as the occasion for forming publics, elaborating common worlds, making the transposition from shame to honor, from hiddenness to the exchange of viewpoints with generalized others, in such a way that the disclosure of self partakes of freedom.

The challenge facing this project in transgender activism, feminism, and queer theory is to understand how world making unfolds in publics that are, after all, not just natural collections of people, not just "communities," but also mediated publics. Arendt's language of "speech" and "action in view of others" sound, in this context, fairly antiquated—an unfortunate faithfulness to the metaphor of the polis rather than a complex understanding of how politics happens. Habermas, meanwhile, pays more careful attention to the practices and structures that mediate publics, including print, genre, architecture, and capital. But he extracts from them such an idealized image of persuasion that the world-disclosing activity of a counterpublic falls out of view. Both thinkers share a strong sense that the utopian ideals of public and private have been contradicted by the social conditions for realizing them in modern mass culture.

What remains, then, is a need for both concrete and theoretical understandings of the conditions that currently mediate the transformative and creative work of counterpublics. Counterpublics of sex and gender are teaching us to recognize in new and deeper ways how privacy is publicly constructed. They are testing our understanding of how private life can be made publicly relevant. And they are elaborating not only new shared worlds and critical languages but also new privacies, new individuals, new bodies, new intimacies, and new citizenships. In doing so, they have provoked visceral reactions, and necessarily so, since the visceral meaning of gender and sexuality is the very matter that they wish to disclose as publicly relevant. It is often thought, especially by outsiders, that the public display of private matters is debased narcissism, a collapse of decorum, expressivity gone amok, the erosion of any distinction between public and private. But in a counterpublic setting, such display often has the aim of transformation. Styles of embodiment are learned and cultivated, and the affects of shame and disgust that surround them can be tested and, in some cases, revalued. Visceral private meaning is not easy to alter by oneself, by a free act of will. It can only be altered through exchanges that go beyond self-expression to the making of a collective scene of disclosure. The result, in counterpublics, is that the visceral intensity of gender, of sexuality, or of corporeal style in general no longer needs to be understood as private. Publicness itself has a visceral resonance.

At the same time, these counterpublics are encountering—without always recognizing—limitations in their public media, their relation to the state and to official publics, their embeddedness in larger publics and larger processes of privatization, and their reliance on distorting models of privacy and intimacy. One doesn't "go public" simply as an act of will—neither by writing, nor by having an opinion, nor by exposing oneself in the marketplace. The context of publicness must be available, allowing these actions to count in a public way, to be transformative. How does that come about? Habermas would have us ask whether it is even possible to be public in the validating sense when the public media are mass media, and to some extent this remains a question for counterpublics as well. Counterpublics are, by definition, formed by their conflict with the norms and contexts of their cultural environment, and this context of domination inevitably entails distortion. Mass publics and counterpublics, in other words, are both damaged forms of publicness, just as gender and sexuality are, in this culture, damaged forms of privacy.[7]

Notes

1. A notable irony in claims to break down the "binary" of public and private is that most major theorists of the terms—notably Hannah Arendt (1958), Jürgen Habermas ([1962] 1989),

and Richard Sennett (1977)—argued that the conditions of mass society were already dissolving the potential for both public action and real privacy.

2. Jane Addams's dictum "A city is enlarged housekeeping" represents an early version of this remapping. "From the beginning of tribal life," Addams writes, "women have been held responsible for the health of the community, a function which is not represented by the health department; from the days of the cave dwellers, so far as the home was clean and wholesome, it was due to their efforts, which are now represented by the bureau of tenement-house inspection; from the period of the primitive village, the only public sweeping performed was what they undertook in their own dooryards, that which is now represented by the bureau of street cleaning" (quoted in Zaretsky 1997, 224–25).

3. See, for example, Landes (1988) and the essays by Mary Ryan, Nancy Fraser, and Geoff Eley in Calhoun (1992). On Landes's claim that the public sphere was "essentially, not just contingently, masculinist," see Baker (1992).

4. This misreading can be found in the essays by Fraser and Eley in Calhoun (1992). It is an easy reading to make and appears even in that close and scrupulous reader of Habermas, Craig Calhoun (1997, 84). What supports it is Habermas's strong emphasis on the way the public is thought to derive an implied unity from its critical opposition to the state and the legislative power.

5. This point has been the subject of some dispute between Bonnie Honig and Seyla Benhabib (I follow Honig's reading here). For a contrasting reading of Arendt, see Benhabib (1993, 1995).

6. This point is made by Zaretsky (1997), particularly in reference to *The Origins of Totalitarianism*. A sticking point in many contemporary debates about Arendt is that in the classical conception, as she interprets it, the private is almost entirely without value, even without content. That, she emphasizes, is the point: the private is privative, a negative category, a state in which one is deprived of context for realizing oneself through action and in free interaction with others. The most private person is the slave. The life of the polis is opposed to all that is one's own (*idion*)—hence a merely private or idiosyncratic person would be an idiot. That Arendt was capable of seeing the expression of a strong value in such a vacuous— or, rather, evacuating—conception of the private is testament to the imaginative strength of her interpretation; but it is not a site of nostalgia or phallocentric commitment, as some feminist critics contend. Privacy for Arendt does have one valuable dimension, however: the sense of rootedness, of place in the world, provided by the classical conception of property as a transgenerational estate. But this sense of the private is unrecoverable in a capitalist economy and in an age with no secular orientation to immortality, and Arendt writes that "the intimate is not a very reliable substitute" for it (1958, 70).

7. An excellent illustration of the latter point is to be found in Berlant (1998). Analyzing women's culture of sentimentality, Berlant shows that it has some counterpublic features but that these are distorted. "When sentimentality meets politics," she writes, "it uses personal stories to tell of structural effects, but in so doing it risks thwarting its very attempt to perform rhetorically a scene of pain that must be soothed politically. Because the ideology of true feeling cannot admit the nonuniversality of pain, its cases become all jumbled together and the ethical imperative toward social transformation is replaced by a civic-minded but passive ideal of empathy. The political as a place of acts oriented toward publicness becomes replaced by a world of private thoughts, leanings, and gestures. Suffering, in this personal-public context, becomes answered by survival, which is then recoded as freedom. Meanwhile, we lose the original impulse behind sentimental politics, which is to see the individual effects of mass social violence as different from the causes, which are impersonal and depersonalizing" (Berlant 1998, 641).

References

Appleby, Joyce. 1992. *Liberalism and Republicanism in the Historical Imagination*. Cambridge, MA: Harvard University Press.

Arendt, Hannah. 1958. *The Human Condition*. Chicago: University of Chicago Press.

Baker, Keith Michael. 1992. "Defining the Public Sphere in Eighteenth-Century France." In Calhoun 1992, 181–211.

Benhabib, Seyla. 1993. "Feminist Theory and Hannah Arendt's Concept of Public Space." *History of the Human Sciences* 6:97–114.

———. 1995. "The Pariah and Her Shadow: Hannah Arendt's Biography of Rahel Varnhagen." In *Feminist Interpretations of Hannah Arendt*, ed. Bonnie Honig, 83–104. University Park: Pennsylvania State University Press.

Berlant, Lauren. 1998. "Poor Eliza." *American Literature* 70 (3): 635–68.

Berlant, Lauren, and Michael Warner. 1994. "Introduction to 'Critical Multiculturalism.'" In *Multiculturalism: A Critical Reader*, ed. David Theo Goldberg, 107–13. Oxford: Basil Blackwell.

———. 1998. "Sex in Public." *Critical Inquiry* 24 (2).

Boydston, Jeanne, Mary Kelley, and Anne Margolis, eds. 1988. *The Limits of Sisterhood: The Beecher Sisters on Women's Rights and Woman's Sphere*. Chapel Hill: University of North Carolina Press.

Brenkman, John. 1993. *Straight Male Modern*. New York: Routledge.

Brinkley, Alan. 1998. *Liberalism and Its Discontents*. Cambridge, MA: Harvard University Press.

Calhoun, Craig, ed. 1992. *Habermas and the Public Sphere*. Cambridge, MA: MIT Press.

———. 1997. "Nationalism and the Public Sphere." In *Public and Private in Thought and Practice: Perspectives on a Grand Dichotomy*. Chicago: University of Chicago Press.

Chartier, Roger, ed. 1989. *A History of Private Life*. Vol. 3, *Passions of the Renaissance*. Trans. Arthur Goldhammer. Cambridge, MA: Harvard University Press.

———. 1991. *The Cultural Origins of the French Revolution*. Trans. Lydia Cochrane. Durham, NC: Duke University Press.

Deutsche, Rosalyn. 1990. "Men in Space." *Artforum* 28.

Dietz, Mary. 1995. "Feminist Receptions of Hannah Arendt." In *Feminist Interpretations of Hannah Arendt*, ed. Bonnie Honig, 17–50. University Park: Pennsylvania State University Press.

Echols, Alice. 1989. *Daring to Be Bad: Radical Feminism in America, 1967–1975*. Minneapolis: University of Minnesota Press.

Elshtain, Jean Bethke. 1981. *Public Man, Private Woman: Women in Social and Political Thought*. Princeton, NJ: Princeton University Press.

Foucault, Michel. 1985. *The History of Sexuality*. Vol. 2, *The Use of Pleasure*. Trans. Robert Hurley. New York: Pantheon.

Fraser, Nancy. 1992. "Rethinking the Public Sphere: A Contribution to a Critique of Actually Existing Democracy." In Calhoun 1992, 109–42.

Graham, Laura. 1993. "A Public Space in Amazonia?" *American Ethnologist* 40 (4): 717–41.

Grimké, Sarah, and Angelina Grimké. 1989. *The Public Years of Sarah and Angelina Grimké: Selected Writings, 1835–1839*. Ed. Larry Ceplair. New York: Columbia University Press.

Habermas, Jürgen. (1962) 1989. *The Structural Transformation of the Public Sphere: An Inquiry into a Category of Bourgeois Society*, trans. Thomas Berger. Cambridge, MA: MIT Press.

——. 1974. "The Public Sphere: An Encyclopedia Article." *New German Critique* 1 (3): 49–55.

Halley, Janet. 1994. "The Politics of the Closet: Towards Equal Protection for Gay, Lesbian and Bisexual Identity." In *Reclaiming Sodom*, ed. Jonathan Goldberg. New York: Routledge.

——. 1999. *Don't: A Reader's Guide to the Military's Anti-Gay Policy*. Durham, NC: Duke University Press.

Hirschman, Albert. 1977. *The Passions and the Interests: Arguments for Capitalism before Its Triumph*. Princeton, NJ: Princeton University Press.

Honig, Bonnie. 1995. "Toward an Agonistic Feminism: Hannah Arendt and the Politics of Identity. In *Feminist Interpretations of Hannah Arendt*, ed. Bonnie Honig. University Park: Pennsylvania State University Press.

Johnson, Paul. 1978. *A Shopkeeper's Millennium*. New York: Hill and Wang.

Kant, Immanuel. 1996. "An Answer to the Question: What Is Enlightenment?" Trans. James Schmidt. In *What Is Enlightenment? Eighteenth-Century Answers and Twentieth-Century Questions,* ed. James Schmidt, 58–64. Berkeley: University of California Press.

Kelley, Mary. 1984. *Private Woman, Public Stage: Literary Domesticity in Nineteenth-Century America*. New York: Oxford University Press.

Kramnick, Isaac. 1990. *Republicanism and Bourgeois Radicalism: Political Ideology in Late Eighteenth-Century England and America*. Ithaca, NY: Cornell University Press.

Landes, Joan. 1988. *Women and the Public Sphere in the Age of the French Revolution*. Ithaca, NY: Cornell University Press.

Laursen, John Christian. 1996. "The Subversive Kant: The Vocabulary of 'Public' and 'Publicity.'" In *What Is Enlightenment? Eighteenth-Century Answers and Twentieth-Century Questions*, ed. James Schmidt, 253–69. Berkeley: University of California Press.

Lee, Benjamin. 1992. "Textuality, Mediation, and Public Discourse." In Calhoun 1992, 402–20.

MacKinnon, Catharine. 1987. "Privacy v. Equality." In *Feminism Unmodified: Discourses on Life and Law*. Cambridge, MA: Harvard University Press.

Macpherson, C. B. 1962. *The Political Theory of Possessive Individualism*. Oxford: Oxford University Press.

Negt, Oskar, and Alexander Kluge. 1993. *Public Sphere and Experience*. Minneapolis: University of Minnesota Press.

Pateman, Carol. 1989. "Feminist Critiques of the Public/Private Dichotomy." In *The Disorder of Women: Democracy, Feminism, and Political Theory*. Palo Alto, CA: Stanford University Press.

Pocock, J. G. A. 1975. *The Machiavellian Moment*. Princeton, NJ: Princeton University Press.

Rawls, John. 1989. *A Theory of Justice*. Cambridge, MA: Harvard University Press.

——. 1996. *Political Liberalism*. New York: Columbia University Press.

Rosaldo, Michelle Zimbalist. 1974. "Woman, Culture, and Society: A Theoretical Overview." In *Woman, Culture, and Society*, ed. Michelle Zimbalist Rosaldo and Louise Lamphere, 17–42. Palo Alto, CA: Stanford University Press.

Ryan, Mary P. 1990. *Women in Public: Between Banners and Ballots, 1825–1880*. Baltimore: Johns Hopkins University Press.

Scott, Joan W. 1988. *Gender and the Politics of History*. New York: Columbia University Press.

———. 1996. *Only Paradoxes to Offer: French Feminists and the Rights of Man*. Cambridge, MA: Harvard University Press.

Sedgwick, Eve Kososfky. 1990. *Epistemology of the Closet*. Berkeley: University of California Press.

Sennett, Richard. 1977. *The Fall of Public Man*. New York: Knopf.

Skinner, Quentin. 1978. *The Foundations of Modern Political Thought*. 2 vols. Cambridge: Cambridge University Press.

Sklar, Kathryn Kish. 1973. *Catharine Beecher: A Study in American Domesticity*. New Haven, CT: Yale University Press.

Sullivan, Andrew. 1995. *Virtually Normal: An Argument about Homosexuality*. New York: Knopf.

Thomas, Kendall. 1992. "Beyond the Privacy Principle." *Columbia Law Review* 92:1359–1516.

Warner, Michael. 1990. *The Letters of the Republic: Publication and the Public Sphere in Eighteenth-Century America*. Cambridge, MA: Harvard University Press.

———. 2002. *Publics and Counterpublics*. New York: Zone.

Wilentz, Sean. 1984. *Chants Democratic*. New York: Oxford University Press.

Zaretsky, Eli. 1986. *Capitalism, the Family, and Personal Life*. Rev. ed. New York: Harper & Row.

———. 1994. "Identity Theory, Identity Politics: Psychoanalysis, Marxism, Post-Structuralism." In *Social Theory and the Politics of Identity*, ed. Craig Calhoun. Oxford: Blackwell.

———. 1997. "Hannah Arendt and the Meaning of the Public/Private Distinction." In *Hannah Arendt and the Meaning of Politics*, ed. Craig Calhoun and John McGowen. Minneapolis: University of Minnesota Press.

17 :: RACE

In a 1961 speech, James Baldwin remarked that "Bobby Kennedy recently made me the soul-stirring promise that one day—thirty years, if I'm lucky—I can be President too. It never entered this boy's mind, I suppose—it has not entered the country's mind yet—that perhaps I wouldn't want to be. And in any case, what really exercises my mind is not this hypothetical day on which some Negro 'first' will become the first Negro President. What I am really curious about is just what kind of country he'll be president of"(quoted in Kenan 2010, xxii). Nearly fifty years later, an African American was indeed elected to the presidency. With Barack Obama's ascendancy, we might well wonder what kind of country we now have and what is to come. Have we reached the "postrace" status that some have claimed? Despite the fact that the current occupants of the White House are a black man and his family, race persists—both the term and its historical-political realities. My discussion of it here serves as a case in point but will also bring into alignment the dual prongs of a certain critical circuitry—the implications of "race" for "gender," and perhaps the other way around.

Also fifty years after Kennedy's prediction, on May 17, 2011, the following headline appeared in the *Huffington Post*: "Satoshi Kanazawa Causes Firestorm after Claiming Black Women Are Less Attractive." The article reported on a post by Kanazawa on his *Psychology Today* blog "The Scientific Fundamentalist," which is billed as "A look at the hard truths of human nature" (Moss 2011). Kanazawa's post (which has since been taken down) posed in its title the question "Why Are Black Women Rated Less Physically Attractive Than Other Women but Black Men Are Rated Better Looking Than Other Men?" It was a familiar, time-worn folk belief, laughable despite its reappearance here in scientific dress, complete with charts and graphs. We were being exposed, once again, to the toxicity of "looks" as a quantifiable measure and as an example of the intersection of gender, race, and skin color.

Kanazawa is a self-described evolutionary psychologist with an appointment in management at the London School of Economics and a long list of publications, including three coauthored books with mainstream publishers. Among the claims in his blog post stands another of the ancient saws: "There are marked race differences in physical attractiveness among women, but not among men." Kanazawa's pseudoscientific exercise involves computing a "latent 'physical attractiveness' factor" using a statistical procedure called factor analysis, then positing that African peoples carry genetic "mutation loads" that "significantly decrease physical attractiveness." None of these claims, however, quite clinches the case in his own mind. "The only thing I can think of that might potentially explain the lower average level of physical attractiveness among black women," he concludes, "is testosterone." Women with higher levels of testosterone "also have more masculine features and are therefore less physically attractive," and "Africans on average have higher levels of testosterone than other races."

Kanazawa's premises and conclusions ultimately have nothing to do with the statistical sciences or his evidentiary maneuvers. The investigator in this case already "knows" the answer to the questions that he purports to advance; his questions are not only posed in bad faith but as rhetorical props for a repetition of social "facts," inherited from mimetic racism and trumped up as science. The value of the entry, then, consists in inadvertently demonstrating how words about "gender," "race," and their interconnectedness are subtly blended to orchestrate what we believe we know already.

Gender, as a carrier and host of race, bundles up the intimations of difference and puts them into play. Even before we reach the question of race—even before race has acquired its powerful means and meanings—it has been traversed and worked over by gender *as sexual difference*. To put it more personally: before I was black, I was female. *But for whom?* In my homogeneous nuclear family, the last child born was myself, a girl, and race need not have been named. But the state of Tennessee (and eventually a repertoire of state apparatuses, including the census) would also have an interest in the matter. It would seem, then, that gender is more "natural" than race, but this conclusion, though not false, does not take us very far. It would also appear that gender sustains greater "intimacy" than race, insofar as it collapses onto sex difference *where we first live* and therefore determines the social pathway that we immediately enter at first birth: the query that we cannot remember but that has already transformed us into a beloved object for someone, even before one knows her name, is the ubiquitous What is it? Boy or girl? "Gender" and "race," as socially decided properties of human and social being, set in motion by genetic coding, find their actual significance in the cultural circumstances that claim them, as both *potentials* will be articulated through social texts that seem to demand the performative "utterance" of attitude, script, and gesture.

Race and gender as social practice both attach to varying levels of order and degree, from family membership to health care and tax structure, just as both translate into objects of study in the research academy. The front lines of critical investigation and the disciplinary protocols since the late 1960s and early 1970s have passed through race and gender studies, among the new curricular objects that have radically redefined knowledge in the human sciences (Wiegman 2012). Though the new humanistic configurations often run in tandem along *theoretical* pathways, they are, off paper and in their referential relationship to living subjects and subjectivities, uneven in their respective historicopolitical and discursive development. Gender, as I have already noted, predates racialized perceptions of identity as a mode of social organization, which perceptions a number of thinkers tether to the emergence of the modern world. "Woman" as a universal category of distinction apparently penetrates cultural, linguistic, ethnic, and spatiotemporal borders in differentiating human interests as *gendered* expression. Maleness certainly constitutes a gender, but in truth the gender dimensions of the male are subsumed by his abstract humaneness so that gender comes to articulate a particularity and peculiarity that mark "otherness." If in this scheme "man" constitutes the general, "woman" suggests the particular. Race, with regard to (white) maleness in the context of the modern West, will work along analogous lines.

It is difficult to decide where and when gender studies begins, or indeed how to constitute a genealogy of the gender problematic (Newman 2002, 141–73). It would be just to say that whatever hermeneutic the investigator chooses will be inadequate or incomplete precisely because of the dual inheritance of our biological legacy (which, for reasons not at all clear, appears to be embarrassing) into which our cultural patrimonies seem to pour. In short, "female" and "male," not altogether conformable to "woman" and "man," are already given with the critical ground that the investigator wishes to turn over, and, as a result, this ground on which we stand is inherited and "in the way." Going behind these apparent givens, then, to some prior state of human and social being is unthinkable on its face. If that is so, then there is no such thing, as far as we can tell, as an untrammeled and uncontested beginning. It is somewhat clearer that we are constituted in and by our present(s), looking toward an infinitely receding horizon. One therefore compromises and conjures with a more or less plausible interpretive schematic. The signal text that marks the beginning of feminist studies both as a curricular object and as "scene of instruction" into the formation of human being as female-ness is Simone de Beauvoir's *The Second Sex* ([1953] 1974). All feminist critique in the Western context has taken at least some of its inspiration from this midcentury work. Though other feminist texts have reached for a definitive statement, Beauvoir's work must be said to have pointed the way (Newman 2002).

First available to English-speaking audiences in 1953, H. M. Parshley's translation of *Le deuxième sexe* not only is well known to generations of feminist scholars but occupies prime status as an inaugural gesture to-ward a feminist historiography in the modern period. The first book of the work situates "woman" as a subject of history from the vantage point of varied analytical foci, from the historical materialist and the psychoan-alytic to the mythic, but the thread of analysis that works its way across the entirety of the project is Beauvoir's inquiry into "that particular form of being which we call human life" (de Beauvoir [1953] 1974, 67). From this perspective, Beauvoir judges each of the analytical lenses that she exam-ines to be inadequate in its confrontation with the concrete conditions of a woman's life—economic, bodily, and psychoanalytic. As an existential-ist philosopher, she adopts concepts that are central to this philosophical protocol—"existent," "immanence," "transcendence," among them—in relationship to the historical situation of women. Even though, as Toril Moi observes, large chunks of Beauvoir's original text disappear from Parshley's translation, the encyclopedic character of *The Second Sex* none-theless contributes to its applicability across cultural and geographical boundaries. For Beauvoir, the route to freedom for woman must pass through flights from "immanence," or the human being in his capture by the given, to acts of "transcendence," in which "being" finds itself "only in estrangement, alienation" (63). Finding herself in the shape of her work, in successive acts of transcendence, woman as "existent" in Beau-voir's conceptual narrative is no longer the embodiment of the dream of man (or existing *for another*) but rather, now existing *for self*, joins the other half of humanity in the participatory and reciprocal remaking of the world.

Beauvoir assigns "woman," deprived of existential freedom and thought of in terms of her "essence," to the realm of "mystery." She is joined there "by the slave, the servant, the indigent, all who depend upon the caprices of a master" (de Beauvoir[1953] 1974, 292). Although Beauvoir does not address race at any length, these "others," traversing the analytical cate-gories of gender and class and quite literally *confusing* them, show a mod-icum of resemblance to "raced" subjects. *Raced* is not a term that would have been available to Beauvoir or her first English translator, having only later entered cultural studies as shorthand for subjects and subjectivities defined by race. The term accords well with the character of race as a discredited social value. Race, however, remains one of the master signs of human and social differentiation, as "raced" implies that it comes in degrees—some people having more of "it" than others. Despite the uncertainties that attend race as an analytical object, it is the only mode of identification that has been declared "dead" even as it thrives. Today, the "leader of the free world" himself is violently subjected to processes of demonization because of his race. In any event, Beauvoir places the essential woman on a par with "the Black" and "the Yellow" to the extent that these perambulatory "attitudes," we might call them, are circumscribed by "mystery," which is "never more than a mirage that vanishes as we draw near to look at it" (de Beauvoir[1953] 1974, 293). In an elaboration of Francophone personality in the iron grip of colonization—"the Negro of the Antilles"—Frantz Fanon similarly positions race as an effect of vision. "Look, A Negro!" the child in its mother's arms cries out in a scenario conjured up by Fanon (Fanon 1967, 111). The child here is responding to the physical features of the *persona*—his hair type and above all, his skin color—and their difference from the child's own physical type. In Ralph Ellison's *Invisible Man,* the protagonist relates that the condition of invisibility has little to do with the object of perception but, rather, aligns itself more nearly with the disposition of the gaze wielded by the other (Ellison 1992). In both the Fanonian instance, drawn from real life, and the Ellisonian scenes, fictionalized to mimic real life, the object of attention draws an emphatic response because he looks different from those around him; in effect, this different appearance, registered at the level of vision, accounts for the "mystery" that Beauvoir, as well as Fanon and Ellison, assigns to the "other."

Gender thinking and race thinking, then, can be said to inhabit the same territory of "mystery." We are left, however, with the problem of defining how they differ. Feminist writers in Beauvoir's wake would wrestle with the question, and none more effectively than Betty Friedan, who located the problematic squarely within the precincts of family and domesticity. The 1963 publication of Friedan's *Feminine Mystique* is celebrated as one of the events that touched off the new women's movement of the 1960s and 1970s. In fact, however, the women's movement might be said to inscribe one long continuous interrogation that first gained momentum in the mid-nineteenth century, pursuant, in the United States, to the growing agitation to end slavery. Such movements may go dormant for a time but regain emergent status in circumstances of historical crisis so that the *impression* that they are new seems inevitable to the success of their reception. In the introduction to a tenth-anniversary reissue of

The Feminine Mystique, which takes up Beauvoir's woman "mystery" in its American context, Friedan herself asserted that "until I started writing the book, I wasn't even conscious of the woman problem" (Friedan [1963] 2001, 43). Thirty years later, Anna Quindlen, introducing another reissue of this germinal text, recalls her twelve-year-old self, watching her mother—"hunched over this paperback"—reading it "in the place usually reserved for cooking." Quindlen herself first read the book nearly a decade later, when it was assigned in a women's studies class at Barnard College. If *The Feminine Mystique* "changed the lives of millions upon millions of other women who jettisoned empty hours of endless housework and found work, and meaning, outside of raising their children and feeding their husbands," it changed Friedan's life as well: transformed into "a celebrity, a pariah, a standard bearer, a target," she would go on to found the National Organization for Women (NOW), as "her name became synonymous with the Equal Rights Amendment and late-twentieth-century feminism" (Friedan [1963] 2001, 12–13).

The year 1963 was also, of course, the year of John F. Kennedy's assassination and consequently one of the most dangerous years of the civil rights movement in the United States. For that reason, my own eye actually missed *The Feminine Mystique*, though it landed solidly on James Baldwin's essays—"The Fire Next Time" in particular. My attention was riveted to the fate of James Meredith and his law school application to "Ole Miss," as well as the chilling uncertainties that accompanied my daily life and that of thirty other black students attending school in the then-hostile environment of the University of Memphis. We made it out, we lived to tell the story, but who knew for sure at the time? Quindlen's "millions upon millions of women," though we take her point, must therefore be modified regarding its racial, demographic, and class dimensions.

This refinement of perspective also inscribes one of the crucial fields of intervention in feminist theory and women's studies of the late 1970s through the turn of the century (Hull, Scott, and Smith 1982). Those almost infinite differences of women's *location* describe the single most consistent feature of feminist engagement and critique from Beauvoir's and Friedan's generation to succeeding ones. *Location* is at once feminism's most redolent and nettlesome aspect, as it hampers generalization, on the one hand, and, on the other, allows the general to emerge, not as a definitive theoretical *summa* but, rather, as a *bare minimum* of theoretical possibility. However, the ambition to achieve a unified field theory of feminist praxis and critique nevertheless defines one of the most energetic intellectual endeavors of "second-wave" practitioners—to make the present speak both for itself and a reconsideration of the past. Second-wave feminism, the term often applied to feminist practice and theory beginning with Friedan and extending to the mid-1990s, marks not only the sustained reanimation of debates on the life of women in US society, but also inaugurates the institutionalization of feminist/women and gender studies—its systematic execution as an aspect of the new curricula in the human sciences (Kolmar and Bartkowski 2010, 38, 335, 475). Certain titles from this era of critique attempt both overview and careful contextualization, as in Nancy F. Cott's *Grounding of Modern Feminism* (1987) and Joan Scott's *Gender and the Politics of History* (1988). Such works have opened the field to refinement in the narrative of women's locational dispositions.

One of its key accomplishments is intersectional theory, which attempts to disaggregate the mutual exclusivity of gender and race analysis. Kimberle Crenshaw argues that the "monocausal" focus on gender, for example, "tends to downplay the interaction of gender subordination with race and class" (Matsuda et al. 1993, 111). The material outcome of the interplay between and among convergent hierarchies "in the lives of women of color" is defined by Crenshaw as a "structural intersectionality" that breaks down into three component parts (114ff). The intersectional thematic not only broadened the reach of women's studies across communities of racial and "raced" subjects, but also generated further refinements on the distinction between the empirical female subjects of history and the philosophical and theoretical "subjects of feminism" (de Lauretis 1987).

When Teresa de Lauretis identifies "subjects of feminism," she is referring not only to feminism as a philosophical and conceptual system to which women are historically related, but also to women as subjects of histories that are defined culturally, geographically, linguistically, and locationally. In other words, women, because they are differently situated by circumstance, do not always relate to feminism or the "woman question" in the same way, and it is precisely this difference in life circumstance and the contingencies of history that Crenshaw's "intersectionality" is meant to address. Intersectionality implies that a generalized and comparative view of race and gender concepts over time and space must be carefully formulated, and this, in fact, remains one of the most difficult tasks of feminist analysis as it is conducted by different women subjects.

In coming to grips with the question of what is different about the experience of gender for black women and other women of color (or, in general, subjects of feminism who are defined by race as well as gender), the investigator is hard put to find a definitive answer, but it seems right to say that such subjects are marked by the effects of *stigma* (which the dictionary defines as a "mark of shame or discredit") that gender is apparently lacking. The stigmata of race—those markings of race in the plural—seem to endure right alongside the attempts to undo race prejudice. What we might call stigmatic effect, or the material outcome of defining persons by the color of their skin, for example, or the shape of their eyes, or the texture of their hair, is measurable—we can locate it in the flight of capital, for instance, and in the ascription of group status to entire communities of subjects—"blacks" and so on. By no means definitive in its power to constrain or define subjects, stigmatic effect, which stimulates and engenders race thinking, or the racialized perception of identity, remains one of the most palpable and perdurable symptoms of disorder in the contemporary world, maintaining distinctions between the woman mystery and other "others," but it is also questionable, given race and gender analyses over the last three decades, intersectionality in particular.

Here it is useful to keep in mind that the category "woman" overlaps women as historical subjects but is not entirely commensurate or synonymous with those subjects, just as "the Black" and "the Yellow" are abstracted from the historicities of "black" and "yellow" peoples; occlusions between abstractions and the actualities supposed to embody them account for one of the most enduring forms of violence exacted at the epistemic level. The attempt to generalize a comparative view of race and gender across a spatiotemporal progression, unmodulated by the contingencies of specific conditions, is of limited use. But we could venture to say that the most telling mark of difference between race and gender categories is the *stigma* that falls on race. And further, that the *stigmata* of race, whether the latter are taken as cause or effect, seem to endure alongside the march of ameliorative gestures. Stigmatic effect does not announce itself *as such* but, rather, can only be addressed as an actual material outcome (for example, the flight of capital and the ascription of group status). Stigmatic effect is by no means definitive in its power to define or constrain subjects. Nevertheless, racist thinking, which takes its cues from stigmatic effect, remains one of the most palpable and perdurable symptoms of disorder in the contemporary world.

+ + +

Historians and culture critics are at variance concerning the origins of race thinking: David Theo Goldberg (2002), for example, argues that the modern state is "nothing less than a racial state. It is a state or set of conditions that assumes varied racially conceived character in different sociospecific milieus." By contrast, Ivan Hannaford (1996) persuasively argues that his work "is an invitation *not* to accept that the history of Western thought has always been, and will always be, a history of racial thought." Hannaford argues that race, as we currently understand it, is a modern invention or fabrication given impetus by seventeenth-century natural history. While other critiques adopt an earlier, even ancient, time frame for the emergence of race thinking (Gossett 1963), there is general agreement that the modern world provides the crucible for its most concentrated and systematic fermentation.

Several studies that advance an etiology of race have surfaced since Winthrop Jordan's seminal 1968 work *White over Black: American Attitudes toward the Negro, 1550–1812*. Within the scholarly alignment of race constructionists, emerging after the 1960s and taking its cue, in part, from the new cultural studies, emphases fall on the concocted character of race and the degree to which raciation or racialization could be described as a "making," not unlike the theatricality inherent in the donning of a mask. These studies treat race as a fiction that is neither time-honored nor endemic to human and historical arrangements. Instead, they have located the impulse to raciation in economic and class turbulence, tethered to gender, and in the velocities of discontent that thrive with possessive individualism (Pocock 1995). As it emerges from the complex historical trajectories of modernity, the concept of race shows the ebb and flow of social practice shaped by competitive pressures.

We cannot avoid, then, the overwhelming sense that as a consequence of the anxieties attendant upon the advent of the modern world, race/racism becomes a strategy for canceling them. In modernity's spectacular contest of gains and losses, advantages and disadvantages, strokes of happiness and outbreaks of misery, it is not written that a given subject will succeed. Enter race, which eliminates significant numbers of competitors, or would-be competitors, and advances others. As a strategy of intervention, race assures that the field of play is uneven and that struggles to make it so will be scored in violence. Theodore Allen's description of "racial oppression," while suggesting an era long gone, outlines nonetheless precisely what remains at stake in the intercessory gestures of racialization:

> The hallmark of racial oppression in its colonial origins and as it has persisted in subsequent historical contexts is the reduction of all members of the oppressed group to one undifferentiated social status, a status beneath that of any member of any social class within the oppressor group. It is a system of rule designed to deny, disregard, delegitimate previous

and potential social distinctions that may have existed or might tend to emerge in the normal course of development of a class society. (Allen 1997, 177)

+ + +

The oppressive "system of rule" described by Allen courses still through our own era. We hear it effectually performed, for example, by plaintiffs in suits against affirmative action, from Bakke to Hopwood to Gratz and Grutter. Affirmative action cases also show the complexities of the relations between race and gender. Members of racial minorities of all genders and women of all races have hoped that affirmative action would help them achieve greater equality of opportunity—economically and educationally. Yet affirmative action can also generate conflict and competition between racial minorities and women, especially white women.

I will focus here on four cases: *Regents of the University of California v. Bakke,* which reached the US Supreme Court in 1977; *Hopwood v. Texas,* launched in 1992 by Cheryl J. Hopwood, joined by three other plaintiffs; and two cases mounted shortly after the turn of the century, both involving the University of Michigan: *Gratz v. Bollinger* and *Grutter v. Bollinger.* In each, the "equal protection" clause of the Fourteenth Amendment of the US Constitution was put to the test. Adopted as an amendment in July 1868, the Fourteenth Amendment guarantees citizenship to *all* persons born and naturalized in the country. Pursuant to the aims of Reconstruction, in light of the Thirteenth Amendment, passed by Congress three years earlier, it secured the rights of the formerly enslaved and ended the human and juridical ambiguity in which persons of African descent had been trapped for nearly two centuries. Not only did these amendments theoretically level the playing field of national life; they also monumentally stamped equality before the law as a touchstone of the American political system.

The extent to which *reaction* against the citizenship amendments with reference to African Americans overshadowed the best of legislative and constitutional intent cannot be briefly summarized here. Suffice it to say that this reaction endured for a century and beyond. Its intractability was even recognized at the level of the US Supreme Court, attendant on *Bakke,* as "tragic." In short, the citizenship amendments had not dispatched race and the racialized perception of identity from the national imaginary but instead had set the stage for an ongoing confrontation between citizen actors, each armed, at least in theory, as a juridical personality with the power and reach of equality before the law. As Justice Lewis F. Powell Jr., in announcing the judgment of the Court in *Bakke,* put the matter, the sweep and "majesty" of the Fourteenth Amendment essentially rendered it a kind of constitutional "man for all seasons":

> Although many of the Framers of the *Fourteenth Amendment* conceived of its primary function as bridging the vast distance between members of the Negro race and the white "majority" ... the Amendment itself was framed in universal terms, without reference to color, ethnic origin, or condition of prior servitude. (*Regents of the University of California v. Bakke* 1978)

The potential universality of judicial motivation, then, has created difficulties, for it stands squarely behind what has become *predictable* opposition to efforts to remedy or ameliorate decades of discrimination against black Americans in particular and to make them whole.

At the level of *practice*, it would seem that the equal protection clause hurls the nation's ethnicities into a zero-sum game in which X loses some benefit if Y gains (and vice versa). Allan Bakke, for instance, applied to the medical school at the University of California, Davis, in 1973 and 1974; denied admission both years, Bakke, a white male, protested that the campus's special admissions program, which set aside sixteen positions for "disadvantaged" students—"Blacks," "Chicanos," "Asians," and "American Indians"—violated his rights as a private citizen under the equal protection clause. The US Supreme Court's decision, written by Justice Powell, affirmed the California Supreme Court's ruling that Davis's special admissions program was "unlawful" and directed that "respondent [Bakke] be admitted to the Medical School." In affirming the lower court but allowing that the university could nevertheless weigh race as a factor, *Bakke* intruded a pirouette into the dance of admissions to the nation's public colleges and universities, already complicated in the aftermath of the 1964 Civil Rights Act and a long succession of gestures that sought to ameliorate the failures of the country's post-Reconstruction regimes. The Powell opinion laid down guidelines wherein race, always a judicially "suspect" category, ever subject to "strict scrutiny," figures as one of many factors that a university can take into consideration in admitting students. Significantly, the *Bakke* decision permits racial consideration *only* as a means to achieve *diversity*, and only in conjunction with other factors: "The diversity that furthers a compelling state interest encompasses a far broader array of qualifications and characteristics, of which racial or ethnic origin is but a single, though important, element. Petitioner's special admissions program, focused solely on ethnic diversity, would hinder, rather than further, attainment of genuine diversity." An admissions program "which considers race only as one factor is simply a subtle and more sophisticated—but no less effective—means of according racial preference than the Davis program." In comparison, Harvard's admissions program, because it allowed race as one of several factors used to achieve diversity in admissions, is cited as an exemplary instance of admissions protocols in the appendix of the Powell opinion.

It is fair to say that a reparative or restorative regime linked to black Americans has never been given the occasion to succeed precisely because of race, which necessitated restorative efforts in the first place. Compensation because of racial prejudice, historically speaking, was as unthinkable in 1978 as it was in 1865 (when the question of the disposition of former Confederate land was most dramatically posed) and remains so. An "amorphous concept of injury that may be ageless in its reach into the past" is beyond adjudication and can never be materially satisfied in a court of law because the law is negotiating betwixt and between claims that are well defined in space and time. As the Court wrote, "We have never approved a classification that aids persons perceived as members of relatively victimized groups at the expense of other innocent individuals in the absence of judicial, legislative, or administrative findings of constitutional and statutory violations." Moreover, in today's reactionary climate, and in light of *Bakke*'s shift away from race to diversity, those "disadvantaged" subjects that the defunct Davis admissions policies sought to redress (though "black" is still haunted by a spectral presence on the American scene) have long since disappeared into the general category of "minorities." They, in turn, have been dispersed and absorbed into an enormous array of diverse "others" (just about everybody else) that melds gender, sexuality, sexual orientation, and ableness with the more traditional ontological features, for example, class, religion, and region.

In this democratic sweepstakes, women, the time-honored ally of black Americans (though it has not been an alliance without grievous complications), have fared relatively well; some would even say that women and gender as *judicial categories* have outpaced all the others. In any event, wherever race is at issue, it seems that gender is never far behind. In the *Bakke* decision, for example, it is disconcerting to see the petitioner's view of applicable standards compared to "gender based classifications" and disposed of in the following manner: "Gender-based distinctions are less likely to create analytical and practical problems present in preferential programs premised on racial or ethnic criteria. With respect to gender, there are *only two* possible classifications." We suppose that the justice means that there are only "men" and "women" and that, as a result, the "incidence of the burdens imposed by preferential classifications is clear. There are no rival groups which can claim that they, too, are entitled to preferential treatment." Here the language of the opinion lapses into obscurity, but, risking a translation, we might say that Justice Powell, assuming that all the "women" would be white, was gesturing toward what he felt was an unarguable clarity of "disadvantage" in the case of women subjects *as a class*: "Classwide questions as to the group suffering previous injury and groups which fairly can be burdened are relatively manageable for reviewing courts." In other words, "class" as a category of analysis regarding advantage and disadvantage yields a transparence that is absent from "race" analysis. The only problem is that some of the applicants to the Davis program were (and will be) black women and women of color. In any event, "the resolution of these same questions in the context of racial and ethnic preferences presents far more complex and intractable problems than gender-based classifications. More importantly, the perception of racial classifications as inherently odious stems from a lengthy and tragic history that gender-based classifications do not share. In sum, the Supreme Court has never viewed such classification as inherently suspect or as comparable to racial or ethnic classifications for the purpose of equal protection analysis."

This remarkable example of judicial discourse is clear with regard to a benign public disposition toward women as historical subjects, and implicitly enunciates the difference between a *stigmatized* or *marked* category of subjects and one that is not—at least in the United States and in an influential judicial rendering. To be sure, public attitudes toward women are not always benign, to say the very least, but what the court's opinion figures as differences between the *perceptual* regard of gender and of race suggests to my mind a *spatial* dimension of the discriminatory regime: women and gender occupy the *least far distance* to be closed between a social deficit and its abrogation; in other words, the best and the worst of lived experience happens to women because of their *nearness* to masculine arrangements—because they embody *intimate* others—and as such, either on account of actuality and practice, or theory and imagination, women have historically tended to escape the objective exactions of public history and accountability. This is not to say that women of the dominant class or white women have always escaped public censure, but it is to say that black women as marked subjects in the traditional arrangements of power have been defined by their group status, or their relationship to black people defined as an alien and alienable group; so defined, black Americans, historically speaking, were assigned their human status on the basis of laws that granted judicial recognition or the lack of it. We would consider such a relationship public, objective, and distant in its resonance.

The women's movement has been devoted to altering this calculus, to bringing what occurs behind the shut doors of private space into the business of daylight and public life; legislation directed at mitigating violence against women, which takes place often enough within the precincts of an individual's home, lends a case in point. So it is that because women are *felt* to be close at hand (e.g., mothers, wives, daughters, lovers), their social presence might be defined as a subject and object of *access*, virtually unlimited, that is palpable and immediate; this access changes the stakes of the game in a radical way: perhaps we could justifiably contend that under these historical conditions, the largest mandate to one's human transformation is becoming *inaccessible*, or at least the clearing of a space marked "unavailable." Women in the professions, women gazing steadily at the horizon, have initiated this long, arduous, ongoing journey toward an achievement that is at once very simple and very complex—that is to say, toward the ability to assert, in light of whatever loneliness such a position might entail, "I am an extension of no one."

Progression toward the larger goal of women's vocation as competitive public actors is riddled with the tensions of risk and uncertainty. In some cases, the aims of individual actors oppose the aims of others, and on occasion might be outright hostile to them. For example, all of the judicial petitioners since *Bakke* and the initial challenge to special admissions programs adopted by public universities have been white women: Cheryl Hopwood (*Hopwood v. State of Texas*, 2000), Jennifer Gratz (*Gratz v. Bollinger*, 2003), Barbara Grutter (*Grutter v. Bollinger*, 2003), and, most recently, Abigail Noel Fisher, whose claims of discrimination at the University of Texas were accepted for appeal by the US Supreme Court in February 2012, and arguments were heard in October 2012. No decision had been rendered as this essay was going to press.

It is doubtful that *Bakke* can be said to have "authorized" the consideration of race in admissions, but it clearly *allows* it, and the decision established a reasonably clear path for public universities to follow—until the US Supreme Court took up *Gratz v. Bollinger* and *Grutter v. Bollinger*, both decided in June 2003. In those decisions, Justice Sandra Day O'Connor's twenty-five-year gauge emerged as the next *arpeggio* in the nation's disheartening orchestration of its race matters.

In both *Gratz* and *Grutter*, the scene shifts to Michigan and the jurisdiction of the US Court of Appeals for the Sixth Circuit. Jennifer Gratz was first denied early admission, in 1995, and, two years later, regular admission to the College of Literature, Science and the Arts (LSA) at the University of Michigan's flagship campus at Ann Arbor. From what the ruling describes of the university's admissions policies, the Office of Undergraduate Admissions took many factors into consideration: "high school grades, standardized test scores, high school quality, curriculum strength, geography, alumni relationships, leadership and race." But the practice that apparently led to difficulties for that office was the automatic assignment of twenty points (out of one hundred "needed to guarantee admission") to "African-Americans, Hispanics, and Native Americans," that is, "underrepresented minorities." Chief Justice William Rehnquist, delivering the opinion in *Gratz* for the Supreme Court, held that the university's "use of race in its current admissions policy is not narrowly tailored to achieve respondents' asserted interest in diversity" and that consequently the policy "violates the Equal Protection Clause." But at the same time, the Rehnquist opinion holds that "for the reasons set forth in *Grutter v. Bollinger*"—a decision handed down the same day—"the Court has today rejected petitioners' argument that diversity cannot constitute a compelling state interest." The Rehnquist opinion thus struck down the use of race in the particular instance before the court, but did not prohibit it as a single factor for the achievement of diversity as a state interest.

When the law school at Michigan denied Barbara Grutter a seat, she too filed suit, alleging violation of her rights under the Fourteenth Amendment. In the Grutter case, Justice O'Connor, rendering the opinion of the court, argued that the law school's "narrowly tailored use of race in admissions decisions to further a compelling interest in obtaining the educational benefits that flow from a diverse student body is not prohibited by the Equal Protection Clause." Furthermore, the ruling in *Grutter* endorsed Justice Powell's view that "student body diversity is a compelling state interest that can justify using race in university admissions." The law school's admissions standard "bears the hallmarks of a narrowly tailored plan." The O'Connor and Rehnquist opinions, handed down the same day by the high court, show the awful tensions at work even in jurisprudence when the question of race is at stake.

The judicial whirligig to which access to the public university has been subjected over the last three decades or so appears to suggest that a special program for minority admissions to a public university for *any* reason is impermissible, and that, *by definition*, any special admissions program cancels out the occasion for a putative nonminority subject to be treated fairly. If this pessimistic reading is correct, then US society, or at least its courts, is poised to resurrect the status quo in higher education that obtained prior to Title VI and the Civil Rights Act of 1964. Given that the current court is far more conservative than its 1978 iteration (as a determinative outcome of Republican presidencies since Ronald Reagan), and given its majority's apparently unabashed embrace of its role as a *political* actor, we await the next twelve months and the Court's ruling with nervous expectation.

In 2003, as Justice O'Connor neared the conclusion of her opinion in *Grutter*, she struck a subjunctive note: "The Court expects that 25 years from now, the use of racial preferences will no longer be necessary to further the interest approved today." 2028, anyone? Race thinking can tie up a community's spiritual, intellectual, and material energies for the long term and to an astonishing degree. Even as the plaintiffs in these cases have every right to seek admission to the university, as well as to share in various aspects of the common good, their competitors are not limited to representative black and colored peoples but, rather, are consonant with all petitioners, right across the race divide; all citizen actors seek the benefits of higher education and training for the professions. The social logic put to work in these instances, embedded in much older historical regimes, is staked out on the idea that hundreds of empirical subjects are, at all times, inferior to hundreds of others. How came these seats to belong to anyone in particular, we might ask? The entanglements of race assure a general consensus that were it not for X, then Y would be able to achieve what is hers by birthright. Repeated often enough, such belief acquires the force of law and, even better, the irrepressible rhythms of natural phenomena.

While mired in the stuff of modern history, race appears to transcend it, given the fact that its conceptual and practical recurrence haunts generations of actors whatever their particular habitude. But the recently closed century also suggests, by way of paradox, that race need not be destiny in light of altered practice and conviction. Enhanced global relatedness, inspired primarily by triumphant market forces, has ushered into ever bolder relief the contradictions of race, insofar as the color that matters now is green. That was arguably always the case, except that the new "primitive accumulations" and consolidations of power, global and otherwise, appear to have reanimated the fiction of race and fired up, once again, the brazen engines of its indispensable mysticisms.

In this uneasy new climate of alienated social relations, race "returns" as the glamorous overlay of a fashionable diversity. What we have learned to our chagrin is that gender cannot help us negotiate this new landscape because it must compete against all the other interested parties. But gender, nevertheless, as well as women, seems perfectly positioned today to be forced to learn, all over again, lessons that it seems to have forgotten—that no advantage is secured and secure for any individual, or social formation, when the blessings of commonwealth are denied to any other; this is the only thing in a democracy that we know for sure.

The 2012 election season, for example, with its radical right-wing challenges to women's rights (placing us perhaps only a president away from the abrogation of many of those rights), places gender, in addition to race, along parallel lines of concern where they have subsisted, in tandem, sometimes pulling together, sometimes pulling away from each other, for many decades now.

References

Allen, Theodore. 1997. *The Invention of the White Race: The Origin of Racial Oppression in Anglo-America*. London: Verso.

Cott, Nancy. 1987. *The Grounding of Modern Feminism*. New Haven, CT: Yale University Press.

de Beauvoir, Simone. (1953) 1974. *The Second Sex*. Trans. and ed. H. M. Parshley. New York: Vintage.

de Lauretis, Teresa. 1987. *Technologies of Gender: Essays on Theory, Film, and Fiction*. Bloomington: Indiana University Press.

Ellison, Ralph. 1992. *Invisible Man*. New York: Modern Library.

Fanon, Frantz. 1967. *Black Skin, White Masks*. Trans. Charles Lam Markmann. New York: Grove Press.

Friedan, Betty. (1963) 2001. *The Feminine Mystique*. With an introduction by Anna Quindlen. New York: Norton.

Goldberg, David Theo. 2002. *The Racial State*. Oxford: Blackwell Publishers.

Gossett, Thomas. 1963. *Race: The History of an Idea in America*. Dallas: Southern Methodist University Press.

Gratz v. Bollinger. 2003. 539 US 244. http://www.law.cornell.edu/supct/html/02-516.ZS.html.

Grutter v. Bollinger. 2003. 539 US 306. 288 F.3d 732, affirmed. http://www.law.cornell.edu/supct/html/02-241.ZS.html.

Hannaford, Ivan. 1996. *The History of an Idea in the West*. Baltimore: Johns Hopkins University Press/Woodrow Wilson Center.

Hopwood v. State of Texas. 2000. 236 F.3d 256, United States US Court of Appeals, Fifth Circuit. http://www.caselaw.findlaw.com/us_5th_circuit/1120774.html.

Hull, Akasha (Gloria), Patricia Bell Scott, and Barbara Smith, eds. 1982. *All the Women Are White, All the Blacks Are Men, but Some of Us Are Brave*. Old Westbury, NY: Feminist Press.

Jordan, Winthrop. *White over Black: American Attitudes toward the Negro, 1550–1812*. Chapel Hill: University of North Carolina Press.

Kenan, Randall, ed. 2010. *James Baldwin: The Cross of Redemption—Uncollected Writings*. New York: Pantheon.

Kolmar, Wendy and Frances Bartkowski, eds. 2010. *Feminist Theory: A Reader*. 3rd ed. Boston: McGraw Hill.

Matsuda, Mari J., Charles R. Lawrence, III, Richard Delgado, and Kimberle Williams Crenshaw. 1993. *Words That Wound: Critical Race Theory, Assaultive Speech, and the First Amendment*. Boulder, CO: Westview Press.

Moss, Hilary. 2011. "Satoshi Kanazawa Causes Firestorm After Claiming Black Women

Are Less Attractive." *Huffington Post*, May 17. www.huffingtonpost.com/2011/05/17
/Satoshi-Kanazawa-black-women-less-attractive_n_863327.html (accessed March 16,
2012)

Newman, Jane O. 2002. "The Present and Our Past: Simone De Beauvoir, Descartes, and
Presentism in the Historiography of Feminism." In *Women's Studies on Its Own*, ed.
Robyn Wiegman. Durham, NC: Duke University Press.

Pocock, J.G.A. 1995. "The Ideal of Citizenship since Classical Times." In *Theorizing Citizenship*, ed. Ronald Beiner. Albany: SUNY Press.

Regents of the University of California v. Bakke. 1978. 438 US 265. 18 Cal.3d 34, 553 P.2d 1152,
affirmed in part and reversed in part. http://www.law.cornell.edu/supremecourt/text
/438/265.

Scott, Joan Wallach. 1988. *Gender and the Politics of History*. New York: Columbia University Press.

Stohr, Greg, and John Hechinger, 2012. "University Affirmtive Action Threatened By US
Top Court Admissions Case." *Bloomberg Business Week*, February 22. http://www
.businessweek.com/news/2012-02-22/college-affirmative-action-threatened-by-u-s
-high-court-case.html.

Wiegman, Robyn. 2012. *Object Lessons*. Durham, NC: Duke University Press.

18 :: REGULATION   JUDITH BUTLER

At first glance, the term *regulation* appears to suggest the institutionalization of the process by which persons are made regular. Indeed, to refer
to "regulations," in the plural, is already to acknowledge those concrete
laws, rules, and policies that constitute the legal instruments through
which persons are made regular. But it would be a mistake, I believe, to
understand all the ways in which gender is regulated in terms of those
empirical legal instances, because the norms that govern those regulations exceed the very instances in which they are embodied. On the other
hand, it would be equally problematic to speak of the regulation of gender in the abstract, as if the empirical instances only exemplified an operation of power that take s place independently of those instances.

Indeed, much of the most important work in feminist and lesbian/gay
studies has concentrated on actual regulations: legal, military, psychiatric, and a host of others. The kinds of questions posed within such scholarship tend to ask how gender is regulated, how such regulations are imposed, and how they become incorporated and lived by the subjects on
whom they are imposed. But for gender to be regulated is not simply for
gender to come under the exterior force of a regulation (Smart 1992). If
gender were to exist prior to its regulation, we could then take gender as
our theme and proceed to enumerate the various kinds of regulations to
which it is subjected and the ways in which that subjection takes place.
The problem, however, for us is more acute. After all, is there a gender
that preexists its regulation, or is it the case that, in being subject to
regulation, the gendered subject emerges, produced in and through that
particular form of subjection? Is subjection not the process by which regulations produce gender?

It is important to remember at least two caveats on subjection and
regulation derived from Foucauldian scholarship: (1) regulatory power
not only acts upon a preexisting subject but also shapes and forms that
subject; moreover, every juridical form of power has its productive effect.

And (2) to become subject to a regulation is also to become subjectivated by it, that is, to be brought into being as a subject precisely through being regulated. This second point follows from the first in that the regulatory discourses that form the subject of gender are precisely those that require and induce the subject in question.

Particular kinds of regulations may be understood as instances of a more general regulatory power, one that is specified as the regulation of gender. Here, I contravene Foucault in some respects. For if the Foucauldian wisdom seems to consist in the insight that regulatory power has certain broad historical characteristics, and that it operates on gender as well as on other kinds of social and cultural norms, then it seems that gender is but the instance of a larger regulatory operation of power. I would argue against this subsumption of gender to regulatory power, and that the regulatory apparatus that governs gender is one that is itself gender-specific. I do not mean to suggest that the regulation of gender is paradigmatic of regulatory power as such, but rather, that gender requires and institutes its own distinctive regulatory and disciplinary regime.

The suggestion that gender is a norm requires some further elaboration. A norm is not the same as a rule, and it is not the same as a law (Ewald 1986, 1991, 1992; Taylor 1993). A norm operates within social practices as the implicit standard of *normalization*. Although a norm may be analytically separable from the practices in which it is embedded, it may also prove to be recalcitrant to any effort to decontextualize its operation. Norms may or may not be explicit, and when they operate as the normalizing principle in social practice, they usually remain implicit, difficult to read, discernible most clearly and dramatically in the effects that they produce.

For gender to be a norm suggests that it is always and only tenuously embodied by any particular social actor. The norm governs the social intelligibility of action, but it is not the same as the action that it governs. The norm appears to be indifferent to the actions that it governs, by which I mean only that the norm appears to have a status and effect that is independent of the actions governed by the norm. The norm governs intelligibility, allows for certain kinds of practices and actions to become recognizable as such, imposing a grid of legibility on the social and defining the parameters of what will and will not appear within the domain of the social. The question of what it is to be outside the norm poses a paradox for thinking, for if the norm renders the social field intelligible and normalizes that field for us, then being outside the norm is in some sense being defined still in relation to it. To be not quite masculine or not quite feminine is still to be understood exclusively in terms of one's relation to the "quite masculine" and the "quite feminine."

To claim that gender is a norm is not quite the same as saying that there are normative views of femininity and masculinity, even though there clearly are such normative views. Gender is not exactly what one "is," nor is it precisely what one "has." Gender is the apparatus by which the production and normalization of masculine and feminine take place along with the interstitial forms—hormonal, chromosomal, psychic, and performative—that gender assumes. To assume that gender always and exclusively means the matrix of the "masculine" and "feminine" is precisely to miss the critical point that the production of that coherent binary is contingent, that it comes at a cost, and that those permutations of gender that do not fit the binary are as much a part of gender as its most normative instance. To conflate the definition of gender with its normative expression is inadvertently to reconsolidate the power of the norm to constrain the definition of gender. Gender is the mechanism by which notions of masculine and feminine are produced and naturalized, but gender might very well also be the apparatus by which such terms are deconstructed and denaturalized. Indeed, it may be that the very apparatus that seeks to install the norm also works to undermine that installation, that the installation is, as it were, definitionally incomplete. To keep the term *gender* apart from both masculinity and femininity is to safeguard a theoretical perspective by which one might offer an account of how the binary of masculine and feminine comes to exhaust the semantic field of gender. Whether one refers to "gender trouble" or "gender blending," "transgender" or "cross-gender," one is already suggesting that gender has a way of moving beyond the naturalized binary. The conflation of gender with masculine/feminine, man/woman, male/female, thus performs the very naturalization that the notion of gender is meant to forestall.

Thus, a restrictive discourse on gender that insists on the binary of man and woman as the exclusive way to understand the gender field performs a *regulatory* operation of power that naturalizes the hegemonic instance and forecloses the thinkability of its disruption.

One tendency within gender studies has been to assume that the alternative to the binary system of gender is a multiplication of genders. Such an approach invariably provokes the question How many genders can there be, and what will they be called? (Trumbach 1998; Fausto-Sterling 2000). But the disruption of the binary system need not lead us to an equally problematic quantification of gender. Luce Irigaray, following a Lacanian lead, asks whether the masculine sex is the "one" sex, meaning not only "the one and only," but the one that inaugurates a quantitative approach to sex. "Sex," in her view, is neither a biological category nor a social one (and is thus distinct from "gender") but a linguistic one that exists, as it were, on the divide between the social and the biological. "The sex which is not one" is thus femininity understood precisely as what cannot be captured by number (Irigaray 1985). Other approaches insist that "transgender" is not exactly a third gender but a mode of passage between genders, an interstitial and transitional figure of gender that is not reducible to the normative insistence on one or two (Bornstein 1994).

Symbolic Position and Social Norms

Although some theorists maintain that norms are always social norms, Lacanian theorists, indebted to the structuralism of Claude Lévi-Strauss, insist that symbolic norms are not the same as social ones, and that a certain "regulation" of gender takes place through the symbolic demand that is placed on psyches from this inception.

The *symbolic* became a technical term for Jacques Lacan in 1953 and became his own way of compounding mathematical (formal) and anthropological uses of the term. In a dictionary on Lacanian parlance, the symbolic is explicitly linked with the problem of regulation: "The symbolic is the realm of the Law which *regulates* desire in the Oedipus complex" (Evans 1996, 202; my emphasis). That complex is understood to be derived from a primary or symbolic prohibition against incest, a prohibition that makes sense only in terms of kinship relations in which various "positions" are established within the family according to an exogamic mandate. In other words, a mother is someone with whom a son and daughter do not have sexual relations, and a father is someone with whom a son and daughter do not have sexual relations; a mother only has sexual relations with the father; and so forth. These relations of prohibition are encoded in the "positions" that each of these family members occupies. To be in such a position is thus to be in such a crossed sexual relation, at least according to the symbolic or normative conception of what that position is.

The consequences of this view are clearly enormous. In many ways, the structuralist legacy within psychoanalytic thinking exerted monumental effect on feminist film and literary theory, as well as feminist approaches to psychoanalysis throughout the disciplines. It also paved the way for a queer critique of feminism that has had, and continues to have, inevitably divisive and consequential effects within sexuality and gender studies. In what follows, I hope to show how the notion of culture that becomes transmuted into the "symbolic" for Lacanian psychoanalysis is very different from the notion of culture that remains current within the contemporary field of cultural studies, such that the two enterprises are often understood as hopelessly opposed. I also argue that any claim to establish the rules that "regulate desire" in an inalterable and eternal realm of law has limited use for a theory that seeks to understand the conditions under which the social transformation of gender is possible. Another concern regarding the symbolic is that the prohibition of incest can be one of the motivations for its own transgression, which suggests that the symbolic positions of kinship are in many ways defeated by the very sexuality that they produce through regulation (Bell 1993). Lastly, I hope to show that the distinction between symbolic and social law cannot finally hold, that the symbolic itself is the sedimentation of social practices, and that radical alterations in kinship demand a rearticulation of the structuralist presuppositions of psychoanalysis, moving us, as it were, toward a queer poststructuralism of the psyche.

To return to the incest taboo, the question emerges, What is the status of these prohibitions and these positions? Lévi-Strauss makes clear in *The Elementary Structures of Kinship* (1969) that nothing in biology necessitates the incest taboo, that it is a purely *cultural* phenomenon. By "cultural," he does not mean "culturally variable" or "contingent" but, rather, according to "universal" laws of culture. Thus, for Lévi-Strass, cultural rules are not alterable rules (as Gayle Rubin subsequently argued) but are inalterable and universal. The domain of a universal and eternal rule of culture—what Juliet Mitchell calls "the universal and primordial law" (Mitchell 1975, 370)—becomes the basis for the Lacanian notion of the symbolic and the subsequent efforts to divide the symbolic from both the biological and social domains. In Lacan, that which is universal in culture is understood to be its symbolic or linguistic rules, and these are understood to support kinship relations. The very possibility of pronominal reference, of an "I," a "you," a "we," and a "they" appears to rely on this mode of kinship that operates in and as language. This is a slide from the cultural to the linguistic, one toward which Lévi-Strauss himself gestures toward the end of *The Elementary Structures of Kinship*. In Lacan, the symbolic becomes defined in terms of a conception of linguistic structures that are irreducible to the social forms that language takes. According to structuralist terms, it establishes the universal conditions under which the sociality, that is, communicability of all language use, becomes possible. This move paves the way for the consequential distinction between symbolic and social accounts of kinship. Hence, a norm is not quite the same as a "symbolic position" in the Lacanian sense, which appears to enjoy a quasi-timeless character, regardless of the qualifications offered in the endnotes to several of Lacan's seminars. The Lacanians almost always insist that a symbolic position is not the same as a social one, that it would be a mistake to take the symbolic position of the father, for instance, which is after all the paradigmatically symbolic position, and mistake that for a socially constituted and alterable position that fathers have assumed throughout time. The Lacanian view insists that there is an ideal and unconscious demand that is made upon social life that remains irreducible to socially legible causes and effects. The symbolic place of the father does not cede to the demands for a social reorganization of paternity. Instead, the symbolic is precisely what sets limits to any and all utopian efforts to reconfigure and relive kinship relations at some distance from the Oedipal scene (Tort 1983; 1989, 46–59; also "Le différend" [on file with the author]).

One of the problems that emerged when the study of kinship was combined with the study of structural linguistics is that kinship positions were elevated to the status of fundamental linguistic structures. These are positions that make possible the entry into language and which, therefore, maintain an essential status with respect to language. They are, in other words, positions without which no signification could proceed, or, in a different language, no cultural intelligibility can be secured. What were the consequences of making certain conceptions of kinship timeless and elevating them to the status of the elementary structures of intelligibility?

Although Lévi-Strauss purports to consider a variety of kinship systems, he does so in the service of delimiting those principles of kinship that assume cross-cultural status. What is offered by structuralism as a "position" within language or kinship is not the same as a "norm," for the latter is a socially produced and variable framework. A norm is not the same as a symbolic position. Moreover, if a symbolic position is more appropriately regarded as a norm, then a symbolic position is not the same as itself but is, rather, a contingent norm whose contingency has been covered over by a theoretical reification that bears potentially stark consequences for gendered life. One might respond within the structuralist conceit with the claim "But this is the law!" What is the status of such an utterance, however? "It is the law" becomes the utterance that performatively attributes the very force to the law that the law itself is said to exercise. "It is the law" is thus a sign of allegiance to the law, a sign of the desire for the law to be the indisputable law, a theological impulse within the theory of psychoanalysis that seeks to put out of play any criticism of the symbolic father, the law of psychoanalysis itself. Thus, the status given to the law is, not surprisingly, precisely the status given to the phallus, where the phallus is not merely a privileged "signifier" within the Lacanian scheme but also becomes the characteristic feature of the theoretical apparatus in which that signifier is introduced. In other words, the authoritative force that shores up the incontestability of the symbolic law is itself an exercise of that symbolic law, a further instance of the place of the father, as it were, indisputable and incontestable. Although there are, as Lacanians will remind us, only and always contestations of the symbolic, they fail to exercise any final force to undermine the symbolic itself or to force a radical reconfiguration of its terms.

The authority of the theory exposes its own tautological defense within the fact that the symbolic survives any and every contestation of its authority. It is not only a theory, that is, that insists upon masculine and feminine as symbolic positions that are finally beyond all contestation and that set the limit to contestation as such, but also one that relies on the very authority it describes to shore up the authority of its own descriptive claims.

To separate the symbolic from the social sphere facilitates the distinction between the Law and variable laws. In the place of a critical practice that anticipates no final authority, and which opens up an anxiety-producing field of gendered possibilities, the symbolic emerges to put an end to such anxiety. If there is a Law that we cannot displace, but which we seek through imaginary means to displace again and again, then we know in advance that our efforts at change will be put in check, and our struggle against the authoritative account of gender will be thwarted, and we will submit to an unassailable authority. There are those who believe that to think that the symbolic itself might be changed by human practice is pure voluntarism. But is it? One can certainly concede that desire is radically conditioned without claiming that it is radically determined, and one can acknowledge that there are structures that make desire possible without claiming that those structures are timeless and recalcitrant, impervious to a reiterative replay and displacement. To contest symbolic authority is not necessarily to return to the "ego" or classical liberal notions of freedom; rather, to do so is to insist that the norm in its necessary temporality is opened to a displacement and subversion from within.

The symbolic is understood as the sphere that regulates the assumption of sex, where sex is understood as a differential set of positions, masculine and feminine. Thus, the concept of gender, derived as it is from sociological discourse, is foreign to the discourse on sexual difference that emerges from the Lacanian and post-Lacanian framework. Lacan was clearly influenced by Lévi-Strauss's *Elementary Structures of Kinship*, first published in 1947, approximately six years before Lacan uses the term.

Jean Laplanche and J.-B. Pontalis write under the entry "Symbolique" in *The Language of Psycho-Analysis* that the "idea of a symbolic order structuring intersubjective reality was introduced into the social sciences most notably by Claude Lévi-Strauss who based his view on the model of structural linguistics taught by F. de Saussure. The thesis of [Saussure's] *The Course in General Linguistics* (1955) is that the linguistic signified does not take place internally to the signifier; it produces a signification because it is part of a system of signifieds characterized by differential opposi-tions" (Laplanche and Pontalis 1973). They cite Lévi-Strauss: "Every cul-ture may be considered as an ensemble of symbolic systems which in the first instance regulate the taking place of language, matrimonial rules, economic relations, art, science, and religion" (Laplanche and Pontalis 1973). Lacan makes use of the symbolic, according to these authors, to establish that the unconscious is structured like a language and to show the linguistic fecundity of the unconscious. The second use to which it is put, however, bears more directly on our inquiry, that is, "to show that the human subject is inserted in a pre-established order which is itself a symbolic nature, in the sense that Lévi-Strauss describes" (Laplanche and Pontalis 1973).

In this view, one which is distinguished from that of other Lacanian expositeurs such as Malcolm Bowie, the sense of the symbolic as a pre-established order is in tension with Lacan's insistence that there be an arbitrary relation between signifier and signified. On some occasions, it seems, Lacan uses "the symbolic" to describe the discrete elements that function as signifieds, but at other times he appears to use the term to describe the more general register in which those elements function. In addition, Laplanche and Pontalis argue that Lacan uses "the symbolic" "to designate the law (la loi) that founds this order." The foreclosure of the "symbolic father" or "the Name of the Father" is such an instance of founding that is irreducible to an imaginary or real father, and which en-forces the law. Of course, no one inhabits the position of the symbolic father, and it is that "absence" that paradoxically gives the law its power.

Although Bowie maintains that the symbolic is governed by the sym-bolic law (1991, 108), he also maintains that "the symbolic is often spoken of admiringly ... it is the realm of movement rather than fixity, and of heterogeneity rather than similarity ... the Symbolic is inveterately so-cial and intersubjective ..." (1991, 92–93). The question remains, though, whether the "social" sphere designated by the symbolic is not governed by "the Name of the Father," a symbolic place for the father, which, if lost (the place, and not the father), leads to psychosis. What presocial con-straint is thereby imposed upon the intelligibility of any social order?

In the Lévi-Straussian model, the position of man and woman is what makes possible certain forms of sexual exchange. In this sense, gender operates to secure certain forms of reproductive sexual ties and to pro-hibit other forms. One's gender, in this view, is an index of the proscribed and prescribed sexual relations by which a subject is socially regulated and produced.

According to Lévi-Strauss, the rules that govern sexual exchange, and which, accordingly, produce viable subject positions on the basis of that regulation of sexuality, are distinct from the individuals who abide by those rules and occupy such positions. That human actions are regulated by such laws but do not have the power to transform the substance and aim of their laws appears to be the consequence of a conception of law that is indifferent to the content that it regulates. How does a shift from thinking about gender as regulated by symbolic laws to a conception of gender as regulated by social norms contest this indifference of the law to what it regulates? And how does such a shift open up the possibility of a more radical contestation of the law itself?

If gender is a norm, it is not the same as a model that individuals seek to approximate. On the contrary, it is a form of social power that produces the intelligible field of subjects and an apparatus by which the gender binary is instituted. As a norm that appears independent of the practices that it governs, its ideality is the reinstituted effect of those very practices. This suggests not only that the relation between practices and the idealizations under which they work is contingent, but also that the very idealization can be brought into question and crisis, potentially undergoing deidealization and divestiture.

The distance between gender and its naturalized instantiations is precisely the distance between a norm and its incorporations. I suggested above that the norm is analytically independent of its incorporations, but I want to emphasize that this is only an intellectual heuristic, one that helps to guarantee the perpetuation of the norm itself as a timeless and inalterable ideal. In fact, the norm only persists as a norm to the extent that it is acted out in social practice and reidealized and reinstituted in and through the daily social rituals of bodily life. The norm has no independent ontological status, yet it cannot be easily reduced to its instantiations; it is itself (re)produced through its embodiment, through the acts that strive to approximate it, through the idealizations reproduced in and by those acts.

Foucault brought the discourse of the norm into currency by arguing, in volume 1 of his *History of Sexuality*, that the nineteenth century saw the emergence of the norm as a means of social regulation that is not identical with the operations of law. Influenced by Foucault, the sociologist François Ewald has expanded upon this remark in several essays (Ewald 1986, 1991, 1992). Ewald argues that the action of the norm is at the expense of the juridical system of the law, and that although normalization entails an increase in legislation, it is not necessarily opposed to it, but remains independent of it in some significant ways (Ewald 1991, 138).

Foucault notes that the norm often appears in legal form and that the normative comes to the fore most typically in constitutions, legal codes, and the constant and clamorous activity of the legislature (Foucault 1978, pt. 5). He further claims that a norm belongs to the arts of judgment and that, although a norm is clearly related to power, it is characterized less by the use of force or violence than by, as Ewald puts it, "an implicit logic that allows power to reflect upon its own strategies and clearly define its objects. This logic is at once the force that enables us to imagine life and the living as objects of power and the power that can take 'life' in hand, creating the sphere of the bio-political" (Ewald 1991, 138).

For Ewald, this raises at least two questions: whether, for instance, modernity participates in the logic of the norm, and what the relation between norms and the law would be. It is perhaps useful to note at this point the important historical work that Georges Canguilhem has done on the history of the normal in *The Normal and the Pathological* (1989). Ewald remarks that the etymology links the norm with mathematical and architectural prototypes. *Norm* is, literally, the Latin word for a T-square; and *normalis* means perpendicular. Vitruvius used the word to indicate the instrument used to draw right angles, and Cicero used the term to describe the architectural regularity of nature; nature, he claimed, is the norm of the law.

Although "the norm" is sometimes used as synonymous with "the rule," it is clear that norms are also what give rules a certain local coherence. Ewald claims that the beginning of the nineteenth century inaugurates a radical change in the relation between the rule and the norm (1991, 140) and that the norm emerges conceptually not only as *a particular variety of rules*, but also as *a way of producing them* and as *a principle of valorization*. In French, the term *normalité* appears in 1834, *normatif* in 1868, and in Germany at the end of the nineteenth century we get the normative sciences (which, I gather, gets carried forward in the name of the division at the contemporary American Political Science Association meetings called "normative political theory"); the term *normalization* appears in 1920. For Foucault as well as Ewald, it corresponds to the normalizing operation of bureaucratic and disciplinary powers.

According to Ewald, the norm transforms constraints into a mechanism, and thus marks the movement by which, in Foucauldian terms, juridical power becomes productive; it transforms the negative restraints of the juridical into the more positive controls of normalization; thus the norm performs this transformative function. The norm thus marks and effects the shift from thinking power as juridical constraint to thinking power as (a) an organized set of constraints and (b) a regulatory mechanism.

Norms and the Problem of Abstraction

This then returns us to the question not only of how discourse might be said to produce a subject (something everywhere assumed in cultural studies but rarely investigated in its own right) but, more precisely, what in discourse effects that production. When Foucault claims that discipline "produces" individuals, he means not only that disciplinary discourse *manages* and *makes use of them* but that it also *actively constitutes them*.

The norm is a measurement and a means of producing a common standard; to become an instance of the norm is not fully to exhaust the norm but, rather, to become subjected to an abstraction of commonality. Although Foucault and Ewald tend to concentrate their analyses of this process in the nineteenth and twentieth centuries, Mary Poovey in *Making a Social Body* dates the history of abstraction in the social sphere to the late eighteenth century. In Britain, she maintains, "The last decades of the eighteenth century witnessed the first modern efforts to represent all—or significant parts—of the population of Britain as aggregates and to delineate a social sphere distinct from the political and economic domains" (Poovey 1995, 8). What characterizes this social domain, in her view, is the entrance of quantitative measurement: "Such comparisons and measurement, of course, produce some phenomena as normative— ostensibly because they are numerous, because they represent an average, or because they constitute an ideal toward which all other phenomena move" (1995, 9).

Ewald seeks a narrower definition of the norm in order to understand its capacity to regulate all social phenomena as well as the internal limits it faces in any such regulation (1992, 170–71). He writes:

> What precisely is the norm? It is the measure which simultaneously individualises, makes ceaseless individualisation possible and creates comparability. The norm makes it possible to locate spaces, indefinitely, which become more and more discrete, minute, and at the same time makes sure that these spaces never enclose anyone in such a way as to create a nature for them, since these individualising spaces *are never more than the expression of a relationship*, of a relationship which has to be seen indefinitely in the context of others. What is a norm? A principle of comparison, of comparability, a common measure, which is instituted in the pure reference of one group to itself, when the group has no relationship other than to itself, without external reference and without verticality. (Ewald 1991, 173; my emphasis)

According to Ewald, Foucault adds this to the thinking of normalization: "Normative individualization is not exterior. The abnormal does not have a nature which is different from that of the normal. The norm, or normative space, knows no outside. The norm integrates anything which might attempt to go beyond it—nothing, nobody, whatever difference it might display, can ever claim to be exterior, or claim to possess an otherness which would actually make it other" (Ewald 1991, 173).

Such a view suggests that any opposition to the norm is already contained within the norm and is crucial to its own functioning. Indeed, at this point in our analysis, it appears that moving from a Lacanian notion of symbolic position to a more Foucauldian conception of "social norm" does not augment the chances for an effective displacement or resignification of the norm itself.

In the work of Pierre Macheray, however, one begins to see that norms are not independent and self-subsisting entities or abstractions but must be understood as forms of action. In "Towards a Natural History of Norms," Macheray makes clear that the kind of causality that norms exercise is not transitive, but immanent, and he seeks recourse to Spinoza and Foucault to make his claim:

> To think in terms of the immanence of the norm is indeed to refrain from considering the action of the norm in a restrictive manner, seeing it as a form of "repression" formulated in terms of interdiction exercised against a given subject in advance of the performance of this action, thus implying that this subject could, on his own, liberate himself or be liberated from this sort of control: the history of madness, just like that of sexuality, shows that such "liberation," far from suppressing the action of norms, on the contrary reinforces it. But one might also wonder if it is enough to denounce the illusions of this anti-repressive discourse in order to escape from them: does one not run the risk of reproducing them on another level, where they cease to be naïve but where, though of a more learned nature, they still remain out of step in relation to the context at which they seem to be aiming? (Macheray 1991, 185)

By maintaining that the norm only subsists in and through its actions, Macheray effectively locates action as the site of social intervention: "From this point of view it is no longer possible to think of the norm itself in advance of the consequences of its action, as being in some way behind them and independent of them; *the norm has to be considered such as it acts precisely in its effects*—in such a way, not so as to limit the reality by means of simple conditioning, but in order to confer upon it the maximum amount of reality of which it is capable" (Macheray 1991, 186; my emphasis).

I mentioned above that the norm cannot be reduced to any of its instances, but I would add: neither can the norm be fully extricated from its instantiations. The norm is not exterior to its field of application. Not only is the norm responsible for producing its field of application, according to Macheray (187), but *the norm produces itself in the production of that field*. The norm is actively conferring reality; indeed, only by virtue of its repeated power to confer reality is the norm constituted as a norm.

Gender Norms

According to the notion of norms elaborated above, we might say that the field of reality produced by gender norms constitutes the background for the surface appearance of gender in its idealized dimensions. But how are we to understand the historical formation of such ideals, their persistence through time, and their site as a complex convergence of social meanings that do not immediately appear to be about gender? To the extent that gender norms are *reproduced*, they are invoked and cited by bodily practices that also have the capacity to alter norms in the course of their citation. One cannot offer a full narrative account of the citational history of the norm: whereas narrativity does not fully conceal its history, neither does it reveal a single origin.

One important sense of regulation, then, is that persons are regulated by gender, and that this sort of regulation operates as a condition of cultural intelligibility for any person. To veer from the gender norm is to produce the aberrant example that regulatory powers (medical, psychiatric, and legal, to name a few) may quickly exploit to shore up the rationale for their own continuing regulatory zeal. The question remains, though: What departures from the norm constitute something other than an excuse or rationale for the continuing authority of the norm? What departures from the norm disrupt the regulatory process itself?

The question of surgical "correction" for intersex children is one case in point. There the argument is made that children born with irregular primary sexual characteristics are to be "corrected" in order to fit in, feel more comfortable, achieve normality. Corrective surgery is sometimes performed with parental support and in the name of normalization, and the physical and psychic costs of the surgery have proven to be enormous for those persons who have been submitted, as it were, to the knife of the norm (Chase 1998, 189–211). The bodies produced through such a regulatory enforcement of gender are bodies in pain, bearing the marks of violence and suffering. Here the ideality of gendered morphology is quite literally incised in the flesh.

Gender is thus a regulatory norm, but it is also one that is produced in the service of other kinds of regulation. For instance, sexual harassment codes tend to assume, following the reasoning of Catharine MacKinnon, that harassment consists of the systematic sexual subordination of women at the workplace, and that men are generally in the position of the harasser, and women, of the harassed. For MacKinnon, this seems to be the consequence of a more fundamental sexual subordination of women. Although these regulations seek to constrain sexually demeaning behavior at the workplace, they also carry within them certain tacit norms of gender. In a sense, the implicit regulation of gender takes place through the explicit regulation of sexuality.

For MacKinnon, the hierarchical structure of heterosexuality, in which men are understood to subordinate women, is what produces gender: "Stopped as an attribute of a person, sex inequality takes the form of gender; moving as a relation between people, it takes the form of sexuality. Gender emerges as the congealed form of the sexualization of inequality between men and women" (MacKinnon 1987, 6–7).

If gender is the congealed form that the sexualization of inequality takes, then the sexualization of inequality precedes gender, and gender is its effect. But can we even conceptualize the sexualization of inequality without a prior conception of gender? Does it make sense to claim that men subordinate women sexually if we don't first have an idea of what men and women are? MacKinnon maintains, however, that there is no constitution of gender outside of this form of sexuality and, by implication, outside of this subordinating and exploitative form of sexuality.

In proposing the regulation of sexual harassment through recourse to this kind of analysis of the systematic character of sexual subordination, MacKinnon institutes a regulation of another kind: to have a gender means to have entered already into a heterosexual relationship of subordination. There appear to be no gendered people who are outside of such relationships; there appear to be no nonsubordinating heterosexual relations; there appear to be no nonheterosexual relations; there appears to be no same-sex harassment.

This form of reducing gender to sexuality has thus given way to two separate but overlapping concerns within contemporary queer theory. The first move is to separate sexuality from gender, so that to have a gender does not presuppose that one engages in sexual practice in any particular way, and to engage in a given sexual practice, anal sex, for instance, does not presuppose that one is a given gender. (This position is put forward by Gayle Rubin in her essay "Thinking Sex" and elaborated upon in Eve Kosofsky Sedgwick's *Epistemology of the Closet*.) The second and related move within queer theory is to argue that gender is not reducible to hierarchical heterosexuality; that it takes different forms when contextualized by queer sexualities, indeed, that its binariness cannot be taken for granted outside the heterosexual frame; that gender itself is internally unstable; that transgendered lives are evidence of the break-down of any lines of causal determinism between sexuality and gender. The dissonance between gender and sexuality is thus affirmed from two different perspectives: the one seeks to show possibilities for sexuality that are not constrained by gender in order to break the causal reductive-ness of arguments that bind them; the other seeks to show possibilities for gender that are not predetermined by forms of hegemonic heterosex-uality. (My own work runs in this direction and is closely allied with that of Biddy Martin, Joan W. Scott, Katherine Franke, and the emergence of transgender theory.)

The problem with basing sexual harassment codes on a view of sexu-ality in which gender is the concealed effect of sexualized subordination within heterosexuality is that certain views of gender and certain views of sexuality are reinforced through the reasoning. In MacKinnon's the-ory, gender is produced in the scene of sexual subordination, and sex-ual harassment is the explicit moment of the institution of heterosexual subordination. What this means, effectively, is that sexual harassment becomes the allegory for the production of gender. In my view, the sexual harassment codes become themselves the instrument by which gender is thus reproduced.

It is the regulation of gender, argues legal scholar Katherine Franke, that remains not only uninterrogated in this view, but unwittingly abetted:

> What is wrong with the world MacKinnon describes in her work is not ex-hausted by the observation that men dominate women, although that is descriptively true in most cases. Rather, the problem is far more system-atic. By reducing sexism to only that which is done to women by men, we lose sight of the underlying ideology that makes sexism so powerful.... The subordination of women by men is part of a larger social practice that creates gendered bodies—feminine women and masculine men. (Franke 1997, 761)

The social punishments that follow upon transgressions of gender in-clude the surgical correction of intersex persons; the medical and psy-chiatric pathologization and criminalization in several countries, includ-ing the United States, of "gender dysphoric" people; the harassment of gender-troubled persons on the street or in the workplace; employment discrimination; and violence. The prohibition of sexual harassment of women by men that is based on a rationale that assumes heterosexual subordination as the exclusive scene of sexuality and gender thus itself becomes a regulatory means for the production and maintenance of gen-der norms within heterosexuality (Alexander 1991).

At the outset of this essay, I suggested several ways to understand the problem of "regulation." A regulation is that which *makes regular*, but it is also, following Foucault, a mode of *discipline and surveillance* within late-modern forms of power; it does not merely constrict and negate and is, therefore, not merely a juridical form of power. Insofar as regulations operate by way of norms, they become key moments in which the ideality of the norm is reconstituted, its historicity and vulnerability temporarily put out of play. As an operation of power, regulation can take a legal form, but its legal dimension does not exhaust the sphere of its efficaciousness. As that which relies on categories that render individuals socially interchangeable with one another, regulation is thus bound up with the process of *normalization*. Statutes that govern who the beneficiaries of welfare entitlements will be are actively engaged in producing the norm of the welfare recipient. Those that regulate gay speech in the military are actively engaged in producing and maintaining the norm of what a man or what a woman will be, what speech will be, where sexuality will and will not be. State regulations on lesbian and gay adoption, as well as single-parent adoptions, not only restrict that activity but refer to and reinforce an ideal of what parents should be, for example, that they should be partnered, and of what counts as a legitimate partner. Hence, regulations that seek merely to curb certain specified activities (sexual harassment, welfare fraud, sexual speech) perform another activity that, for the most part, remains unremarked: the production of the parameters of personhood, that is, making persons according to abstract norms that at once condition and exceed the lives they make—and break.

References

Alexander, Jacqui. 1991. "Redrafting Morality: The Postcolonial State and the Sexual Offenses Bill of Trinidad and Tobago." In *Third World Women and the Politics of Feminism*, ed. Chandra Talpade Mohanty, Ann Russo, and Lourdes Torres. Bloomington: Indiana University Press.

Bell, Vikki. 1993. *Interrogating Incest: Feminism, Foucault, and the Law*. London: Routledge.

Bornstein, Kate. 1994. *Gender Outlaw*. New York: Routledge.

Bowie, Malcolm. 1991. *Lacan*. Cambridge, MA: Harvard University Press.

Canguilhem, Georges. 1989. *The Normal and the Pathological*. Trans. Carolyn Faucett and Robert S. Cohen. New York: Zone Books.

Chase, Cheryl. 1998. "Hermaphrodites with Attitude: Mapping the Emergence of Intersex Political Activism." *GLQ* 4 (2).

Evans, Dylan. 1996. *An Introductory Dictionary of Lacanian Psychoanalysis*. London: Routledge.

Ewald, François. 1986. "A Concept of Social Law." In *Dilemmas of Law in the Welfare State*, ed. Gunter Teubner. Berlin: Walter de Gruyter.

———. 1991. "Norms, Discipline, and the Law." In *Law and the Order of Culture*, ed. Robert Post. Berkeley: University of California Press.

———. 1992. "A Power without an Exterior." In *Michel Foucault, Philosopher*, ed. Timothy Armstrong. New York: Routledge.

Fausto-Sterling, Anne. 2000. *Sexing the Body: Gender Politics and the Construction of Sexuality*. New York: Basic Books.

Foucault, Michel. 1978. *The History of Sexuality*. Vol. 1. Trans. Robert Hurley. New York: Pantheon.

Franke, Katherine. 1997. "What's Wrong with Sexual Harassment?" *Stanford Law Review* 49:691–772.

Irigaray, Luce. 1985. *This Sex Which Is Not One*. Trans. Catherine Porter and Carolyn Burke. Ithaca, NY: Cornell University Press.

Laplanche, Jean, and Jean-Bertrand Pontalis. 1973. *The Language of Psycho-Analysis*. Trans. Donald Nicholson-Smith. London: Hogarth Press.

Lévi-Strauss, Claude. 1969. *The Elementary Structures of Kinship*. Rev. ed. Ed. Rodney Needham. Trans. James Harle Bell et al. Boston: Beacon.

Macheray, Pierre. 1991. "Towards a Natural History of Norms." In *Michel Foucault, Philosopher*, ed. Timothy Armstrong. New York: Routledge.

MacKinnon, Catharine. 1987. *Feminism Unmodified: Discourses on Life and Law*. New York: Routledge.

Mitchell, Juliet. 1975. *Psychoanalysis and Feminism: A Radical Reassessment of Freudian Psychoanalysis*. New York: Vintage.

Poovey, Mary. 1995. *Making a Social Body: British Cultural Formations, 1830–1864*. Chicago: University of Chicago Press.

Rubin, Gayle. 1984. "Thinking Sex: Towards a Political Economy of 'Sex.'" In *Pleasure and Danger*, ed. Carol Vance. New York: Routledge.

Sedgwick, Eve Kosofsky. 1991. *Epistemology of the Closet*. Berkeley: University of California Press.

Smart, Carol, ed. 1992. *Regulating Womanhood: Historical Essays; on Marriage, Motherhood, and Sexuality*. London: Routledge.

Taylor, Charles. 1993. "To Follow a Rule ..." In *Bourdieu: Critical Perspectives*, ed. Craig Calhoun et al. Chicago: University of Chicago Press.

Tort, Michel. 1983. "Le nom du père incertain: La question de la transmission du nom et la psychanalyse." Work carried out at the request of the Service of Coordination of Research, Ministry of Justice, Paris.

———. 1989. "Artifice du père." In *Dialogue-recherches cliniques et sociologiques sur le couple et la famille*, no. 104.

Trumbach, Randolph. 1998. *Sex and the Gender Revolution*. Vol. 1, *Heterosexuality and the Third Gender in Enlightenment London*. Chicago: University of Chicago Press.

19 :: RELIGION REGINA M. SCHWARTZ

The fury that has been released upon religion, from the perspective of gender, has been considerable, including the charge that "God is male: his cult is male, their liturgy is male, cosmogony is male ... it is a wonder that salvation does not leave women out altogether." Since the nineteenth century, many critics of religions have claimed that definitions that purported to be universal and gender-neutral were in fact androcentric. Elizabeth Cady Stanton, one of the writers of *The Woman's Bible*, claimed that women could thank religion for stressing their "inferiority and subjection" (Stanton [1898] 1987, 357). Feminist complaints have included that these religions sanction silencing women, controlling their sexuality, removing them from the public sphere, denying them equal rights of participation, denying them leadership roles in the church, and, at the most extreme, even denying access to the blessings conferred by divinity. Some have also argued that because the pronouns referring to the deity are all masculine, not only does this suggest that absolute power is male, but that maleness itself is divinized; maleness is the absolute value. Many of these same charges are now being leveled against religion by gay activists, deepened by the objection that in Western religions, gays are not only considered inferior to heterosexuals, but they and their sexual practices are completely anathema. Controversies over church leadership and sacraments, over a gay priesthood and gay marriage, have galvanized nations and divided churches. In this field of ferocious contention, we might well ask, does religion generate social constructs of gender or does it only reflect the gender constructions that it receives? Or is this a false dichotomy, for if gender is constituted, as Judith Butler has said, by the "reiterative power of discourse to produce the phenomena that is regulates and constrains," then perhaps so too is religion (Butler 1993, 2).

Definitions

If religion both prescribes and codifies cultural norms, then surely it touches upon every aspect of gender. How, then, to begin? Perhaps it is best to approach the subject with an explicit recognition of the many difficulties. The topic "Religion and Gender" cries out for cultural specificity: which religion, which sect in that religion? Which moment in its long complex tradition, and where in its marked global variations? Then, too, which ritual or practice, and which belief or dogma? Which authority or institution? Which liturgy or sacred text? Defining religion poses another peculiar problem, for cultures are often reluctant to ask the question "what is religion?" as such, because they assume that their own religion is religion. In a legitimate way, "for the religious person the definition of religion could be only that of her/his own "religion'" (Goetz 1967, 240).

The converse, a universal definition of religion, is always suspect in light of the stubborn evidence of the enormous diversity *among* religions. Some religions, but not all, include belief in supernatural beings (gods). Some, not all, distinguish between sacred and profane objects in the world. Some, not all, include ritual acts that focus on sacred objects. Some, not all, tend to arouse "religious feeling," but while Rudolf Otto famously defined religious feeling as a combination of dread and fascination, this *mysterium tremendum* may not fully encompass the variety— the sense of mystery, debt, piety, or adoration that can emerge during rituals associated with the gods. In addition, religions can bind together a social group based on many of the above characteristics (Alston 1967, 141), groups with a common deity, commonly held sacred objects, common rituals, common worldviews and life-organization. Just to complicate the conundrum further, all of the above characteristics of religion can be related in reciprocal ways: some objects (i.e., the Torah scroll in Judaism and Host in Christianity) arouse feelings of awe and are therefore held to be sacred, but inversely, the prior belief that those objects are associated with the gods or God can be what endows them with the sacrality that inspires the feelings of awe. Some religions, not all, include communication with the gods, for instance, in prayer or song. And while it may sound ambitious, most religions, not all, also offer a worldview; this *weltenschaung* "contains some specification of an over-all purpose or point of the world and an indication of how the individual fits into it" (Alston 1967, 141). Of course, this ambition also poses another of the difficulties of defining religion: through which worldview do the definers look when they engage in describing an entire worldview? The final claim of religion sounds even more grandiose, for if many religions offer an entire worldview, many, not all, offer a more or less complete organization of one's life based on that worldview. As such, both the difficulties of defining religion and its consequences for gender are difficult to overstate.

As the historical examples below will demonstrate, the effort to define "religion" or to distinguish the "religious" from other spheres of life is a chiefly Western preoccupation, reflecting the West's emphasis on the scientific, the classificatory, and the speculative. The essential dualism marking the Western traditions—between the Creator and his creation, between the transcendent deity and the immanent world, between the sacred and the profane—are foreign to Hinduism where everything is divine and Buddhism where the notion of a radically other, transcendent Creator is alien, and where instead the immanence of the sacred is experienced as the depth of human inwardness (King 1995, 283). Western religions, with their equation of religion with belief in a transcendent supreme being, their frequent separation of the "religious" from the "non-religious" spheres, and their corollary separation of community into believers and nonbelievers, frustrate attempts at definition that would also embrace many Asian religions. Definitions of religion in the context of gender require further delimitation than the wide umbrella under "Western" religion, for as most of the characterizations of Western religion fail to encompass Asian religions, so many of the generalizations that can be made about Christianity do not apply to Judaism, chief among them, the questions of how marriage and procreation are regarded, and Islam also has its unique set of concerns stemming from its own scripture, law codes, and honored traditions. Because Judaism, Christianity, and Islam are all monotheistic and trace their inspiration to the same revelation, they are often grouped together, but because the social organization of gender and the impact of feminism have been inflected in them differently, they undoubtedly deserve separate treatment. Nonetheless, for the purview of this brief essay, we are confining our scope to the Judeo-Christian tradition, with the caveat that such a hyphenated construction is a construction of Christianity and of Western secular intellectual traditions, but not of Judaism.[1]

Because it has had an impact on so many different aspects of life, religion has been approached historically under the rubric of several disciplines, with each of their methodologies and assumptions coloring their definitions. Anthropological discussions of religion have been preoccupied with "primitive" religion, viewing this notion from the wider context of evolutionary theory, that is, the assumption of evolution from primitive into civilized thought. And so for a nineteenth-century anthropologist of cultural evolution like E. B. Tylor, the elementary form of religion was animism, a "belief in spiritual beings," which developed later into monotheism; for Sir James Frazer, it was magic, which progressed to religion and then to science. In general, these thinkers asserted that the "diffuse, all-embracing, but rather unsystematic and uncritical religious practices of primitive peoples are transformed into the more specifically focused, more regularized, less comprehensively authoritative practices of more advanced civilizations" (Geertz 1968, 400).

Subsequent psychological, phenomenological, and sociological approaches to religion reacted against this emphasis on evolution. Freud understood religion as springing from the same source as private obsessions and neuroses, with the difference that in religion, these assume a collective life. His claim that religious practices can be understood as manifestations of unconscious psychological forces has since been nuanced to take into account the social and institutional character of religion, but Freud's emphasis on the ambivalence of the sacred—as both dangerous and attractive—has proved remarkably tenacious. Emile Durkheim's sociological approach to the sacred also included this ambivalence; for him, the collective veneration of the sacred constituted social solidarity, with an attendant system of rights and obligations. If for Freud, God was a projection of infantile phantasies of dependency and helplessness, for Durkheim, God was the "symbol of society."

This spawned a whole movement to connect social to religious norms, a "functionalism" that argued that the main function of religion was to uphold the norms that integrate a society. For Alfred R. Radcliffe-Brown, religion endowed things that had a practical social value with a spiritual, ritual value. Even those who wanted to stress structure over function, like Arnold van Gennep, still saw social and religious categories as mutually constitutive. Clifford Geertz makes this apparent:

> In religious belief and practice a people's style of life, what Clyde Kluckhohn called their *design for living,* is rendered intellectually reasonable; it is shown to represent a way of life ideally adapted to the world as it "really" (i.e., "fundamentally," "ultimately") is. At the same time, the supposed basic structure of reality is rendered emotionally convincing because it is presented as an actual state of affairs uniquely accommodated to such a way of life and permitting it to flourish. Thus do received beliefs, essentially metaphysical, and established norms, essentially moral, confirm, support one another. (Geertz 1968, 406)

This mutual confirmation makes religious beliefs difficult to change for they can only change along with changes in the *design for living* that supports and confirms them. This deep interrelation between a way of life and religion goes a long way toward explaining not only the enormous impact religion has had on thinking about gender, but also the ways that challenging gender definitions inevitably challenges definitions of religion.

Jonathan Z. Smith's entry "Religion, Religions, Religious," in *Critical Terms in Religious Studies* (Taylor 1998), reflects this Western preoccupation. He notes that in Roman and early Christian Latin, *religio/religiones* (as noun forms), *religiosus* (adjectival), and *religiose* (adverbial) were used to designate the careful performance of ritual obligations in the cult. By the fifth century, Christianity had extended this usage to a way of life: "to enter religion" was to join a monastery. And the term also referred to religious orders in the literature of exploration in the sixteenth century: Cortes writes that in Tenochtitlan he encountered monks (*religiosos*) who dress in black from the time they enter their order (*entran en la religion*). The meaning of religion was always in close proximity to ritual, even until the eighteenth century. When this understanding of religion began to be superseded by a less performative one, religion came to be associated with belief. Samuel Johnson's *Dictionary of the English Language* (London, 1755) defines religion as "virtue, as founded upon reverence of God, and expectations of future rewards and punishments." The *Encyclopaedia Britannica* (first edition, Edinburgh, 1771) defines "Religion, or Theology" (the terms are apparently synonymous to its editors) in this way: "To know God, and to render him a reasonable service are the principle objects of religion .... Man appears to be formed to adore, but not to comprehend, the Supreme Being." In eighteenth-century debates about religion, "the goal of the inquiry was to make religion intelligible" by identifying it either with "rationality, morality or feeling" (Capps 1995, 9). Rousseau and Kant believed in a reasonable universal (as opposed to historical) religion; Herder and Schleiermacher insisted religion was grounded, not in reason or morality, but in feeling. In the nineteenth century, the activity of missionaries and the new data gleaned by colonial officials and travelers contributed to ethnography; handbooks often titled "history of religions" began to multiply, and classifications that began in the seventeenth century—when the categories were Jewish, Christian, Muslim, and Idolatry—also multiplied.

Today, the term *religion* has many meanings—if it refers to rituals, traditions of the ancestors, a cult, and a religious order, it also refers to a set of beliefs, a system of doctrines, and a spirituality that resists systemization. In the former, praxis is usually supported by a theology, and in the latter, theologies are reflected in praxis. But are these really two categories; that is, are prescribed rituals separable from prescribed beliefs? And if we resolve that riddle, which rituals and which beliefs comprise a given religion? Because these answers are contestable, religious authorities are perpetually called upon to define and prescribe, but which authorities? And when the authorities conflict, as they inevitably do, whose interpretations prevail? Aye, there's the rub, for it quickly becomes apparent that the question of religious authority is implicated in the question of the definition of religion, and when religious authority is a male preserve, as it largely has been in Western religions, definitions tend to be androcentric. Will the traditional doctrines persist in their androcentrism? If male-dominant liturgies and beliefs are so deeply embedded in the very structures of Western religion, will women feel forced either to acquiesce to such dominance or to leave their churches, their synagogues, their mosques, and establish their spiritual communities elsewhere? The answers to these questions depend upon deeper assumptions about the relation of religion to gender, the possibility for change, and the possibility for refiguring religious authority and with it, definitions of religion.

In general, the wide range of meanings of religion has tended to be more productive than confusing for religions, affording opportunities for change within cultural formations that would otherwise be stable and conservative. If Christianity has been defined variously over time—as a cult, as a community who practice prescribed rituals in prescribed ways, as a group who read the scripture, as individuals who have an inward, spiritual understanding of a religious life, as an institution with hierarchy and councils, as a group that is sometimes difficult to distinguish from secular charitable ones, as virtually synonymous with morality— that means that religion's ability to offer identity and identifications to its adherents is remarkably capacious.[2]

On the other hand, the forces against change are powerful: authorized scriptures, inherited rituals, etiologies, genealogies, apostolic succession, ecclesiastical authority—all reinforce the value of tradition, tying religions to the past. And yet, Western religions all embrace foundational myths of radical rupture from the past: the call to Abraham, the incarnation of Christ, and the revelation to Mohammed break into history with a sudden revelation that changes the course of events irrevocably. And then, for all their catastrophic suddenness, these originating accounts of revelation are followed by institutional structures designed to make them stick: to preserve the cult, to maintain the lineage, to authorize the priesthood. The challenge thereafter becomes how to introduce *change* in religion, short of beginning a new one with a new revelation—although that has continued to be a viable option, as the revelations to Joseph Smith and Mary Baker Eddy, among others, attest.

If religion has produced or reproduced the constructions of two genders and reinforced the ubiquity of those binary categories along with male dominance, it has also covered its tracks, for these reproductions have not always been seen as human inventions or choices, subject to reason and revisable. They have more often been regarded as the order of the universe, the will of God, and hence, the purview of faith. "Religion structures reality—all reality, including that of gender—and encompasses the deepest level of what it means to be human." What gives religion cultural strength is also the ground of its potential danger: its claim to embody the prevailing organization of knowledge, to deliver, in short, Truth. Yet while the source of truth in the Western religions is revelation, as received in scripture conveyed through the wisdom of the Fathers (or Elders, Priests, or Rabbis), the scriptures are also open to new interpretations, and who, exactly, constitutes the "Fathers" can even change radically, to include "Mothers,"[3] allowing many heretofore "unchangeable" truths also to change. An edict by Pius X against abortion can be challenged on the grounds that it is not scriptural; the limitation of marriage to heterosexual couples can undergo intense theological scrutiny. Furthermore, official doctrines can be revised: on marriage and divorce, on sexual practices, on abortion and reproduction, and on the gender of clergy.

Religion and Gender

Throughout the history of Christianity, a woman could still embrace her self-description "as Christian" despite (1) not being a member of a religious order, (2) not administering the rituals of the church, and (3) not interpreting scripture. Even now, when Catholic women hold a "Woman-Eucharist," in theory they could be, under canon law, excommunicated, but instead more than one-hundred communities of women conducting the Eucharist in several countries are challenging the traditional church to rethink the assumption that the liturgical role is the preserve of men. Once again, we see that the polysemic nature of religion ensures not only endless conflicts, but also the flexibility that makes religions endure.

This sounds more accommodating, more peaceful, than it has often been. The pressure to change has erupted at many moments in the history of Western religion, producing ruptures, convulsions, sects, and schisms. As each splintered from the parent church, the charge was leveled against the innovators that they had departed from the one true religion, while the so-called innovators (Protestants, Reform Jews, et al.) consistently claimed that they were the genuine adherents of the original religion. This impulse to claim the status of the original and the genuine is evident in much feminist research on religion, marked by a persistent drive to claim that an original cult worshipped a goddess, that the true history of Christ included prominent women, that the original role of women in the early church was of vital importance, and that the medieval voices of women (e.g., Julian of Norwich, Hildegard of Bingen, Catherine of Siena) must be recovered. This revisionary project has been devoted to demonstrating that the androcentric Western religious traditions are really corruptions of more original traditions that honored women—a project pursued by many theologians, archeologists, textual scholars, and historians of religion.[4] For these scholars, religion as such need not be androcentric; rather, the history that represents it has been the culprit. They have called for a complete reconceptualization of religion in which male and female roles are reexamined and religious beliefs are reconstructed—complete with rewritten liturgies, reinterpreted scriptures, revised histories of men and women, reconceived divinity as gender-neutral, as well as demands for women and gays to assume religious authority as ministers, priests, and rabbis.[5] In her survey of feminist research on religion, June O'Connor (1989) characterized the research as falling into the categories of (1) rereading the traditions "with an eye attuned to women's presence and absence, women's words and women's silence, recognition given and denied women"; (2) reconceiving women in the different religious traditions through the "retrieval and recovery of lost sources and suppressed visions"; and (3) reconstructing the past on the basis of "new information and creating new paradigms for understanding and valuing."[6] Others have felt the need to abandon traditional religion, having felt that it has abandoned them (O'Connor 1989, esp. 102–4). And this spectrum also describes gay responses to religion: from rereading traditions with attention to valuation of gays, to reviving lost traditions, to revaluing the past, and radically, to abandoning religion as hopelessly intolerant.

One of the most enduring effects of Western religion has been its contribution to gender dualism and the heterosexual norms that this dualism helps to endorse. Many rituals and myths are designed to create a distinction between men and women, to exaggerate that distinction, and to claim it as the order of the universe, divinely decreed from the beginning: "Male and female he created them." In Islam, women are veiled, closed, owned; men are exposed, open, the owners. In Judaism, circumcision is the sign of the covenant, excluding women from that mark of membership in the cult, and a collection of levitical laws define and regulate male and female impurity differently. In Christianity, the religious orders were male until women were cloistered—or cloistered themselves—*separately.*

The polarizations in religion are not confined to masculine and feminine. In a powerful essay written in the early 1970s, Rosemary Ruether argued that these are part of an ever-widening structure of dualism inherited from Greek philosophy and Hebraic monotheism in which the first term is always valued over the second:

mind	over	body
spirit	over	matter
reason	over	passion
active	over	passive
penetrator	over	penetrated
male	over	female

This bold argument has been nuanced by those who emphasize the carnality of Talmudic thought—here domination of males is linked to the flesh, not to the spirit. The cliche has long been attributed to the Hebraic tradition that God is exclusively male, but references to "EI Shaddai" are associated with *shadayim*—breasts (Biale 1982)—and in the middle ages, Jewish mysticism described emanations of God as an interaction between female and male principles. Christianity seems to offer another exception to the spirit/matter hierarchy with its doctrine of the incarnation of God; that is, a doctrine that describes God assuming flesh deliberately inverts a hierarchy already in place, embracing the categories in the second column and making that subversion central to Christianity. If so, then imagining Christ as a woman would be the next logical step, and Caroline Bynum has shown that this was not lost on medieval devotees who focused on the penetrated, punctured body of God along with his submission. Is religion inscribing dualisms received from elsewhere, or is it subversively inverting a received hierarchy?

Gendering God

Any discussion of gender and religion would need to take up the question of the gendering of God, for social orders, gender roles, and even sexual practices all unfold from the premise of a deity's dominion over creation and community, of a deity authorizing a priesthood and conferring blessings and obligations onto a cult. But in what sense? That is, what is the relation of the social order to the sacred? Is it transparent? The danger is to draw easy analogies, even equations, between the sphere of the sacred and the social sphere or to oversimplify the complex causes and effects that flow between them. Examples demonstrate the difficulties: does a pantheon of divinities that includes a powerful goddess of wisdom reflect a social order in which women are the powerful keepers of wisdom? Does the cult of Mary in the early middle ages indicate that a high social status was afforded to mothers? Does the incarnation of Christ suggest that the body was of highest value—so important that it could even be divinized? Or in Genesis, when Rebecca dupes her husband into blessing Jacob, should we infer that women in Talmudic Judaism felt divine justification for defying their husbands? Just how can we infer a social order from the symbolic order of the sacred?

Fortunately, because social history is not entirely lost to us, we know such easy conclusions are absurd. But conversely, we would be mistaken to conclude that the social order is unrelated to imaginings of the sacred. Religion is a cultural production, and as such it does encode collective values, cherished by some, especially those who managed to seize control of cultural production. However, because the values and categories of religions are not cherished by everyone, and especially by those who feel excluded or oppressed by the hegemony, resistant voices perpetually emerge to subvert the dominant order, overtly, in challenges to authority, but also through disguise, parody, and play. And while the cults of Athena and Mary and the biblical narrative about Rebecca failed to reflect or engender social orders dominated by wise women, mother-worshipping men, or rebellious wives, these very images do stand ready as imaginative possibilities to subvert the predictable patriarchy for believers.

Women were not the first to associate female imagery with the body of God. Twelfth-century Cistercian monks, among them Bernard of Clairvaux, Aelred of Rievaulx, Adam of Perseigne, William of St. Thierry, and Anselm of Canterbury, used explicitly maternal imagery to describe Jesus, associating nursing with Christ the bridegroom, the womb with divine fertility and union. Still, it was Julian of Norwich's fourteenth-century trinitarian theology of "Fatherhood, Motherhood, and Lordship" in one God which most extensively used the theme; for her, the second person of the trinity "is our Mother substantial. For in Mother Christ, we have profit and increase; and in mercy he re-formeth and restoreth us: and by the power of his passion, his death and his uprising, gave us to our substance.... And thus is Jesus our true Mother in kind of our first making; and he is our true Mother in grace by his taking of made kind" (Julian of Norwich 1961, 49, 51, 144, 158–67).

What conclusions can we draw about a religion that can harbor such subversions of gender norms? Could it be an instrument for social reform? Despite the wealth of feminine imagery in religious discourse, we know women's social status in the high middle ages remained unambiguous: "the female sex is forbidden on apostolic authority [I Timothy 2:12] to teach in public that is either by word or by writing.... The reason is clear: common law—and not any kind of common law, but that which comes from on high—forbids them. And why? Because they are easily seduced, and determined seducers; and because it is not proved that they are witnesses to divine grace" (Gerson 1706, 1:14–26, quoted in Bynum 1982, 136). Ironically, then, "alongside the theory of women as inferior, we find an increasing presence in later medieval religious literature of images taken from uniquely female experiences (childbearing, nursing, female sexual surrender or ecstasy), ... who equate motherhood or the Virgin Mary with compassion and nurture [and] also use woman as a symbol of physical or spiritual weakness, of the flesh, of sin, of inability to bear burdens or resist temptation" (Bynum 1982, 136, 144). Caroline Bynum has discerned that in the twelfth century males who were recognizable authority figures were often referred to as mother or described as nursing, conceiving, and giving birth. But she astutely sees this gender-bending as only reinscribing gender stereotypes: marking the female and maternal as characterized by "gentleness, compassion, tenderness, emotionality and love, nurturing and security" while coding male and paternal as "authority, judgment, command, strictness, and discipline." Bynum concludes that this surge of feminine imagery reflects less about a changing evaluation of women than an anxiety about authority; perhaps religious leaders wanted to temper their command with compassion. In this case (and it is one among many) both the religious discourse and the scholarship that initially may have looked like a liberating gesture for women— recovering feminine imagery—turns out only to confirm the tenacity of gender binarism.

The God of Israel, "unlike many of his contemporaries among the deities of the ancient Near East, shares his power with no female divinity, nor is he the divine Husband or Lover of any such divinity. He scarcely can be characterized in any but masculine epithets: King, Lord, Master, Judge, and Father" (Pagels 1976, 293). According to one distinguished biblical scholar, "the Bible records the biased view of the dominant party" (Davies 1992)—but the other voices were not silenced. The worship of God the Father may have been in the interest of that dominant party, but those who were committed to the fertility cults of polytheism in ancient Israel posed enough of a problem to evince dire warnings and curses against them; still, their resistance was not quelled altogether. Some of the functions of the fertility deities were subsumed by the father-god who, while he does not copulate to create, does confer, as his first blessing, "Be fruitful and multiply." Some Christian Gnostic works that were condemned as heretical as early as 100–150 CE refer to a God who is not monistic and masculine, and to prayers that were offered to both God the Father and God the Mother, "From Thee, Father, and through Thee, Mother, the two immortal names, Parents of the divine being, and thou, dweller in heaven, mankind of the mighty name ..." (Hippolytus 1859, 5.6; cited in Pagels 1976, 293). In one version of the Gnostic creation, the Valentinian

Gnostic scheme, the Forefather, Abyss, mates with a primordial female, Thought, to bring forth a male aeon, Mind, and a female one, Truth. Male and female principles continue procreating until Sophia, Wisdom, causes a disturbance with her passion to know Father Abyss—resulting in the creation of the universe. In the Gnostic *Apocryphon* of John, John receives a revelation in which he is informed by God, "I am the Father, I am the Mother, and I am the Son" (*Apocryphon Johannis* 1963, 47.20–48.14; cited in Pagels 1976, 296).

In orthodox Christianity, devotion to Mary reached such a high pitch from the twelfth century through the Counter-Reformation that the Church, fearing "goddess-worship," created a distinction between "worship" of the Father and Son and "veneration" of the Virgin. In homilies, she is portrayed as loving mother, majestic Queen, and powerful intercessor for prayers, with her Immaculate Conception and her Assumption celebrated for centuries before they became official doctrine. Any assumption that rituals, theologies, and religious institutions only reflect the dominant social order clearly demands revision; for subversions have survived too—whether hidden on papyrus in clay jars for sixteen hundred years, practiced in ritual by the faithful (sometimes unofficially), or leaking through cracks in an authorized scripture—as an image here, an episode there. When we move from theology to sacred texts, we encounter the many ways in which interpretations can uphold or defy the status quo, in which the sacred text is used to justify the norms of gender and to challenge them.

Male and Female: The Politics of Scriptural Hermeneutics

How does one read the sacred texts? The biblical story of the creation of man and woman has been continuously interpreted, and because myths of origin are used to justify or encode social norms, those interpretations have inevitably been a crux in the religious discourse about gender. The scriptures offer two accounts of the creation of man and woman. Taken together, these narratives reflect the anthropology of a priesthood in the distant past, one in which gender binarism is woven into the very fabric of creation—"male and female He created them"—and in which male priority is decreed from the beginning of time—"he called her woman because she was taken from man." In the first account of creation, Genesis 1:1–2:4a (the Priestly narrative), the narrative describes the creation of male and female together, "in the image of God he created them, male and female he created them." Does that mean that they are both "in the image of God," equally dignified by that image?[7] One biblical scholar argues that, to the contrary, read in its context, being "created in the image of God" signals having dominion over the creatures, like God has over his creation. "Male and female he created them" signals the reproductive function he gave to all living things. Phyllis Bird writes that according to the Priestly author, "for living things, with their observable styles of life, permanence must be conceived in dynamic terms, as a process of replenishment and reproduction. Thus for each order of living thing, explicit attention is given to the means by which it is to be perpetuated." If this verse refers to the provision for reproduction, then it may well stubbornly resist the feminist rehabilitations that would see it asserting the equal dignity of male and female in the image of God.[8]

The second creation account, Genesis 2:7–24, complicates this picture further. There, the text seems to endorse a hierarchical approach to gender binarism. Here, woman is created after man, from a rib taken from him, and the narrative alludes to her as a "help-mate" to him—all seeming to give scriptural sanction to women's secondary status. "Then the rib which the Lord God had taken from man He made into a woman, and He brought her to the man. And the man [adam] said":

> This is now bone of my bones
> And flesh of my flesh
> She shall be called Woman [ishah],
> Because she was taken out of Man [ish]. (Genesis 2: 18–23)

Feminist critics have reread these verses too. Phyllis Trible has argued that the first creature (adam) should not be translated "man" (who is instead designated as ish, woman as ishah). She translates adam as a generic "earth-creature" and translates "helpmate" (ezer), not as an assistant or helper, but a companion.[9] The two accounts taken together—one of a simultaneous creation of male and female, the other of woman as a second and secondary creation—have offered room for the reinterpretations of the genesis of woman that have been part of the larger work of reinterpreting gender in Judeo-Christian traditions. Scriptural exegesis has functioned as both a deeply conservative force—biblical narratives still command authority in Judaism and Christianity—as well as the vehicle for radical revision in the founding story of male dominance."[10]

When the question of gender is explored in Pauline texts, questions about dualism and domination emerge again. The Pauline text "There is no longer Jew or Greek, there is no longer slave or free, there is no longer male and female for all of you are one in Christ Jesus" (Galatians 3:28) has been used to demonstrate that "every distinction between man and woman has been overcome in principle, that equality in Christ has been established as a theological fact, and that gender-critical questions are no longer needed among human beings in Christ" (see Fatum 1991,

51). And yet this verse contrasts markedly with another Pauline passage where women's inferior rank and secondary role in creation and salvation are explicit:

> But I want you to understand that Christ is the head of every man, and the husband is the head of his wife, and God is the head of Christ. Any man who prays or prophesys with something on his head disgraces his head, but any woman who prays or prophesys with her head unveiled disgraces her head—it is one and the same thing as having her head shaved For a man ought not to have his head veiled, since he is the image and reflection of God; but woman is the reflection of man. Indeed, man was not made from woman, but woman from man. Neither was man created for the sake of woman, but woman for the sake of man.... Nevertheless, in the Lord woman is not independent of man or man independent of woman. For just as woman came from man, so man comes through woman but all things come from God. (I Corinthians 11:2–16).

The contrast between the theological, eschatological ideal and the endorsement of social conditions that reinforce dominance seems stark. But at least one critic has registered weariness with reducing this contrast to theory versus practice. Galatians, with its obliteration of difference, is often seen as absolutely valid and, in a move of Christian apologetics that defends the position that Christianity is not guilty of suppressing women, is used to neutralize and even justify the Corinthians passage—which is then regarded as only a contingent social compromise.[11] Another interpretation of the different passages produces a more coherent Paul: the vision in Galatians is of the life of the spirit, "an ideal universal human essence, beyond gender and hierarchy," while Corinthians is about the life of the body, gendered male and female. Many early church writers interpreted Paul's egalitarian notions as pertaining to the spirit only. The binaries of male and female are now implicated in another dualism, of spirit and body, which continues to inflect our understanding of gender (Boyarin 1994, 180–200; see also MacDonald 1983).

An influential scriptural exegete, Philo, offers a clear example of this dualism: for him, the first human of Genesis was the singular, embodied *adam*-creature in the image of God. "There is a vast difference," wrote Philo, "between the man thus formed and the man that came into existence earlier after the image of God [the spiritual androgyne]: for the man so formed is an object of sense perception, partaking already of such or such quality, consisting of body and soul, man or woman, by nature mortal; while he that was after the Image was an idea or type or seal, an object of thought, incorporeal."

By and large, Judaism has valorized the body and sexuality: celibacy is rejected. But does this lead to the concomitant valorization of the feminine? Women's roles have often been constrained to maternity and domesticity, while men were granted the privilege of studying Torah. Some would argue that this gender difference is only "separate but equal." Another scholar has asserted that while "the two creation stories in Genesis are treated as statements on one and the same event, the Yahwistic account sets the interpretive norm and provides justification for the subordinate role assigned to women by the Jewish society and its male-shaped ideology" (Hultgård 1991, 44).

Regardless, the interpretation of the creation of male and female informed lives in direct ways: in early Judaism, the creation stories of Genesis are invoked to explain the purity laws that govern women's sexuality. *The Book of Jubilees*, written by the Zadokites in Palestine during the Hellenistic period, depicts Adam as created in the first week and brought to the garden of Eden on the fortieth day—this explains why ritual laws stipulate that when a woman bears a male child, she is considered unclean for seven days and must be purified for thirty-three more days, for a total of forty, while Eve, born in the second week and brought to Eden on the eightieth day, explains why, upon the birth of a female child, the mother is considered unclean for fourteen days and her total time for purification is eighty days.

To delve further, the binary-gendering of mankind as the very will of God is accompanied by the injunction that male and female will combine: "therefore a man shall leave his father and mother and be joined to his wife, and they shall become one flesh." Is this endorsing heterosexuality or doing something radically different, like offering an androgyne as the ideal goal? Religion has taken as its purview not only the definition of gender roles but also of sexual practices, legislating which are legitimate. In the Bible, the levitical legislation against same-sex practices conforms to the approbation that seems to be expressed in narratives—Noah's son is cursed for "seeing his father's nakedness" (presumably some mysterious sexual advance), and Sodom is scorched from the face of the earth because its wickedness grew so great (again, the implication of sexual license includes male-male desire). And yet one scholar has shown that while the narrative of Sodom was invoked throughout the Hebrew Bible as an instance of divine judgment, "there is no text that determines the reading of Sodom as a story about same-sex copulation" (Jordan 1997, 32). Furthermore, while in the Hebraic tradition, the valorization of procreation may have repressive effects on same-sex practice, the prominence of male devotion to other males—to the exclusion of women—suggests another valorization, of filial and brotherly love. The narratives of fathers and sons, of David's love of Jonathan, exemplify this kind of devotion, where so much energy flows between males that, rather than an Oedipal drive haunting the Hebraic narrative, it seems grounded in a "Noah complex" in which sons yearn not only for their father's blessing, but for his mantle as well.[12]

In Christianity, "there are, and have always been, familial communities of men who lived together, prayed together, ministered together, and loved one another in complete rejection of heterosexist conceptions of family" (Jordan 1997, 175). "Sodomy"was not turned into a classification by theologians until the eleventh century, by Peter Damian. He coined the term *sodomia* on analogy to *blasphemia* ("blasphemy"), the sin of denying God. Damian's association of same-sex practices with sodomy occurred in the context of penitentials: Damian thought the penance assigned was not consistent with the gravity of the sin, and so he produced a booklet, *The Book of Gomorrah*, in which he does something completely contrary to Christian theology: he conceives of a fleshly sin that cannot be repented or forgiven (Jordan 1997, 66). It has been argued that Damian made a double mistake when he produced the abstraction "sodomy"—with fateful consequences. The first part of the mistake was to interpret the story of Sodom as centrally about same-sex pleasure, and the second was giving the moral lessons emerging from this allegorical reading of scripture the force of legal prescription. *Contra* Foucault, Mark Jordan argues that the very idea of identity built around the genital configuration of one's partner is not a nineteenth-century invention but the product of Latin theologians who thought in terms of Sodomites, and who ended up pitting theology against itself. But as theologically bent scholars point out the deep contradiction between the Gospel and official church teachings on same-sex pleasure,[13] historians of religion are quick to point out that the early Christian church "does not appear to have opposed homosexual behavior per se." At the end of his extensive treatment of the problem of tolerance and homosexuality, John Boswell concludes that "neither Christian society nor Christian theology as a whole evinced or supported any particular hostility to homosexuality, but both reflected and in the end retained positions adopted by some governments and theologians which could be used to denigrate homosexual acts" (Boswell 1980, 333). He regards intolerance toward homosexuality as part of a general rise in intolerance in both ecclesiastical and secular institutions in thirteenth- and fourteenth-century Europe. One central question that haunts the scholarship about homosexuality and religion is familiar from the feminist debates about religion: to what extent is the definition of gender roles the product of religion, and to what extent has religion been used to justify roles that are legislated in nonreligious cultural institutions?

In any discourse about gender, apart from the familiar role religions have played in the production and reproduction of gender binarism and hierarchy, religion has held forth another promise: the promise to go beyond gender. Can a theology that once valorized the spirit over the flesh now rise to the challenge of imagining both flesh and spirit beyond gender?[14] Intimations of this movement beyond gender are offered through mystical traditions, which offer love as transcending the violence of gender distinction.[15] The thirteenth-century Beatrijs of Nazareth eloquently suggests what this "beyond" might be in her *There Are Seven Manners of Loving*:

> Yet the blessed soul has a seventh manner of yet higher loving, in which it will experience little activity of itself. For it is drawn, above humanity, into love, and above human sense and reason and above all the words of the heart, and it is drawn along with love alone into eternity and incomprehensibility, into the vastness and the unattainable exaltation and into the limitless abyss of Divinity, which is all in all things, remaining incomprehensible in all things, immutable in all being, all-powerful, all-comprehending, all-doing in its might. (Beatrijs of Nazareth 1965; cited in Petroff 1986, 200–206)

And then this love takes flight in desire. Here, flesh is not reviled, it is perfected:

> And in this the blessed soul sinks down so deeply and softly in love, it is so mightily led in desire, that the heart fails and is within full of disquiet ... the spirit is possessed with the violence of great longing. All the senses prompt the soul to long for the delight of love. The soul begs and entreats this from God, it seeks it ardently in God, it cannot but long for it above all, for love will not allow the soul to dally or rest or be at peace. Love draws it on, love thrusts it back, love gives it death and brings it life, love heals it, wounds it again, love makes it sorry and then glad again: and so love draws the soul up into a higher life. Its life and its longing, its desires and its love are all there in the unshakable truth that is pure brightness, that noble exaltations and that transfiguring beauty in the sweet company of those brightest spirits who all flow out of the superabundance of love, who have their being in the brightest knowledge, the possession and the delight of their love.

Notes

1. For a selected introduction to the extensive scholarship on gender and Islam, see Ahmed 1992; Ali 2010; Hughes 2012; Mahmood 2005; Mernissi 1991; Mir-Hosseini 1999; Spellberg 1994; Stowasser 1996.

2. As I note in Schwartz 1997, there are at least five different categories of community well delineated in the Hebrew Bible alone.

3. See "Matristics: Mothers of the Church," chap. 3 (243–340) in Borresen and Vogt 1993.

4. See, for example, Ruether 1983; Meyers 1991; Trible 1978; and Clark and Richardson 1996.

5. Mary Daly (1973) finds Christianity irredeemably misogynistic.

6. Christ and Plaskow (1979) classified responses as "reformist" (those who continue to identify with Christianity and Judaism and seek to transform them) and "revolutionary" (those who reject inherited traditions).

7. This is the thrust of Phyllis Trible's argument (1978, 15–23).

8. Bird 1991b, 10. The contrast between the interpretations of the two feminist biblical scholars nicely illustrates that some see the text itself as comparable with feminism, while others realize their feminist purposes precisely in showing that the text is not.

9. Trible 1978, 78. This reading has been countered by others who have argued that even if *adam* does refer to a generic human, that human is conceived as male; in an androcentric culture, when gender is not designated, the meaning for "human" is virtually man.

10. It is impossible to produce an exhaustive account of the many projects devoted either (1) to reinterpreting the scriptures to correct the androcentric cultural bias that has interpreted it in the past or (2) to exposing that bias in the scriptures themselves. Among them are Bach 1997; Bird 1991a; Bal 1987, 1988, 1989; Day 1989; Pardes 1992; Boyarin 1993; Fiorenza et al. 1992; Russell 1985; Trible 1984; Weems 1995; Brenner 1993, 1995; Stackhouse 2005; and Bilezikian 2006.

11. Fatum 1991, 50–57. But Corinthians includes its own theology, one in which the hierarchy God, Christ, husband, wife is articulated (but this too must be qualified, by contrast with I Corinthians 12:12–31).

12. Aspects of the question of gender in the Bible are further elaborated in Schwartz 1997, 102–19.

13. Although even moral theology is more complex on the issue than is generally noted, with Aquinas, who was used as justification for intolerance, misreading Augustine on the meaning of "disgraceful acts" (Jordan 1997, 148).

14. For further discussion of both religious and secular move to transcend received categories, see Schwartz 2004.

15. See Bernard McGinn 1992–2008; Cupitt 1997; Carlson 1999.

References

Ahmed, Leila. 1992. *Women and Gender in Islam: Historical Roots of a Modern Debate*. New Haven, CT: Yale University Press.

Ali, Kecia. 2010. *Marriage and Slavery in Early Islam*. Cambridge, MA: Harvard University Press.

Alston, William P. 1967. "Religion." In *Encyclopedia of Philosophy*, vol. 7, ed. Paul Edwards. New York: Macmillan/Free Press.

Apocryphon Johannis. 1963. Ed. S. Giversen. Copenhagen: Prostant Apud Munksgaard.

Bach, Alice. 1997. *Women, Seduction, and Betrayal in Biblical Narrative*. Cambridge: Cambridge University Press.

Bal, Mieke. 1987. *Lethal Love*. Bloomington: Indiana University Press

———. 1988. *Murder and Difference: Gender, Genre, and Scholarship on Sisera's Death*. Trans. Matthew Gumpert. Bloomington: Indiana University Press.

———. 1989. *Death and Dissymmetry: The Politics of Coherence in the Book of Judges*. Chicago: University of Chicago Press.

Beatrijs of Nazareth. 1965. *There Are Seven Manners of Loving*. In *Medieval Netherlands Religious Literatures*, trans. and intro. Eric Colledge. New York: London House and Maxwell.

Biale, David. 1982. "The God with Breasts: El Shaddai in the Bible." *History of Religions* 20 (3): 240–56.

Bilezikian, Gilbert. 2006. *Beyond Sex Roles: What the Bible Says about a Woman's Place in Church and Family*. Grand Rapids, MI: Baker Academic.

Bird, Phyllis A. 1991a. *Missing Persons and Mistaken Identities: Women and Gender in Ancient Israel*. Minneapolis: Fortress Press.

———. 1991b. "Sexual Differentiation and Divine Image in the Genesis Creation Texts." In Borresen 1995.

Borresen, Kari Elisabeth, ed. 1995. *The Image of God: Gender Models in Judeo-Christian Tradition*. Minneapolis: Augsburg Fortress.

Borresen, Kari Elisabeth, and Kari Vogt, eds. 1993. *Women's Studies of the Christian and Islamic Traditions: Ancient, Medieval and Renaissance Foremothers*. Dordrecht: Kluwer Academic Publishers.

Boswell, John. 1980. *Christianity, Social Tolerance, and Homosexuality*. Chicago: University of Chicago Press.

Boyarin, Daniel. 1993. *Carnal Israel*. Berkeley: University of California Press.

———. 1994. *A Radical Jew: Paul and the Politics of Identity*. Berkeley: University of California Press.

Brenner, A. 1993. *On Gendering Texts*. Leiden: E. J. Brill.

———, ed. 1995. *A Feminist Companion to Esther, Judith, and Susanna*. Peabody, MA: Sheffield Academic Press.

Butler, Judith. 1993. *Bodies That Matter*. New York: Routledge.

Bynum, Caroline Walker. 1982. *Jesus as Mother: Studies in the Spirituality of the High Middle Ages*. Berkeley: University of California Press.

Capps, Walter H. 1995. *Religious Studies: The Making of a Discipline*. Minneapolis: Augsburg Fortress.

Carlson, Thomas. 1999. *Indiscretion: Finitude and the Naming of God*. Chicago: University of Chicago Press.

Christ, Carol P., and Judith Plaskow, eds. 1979. *Womanspirit Rising: A Feminist Reader in Religion*. New York: HarperCollins.

Clark, Elizabeth A., and Herbert Richardson, eds. 1996. *Women and Religion: The Original Sourcebook of Women in Christian Thought*. New York: HarperCollins.

Cupitt, Don. 1997. *Mysticism after Modernity*. Oxford: Wiley-Blackwell

Daly, Mary. 1973. *Beyond God the Father: Toward a Philosophy of Women's Liberation*. Boston: Beacon.

Davies, Phillip R. 1992. *In Search of "Ancient Israel."* Peabody, MA: Sheffield Academic Press.

Day, Peggy, ed. 1989. *Gender and Difference in Ancient Israel*. Minneapolis: Fortress Press.

Fatum, Lone. 1991. "Image of God and Glory of Man: Women in the Pauline Congregations." In Borresen 1995.

Fiorenza, Elisabeth Schüssler, et al. 1992. *The Women's Bible Commentary*. Louisville, KY: Westminster/John Knox Press.

Geertz, Clifford. 1968. "Religion: Anthropological Study." In *International Encyclopedia of the Social Sciences*, vol. 13, ed. David L. Sills. New York: Macmillan/Free Press.

Gerson, John. 1706. *De examinatione doctrinam, pt. 1 considerations 2a and 3a, Joannis … omnia opera*. 5 vols. Ed. Louis Ellis-Dupin. Antwerp.

Goetz, J. 1967. "Religion." In *The New Catholic Encyclopedia*, vol. 12. New York: McGraw Hill.

Hippolytus. 1859. *Refutationis Omnium Haeresium*. Ed. L. Dunker and F. Schneidewin. Gottingen.

Hughes, Aaron W. 2012. "Toward a Reconfiguration of the Category 'Muslim Women.'" In *Theorizing Islam: Disciplinary Deconstruction and Reconstruction*, ed. Aaron W. Hughes, 81–99. London: Equinox.

Hultgård, Anders. 1991. "God and Image of Woman in Early Jewish Religion." In Borresen 1995.

Jordan, Mark D. 1997. *The Invention of Sodomy in Christian Theology*. Chicago: University of Chicago Press.

Julian of Norwich. 1961. *Revelations of Divine Love*. Trans. James Walsh. New York: Harper & Row.

King, Ursula, ed. 1995. *Religion and Gender*. Oxford: Basil Blackwell.

King, Winston L. 1987. "Religion." In *Encyclopedia of Religion*, ed. Mircea Eliade. London: Macmillan.

MacDonald, Dennis Ronald. 1983. *The Legend and the Apostle: The Battle for Paul in Story and Canon*. Philadelphia: Westminster Press.

Mahmood, Saba. 2005. *Politics of Piety: The Islamic Revival and the Feminist Subject*. Princeton, NJ: Princeton University Press.

McGinn, Bernard. 1992–2008. *The Presence of God: A History of Western Christian Mysticism*. New York: Crossroad. Vol. 1, *The Foundations of Mysticism: Origins to the Fifth Century* (1992); vol. 2, *The Growth of Mysticism: Gregory the Great through the 12th Century* (1994); vol. 3, *The Flowering of Mysticism: Men and Women in the New Mysticism—1200–1350* (1998); vol. 4, *The Harvest of Mysticism in Medieval Germany* (2008).

Mernissi, Fatima. 1991. *The Veil and the Male Elite: A Feminist Interpretation of Women's Rights in Islam*. Trans. Mary Jo Lakeland. Reading, MA: Addison-Wesley.

Meyers, Carol. 1991. *Discovering Eve: Ancient Israelite Women in Context*. Oxford: Oxford University Press.

Mir-Hosseini, Ziba. 1999. *Islam and Gender: The Religious Debate in Contemporary Iran*. Princeton, NJ: Princeton University Press.

O'Connor, June. 1989. "Rereading, Reconceiving, and Reconstructing Traditions: Feminist Research in Religion." *Women's Studies* 17 (1): 101–23.

Pagels, Elaine H. 1976. "What Became of God the Mother? Conflicting Images of God in Early Christianity." *Signs* 2 (2).

Pardes, Ilana. 1992. *Countertraditions in the Bible: A Feminist Approach*. Cambridge, MA: Harvard University Press.

Petroff, Elizabeth. 1986. *Medieval Women's Visionary Literature*. New York: Oxford University Press.

Ruether, Rosemary Radford. 1983. *Sexism and God-Talk: Toward a Feminist Theology*. Boston: Beacon.

Russell, Letty M. 1985. *Feminist Interpretation of the Bible*. Philadelphia: Westminster Press.

Schwartz, Regina M. 1997. *The Curse of Cain: The Violent Legacy of Monotheism*. Chicago: University of Chicago Press.

———, ed. 2004. *Transcendence: Philosophy, Theology and Literature Approach the Beyond*. New York: Routledge, 2004

Smith, Jonathan Z. 1998. "Religion, Religions, Religious." In *Critical Terms for Religious Studies*, ed. Mark C. Taylor. Chicago: University of Chicago Press.

Spellberg, D. A. 1994. *Politics, Gender, and the Islamic Past: The Legacy of 'A'isha bint Abi Bakr*. New York: Columbia University Press.

Stackhouse, John G., Jr. 2005. *Finally Feminist: A Pragmatic Christian Understanding of Gender*. Acadia Studies in Bible and Theology. Grand Rapids, MI: Baker Academic.

Stanton, Elizabeth Cady. (1898) 1987. *Eighty Years and More: Reminiscences, 1815–1897*. New York: Schocken Books.

Stowasser, Barbara Freyer. 1996. *Women in the Qur'an, Traditions, and Interpretation*. New York: Oxford University Press.

Taylor, Mark C., ed. 1998. *Critical Terms for Religious Studies*. Chicago: University of Chicago Press.

Trible, Phyllis. 1978. *God and the Rhetoric of Sexuality*. Philadelphia: Fortress Press.

———. 1984. *Texts of Terror: Literary Feminist Readings of Biblical Narratives*. Philadelphia: Fortress Press.

Weems, Renita. 1995. *Battered Love, Marriage, Sex and Violence in the Hebrew Prophets*. Minneapolis: Fortress Press.

20 :: SEX/SEXUALITY/ SEXUAL CLASSIFICATION

DAVID M. HALPERIN

In a deceptively bland tone—the sort of tone adopted by those who foresee no possible objection to what they are about to say—Sigmund Freud opened a discussion of "femininity" in 1932 by making a mischievous observation: "When you meet a human being, the first distinction you make is 'male or female?' and you are accustomed to make the distinction with unhesitating certainty" (1953–1974, 22:113). By means of that deliberate provocation, Freud invited the question later put to him by the French psychoanalyst Luce Irigaray, one of his more literal readers: "How?" *How can they immediately be so sure?* (1985, 13–14). Many practitioners of gender studies have in fact been trying, for many years and in many different ways, to answer that question.

If the categories of sex seem at first glance to be as self-evident and secure as the grounds of immediate certainty are mysterious, the categories of sexuality appear scarcely less imposing: heterosexual and homosexual, normal and perverted, active and passive are all obvious and commonsensical classifications, even if we may be unsure at times how to apply them to specific cases. And those classifications can easily be expanded to include a number of more recent taxonomic refinements, such as bisexual versus monosexual, egalitarian versus hierarchical, real versus virtual. Despite the apparent clarity of these distinctions, and despite the vast amount of useful work they do in making sense of our erotic experiences, the currently reigning systems of sexual classification actually contain a number of unexamined contradictions and conceal remarkable gaps in contemporary thinking about sex and sexuality. The result is a state of conceptual crisis that is less a matter of conscious perplexity than it is a source of ineradicable incoherence in both social and intellectual life. At this point, the best we can do is to begin to describe that crisis and to account for it; we cannot hope to resolve it or to make it go away.

A few things about our terminology and concepts are generally accepted. "Sex" refers in English to at least four different entities. It can refer collectively to the *two classes of human beings* who are said to differ from each other according to sex: namely, "the male sex" and "the female sex." That is by far its oldest meaning in English. Next (in chronological order), it can refer to *the male and female genitals,* or "sexual organs," of both plants and animals—as it does, for example, in a seventeenth-century poem by Andrew Marvell, in which an agricultural laborer protests against a horticulturalist's artificial creation, through grafting, of "eunuch" species of plants: "And in the Cherry he does Nature vex, / To procreate without a Sex" ("The Mower against Gardens," 29–30). Third, "sex" was used increasingly in the twentieth century to refer to *the act of sexual intercourse*—as in phrases such as "to have sex"—and more generally to any genital activity, as well as to all aspects of personal and social life affected by sexual desire, erotic pleasure, or human reproduction. Finally, "sex" can refer to what practitioners of feminist and gender studies have called *sexual difference*: the sum of anatomical, morphological, or chromosomal properties that constitute maleness and femaleness, the sets of physical differences in many living things that correspond to the phenomenon of sexual dimorphism and to the function of sexual reproduction—in short, the very criteria according to which the male sex and the female sex were distinguished in the first place.

In this, "sex" can be differentiated from "gender," which refers to qualities *not* necessarily connected to the natural or embodied differences of sex. Gender signifies the difference that sexual difference makes: the *cultural meanings* of "man" and "woman," or "masculinity" and "femininity," as over against the *natural facts* of "male" and "female." The anthropologist Gayle Rubin, using an economic metaphor, speaks of sex or sexual difference as "raw material" that is processed by culture into gender. On this view, every human society begins with differently sexed bodies and turns them into gendered beings, transforming males and females into men and women according to its own specific, culture-bound notions of what "men" and "women" are (Rubin 1975, 165–67, 178–79). Thus, all human societies contain males and females (sex) and all human societies make them into men and women (gender), but what "men" and "women" actually are in any given society depends on how that society defines the categories of "man" and "woman."

The intellectual and political move that consists in distinguishing gender from sex has been critically important both for feminist studies and for gender studies, because it makes possible the task of detaching the social and cultural meanings assigned to human bodies (gender) from those bodies themselves (sex), and so helps to isolate, conceptually at least, the cultural meanings attached to sex, our differing interpretations of sex, and the cultural ideas bound up with masculinity and femininity, from some supposedly objective truth about male and female bodily differences. It is upon the differentiation of gender from sex that the interdisciplinary field of gender studies is based.

At the same time, the relation between sex and gender is more complicated than the preceding account indicates. The philosopher Judith Butler has pointed out that sexual difference itself is not an uninterpreted bodily fact but the discursive or ideological projection onto bodies of an originary gender dualism—an effect of that very primitive and unshakable habit of thought, which, as Freud remarked, impels us to conceive humanity as divided from the outset into males and females. On this latter view, it is the ritualized repetition of gender norms, the operation of "highly gendered regulatory schemas," that constructs "the materiality of sex" (Butler 1993, x–xi).

Human beings are indeed born with sexed bodies, but they are born with many different sorts of sexed bodies, with bodies that possess different degrees of maleness and femaleness, and sometimes with bodies that contain intersexual combinations of the two (see Fausto-Sterling 1993, 20–24). It is not bodies, in other words, that come in two, and only two, kinds (namely, male and female). It is the bipolar notion of gender itself, with its binary opposition of "man" and "woman," that functions as a device with two, and only two, default settings, and thereby provides two, and only two, alternatives for interpreting bodies (either "male" or "female"), instead of generating a spectrum with two ends and many gradations in between. That, at least, is how gender operates in modern Western societies. Other societies have multiple gender categories to accommodate finer variations of bodily difference along with other sorts of sexual betweenness. Some societies have a third gender; some have nine genders. Modern Western societies have only two genders. And therefore they have only two sexes.

Thus, sex—insofar as it is defined as the binary difference between male and female—is a product of human thought, not a fact of nature. The bipolar concept of male/female is projected onto human bodies, which are then interpreted in terms of that projection and taken, or mistaken, as the origin and cause of the habit of thought that constituted them as male and female in the first place. Gender dualism sexes as male or female the variously sexed beings that fall along a female-to-male continuum, and then treats the male/female polarity that results from the imposition of gender dualism as the origin and cause of gender dualism—so that gender dualism appears to be based on the male/female polarity, a mere reflection of it, an effect of sexual difference, instead of its cause. Human culture thereby installs in nature what it pretends to discover in nature as the purely natural origin of human culture.

In short, according to Rubin, human societies begin with sexed bodies and produce gender. According to Butler, human societies begin with gender and impose it on human bodies as sex. Both views may be considered correct, if we take them to be descriptions of different phases in the circular and never-ending process by which material and cultural realities reciprocally constitute each other.

Wherever we draw the line between sex and gender, and whatever view we take of their priority or their relative ordering in discourse, we are likely to be presupposing a historically recent formulation of "sex." For, according to some historians at least, the very notion of sex as a natural human endowment common to males and females alike is itself a cultural artifact of the modern age. The ancient Mediterranean societies of the classical world, by contrast, do not seem to have acknowledged the existence of sex in quite our conceptualization of it, despite the existence of an infrequently used Latin word, *sexus,* which corresponds to the English word *sex* in the first and oldest of its four meanings. For the ancient model of sexual difference was so extreme, so polarized, that it tended to militate against a notion of sex as a single overarching category applicable to males and females alike. In ancient Greek gynecological writings, for example, "the notion of sex never gets formalized as a functional identity of male and female but is expressed solely through the representation of asymmetry and of complementarity between male and female, indicated constantly by abstract adjectives (*to thêly* [the female], *to arren* [the male])" (Manuli 1983, 151, 201n). Rather than conceiving of males and females as different with respect to sex, with "sex" being defined as an organic property common to each, the ancient Greeks tended to think of "men" (*andres*) and "women" (*gynaikoi*) as belonging to different "species" or "races" of human beings: from Hesiod on, Greek texts typically speak of the separate "race" (*genos*) of women (Zeitlin 1996, 56–61, 140, 362). This emphatically dichotomous model of sexual difference extended even to ancient theories of human reproduction. Thus, in Aeschylus's *Oresteia,* Apollo (the god of medicine) insists that the female is not a true parent but rather a human incubator who merely nurtures the male seed, while Aristotle in the *Generation of Animals* and elsewhere similarly claims that in the reproductive act male spirit imparts form and activity to passive female matter. For some ancient authors, in short, male and female are so different as to defeat any abstract term, such as "sex," that would apply equally to both: they are like apples and oranges, in a world without "fruit."

At the same time that some ancient models of sexual difference sacrificed our notion of sex to a polarized conception of male and female, other ancient models simply abolished it by going to the opposite extreme and collapsing sexual polarities in favor of a unitary, almost sexless concept of the body and gender. On this latter view, male and female were merely endpoints of a sliding scale, the result of relative degrees of difference in an otherwise uninterrupted spectrum (see Winkler 1990; Gleason 1995). An alternate view of human reproduction, which may in fact have been the dominant one in classical antiquity, accordingly emphasized the correspondences between male and female in the anatomy and morphological configuration of the genitals as well as in the procreative process. Hippocratic medicine, along with other (though by no means all) traditions in Greek embryology, taught that males and females made similar contributions to the generation of offspring—holding, for example, that both men and women produced seed, which they alike ejaculated in the reproductive act. On this view, the woman's pleasure in intercourse was no less necessary to conception than the man's, because unless she achieved an orgasm she would not ejaculate her seed and therefore would not conceive (Halperin 1990, 139–41). Although Galen (like Aristotle) did not subscribe to the Hippocratic view that female pleasure was necessary for conception, he did affirm the existence of (an inferior) female seed, and, significantly, he treated the male and female genitals as essentially the same organ turned inside out. Males and females continued to be differentiated within these unitary theories of sexual function by the relative degrees to which they embodied natural polarities of dry and moist or hot and cold (though experts could not always agree as to which sex was the hotter) as well as metaphysical polarities of activity and passivity, form and matter, perfection and imperfection. The Hippocratic and Galenic traditions, along with their various folk equivalents, continued to attract adherents in Europe into the eighteenth century and even beyond it, though they had constantly to contend with the rival Aristotelian tradition. The more familiar notion of male and female as entirely separate, dissimilar, autonomous but complementary *sexes* came to dominate medical discourse and popular culture alike only in the course of the eighteenth century (Laqueur 1990).

The result is the modern conception of sex as an organic property of both males and females, applicable equally to each, though constituting (paradoxically) the common basis of the difference between them. Such a conception of "sex" made possible the subsequent development of a notion of "sexuality," similarly understood as common to both men and women, as well as the corresponding notions of "homosexuality" and "heterosexuality," both also applicable equally to men and to women. Although men and women may be different with respect to sexuality, "female sexuality" being considered different from "male sexuality" (just as the female sex is considered different from the male sex), sexuality itself is defined as a property that belongs to women and men alike. The paradox of both "sex" and "sexuality" is that they foreground sexual difference, insisting on the *differences* between men and women, even reducing those differences to differences of sex and sexuality, and yet they apply *indifferently* to men and women, eclipsing the differences that constitute the two sexes as such in favor of the common features that they share.

In fact, contemporary notions of both sex and sexuality produce a *homogenizing effect,* insofar as they posit common properties on the parts of women and men (albeit on the basis of their difference), at the same time as they also enforce a *heterosexualizing imperative,* constructing "sex" and "sexuality" as categories that require the joining together of male and female, man and woman, within an inclusive system of classification that embraces them both. One way to measure the persistent, if hidden, normative force of the homogenizing and heterosexualizing design of our sexual categories is to notice how inadequate any account of sex, sexuality, and sexual classification will appear *if it does not refer to males and females in equal proportion.* The account offered here will be vulnerable to precisely such a criticism, for it will focus specifically on male sexual classification—for the reason that male sexual practices and identities have been complexly elaborated over time and so provide plentiful and salient material for the study of sexual classification in general. It may well be worth asking whether "sex," "sexuality," and "sexual classification" in modern Western discourses bear a special and privileged relation to men—even when they seem to comprehend definitions of femininity or female sexuality—despite the standard understanding of them as equal opportunity categories open indifferently to men and women.

+   +   +

The meaning of "sex," in short, proves to be rather less straightforward than might have been expected. With "sexuality" we move into even more disputed territory. Originally understood in eighteenth- and nineteenth-century medical writing as the organic system responsible for the sexual "drive" or "instinct" (defined as a functional property of the organism, like nutrition and respiration), sexuality came rapidly to be conceptualized as a psychological and physiological entity, as "a systematic organization and orientation of desire" (Edelman 1994, 8). It thereby furnished a quasi-scientific basis for differentiating among degrees of normality or deviance in matters of sexual desire and behavior, and it now provides a kind of shorthand for registering differences among human beings in *sexual object-choice* and in *sexual aim.* "Sexual object-choice" refers to the kind of object intended by any particular sexual desire and, more specifically, to the sex of the sexual object, especially its relation of sameness (homo-) or difference (hetero-) to the sex of the desiring subject. "Sexual aim" refers to what the desiring subject wishes to do with the sexual object, whether the relation to the object is "active" or "passive," what kind of contact—genital, visual, oral, anal, mental—is desired, and so on. The various distinctions of sexual object and sexual aim contribute to defining the different sexual "orientations," which in turn account for both large-scale variations in personality types and many finer distinctions in sexual taste on the part of human beings. Sexuality, then, does not classify sexual practices so much as describe the psychological/physiological condition, and ultimately the sexual character or identity, of those who practice them.

Sexuality is conventionally thought of as a "deep" or "basic" feature of the human personality—in three senses: first, it is supposedly established early in human life, as a result of biological or cultural influences at work from the time of infancy, or even conception; second, it is thought of as an aspect of the personality that powerfully shapes or even determines human feeling and behavior; and third, although it is the cause of overt sexual and emotional expression, it is not immediately visible in its own right, and its exact nature may remain mysterious even to its possessor. Hence, it is commonplace to speak of exploring one's sexuality, or discovering one's "true" sexuality. Sexuality is conventionally thought to be the feature of a person that is most difficult for others to get to know, and once others know it they are in a significantly better position to account for many other features of that person that might otherwise have remained inexplicable. Sexuality nowadays, at least among the more prosperous inhabitants of the industrialized world, is at the center of the human personality.

Yet "sexuality" represents only one way of making sense of human erotic life. It purports to refer to an objectively true and natural feature of human beings, but it is itself the historical outcome of a relatively recent process of social transformation. As a concept, sexuality is largely the product of nineteenth-century French and German medical thought. However, as an experience, a form of consciousness, an operative category of social life, and a source of personal identity, it appears to derive from the massive cultural reorganization that accompanied the transition from a traditional, hierarchical society to a modern, mass society in Europe during the period of industrialization and the rise of a capitalist economy. The medical experts did not simply invent the categories of sexuality; they described and systematized the experiences of their patients, and they sometimes reproduced the sexual categories current in contemporary popular culture. Sexology encoded many underlying assumptions about sexual life that had developed in the course of the modern period, and its preoccupations were shared by contemporary philosophers, novelists, and journalists (Rosario 1997). The production of sexuality was a centuries-long process in which many parts of society participated.

How did the process of modernization produce sexuality? Here, in very rough outline, is a story that social historians inspired by Marxist thought tell. As the family-based economy declined with the rise of industrial capitalism, the household and family ceased to be a unit of economic production or reproduction and family members became less dependent on one another's labor for their subsistence. Children, in particular, were needed less as helpers around the house; rather than being more or less willing domestic laborers, they became expensive consumers—and the result was a sharp fall in the birthrate, which began first among the propertied classes in the United States and France during the early decades of the nineteenth century, then accelerated in Europe after midcentury, and eventually spread to the working classes by the century's end. Increasingly stripped of their economic functions, the household and family came to be largely symbolic or emotional entities: they were gradually transformed into a locus of personal feeling, of private life, of individual choice and expression. Instead of producing commodities or domestic services, they produced—supposedly—happiness (see D'Emilio 1993, 467–76).

Along with the invention of vulcanized rubber in the 1840s, which made contraception easy and reliable and affordable for the first time in human history (although other methods of birth control, such as douching, continued to be preferred to condoms and diaphragms throughout the nineteenth century), these developments permitted the detachment and isolation of something called "sexuality" from family life, from the relations of the sexes, from gender, and from the imperative to procreation. Sexuality could now become an independent sphere of life. Doctors discussed its manifestations, and wrote case histories of their patients. Scientists discovered the existence of a separate sexual instinct, of a distinct human function without an organ, whose existence had never before been suspected (see Davidson 1990, 295–325). Anthropologists cataloged human sexual practices. Demographers worried about the sexual health of the population and kept careful track of marriages, birthrates, and venereal diseases using fancy new statistical methods. Philosophers and moralists worried about the effect of civilization and, particularly, of urban life on the sexual instinct, and politicians worried about which nations might be getting an edge over the others in terms of their populations' sexual vigor.

Even as sexuality came increasingly to be considered the core of the human personality, the most intimate, secret, mysterious, intractable part of a person, the most private part of private life, a whole new arsenal of techniques was developed to monitor it. The new liberal states of western and northern Europe made stricter divisions between public life and private life, no longer regulating what sorts of fabric people might wear (depending on their social rank), for example, or what opinions they might hold, seeking instead to protect the sanctity of personal choice within the private sphere from unreasonable interference by public authorities. But at the same time, the liberal state also evolved a series of new methods for governing private life and—if not regulating it directly—persuading people to regulate it themselves, and to regulate one another (see Foucault 1978). Laws enforced by the state, once relatively few in number, were now reinforced by a multiplicity of norms—medical and moral, professional and personal, institutional and individual—that were produced and could be applied both formally and informally by agencies ranging from schools, bureaucracies, and public health organizations to the mass media, families, and networks of friends and lovers. The outcome is a paradoxical one long familiar to modern folk: we are all left procedurally free to make certain kinds of choices about how to conduct our personal lives, with the result that we all, freely and spontaneously, conduct our personal lives more or less exactly alike (we fall in love, we form couples, we create private social worlds based shared sentiments and styles of life, etc.). Those who don't behave like everyone else will find that they pay a high price for their social deviance in terms of stigmatization or marginalization, and they also run the risk of incurring other penalties, which may be considerably more severe.

In the course of this process of modernization, gender ceased to be a public status, an outward insignia of difference between higher and lower sorts of social beings, a marker of their rank in a formal ordered hierarchy of life. The old status-based feudal society organized by a hierarchy of ranks was gradually replaced by a mass society made up of notionally identical, unmarked individuals, who could be either male or female, but who were now endowed with an array of human and personal differences, including sex and sexuality, which served as the basis for a new, more informal and decentralized system of social controls. There emerged a set of modern classifications, ranks, and hierarchies, based no longer on the group but on the individual, looking not to formal social status but to such measurable personal criteria as health, intelligence, social integration, and normality. Sexuality, as the most private part of private life, was thought particularly difficult to regulate, and therefore all the more important to regulate. Manifold procedures were invented, accordingly, by different agencies and authorities, for inquiring into it, keeping track of it, measuring it, evaluating it, discovering whether it was normal or abnormal, healthy or diseased. Modern sciences of education, orthopedics, neuroanatomy, forensic medicine, psychiatry, psychoanalysis, social psychology, political science, sociology, and criminology all concerned themselves with the study of human sexuality—and with ensuring that it expressed itself in healthy, normal ways. The state intervened at various points in order to regulate prostitution, combat venereal diseases, foster healthy diets, reduce illegitimate births, stop abortion, and prevent modern males in particular from becoming enervated or debilitated by the nature of modern indoor work. And scientists identified a great number of newly discovered perversions.

The sexual instinct, it turned out, could be normal or deviant, healthy or diseased. There was no name for the healthy expression of the sexual instinct. The names of its various pathologies, however, were legion. Beginning in the middle of the eighteenth century, and accelerating with the establishment of the concept of perversion in the 1840s, medical experts identified increasing numbers of "deviations of the sexual instinct" and made increasingly fine distinctions among them. Prominent among the perversions, in order of appearance, were onanism (that is, masturbation), pathologized circa 1710 in popular literature and medicalized in 1758; erotic monomania (1810); necrophilia (1861); contrary sexual feeling (1869); exhibitionism (1877); inversion (1878); coprophagia (1884, in a work of fiction); sadism and masochism (1890); and transvestism (1910). In addition, a vast multitude of other bizarre and now-forgotten species and subspecies of sexual deviation were named and studied with an almost botanical fascination. By the end of the century, virtually the entirety of human erotic life had been brought under the aegis of perversion—with the all-embracing concept of fetishism, first identified as a sexual deviation in 1887, completing the picture (see Rosario 1997). All types of sexual expression could now be encompassed by notions of pathology.

These developments can be illustrated by the history of the term *lesbian*. The word itself is originally the adjectival form of the Greek place-name Lesbos, a large island in the Aegean Sea six miles off the northwest coast of Asia Minor, probably settled by Aeolian Greeks in the tenth century BCE. Originally, then, the word *Lesbian* referred to any inhabitant of Lesbos, whether male or female. Lesbos was also the birthplace and home of the Greek lyric poet Sappho, who flourished toward the end of the seventh century BCE and the beginning of the sixth. Her poems, many of which express love and desire for women and girls, were greatly admired in the male literary culture of classical antiquity, and sufficient numbers of them survived by the third century BCE to fill nine books; unfortunately, they have come down to us, with a few possible exceptions, only in fragments. Nonetheless, Sappho's poetry and her fame have proved sufficiently powerful to impart to the adjective "lesbian" its now-familiar sexual meaning. "Lesbian" is by far the most ancient term in our current lexicon of sexuality.

But the transformation of "lesbian" into the proper name of a particular sexual orientation, into a conceptual shorthand for "female homosexual," took a very long time. It is a curious fact that no extant ancient writer of the classical period in Greece found the homoeroticism of Sappho's poetry sufficiently remarkable to mention it. Either Sappho's earliest readers and auditors saw nothing homoerotic in her poems or they saw nothing remarkable in Sappho's homoeroticism. Nor is the island or people of Lesbos associated with "lesbianism" in our sense of the term before Lucian's *Dialogues of the Courtesans* (5.2) in the second century CE (with the possible exception of an enigmatic allusion in the work of the Greek poet Anacreon in the later sixth century BCE; see his fragment 358). In other words, it took nearly a thousand years for a link to be made between Lesbos and "lesbianism." The women of Lesbos acquired very early a reputation for sensuality, even licentiousness, but from at least the fifth century BCE the sexual act associated with "Lesbianism" in antiquity was a rather unlesbian one by our criteria: namely, fellatio. Sappho was represented in classical Athenian comedies of the fifth and fourth centuries BCE as the lover of various men, sometimes as a prostitute. The first writers to touch on the question of Sappho's sexual and gender deviance were the Roman poets of the late first century BCE and early first century CE (Horace, *Odes* 2.13.24–5; Ovid, *Heroides* 15.15–9, *Tristia* 2.365).

From that period onward, Sappho and Lesbos could be associated at times with certain aspects of female same-sex love and desire, with certain female same-sex sexual practices, and with certain forms of female sexual and gender deviance. In addition to being portrayed as an exemplary poetess, a passionate lover of men, and a whore, Sappho could now qualify as a "tribade." This term, an ancient Greek word borrowed by Roman writers and first attested in Latin in the first century CE, was originally understood in antiquity to signify a phallic woman, a hypermasculine or butch woman, and/or a woman who sought sexual pleasure by rubbing her genitals against those of other women. The identification of Sappho as a tribade therefore led to the word "Lesbian" being *applied* to acts or persons we might qualify as "lesbian" today, although the referents of that term were not exactly coextensive with the referent of the modern word. In the early tenth century, a Byzantine bishop of Caesarea by the name of Arethas included the plural noun *Lesbiai* (Lesbians), along with *tribades* and other Greek words for female sexual deviants, in a gloss on a text by the second-century Christian writer Clement of Alexandria

(Brooten 1996, 5), though Arethas himself probably did not have much understanding of the ancient terminology. A variety of ways of referring to female-female sex existed in the medieval period, but they were often quite confused and modeled on male sexual practices.

A vocabulary for describing sexual relations between women was gradually consolidated, first in France and then in England, from the sixteenth through the eighteenth centuries. "Tribade" and its derivatives were the terms most commonly used to refer to female same-sex eroticism from at least 1566, especially in medical or anatomical texts, though also in poetry, moral philosophy, and other learned discourses. Although early modern authors first employed "tribade" when speaking about those ancient women who had already been labeled tribades in classical texts, the word soon achieved a more contemporary application. But it remained tied to specific sexual practices or anatomical features and it continued to refer to masculine or phallic women or to women who engaged in genital rubbing with other women. "Lesbian," by contrast, occurred less frequently and remained largely a proper name, a place-name, a geographical designation—though one strongly associated with sexual relations between women and often embedded in discourses pertaining to female same-sex erotic practices (see, generally, Wahl 2000; Traub 2002). For example, a 1646 libertine poem in French by François de Maynard, preoccupied with female finger-fucking, is entitled, in discreet Latin, "Tribades seu Lesbia" (Tribades, or Lesbia). In *The Toast*, a mock-epic poem by William King published in 1732, the geographical reference shades into the sexual: "What if *Sappho* was so naught? / I'll deny, that thou art taught / How to pair the Female Doves, / How to practice *Lesbian* Loves." The expanded 1736 edition of the poem refers to "Tribades or Lesbians," demonstrating that "'Lesbian' could be used both as an adjective and as a noun" in English in the early eighteenth century (Donoghue 1995, 3, 258–59), though not yet that it had become the name of a full-scale sexual identity rather than a topographical one. By the end of the eighteenth century in France and England, "Sappho," "Sapphic," "Sapphist," "Lesbos," and "Lesbian" had become virtually interchangeable with "tribade" and its derivatives. But although "Lesbian" could be *applied* to love between women in the early modern period, it is probably not until the latter part of the nineteenth century that the word acquired an autonomous meaning, becoming almost a technical term, a proper name for a particular kind of erotic practice or sexual orientation. As late as 1923, a society lady in Aldous Huxley's novel *Antic Hay* could still ask a heterosexual man of her acquaintance to tell her and her guests "all about [his] Lesbian experiences"—invoking, apparently, the archaic association of the word with female sexual abandon in order to refer to this man's *hetero-*

sexual conquests. Despite the antiquity of the term, then, the mutation of the word "lesbian" into a standard designation for "female homosexual" seems to be a relatively recent development (Halperin 2002, 48–53).

The term *homosexuality* itself appeared in print for the first time in German (as *Homosexualität*) in 1869 in a pamphlet calling for the decriminalization of same-sex sexual relations among males. The word was later taken up by the great German sexologist Richard von Krafft-Ebing, thereby entering the specialized vocabulary of forensic medicine and psychopathology, and was popularized by French newspapers in the first decade of the twentieth century. It took even longer for a word for its antithesis, designating normal sexual object-choice, to gain currency. When *heterosexual* first appeared in print in the United States in May 1892, in a learned summary of Krafft-Ebing's work undertaken by an American psychiatrist, it designated one of several "abnormal manifestations of the sexual appetite" that found their way into a list of "the sexual perversions proper." The rare and unfortunate heterosexual condition was one of "psychical hermaphroditism," explained the doctor: "In these [heterosexuals] inclinations to both sexes occur—as well as [inclinations] to abnormal methods of gratification." So the *hetero* in "heterosexuality" initially referred to the two *different* sexes to which this kind of pervert was attracted and to the two *different* modes—"male" and "female," or "active" and "passive"—of being attracted to them (Katz 1995, 19–20).

The meaning of "heterosexuality" continued to shift, however. As late as 1923, Merriam-Webster's *New International Dictionary* could still define it as follows: "Med. [A] morbid sexual passion for one of the opposite sex." Only in Webster's *Second Unabridged Dictionary* of 1934 was heterosexuality finally jockeyed into position as the polar opposite of homosexuality, and thus as the designation of normative sexual desire, psychology, object-choice, and orientation (Katz 1995, 92). Then at last could the training wheels be taken off the sexual bicycle, as it were: with the invention and implementation of heterosexuality, modern citizens could be left to make their sexual choices in the private sphere in greater freedom, with the help of the notion of heterosexuality to steady them should they start to lose their balance.

+   +   +

Which they never cease to do, as the curious story of a sex scandal in 1919 at the United States Naval Training Station in Newport, Rhode Island, clearly demonstrates. In an effort to eradicate "immoral conditions" in the vicinity of the base, military staff in Newport undertook a sting operation, recruiting from among the younger enlisted men a number of sailors who volunteered to serve as decoys. The decoys agreed to seek out and identify men they suspected of being sexual perverts, to have sex with such men, to infiltrate their social networks, and ultimately to find out as much as possible about the extent and organization of male homosexual activity in Newport. The decoys soon discovered that the Army and Navy YMCA was the most popular hangout for "fairies," by which they referred to men who violated masculine norms of both gender and sexuality—in the first case by displaying "effeminate" mannerisms or adopting feminine nicknames, cosmetics, and dress, and in the second case by manifesting a preference for a "passive," or receptive, role in sexual relations with other men. The decoys also identified as fairies a number of local clergy who ran sailors' homes and otherwise ministered to the fleet. After repeated personal and sexual contact with these men, the decoys turned their evidence over to the authorities, and as a result of their testimony more than twenty sailors were arrested in April 1919, along with another sixteen civilians in July. In 1920 the navy opened a second inquiry into the methods employed in the first investigation. And in 1921 a United States Senate Committee issued a report of its own (see Murphy 1988; Chauncey 1989a, 294–317, 541–46).

The massive documentary record left by those various proceedings reveals a moral universe that may strike veterans of recent debates over "gays in the military" as remote and bizarre. (GI drag shows, which produced plenty of offstage romance between the male transvestite performers and the troops, continued to be an integral feature of American military life throughout World War II; see Bérubé 1990, 67–97.) Not only did some military personnel in Newport—including both officers and enlisted men—not consider oral and anal sex among men incompatible with military service; they also did not consider it incompatible with normal masculinity or normal male sexuality—so long, that is, as a man continued to exhibit a normatively masculine gender style and played an "active," or insertive, sexual role in homosexual intercourse. It does not appear ever to have occurred to the military higher-ups in Newport that what they were asking the decoys to do was deviant, perverted, or sexually repugnant—in short, something that any normal man could not naturally be brought to do—and the decoys, for their part, did not regard themselves as differing in their sexual makeup from normal men. It was only in 1920, when the Episcopal bishop of Rhode Island and the Newport Ministerial Union entered the fray, coming to the defense of their beleaguered fellow clergy, that the terms of the discourse shifted. Now the navy itself was charged with using immoral methods, with instructing young enlisted men "in details of a nameless vice" and dispatching them into the community to entrap innocent citizens, while the decoys suddenly found themselves subjected to humiliating cross-examination, forced to describe minutely the nature and extent of their sexual motives for volunteering for this dubious assignment and the degree of their sexual pleasure in carrying it out—a cross-examination plainly designed to impugn their own claims to a normative sexual identity.

More was at stake in this dispute between the navy and the church than a mere difference of opinion about sexual morals or about the relative uprightness of the two institutions' respective personnel. The military men and the bishops held radically divergent and even incommensurate notions about what constituted the normal and the deviant in matters of sex and gender, and this difference in outlook reflected profound divisions between them in social class as well as in—for lack of a better word—sexuality itself. The mostly working-class sailors and their petty officers had yet to feel the effects of a cumulative historical process of "heterosexualization" that had already overtaken the mostly middle-class churchmen: in the working-class culture of the navy, what distinguished a normal male from a deviant was not the sex of his sexual partners per se—not, that is, his (hetero)sexuality—but his masculinity: the extent to which he displayed a normatively masculine gender style of personal self-assertiveness, both on the street and between the sheets (or in the public parks). Judged according to those high standards of masculine comportment, the local ministers—with their deferential middle-class manners, their ethic of humility and submissiveness, and their sometimes extravagant expressions of affection and concern for the sailors—fell considerably short of the minimal requirements of normal manhood. By contrast, the ecclesiastical authorities were concerned less with gender style than with what we would now call sexuality: they considered any genital contact between two persons of the same sex to be a sign of pathological tendencies in *both* partners, no matter who did what to whom; they disputed the sailors' claims to be able to identify "fairies" on the basis of personal mannerisms alone; and they denied that what the sailors called effeminacy was in and of itself a symptom of sexual deviance. What is striking about the Newport affair is that the disagreement between the navy men and the churchmen was not conceptual but sexual: that is, it was not just a dispute about what *classifications* to use in categorizing sexual behavior; it was a clash over what sorts of *desires* and *pleasures* were normal for men—what objects might stimulate a sexually normal or healthy man, what sexual acts a normal man might enjoy.

Alfred Kinsey attempted to settle the question of homo/heterosexual definition three decades later in *Sexual Behavior in the Human Male* (1948), the first "Kinsey Report." In a famous chapter on "Homosexual Outlet," Kinsey wrote, "The homosexuality of certain relationships between individuals of the same sex may be denied by some persons.... Some males who are being regularly fellated by other males without, however, ever performing fellation themselves, may insist that they are exclusively heterosexual and that they have never been involved in a truly homosexual relation" (let that be a warning to those who conduct sex research by means of general surveys or questionnaires). What this passage indicates is that a number of Kinsey's informants came from the same sort of background, had the same sort of sexual histories, and exhibited the same sort of sexual attitudes as the Newport decoys. Kinsey, however, took the position of the Newport ministers and inscribed it in the deceptively neutral, descriptive, objective language of behavioral social science. Dismissing his informants' claims to heterosexuality as mere "propaganda," Kinsey stalwartly maintained that "few if any cases of sexual relations between males [can] be considered anything but homosexual," adding that all "physical contacts with other males" that result in orgasm are "by any strict definition ... homosexual." By attempting to solve the conceptual and definitional conundrum in that way, Kinsey simply buried it, because his new methodology and system of classification effectively screened out the criteria that had defined for his subjects the difference between normal and abnormal sex, and that accordingly had shaped their attitudes, their behavior, their identities, their pleasures, and their desires—in short, their very sexuality. Kinsey's hard-and-fast homosexual/heterosexual division, even though it was based on a categorization of sexual acts rather than on a typology of personal identities, ultimately made it *more* difficult to understand the sexual careers of those who had lived before those sexual classifications rose to their present position of dominance or those whose sexual experiences would seem to fall outside them—including the 37 percent of Kinsey's white male respondents who admitted to having had "some homosexual experience to the point of orgasm" in the course of what, for many of them, were otherwise quite heterosexual lives (Kinsey, Pomeroy, and Martin 1948, 615–17, 623).

At the root of all these difficulties lies a basic conceptual impasse. Only a fraction of human sexual behavior may be determined by sexual orientation, or may be explicable in terms of "sexuality," but "sexuality" happens to be the central term we currently employ to explicate sexual behavior. We cannot dispense with notions of sexual orientation nowadays, but neither can we make those notions do all the explanatory work we need them to do. Hence the present state of conceptual, social, and discursive crisis. Symptomatic of this crisis is "the unrationalized coexistence of different models" of sex and gender (Sedgwick 1990, 47), and the wide circulation and simultaneous (though largely unrecognized) occurrence of many different concepts of sexuality—defined variously according to conduct, status, orientation, psychology, identity, and combinations thereof—none of which has managed to succeed in achieving a definitive ideological or cultural victory over the others.

+   +   +

"All concepts in which an entire process has been semiotically gathered escape definition," Nietzsche remarked with typical acuity; "only what is without history is definable" (*On the Genealogy of Morals* 2.13). Let us turn to history, then, not in order to define sexuality, but to explain why it is now impossible to arrive at a satisfactory definition of it. As a modern invention, sexuality still has to compete with a number of other ways of understanding sexual life that evolved earlier, that derive from different systems of thought, and that modern people have retained, despite the resulting inconsistencies with more recent notions of sexuality. Perhaps the best illustration of how these historical overlays complicate thinking about the nature of sexuality today is provided by examining the different historical modes of conceptualizing male same-sex sexual contacts. For it is this department of sexual classification, as the Newport incident suggests, that has received a particularly detailed and complex historical elaboration.

There is no such thing as a history of male homosexuality. Instead, what we find are at least five different but simultaneous themes or traditions of discourse pertaining to what we would now call male homoeroticism and gender deviance, each with its own density, particularity, and history, and each subsisting more or less independently of the others—though regularly interacting with them over time. These discourses can be identified, provisionally, as discourses of (1) effeminacy, (2) pederasty or "active" sodomy, (3) friendship or love, (4) passivity or inversion, and (5) homosexuality. Each requires separate description (for additional details, see Halperin 2002, 110–36, from which the following survey is derived).

Effeminacy. Effeminacy has often functioned as a marker of so-called sexual passivity or sexual inversion in men, of sexual role reversal or transgenderism, and ultimately of homosexual desire. Nonetheless, it is useful to distinguish effeminacy from male passivity, inversion, and homosexuality. In particular, effeminacy should be clearly distinguished from homosexual object-choice or same-sex sexual preference in men— and not just for the well-rehearsed reasons that it is possible for men to be effeminate without being homosexual and to be homosexual without being effeminate. Rather, effeminacy deserves to be treated independently because it was seen for a long time as a symptom of what we would now call heterosexual desire as well as homosexual desire. It is therefore a category unto itself.

Effeminacy nowadays implies homosexuality, but that was not always the case. In a number of European cultural traditions, men could be designated as "soft" or "unmasculine" (*malthakos* in Greek, *mollis* in Latin and its Romance derivatives) *either* because they were inverts or "pathics"— because, like the Newport "fairies," they had womanly mannerisms and derived erotic enjoyment from submitting their bodies (in supposedly womanly fashion) to sexual penetration by other men—*or* because they were womanizers, who deviated from masculine gender norms insofar as they preferred the soft option of love to the hard option of war. In the culture of the military élites of Europe, at least from the ancient world through the Renaissance, normative masculinity entailed austerity, resistance to appetite, and mastery of the impulse to pleasure. A man displayed his true mettle in war, and more generally in struggles with other men for honor—in politics, business, or other competitive enterprises. Men who refused to rise to the challenge, who abandoned the competitive society of men for the amorous society of women, who pursued a life of pleasure, who made love instead of war—they incarnated the classical stereotype of effeminacy. (The once-fashionable American stereotype of the Big Man on Campus, the football jock who gets to indulge limitlessly his love of hot showers, cold beer, fast cars, and faster women, would appear in this context not as an emblem of masculinity but as its degraded opposite, a monster of effeminacy.)

The paradigmatic case of this tension between hard and soft styles of masculinity is Hercules (Loraux 1990, 21–52). Hercules is a hero who oscillates between extremes of hypermasculinity and effeminacy: he is preternaturally strong, yet he finds himself enslaved by a woman (Queen Omphale); he surpasses all men at feats of strength, yet he is driven mad by love, either for a woman (Iole) or for a boy (Hylas). Hercules sets the stage for such modern figures as Shakespeare's Mark Antony, who claims Hercules as his literal ancestor in *Antony and Cleopatra* and who incurs similar charges of effeminacy when he takes time out from ruling the Roman Empire to live a life of passion and indulgence with Cleopatra. The roles of ruler and lover are made to contrast from the very opening of the play, when Antony is described as the "triple pillar of the world transform'd / Into a strumpet's fool" (I.i.12–13). Antony is not unique in Shakespeare. Othello also voices anxieties about the incapacitating effects of conjugal love on a military leader. But it is Romeo, appropriately enough, who dramatizes most vividly the connection between the love of women and effeminacy. Although he may qualify nowadays as an icon of heterosexuality, Romeo himself saw his romantic ardor in a rather less normative light: blaming a momentary lack of martial vigor on the effects of erotic passion, he exclaims: "O sweet Juliet, / Thy beauty hath made me effeminate, / And in my temper softened valor's steel!" (III.i.118–20; see Orgel 1996, 25–26).

Effeminacy can function, then, as a marker of heterosexual excess in men. True to this type, the classical literary representation of a man passionately attracted to women foregrounds his effeminacy. In an effort to appear smooth instead of rough, graceful instead of powerful, a man who wishes to seduce women is typically distinguished by his use of makeup and perfumes, by his elaborate grooming, by his prominent jewelry. Here, for example, is what an adulterer is supposed to look like, according to a description by the ancient Greek novelist Chariton: "His hair was gleaming and heavily scented; his eyes were made up; he had a soft cloak and fine shoes; heavy rings gleamed on his fingers" (1.4). Although this stereotype of the womanizer as pansy has largely died out, and although effeminacy now tends to be associated with homosexual rather than heterosexual desire, the old discourse of effeminacy is not altogether defunct. A recent ethnographer of the American South defines what she calls "a redneck queer" as a traitor not to heterosexuality (unthinkable, perhaps) but to masculinity: namely, "a boy from Alabama who laks girls better'n football" (Daniell 1984, 71). And in contemporary Australia, conversely, normative masculinity is represented by the sort of bloke who avoids the company of women and prefers to spend time with his "mates." The survival and interplay of these different notions of effeminacy may help to explain the persistent sexual ambiguity that attaches, even today, to male single-sex institutions, such as fraternities, the armed forces, the church, the corporate boardroom, the United States Congress: is the sort of manhood fostered and expressed there to be considered the truest and most essential form of masculinity or an exceptional and bizarre perversion of it?

Pederasty/sodomy. Nineteenth-century sexologists differentiated sharply between what they called pederasty or sodomy and "contrary sexual feeling" or "sexual inversion" (to which we shall return). Pederasty and sodomy referred to male sexual penetration of a subordinate male— subordinate in terms of age, gender style, social class, and/or sexual role (the receptive sexual role was variously constructed as "passive," "submissive," or "feminine" and in that sense it was deemed inferior or "subordinate" in relation to the "active," "masculine," insertive role). These experts fortified their distinction between pederasty or sodomy, on the one hand, and inversion or male passivity, on the other, by grounding it in an even more fundamental distinction between "perversity" and "perversion," according to which an inverted, passive sexual orientation always indicated perversion, whereas the sexual penetration of a subordinate male might qualify merely as perversity.

This distinction between perversity and perversion was felt to be decisive. For Victorian medical writers, still largely untouched by the distinction between homo- and heterosexuality, which had yet to assert its ascendancy over earlier modes of sexual classification, it was supremely important to determine whether deviant sexual acts proceeded from an individual's morally depraved character—whether, that is, they were merely the result of vice, which might be restrained by laws and punished as a crime—or whether they originated in a pathological condition, a mental disease, a perverted "sexuality," which could only be medically treated. The distinction is expounded by Krafft-Ebing as follows:

> *Perversion* of the sexual instinct . . . is not to be confounded with *perversity* in the sexual act; since the latter may be induced by conditions other than psychopathological. The concrete perverse act, monstrous as it may be, is clinically not decisive. In order to differentiate between disease (perversion) and vice (perversity), one must investigate the whole personality of the individual and the original motive leading to the perverse act. Therein will be found the key to the diagnosis. (quoted in Davidson 1990, 315)

Male sexual penetration of a subordinate male certainly represented a perverse act, but it might not in every case signify a perversion of the sexual instinct, a mental illness affecting "the whole personality"; it might indicate a morally vicious character rather than a medical condition.

Implicit in this doctrine was the premise that there is not necessarily anything sexually or psychologically *abnormal* in itself about male sexual penetration of a subordinate male. If the man who played an "active" sexual role in sexual intercourse with other males was conventionally masculine in both his appearance and his manner of feeling and acting, if he did not seek to be penetrated by other men, and/or if he also had sexual relations with women, he might not be sick but immoral, not perverted but merely perverse. His penetration of a subordinate male, reprehensible and abominable though it might be, could be reckoned a manifestation of his excessive but otherwise normal male sexual appetite. Like the somewhat earlier, aristocratic figure of the libertine, rake, or *roué,* such a man perversely refused to limit his sexual options to those pleasures supposedly prescribed by nature and instead sought out more unusual, unlawful, sophisticated, or elaborate sexual experiences in order to gratify his jaded sexual tastes. In the case of such men, pederasty or sodomy ("Greek love") was a sign of immoral character, but it was not a symptom of a personality disorder, "moral insanity," or psychological abnormality.

The sexologists' distinctions between the perverse and the perverted, the immoral and the pathological, the merely vicious and the diseased, may strike us as quaintly Victorian, but prominent psychologists, sociologists, and jurists today continue to draw similar distinctions between "pseudo-homosexuality" and "homosexuality" or between "situational," "opportunistic" homosexuality and what they call (for lack of a better word) "'real'" homosexuality (e.g., Posner 1992). The acts of homosexual penetration performed in prison by men who lead heterosexual lives when they are out of prison, for example, are often regarded not as symptoms of a particular psychosexual orientation, as expressions of erotic desire, or even as "homosexuality," but rather as a mere behavioral adaptation by men to a society without women (for an excellent survey of disputes about this issue, see Kunzel 2008). Such behavior, it is often believed nowadays, simply vouches for the male capacity to enjoy various forms of perverse gratification and, further, to eroticize hierarchy, to be sexually aroused by the opportunity to play a dominant role in structured relations of unequal power. We have already seen an example of how such an outlook can shape both the desires and the self-conceptions of real historical subjects: the Newport decoys and the naval authorities who recruited them shared the belief that "normal men" can have sex with "fairies" without becoming fairies themselves—without, that is, compromising either their masculinity or their sexual normality.

Radically different sexual discourses applied to the Newport decoys and to the fairies in the social world of the United States Navy; without a unitary notion of homosexuality to embrace them, the two groups were evaluated and classified very differently, as if they belonged to separate sexual species. But this radical separation of pederasty or sodomy from sexual inversion or male passivity, whether it is explained and justified by some accompanying distinction between perversity and perversion (as in the case of nineteenth-century sexology) or between pseudo-homosexuality and homosexuality (as in the case of modern psychology), has in fact a much longer history, and it reflects a very old and persistent habit of thought. It did not originate in the nineteenth century. Rather, it derives from the age-old practice of classifying sexual relations in terms of penetration versus being penetrated, superordinate versus subordinate status, masculinity versus femininity, activity versus passivity—in terms of hierarchy and gender, that is, rather than in terms of sex and sexuality. By the time of the Newport affair in 1919, such a classificatory scheme had been around for at least three and a half thousand years. Possible evidence for the existence of an age-structured, role-specific, hierarchical pattern of sexual relations among males can be found in the Mediterranean basin as early as the Bronze Age civilizations of Minoan Crete in the late second millennium BCE and as late as the Renaissance cities of Italy in the fifteenth and sixteenth centuries CE. The best known and most thoroughly documented historical instances of this hierarchical model of male sexual relations are probably ancient Greek and Roman pederasty and early modern European sodomy, but the hierarchical pattern seems to have preexisted them and, as the Newport decoys testify, also to have outlived them. Indeed, it persists in various forms to this day.

The term *pederasty* comes from the ancient Greek word *paiderastia*, and it refers to the erotic pursuit (*-erastia*) and sexual penetration of "boys" (*paides* or *paidika*) by "men," usually young men. The conventional use of the term *boy* in classical and early modern European cultures to designate a male in his capacity as an object of male desire is somewhat misleading, because males were customarily supposed to be sexually desirable to other males mostly in the period of life that extended from around the time of puberty to the arrival of well-developed hair on the face, thighs, and buttocks. To say, as it is often said, that pederasty signifies the pursuit of "young boys" is therefore quite wrong; the "boys" in question are teenagers rather than children.

Sodomy was coined by Peter Damian, a medieval Catholic theologian, in the middle of the eleventh century. It refers to the "vice" or "manner of copulation" allegedly practiced by the inhabitants of the biblical city of Sodom, which was destroyed by God according to the memorable if enigmatic narrative of Genesis 18:16–19:29. In Peter Damian's formulation, "sodomy" comprises masturbation, mutual masturbation among males, intercourse between the thighs, and anal intercourse. As such, sodomy was not limited in its application to male same-sex sexual activity, and it came to be applied to anal intercourse between male and female partners and to nonprocreative sexual acts in general, including oral sex. Nonetheless, the word retained a special association with sexual relations among males and with anal intercourse. The evidence from judicial records in fifteenth-century Florence is sufficiently detailed to afford us a glimpse of the extent and distribution of sodomitical activity in one (admittedly notorious) premodern European community. Between 1432 and 1502 as many as seventeen thousand individuals in Florence, most of them males, were formally incriminated at least once for sodomy, out of a total population of forty thousand men, women, and children: on average, two out of every three men who reached the age of forty in this period were formally incriminated as having committed sodomy. Among those who were indicted, approximately 90 percent of the "passive" partners (including, according to Florentine notions, the insertive partners in oral copulation) were aged eighteen or younger, and 93 percent of the "active" partners were aged nineteen or older—the vast majority of them under the ages thirty to thirty-five, the age at which men customarily married (Rocke 1996, 4, 96–97).

This is sex as hierarchy, not as mutuality, sex as something that is done by someone to someone else, not a common search for shared pleasure or a purely personal, private experience in which larger social identities based on age or social status are swallowed up and lost. Greek usage distinguishes sharply, for example, between the roles of the older, superordinate, and desiring "lover" (*erastês*) and the younger, subordinate, and desired "beloved" (*erômenos*); both Greek and Roman usage differentiates "boys" and "slaves" (designated indifferently by the same word) from "men." Fourteenth- and fifteenth-century Italian usage applies the terms *sodomy* and *sodomite* only to the "active" partner in sodomitical relations. There is a clear division of sexual labor here: it is the younger partner who is considered beautiful and who attracts the older one, while it is the older one who experiences erotic desire for the younger one. Although love, emotional intimacy, and tenderness are not necessarily absent from the relation, the distribution of erotic passion and sexual pleasure is assumed to be more or less lopsided, with the older, "active" partner being the subject of desire and the recipient of the greater share of pleasure from a younger partner who feels no comparable desire and derives no comparable pleasure from the contact (unless he is an invert or pathic), and whose reward must be measured out in other currencies: praise, assistance, gifts, or money. As an erotic experience, pederasty or sodomy refers to the "active" partner only.

What distinguishes this hierarchical model of male sexual relations further is that it represents sexual preference without sexual orientation. Like the nineteenth-century sexologists, like the naval authorities in Newport, and like contemporary prison wardens, the ancient Greeks and Romans and the Renaissance Florentines did not consider the older, masculine males who sexually penetrated younger, subordinate, submissive, or effeminate males to be necessarily deviant or abnormal, or to have erotic desires that were oriented in a different way from those of normal men. If such men refused to marry, avoided sexual contact with women, and pursued sexual contacts with boys exclusively, then Renaissance Italians might view them as "inveterate" sodomites. Otherwise, pederasty or sodomy, as a feature of the world of young males on their way to marriage and fatherhood, was not a deviant or even a minority practice. But it did provide a forum in which "men," the "active" subjects of erotic desire, could express and discuss their sexual tastes, explore their erotic subjectivities, and compare their sexual preferences. It is in the context of erotic reflection by socially empowered, superordinate, conventionally masculine males that "men" were able to articulate conscious erotic preferences, sometimes to the point of exclusivity, for sexual relations with boys or sexual relations with women, as well as for sexual relations with certain kinds of boys or certain kinds of women.

There is even a venerable subgenre of erotic literature consisting of a formal debate between two "men" about whether women or boys are superior vehicles of male sexual gratification. Such playful debates are widely distributed within the luxury literatures of traditional male societies: surviving examples can be found in Greek prose works from late antiquity, in medieval European and Arabic poetry and prose, in late imperial Chinese writings, and in the literary productions of the "floating world"—the sophisticated literature of town life in seventeenth-century Japan (see Halperin 2002, 81–103). The explicit and conscious erotic preferences voiced in such contexts should not be equated with declarations of sexual orientation, for they represent the chosen tendencies of "men" who see themselves as at least nominally capable of responding to the erotic appeal of both good-looking women and good-looking boys. Instead of testifying to some involuntary psychosexual condition, such preferences express the male subject's values, aesthetics, and chosen way of life: this is sexual object-choice not as a reflex of sexuality but as an exercise in erotic connoisseurship. Homosexual object-choice in and of itself does not function here as a marker of difference. Nor does it impugn a man's masculinity or mark itself visibly on his physical appearance or personal deportment. Boy-love simply represents one of a number of erotic options available to socially empowered males, and the highly elaborate, ritualistic, conspicuously public practice of courtship and lovemaking provides them with a traditional, socially sanctioned discursive space in which they can give voice to a range of conscious erotic preferences. In this context, sexual preference does not correlate with, much less express, sexual orientation.

Friendship/love. Far removed from the hierarchical world of the sexual penetration of subordinate males by superordinate males is the world of male friendship and love, which can claim an equally ancient and long-lived discursive tradition. To be sure, hierarchy is not always absent from social relations between male friends: from the heroic comradeships of Gilgamesh and Enkidu in the Babylonian *Gilgamesh Epic*, David and Jonathan in the biblical books of Samuel, or Achilles and Patroclus in Homer's *Iliad* (see Halperin 1990, 75–87) to the public displays of royal affection by England's James I and his male courtiers or the latest Hollywood biracial cop thriller, male friendships often reveal striking patterns of asymmetry. Precisely to the extent, however, that such friendships are structured by social divisions or by inequalities of power, to the extent that they approximate to patron/client relationships in which the two "friends" are assigned radically different and dissimilar duties, postures, and roles, to just that extent do such friendships open themselves up to the possibility of being interpreted, then as now, in pederastic or sodomitical terms (Bray 2003). Within the horizons of the male world, as we have seen, hierarchy itself is "hot"—it is indissociably bound up with at least the potential for erotic signification: disparities of power between male intimates take on an immediate and inescapable aura of eroticism. Hence, three and four centuries after the composition of the *Iliad*, some Greeks of the classical period interpreted Achilles and Patroclus as a pederastic couple (though they couldn't always agree as to who was the man and who was the boy), while more recently scholars have disputed whether James I was homosexual or David and Jonathan were lovers. Such disputes, which often have a very long history, tend to conflate notions of friendship with notions of erotic hierarchy or sodomy and with notions of homosexuality. It may be useful, therefore, to make an effort to distinguish friendship both from erotic hierarchy and from homoerotic desire.

In addition to the tradition of the heroic warrior with his subordinate male pal or sidekick (who inevitably dies), in addition to the patron/client model of male friendship, there is another tradition, this one emphasizing equality, mutuality, and reciprocity. Such an egalitarian and reciprocal relation can obtain only between two men who occupy the same social rank, usually an elite one, and who can claim the same status in terms of age, masculinity, and social empowerment. In the eighth and ninth books of his *Nicomachean Ethics,* Aristotle championed such a reciprocal model of friendship between equals, and he wrote, most influentially, that the best sort of friend is "another self," an *alter ego* (*allos autos:* 9.4 [1166a31]). The sentiment is echoed repeatedly through the centuries: a true friend is another self, part of oneself, indistinguishable from oneself. True friends have a single mind, a single heart in two bodies. As the sixteenth-century French aristocrat Michel de Montaigne writes in his essay *On Friendship,* "Our souls mingle and blend with each other so completely that they efface the seam that joined them, and cannot find it again." The friendship of virtuous men is characterized by a disinterested love that leads to a merging of individual identities and, hence, to an unwillingness to live without the other, a readiness to die with or for the other. We find this theme of male friends inseparable in life and death repeated time and again, from representations of Achilles and Patroclus, Orestes and Pylades, and Theseus and Pirithous in the ancient world to *Lethal Weapon*'s Mel Gibson and Danny Glover in the modern world.

The language used to convey such passionate male unions often appears to modern eyes suspiciously overheated, if not downright erotic. Thus Montaigne can write:

If you press me to tell why I loved him, I feel that this cannot be expressed, except by answering: Because it was he, because it was I.... [I]t is I know not what ... which, having seized my whole will, led it to plunge and lose itself in his; which, having seized his whole will, led it to plunge and lose itself in mine, with equal hunger, equal rivalry. I say lose, in truth, for neither of us reserved anything for himself, nor was anything either his or mine.... Our souls pulled together in such unison, they regarded each other with such ardent affection, and with a like affection revealed themselves to each other to the very depths of our hearts, that not only did I know his soul as well as mine, but I should certainly have trusted myself to him more readily than to myself.

Similarly, in *All for Love* (1677), a neoclassical drama on Roman themes by the English poet John Dryden, Antony can say about his noble friend Dolabella:

I was his soul, he lived not but in me.
We were so closed within each other's breasts,
The rivets were not found that joined us first.
That does not reach us yet: we were so mixed
As meeting streams, both to ourselves were lost;
We were one mass; we could not give or take
But from the same, for he was I, I he. (3.90–96: see Haggerty 1999)

It is difficult for us moderns, with our heavily psychologistic model of the human personality, of conscious and unconscious desire, and our heightened sensitivity to anything that might seem to contravene the strict protocols of heterosexual masculinity, to avoid reading into such passionate expressions of male love a suggestion of "homoeroticism" at the very least, if not "latent homosexuality." But, quite apart from the difficulty of entering into the emotional lives of premodern subjects, we need to reckon with the discursive contexts in which such passionate declarations were produced. The thematic insistence on mutuality and the merging of individual identities, though it may invoke in the minds of modern readers the formulas of heterosexual romantic love, in fact serves to situate avowals of reciprocal love between male friends in an honorable, even glamorous tradition of heroic comradeship; by banishing any hints of the subordination of one friend to the other, and thus any suggestion of hierarchy, the emphasis on the fusion of two souls into one actually *distances* such a love from erotic passion. Montaigne never betrays the slightest doubt, in writing about his love for his friend, that the sentiments he expresses are entirely normative, even admirable and boastworthy (though, of course, unique in their specifics). Far from offering us clues to his personal psychopathology, inadvertently revealing to us traces of his suppressed or unconscious desires, or confessing his erotic peculiarities (as he does freely elsewhere in his *Essays*), Montaigne seems to have understood that the account of friendship he offers would be immune to any disreputable erotic interpretation, in part because it is so elaborately presented as egalitarian, nonhierarchical, and reciprocal. For by that means he detaches it from the erotic realms of difference and hierarchy, setting it explicitly *against* the sexual love of men and women as well as the male sexual enjoyment of boys.

Some male lovers could appeal to the discourse of friendship as a cover for same-sex desire or as means of ennobling it. Edward II, for example, in Marlowe's play of the same name, declares himself to Piers Gaveston "thy friend, thy self, another Gaveston" (I.i.141–42). What makes the discourse of friendship a safe refuge for relations susceptible of being seen as sodomitical is precisely its perceived dissimilarity to the language of sex. Sexual love, at least as it is viewed within the cultural traditions of the male world, is all about penetration, and therefore all about position, superiority and inferiority, rank and status, gender and difference. Friendship, by contrast, is all about sameness: sameness of rank and status, sameness of sentiment, sameness of identity. It is this very emphasis on identity, similarity, and mutuality that distances the friendship tradition, in its original social and discursive context, from the world of sexual love. In such a context, in fact, "sexual love" sounds like a contradiction in terms: sex is not something you would do to someone you really love. In this way, the friendship tradition provided socially empowered men with a discursive venue in which to express, without social reproach, sentiments of passionate and mutual love for one another.

Passivity/inversion. Both pederasty/sodomy and friendship/love are consonant with masculine gender norms, with conventional masculinity as it has been defined in a number of European cultures. If anything, pederasty and friendship are traditionally masculinizing, insofar as they express the male subject's virility and imply a thoroughgoing rejection of everything that is feminine. Both can therefore be seen as consolidating male gender identity (though not, of course, in every instance). As such, they belong to a different conceptual, moral, and social universe from what the Greeks called *kinaidia*, the Romans *mollitia*, the nineteenth-century sexologists "contrary sexual feeling" or "sexual inversion," and the Newport decoys a "fairy." All these terms refer to the male "inversion" or reversal of masculine gender identity, a wholesale surrender of masculinity in favor of femininity, a transgendered condition expressed in everything from personal comportment and style, to physical appearance, manner of feeling, sexual attraction to "normal men," and preference for a receptive or "passive" role in sexual intercourse with men.

The fact of being sexually penetrated by a man is much less significant for the sexual classification of passives or inverts than the question of the penetrated male's pleasure. In the premodern systems of pederasty and sodomy, as we have seen, boys are the more or less willing objects of adult male desire, but they are not conventionally assigned a share of desire equal to that of their senior male partners, nor are they expected to derive much sexual pleasure from the contact. They are "passive" in their behavior, but such "passivity" does not extend to their desire, which, by remaining unengaged, can claim to be uncontaminated by any impulse to subordination. They have to be motivated to submit to their male lovers by a variety of largely nonsexual inducements, such as gifts or threats. *Cinaedi* and inverts, by contrast, actively desire to submit their bodies "passively" to sexual penetration by "men," and in that sense they are seen as having a woman's, not a man's, desire, subjectivity, and gender identity. A pederast or sodomite may enjoy the sexual favors of either a normatively masculine (and therefore comparatively unimpassioned) male subordinate or a gender-deviant, "feminine," inverted, and sexually enthusiastic male subordinate: the "active" partner's status and masculinity are unaffected by the degree to which his male object enjoys being penetrated or is motivated by erotic desire. By contrast, the subordinate partner's social and moral status, though always at least potentially undermined by the shaming fact of his undergoing sexual penetration, often depends crucially on his motives and attitude. The category of male passive or invert applies specifically to those subordinate males whose willingness to submit themselves to sexual penetration by men proceeds from their own erotic desires and/or from their assumption of a feminine gender identity rather than from essentially nonsexual motives.

Although the pleasure he takes in being sexually penetrated may be the most flagrant, the most extreme expression of the overall gender reversal that characterizes the male invert, inversion is not necessarily, or even principally, defined by the enjoyment of particular sexual acts. Nor does it have to do strictly with homosexual desire, because inverts may also have insertive phallic sex with women without however ceasing to be considered inverts. Rather, inversion has to do with deviant gender identity, sensibility, and personal style, one aspect of which is the "womanly" liking for a passive role in sexual intercourse with other men. Therefore, notions of inversion do not tend to make a strict separation between specific sexual manifestations of inversion and other, equally telling deviations from the norms of masculinity, such as the adoption of feminine dress. The emphasis falls on a violation of the protocols of manhood, a characterological failure of grand proportions that cannot be redeemed (as sodomy can) by the enjoyment of sexual relations with women. Inversion is not about sexuality but about gender, insofar as the two can be distinguished in this context.

What, then, is the difference between effeminates and passives? What distinguishes those men (belonging to our first category) who prefer making love to making war and who favor a "soft" style of masculinity from those men who have effeminate mannerisms and who wish to submit their bodies, in "womanly" fashion, to the phallic pleasures of other men? The distinction between the two categories is a subtle one, and it is easily blurred. After all, some stigma of gender deviance, of effeminacy, applies to both types of men. And polarized definitions of the masculine and the feminine, along with the hyperbolic nature of sexual stereotyping, enable the slightest suggestion of gender deviance to be quickly inflated and transformed into an accusation of complete and total gender treason. From liking women to wanting to be like women is, according to the phobic (il)logic of this masculinist ideology, only a small step. Which is why both effeminates and passives ("pathics") can be characterized as "soft" (*mollis*) or unmasculine.

One way to describe the difference between effeminates and passives is to contrast a universalizing notion of gender deviance with a minoritizing one. "Softness" may represent either the specter of potential gender failure that haunts all normative masculinity, an ever-present threat to the masculinity of every man, or the disfiguring peculiarity of a small class of deviant individuals (see Sedgwick 1990, 1, 9, 85–86). Effeminates are men who succumb to a tendency that all normal men have and that all normal men have to guard against or suppress in themselves, whereas passives are men who are so unequal to the struggle that they can be seen to suffer from a specific constitutional defect—namely, a constitutional lack of the masculine capacity to withstand the appeal of pleasure (especially pleasure deemed exceptionally disgraceful or degrading), as well as a constitutional tendency to adopt a specifically feminine attitude of surrender in relations with other men.

It is these features that define the invert, even more than his desire or his sexual object-choice, because those are not unique to him. The desire for a male partner, for example, is something the invert has in common both with the pederast and with the heroic friend, figures vastly removed from him in social and moral status. Inversion also differs from pederasty and friendship in that the love of boys and the love of friends are not necessarily discreditable sentiments, and they may well be confessed or even championed by the subjects themselves, whereas inversion is a shameful condition, never proclaimed about oneself, almost always ascribed to some *other* by an accuser whose intent is to demean and to vilify.

Traditional representations of "active" pederasts or sodomites do not necessarily portray them as visibly different in their appearance from normal men. You can't always tell a pederast or sodomite by looking at him. But an invert usually stands out, because his reversal of his gender identity affects his personal demeanor and shapes his attitude, gestures, and manner of conducting himself. Unlike the active penetration of boys, which might differentiate the lover of boys from the lover of women in terms of his erotic preference but does not mark him as a visibly different sort of person, passivity or inversion stamps itself all over a man's social presentation and identifies him as a spectacularly deviant social type. There is "a plague-spot visibly imprinted on all that are tainted" with this passion, as a character emphatically puts it in *Fanny Hill* (John Cleland's 1748 *Memoirs of a Woman of Pleasure*). It is in the context of inversion, then, that we most often find produced and elaborated representations of a peculiar character type or stereotype, a phobic caricature embodying the supposedly visible and flagrant features of male sex/gender deviance. Although this type is attached to homosexual sex, it is not attached to homosexual sex absolutely, for as we have seen it is seldom connected with "active" pederasty or sodomy; rather, it seems to be associated more readily with passive or receptive homosexual sex, seen as merely one aspect of a more generalized gender reversal, an underlying betrayal of masculinity. There is a remarkably consistent emphasis throughout the history of European sexual representation on the deviant morphology of the invert, his visibly different mode of appearance and dress, his feminine style of self-presentation. Inversion manifests itself outwardly.

It doesn't take one to know one. Everybody seems to know what an invert looks like and how he behaves, even if no normal man could possibly impersonate one. As a character in an ancient Greek comedy says, "I have absolutely no idea how to use a twittering voice or walk about in an effeminate style, with my head tilted sidewise like all those pathics that I see here in the city smeared with depilatories." Ancient physiognomists, experts in the learned technique of deciphering a person's character from his or her appearance, provide a more detailed description of the type:

> You may recognize him by his provocatively melting glance and by the rapid movement of his intensely staring eyes. His brow is furrowed while his eyebrows and cheeks are in constant motion. His head is tilted to the

side, his loins do not hold still, and his slack limbs never stay in one position. He minces along with little jumping steps; his knees knock together. He carries his hands with palms turned upward. He has a shifting gaze, and his voice is thin, weepy, shrill, and drawling.

All attempts at concealment are useless: "For it is by the twitching of their lips and the rotation of their eyes, by the haphazard and inconsistent shifting of their feet, by the movement of their hips and the fickle motion of their hands, and by the tremor of their voice as it begins with difficulty to speak, that effeminates are most easily revealed" (the quoted passages are from Gleason 1995, 68, 63, 78). Although the particular markers of inversion may be culture-bound and therefore susceptible to change over time, the legibility of inversion is one of its perennial features, as the Newport fairies vividly illustrate.

It is this character type, the male passive or invert, who in the latter part of the nineteenth century provided medical doctors and psychiatrists with the clinical basis for the first systematic scientific definition and conceptualization of pathological (or perverted) sexual *orientation*. In August 1869, the same year that witnessed the first printed appearance of the word *homosexuality*, Karl Friedrich Otto Westphal, a German expert on "the diseases of the nerves" or "nervous system," published in a new journal of psychiatry an article on "contrary sexual feeling" or "sensibility" (*conträre Sexualempfindung*), which he presented as a symptom of a neuropathic or psychopathic condition (Westphal 1870, 73–108). "Contrary sexual feeling" signified a sexual feeling contrary to the sex of the person who experienced it—that is, a feeling of belonging to a different sex from one's own, *as well as* a feeling of erotic attraction at odds with the sex to which one belonged (because its object was a member of the same sex as oneself and because it expressed a masculine or feminine attitude proper to members of a sex different from one's own). Similarly, "inversion of the sexual instinct," a formula coined by the Italian psychiatrist Arrigo Tamassia in 1878 (97–117), also treated same-sex sexual desire and object-choice as merely one of a number of pathological symptoms exhibited by those who reversed, or "inverted," the sex roles thought appropriate to their own sex: such symptoms, indicating masculine identification in women and feminine identification in men, comprised many different elements of personal style, ranging from the ideologically loaded (women who took an interest in politics and campaigned for the right to vote) to the trivial and bizarre (men who liked cats), but the common thread linking them was sex-role reversal or gender deviance. According to this model, sexual preference for a member of one's own sex was not clearly distinguished from other sorts of noncon-formity to one's gender identity, as defined by prevailing cultural norms of manliness and femininity.

One implication of this model, which differentiates it strikingly from notions of homosexuality, is that the conventionally masculine and femi-nine same-sex partners of inverts are not themselves necessarily abnor-mal or problematic: like the decoys at Newport in the eyes of the United States Navy, the femme who allows herself to be pleasured by a butch or the straight-identified male hustler is merely acting out a proper sexual scenario with an improper partner and may well be sexually normal in her or his own right (see Chauncey 1989b, 87–117).

If pederasty/sodomy was traditionally understood as a sexual prefer-ence without a sexual orientation, inversion was defined as a psychosex-ual orientation without a sexuality. In a footnote at the end of his article, Westphal emphasized "the fact that 'contrary sexual feeling' *does not al-ways coincidentally concern the sexual drive as such* but simply the feeling of being alienated, with one's entire inner being, from one's own sex—a less developed stage, as it were, of the pathological phenomenon" (West-phal 1870, 107n; emphasis added). For Westphal and his colleagues, con-trary sexual feeling or sexual inversion was an essentially psychological condition of gender dysphoria affecting the inner life of the individual, not necessarily expressed in the performance or enjoyment of particular (homo)sexual acts. In fact, one of Westphal's star examples of contrary sexual feeling was a male cross-dresser who strictly avoided—or at least claimed to avoid—all sexual contact with members of his own sex and who was diagnosed as suffering from "contrary sexual feeling" on the ba-sis of his gender style alone, not on the basis of homosexual desire.

Sexual inversion, then, does not represent the same notion as homo-sexuality, because same-sex sexual object-choice, or homosexual desire, is not essential to it: one can be inverted without being homosexual and one can have homosexual sex, as the Newport decoys did, without qual-ifying as sexually inverted. Hence, as Kinsey insisted, "Inversion and homosexuality are two distinct and not always correlated types of be-havior" (Kinsey, Pomeroy, and Martin 1948, 615). Rather, the notions of contrary sexual feeling and sexual inversion seem to glance back at the long tradition of stigmatized male passivity, effeminacy, and gender de-viance, which focuses less on homosexual sex or homosexual desire per se than on an accompanying lack of normative masculinity in one or both of the partners.

Homosexuality. The term *homosexuality* appeared in print for the first time in 1869, in two pamphlets published in Leipzig as open letters to the Prussian minister of justice, whose task it was to supervise the redrafting of the Prussian penal code so as to adapt it to the needs of the newly formed North German Federation. The anonymous author of these pamphlets was an obscure Austro-Hungarian translator and littérateur of Bavarian extraction by the name of Karl Maria Benkert, who wrote in German under the inverted Hungarianized pseudonym of Kertbeny and who claimed (rather unconvincingly), in the second of the two tracts, to be sexually normal himself. Nonetheless, he argued that a number of great men had been homosexual, that the condition was innate, not acquired, and that it was therefore pointless to criminalize it—as the new imperial German legal code proceeded to do nonetheless, defining "unnatural lewdness" (*widernatürliche Unzucht*) as a criminal act in its infamous Article 175 (modified in West Germany in 1969 but repealed only with German reunification in 1994). In any case, "homosexuality" began life as a progay, politically activist coinage.

It did not retain that character for long. The word itself might have been forgotten had not Kertbeny's friend Gustav Jaeger, a zoologist, allowed Kertbeny to ghost-write a chapter in the second edition of his book *The Discovery of the Soul* (*Entdeckung der Seele*) in 1880. There the newfangled term attracted the attention of the great forensic sexologist Richard von Krafft-Ebing. Krafft-Ebing borrowed the word from Jaeger in 1887 for the second edition of his massive encyclopedia of sexual deviance, the *Psychopathia Sexualis,* and he employed it with increasing frequency and freedom in the many later editions of that influential work. That is how the word acquired its medical and forensic connotations, mutating from a gay-friendly affirmation into a clinical designation. The popularization of the terms *homosexuality* and *heterosexuality* in their modern senses was not fully achieved until the publication of the first Kinsey report in 1948 (though it should be emphasized that Kinsey treated homosexuality as a behavior, which may be practiced with greater or lesser frequency, rather than as quasi-permanent sexual orientation, psychological condition, or category of being).

In fact, what distinguishes the modern category of "homosexuality" as a sexual classification is its unprecedented combination of at least three distinct and previously uncorrelated conceptual entities: (1) a psychiatric notion of perverted or pathological *orientation,* derived from Westphal and his nineteenth-century medical colleagues, which is an essentially psychological concept that applies to the inner life of the individual and does not necessarily presume same-sex sexual behavior; (2) a psychoanalytic notion of same-sex *sexual object-choice* or desire, derived from Freud and his successors, which is a category of erotic intentionality and does not necessarily imply a permanent sexual orientation, let alone a deviant or pathological one (since, according to Freud, most normal individuals make an unconscious homosexual object-choice at some point in their fantasy lives); and (3) a sociological notion of *sexually deviant behavior,* derived from nineteenth- and twentieth-century forensic inquiries into "social problems," which focuses on nonstandard sexual practice and does not necessarily refer to erotic psychology or sexual orientation (since same-sex sexual behavior, as Kinsey showed, is not the exclusive property of those with a homosexual sexual orientation, nor is it necessarily pathological, since it is widely represented in the population). So neither a notion of orientation, nor a notion of object-choice, nor a notion of behavior alone is sufficient to generate the modern definition of "homosexuality"; rather, the notion seems to depend on the unstable conjunction of all three. "Homosexuality" is at once a psychological condition, and an erotic desire, and a sexual practice (which are three quite different things).

Beyond that, homosexuality—both as concept and social practice—significantly rearranges and reinterprets earlier modes of formulating erotic relations among members of the same sex, and as such it has a number of important practical consequences (for what follows, see Adam 1996, 111–26). First of all, the significance of gender and of gender roles for categorizing sexual acts and sexual actors fades in significance. That is not to deny that gender deviance continues to serve as a marker of deviant sexuality, and that homosexuals are often thought to be defined by inappropriate excesses and deficiencies of masculinity and femininity. Even so, one effect of the concept of "homosexuality" is to detach sexual object-choice from any necessary connection with gender identity, making it possible to ascribe "homosexuality" to women and to men whose gender styles and outward appearance or manner are perfectly normative. It also means that *any sexual contact between two members of the same sex* may be classed as homosexual, even if one partner is cross-gendered and the other partner seems entirely normal in terms of gender and plays an insertive or receptive sexual role in conformity with what is deemed proper to his or her sex: as the Newport decoys discovered, a conventionally masculine gender style does not protect you from imputations of abnormality or deviance once you willingly engage in sexual relations with a person of the same sex, even if that person is a "fairy."

Another result of this degendering of sexual relations has been to group homosexual women and men together, in the same category, as homosexuals, and to differentiate them from heterosexual women and men, classified together in a separate category as heterosexuals. The implication is that a lesbian has more in common with a gay man, in terms of her "sexuality," than she has in common with a straight woman, with whom she shares merely her "sex." The homogenizing and heterosexualizing effects that, as we have seen, are produced by the very notion of sexuality extend to politics no less than to discourse: they propel lesbians and gay men to join together in a single social movement for the liberation of "sexuality" or "homosexuality," even as the differences between lesbian and gay-male sexual and political cultures often make the basis for their collaboration seem mysterious if not simply bogus. The resulting tensions and misunderstandings between and among lesbians and gay men indicate just how strongly even those who are most sharply critical of contemporary sexual categories share a belief in (homo)sexuality as a classification that includes women and men alike.

Earlier discourses, whether of sodomy or inversion, referred to only *one* of the sexual partners—to the "active" partner in the case of sodomy, to the effeminate male or masculine female in the case of inversion. The other partner—the one who was not motivated by sexual desire in the first case, the one who was not gender-deviant in the second—did not qualify for inclusion in the category. "Homosexuality" applies to *both* partners, whether active or passive, whether gendered normatively or deviantly. The hallmark of homosexuality, in fact, is the refusal to distinguish between same-sex sexual partners, or to rank them by treating one as more (or less) homosexual than the other.

Homosexuality thus translates same-sex sexual relations into the register of sameness and mutuality. Like heterosexual romantic love, and like the earlier tradition of male friendship, the notion of homosexuality implies that it is possible for sexual partners to bond with one another not on the basis of their difference but on the basis of their sameness, their identity of desire and orientation and sexuality. Homosexual relations no longer require a polarization of roles (active/passive, insertive/receptive, masculine/feminine, man/boy). Exclusive, life-long, companionate, romantic, and mutual homosexual love becomes possible for both partners.

Homosexuality generates its own forms of identity and sociality. Homosexual relations are not simply determined or prescribed by kinship systems, age classes, or initiation rituals; rather, they give rise to independent and freestanding social networks. Homosexuality is now set over against heterosexuality, and homosexual object-choice, in and of itself, is seen as marking a difference from heterosexual object-choice. Finally, sexual object-choice attaches to a notion of sexual orientation, such that sexual behavior is seen to express an underlying and permanent psychosexual feature of the human subject, and homo- and heterosexuality become more or less mutually exclusive forms of human subjectivity, different *kinds* of human sexuality. People are thought to belong to one or the other of those two sexual species, and any feeling or expression of heterosexual desire is thought to rule out the likelihood of any feeling or expression of homosexual desire on the part of the same individual.

In short, homosexuality is more than same-sex sexual object-choice, more even than conscious erotic same-sex preference (which, after all, is nothing new). Homosexuality is the specification of same-sex sexual object-choice in and of itself as an overriding principle of sexual and social difference. Homosexuality is part of a new system of *sexuality,* which assigns to individuals a sexual orientation and a sexual identity. As such, sexuality introduces a novel element into social organization, into the social articulation of human difference, into the social production of desire, and ultimately into the social construction of the self.

+ + +

Perhaps the final irony in all this is that the very word *sex,* which itself may derive from the Latin *secare,* to cut or divide, and which originally signified the sharpness and cleanness of the division between the natural categories of male and female, has had the fine edge of its precise meaning so thoroughly blunted by historical shifts, conceptual muddles, and rearrangements in the forms of sexual life that it now represents that which is most resistant to clear classification, discrimination, and division.

References

Adam, Barry D. 1996. "Structural Foundations of the Gay World." In *Queer Theory/Sociology,* ed. Steven Seidman. Oxford: Blackwell.

Bérubé, Allan. 1990. *Coming Out under Fire: The History of Gay Men and Women in World War Two.* New York: Free Press.

Bray, Alan. 2003. *The Friend.* Chicago: University of Chicago Press.

Brooten, Bernadette J. 1996. *Love between Women: Early Christian Responses to Female Homoeroticism.* Chicago: University of Chicago Press.

Butler, Judith. 1993. *Bodies That Matter: On the Discursive Limits of "Sex."* New York: Routledge.

Chauncey, George, Jr. 1989a. "Christian Brotherhood or Sexual Perversion? Homosexual Identities and the Construction of Sexual Boundaries in the World War One Era." In *Hidden from History: Reclaiming the Gay and Lesbian Past,* ed. Martin Bauml Duberman, Martha Vicinus, and George Chauncey Jr. New York: New American Library.

———. 1989b. "From Sexual Inversion to Homosexuality: Medicine and the Changing Conceptualization of Female Deviance." In *Passion and Power: Sexuality in History,* ed. Kathy Peiss and Christina Simmons. Philadelphia: Temple University Press.

Daniell, Rosemary. 1984. *Sleeping with Soldiers: In Search of the Macho Man.* New York: Holt, Reinhart and Winston.

Davidson, Arnold I. 1990. "Closing Up the Corpses: Diseases of Sexuality and the Emergence of the Psychiatric Style of Reasoning." In *Meaning and Method: Essays in Honour of Hilary Putnam*, ed. George Boolos. Cambridge: Cambridge University Press.

D'Emilio, John. 1993. "Capitalism and Gay Identity." In *The Lesbian and Gay Studies Reader*, ed. Henry Abelove, Michèle Aina Barale, and David M. Halperin. New York: Routledge.

Donoghue, Emma. 1995. *Passions between Women: British Lesbian Culture, 1668–1801*. New York: HarperCollins.

Edelman, Lee. 1994. *Homographesis: Essays in Gay Literary and Cultural Theory*. New York: Routledge.

Fausto-Sterling, Anne. 1993. "The Five Sexes: Why Male and Female Are Not Enough." *Sciences* 33 (2) (March/April).

Foucault, Michel. 1978. *The History of Sexuality*. Vol. 1, *An Introduction*. Trans. Robert Hurley. New York: Random House.

Freud, Sigmund. 1953–1974. *The Standard Edition of the Complete Psychological Works of Sigmund Freud*. 24 vols. Ed. James Strachey. London: Hogarth.

Gleason, Maud. 1995. *Making Men: Sophists and Self-Presentation in Ancient Rome*. Princeton, NJ: Princeton University Press.

Haggerty, George. 1999. *Men in Love*. New York: Columbia University Press.

Halperin, David M. 1990. *One Hundred Years of Homosexuality and Other Essays on Greek Love*. New York: Routledge.

———. 2002. *How to Do the History of Homosexuality*. Chicago: University of Chicago Press.

Irigaray, Luce. 1985. *Speculum of the Other Woman*. Trans. Gillian C. Gill. Ithaca, NY: Cornell University Press.

Katz, Jonathan Ned. 1995. *The Invention of Heterosexuality*. New York: Dutton.

Kinsey, Alfred C., Wardell B. Pomeroy, and Clyde E. Martin. 1948. *Sexual Behavior in the Human Male*. Philadelphia: W. B. Saunders.

Kunzel, Regina. 2008. *Criminal Intimacy: Prison and the Uneven History of Modern American Sexuality*. Chicago: University of Chicago Press.

Laqueur, Thomas. 1990. *Making Sex: Body and Gender from the Greeks to Freud*. Cambridge, MA: Harvard University Press.

Loraux, Nicole. 1990. "Herakles: The Super-Male and the Feminine." In *Before Sexuality: The Construction of Erotic Experience in the Ancient Greek World*, ed. David M. Halperin, John J. Winkler, and Froma I. Zeitlin. Princeton, NJ: Princeton University Press.

Manuli, Paola. 1983. "Donne mascoline, femmine sterili, vergini perpetue: La ginecologia greca tra Ippocrate e Sorano." In *Madre materia. Sociologia e biologia della donna greca*, ed. Silvia Campese, Paola Manuli, and Giulia Sissa. Turin: Bollati Boringhieri.

Murphy, Lawrence R. 1988. *Perverts by Official Order: The Campaign against Homosexuals by the United States Navy*. New York: Harrington Park Press.

Orgel, Stephen. 1996. *Impersonations: The Performance of Gender in Shakespeare's England*. Cambridge: Cambridge University Press.

Posner, Richard A. 1992. *Sex and Reason*. Cambridge, MA: Harvard University Press.

Rocke, Michael. 1996. *Forbidden Friendships: Homosexuality and Male Culture in Renaissance Florence*. New York: Oxford University Press.

Rosario, Vernon A., II. 1997. *The Erotic Imagination: French Histories of Perversity*. New York: Oxford University Press.

Rubin, Gayle. 1975. "The Traffic in Women: Notes on the 'Political Economy' of Sex." In *Toward an Anthropology of Women*, ed. Rayna R. Reiter. New York: Monthly Review Press.

Sedgwick, Eve Kosofsky. 1990. *Epistemology of the Closet.* Berkeley: University of California Press.

Tamassia, Arrigo. 1878. "Sull' inversione dell' istinto sessuale." *Rivista sperimentale di freniatria e di medicina legale* 4.

Traub, Valerie. 2002. *The Renaissance of Lesbianism in Early Modern England.* Cambridge: Cambridge University Press.

Wahl, Elizabeth. 2000. *Invisible Relations.* Palo Alto, CA: Stanford University Press, 2000.

Westphal, Karl Friedrich Otto. 1870. "Die conträre Sexualempfindung, Symptom eines neuropathischen (psychopathischen) Zustandes." *Archiv für Psychiatrie und Nervenkrankheiten* 2.

Winkler, John J. 1990. *The Constraints of Desire: The Anthropology of Sex and Gender in Ancient Greece.* New York: Routledge.

Zeitlin, Froma I. 1996. *Playing the Other: Gender and Society in Classical Greek Literature.* Chicago: University of Chicago Press.

21 :: UTOPIA SALLY L. KITCH

Think about all the suffering and inequity in the world. Feel the pain of poverty and despair in your own neighborhood or city and around the globe. Tally all the greed, corruption, and injustice that exist where you would hope to see generosity, honesty, and equality. Now, consider what to do. If your first response is to imagine a "happy island far away, where perfect social relations prevail, and human beings, living under an immaculate constitution and a faultless government, enjoy a simple and happy existence, free from the ... endless worries of actual life," then you may be—or at least think like—a classic utopian (Kaufmann 1879, 1). If it crossed your mind that the world would improve if women were in charge, or if women's and men's roles were identical or at least of equal value, or if sexual distinction could disappear altogether, then you might be or think like a classic "gender utopian." That is, you believe that changed gender relations and identities or equitable sexual practices constitute the core of needed social change. If you think like a "gender utopian," then you are in good company, since sex and gender have been organizing principles of many Western utopian visions—both literary and historical—since at least the fifteenth century. Not coincidentally, gender identities and relations have also been organizing principles for many dystopian visions.

Gender utopianism has historically shared the general characteristics of classic utopian thought. One common theme is the idea that humans are meant to live in a perfect state, which has either been lost or is yet to be achieved (Berlin 1990, 23–24). Most utopians also believe that human nature is the product rather than the cause of prevailing social conditions and, therefore, that good (fair, equitable, efficient) societies or social systems will produce universally good (fair, equitable, efficient) people. In addition, classic utopians tend to believe that the clash of values and the ills and foibles that plague humanity can end, and that everyone can be "virtuous and happy, wise and good and free ... forever"

(Berlin 1990, 47). Because utopians think (or hope) that the values and outcomes of social systems can be formulated in advance of their enactment, they typically analyze the conditions of the present and prescribe conditions for the future that they hope will improve (or even perfect) social organizations and human behavior.

Such perspectives on the human condition and on social possibilities can be appealing, but they are often fraught with peril. Therein lies the utopian paradox. For example, despite its focus on the future, utopian thought is typically and almost inevitably grounded in "histories of the present ... [and] laden ... with conceptual anchors that fix" utopian visions in time and space, thereby unwittingly reinforcing current cultural formations (Gordin, Tiley, and Prakash 2010, 1, 4). Equally ironic, dystopias, usually considered the antitheses of utopias, often emerge from within utopian plans that fail to recognize their own limitations or to calculate their unintended consequences. Of particular concern is the track record of those who try to predict or even imagine what the future will be like. Many technological visions of earlier futurists, such as personal jet packs to power rush-hour traffic, have gone unrealized, for example, while technological innovations, such as personal computers and the smart phone, that have truly transformed the way people work and interact, were not foreseen. Even more troubling for utopian thinkers than the probability that their visions will *not* materialize (or will miss immanent trends) are the difficulties that would accompany their realization. Indeed, fulfilled desires can be just as problematic as dashed hopes. As we shall see, transformative visions for gender roles and sex are particularly vulnerable to those fates.

Because classic utopian thought (or utopianism) is as much about an expansive, even all-encompassing, worldview as it is about explicit plans for new social designs, it has seeped into mainstream ideas about culture, politics, and even consumer products. In the United States in particular, *utopia* is often invoked to accentuate the positive side of any change or challenge, from advertising to AIDS, architecture to artificial insemination, birth control to the broadcast industry, California (the "American Eden") to celibacy, and factories to free love. In recent years, a beverage called Fruitopia hopped onto the utopian bandwagon, and the George Lucas Educational Foundation signaled its idealism with regard to K–12 education by naming its primary project Edutopia.[1] In such usages, *utopia* connotes innovation, considered good in itself, or admirable or pleasurable outcomes. Such perspectives on change, of course, are also subject to the utopian paradox.

This essay's analysis of gender and utopia/dystopia will consider actual, narrative, and theoretical sources of utopianism in Western cultures, especially the United States. It will focus on experimental communities, social commentary, and fictional texts. The essay will not consider utopian or dystopian visions in drama, film, and the visual arts, or in social movements like Romanticism, Nazism, communism, and neoliberal capitalism, which contemporary scholars consider utopian in their "direct engagement with radical change" (Gordin, Tiley, and Prakash 2010, 2). But the general principles of this discussion apply to all kinds of utopian/ dystopian approaches to and perspectives on social movements or changes.

The Utopian Past

Human beings have long enjoyed the idea of utopia. It has appeared in theoretical, philosophical, and literary works and inspired social experiments, some of which evolved from utopian texts, including religious ones. Western utopian literary and philosophical thought goes back at least to Homer's *Odyssey* (especially the land of the Phaeacians), written in the ninth century BCE and to Plato's *Republic,* written in the fourth century BCE. Some would argue for locating the origins of Western utopias in the Hebrew Bible's Garden of Eden or the prophet Isaiah's prediction that, at the end of time, men will beat their swords into plowshares and nations will practice war no more (Berlin 1990,21). Christianity's later goals of regaining Edenic perfection on earth and achieving heaven after death also qualify Christian theology as a source of utopian thought. St. Augustine's *City of God,* written in the fifth century CE, is arguably the first Christian utopian text, since Augustine framed his ideal city as a holy alternative to the hedonistic, "heathen" Roman Empire. Christian Crusaders pursued utopian visions several centuries later as they fought the Muslim "infidels," who were simultaneously yearning for the after-death perfections of Paradise. Thus, utopia was linked with religion early in Western thought.[2]

The real flowering of the Western utopian literary genre occurred during the humanistic period of the Renaissance. That timing has philosophical significance, since utopian thought attributes the success of human social systems to human effort, even if it is divinely inspired. The Renaissance produced one of the first gender-focused utopian literary works by a European—Christine de Pisan's *The Book of the City of Ladies,* written in French (with a bow to St. Augustine) in 1404–1405. Known primarily for its defense of women's intelligence, Christine's work established early that women's hopes for social justice were good partners for utopian ideas.

The word *utopia* first appeared during the Renaissance as well, in the title of Englishman Sir Thomas More's famous text *Utopia,* published in

1516. More constructed the term from two Greek words—*eutopia*, meaning a good place, and *outopia*, meaning no place. Thus, utopia's very etymology suggests that perfect societies, while imaginable, are probably unattainable (Sullivan 1983, 32). Following More's *Utopia* were other improbable English utopian visions, such as Sir Philip Sidney's *Arcadia*, Edmund Spenser's *The Faerie Queene*, and myriad utopian vignettes, such as Shakespeare's Forest of Arden in *As You Like It*, Francis Bacon's Platonic legend in *New Atlantis*, John Bunyan's New Jerusalem in *Pilgrim's Progress*, and John Milton's Christian-classical vision in *Paradise Lost* and *Paradise Regained* (Johnson 1968, 131–34).

That the definition of utopia entered the secular European imagination in literary form suggests its early identification with fantasy, theory, and irony rather than with practical implementation. That situation changed during the eighteenth century, when theorists in Europe and the United States began experimenting with their ideas for social organization. Spurred by the Enlightenment, which also inspired the American and French Revolutions, eighteenth-century European thinkers planned and financed socialist or communist intentional communities predicated on the new values of liberty, equality, and "brotherhood." Like many of their literary predecessors, some were motivated by religious convictions. Many looked to the so-called New World of North America as the perfect venue for practicing their sometimes unorthodox beliefs undisturbed. To them the New World presented an opportunity to reinvent humankind and to fulfill the Christian biblical destiny—implicit in Genesis—to regain Paradise lost.

North America's role as inspiration for utopia peaked in the nineteenth century, when the United States attracted not only streams of hopeful immigrants but also several hundred imported and home-grown religious and secular utopian experiments. Some names of such groups remain familiar today—Oneida, the Shakers, Amana, and New Harmony—and their legacies are surprisingly durable. Many Americans can identify Shaker rocking chairs and wooden boxes, for example, while the name of Amana endures in a line of freezers and microwave ovens. Oneida's entrepreneurial legacy echoes in the trademark of a silverware company. New Harmony, Indiana, has become a charming convention site. Many more experimental communities left less of a mark—Ephrata, the Woman's Commonwealth, Koreshan Unity, Nashoba, Brook Farm, The Kingdom, Fruitlands, Zoar, Aurora, Icaria. (For an analysis of the Woman's Commonwealth, see Kitch 1993.)

Significantly, the populations of US utopian communities in the nineteenth and twentieth centuries were overwhelmingly white. Among the few African American utopians was Rebecca Jackson, a Philadelphia seamstress who moved to the Watervliet Shaker community in 1847, only to become discouraged by the Shakers' disinterest in working with urban blacks. Isabella Van Wagener, known to history as Sojourner Truth, also spent time in utopian communities, including The Kingdom, the Northampton Association of Education and Industry (an Owenite-Fouierist community in Massachusetts), and Harmonia (a spiritualist Quaker seminary and community near Battle Creek, Michigan). Her serial experience in mixed-race communities was mostly negative, however. After the 1850s, Truth was traveling and speaking too much to settle down in a community again, but she was instrumental in creating the Freedmen's Village in Arlington, Virginia, for escaped slaves from the southern states after the Emancipation Proclamation of 1863. She even advocated starting a Negro state on public lands in the West. (For more on Sojourner Truth's utopian connections, see Chmielewski 1993. Perhaps inspired by Truth's vision, after Reconstruction a small group of African Americans founded an all-black town, Nicodemus, in Graham County, Kansas, in 1877.)

The early identification of the New World with utopia also endures in the United States through the legacy of utopian literature and the continued presence of utopia in social thought (as in Edutopia noted earlier). US writers, including women, have produced hundreds of utopian novels and stories, several hundred at the turn of the twentieth century alone. Women once again dominated the US utopian literary genre in the late twentieth century. In the twenty-first century, the United States remains a utopian site—a land of opportunity—to many, while at home writers and thinkers have retreated from the classic utopian vision to a more postmodern fascination with possibilities.

US Gender Utopianism

Gender is a foundational idea in most national imaginaries, in which men are typically seen as the agents of national identities and projects, and women as the containers of national values and reproducers of future citizens (Williams 1996, 6–10). The United States is no exception. This foundational status of gender has had a contradictory effect on the US utopian imagination. On the one hand, traditional roles, heterosexual practices, and male dominance were so prevalent that they were invisible to some utopian thinkers as problems needing solutions. On the other hand, such prevalence inspired many utopian thinkers to make gender roles and sexual norms the centerpiece of their visions.

Not surprisingly, most nineteenth-century utopian fiction written by US women depicted sex and gender as central social and symbolic national features in dire need of change. In the twentieth century, that focus was even more pronounced in utopian fictional works by women (and some men), as well as in separatist (sometimes lesbian) and deliberately egalitarian communal plans (both fictional and actual). Gender was especially central to texts that promoted technological advances to transform reproduction and domestic labor. For example, Robert Francoeur's *Utopian Motherhood* argued that reproductive technology increased options and possibilities and made clear that "we do not yet know what it means to be male or female," in a world in which reproduction, once the defining moment of sexual identity, could be entirely separated from the sexual experience (Francoeur 1970, vii).

Later twentieth- and twenty-first-century treatises on transhumanism contain similar messages. By transcending nature, transhumanists claim, cyborgs that blend biology and technology in synthetic or simulated bodies offer a technological utopian alternative to nature's limitations in terms of human identity, psychology, reproduction, social interaction, and even mortality. Joan Gordon, for example, praised cyberpunk as a "postorganic" utopia far superior to nostalgic pastoral utopian visions (Cherniavsky 1993, esp. 33).

Some feminist theorists of the late twentieth century identified gendered speculative and fictional work as the vanguard of feminist thinking. They even suggested that the purposes of feminism itself are inherently utopian. For example, Marleen Barr and Nicholas Smith claimed in the 1980s that conceptions of utopia that "reconstruct human culture" are precisely what feminism should promote (Barr and Smith 1983, 1). Frances Bartkowski declared toward the end of the 1980s that feminist theory is necessarily utopian since it privileges the "not-yet as the basis for feminist practice, textual, political, or otherwise" (Bartkowski 1989, 12). Drucilla Cornell argued in the early 1990s that "without utopian thinking, feminism is inevitably ensnared in the system of gender identity that devalues the feminine" (Cornell 1991, 169). And a few years later, Lucy Sargisson (1996) declared the imaginative models of feminist utopian fiction as the most effective challenge to a sexist social order.

Critiques of Utopia: Dystopias and the Utopian Paradox

As widespread and popular as utopian thinking has been, however, both in general and in terms of gender theory and feminist theory, the concept of utopia has also had many critics. Some argue that the not-yet too easily slips into the never-should—the quintessence of the utopian paradox. For them, *utopia* means unrealistic dreams and the denial of actual material conditions and realities, which makes writing and thinking about utopias a waste of time and energy. Even more skeptical critics note how many utopian experiments have failed. The late twentieth century offered far too many examples of that. Famous among them were the mass suicide of 913 disciples of Jim Jones's Peoples Temple in Jonestown, Guyana, in 1978 and the immolation of 78 Branch Davidians, followers of David Koresh, in Waco, Texas, in 1993.

The Branch Davidian tragedy followed a weeks-long standoff with the FBI, which suspected Koresh of child sexual abuse and other crimes. Jones led his followers to suicide because of his paranoia about government interference in his community. (For more about these communities, see Kitch 2000, 43–46.) The twenty-first century has also seen the rise of a deadly utopian quest to restore an alleged golden age of Islamic power by a small group of *jihadist* extremists whose methods for achieving Paradise include both individual martyrdom and mass murder.

Such troubling tragedies and trends have demonstrated clearly how utopian visions can become excuses for oppression and violence, from which adherents or even witnesses may have no means of escape. In such cases, decline and defeat result from some of the same principles and forces that inspire utopian visions and experiments—the desire to transcend the ordinary, establish justice, live according to deeply held convictions, or follow a charismatic leader. Such tragedies suggest the potential of the utopian impulse to create its own alleged opposite—a dystopia in which ideals become destructive parodies of themselves or ultimately serve only a small, often elite, segment of the population.

Several twentieth-century dystopian texts cataloged this effect. For example, Aldous Huxley's *Brave New World* (1932) chronicles the ironic translation of socialist ideals into mechanisms of oppression and iron-fisted control. George Orwell's *1984*, published in England in 1948, describes Oceania, an allegedly egalitarian society that has descended into totalitarian rule, which benefits the few and grinds the many into an efficient but rigid conformity under the watchful eye of its absolute rulers. Orwell recognized the basic utopian premise that societies can mold the thoughts and behaviors of the people who live in them, but he was suspicious of systems that overhaul human desire and indoctrinate everyone to the needs of the alleged collective (who are often just the powerful). Through his fiction, Orwell probed the difficulty of determining what the common good really is and how it should be pursued. Echoing that concern, twenty-first-century dystopian visions may document the similarly paradoxical translation of religious ideals into violent anarchy.

Dystopian visions frequently center on manipulations of sexual behavior and gender identities in which the promise of gender liberation betrays innocent believers. Such gender manipulations can be as emblematic of dystopian social control as they are of progress in utopian texts. In many twentieth-century dystopian novels written by men, sexual freedom, a famous hallmark of utopia, epitomizes hell. For example, in Yevgeny Zamyatin's *We* (1921), often considered the first genuinely modern dystopian text, citizens of the One State—a Soviet clone projected a thousand years into the future—believe they have sexual freedom, even though all sexual encounters must be authorized by the state, and family forms, including marriage, are banned because they might inspire noncollective notions of individual worth. Zamyatin's dystopian sexual vision acknowledges the differing effects of the sexual system on men and women, since women's sexual transgressions—such as becoming pregnant illegally—result in stricter sanctions than do men's. Zamyatin fell prey to utopian presentism by not interrogating some of his own ideas about women, however. Instead, his novel attributes women's social power to their sexual allure and romanticizes motherhood (Booker 1994a, 25, 34–35).

Sexuality is also central to dystopian gender identities in Georges Perec's *W, or the Memory of a Childhood* (1975). The island society, W, is intensely competitive, especially in athletics. Women are excluded from athletics, however, and restricted to housewifery and childbearing. Pregnancies are orchestrated by the state, which mandates public rapes by gangs of male athletes who chase nude women around a track (Booker 1994b, 214). This sexual aggression parodies "survival of the fittest" mentalities through its promise that the best athletes will have the most reproductive success.

Thomas Berger's *Regiment of Women* (1973) defies the dystopian norm a bit by incorporating women's increased social power into its vision of transformed gender relations in twenty-first-century New York. The novel also distinguishes between biological women and the trappings of femininity and between biological men and the performance of masculinity. Indeed, conventionally feminine occupations, clothing, hairstyles, and body parts still signify social subordination, but they are adopted and performed by cross-dressed men with long hair, makeup, and silicone breasts rather than by women. At the same time, women in Berger's society can enjoy all the social power typically ascribed to men, but only if they bind their breasts and dress and behave in conventionally masculine ways. The power they acquire through cross-dressing is absolute and tyrannical, however, as illustrated by the society's predominant form of sex—in which the female-men strap on dildos and rape the male-women. Otherwise, organ-to-organ heterosexual sex has been replaced by incubator reproduction.

The exact gender implications of Berger's dystopian vision remain ambiguous. Is his portrayal of male-women and female-men a spoof of feminism? Or (as a critic for *Ms.* magazine opined) does it indict masculinity and conventional male behavior, since tyranny still wears masculine dress (Landon 1983, esp. 22–23)? Whichever is the better interpretation, Berger's novel stands out among men's dystopian texts because it considers gender a factor in social and political power apart from sexuality and reproduction.

Gender typically plays an even larger role in women's late twentieth- and early twenty-first-century dystopian novels. For example, the source of the dystopian militaristic police state in Margaret Atwood's *The Handmaid's Tale* (1985) is excessive male power, a logical extension of the extremist Christian fundamentalism Atwood witnessed in her own time. In Gilead—a variant of US society in the not too distant future—women are defined solely by their sexual relationships to men and by their reproductive roles: as wives, servants (Marthas), baby breeders (Handmaids), trainers of Handmaids (Aunts), or prostitutes to government officials (Jezebels). Women who fail at or refuse those roles become Unwomen, condemned to clean up fatally toxic waste sites.

Atwood later explored the dystopian implications of reproductive technology (via drugs) and genetic engineering in *Oryx and Crake* (2003). In that work, Glenn Crake's scheme to manipulate human sexual attraction and reproductive cycles and to create human beings to order, based on specified genetic characteristics, is clearly a misdirected utopian scheme. The novel links unchecked technology—specifically the Internet—with pornography, rampant sexuality, and violence, and it illustrates the fine line between a utopian and a megalomaniacal criminal imagination. The novel also explores the ironies of the cyborgian dream and promotes the very nonutopian idea that art, creativity, and even genius are more likely to result from the processes of natural reproduction than from engineered human genomes.

The Utopian Paradox: Overview

As such dystopian visions illustrate, the utopian paradox arises from failures to account for the full range of consequences, complexities, contingencies, and nuances of human life and relationships, mistaking specific individual or group visions of social perfection for a universal ideal, and believing in the promise of perfection rather than in the value of engagement with ever-changing and competing social goods. Utopian constructions—in both fact and fiction—also divide and categorize individuals and ideas while ignoring important connections among them (or vice versa), exclude mechanisms for dissent and democratic transfers of power, and assume incorrectly that the future is either finite or fully knowable. In light of those difficulties, utopia's lure must always be tempered by the familiar caveat: Be careful what you wish for; it might come true.

The seeds of the utopian paradox were already germinating in Thomas More's *Utopia,* since that novel's "ideal" society is founded on natural reason rather than on the author's own firmly held belief in divine law. More left his readers to determine whether Utopia's embrace of euthanasia, divorce, and religious pluralism, among other reforms, along with its preference for natural pleasures, produced intended or unintended consequences (Ackroyd 1998, 168–69).

Long-standing evidence of the paradox is also apparent beyond literary constructions like More's, Orwell's, Berger's, or Atwood's, as groups or individuals have actually pursued heaven on earth, according to their own lights, only to induce hell on earth for others. This real-life version of the utopian paradox is famously illustrated in the United States by the settlement—some would say invasion—of North America by white Europeans who identified the "New World" as a land of utopian promise for themselves in the seventeenth century. By overlooking the fact that their new frontier was already populated, those Europeans underestimated the resistance they would encounter from Native Americans, who would soon come to regard them as interlopers in their own Eden, crafted by their own gods, and requiring no improvements from outsiders. European utopian desires also produced dystopian results for African slaves, who were forced to play a dehumanized and perilous role in a paternalistic economic fable fabricated by white masters. For Indians, slaves, and free blacks, America's utopian promises of freedom and self-determination became hollow mockeries. Those in US-forged chains constructed their own utopian image, of Canaan—by which they meant Canada—as they fantasized and planned their escape from the US south. Such paradoxes illustrate why utopias may be more valuable as social critique than as blueprints for change.

Nonutopian strategies for social change are more likely to avoid the paradox to the extent that they probe multiple truths and incremental outcomes rather than design wholesale solutions to predetermined problems. Such strategies recognize ambiguity and contingency, question categories and labels, acknowledge the limitations of present-day understanding for future social planning, respect counterarguments and dissident voices, and reexamine their own foundational ideas over time.

They further seek to incorporate the inevitability of unpredictable change into their approach.

The Utopian Gender Paradox

Because of its centrality to the structures of both narratives and experimental societies, gender serves as a magnifying lens for the utopian paradox. Indeed, in many ways, gender is the crux of the utopian paradox, since attitudes toward sex, women's status, gender roles, family, marriage, and motherhood are deeply held and easily reside in the ideological blind spots of those who would reconceptualize social arrangements. The vulnerability of gender innovations to the hazards of utopian thinking— its present-focus, its failure to reexamine foundational principles over time, its tendency to concentrate power in a single leader, and its intolerance of dissent, among other characteristics—often derail daring and revolutionary plans for sexual practices and gender-role innovations or cause them to backfire. (For more on the hazards of utopian thought, see Kitch 2000, 21–116.) Even those who understand the utopian paradox often miss the pitfall of gender: recall Zamyatin's limited ideas about gender norms, mores, and behaviors that would challenge his own dystopian vision. The best Zamyatin could do when it came to gender was to perpetuate his own conventional understanding of heterosexual seduction and the bonding of idealized mothers to their idealized babies.

Indeed, the inevitable limitations of utopian change agents' perspectives on gender conventions, as well as innovations, may also make them unconsciously replicate the gender conditions they set out to change. For example, although few nineteenth-century utopian communities intended to reinforce the underlying gender attitudes of their time, Carol Kolmerten has concluded, after years of studying American utopian communities, that "utopian visions, with few exceptions, have always been grounded firmly in ... patriarchal power," which "infuses all of [our] culture's institutions" (Kolmerten 1990, 2). Invisible preconceptions limit the social solutions utopian thinkers can imagine and may prevent them from identifying the key social problems their future visions should address.

Even female and feminist utopian thinkers can fall into this presentist trap with regard to gender. For example, nineteenth-century utopian novelist Mary Griffith constructed a utopian society in which women's poverty would be eliminated by guaranteed sewing jobs for poor women. An income-producing solution to women's economic dependence on men seemed radical to Griffith in 1836 but appears ludicrous in hindsight.

More contemporary utopian visions are likely to seem equally quaint in fewer years than their designers might suppose.

Examples of the Gender Paradox

Plato's *Republic* provides an early example of the utopian gender paradox. That text's revolutionary claims about male and female leadership potential were almost equally matched by its simultaneous prescriptions for gender hierarchy. For example, book 5 asserts that nothing intrinsic in women's nature prevents them from governing the ideal state. Indeed, in Plato's plan for the perfect *polis,* a female philosopher-guardian can theoretically become a philosopher-queen, providing she has been trained like her male counterparts. But Plato's acceptance of social hierarchy and stratified classes in his own day prevented him from recommending social reforms for ordinary citizens that might reduce male control over women and children (Halliwell 1993, 53). The *Republic* also persists in differentiating the skills (versus the nature) of men and women. Thus, although proper training could enable women to perform the same tasks as men, Plato suggested that men would likely continue to perform their gender-related tasks better than women (Bluestone 1987, 117; Nielsen 1984, esp. 153).

More's *Utopia* offers another historic example of the utopian gender paradox. Although that text is arguably a sixteenth-century revision of the *Republic,* the ensuing centuries, and More's own experience (especially his years among Carthusian monks), did little to immunize his text from paradox. Although More envisioned much more limited social roles for women than did Plato, *Utopia*'s rare attempts at gender innovation illustrate both the presentist limitations of the utopian genre and the paradox of apparent reforms. For example, women in More's *Utopia* have little sanctioned social function beyond "the office and charge of cookery" in communal dining halls and the care of children. Communal dining halls were innovative in their reduction of individual women's food preparation burdens, but the novel contradicts that innovation by urging women to eat their dinners by the dining room doors so "they may rise without trouble or disturbance of anybody [men?], and go thence into the nursery" (More [1516] 1963, 84). In addition, the novel criticizes the practice of arranged marriages by suggesting that prospective wives and husbands in Utopia view one another in the nude before betrothal— the woman chaperoned by a "sad and honest matron" and the "wooer" by a "sage and discreet man" (116). Given More's complex relationship to ideas in *Utopia*, it is difficult to determine his personal views about such matters (including why the matron should be sad rather than wise), but the novel's attention to an epiphenomenon of arranged marriages rather than to their deeper difficulties reflects not real innovation but rather moderate—and possibly ironic—revision of the conventions of his time. Mired in the sixteenth century, *Utopia's* gender agenda pales by comparison with Plato's vision of women as prospective philosopher-queens, even as both texts suffer from the gender paradox (Ackroyd 1998, 114).

Nineteenth- and twentieth-century fictional utopias and utopian communal experiments encountered similar imaginative limitations when they attempted to address gender issues and promote women's rights. Edward Bellamy's enormously popular *Looking Backward, 2000–1887* provides a literary example. Bellamy explicitly advocated sexual equality, declaring at one point that woman's "personal dependence upon man for her livelihood" was the root of her historical disadvantage. Instead of blaming women for being deficient in skills, as many of his contemporaries might have done, Bellamy acknowledged men's culpability for women's condition: "Men [have] seized for themselves the whole product of the world and left women to beg and wheedle for their share" (Bellamy [1888] 1982, 192–93). But his understanding of one root cause of women's subordination to men did not prevent him from overlooking others. Indeed, Bellamy maintained his belief that male and female natures are not only different but also unequal. Therefore, his text falls into the utopian gender paradox, as women's work outside the home in Bellow's utopia is limited to "labor of a sort adapted to their powers" (188), which the novel assumes are inferior to and less enduring than men's.

Nineteenth-century experimental communities that advocated stretching or even shattering conventions concerning gender roles and sexuality also exhibit signs of the gender paradox, and in those cases an ironic sensibility was not the cause. For example, Robert Owen's New Harmony, founded in Indiana in 1825, was dedicated to women's independence and education, egalitarian marriages, and simplified divorce procedures. Owen also eschewed what he considered irrational religion, because of its role in perpetuating women's subordination (Kolmerten 1990, 71–76). However, evidence from women who lived at New Harmony reveals the community's gender paradox. Despite the alleged centrality of women's education to the community's goals, women were not allowed to read the newspapers that arrived daily. Furthermore, all New Harmony women were relegated to domestic work. Even one highly trained female teacher who came to New Harmony from Paris in order to pursue her educational ideals was required to spend more than seven hours a day on housework on top of her eight hours of teaching (Kesten 1993, 104).

The Oneida Community, which flourished from 1850 to 1880, also partook of the utopian gender paradox. John Humphrey Noyes founded

Oneida specifically to overhaul conventional sexual practices and gender roles. Indeed, some historians have regarded Oneida as "one of the most radical institutional efforts to change relations between the sexes and improve women's status in America." Oneidan "Perfectionists" practiced male continence or *coitus interruptus*, which made men responsible for birth control and encouraged women to enjoy sex without fear of pregnancy. The community also established communal forms of child-rearing and eliminated monogamous marriage in favor of "complex" or group marriage in which all community members considered themselves married to all others of the opposite sex. Reproduction was regulated to serve community needs. The stated intention of complex marriage was to eliminate the sexual double standard and promote female sexual expression (Foster 1991, 91–92).

Despite those liberating intentions, however, Oneida became a sexually oppressive dystopia for many women and girls who lived there. While nonmonogamous complex marriage dramatically altered women's wifely and maternal roles and theoretically freed women for a variety of community activities, Oneidan women were still expected to defer to men and to serve as helpmates to all men in the community. Complex marriage also resulted in female sexual exploitation. Noyes insisted on sexually initiating all female virgins himself after their first menses, and other older men had sexual access to their pick of young women, aged twelve to twenty-five, on a daily basis (Klee-Hartzell 1993). Male community elders also determined which couples could reproduce. Women could refuse but not actively choose their sexual partners (Kern 1981, 245). Thus, women's freedom from both marriage and excessive childbearing entailed systematic subordination to and forced sexual activity with multiple partners.

What resulted was a nightmarish, dystopian replication of the same problems the community originally hoped to solve, plus a few others. Oneidan practices inflicted emotional harm through the oversexualization of many female childhoods, as documented in women's letters and diaries. Adding insult to injury, community policy further sexualized the same girls by restricting their access to education. No girls at Oneida were allowed to attend college or to receive formal instruction after age twelve. Such restrictions ensured that Oneidan girls would develop only domestic, sexual, and reproductive identities and roles (Klee-Hartzell 1993, 198).

To an important degree, celibacy provided a mechanism for forestalling the utopian gender paradox in some nineteenth-century communities. Celibacy effectively equalized women and men by eliminating the disparity in their reproductive roles and removing the disruptive possibility of sex from male-female relationships. It thereby served as a material basis for women's elevated cultural status. In addition, celibacy transformed a sign of women's alleged need for male protection—sexual purity—into a positive, empowering community value. (For more on celibacy's role in transforming gender roles in nineteenth-century communities, see Kitch 1989.)

For example, the Shakers' commitment to celibacy from the group's eighteenth-century inception was tied to the unusual empowerment of women, starting with Shaker founder Ann Lee's divine revelation that she was the second coming of Christ in the female line. Thus, Lee had divine authority for claiming lifelong celibacy, despite having had eight pregnancies. (Lee's claim was based on the fact that all of her children died either in utero or in early childhood.) Lee's revelation also inspired the group's official name—the United Society of Believers in Christ's Second Appearing. Moreover, the dual Christhead was indicative in Shaker belief of a dual Godhead—Mother and Father God. On that heavenly example, Believers established a dual-sex community-governance structure in which both sexes were represented at every level—Brothers, Sisters, Mothers, and Fathers. Celibacy and gender segregation allowed Believers to maintain their gender-balanced structure without reinforcing the inequities inherent in mainstream society's sexual and marital relationships and parenthood. The Shakers were ultimately thwarted in maintaining the dual-sex leadership structure, however, because they had more trouble recruiting men than recruiting women. It was that difficulty, and not the group's commitment to celibacy (as is widely believed), that eventually made the Shakers decide to stop taking in members in 1920. (See Kitch 1989, 202.)

Celibacy also invested Shaker women with greater spiritual power than Shaker men. Believers recognized men as historically more sinful than women in sexual matters—a reversal of the mainstream Christian idea of woman as first in sin. Therefore, even celibate men needed women's leadership to atone for their sex's (and possibly their own) shameful history. Sexually purer to begin with, the celibate woman could, in the words of Shaker Alonzo Hollister, "comprehend [man's] lost and captive state, the causes which brought him into it, and compass him with wisdom and knowledge to rise out of it" (quoted in Kitch 1989, 90–91). Celibacy thereby "feminized" Shakers as a whole and reinterpreted the mainstream value of female sexual purity in ways that promoted women's social power.

Celibacy did not eliminate the conventional sexual division of labor in Shaker communities, however, which confirms that sex reform alone does not transform all gender conventions. Sisters still cooked the food and mended the men's clothes. Jobs were also sex-specific in Shaker industries, although the inequities implied by those gender conventions were at least somewhat mitigated by the Shakers' belief that male and female jobs were complementary. Therefore, Believers of both sexes could take credit for the community's economic success (Kitch 1989, 126–41).

Celibacy also defused the utopian gender paradox in another, less well-known nineteenth-century community, the Woman's Commonwealth, organized in the 1870s in Belton, Texas. The Commonwealth's founder was also a woman, Martha McWhirter, who was divinely inspired to become celibate (after giving birth to twelve children). McWhirter's mostly female followers also committed themselves to celibacy, which, not coincidentally, put an end to the women's unsatisfactory marriages and legally reclassified them as *femes soles*. That change allowed the women to own property and conduct business without male approval or interference, rights denied to married women in Texas until 1913, when the state's married women's property act was finally passed (the last such act in the United States). Thus, Commonwealth members, also known as Sanctificationists, extended the personal power they achieved through celibacy into the world of business. (For a full history and analysis of the Woman's Commonwealth, see Kitch 1993.)

Although these celibate communities were less implicated in the utopian gender paradox than other utopian experiments, they did not completely escape it. That's because women's empowerment and agency achieved through their commitment to celibacy actually reinforced the notion that women's reproductive roles and sexual identities are an obstacle to their full humanity, freedom, and social power. Moreover, celibacy exacted a high price for equality by requiring of women what many would (and did) consider a dystopian sacrifice in order to gain simple recognition of their personhood.

Lesbian separatist groups of the 1960s through the 1980s, such as Adobeland, Silver Circle, Wildfire, Green Hope Farm, La Luz, the Gutter Dyke Collective, and the Lavender Collective, suffered from a related version of the utopian gender paradox, despite their commitment to women's empowerment and rejection of heterosexual norms. That is, by making sexual characteristics the primary—if not the exclusive—criterion for membership, lesbian communities (like the celibate groups of the previous century) often set themselves up to falter on the same sex-defined grounds on which they were founded.

Lesbian communities typically regarded single-sex living arrangements as key to developing women's identities beyond male definitions. Alix Dobkin explained the concept of separatism by saying that men's presence inhibited her feelings about herself, while "conversely, when I know that I am in the exclusive company of women I feel safe enough to 'open up'" (Dobkin 1988, 287). Although the goals of lesbian communities and collectives varied, most sought to create a place where "murderous patriarchal oppression is unknown" (Moontree 1988, 248).

In practice, however, many lesbian communitarians found that achieving their gender and sexual goals did not necessarily produce harmonious power-sharing or complete equity. Two common bones of contention were money and child-rearing practices. As early as 1973, a member of the Gutter Dyke Collective concluded that "the oppression we share as lesbian women in a burning patriarchal world was not enough to bind us together" (quoted in Shugar 1995, 52). Lesbian assumptions about fixing society through sexual practices often proved as limited and paradoxical a foundation for community organization as celibacy and complex marriage.

Feminist Utopian Fiction and the Utopian Paradox

Because so few experimental communities in US history had any feminist intent, let alone success, the primary source of feminist utopian rumination and experimentation has been textual, much of it fictional. In such texts, *feminist* has typically signified a wish to increase women's power over their own identities, roles, and choices and to promote their leadership of social systems. For some writers, like Suzy McKee Charnas in her *Holdfast* series, it meant "parity" between the sexes and the elimination of all dualisms (Mohr 2005, 145). For others, it meant reconceptualizing and rebuilding basic social institutions from the ground up, from the family to the nation, in order to rewrite and equalize or even eliminate gender scripts. For most, *feminism* meant at the very least recognizing that women are fully human.

Most explicitly US feminist utopian texts were produced in the nineteenth and twentieth centuries, although there is technically a three-hundred-year history of Western feminist utopian literature. Consistent with the hazards of classic utopian thought, many feminist texts produced in those centuries suffer from the utopian gender paradox, with unintentionally presentist prescriptions for changes in sexual practices and gender norms, naïve beliefs in the universality of solutions and ideals, undemocratic charismatic leaders, intolerance for dissent, and blind spots regarding gender, as well as race and class. With the approach of the twenty-first century, feminist writers began to recognize their own implication in the utopian gender paradox and to acknowledge and lament the dystopian underside of even feminist ideas for social transformation. The full range of texts that constitute the feminist utopian fictional heritage helps to explain how that awareness developed.

From 1405 to 1920: Separatist, Maternal, and Reformist Utopias

As noted earlier, arguably the first feminist utopian vision in Western literature was Christine de Pisan's fifteenth-century *Book of the City of Ladies*. Her main purpose was to defend women's virtues from misogynist attacks, especially by Catholic clerics, and to establish a world based on female worth. French *précieux* works followed in the seventeenth-century, including Marie-Catherine D'Aulnoy's "L'Isle de la Félicité" (1690). That text depicted a utopian sanctuary in which wealthy, educated women could enjoy a life of intellectual, aesthetic, and sensual pleasure without male interference (Capasso 1994, 44–47). Although there were male *précieux*, the movement appealed primarily to women. Its goals included aesthetic and moral reform, specifically the purification of language and manners and the appreciation of the arts (Capasso 1994, esp. 35–36).

Three-quarters of a century later, British writer Sarah Robinson Scott's *Millennium Hall* (1762) described a separatist feminist utopian community free from the threat of male power and violence and dedicated to women's pursuit of their own spiritual and intellectual interests. The model of female friendship in the novel is the idealized mother-daughter relationship, which forms the basis of a functional home and, by extension, a successful community (Dunne 1994, esp. 65–71). Clearly rooted in their writers' class-bound visions, such sources helped sow the seeds of the utopian gender paradox.

US feminist writers joined the utopian parade between 1840 and 1920, when suffrage activism nourished hopes (but not real plans) for gender equality in mainstream society. Some novels from this period adopted the all-female society as a mechanism for women's liberation. For example, Mary E. Bradley Lane's *Mizora: A Prophecy* (1880–1881) depicted a land that had been without men for so long—more than two thousand years—that Mizoran women had forgotten what men are. Because their all-female civilization had eliminated everything men seemed to care about, such as war, males eventually became superfluous to the society and disappeared. Without male domination, Mizoran women discovered that mothers are the "only important part of all life" and that asexual reproduction is not only possible but also more conducive than ordinary reproduction to the improvement of the human species (Lane [1880–1881] 1984, 124–35).

Charlotte Perkins Gilman's *Herland* (1915) also depicted a two-thousand-year-old female society left without men, in their case because war and an accompanying natural disaster eliminated men from their isolated territory. The women developed the ability to reproduce through parthenogenesis, just as certain insect species do in the absence of males. Each woman produced at most a single child, a daughter, and the urge to procreate came upon her only when she was emotionally mature. As in Mizora, Herland's organizing principle was motherhood, which was considered less an instinct than an art and a science that only the most gifted Herlanders were allowed to practice directly by caring for and educating children. Other Herlanders did work that indirectly promoted the growth and well-being of the children, such as producing food, tending the forests, and building houses.

These and other maternally based utopian visions, such as Alice Ilgenfritz Jones's *Unveiling a Parallel: A Romance* (1893) and Lois Waisbrooker's *A Sex Revolution* (1894), reflect what is now called "gender feminism," which promotes women's rights by accentuating their allegedly unique attributes and capabilities. Yet, despite the arguably feminist qualities of such novels, including their depiction of expanded work roles and social activity for mothers, the feminist utopian paradox lurked just beneath their surfaces. Like celibacy, maternal versions of utopia tacitly concede the primacy of reproduction to women's identities and roles. While they glorify rather than eliminate women's unique capacity to bear and nourish children, maternal utopian novels not only promote traditional values but virtually equate *woman* and *mother*. At the same time, by disassociating motherhood from sexual activity, maternal utopias suppress an important element of women's humanity. They therefore, and paradoxically, diminish women's identities even as they expand their behavioral repertoires. Moreover, these maternal visions often depict women of the writer's own (typically white) race and class, thereby associating feminism with a near-eugenicist approach to the ideal future. Gilman in particular has been harshly criticized for that aspect of her thinking.

The majority of nineteenth- and early twentieth-century feminist utopian novels did not, however, promote maternal separatism, invent new societies from scratch, or eliminate men. Rather, most were more reformist in spirit. They offered enlightened social programs that would allegedly eliminate the inequities of marriage and traditional family life and revise assumptions about women's capabilities in sexually integrated societies (Lewes 1995, 44).

The reformist character of such visions did not eliminate their risk of the feminist utopian paradox, though. For example, Mary Griffith's *Three Hundred Years Hence* (1836) focuses on eliminating war, elevating the importance of religion, reforming the insurance industry, and modifying building codes. Having gained political power sometime after 1836 in the novel, the women of 2136 institute general reforms and transform women's lives via inheritance rights for wives and the (myopic) guarantee of sewing jobs or vocational training for poor girls (Griffith [1836] 1984, 42–45). Jane Sophia Appleton's "Sequel to the 'Vision of Bangor in the Twentieth Century'" (1848) and Marie Stevens Case Howland's *Papa's Own Girl; A Novel* (1874) provide additional paradoxical examples of the reformist feminist utopia.

Many of Gilman's early twentieth-century texts, including "A Woman's Utopia" (1907) and its revision, *Moving the Mountain* (1911), are also reformist, but perhaps more pointedly focused on changing women's economic roles than many other works. (Gilman had laid out her analysis of women's economic dependence in 1898, in her groundbreaking *Women in Economics: A Study of the Economic Relation between Men and Women as a Factor in Social Evolution*.) Gilman's reformist utopian plans substituted public nurseries, communal kitchens, and woman-centered apartment houses for the private home and replaced the domestic drudgery of individual women with professionalized household services. Gilman's works also envision meaningful paid work for women and reduced prerogatives for men (Kolmerten 1990, 110–11). Such visions converge in *Moving the Mountain*, where a visitor to the future world of 1940 is told about the riches women have amassed by commercializing their domestic skills: "We were so used to the criminal waste of individual housekeeping that it never occurred to us to estimate the amount of profit there really was in the business" (Gilman [1910] 1980, 185).

The focus of these novels on diverse roles for women in a recognizable, sexually integrated society reflects reformist feminist agendas in which power and privilege are redistributed within an existing but improved social system. That sounds reasonable enough, but it produces its own form of feminist utopian paradox by associating women's progress with a particular social agenda that may miss or oversimplify the deepest causes of gender inequities. A century later, we can see how the paradox works: "improvements" in public health and safety and professionalized domestic services, while socially progressive from one perspective, cannot transform all gender relations or ensure all women's economic well-being. Most egregiously, the reformist feminist utopian agenda often entails liberating one class of women through services performed by women of another, thereby predicating a middle-class white utopia on a working-class dystopia (or status-quopia!). Gilman's visions, admittedly, were somewhat less subject to this paradox than others', in part because she imagined that every woman would become an entrepreneur of household skills through collective effort. Nevertheless, attention to the racial implications of implicit class disparities was also absent from her reformist works.

Reformist novels that prescribed nontraditional work for women were especially susceptible to the feminist utopian paradox. Included in this group are novels in which women fly airplanes, as in Anna Adolph's *Arqtiq* (1899) and M. Louise Moore's *Al Modad* (1892); work as farmers, as in Eloise O. Richberg's *Reinstern* (1900); and perform physical labor, as in Martha Bensley Bruère's *Mildred Carver, USA* (1919). Even more than other reformist works, such novels assume that a single social change— typically women's greater access to careers—will in and of itself improve gender relations and eliminate gender hierarchy throughout society. But such reforms overlook many other aspects and causes of women's oppression. For example, Gertrude, the main character of Helen Winslow's *A Woman for Mayor* (1909), becomes politically active and runs for mayor. But when her fiancé enters the race, she withdraws to live happily ever after with him, in the belief that "the loving heart of the woman was to stand alongside the strong desire of the man" (quoted in Kolmerten 1990, 118). Gertrude's career opportunity does little to challenge even her own deeply ingrained, presentist gender identity or relationship values. Her entry into political life, had she followed it through, was even less likely to alter society as a whole. The last century has demonstrated only too well that women's political presence, even in leadership positions, does not necessarily transform either politics or gender hierarchies, behaviors, or values. (Think Sarah Palin.)

After 1960: Communitarian Values and Separatism

After a forty-year hiatus, reflecting a parallel lull in overt political action for women's rights, the production of feminist utopian fiction once again surged after the mid-1960s and peaked during the feminist activism of the 1970s and 1980s. Well-known examples from this period include Ursula Le Guin's *The Left Hand of Darkness* (1969) and *The Dispossessed* (1974); Marge Piercy's *Woman on the Edge of Time* (1976); Mary Staton's *From the Legend of Biel* (1975); Suzy McKee Charnas's *Motherlines* (1978); Doris Lessing's *Canopus in Argos* series (1979–1983); Suzette Elgin's *Native Tongue* series (1984–1994); Katherine V. Forrest's *Daughters of a Coral Dawn* (1984); Joan Slonczewski's *A Door into Ocean* (1986); and Pamela Sargent's *The Shore of Women* (1986). Evidence of the feminist paradox in such works has special significance since so many feminist theorists of that period believed along with Frances Bartkowski that "utopian thinking is crucial to feminism" (1989, 12). (For more on utopianism as a feature of late twentieth-century US feminist thought, see Kitch 2000, 97–160.)

Motherhood is less central to woman's identity in late twentieth-century feminist utopian works than in earlier novels, but the mother-daughter relationship often remains a model for women's relationships to one another and for society as a whole, as exemplified by the novels' preference for consensual political decision-making. In addition, communitarian, almost tribal, values dominate the texts (Kessler 1984, 17–18; Kelso 2008, 3–19). Several utopian works of the period, such as Dorothy Bryant's *The Kin of Ata Are Waiting for You* (1976) and Sally Gearhart's *The Wanderground* (1979), glorify women's traditional association with nature, depicting it as both the source of social life and a form of feminine spirituality that could replace conventional, androcentric religion (Kiser and Baker 1984, esp. 33; Kessler 1984).

Many of these characteristics can be found in Marge Piercy's *Woman on the Edge of Time* (1975). Piercy's text contrasts the brutality, individualism, materialism, classism, racism, sexism, and competitiveness of the twentieth-century United States with a future time in which small, ecologically sensitive, egalitarian communities thrive on a model of cooperative, decentralized local governments and deregulated familial relationships. In those qualities, the novel reflects the critique of patriarchy and capitalism as tools for oppressing women found in many feminist utopian works of the period.

The text's future society, Mattapoisett, appears to be a very different place from Piercy's present. It imposes no restrictive sex roles or fixed gender identities. Indeed, conventional masculinity has disappeared, and a universal femininity reigns. Motherhood is important, but it is no longer solely a female value or experience. Ova are fertilized and fetuses gestated in artificial wombs, and men take hormones that enable them to breastfeed the babies they then help to raise. Each child has three "mothers," male and/or female. To reinforce the blurring of gender roles and the elimination of gender hierarchy, Piercy introduced nonsexist pronouns, such as *per* (for "person") instead of either *him* or *her*. Piercy's concern with the role of language in both maintaining and exterminating oppressive gender relations echoed many feminists' preoccupation with the same issue, as well as other utopian writers' experiments with new language.[3]

Piercy's work was immensely influential as a feminist model, but that did not immunize it from paradox (or criticism). As in other works of its type, the novel posits an ideal future in reaction against present conditions, but it follows a universalist feminist script very rooted in its time.

Later readers might wonder how feminine qualities can still be identified after gender disappears, for example. And in an era when body morphology has become increasingly important to human identity, today's readers might wonder about the effects of Piercy's desire to divorce the two completely. Piercy could also be criticized for misunderstanding the idea of parental bonding and, in general, throwing the baby of sexuality out with the bathwater. The novel also ignores racial differences in its blanket assumptions about women's ideals (a utopian tendency that may explain why few US women of color have written utopian fiction in any period).[4]

In Piercy's work, as elsewhere, utopian "solutions" to the "problem" of womanhood seem unable to accommodate women's diverse identities and desires. Assumptions in the novels about universal feminine or feminist values also prevent close scrutiny of those values and promote idealization. Why perpetuate the myth that women are experts at relationships, for example? Few novels interrogate the validity of that claim, and some even make it a premise for an entire social system. At the same time, why assume that conventionally masculine characteristics are necessarily bad? Yet many utopian texts of the period overlook the possible benefits to society and to women of such tainted concepts as self-reliance, ambition, and dissent.

Lesbian feminist utopian novels of the period offer interesting variations on the feminist utopian paradox. Among the best known are Monique Wittig's *Les guérillères* (1969), Sally Gearhart's *The Wanderground* (1979), Katherine Forrest's *Daughters of a Coral Dawn* (1984), and Jewelle Gomez's *The Gilda Stories* (1991). The themes of such novels include variations on communal social systems, with controlling metaphors from warriors (Wittig) to vampires (Gomez). The lesbian novels also resemble certain maternal and celibate utopian designs from the nineteenth century by offering women self-definition and self-determination through reconceptualized sexuality and sexual practices and allowing them to transform conventional sources of disparagement into sources of female strength. But lesbian utopian texts of the period are also subject to paradox. Universalist lesbian visions, for example, exclude women who cannot or do not wish to fit particular definitions of lesbian womanhood and idealize those who did, thereby ignoring internal diversity and suppressing dissent.

The Feminist Retreat from Utopia

The paradoxes and contradictions in maternal, communal, reformist, separatist, lesbian, and other classic feminist utopian visions became more apparent as the twentieth century drew to a close, even among writers of utopian (or speculative) feminist fiction themselves. Some disavowed the utopian genre altogether, although they continued to contemplate the future of feminist issues and gender relations. As Tom Moylan concluded in 1986, feminist texts were beginning to "reject utopia as blueprint while preserving it as dream" (quoted in Teslenko 2003, 164).

Examples of the fictional retreat from utopian feminism multiplied in the mid-1980s, coincident with a political backlash against feminism itself (commemorated by Susan Faludi's *Backlash: The Hidden War against Women* in 1991). But the retreat was prefigured in earlier works, such as Joanna Russ's 1975 *The Female Man* and Ursula Le Guin's 1974 *The Dispossessed*. Le Guin's novel is even subtitled *An Ambiguous Utopia*, referring to the text's deliberate complication of utopian feminist expectations: its utopian planet, Gethen, remains a troubled place despite liberated gender roles and sexual identities and the total absence of rape and war (Peel 1990, esp. 39–41). Suzy McKee Charnas's *Motherlines* stuck pins in utopian feminist notions of sisterhood by depicting jealous and contentious female "tribes." The novel's protagonist, Alldera, is disappointed by the acrimony because she "wanted the women to be perfect, and they were not" (Barr 1983, 62).

Other retreats from feminist utopias in that period include Doris Lessing's *Marriages between Zones Three, Four, and Five* (1980), Ursula Le Guin's *Always Coming Home* (1985), and Sheri Tepper's *Beauty: A Novel* (1991).[5] Lessing portrayed her feminist utopia (Zone 3), which looked ideal on the surface, as an insular, self-satisfied, and complacent society (White 1983, esp. 138; Peel 2002, 92), whose lack of imagination contributed to women's oppression without their realizing it (Peel 2002, 36–38). The novel begins with a utopia, then dares readers "to appreciate the taxing process of shedding parochialism," as it redefines utopia from a "static place to a pragmatic process that questions any individual place" (Peel 2002, 108). Le Guin's *Always Coming Home* went even further to express contempt for utopian thinking in general. Pandora, the voice of Le Guin in the novel, says, "I never did like smartass utopians. Always so much healthier and saner and sounder and fitter and kinder and tougher and wiser and righter than me and my family and friends. People who have the answers are boring, nice. Boring, boring, boring" (Le Guin 1985, 335).

Sheri Tepper's plucky, time-traveling character, Beauty, recognizes the sexist evils of all ages, including her own fourteenth-century aristocratic life. Because she has spent much of her childhood disguised as a boy and working in her father's stables, with her look-alike half-sister playing her role in the castle, Beauty manages to escape the curse inflicted on her at birth (as in the fairy tale Tepper rewrites). As Beauty's beloved castle is overtaken by the hundred-year sleep and the thorny rose vine predicted in the curse, Beauty escapes, only to be absconded into the future—the late twenty-first century—where she learns that things will only get worse. The future is riddled with unintended consequences and good intentions gone badly awry. In the name of feeding the poor, for example, almost everyone is starving except the leaders, and the earth is so depleted that "all the people had to be shut up in great tall, half-buried towers," where they live in windowless bunkers and get disposed of at will by unseen leaders (Tepper 1991, loc. 1539). The loss of gender distinction, in particular, has become a tool of oppression. Beauty wonders what the social planners could possibly have been thinking beyond their own greed.

Such anti-utopian speculative novels foreground the continuum between desire and disaster by suggesting the slippery relationship between utopian and dystopian outcomes of human visions and plans. They also emphasize the necessity for multiple forms of female subjectivity and nuanced and varied alternatives to the patriarchal social order (Teslenko 2003, 173). These works thereby expose the utopian paradox, especially its gendered and feminist forms.

Margaret Atwood's *Handmaid's Tale* is the primary evidence of that exposé. It depicts a dystopian world that has, in some ways, fulfilled certain feminist dreams but with chilling results. Offred, the novel's Handmaid narrator, is the daughter of a 1960s radical feminist whose agenda alienated her as a child. Offred sees how feminist desires for women's power, sisterhood, and state-supported maternity have been twisted by demonic forces of social change. She thinks wryly that the new regime's communalized birthings, in which all Handmaids gather for the delivery of babies they have been forced to bear for Commanders and their infertile wives, are (among other affronts) a distorted version of maternal-based feminism. Offred thinks, "Mother ... Wherever you may be. Can you hear me? You wanted a women's culture. Well, now there is one" (Atwood 1985, 164).

This feminist retreat from classic utopian visions in the late twentieth century illustrates their ultimate failures as models of feminist social change. If they project fixed or universalist ideals of identity or social organization, pretend to comprehend all the complexities that constitute successful societies or human happiness, and assume that all positive values are compatible with one another, utopian visions not only risk inflicting "oppression, cruelty, [and] repression" but may also promote a "conceptual (and not merely practical) impossibility" (Berlin 1990, 47). The values of feminism are themselves diverse and heterogeneous. *Good* and *bad* may exist on a continuum. *Women* and *men* are complicated categories. Even obvious variations within and between them, such as race, ethnicity, class, age, and level of physical ability, are not easily address-able, and certainly not with blanket solutions. Other, more conceptual differences and values may not be reconcilable at all. Those complexities render *women* itself a somewhat utopian term, to the extent that it imposes coherent identities, distinct gender boundaries, and dreams of consensual alliances that characterize many utopian visions. Twenty-first-century politics render the idea of women's universally shared social and personal values and goals a cruel joke.

Rather than privileging particular feminist perspectives in a uniform utopian vision, by the 2000s feminist theorists had begun recognizing the value of diverse feminist theoretical approaches to problems of gender and power in different contexts and political moments. They saw the future of feminism in healthy disagreements and internal conflicts, as well as in respect for women's diversely focused lives and values. In rejecting the classic utopian solution, they sought another way to preserve feminism's vitality as an analytical and political tool. (For more on the pitfalls of utopian thinking for feminist discussions of social change, see Kitch 2000.)

Reproductive Technology: A Feminist Utopian Test Case

Because reproductive technology features in so many feminist utopian visions, its evolution in the real world offers an opportunity to investigate the feminist utopian paradox in a material practice. This investigation is especially pertinent as reality closes in on classic utopian speculations about nonsexual reproduction, *in vitro* fertilization, and extrauterine gestation.

Feminist theorist Shulamith Firestone was a strong voice in favor of reproductive technology in 1970. Paralleling Robert Francoeur's optimism about the utopian possibilities for motherhood through reproductive technology, Firestone's *The Dialectic of Sex* recommended that women abandon reproduction—which she identified as the cause of their social subordination—as the best route to sexual equality. (Unlike celibate utopians, Firestone did not recommend abandoning sex.) Firestone claimed that without biological reproduction, "genital distinctions between the sexes would no longer matter culturally" (1970, 11). She thereby challenged Freudian theory and echoed many feminist utopians before her.

Firestone jumped on the technological bandwagon just as early reproductive technologies were becoming available. She and other feminists at the time, including Simone de Beauvoir, believed the new technologies would improve women's lives by providing greater reproductive flexibility, through donated sperm or transferred ova, and by extending the reproductive limits of women's bodies. Firestone's work inspired Marge Piercy's depiction of extrauterine gestation in *Woman on the Edge of Time*. Other feminists also hoped for the day when the extracorporeal membrane oxygenation—a version of the heart-lung machine—that now keeps prematurely born fetuses alive might eventually replace the functions of the placenta and render the womb technically obsolete (Donchin 1986).

In practice, the reproductive technologies envisioned by such thinkers have subsequently garnered both support and criticism from feminists. Supporters point out that technological advances have made motherhood available to more women, including lesbians, and reduced the male role in reproduction by making fatherhood anonymous, at least in the case of donated sperm. Such changes have challenged the social conventions of patriliny and male control of women's reproductive lives. In addition, they have supported the idea that children born to intentional mothers will be better cared for than those whom nature brings unbidden.

Critics like Donna Haraway, however, reply that most reproductive technologies are "heavily embedded in the history of misogyny, medicalization and control of the female body" (Handlarski 2010, 97). Shelley Tremain further connects the indignities and invasiveness of prenatal impairment diagnoses and genetic counseling to the "form of power that began to emerge in the late eighteenth century" (Tremain 2006, 35). Other theorists recognize that the consequences of reproductive technologies are unpredictable with regard to gender relations and hierarchies.

Critics also argue that artificial fertilization has reinforced racial and class hierarchies by remaining virtually unavailable to all but the rich, and has in some circumstances ironically increased paternal authority. In facilitating surrogate motherhood, for example, artificial fertilization and egg transplantation make a fetus's paternity clearer than its maternity. Biological and social mothers may now quarrel over their rights and relationships to a child, whom one may have conceived and the other gestated, while the fathers enjoy paternal certitude (Stolcke 1988, 14). In that way, reproductive technologies can undermine what was once considered both the primary human biological link and a source of women's power—the biological clarity of motherhood.

Critics further point out that reproductive technology, again paradoxically, renders childbearing even more essential to female gender identity. When infertility need not be accepted as God's will or the luck of the draw, women are more likely to regard childbearing as part of their biological destiny and infertility as symptomatic of their own failure to solve a technological problem. In its efforts to cheat time, critics argue, reproductive technology has transformed much early feminist ranting against unlimited childbearing into the fervent pursuit, even by career-minded women, of the one perfect biological child in their late thirties or even forties. What was once "choice" has morphed into "creeping non-choice" (Stolba 2003, 34).

In addition, the fact that infertility treatments are far from simple or universally successful does little in a technologized climate to stop women (and men) from exhausting themselves and their savings in their drive to produce their "own" child. It is also possible that reproductive technologies have helped to make US society more pronatalist, racist, and classist, and less supportive of abortion rights. Such technologies may also have rendered infertile women more socially unacceptable (Donchin 1996, 477; Lublin 1998, 98, 104). Moreover, who can say how such dynamics would affect social attitudes and structures if women's wombs eventually became entirely superfluous to the reproductive process, as second-generation reproductive technologists are working in Japan and the United States to make possible?[6] Would women themselves become obsolete rather than men's equal parenting partners, as Piercy imagined? Indeed, critics ask, is reproductive technology already making women obsolete? In India in 2011, for example, there were 7.1 million fewer girls than boys between zero and six years old, a gap that has increased even since 2001, when it was 6.0 million.[7]

Feminists over the last half century have debated these developments and their implications as they have witnessed the transformation of utopian visions of birth-without-burden into a potentially dystopian nightmare. Feminist fiction writer Angela Carter (*Heroes and Villains*, 1969; *The Passion of New Eve*, 1977) worried decades ago that the turn to reproductive technology would reinforce women's reproductive identities and further oppress women in its continued reliance on the language and concepts of patriarchy (Jennings 2008, 66). More recently, Donna Haraway has touted cyborgian *regeneration* rather than conventional reproductive technology as a way to free women from the burdens of childbirth and create a genderless society—her idea of a utopia (Handlarski 2010, 75–76, 92). (Haraway hopes that the way salamanders can regenerate a limb could eventually be extended to human-machine cyborgs.) The prospect of a womanless world, or a world in which women's value is increasingly subordinated to the value of babies and the decisions of politicians and physicians, is a contemporary feminist concern about reproductive technology. So is women's commoditization by competitive fertility providers driven more by demand than by safety, reliability, or feminist principles (Lublin 1998, 98).

Single feminist solutions are not clear. Suppressing all reproductive technologies would deprive involuntarily infertile women of their possibility to experience motherhood, which cannot be entirely attributed to sexist socialization. In addition, the capacity to create a family is the only form of social power for many women around the world. But doing nothing about the proliferation of technologies means abandoning vulnerable women to exploitation and allowing society as a whole to become ever more focused on women's reproductive and sexual identities and roles, while at the same time depriving marginalized groups of technology's benefits (Donchin 1996, 482).

Both pro- and antitechnology feminist positions on reproductive technology illustrate the liabilities of utopian approaches to social issues. On the one hand, putting complete faith in technological alternatives to natural reproductive processes can reflect the utopian assumption that a specific social change will have only positive consequences for everyone. On the other hand, disavowing all technology can imply a utopian idealization of "nature" or an evocation of a golden age when all pregnancies and childbirths were allegedly unproblematic and free of power relations. Hilary Rose calls such hopes a form of "feminist fundamentalism"; others see them as ecofeminist utopianism (Donchin 1996, 483; Lublin 1998, 52–54). By the same token, romanticizing the mother-child relationship as the epitome of natural loving human relationships, demonizing all "artificial" interventions in conception or birthing, or equating all fertility specialists with shysters and powermongers or, conversely, with saviors, are also utopian perspectives, with arguably conservative implications (Briggs and Kelber-Kaye 2000).[8] Like many utopian analyses, they present only polarized alternatives and absolutist solutions.

Recent feminist approaches to reproductive technology have avoided classic utopianism/dystopianism by starting from the premise that women are not a monolithic category and that they are unlikely to unite around any single policy position or theoretical perspective on any issue. Instead of seeking a singular answer, therefore, some feminists break down the larger topic into smaller questions and address each of them with flexible solutions. For example, Anne Donchin suggests that a feminist approach to reproductive technology should begin by assessing fertility-services delivery systems in the United States and abroad. Open processes of decision-making about the uses of technology, as well as adequate monitoring and oversight of its delivery, would benefit all women, no matter what their views. Donchin also suggests that the major alternative to fertility services—adoption—should be made easier. Many couples and individuals who seek fertility services have already been turned down by adoption agencies. Finally, Donchin calls for more research on the causes of infertility in an effort to reduce the need for medical intervention (1996, 492–94). Nancy Lublin argues that a "praxis feminist assessment" of reproductive technologies requires not a sweeping judgment of all technologies but rather "a set of standards against which particular technologies can be measured" (1998, 55). Such reasonable and incremental feminist approaches counter both utopian and dystopian views of reproductive technology.

Postdystopian Gender Utopias

Despite the deflated state of the classic feminist/gender utopia in the 1980s and 1990s, feminist thinkers and writers did not completely abandon utopian perspectives. Gender, feminism, and utopia have remained a resilient combination in the new century—but with a twist. In this postdystopian era, more writers and thinkers are embracing utopia's impossibilities and inconsistencies as they reinterpret it through a postmodern lens: paying attention to parts rather than wholes, to desire as well as politics, and to heterogeneity, contradiction, diversity, and playful juxtapositions (Siebers 1994, 7). The "happy island far away, where perfect social relations prevail, and human beings … enjoy a simple and happy existence," may be gone, but the idea of utopia as a tool of feminist critique and contemplation still exists in speculative and science fiction, political thought, and social analysis.[9]

In the late twentieth and early twenty-first centuries, "heterotopian" fictional worlds (to use Tobin Siebers's term), instability, and fragmentation have replaced stability and unity as key characteristics of utopian thought, according to literary critic Jennifer Wagner-Lawlor. The fictional texts Wagner-Lawlor analyzes continuously disrupt and reconstruct literary as well as social conventions and intertwine reality and fantasy. Speculation becomes a standpoint for gendered inquiry, although feminist dogma may be less explicitly claimed (and more parodied). The texts rewrite history from future perspectives and judge the future via historical virtues and values. Art and the imagination become new sources of a truth that is larger than fact. Instead of a specified place of social organization, utopia persists in disjointed moments of possibilities—the "nowhere" of *utopia*'s Greek etymology (Wagner-Lawlor 2012). Irony also reappears as a defining characteristic of utopian thinking, thereby reconnecting utopianism to its generic origins.

Novels adopting this postmodern speculative neofeminist perspective, in which utopia is an unresolved, open-ended world of regendered possibilities, and art and the imagination intervene in history, include Toni Morrison's *Paradise* (1998), Octavia Butler's *Parable* series (1993, 1998), Susan Sontag's *In America* (2000), Ursula Le Guin's *The Telling*

(2000), Doris Lessing's *The Cleft* (2007), Jeanette Winterson's *The Stone Gods* (2009), and Margaret Atwood's *The Year of the Flood* (2009).

Morrison's *Paradise* is a prime example of the heterotopian genre. The novel clearly rejects classic utopian solutions in its portrayal of an all-Negro racial utopia, Ruby, as a male-controlled near-prison for its women (in ironic affirmation of its idealized female namesake). The town's insularity has weakened its denizens' genetic constitutions so much that children sicken at an alarming rate. Men's exaggerated power has corrupted them, silenced women, and created a breeding ground for violence. The novel juxtaposes this "backward noplace ruled by men" (1998, 306) to an indeterminate utopian world inhabited by women. Located fifteen miles outside of Ruby's borders, the Convent is a place where all who come—regardless of color—are welcomed and given what they need. The motley collection of abandoned, disaffected, even criminal women who gravitate toward the Convent and its doyenne, Connie—including several from Ruby—learn to create a different kind of community, based on deep understanding of and empathy for one another and absolute freedom to come and go.

It is perhaps inevitable that the Convent's loose and self-directed female space would get entangled in the utopian paradox being bred in Ruby. So it was that the Convent women were attacked and killed one morning by men from Ruby, whose fear of female power erupted in an almost erotic burst of violence. But that is not the end of Morrison's story. After the women's dead bodies simply disappear, their children and friends begin to see them again. Reconciliation is the goal of these ghostly encounters, as the women who have opened themselves to change, self-knowledge, and authentic relationships provide new opportunities for and with others. The fleeting suggestion of an opening in the air around the decimated Convent makes the prospect of opportunity visible to the town's open-minded minister, Reverend Misner, and its librarian, Anna: "There was nothing to see. 'A door,' she said later. 'No, a window,' he said, laughing.... Whether through a door needing to be opened or a beckoning window already raised, what would happen if you entered?" (Morrison 1998, 305). What, indeed?

Other heterotopian novels ask similar questions of cyberspace, the theater, and history, according to Wagner-Lawlor. They disrupt conventions of power and domesticity. Though gender is part of the vision, it may not be all of it. Feminism is a set of possibilities rather than a fixed ideology. Twentieth-century novels by Le Guin, Winterson, Sontag, Atwood, and others, in which utopia is the pursuit of potential "at the horizon of a voyage," adopt multiple perspectives as they fragment time, space, and place (Marin 1993, 413). They invent new ways of seeing the old, and old ways of seeing the new. They celebrate speculation as they stretch boundaries and challenge binaries. They embody the transformative powers of art, love, and language (Wagner-Lawlor 2012). In Fredric Jameson's terms, these utopias force "a meditation on the impossible, on the unrealizable in its own right" (Jameson 2005, 232).

The persistence of utopia as a feminist tool of both possibility and critique rather than a coherent vision is also evident among recent lesbian feminist theorists, such as Kath Browne (2011), Rosie Harding (2010), and Lucy Nicholas (2009). In addition, utopian possibilities rather than utopian worlds characterize feminist ecocritical texts, such as Marisa Pereyra's essay, in which she uses feminist utopian novels to interpret Nicaraguan writer Gioconda Belli's ecocritical utopian novel *Wasala* (Pereyra 2010, 136–53). Such approaches reinforce Ruth Levitas's observation that utopianism "allows for the possibility of a radical break from the present" in order to "pose the questions of what would be necessary to live within ecological constraints" (Levitas 2008, 8). Attention to gender may itself constitute such a "radical break" in redefining humanity's relationship to nature and reenvisioning a world built on respect and caring for a complex ecosystem that humans do not fully understand.

Some theoretical texts further illustrate this feminist embrace of utopia as a tool for probing possibilities. Valerie Bryson's *Gender and the Politics of Time*, for example, examines the role of utopian thought in transforming feminist theorizing about temporality as a way to understand political disputes. Though critical of classic utopias' presentist tendencies, Bryson believes that utopianism offers an "element of strategic thinking" that balances "short-term practical gains against women's longer term strategic interests" (Bryson 2007, 102–3).

Karin Schönpflug's *Feminism, Economics, and Utopia: Time Travelling through Paradigms* similarly harnesses utopian yearnings, in her case as a framework for feminist economic theory. "Femeconomist" Schönpflug does not envision a wholesale utopian transformation of all social institutions, but she seeks "utopian moments" to light the way forward for economics (2008, 135). She defines *utopia* as considering or taking "action to create alternative structures" and embracing "the necessity to think the unimaginable" (2008, 137–38). Although Schönpflug recognizes the historical pitfalls—especially the gender paradoxes—of historical utopian visions (specifically the Saint-Simonians'), she believes that feminist economic theory needs utopian inspiration in order to free itself from the androcentric assumptions of Adam Smith. For inspiration, Schönpflug and other femeconomists she cites use Charlotte Perkins Gilman's *Women in Economics* (1898) as a key reference. Schönpflug also applauds femeconomist Nancy Folbre for seeking alternative economic theory in the works of fictional writers such as Marge Piercy and Sheri Tepper (Schönpflug 2008, 150, 154).

Young adult fiction aimed at female audiences (and appealing to both teens and their mothers) is another arena for postdystopian gender speculation. Perhaps inspired by the concept of alternative worlds in cyberspace, such as "Second Life," these works have absorbed the fantasy and the warrior mentalities of the Internet and embraced the speculative standpoint of heterotopia. One example, *The Hunger Games*, both the print and e-book series (2008–2010) and the films (the first released in 2012), depicts a cruel, dystopian postapocalyptic world (in the country of Panem, where North America once stood). But *The Hunger Games* presents a nuanced interplay between dystopia and hope, according to Sarah Seltzer. The novels' heroine, Katniss, lives on the brink of starvation and must literally fight for her life, while she constantly confronts the ugliness of the ruined world (Seltzer 2011). Katniss has agency as well as sex appeal in the novels, but any view of those characteristics as utopian panaceas is "limited by the intersectional oppressions of poverty, her obligation to those she loves, and her body's appropriation as a symbol" for the revolution she leads. The novels locate greater hope in the heroine's engagement with "difficult moral and philosophical questions" that also plague readers in their own world (Seltzer 2011, 38–42).

The Hunger Games stands in stark contrast to an equally popular classic utopian holdover, according to Seltzer—the *Twilight* vampire series, which depicts a utopia of "sparkly, supernatural stalker boyfriends, glorified abstinence, [and] skipping college to be impregnated with vampire spawn" (Seltzer 2011, 39). The *Twilight* heroine, Bella Swan, seeks love, sexual fulfillment, and motherhood in her fantasy vampire utopia, where she can live a purely personal, protected life as long she doesn't worry about what happens to everyone else. The history of utopia suggests that such a classic vision can only produce the heartbreak of paradox.

Conclusion

Utopias have inspired social reformers and revolutionaries for centuries. In their classic form, they offer hope that venal human nature is an aberration and that humanity can be improved through its own efforts to achieve a lost ideal state. But such classical utopian approaches to social change miss complexities and overlook the value of diversity in human relations, values, and social forms. Classic utopias often eschew incremental, conditional, and context-sensitive solutions that are revisable over time. Thus, they typically produce paradoxes—changes that create no change, heavens that contain hells, and finite solutions to the wrong problems.

Gender issues only magnify the classic utopian tendency toward paradox. Presentist gender blinders have betrayed women in men's utopian plans and shortchanged them in their own. Transforming such highly charged cultural domains as family, sexualities, and reproduction risks devaluing viable present realities and overlooking the need for continual revision, competing perspectives, and the flexibility necessary for an essentially unforeseeable future.

For feminists, the utopian gender paradox has been especially egregious, since feminism is historically dedicated to revealing the pitfalls of considering men's values and worldviews as universal. Feminists have also struggled to embrace women's cultural, racial, and geographic diversity, as well as a variety of perspectives on the causes of and appropriate responses to misogyny, patriarchy, and sexism. Given those goals of multiplicity and diversity, the dogmas of classic utopias produced a logical inconsistency that drove many feminists in the other direction.

Yet the feminist utopian impulse did not disappear. Instead, in recent decades feminist theorists and writers have adopted what many critics consider a more appropriate perspective on utopia—"heterotopia," or the utopia of fragmentation and possibilities rather than unified visions, open-ended rather than definitive resolutions, continuously advancing horizons rather than destinations, and self-reflexivity for all who empower their imaginations to intervene in history. For the twenty-first century, utopia makes a better muse than an architect for gendered social change.

Notes

1. The Edutopia project produces media-based materials that help teachers and school districts "change education for the better" by being "a place where … innovation is the rule, not the exception; a place where students become lifelong learners and develop 21st-century skills" (http://www.edutopia.org/mission-vision).

2. Many historians argue that utopian visions are uniquely Western and have depended on Renaissance humanistic beliefs in the perfectibility of human nature, in contrast to medieval and Augustinian religious ideas about original sin. Indeed, such utopianism has been influential in non-Western societies, including on Nkrumaism in Ghana (Smith 1991, 31–36). But Zhang Longxi argues that the correlation of utopian visions with secular concerns for the here and now and belief in human perfectibility is evident in Chinese Confucianism as well. Confucius himself (551–449 BCE) regarded the ancient kingdom of Zhou under the rule of King Wen (Ji Chang, 1099–1050 BCE) as the ideal moral and political society that humans should strive to emulate through diligent moral training and hard work. Confucian respect for ancient rituals did not contradict his secularism, since he regarded rituals as outer forms designed "to bring individual and social ethics to perfection." Zhang also describes a Chinese utopian literary tradition, starting in the second century CE, which included at least one feminist novel, *The Flowers in the Mirror* by Li Ruzhen (1768–1828) (Zhang 2002, 6–8, 12–17).

3. See, for example, Monique Wittig's use of "the women" in *Les guérillères* (1969), Sally Gearhart's invention of "rapists" and "gentles" as categories of men in *The Wanderground* (1979), and Ursula Le Guin's invention of an entire language for her Kesh society in *Always Coming Home* (1985). For a discussion of language in twentieth-century feminist dystopian texts, see Ildney Cavalcanti (2000, 152–80).

4. Among the rare nineteenth-century utopian novels by an African American woman is Lillian B. Jones's *Five Generations Hence* (1916). Twentieth-century African American utopian novelists include Jewelle Gomez and Octavia Butler. Butler's arguably feminist works include *Kindred* (1979), *Parable of the Sower* (1993), and *Parable of the Talents* (1998). Gomez died in 2004.

5. Critic Ellen Peel suggests that some novels, such as Lessing's *The Marriages between Zones Three, Four, and Five* and Le Guin's *Left Hand of Darkness*, which seem to retreat from utopia are simply moving beyond the static and unidimensional version of utopia to a more pragmatic, process-oriented approach to feminist persuasion. Yet Peel admits that this move entails a critique of utopia itself, which may amount to a retreat (2002, 173–74).

6. According to Christine Stolba, "The near future will bring uterus transplants and artificial wombs. Scientists at Cornell University are perfecting the former, while researchers at Juntendou University in Tokyo, who have had success keeping goat fetuses alive in artificial wombs ... predicted the creation of a fully functional artificial womb for human beings" by 2010, which did not occur. Cloning might even make parthenogenesis, touted by feminist utopians for more than a century, a possibility (Stolba 2003, 32). More recent sources predict that the artificial human womb won't be developed until 2050 (Bulletti et al. 2011, 124–28).

7. Reproductive technologies that have led to selective abortion of female fetuses and other procedures are not entirely responsible for this gap. Other factors include female infanticide, the neglect of baby girls, and better health care for boys ("Technology" 2000, 6; Jha et al. 2011, 1921–28).

8. The belief that genetic manipulation is "unnatural" and the romanticization of "natural" motherhood can be profoundly unfeminist positions that prescribe breeding as "women's work" and pit genetic technologies against the "right kind" of reproduction (Briggs and Kelber-Kaye 2000, 111).

9. Peter Fitting suggests that utopian fiction and science fiction are drifting apart and that science fiction is proving more popular. "The utopian moment of the 1960s and 1970s has passed" (Fitting 2010, 150), he explains. Utopian fiction is now a subset of science fiction.

References

Ackroyd, Peter. 1998. *The Life of Thomas More*. New York: Nan A. Talese.

Adolph, Anna. 1899. *Arqtiq: A Study of Marvels at the North Pole*. Hanford, CA: Author.

Appleton, Jane Sophia. (1848) 1971. Sequel to "The 'Vision of Bangor in the Twentieth Century.'" In *American Utopias: Selected Short Fiction*, ed. Arthur O. Lewis. New York: Arno.

Atwood, Margaret. 1985. *The Handmaid's Tale*. New York: Fawcett.

———. 2003. *Oryx and Crake*. New York: Anchor.

———. 2009. *The Year of the Flood*. New York: Doubleday.

Barr, Marleen. 1983. "Utopia at the End of a Male Chauvinist Dystopian World: Suzy McKee Charnas's Feminist Science Fiction." In *Women and Utopia: Critical Interpretations*, ed. Marleen Barr and Nicholas D. Smith. Lanham, MD: University Press of America.

Barr, Marleen, and Nicholas D. Smith, eds. 1983. *Women and Utopia: Critical Interpretations*. Lanham, MD: University Press of America.

Bartkowski, Frances. 1989. *Feminist Utopias*. Lincoln: University of Nebraska Press.

Bellamy, Edward. (1888) 1982. *Looking Backward, 2000–1887*. New York: Random.

Berger, Thomas. 1973. *Regiment of Women*. New York: Simon & Schuster.

Berlin, Isaiah. 1990. *The Crooked Timber of Humanity*. Princeton, NJ: Princeton University Press.

Bluestone, Natalie Harris. 1987. *Women and the Ideal Society: Plato's Republic and Modern Myths of Gender*. Amherst: University of Massachusetts Press.

Booker, M. Keith. 1994a. *The Dystopian Impulse in Modern Literature: Fiction as Social Criticism*. Westport, CT: Greenwood.

———. 1994b. *Dystopian Literature: A Theory and Research Guide*. Westport, CT: Greenwood.

Briggs, Laura, and Jodi I. Kelber-Kaye. 2000. "'There is No Unauthorized Breeding in Jurassic Park': Gender and the Uses of Genetics." *NWSA Journal* 12 (3) (Fall): 92–113.

Browne, Kath. 2011. "Beyond Rural Idylls: Imperfect Lesbian Utopias at Michigan Womyn's Music Festival." *Journal of Rural Studies* 27.

Bruère, Martha Bensley. 1919. *Mildred Carver, USA*. New York: Macmillan.

Bryant, Dorothy. 1976. *The Kin of Ata Are Waiting for You*. New York: Moon Books.

Bryson, Valerie. 2007. *Gender and the Politics of Time: Feminist Theory and Contemporary Debates*. Bristol: Policy Press.

Bulletti, Carlo, Antonio Palagiano, Caterina Pace, Angelica Cerni, Andrea Borini, and Dominique de Ziegler. 2011. "The Artificial Womb." *Annals of the New York Academy of Sciences: Reproductive Science Issue*, 1221 (March): 124–28.

Butler, Octavia. 1979. *Kindred*. New York: Doubleday.

———. 1993. *Parable of the Sower*. New York: Aspect.

———. 1998. *Parable of the Talents*. New York: Seven Stories Press.

Capasso, Ruth Carver. 1994. "Islands of Felicity: Women Seeking Utopia in Seventeenth-Century France." In *Utopian and Science Fiction by Women*, ed. Jane L. Donawerth and Carol A. Kolmerten, 35–53. Syracuse: Syracuse University Press.

Cavalcanti, Ildney. 2000. "Utopias of/f Language in Contemporary Feminist Literary Dystopias." *Utopian Studies* 11 (2): 152–80.

Charnas, Suzy McKee. 1978. *Motherlines*. New York: Berkley.

Cherniavsky, Eva. 1993. "(En)Gendering Cyberspace in Neuromancer: Postmodern Subjectivity and Virtual Motherhood." *Genders* 18 (Winter): 33–46.

Chmielewski, Wendy. 1993. "Sojourner Truth: Utopian Vision and Search for Community, 1797–1883." In Chmielewski, Kern, and Klee-Hartzell 1993, 133–49.

Chmielewski, Wendy, Louis J. Kern, and Marlyn Klee-Hartzell, eds. 1993. *Women in Spiritual and Communitarian Societies in the United States*. Syracuse: Syracuse University Press.

Cornell, Drucilla. 1991. *Beyond Accommodation: Ethical Feminism, Deconstruction, and the Law*. London: Routledge.

Dobkin, Alix. 1988. "Why Be Separatist? Exploring Women-Only Energy," 286–90. In *For Les-*

bians Only: A Separatist Anthology, ed. Sarah Lucia Hoagland and Julia Penelope. London: Onlywomen.

Donchin, Anne. 1986. "The Future of Mothering: Reproductive Technology and Feminist Theory." *Hypatia* 1(Fall): 121–38 .

———. 1996. "Feminist Critiques of New Fertility Technologies: Implications for Social Policy." *Journal of Medicine and Philosophy* 21 (October): 475–98.

Dunne, Linda. 1994. "Mothers and Monsters in Sarah Robinson Scott's *Millennium Hall.*" In *Utopian and Science Fiction by Women*, ed. Jane L. Donawerth and Carol A. Kolmerten, 54–72. Syracuse: Syracuse University Press.

Elgin, Suzette. 1984. *Native Tongue*. New York: DAW.

———. 1987. *Native Tongue II: The Judas Rose*. New York: DAW.

———. 1994. *Native Tongue III: Earthsong*. New York: DAW.

Faludi, Susan. 1991. *Backlash: The Undeclared War against American Women*. New York: Doubleday.

Firestone, Shulamith. 1970. *The Dialectic of Sex: The Case for Feminist Revolution*. New York: Morrow.

Fitting, Peter. 2010. "Utopia, Dystopia and Science Fiction." In *The Cambridge Companion to Utopian Literature*, ed. Gregory Claeys, 135–54. Cambridge: Cambridge University Press.

Forrest, Katherine V. 1984. *Daughters of a Coral Dawn*. Tallahassee, FL: Naiad.

Foster, Lawrence. 1991. *Women, Family, and Utopia: Communal Experiments of the Shakers, the Oneida Community, and the Mormons*. Syracuse: Syracuse University Press.

Francoeur, Robert. 1970. *Utopian Motherhood: New Trends in Human Reproduction*. Garden City: Doubleday.

Gearhart, Sally. 1979. *The Wanderground*. Watertown, MA: Persephone.

Gilman, Charlotte Perkins. 1907. "A Woman's Utopia." Chaps. 1–4 in *The Times Magazine* 1 (January–March): 215–20, 369–76, 498–504.

———. (1910) 1980. *Moving the Mountain*. In *The Charlotte Perkins Gilman Reader: The Yellow Wallpaper and Other Fiction*. Ed. Ann J. Lane. New York: Pantheon.

———. (1915) 1979. *Herland*. New York: Pantheon.

Gomez, Jewelle. 1991. *The Gilda Stories: A Novel*. Ithaca, NY: Firebrand Books.

Gordin, Michael D., Helen Tiley, and Gyan Prakash. 2010. *Utopia/Dystopia: Conditions of Historical Possibility*. Princeton, NJ: Princeton University Press.

Griffith, Mary. (1836) 1984. *Three Hundred Years Hence*. In *Daring to Dream: Utopian Fiction by United States Women, 1836–1919*, ed. Carol Farley Kessler. Boston: Pandora Press.

Halliwell, S., trans. 1993. *Republic V* by Plato. Warminster: Aris and Phillips.

Handlarski, Denise. 2010. "Co-Creation—Haraway's 'Regeneration' and the Postcolonial Cyborg Body." *Women's Studies* 39 (2) (March): 73–99.

Harding, Rosie. 2010. "Imagining a Different World: Reconsidering the Regulation of Family Lives." *Law and Literature* 22 (3).

Hollister, Alonzo Giles. 1887. *Divine Motherhood*. Mt. Lebanon, NY: n.p.

Howland, Marie Stevens Case. 1874. *Papa's Own Girl; A Novel*. New York: John P. Jewett.

Huxley, Aldous. 1932. *Brave New World*. New York: HarperCollins.

Jameson, Fredric. 2005. *Archaeologies of the Future: The Desire Called Utopia and Other Science Fictions*. London: Verso.

Jennings, Hope. 2008. "Dystopian Matriarchies: Deconstructing the Womb in Angela Carter's *Heroes and Villains* and *The Passion of New Eve.*" *Michigan Feminist Studies* 21:63–84.

Jha, Prabhat, Maya A. Kesler, Rajesh Kumar, Faujdar Ram, Usha Ram, Lukasz Aleksand-
rowicz, Diego G. Bassani, Shailaja Chandra, and Jayant K. Banthia. 2011. "Trends in Selective Abortions of Girls in India: Analysis of Nationally Representative Birth Histories
from 1990 to 2005 and Census Data from 1991 to 2011." *Lancet* 377.

Johnson, J. W., ed.1968. *Utopian Literature*. New York: Modern Library.

Jones, Alice Ilgenfritz.1893. *Unveiling a Parallel: A Romance*. Boston: Arena.

Jones, Lillian B. 1916. *Five Generations Hence*. Fort Worth, TX: Dotson Jones.

Kaufmann, Rev. M. 1879. *Utopias; or, Schemes of Social Improvement from Sir Thomas More
to Karl Marx*. London: Kegan Paul.

Kelso, Sylvia. 2008. "'Failing That, Invent': Writing a Feminist Utopia in the 21st Century."
Femspec 9 (1): 3–19.

Kern, Louis. 1981. *An Ordered Love: Sex Roles and Sexuality in Victorian Utopias: The Shakers,
the Mormons, and the Oneida Community*. Chapel Hill: University of North Carolina Press.

Kessler, Carol Farley, ed. 1984. *Daring to Dream: Utopian Fiction by United States Women,
1836–1919*. Boston: Pandora Press.

Kesten, Seymour. 1993. *Utopian Episodes: Daily Life in Experimental Colonies Dedicated to
Changing the World*. Syracuse: Syracuse University Press.

Kiser, Edgar V., and Kathryn A. Baker. 1984. "Feminist Ideology and Utopian Literature."
Quarterly Journal of Ideology (October), 29–36.

Kitch, Sally L. 1989. *Chaste Liberation: Celibacy and Female Cultural Status*. Champaign-
Urbana: University of Illinois Press.

———. 1993. *This Strange Society of Women: Reading the Letters and Lives of the Women's
Commonwealth*. Columbus: Ohio State University Press.

———. 2000. *Higher Ground: From Utopianism to Realism in Feminist Thought and Theory*. Chicago: University of Chicago Press.

Klee-Hartzell, Marlyn. 1993. "Family Love, True Womanliness, Motherhood, and the Socialization of Girls in the Oneida Community, 1848–1880." In Chmielewski, Kern, and Klee-
Hartzell 1993, 187–97.

Kolmerten, Carol A. 1990. *Women in Utopia: The Ideology of Gender in the American Owenite
Communities*. Bloomington: Indiana University Press.

Landon, Brooks. 1983. "Language and the Subversion of Good Order in Thomas Berger's
Regiment of Women." *Philological Quarterly* 62 (1) (Winter): 21–30.

Lane, Mary E. Bradley. (1880–1881) 1984. "Mizora: A Prophecy." In *Daring to Dream: Utopian Fiction by United States Women, 1836–1919*, ed. Carol Farley Kessler. Boston: Pandora Press.

Le Guin, Ursula. 1969. *The Left Hand of Darkness*. New York: Walker.

———. 1974. *The Dispossessed: An Ambiguous Utopia*. New York: Harper & Row.

———. 1985. *Always Coming Home*. Toronto: Bantam.

———. 2000. *The Telling*. Orlando, FL: ACE.

Lessing, Doris. 1980. *The Marriages between Zones Three, Four, and Five*. Book 2 of *Canopus
in Argos*. New York: Knopf.

———. 1981a. *Shikasta: re, colonised planet 5: personal, psychological, historical documents
relating to visit by Johor (George Sherban) emissary (grade 9) 87th of the period of the last
days*. Book 1 of *Canopus in Argos*. New York: Vintage.

———. 1981b. *The Sirian Experiments: The Report by Ambien II, of the Five*. Book 3 of *Canopus
in Argos*. New York: Knopf.

———. 1982. *The Making of the Representative for Planet 8*. Book 4 of *Canopus in Argos*. New York: Knopf.

———. 1983. *Documents Relating to the Sentimental Agents in the Volyen Empire*. Book 5 of *Canopus in Argos*. London: J. Cape.

Levitas, Ruth. 2008. "Be Realistic: Demand the Impossible." *New Formations* 65, Autumn: 78–93.

Lewes, Darby. 1995. *Dream Revisionaries: Gender and Genre in Women's Utopian Fiction, 1870–1920*. Tuscaloosa: University of Alabama Press.

Lublin, Nancy. 1998. *Pandora's Box: Feminist Confronts Reproductive Technology*. Lanhan, MD: Rowman & Littlefield.

Marin, Louis. 1993. "Frontiers of Utopia: Past and Present." *Critical Inquiry* 19 (3).

Mohr, Dunja. 2005. *Worlds Apart: Dualism and Transgression in Contemporary Female Dystopias*. Jefferson, NC: McFarland and Company.

Moontree, Iandris. 1988. "An Interview with a Separatist, January 23, 1983." In *For Lesbians Only: A Separatist Anthology*, ed. Sarah Lucia Hoagland and Julia Penelope. London: Onlywomen.

Moore, M. Louise. 1892. *Al Modad; or, Life Scenes beyond the Polar Circumflex. A Religio-Scientific Solution of the Problems of Present and Future Life*. Shell Bank, LA: Moore and Beauchamp.

More, Thomas. (1516) 1963. *Utopia*. Norwalk, CT: Easton Press.

Morrison, Toni. 1998. *Paradise*. New York: Knopf.

Nicholas, Lucy. 2009. "A Radical Queer Utopian Future: A Reciprocal Relation beyond Sexual Difference." *Thirdspace: A Journal of Feminist Theory and Culture* 8 (2).

Nielsen, Joyce McCarl. 1984. "Women in Dystopia/Utopia: 1984 and Beyond." *International Journal of Women's Studies* 7 (2) (March/April): 144–54.

Orwell, George. 1949. *1984*. New York: Milestone Editions.

Peel, Ellen. 1990. "Utopian Feminism, Skeptical Feminism, and Narrative Energy." In *Feminism, Utopia, and Narrative*, ed. Libby Falk and Sarah Webster Goodwin, 34–49. Knoxville: University of Tennessee Press.

———. 2002. *Politics, Persuasion, and Pragmatism: A Rhetoric of Feminist Utopian Fiction*. Columbus: Ohio State University Press.

Perec, Georges. (1975) 1988. *W, or the Memory of a Childhood*, trans. David Bellos. Boston: Godine.

Pereyra, Marsia. 2010. "Paradise Lost: A Reading of *Wasala* from the Perspectives of Feminist Utopianism and Ecofeminism." Trans. Diane J. Forbes. In *The Natural World in Latin American Literatures: Ecocritical Essays on Twentieth-Century Writings,* ed. Adrian Taylor Kane. Jefferson, NC: McFarland and Company.

Piercy, Marge. 1976. *Woman on the Edge of Time*. New York: Knopf.

Plato. 1993. *Republic*. Trans. Robin Waterfield. New York: Oxford University Press.

Richberg, Eloise O. 1900. *Reinstern*. Cincinnati: Editor Publishing.

Russ, Joanna. 1975. *The Female Man*. Boston: Beacon.

Sargent, Pamela. 1986. *The Shore of Women*. New York: Crown.

Sargisson, Lucy. 1996. *Contemporary Feminist Utopianism*. New York: Routledge.

Schönpflug, Karin. 2008. *Feminism, Economics and Utopia: Time Travelling through Paradigms*. New York: Routledge.

Seltzer, Sarah. 2011. "Hunger Pangs," *Bitch Magazine* 51:38–42.

Shugar, Dana R. 1995. *Sep-a-ra-tism and Women's Community*. Lincoln: University of Nebraska Press.

Siebers, Tobin. 1994. "Introduction: What Does Postmodernism Want? Utopia." In *Heterotopia: Postmodern Utopia and the Body Politic*, ed. Tobin Siebers, 1–38. Ann Arbor: University of Michigan Press.

Slonczewski, Joan. 1986. *A Door into Ocean*. New York: Avon.

Smith, Curtis. 1991. "Nkrumaism as Utopianism." *Utopian Studies* 3.

Sontag, Susan. 2000. *In America: A Novel*. New York: Picador.

Staton, Mary. 1975. *From the Legend of Biel*. New York: Ace.

Stolba, Christine. 2003. "Overcoming Motherhood: Pushing the Limits of Reproductive Choice." *Policy Review* (December 2002–January 2003), 31–41.

Stolcke, Verena. 1988. "New Reproductive Technologies: The Old Quest for Fatherhood." *Reproductive and Genetic Engineering* 1 (1): 5–19.

Sullivan, E. D. S., ed. 1983. *The Utopian Vision: Seven Essays on the Quincentennial of Sir Thomas More*. San Diego: San Diego State University Press.

"Technology Causing Drop in Proportion of Females." 2000. *Women in Action* 3 (3).

Tepper, Sheri S. 1991. *Beauty: A Novel*. New York: Doubleday (Spectra Special Editions; Kindle Edition).

Teslenko, Tatiana. 2003. *Feminist Utopian Novels of the 1970s: Joanna Russ and Dorothy Bryant*. New York: Routledge.

Tremain, Shelley. 2006. "Reproductive Freedom, Self-Regulation, and the Government of Impairment in Utero." *Hypatia* 21 (1): 35–53.

Wagner-Lawlor, Jennifer A. 2012. "Ways of Being Nowhere: Forms of Speculation in Twentieth-First-Century Feminist Fiction." Unpublished manuscript.

Waisbrooker, Lois. 1894. *A Sex Revolution*. Topeka, KS: Independent.

White, Thomas I. 1983. "Opposing Necessity and Truth: The Argument against Politics in Doris Lessing's Utopian Vision." In *Women and Utopia: Critical Interpretations*, ed. Marleen Barr and Nicholas D. Smith, 134–47. Lanham, MD: University Press of America.

Williams, Brackette F. 1996. "Introduction: Mannish Women and Gender after the Act." In *Women Out of Place: The Gender of Agency and the Race of Nationality*, ed. Brackette F. Williams. New York: Routledge.

Winslow, Helen. 1909. *A Woman for Mayor: A Novel of Today*. Chicago: Reilly and Britton.

Winterson, Jeanette. 2009. *The Stone Gods*. Orlando, FL: Houghton Mifflin Harcourt.

Wittig, Monique. (1969) 1973. *Les guérillères*. Trans. David Le Vay. New York: Avon.

Zamyatin, Yevgeny. (1921) 1972. *We*. Trans. Mirra Ginsburg. New York: Avon.

Zhang Longxi, Zhang. 2002. "The Utopian Vision, East and West." *Utopian Studies* 13 (1).

Contributors

LAUREN BERLANT is the George M. Pullman Distinguished Service Professor of English at the University of Chicago. She is the author or editor of several books, including *Desire/Love* (2012), *Cruel Optimism* (2011), and *The Female Complaint: The Unfinished Business of Sentimentality in American Culture* (2008). She is also coeditor of the journal *Critical Inquiry*.

WENDY BROWN is the Class of 1936 First Professor of Political Science at the University of California, Berkeley, where she is an affiliated faculty member in the Department of Rhetoric and the Program in Critical Theory. She is the author of several books, including *Edgework: Essays on Knowledge and Politics* (2005), *Regulating Aversion: Tolerance in the Age of Identity and Empire* (2008), *Walled States, Waning Sovereignty* (2010), and, with Rainer Forst, *The Power of Tolerance* (2014).

JUDITH BUTLER is the Maxine Elliot Professor in the Departments of Rhetoric and Comparative Literature and the codirector of the Program of Critical Theory at the University of California, Berkeley. She is the author or coauthor of several books, including *Antigone's Claim: Kinship between Life and Death* (2000), *Precarious Life: Powers of Violence and Mourning* (2004), *Undoing Gender* (2004), and, with Gayatri Spivak, *Who Sings the Nation-State? Language, Politics, Belonging* (2008).

DEBORAH CAMERON is the Rupert Murdoch Professor in Language and Communication at the University of Oxford. She is the author or editor of several books, including *The Myth of Mars and Venus: Do Men and Women Really Speak Different Languages?* (2007), *Language and Sexuality* (2003), and *Working with Spoken Discourse* (2001).

JANET CARSTEN is professor of social and cultural anthropology at the University of Edinburgh. She is the author of *The Heat of the Hearth: The Process of Kinship in a Malay Fishing Community* (1997) and *After Kinship* (2004), and the editor of *Cultures of Relatedness: New Approaches to the Study of Kinship* (2000), *Ghosts of Memory: Essays on Remembrance and Relatedness* (2007), and *Blood Will Out: Essays on Liquid Transfers and Flows* (2013).

RAEWYN CONNELL is University Professor at the University of Sydney and a fellow of the Academy of Social Sciences in Australia. She is the author of several books, including *Southern Theory* (2007), *Gender: In World Perspective* (2009), and *Confronting Equality* (2011). See www.raewynconnell.net.

KATE CREHAN is professor of anthropology at the College of Staten Island and the Graduate Center, City University of New York. She is the author of *Community Art: An Anthropological Perspective* (2011), *Gramsci, Culture, and Anthropology* (2002), and *The Fractured Community: Landscapes of Power and Gender in Rural Zambia* (1997).

WENDY DONIGER is the Mircea Eliade Distinguished Service Professor in the Divinity School at the University of Chicago. She is the author of over thirty books, including *Splitting the Difference: Gender and Myth in Greece and India* (1999), *The Woman Who Pretended to Be Who She Was* (2005), and *The Hindus: An Alternative History* (2009).

ANNE FAUSTO-STERLING is the Nancy Duke Lewis Professor of Biology and Gender Studies at Brown University. She is the author of *Sex/Gender: Biology in a Social World* (2012), *Sexing the Body: Gender Politics and the Construction of Sexuality* (2000), and *Myths of Gender: Biological Theories about Women and Men* (1985; rev. ed., 1992).

CARLA FREEMAN is the Winship Distinguished Research Professor of Women's, Gender, and Sexuality Studies and associated faculty in Anthropology and Latin American and Caribbean Studies at Emory University. She is the author of *High Tech and High Heels in the Global Economy: Women, Work, and Pink-Collar Identities in the Caribbean* (2000), co-editor of *Global Middle Classes: Theorizing through Ethnographic* (2012), and editor of the book series Issues of Globalization.

ELIZABETH SWANSON GOLDBERG is professor of English at Babson College. Along with many articles on literature, human rights, and gender, she is the author of *Beyond Terror: Gender, Narrative, Human Rights* (2007) and coeditor of *Theoretical Perspectives in Human Rights and Literature* (2011).

DAVID M. HALPERIN is the W. H. Auden Distinguished University Professor of the History and Theory of Sexuality at the University of Michigan. He is the author or editor of a dozen books, most recently *How to Be Gay* (2012), *Gay Shame* (2009), *What Do Gay Men Want?* (2007), and *How to Do the History of Homosexuality* (2002).

GILBERT HERDT is professor of human sexuality studies and anthropology, and a founder of the Department of Sexuality Studies National Sexuality Resource Center at San Francisco State University. He is the author or editor of several books, including *Secrecy and Cultural Reality* (2001); *Sexual Inequalities and Social Justice*, coedited with Niels Teunys (2006); and *21st-Century Sexualities: Contemporary Issues in Health, Education, and Rights* (2007), coedited with Cymene Howe (2007).

SALLY L. KITCH is the founding director of the Institute for Humanities Research and Regents' Professor of Women's and Gender Studies at Arizona State University. She is the author of several books, including *The Specter of Sex: Gendered Foundations of Racial Formation in the U.S.* (2009) and *Higher Ground: From Utopianism to Realism in American Feminist Thought and Theory* (2000).

JANE MANSBRIDGE is the Adams Professor of Leadership and Democratic Values at the John F. Kennedy School of Government, Harvard University. She is the author or editor of several books, including *Beyond Self-Interest* (1990), *Why We Lost the ERA* (1986), and *Beyond Adversary Democracy* (1983).

RUTH A. MILLER is professor of history at the University of Massachusetts, Boston. She is the author of several books, including *Snarl: In Defense of Stalled Traffic and Faulty Networks* (2013), *Seven Stories of Threatening Speech: Women's Suffrage Meets Machine Code* (2011), *Law in Crisis: The Ecstatic Subject of Natural Disaster* (2009), *The Erotics of Corruption: Law, Scandal, and Political Perversion* (2008), and *The Limits of Bodily Integrity: Abortion, Adultery, and Rape Legislation in Comparative Perspective* (2007).

ANNA SAMPAIO is associate professor of ethnic studies and political science at Santa Clara University. She is coeditor of *Transnational Latino/a Communities: Politics, Processes, and Cultures* (2002) and a member of the editorial board of *PS: Political Science and Politics* and *Latin American Perspectives*.

REGINA M. SCHWARTZ is professor of English at Northwestern University. She is the author of several books, including *Sacramentality at the Dawn of Secularism: When God Left the World* (2007), *Transcendence: Philosophy, Literature, and Theology Approach the Beyond* (2004), and *The Curse of Cain: The Violent Legacy of Monotheism* (1997).

JOAN W. SCOTT is the Harold F. Linder Professor in School of Social Science at the Institute for Advanced Study, Princeton. She is the author of several books, including *Parité: Sexual Equality and the Crisis of French Universalism* (2005), *The Politics of the Veil* (2007), and *The Fantasy of Feminist History* (2011).

CARROLL SMITH-ROSENBERG is Mary Frances Berry Collegiate Professor Emerita at the University of Michigan. She is the author of three books, including *This Violent Empire: The Birth of an American National Identity* (2010) and *Disorderly Conduct: Visions of Gender in Victorian America* (1986).

HORTENSE SPILLERS is the Frederick J. Whiton Professor of English at Cornell University. She is the author of *Black, White, and in Color: Essays in American Literature and Culture* (2003), editor of *Comparative American Identities: Race, Sex and Nationality in the Modern Text* (1991), and coeditor of *The Norton Anthology of African American Literature* (2003).

CATHARINE R. STIMPSON is University Professor, professor of English, and dean emerita of the Graduate School of Arts and Science at New York University. Her many books include *Where the Meanings Are* (1988) and *Class Notes* (1979). She is also the founding editor of *Signs: Journal of Women in Culture and Society*.

MICHAEL WARNER is the Seymour H. Knox Professor of English Literature and American Studies at Yale University. He is the author of several books, including *Varieties of Secularism in a Secular Age* (2010), *Publics and Counterpublics* (2002), and *The Trouble with Normal* (1999), and the editor of *The Portable Walt Whitman* (2003).

Index

American Kinship (Schneider), 217–18

American Political Science Association, 420

American Progressives, 184

American Revolution, 190, 490

Anacreon, 459

Ancient Society (Morgan), 211

Anderson, Benedict, 36

androgyny, 6; myth of, 288–91

animism: Native Americans, 298; and nature, 298; and religion, 430–31

Anselm of Canterbury, 437

anthropology, 211, 216; and culture, 42–44, 47, 62; feminism, relationship between, as awkward, 46; feminist anthropologists, critique of, 45; gender, study of, 46, 210, 220–21; kinship, study of, 207–9, 212, 218–20, 222, 225–27; male bias within, 45; marriage, relations between groups, 216; political-economy approach in, 47; as practice-based, 219; reproductive technologies, 227; second-wave feminism, effect on, 45, 208; women, "honorary men" status of in, 208; women, as open to, 45

Antic Hay (Huxley), 460

anticolonialism, 218

Anti-Federalists, 190

Antony and Cleopatra (Shakespeare), 466

Anzaldúa, Gloria, 109

Appleton, Jane Sophia, 506

Apter, Emily, 81

Aquinas, Thomas, 445n13

Arcadia (Sidney), 490

Arendt, Hannah, 143, 363, 376, 388–89nn1, 389n6; private, as word, understanding of, 385; and public action, 386–87

Arethas, 459–60

Aristophanes, 7, 289

Aristotle, 366, 452–53; friendship, reciprocal model of, 473; and justice, 180

Arlington (Virginia), 491

Arnow, Harriet, 295–96

Arqtiq (Adolph), 507

art: modern meaning of, 60

Asdal, Kristin, 323

"Ashes" (Sedaris), 264

Asia, 154, 207, 219

Asian Americans, 98, 106; Asian American studies, 12

assimilation: Americanization, push toward, 103; and assimilationists, 101; and ethnicity, 97–98, 100–103, 105–8, 111; resistance to, 107–8

assisted reproductive technology (ART), 307–8

Association of Women Surgeons (AWS), 59

Astell, Mary, 372

As You Like It (Shakespeare), 490

Athens (Greece), 180, 361

Atwood, Margaret, 495–96, 511, 517

Augustine, 445n13, 489

Aurora, 490

Austin, J. L., 241

Australia, 467; Central Desert paintings in, 164; and White Australia policy, 165

Author, Art, and the Market, The (Woodmansee), 60

Bachofen, Johannes, 213, 277

Backlash (Faludi), 510

Bacon, Francis, 490

Bacon, Lloyd, 259

Bailey (Colorado), 153

Bakke, Allan, 402–3

Bakunin, Mikhail, 200–201n6

Baldwin, James, 23, 393, 398

Barbados: higglers in, 117, 127–30, 133; informatics employers in, 126, 128, 133–34; pink-collar workers, 129. *See also* Caribbean

Barr, Marleen, 492

Barry, Kathleen, 345–46

Bartkowski, Frances, 492, 507–8

Battle Creek (Michigan), 491

Beatrijs of Nazareth, 444

Beauty (Tepper), 510

Beauvoir, Simone de, 5, 45, 336, 347, 396–98, 512

Beecher, Catharine, 358–59, 360, 362, 364, 369–70

Before Midnight (film), 251

Before Sunrise (film), 251

Before Sunset (film), 251

Beijing Declaration and Platform for Action, 139

Bellamy, Edward, 499

Belli, Giaconda, 518

Belton (Texas), 502

Benedict, Ruth, 44

Canada, 496

Canguilhem, Georges, 420

Canopus in Argus series (Lessing), 507

capitalism, 371–72; and desire, 268

Caribbean, 121; "cutting and contriving," tradition of in, 128; globalization, research on in, 126; higglers in, 117, 124–25, 127–30, 133–35; pink-collar workers in, 116; respectability vs. reputation in, 124. *See also* Barbados

Carter, Angela, 514

Cassell, Joan, 49, 55–59, 61–63

Castries (St. Lucia), 131

Catalina (La Monja Alférez, the Lieutenant Nun), 1–2, 7

category crisis, 7

Catherine of Siena, 435

celibacy: and Judaism, 441–42; and religion, 441–42; and Shakers, 501; and utopia, 500–502; women, as empowering to, 501

Chaitanya (Hindu saint), 288

Chalice and the Blade, The (Eisler), 277

Chariton (Greek novelist), 467

Charnas, Suzy McKee, 503, 507, 510

Cherokee, 295–96

Chicago (Illinois), 182, 218

Chicana and Latina feminism, 108–9

Chicana Service Action Center Newsletter (publication), 108

Chicanismo, 106–7; Chicana feminists, and gendered bias within, protesting of by, 108

Chicano movement, 106–7; masculine rhetoric, privileging of in, 108

Chicano studies, 12; Chicano cultural nationalism, 107

Chickasaw, 296

Childhood and Society (Erikson), 160

childhood development: childhood, as sexualized, 26; and Freud, 348; Lacan, castration theory of, 348–49; Oedipus complex, 348–49

"Child Is Being Beaten, A" (Freud), 254

Chile, 165

China, 153

Choctaw, 296

Chodorow, Nancy, 81, 194, 351

"Choreographies of Gender" (Foster), 38

Chow, Rey, 354

Christianity, 156, 273, 281, 386, 429–30, 432–36, 443; Christian Crusaders, and utopia, 489; Gnostics, 438–39; and Jesus, 437, 440–41; Mary, devotion to, 439. *See also* Genesis; New Testament; Old Testament

Cicero, 420

cinaedi, 476

City of God (Augustine), 489

Civilization and Its Discontents (Freud), 341

Civilization of the Goddess, The (Gimbutas), 278

Civil Rights Act (1964), 403, 407

civil rights movements, 101, 106, 110, 146, 162, 184–85, 366

civil society, 379

Civil War, 23

class: concept of, 48–49; and culture, 46; and gender, 50–52; and globalization, 122; and power, 337

Cleft, The (Lessing), 517

Cleland, John, 478

Clement of Alexandria, 459–60

Clifford, James, 47–48

Code of Hammurabi, 141

Cohen, Ronald, 202n10

Collier, Jane Fishburne, 46

Collins, Patricia Hill, 202n10

colonialism: and nature, 299; and third-world women, 300

Comisíon Feminil Mexicana Newsletter (publication), 108

Commission of Immigration and Housing, 104

commodity culture, 258; and power, 340

Comparative Mythology (Müller), 274

Confederacy, 252

Confessions (Rousseau), 361

Confucius, 520–21n2; and Confucianism, 189–90

Connery, Sean, 256

constructivists, 12

Convention on the Elimination of All Forms of Discrimination against Women, 143

Coole, Diana, 321

Copelon, Rhonda, 149

Copenhagen (Denmark), 245

Cornell, Drucilla, 35, 38, 492

Coronel, Paul, 105

Cortes, Hernán, 432
Cott, Nancy F., 399
Counter-Reformation, 439
Course in General Linguistics, The (Saussure), 417–18
Crenshaw, Kimberle, 399
Crete, 469
Critical Terms in Religious Studies (Taylor), 432
critical theory, 67, 232. *See also* poststructuralism
Critique of the Study of Kinship (Schneider), 221
Crockett, Davy, 29–31
Crockett Almanacs (Crockett), 30
Crusade for Justice, 107
cultural feminism, 300, 305, 307
cultural ideologies: kinship arrangements, 4; labor market, 4; social institutions, 4
cultural nationalism, 106–7
cultural pluralism, 101
cultural studies, 365, 401
culture, 55; and anthropology, 42–44, 47, 62; artistic creation, as practice and products of, 41, 44, 59–60, 63; body, as preeminent object of, 313; civilization and, 42–43; and class, 46; concept of, 47–48; and conformity, 59; cultures, as systems, 46; cultures, concept of, 43, 47; definitions of, 46; economic relations, 49; as fluid, 63; and gender, 46, 48, 60, 63; gender, representations of, 60; groups of people, 59; and history, 49, 60, 63; individuals in, as gendered beings, 63; and inequality, 100; and language, 17, 58; meanings of, 41–42, 62–63; and nationalism, 42–44, 46; and nature, 17; as particular group of people, 41; and race, 46; and Romanticism, 46
cybernetic writing, 321
cyberpunk, 492
cyberspace, 320–21, 333
"Cyborg Manifesto" (Haraway), 322
cyborgs, 314, 333–34, 492; as cybernetic organism, 321–22; and feminism, 321–22; and gender, 323; process vs. identity, 323. *See also* posthuman

Daly, Mary, 277
Damian, Peter, 443, 470

Daniels, Cynthia, 307
Dano, Paul, 265
Darfur, 21
Darwin, Charles, 311
Darwinian feminists, 311–12
Daughters of a Coral Dawn (Forrest), 507, 509
D'Aulnoy, Marie-Catherine, 504
Davis, Elizabeth Gould, 277
Declaration of Independence, 142
Declaration of the Rights of Man and of the Citizen, 142
de Lauretis, Teresa, 81–82, 399
Deleuze, Gilles, 71, 338
de Pisan, Christine, 489, 504
Derrida, Jacques, 16, 170, 338
Descartes, René, 147
desire, 250; aggression, as integral to, 75; and attachment, 67, 73, 91, 258; as "bad," 83; as "becoming," states of, 91; and capitalism, 268; creativity, as source of, 82; and critical thought, 72, 80; and "deterritorialization," 91; and fantasy, 251–55, 258–59, 262; female masochism, 80; forms of, 84; Freudian theory, 72–82; and gender, 90; and ideology, 80; and identification, 268; and identity, 75, 85–86, 91; infantile desire, as allosexual, 75; infantile desire, as autoerotic, 75; and infidelity, 254; and intimacy, 258, 260–61; Lacanian model, 72; and love, 66–67, 72, 75, 82, 257–59, 269–70; "love at first sight," trope of, 259; love, paradox of, 70; 1960s, radical upheavals of, 83; as nonnormative, 73–74; as "normal," 73–74; *objet a*, woman as, 88; Oedipal complex, 79, 88, 91; as political, 70; populations, practices of, 92; and power, 267–68, 341, 349; and psychoanalysis, 71–73, 84–86, 91; public and private, 70; and repetition, 73; "reterritorialization" of, 91; "rhizomatics" of, 91; romantic love, 261; self-help discourse, 264; sexual difference and sexuality, as property of, 87; and sexuality, 92; sexual revolution, 84; in situation comedies, 70; zoning of, 70–71
Dewey, John, 185
Diagnostic and Statistical Manual (*DSM*) (American Psychiatric Association), 168

feminist theory: public and private spheres in, 365–71

Feminist Theory from Margin to Center (hooks), 110

feminist utopian texts, 503, 508; paradox in, 507, 509; as reformist, in nature, 505–7; suffrage activism, 504

fetishism, 78–79, 458; and women, 81–82

"Fetishism" (Freud), 78, 350

"Fire Next Time, The" (Baldwin), 398

Firestone, Shulamith, 304–5, 346, 512–13

First Amendment, 341

First Sex, The (Davis), 277

First Sex, The (Fisher), 8

Fisher, Abigail Noel, 406

Fisher, Helen, 8

Fishman, Pamela, 246

Fitting, Peter, 521n9

Five Generations Hence (Jones), 521n4

Florence (Italy), 470

Folbre, Nancy, 519

Forrest, Katherine V., 507, 509

Fortes, Meyer, 208, 212; "axiom of amity," 214; domestic domain and politico-jural domain, distinction between, 213–14

Foster, Susan, 38

Foucault, Michel, 14, 16, 28, 29, 38, 91, 219, 250, 255, 347, 353–54, 374, 426, 443; bodies, political and social construct of, 24–25; bodies of knowledge, as multidirectional, 26; body, discursive construction of, 25; discourse, concept of, 342–44, 421; and fantasy, 250; feminist scholars, as critical of, 33; gender and regulatory power, 412; and Marx, 340–41; and norm, 419; norm, and legal codes, 420; and normalization, 421–22; and performance criticism, 358; and power, 25–27, 197, 338, 340, 342–45, 349; power, analytics of, 339, 344; power, negative view of, 341; repressive hypothesis of, 339, 341; sex, and power, linkage of by, 33; sexuality, as normative bodily and affective practices, 92; sovereignty, critique of, 339–40; and subjectivization, 339

Four Archetypes (Jung), 277

1491 (Mann), 296

Fourteenth Amendment, 402–3; and Equal Protection Clause, 407

Fourth United Nations Conference on Women, 139–40

France, 26, 214, 456, 460

Francoeur, Robert, 492, 512

Franke, Katherine, 425

Frankfurt School, 376

Fraser, Nancy, 163, 364, 369

fraternity, 197

Frazer, James, 431

Freedmen's Village, 491

freedom: as negative liberty, 372

French Revolution, 42–43, 490

Freud, Sigmund, 11, 15–16, 83, 85–86, 89, 166, 275, 279, 338, 341, 350, 353–54, 449, 451, 481–82; anaclitic or propping relation, 77; apotropaic effect, 350; biological determinism of, 345; castration anxiety, 78, 87; on childhood development, 348; critical feminist thought, 80–82; desire, forms of, 74; desire, therapeutic model of, 75; and drive, 353; on female masochism, 80; fetishism, development of, 78–79; and id, 160; and identification, 77, 159; infantile sexuality, 74, 76–77; melancholia, concept of, 76; modern thought, influence on, 158; and *Nachträglichkeit*, 86; and Otherness, 76, 81; and object-choice, 79; object-choice, as metonymic relation, 77; Oedipal complex, 74, 76–77, 79, 159, 348; and overdetermination, 254; and psychoanalysis, 346; "Rat Man," 159; and religion, 431; and sexuality, 346–47; subjectivity, formation of, 76; and super-ego, 77–78, 160

Friedan, Betty, 397–99

From Ritual to Romance (Weston), 277

From the Legend of Biel (Staton), 507

Frost, Samantha, 321

Fruitlands, 490

Frymer-Kensky, Tikva, 281

Gal, Susan, 247

Galarza, Ernesto, 107

Galen, 453

Gandhi, Mohandas K., 158

Garber, Marjorie, 7, 287

Garrison, William Lloyd, 190

gay and lesbians: and religion, 428; rights of, 150; same-sex marriage, 150; therapy culture, 263

gender theory, 13

gender traditionalists: and codependencies, 9; contrasts, maximizing of, 9; gender structure, as universal, 9; relations, patterns of, 9; same-sex marriage, opposition to, 8–9

gender utopianism, 487, 491

Generation of Animals (Aristotle), 452

Genesis, 8, 437, 439–42, 470, 490. *See also* Christianity; New Testament; Old Testament

Geneva Convention on the Status of Refugees, 149

Geneva Conventions, 149

George Lucas Educational Foundation, 488

German Americans, 101

Germany, 60, 100, 161, 420

Ghana: Nkrumaism in, 520–21n2

Gibson, Mel, 473

Gibson, William, 320, 334

Gilda Stories, The (Gomez), 509

Gilgamesh Epic, 472

Gilligan, Carol, 13, 194–96

Gilman, Charlotte Perkins, 504–6, 518

Gimbutas, Marija, 277, 278–79

Girls (television series), 251

Glazer, Nathan, 100

GLBTIQ (gay, lesbian, bisexual, transgender, intersex, and queer), 141; personal identity construction, and suicide rates of, 151; rights of, 150; violence against, 153–54. *See also* gay and lesbians; homosexuality; LGBTQ

globalization, 17, 117; affective economy of, 122–23; and agency, 135; as agentive, 131; "body-shopping," 122; "care-work" of, 122; contemporary global femininity of, 120–21; feminist critiques of, 118; feminist reconceptualization of, 119; feminization of, survival in, 122; Filipina and Indonesian domestic workers and, 121; flexibility and mobility of, 120; gender, as powerful force in, 134; gender and class, 122; gendered qualities of, 116, 118; gendering of theory, 115, 118; and higglers, 124, 128–29, 134–35; and informatics, 126, 127–31; labor and migration, 122; "late" capitalism, 117; local, feminization of, 115; local contexts of, 117; love and, 122–23; methodological approaches to, 118; and mobility, 123; new communications technologies, 121; off-shore informatics, 127; peasant garb, and otherness, 121; pink-collar workers, 124; as plural, 119; processes of, as distinctly local, 132; production and consumption, gendered opposition between, 123; public spaces, and private venues, 123; "tomboyism," identity, adoption of, 121; transnational migration, 116, 120, 127–28; and travel, 121; "virtual migration," 122; women, as threatening, to gendered configuration, 121

globalization scholarship, 116

globalization studies, 12; and labor, 121; Mexican maquiladoras, 121

globalization theory: as masculine, 115

global North, 21, 37, 42, 47; identity discourse in, 165, 171

Global Sex (Altman), 175

global South, 21, 42, 47, 171

Global Tribunal on Accountability for Women's Human Rights, 139–41, 154

Glover, Danny, 473

Goddess: mythology of, 276–77, 279, 281; Goddess-feminists, 276–79, 281–82

Goddesses and Gods of Old Europe 7000– 3000 BC, The (Gimbutas), 277

Goethe, Johann, 61

"Going to Meet the Man" (Baldwin), 23

Goldberg, David Theo, 400

Goldman, Emma, 303

Gomez, Jewelle, 509, 521n4

Gone with the Wind (Mitchell), 251–52

Gonzalez, Rodolfo "Corky," 107

Goody, Jack, 219

Gordon, Joan, 492

Graham, Laura, 361

Gramsci, Antonio, 44, 50, 52–53, 57; class, concept of, 48–49; culture, role of, 48–49, 58–59, 63; hegemony, meaning of in, 56; on power, 48, 55–56; prison notebooks of, 48–49, 58

Gramsci, Culture and Anthropology (Crehan), 48

Gratz, Jennifer, 402, 406

Gratz v. Bollinger, 402, 406–7

Graves, Robert, 277

Great Mother, The (Neumann), 277

Greece, 459, 278; mother goddess theory in, 279

Green Belt Movement, 301

Green Hope Farm, 502

Gresham's Law, 279

Griffith, Mary, 497, 505

Grimké, Angelina, 373

Grimké, Sarah, 372–73

Griswold v. Connecticut, 364

Grosz, Elizabeth, 313–14, 354

Grounding of Modern Feminism (Cott), 399

group psychology, 382

Grutter, Barbara, 402, 406–7

Grutter v. Bollinger, 402, 406–8

Guantánamo Bay, 144

Guérillères, Les (Wittig), 509, 521n3

Gutter Dyke Collective, 502–3

Gyn-ecology (Daly), 277

Habermas, Jürgen, 363, 378, 388, 388–89nn1, 389n4; mass culture and civil society, 379; public/private spheres, influence on, 365, 376–77, 384; public sphere, "refeudalization" of, 379; reason, public use of, 380; unitary public, adoption of by, 383

Habermas and the Public Sphere (Calhoun), 378

Haiti, 35

Hall, Kim, 34

Hall, Kira, 240–41, 242

Hall, Stuart, 36

Hamlet (Shakespeare), 3

Handmaid's Tale, The (Atwood), 495, 511

Hannaford, Ivan, 401

Haraway, Donna, 314, 321–23, 513; cyborgian regeneration, touting of, 514

Harding, Rosie, 518

Harding, Sandra, 301; and "counter-histories," 302

Harmonia, 491

Harris, Lyle Ashton, 4

Harvard University, 404

Hawkesworth, Mary, 12–13

Hayles, N. Katherine, 326

Hedren, Tippi, 256

Hegel, Georg, 148, 195; recognition, and construction of self, 147

hegemony: and coercion and consent, 56–57; and control, 58

Heidt-Forsythe, Erin, 307

Hennes (god), 355n4

Hercules, 466

Herder, Johann, 61, 432; cultures, concept of, 43

Herland (Gilman), 504–5

Herodotus, 274

Hertz, Neil, 350

Hesiod, 271

heterosexuality, 453; as category, invention of, 92; as term, 10, 461

heterotopia, 520; novel genre of, 517, 519

Heyzer, Noeleen, 140

Higginbotham, Evelyn Brooks, 33

higglers (marketers), 116–17; in Afro-Caribbean history, as powerful figure, 124; agency, evolving sense of, 133; and consumption, 128–29; femininity, as embodiment of, 132–33; and globalization, 126, 134–35; globalization, as agents of, 133; locality and movement, as symbol of, 125; and neoliberalism, 133; professionalism of, 127–30, 132; respectability vs. reputation, 124, 131–32; sugar industry, historical roots in, 126; as suitcase traders, 125, 128, 134; as transnational, 119, 127–28, 132, 134–35; weekend higglers, 125–26; West Indian country higgler, style of, 124–25; womanhood, as embodiment of, 124; work of, as global processes, 119. *See also* informatics

Hijas de Cuahtemoc, Las (publication), 108

Hildegard of Bingen, 435

Hinduism, 189, 273, 430; Hijras in, 283

Hindu mythology, 276, 281, 283; Amba, myth of in, 286–87; asymmetry, of gender in, 286–87; Bhima in, 286–87; cross-dressing in, and politics, as motivated by, 287; and *dharma*, 284; Draupadi, story of in, 286; female-to-male (FTM) transformations in, 286–87; Ila, myth of, 285–86; Kichaka in, 286–87; male-to-female (MTF) in, 284–87; Mohini, myth of, 285; Narada, story of, 284–85; Vedantic theory of illusion, 284; and Vishnu, 284–85, 289

Hirschfeld, Magnus, 11

History of Sexuality, The (Foucault), 341, 419

Hitchcock, Alfred, 256, 266

Hitler, Adolf, 165

Hobbes, Thomas, 34, 145, 341

Hochschild, Jennifer, 183

Hocquenghem, Guy, 169, 173

Holdfast series (Charnas), 503

Hollister, Alonzo, 501

Homer, 271

homosexuality, 163, 167, 453; as category, invention of, 92; concept of, 482; "contrary sexual feeling," 479–80; creation of, 168; hallmark of, 483; homosexual acts, criminalization of, 169; homosexual identity, creation of, 168–69; homosexual men and women, and heterosexual men and women, differentiating from, 482–83; identities of, as multiple, 172–73, 483; intolerance toward, rise in, 443; and Marxism, 162; as medical condition, 169; as mental illness, 168; modern category of, 481–82; object-choice, 472, 483–84; perverted or pathological orientation, psychiatric notion of, 481; and privacy, 381; and pseudo-homosexuality, 468–69; recategorizing of, 174–75, 482; and religion, 443; same-sex sexual object-choice, psychoanalytic notion of, 481–82; sexual instinct, inversion of, 479; sexual inversion, difference between, 480; sexuality, as part of new system of, 484; sexually deviant behavior, sociological notion of, 482; as term, 10, 461, 480–81; as word, first appearance of, 479. *See also* gay and lesbians; GLBTIQ; lesbians; LGBTQ; sexuality

Hong Kong (China), 121

Honig, Bonnie, 385

hooks, bell, 109–10

Hopwood, Cheryl J., 402, 406

Hopwood v. Texas, 402, 406

House Committee on Immigration and Naturalization, 104

Howland, Marie Stevens Case, 506

Hugo, Victor, 350

Human Condition, The (Arendt), 385–86

human rights, 17, 150; asylum, and gender-based persecution, 149; and asylum seekers, 143, 149; democracy, emergence of, 145; and dignity, 151; and displaced, 143; domestic violence, 148–49; and Enlightenment, 147; female genital mutilation (FGM), 149; of gender and sexual minorities, 148–51; gender violence, 152–53; and identity formation, 148; origins of, 141–45; paradox of, 143–44; personal identity, and worth, 151; personhood, legal category of, 143–44; and rape, 148–49; and recognition, 151; recognition, and Hegelian concept of self, 147–48; recognition, of individuals, 147; of refugees, 143; of sex and gender minorities, 148; sex trafficking, 152; as term, 141; and women, 144, 148; as women's rights, 139–41, 153

human rights movement, 141–42; Convention on the Elimination of All Forms of Discrimination against Women, resistance to, 143; as global, 140, 154; "human being" and "legal" person, gap between, 143

Humphrey, Hubert H., 304

Hunger Games, The (Collins) series, 519

Hunger Games, The (film) series, 519

Huxley, Aldous, 460, 493

Ibn Khaldûn, 188

Icaria, 490

Ideas on the Philosophy of the History of Mankind (Herder), 43

identity, 5, 71, 156, 159–60, 175; assertive and affirmative concept of, 361; classifying and labeling of, 168; community, membership in, 161; concept of, 156; and desire, 75, 85–86, 91; Erikson, concept of, 160; and ethnicity, 100, 106; identities, as fluid, 4; and identity card (ID), 167–68, 174; identity fraud, 167; and ideology, 86; meaning, changes in, 156; as mirage, 86; as multiple, 171, 172; as national, 161; and nationalism, 172; and personhood, 174; security risks, 167; and subjectivity, 10; surveillance and regulation, as matter of, 168; as term, 157, 167, 173; unity, theme of, 156; as unstable, 170–71

Identity, Youth and Crisis (Erikson), 160

identity politics, 162, 175, 366, 368; cultural diversity, 164; difference, acceptance of in, 164; of dominant groups, 165–66; essentialism, retreat into, 167; and "gay

justice (*continued*)
    ment, 188; oppositional usage of, 185,
191, 199–200; and oppression, 187–88,
190–91, 201n7; as political weapon,
186–87; private property, 184; as procedural, 200n3, 200n4; public and private
spheres of, 185; and Qur'an, 188; and
Reason, 198; reason vs. sympathy, dichotomy of, 194–95; as retributive, 188,
200n3; rights orientation, as masculine, 196; rule of law, 184; and rules, 181;
social justice, 185, 188; as substantive,
180; and suffrage, 200n1; tactics,179; in
Taoism, 189; terrorism, 179; and truth,
189; as umbrella term, 182–83; universality of, as masculine, 195; and the
weak, 198; wealth and income, distribution of, 184; women's experience, neglect of, 185–86, 193

Kallen, Horace, 100
Kamasutra, 283
Kanazawa, Satoshi, 393–94
Kant, Immanuel, 147, 194, 363, 378, 432;
    different publics, notion of, 375–76; and
Gelehrter (scholar), 375–76; men and
women, different characterizations of
by, 195; public and private, distinction
between, 375; and reading public, 375,
383; "two hats" theory of, 375
Kaplan, Cora, 246
Kaufman, Charlie, 266
Kazan, Zoe, 265
Keates, Debra, 353
Keller, Evelyn Fox, 299
Kennedy, John F., 398
Kennedy, Robert F., 393
Kentucky, 295–96
Kertbeny. *See* Benkert, Karl Maria
Keywords (Williams), 41
Khanna, Ranjana, 354
kinaidia, 475
Kindred (Butler), 521n4
King, Martin Luther, Jr., 158, 185
King, William, 460
Kingdom, The, 490–91
Kin of Ata Are Waiting for You, The (Bryant),
    508
Kinsey, Alfred C., 11, 480–82; on homo-
sexual/heterosexual divisions, 464; on

homosexuality, 463–64; and "Kinsey
Report," 463
kinship, 17; alliance theory, 214–17; American kinship, sexual procreation, as
core symbol of, 218; and anthropology,
207–9, 212, 218–20, 222, 225–27; classificatory system, 210; culturalist critique
of, 217, 226; descent system, 212–13,
217; descriptive system, 210; domestic
domain, feminist critique of, 217; economics of, 219; and evolutionism, 209,
211–12; exchange and marriage, 216; exogamy, 209; family, nature of, 225–27;
family, as universal social institution,
213–14; family forms, evolution of, 211;
feminist critique of, 217, 226; and filiation, 224; and gender, 207–9, 213, 220–
21, 225–27; group marriage, 209–11; as
ideological system, 218; kinship theory,
46; and labor, 227; labor, division of, between men and women, 220; and law,
218; Marxist critique of, 219; and matriarchy, 209, 211; and "matrilineal puzzle,"
213; matriliny, and matriarchy, distinction between, 213; meaning, as system
of, 217; monogamy, 211; moral force of,
214; and nature, 218, 228; patriarchal
despotism theory, 209; patriarchy, 211;
and political authority, 212–13; polyandry, 209; polygamy, 209, 211; primitive matriarchy theory, 210; primitive
promiscuity theory, 209–11; in primitive societies, 208; and private domain,
208; religion and politics, as based in,
212; reproductive technologies, 210, 227;
social uses of, significance of in, 219;
structural linguistics, 416; symbolic position, 415–16
kinship studies, 208, 214, 217, 219–20, 221;
    "biological" and "social," relation be-
tween, 227–28; changes in, 218; resurgence of, 225–26
Kirene (Senegal), 53–54
Klein, Melanie, 351
Kluckhohn, Clyde, 431
Kluckhohn, Florence, 102
Kohlberg, Lawrence, 193–95
Kolmerten, Carol, 497
Komarovsky, Mirra: sex roles, concept
    of, 11

Lesbos, 458–59

Lesser Antilles, 245

Lessing, Doris, 507, 510, 517, 521n5

Lethal Weapon (film), 473

Letters on the Difficulty of Religion (Beecher), 358

Letters on the Equality of the Sexes and the Condition of Woman (Grimké), 372

Lévi-Strauss, Claude, 208, 214, 272, 414, 416–18; critics of, 216; elementary systems, 216; exchange, importance of to, 215; incest taboo, 215, 415; sexual exchange, 419; social entities, importance of relations between, 215

Levitas, Ruth, 518

LGBTQ (lesbian gay bisexual transgender queer) studies, 14. *See also* GLBTIQ

LGBTQ couples, 74. *See also* GLBTIQ

liberal feminism, 299, 305, 307

liberalism, 34, 336, 373–74; difference, view of, 35

liberal political culture, 258, 268; and liberal political theory, 341

liberal state, 339; private lives, governing of, 457

liberal tradition, 372–74, 378; patriarchy, as critique of, 371

liberation movements, 110

Liebestod, 287

Lincoln, Abraham, 190

Lincoln, Bruce, 274

Linklater, Richard, 251

Linnaeus, Carl, 302

literary studies, 62

Little Deer, 295

Locke, John, 34, 38, 145, 156, 329, 371

Looking Backward (Bellamy), 499

Los Angeles (California), 105, 109

Louis XIV, 377

love: aggression, as integral to, 75; commodities, identifying with, 268; death drive, 75; and desire, 66, 72, 75, 82, 257–59, 269–70; desire, paradox of, 70; expressions of, as conventional, 67; and fantasy, 68, 250, 264, 266; and globalization, 122–23; and intimacy, 263; and longing, 261; nonnormative forms of intimacy, public explicitness of, 264; Otherness, attempt to destroy, 75; pleasure principle, 75; popular romance, 260;

reciprocity, 67; and romantic lobe, 263; romantic narrative conventions, 263; seduction, "rules" of, 263; self-help discourse, 263–64; sex, as natural, ideology of, 263–64; therapy culture, 263

Lublin, Nancy, 515–16

Maathai, Wangari, 301

Macheray, Pierre, 422–23

Machiavelli, Niccolò, 374

MacKinnon, Catharine, 197, 337, 366–69, 374, 423, 425; heterosexuality, hierarchical structure of, and gender, 424

Mackintosh, Maureen, 49–56

Madonna, 60

Madsen, William, 102

Mahabharata, 283, 286, 288

Maine, Sir Henry, 209

Mair, Lucy, 45

Making a Social Body (Poovey), 421

Malay, 228; feeding, importance of in, 223; kinship, notions of, 222–25; siblingship, as central to in, 223–24

male friendship, 472; and homoeroticism, 474; reciprocal relations between, 473; same-sex desire, as cover for, 475; sexual love, difference between, 475. *See also* masculinity

Malinowski, Bronislaw, 44, 208, 212–13, 221

Malleus Maleficarum, 290

Mandeville, Bernard, 371–72

Man Made Language (Spender), 235

Mann, Charles, 296

Marlowe, Christopher, 475

Marnie (film), 256–57, 266

Marriages between Zones Three, Four, and Five (Lessing), 510, 521n5

Martin, Biddy, 425

Marvell, Andrew, 450

Marx, Karl, 157, 191–92, 201n7, 210, 211, 219, 26, 337, 343, 378; and Foucault, 340; on justice, 200–201n6

Marxism, 161–62, 336–37; homosexuality, and decadence as sign of, 162; and justice, 191–92; labor power, notion of, 340; and Marxist feminists, 299–300

masculinity, 5, 156, 243, 349, 413; art, identification with, 62; contradiction within, 88; erotic literature, 472; "float-ing world," literary productions of, 472; GI drag shows, 462; hard and soft styles of, 466; hierarchical model, of male sexual relations, 469–73; hierar-chy, eroticizing of, 469; identity, mirage of, 88; libertine, figure of, 468; male inversion, stereotype of, 478–79; male single-sex institutions, 467; masculini-ties, as plural, 171; men and women, dif-ferences between, approaches to, 12–13, 46; nature, association with, 298; New-port, gay decoys in, 461–66, 469–71, 475, 479–80, 482; as normative, 467; and passivity, 475–77, 480; pederasty and friendship, as masculinizing, 475; phallus, castration myth and law of the father, 349; public space, associations with, 360, 366, 385; as rational, stereo-type of, 195; reason and science, asso-ciation with, 298; "redneck queer," 467; and working-class culture, 463. *See also* male friendship

Massachusetts, 491

Mauss, Marcel, 215

Maynard, François de, 460

McLellan, John Ferguson, 209

McWhirter, Martha, 502

Mead, Margaret, 11, 44

"Medusa's Head" (Freud), 78

"Medusa's Head: Male Hysteria under Po-litical Pressure" (Hertz), 350

Melanesia, 46, 207

men's studies, 13

Merchant, Carolyn, 297, 299–300

Merck, Mandy, 354

Meredith, James, 398

Merian, Maria Sybylla, 302

Mexican-American Movement Incorpo-rated, 105

Mexican Americans, 29, 98–99, 111; Amer-icanization of, 103–4; Americaniza-tion schools, 105; and assimilation, 105; collective disenfranchisement of, 107; cultural nationalism, theory of, 106; "culture of poverty" theory, as ap-plied to, 102–3, 106; "fictive ethnicity" of, 105; and *machismo,* 103; Mexican American women, and Americaniza-tion programs, as targets of, 104; self-determination of, 107–8; social science inquiry, as passive objects of, 103

Mexican and Latin American culture: and self-determination, 107

Mexican Voice, 105

Mexico, 106–7; Mexican immigrants, guest worker program for, 104

Mildred Carver, USA (Bruère), 507

Mill, John Stuart, 341, 378

Millennium Hall (Scott), 504

Milton, John, 490

Mitchell, Juliet, 345, 415

Mitchell, Margaret, 251

Mizora (Lane), 504

modernization, 42, 47; and gender, 457; sexuality, and industrial capitalism, 456; social controls, 457

Moi, Toril, 396

mollitia, 475

Money, John, 3–4

monotheism, 282, 431

Montaigne, Michel de, 473–75

Montecino, Sonia, 164–65

Moore, M. Louise, 507

Moraga, Cherríe, 109

More, Sir Thomas, 489–90, 496, 498–99

Morgan, Jennifer, 34

Morgan, Lewis Henry, 209, 212, 219; clas-sificatory system of, 210; descriptive system of, 210; family forms, evolution of, 211

Morris, Jan, 7

Morrison, Toni, 260, 516–17

Moses, 187

Motherlines (Charnas), 507, 510

Motherpeace (Noble), 279

mothers' movements, 165

Movimiento Estudiantil Chicano de Aztlán (MEChA), 107

Moving the Mountain (Gilman), 506

Moylan, Tom, 510

Mujeres Activas en Letras y Cambio Social (MALCS), 109

Müller, Friedrich Max, 274

multiculturalism, 55

Mulvey, Laura, 84

Mumbai (India), 152

Munby, Arthur, 21

Murdock, George Peter, 208, 212

Murray, Judith Sargent, 372

popular culture: commodity culture, 258; liberal political culture, 258; therapy culture, 258, 267

postcolonial science and technology studies (STS), 301

postcolonial studies, 12, 209

posthuman: and agency, 329, 331–32; as ambivalent term, 320; and the body, 327–29; as concept, 320–21; dystopian science fiction, 327–28; feminist writing, as response to, 322; gender, 334; and gender/gender studies, 320–23, 327, 332–34; hybridity of, 323; language, play of, 325; materialist vs. new materialist, 321; "nothing more than" critique, 327–28; and speech, 324; as term, 17, 333–34. *See also* cyborgs

postmodernism, 17, 248

poststructuralism, 232, 235–36, 248. *See also* critical theory

poverty, 163

Powell, Lewis F. Jr., 402–5, 407

power: and class, 337; commodity model of, 340; desire, containment of, 341, 349; and feminism, 336–38, 344–45; and gender, 16, 56, 336, 345–46, 351, 355; and knowledge, 342; and labor, 337; and language, 243; and law, 349; male dominance, as system of stratification, 337; and masculinity, 335; phallus, association with, 350–51; political notion of, 339; and powerless, 340; and regulation, 426; repressive model of, 341; second wave feminism, 335; sexual discourses, 33; as signified symbolically, 351; social construction, 338; sovereignty, 31, 336, 339–41; and subjectivity, 354; as transferable good, 340; as ubiquitous, 339; will, design of, 336; and women, 336–37

Predicament of Culture, The (Clifford), 47

prehistory, 8

privacy: meanings of, 363; protection, feelings of, 381; right to, 363; and self-determination, 363, 381

Promise Keepers, 387

prostitution: women, powerlessness of, 32

psychoanalysis, 11, 15, 80–81, 88, 258, 269, 338, 345, 351; castration, fear of, 350; as cultural phenomenon, 382; and desire, 71–73, 84–86, 91; and the drive, 352–54;

drive, as border concept, 352; feminist use of, 347; and gender, 11; gender and power, 346; law of the father, 346–47; as liberal discourse, 71; normative distinctions of, 84; Oedipal complex, 91, 352; phallus, as symbolic representative, of law, 352; popularization of, 263; and sexual identity, 346; and sexuality, 73, 84–85

Psychoanalysis and Feminism (Mitchell), 345

psychology, 158–59, 161; and subjectivity, 17

Psychopathia Sexualis (Krafft-Ebing), 169, 481

psychotherapy, 267; and lovesickness, 265; romance, as therapy, 265

public and private spheres, 375, 382, 386; and the body, 361; as bourgeois, 384–85; and bracketing, 372; civil society, public sphere of, 377; and "the closet," 380–81; in competition with, 363; as complementary, 363; conflicting meanings of, 364; and counterpublics, 383–85, 387–88; and desire, 70; as distinct zones, 362; division between, 457; family, public significance of, 370; in feminist theory, 365–71; habitus, as rooted in, 360, 380; identity politics, 379; labor, gendered division of, 369–71; and language, 361; legal contexts of, 363–64; and liberal tradition, 371–74; mass culture and civil society, 379; and mediated publics, 387; and multiple publics, 383; "personal is political" slogan, 367–68, 387; polis, as model of, 376; and politics, 366–67, 373–74; and professionalism, 370; public, as word, origins of, 360, 364–65; publicness and privacy, different places, as belonging to, 363; public space, and physical boundaries, 362; public space, as spatial concept, 362; public space, as term, 362; public voice, and private selfhood, notion of, 371–72; public sphere, Marxist critique of, 378; and rational-critical debate, 380, 382; reason, private use of, 375; reason, public use of, 375; and salons, 378; social contexts of, 362; social movements, challenging of, 365–66; space, public

Sennett, Richard, 388–89nn1

"Sequel to the 'Vision of Bangor in the Twentieth Century'" (Appleton), 506

sex: as cultural artifact, of modern age, 452; and education, 309–10; and gender, 11, 313–14, 384, 452, 463–64; gender, distinction between, 5, 221, 450–51; heterosexualizing imperative of, 454; homogenizing effect of, 454; human reproduction, 452–53; materiality of, 451; meaning of, 454; modernization of, 11; sexless concept of, 452; sexual difference, 450–52, 454, 457; study of, 11; terminology of, 449–50, 452; as word, 484. *See also* sexuality

sexology, 455–56

Sex Revolution, A (Waisbrooker), 505

sex trafficking, 152

Sexual Behavior in the Human Female (Kinsey), 11

Sexual Behavior in the Human Male (Kinsey), 11, 463

sexual difference, 1–2, 454, 457; and castration, 348–49; and fantasy, 259; and gender, 394, 450–51; gendering of anxiety, as organized around, 88; and hierarchy, 90; Oedipus complex, 348; Other, desire of, 349; phallus and penis, distinction between, 88

sexual differences, 6–7; conundrum of, 310–11; femininity and masculinity, culturally available symbols of, 4; and gender, 4, 9, 12; relations, patterns of, 9

sexuality, 71–72; classification of, 449–50, 463, 465, 468–69; degenerate groups, 84; and desire, 92; different concepts of, 464–65; and Freud, 75; and gender, 3, 10, 14, 66, 171, 258, 360, 365, 372, 380, 382–84, 387, 424–25; as gender performance, 168–69; and guilt, 11; homogenizing effect of, 454; homosexuality, new system, as part of, 484; heterosexualizing imperative of, 454, 463; human personality, as basic feature of, 455; inversion, as psychosexual orientation, 480; male inversion, 478–79; male same-sex sexual contacts, historical modes of, 465–84; as masochistic, 75; meaning of, 454; and modernization, 456; notion of, 453–54; object-choice, and sexual orientation, 483; pathologies of, 458; and pederasty, 467; perversions, discovery of, 458; and physical body, 23; and psychoanalysis, 11, 73, 84–85; as psychological and physiological entity, 454–55; public and private space, 360; regulation of, 457–58; sexual aim, 454–55; sexual behavior, study of, 11; sexual deviation, 458; sexual identity, 92; sexual instinct, 458; sexual instinct, perversion of, 468; sexual inversion, and gender dysphoria, 480; sexual inversion, and homosexuality, difference between, 480; sexual object-choice, 454–55; sexual orientation, 455, 464; social transformation, as historical outcome of, 455; study of, 458. *See also* homosexuality; sex

sexuality and gender studies, 414

sexual politics, 169–70. *See also* queer politics

Shakers, 490–91; celibacy, commitment to, 501; labor, sexual division of, 501–2

Shango, 187

Shakespeare, 466, 490

Shepherdson, Charles, 353

Shore of Women, The (Sargent), 507

Sidney, Sir Philip, 490

Siebers, Tobin, 516

Signs (journal), 14

silence: femininity and, 247; and language, 245–46; meanings of, 246; and powerlessness, 247; of women, 245–46

Silver Circle, 502

Slaughter, Joseph, 142

slavery, 26, 29, 30–31, 34–35, 99, 145, 153, 163, 185, 190–91, 397, 496

Slonczewski, Joan, 507

Smith, Adam, 372, 518

Smith, Anna Deavere, 4

Smith, Jonathan Z., 432

Smith, Joseph, 433

Smith, Nicholas, 492

Smith, Valerie, 13

Smuts, Barbara, 312

social Darwinism, 99, 107

socialism, 161

socialist feminism, 300, 305

Social Gospel, 184

social movements, 365

Tocqueville, Alexis de, 350, 378

Totem and Taboo (Freud), 275

"Towards a Natural History of Norms"
(Macheray), 422

transgender: as mode of passage, between
genders, 414

transgendered, 6; in public-private sphere,
381–82; word, as umbrella term, for
transsexuals, 15

transgender theory, 425

transhumanism, 492

transsexuals, 14–15; and transsexuality,
282–86, 288

Traub, Valerie, 34

Tremain, Shelley, 513

"Tribades seu Lesbia" (Maynard), 460

tribes, 161

Trible, Phyllis, 440

Trinh Minh-ha, 247

Trobriand islanders, 221

True Woman: myth of, 32

Truth, Sojourner, 145, 167, 491. *See also*
Van Wagener, Isabella

Tuck, Ruth, 102–3

Tucson (Arizona), 103

Turner, Victor, 27–28

"Twilight of the Goddess, The" (Lefkowitz),
280

Twilight series (Meyer), 519

Two Spirit, 6

Tylor, E. B., 430–31

UNICEF, 21

Union of Mexican American Students
(UMAS), 107

United Kingdom, 162. *See also* Britain;
England

United Nations, 139–40

United Nations Commission on Human
Rights, 148

United Nations Development Fund for
Women (UNIFEM), 139–40

United Nations Security Council, 149

United Nations Universal Declaration of
Human Rights (UDHR), 141–43, 145,
148; and brotherhood, 144; human beings, description of, 144

United States, 2, 5, 11, 33, 35, 44, 48, 60, 83,
109, 127, 143, 149, 163, 166, 169, 171, 174,
196, 200n1, 202n10, 217, 225, 258, 260,
271, 282, 304, 307, 309, 313, 361, 368, 381,
397–98, 405, 425, 456, 461, 508, 514–15;
abolition movement in, 145; American
identity, and whiteness, as tethered to,
111; Anglo-Saxon traditions, as quintessentially American, 101; ethnic divisions in, 98–99; ethnic enclaves in, 98;
gender difference in, 195; gender systems in, 7, 9; gender traditionalists in,
8–9; HIV/AIDS policies in, 15; identity politics in, 162; immigration in, 97,
101–2; Jacksonian era, men and women
of in, 29–30; Latinos in, 106; marginalization in, 99; Mexican American youth
in, 105; postrace in, 393; psychoanalysis in, 71; rock and roll, and youth subculture in, 161; self-help culture in, 71;
social change in, 28–29; therapy culture
in, 263; utopias in, 488–91, 496–97, 503;
violence, cultural tradition of in, 154; violence, against women in, 154; "white"
self-images in, 165; women's income in,
as less than men, 146; women's movement in, 192–94

universal human rights, 43

University of California, Davis, 403–5

University of Memphis, 398

University of Michigan at Ann Arbor, 406

University of Texas, 406

Unveiling a Parallel (Jones), 505

Upanishads, 288–89

utopia: and celibacy, 500–502; critics of,
492–95; experimental communities,
499–500; fantasy, earlier identification
with, 490; feminist embrace of, 518;
feminist retreat from, 509–12; feminist
utopian paradox, 506; feminist utopian
works, 508; and gender, 491–92, 518,
520; heterotopian fictional worlds, 516–
17; intentional communities, 490, 497;
lesbian separatist groups, 502–3; maternal utopias, 505; in New World, 490–91;
oppression and violence, as excuse for,
493; postdystopian gender utopias, 516;
religion, linked with, 489; social issues,
utopian approaches to, 515; social organization, experimentation with, 490;
and social thought, 491; utopian experiments, as failures, 493; utopian female
fiction, 491–92; utopian literature, 489–

utopia (*continued*)

91; and utopian paradox, 488, 492–93, 495–96, 519–20; and women, 491; as word, 489–90. *See also* utopian gender paradox; utopianism

Utopia (More), 489–90, 496, 498–99

utopian gender paradox, 497, 520; and celibacy, 502; examples of, 498–502; and feminist utopian fiction, 503–4. *See also* utopia; utopianism

utopianism, 488, 518; in non-Western societies, 520–21n2

Utopian Motherhood (Francoeur), 492

Vance, Carole, 6

van Gennep, Arnold, 431

Van Wagener, Isabella, 491. *See also* Truth, Sojourner

Vespucci, Amerigo, 296

video games, 38

Vienna (Austria), 158

Virtually Normal (Sullivan), 373

Vishnu, 284–85, 289

Vitruvius, 420

W, or the Memory of a Childhood (Perec), 494

Wagner-Lawlor, Linda, 516–17

Waisbrooker, Lois, 505

Waller, Robert James, 259

Walzer, Michael, 183

Wanderground, The (Gearhart), 508–9, 521n3

Wasala (Belli), 518

Watervliet Shakers, 491

We (Zamyatin), 494

Weber, Max, 342

Webster's Collegiate Dictionary, 234

Weed, Elizabeth, 353

Weeks, Jeffrey, 169

Weiner, Annette, 46

Weld, Theodore, 373

Wen, King, 520–21n2

West, Candace, 246

Weston, Jessie, 277

Westphal, Karl Friedrich Otto, 479–80

Wexler, Philip, 175

"What Is Enlightenment?" (Kant), 375, 378, 383

When God Was a Woman (Stone), 277

White Goddess, The (Graves), 277

White over Black (Jordan), 401

Whorf, Benjamin Lee, 235, 238

Whorfianism, 235; utopian element in, 236

Wieland, Christopher Martin, 60–62

Wildfire, 502

William of St. Thierry, 437

Williams, Raymond, 41, 63

Wilson, Elizabeth, 314

Winnicott, Donald, 81

Winslow, Helen, 507

Winterson, Jeanette, 517

Wittgenstein, Ludwig, 361

Wittig, Monique, 509, 521n3

Wollstonecraft, Mary, 341, 372–73

"Woman, Culture, and Society" (Rosaldo), 366

Woman on the Edge of Time (Piercy), 305, 507–8, 513

Woman for Mayor, A (Winslow), 507

Woman in the Surgeon's Body, The (Cassell), 49, 55–56

Woman's Commonwealth, 490, 502

"Woman's Utopia, A" (Gilman), 506

women, 171; and alliance theory, 215; Beauvoir, as second sex, 396; and birth control, 303–4, 306; bodies of, 26, 148; brotherhood, exclusion from, 145; caring, association with, 195; celibacy, as empowering, 501; as chattel, 145; as a class, 405; devaluation of, 152–53; differences among, 13; domestic violence toward, 148, 153; female surgeons, 55–59, 62–63; and gendered expression, 395; global capitalism, as crafting multiple modes of, 134; globalization, democratization of, as signifier, 134; as higglers/informatics workers, 126–35; as historical subjects, 405; home/family, private sphere of, 148; "housework debates," 355n1; human beings, as described, 144–45; and hysteria, 314–15; and identity, 171; as judicial category, 404; liberal legal theory, 35; male violence against, 312; marginalization of, 99; men's dominance over, 12, 34; mother, and breast, symbolic importance of, 351; mystery, in realm of, 396–98, 400; nature of, identification with, 62; nature of, male dominance, repressed by, 341; nature of, and role in life, 309; as other, 400; patriarchal family institution, and oppression of, 211; physical bodies of, reconnecting with, 24; and power, 336–37, 344; power and authority, as lacking, 163; as property, 145–46; public and private spheres, split between and, 144–46, 183–84, 359–60; and rape, 148, 153; and religion, 428, 434–35, 438; reproductive technology, 306; roles and status of, as changing, 10–11; and science, 301–3; self-empowerment, lack of, 12; "separate spheres" of, 351; and serial killing, 153; silence of, 245–46; social roles of, 144–45; suffrage movement, 11, 182, 191; violence against, 153–54; as weak, 100; women's literature, 60–62; women's literature, and female readership, 62; young girls, seduction and exploitation of, 30

"Women and Life on Earth" conference, 299

Women in Economics (Gilman), 506, 518

women of color: and birth control, 304; cautious pluralism of, 110–11; and ethnicity, 98–99; and gender, 399; intersectional identity of, 110, 112; marginalization of, 110; oppositional consciousness of, 110; and power, 405; and women's studies, 13

women's human rights movement, 139–41, 148, 409; rape, as act of genocide, 149; rape, as crime against human-

ity, 149; violence against, as rampant, 153–54

women's movements, 11, 146, 162, 192, 304, 365–66, 397, 405–6; collective identities in, 165

Women's Rights Convention, 145

women's studies, 12–15; multiple identities in, 171; women, differences among, 13; and women of color, 13. *See also* feminist studies

Woodmansee, Martha, 60–62

World War II: gender and race, disruption of, 7; GI drag shows during, 462

Wounded Knee, 22

Wretched of the Earth, The (Fanon), 166

Wright, Fanny, 358, 360, 364, 367, 369, 373

Xavante tribe, 361

Yama, 187, 189

Yanagisako, Sylvia Junko, 46

Year of the Flood, The (Atwood), 517

YMCA Mexican Youth Conference, 105

You Just Don't Understand (Tannen), 243

youth studies, 161

Yugoslavia, 21, 162

Zakin, Emily, 353

Zamyatin, Yevgeny, 494, 497

Zaretsky, Eli, 373, 382, 389n6

Zhang Longxi, 520–21n2

Zhou, 520–21n2

Zimmerman, Don, 246

Zionism, 162

Zoar, 490